CONTENTS

ACKNOWLEDGEMENTS

Blackwell Publishers for Ash Amin and Nigel Thrift, 'Neo-Marshallian Nodes in Global Networks', *International Journal of Urban and Regional Research 16* (1992), pp. 571–87; the excerpts from Denis Cosgrove, 'Contested Global Visions: *One-World, Whole-Earth* and the Apollo Space Photographs' from *Annals of the Association of American Geographers* 84 (1994), pp. 270–94; the excerpts from Jon Goss, 'The "Magic of the Mall": An Analysis of Form, Function, and Meaning in the Contemporary Retail Built Environment' from *Annals of the Association of American Geographers* 83 (1993), pp. 18–47; David Harvey, 'Monument and Myth' from *Annals of the Association of American Geographers* 69 (1979), pp. 362–81; David Harvey, 'Between Space and Time: Reflections on the Geographical Imagination' from *Annals of the Association of American Geographers* 80 (1990), pp. 418–34; and for the excerpts from Cindi Katz, 'Sow What You Know: The Struggle for Social Reproduction in Rural Sudan' from *Annals of the Association of American Geographers* 81 (1991), pp. 488–514; Cambridge University Press for 'Maps, Knowledge and Power' by J. B. Harley from *The Iconography of Landscape* edited by D. Cosgrove and S. Daniels (1988); Professor Leonore Davidoff and Professor Howard Newby for the excerpts from 'Landscape with Figures: Home and Community in English Society'. Chapter 4 from *The Rights and Wrongs of Women* edited by Judith Mitchell and Ann Oakley (Penguin, 1977); Elsevier Science Ltd for Gearóid ÓTuathail and John Agnew, 'Geopolitics and Discourse: Practical Geopolitical Reasoning in American Foreign Policy' from *Political Geography* 11 (1992), pp. 190–204; The Institute of British Geographers for the excerpts from Stephen Daniels and Simon Rycroft, 'Mapping the Modern City: Alan Sillitoe's Nottingham Novels', *Transactions of the Institute of British Geographers* NS 18 (1993), pp. 460–80; Mona Domosh, 'Towards a Feminist Historiography of Geography', *Transactions of the Institute of British Geographers* NS 16 (1991), pp. 95–104; John Langton, 'The Industrial Revolution and the Regional Geography of England', *Transactions of the Institute of British Geographers* NS 9 (1984), pp. 145–67; Susan J. Smith, 'Social Landscapes: Continuity and Change'. Chapter 3 from *The Challenge for Geography* edited by R. J. Johnston (1993); David Stoddart, 'To Claim the High Ground: Geography for the End of the Century', *Transactions of the*

Institute of British Geographers NS 12 (1987), pp. 327–36; Longman Australia for David Sibley, 'Outsiders in Society and Space', Chapter 7 from *Inventing Places: Studies in Cultural Geography* edited by Kay Anderson and Fay Gale (1992); Doreen Massey for her article 'A Global Sense of Place' from *Marxism Today* (June 1991). This article is also included in Doreen Massey, *Space, Place and Gender* (Polity Press, 1994); The Pennsylvania State University Press for *The New Global Economy in the Information Age* edited by M. Carnoy, M. Castells, S. S. Cohen and F. H. Cardoso, pp. 15–44 © 1989 by The Pennsylvania State University Press. Reproduced by permission of the publisher; Rutgers University Press for Allan Pred and Michael John Watts, *Reworking Modernity: Capitalisms and Symbolic Discontent*, pp. 21–63, copyright © 1992 by Rutgers, The State University; Pion Limited, London for the excerpts from John Allen and Michael Pryke, 'The Production of Service Space', *Environment and Planning D: Society and Space* 12 (1994), pp. 453–75; Felix Driver, 'Geography's Empire: Histories of Geographical Knowledge', *Environment and Planning D: Society and Space* 10 (1992), pp. 23–40; the extract from the preface to *Wrecking a Region* by Ray Hudson (1989), pp. i–vii; and Peter Jackson, 'Street Life: The Politics of Carnival', *Environment and Planning D: Society and Space* 6 (1988), pp. 213–77; Sage Publications for the extract from S. Lash and J. Urry, *Economies of Signs and Space* (1994), pp. 198–203; Verso/New Left Books for the extract from *City of Quartz* by Mike Davis (1991), pp. 293–317.

INTRODUCTION

This book presents human geography as a dynamic domain. It does so in a double sense. There is human geography as a field of inquiry, an academic discipline with its traditions, objectives and approaches, a changing and highly contested terrain. And there is human geography as the world at large, the places where people make their livelihood, a world subject to a continual process of struggle and transformation. The writings in this volume address the intersection of these two domains. They view the discipline of human geography as more than an intellectual endeavour, as part of a wider social world with a variable distribution of power and resources. They view the places they study as more than material and social territories waiting to be discovered and known, as complex cultural worlds with their own fields of knowledge and imagination.

The writings included within address a variety of topics from a variety of perspectives. They chart the creation, reshaping and destruction of places, the cultural meanings and social inequalities of geographical change, the relations between large-scale spatial forces and local lived experience, the medium of geography in the making of human identities and constitution of social processes, the role of time and history in geographical understanding, the power of geographical imagery to reflect and shape the world. These issues are now of interdisciplinary concern, addressed by scholars from a broad range of social sciences and humanities (Shields, 1991; Carter *et al.* 1993; Mitchell, 1993). In grouping the writings we have avoided conventional categories such as 'urban geography' or 'social geography' if only because the writings cut across them. We have chosen contributions which in their very concern with a particular place, period or topic range broadly and imaginatively in source material, subject matter, method and theory. Above all, each of these writings charts interconnections between a variety of arenas: global and local, economic and cultural, historical and contemporary, representational and real. Through all this rich variety they raise a fundamental challenge: how can human geography as a changing discipline best represent and participate in a changing world?

Worlds apart? The dynamics of geography

At times like the present, the speed of change in the discipline of human geography can seem bewildering. As David Harvey remarks, 'It is easier to keep pace with the changes in Benetton's colors than to follow the gyrations of ephemeral ideas now being turned over within the academic world' (Harvey, 1990, p. 431 and this volume). This may, as Harvey suggests, reflect recent developments in conditions in the world at large, in the accelerated turnover time of an economic system which rapidly transforms places and livelihoods as well as academic ideas. A century after the institution of geography as a formal academic discipline in Europe, and with the end of the imperial world and vision which gave geography intellectual coherence and political power, human geography may seem fragmented. Some contributors to this volume maintain that such fragmentation should be welcomed, that a post-imperial world demands a pluralistic human geography, deconstructing grand intellectual and practical schemes, giving voice to those so long subordinated or silenced in geographical texts. This has not entailed the abandoning of grand theoretical or conceptual visions, but it has required an enhanced awareness to the way people under study envisage and explain their world.

The history of human geography this century cannot be seen merely as the breakup of a single, monolithic vision. There have been many times when little intellectual consensus has prevailed, when, for reasons both inside and outside the academy, various aims and approaches, concepts and theories have competed for attention (Livingstone, 1992). How could consensus prevail across a complex field of inquiry with so many links to other disciplines and so many places where geography is practised professionally? It is not just at different times that human geography shows affinities with other subjects – geology, economics, social theory to name but a few – but in different places. Given the practical implications of the subject these places have included sites of government, business and community activism as well as universities, colleges and schools. There is, in short, a geography of geography (Gregory, 1994, pp. 15–18). This not just a matter of where you are, but who you are. Professional geography has been largely a white man's world, arguably taking a largely Euro-American, masculine view of the world at large (Rose, 1992; Jackson, 1993).

While the work of feminist geographers is represented in this volume, the authors comprise a largely Anglophone and transatlantic community. They are from leading British and North American universities, their writings selected from prominent Anglo-American academic journals and books of the past fifteen years. The disciplinary affinities are varied – anthropology, economics, literary theory, cultural studies, social history – but tend towards an intellectual perspective which is critical of established power structures. The intellectual realm of these writings is international except, perhaps ironically, for the discipline of geography. French and German social theory, at least in translation, is now fashionable but the past few decades of human geography in Britain and North America have seen a diminishing influence of French and German human geography (Johnston, 1991, p. viii) and relatively little exchange with human geography elsewhere – this despite some shared concerns of subject and method (e.g. Zanetto, 1987).

If the writers in this collection are largely from one world, their writings are about many. It is often the cultural distinctiveness and resilience of these worlds which engage their attention. This raises a serious question for contemporary human geography, especially one which is consciously post-colonial. Edward Said has influentially shown how much Western colonial rhetoric was predicated on the stereotyping of subject territories as an exotic 'other'. In particular, a powerful 'imaginative geography' held the West to be normal, rational and mature and the Orient to be exotic, irrational and backward (Said, 1978). Such thinking of course persists, especially in media images of underdeveloped parts of the world and Western dealings with them. One response, and it is discernible in Anglo-American geography, is to retreat from dealing with far-away places, to focus attention on the subtle patterns and global resonances of urbane Western life. That can be revealing. A worldly geography which explored the ends of the earth tended to overlook the domestic and commonplace nearer home. Familiar places such as shopping malls and suburban gardens emerge, on close inspection, as complex and strangely unsettling cultural landscapes. The challenge for those who focus on places outside the affluent world – and that includes the poorer quarters of that world – is to try to understand such places from within. This can never mean relinquishing the position of outsider, but it can generate a dialogue between the world of the geographer and the world under study (Taylor, 1994, p. 194).

Other worlds are not just far away; they may be long ago. 'The past is a foreign country', as L. P. Hartley's novel The *Go-Between* begins; 'they do things differently there'. A number of contributions to this volume address worlds of the past, generating a dialogue between past and present (Taylor, 1993). Inevitably they discover contemporary concerns and interests in the pasts they describe, but these pasts are not merely prelude to the present, rather they provide contrast and perspective (Harris, 1978). The geographies of the past are not the same as those of the present, nor are they absolutely different; if they were either it would difficult to recognize them. 'The value of historical study lies in the opportunity for self-estrangement, the chance to recognize ourselves in what we are not' (Barrell, 1992, p. 5).

Whose geographies? Geographies of dynamics

Geographical knowledge, as these writings show, extends well beyond the academy. 'From the classroom to the living-room, the newspaper office to the film studio, the pulpit to the presidential office, geographical knowledge about a world is being produced, reproduced and modified' (Ó Tuathail and Agnew, 1992, pp. 194–5 and this volume). As David

Lowenthal once observed, 'anyone who inspects the world . . . is in some measure a geographer' (Lowenthal, 1961, p. 241). How does academic geography position itself with regard to these various forms of geographical knowledge, both official and popular, institutional and everyday? Such geographical knowledge may not conform to conventional standards of academic inquiry, may be shaped by myth and imagery. One academic strategy, especially in relation to official or commercial discourse, is to dismantle images and myths, to rend the veil of ideology to disclose a real world of hard facts. But myth and image may be seen as more than surface decoration, as implicated in basic structures of knowledge, including academic claims to factual knowledge of the real world. It is through analysing literary works that some geographers have come to appreciate how geographical texts are configured by rhetoric, metaphor, image and myth. This is not just in striking similes or graphic illustrations, but in story lines of historical development and structural analogies for society, such as 'system', 'organism' and 'text' (Barnes and Duncan, 1992). To put into question a simple distinction between representation and reality is not to abandon the claims of the real world, nor to slide into some subjective free-for-all. It is to take seriously the way the very words people use shape how they see the world and decide to act.

What is human about human geography? Few geographers now subscribe to categories like 'economic man', or indeed 'man' itself. The contributors to this volume chart varying patterns of human identity, of class, ethnicity, nationality, gender, generation and sexuality, and examine the implications of a variety of human conduct and motivation, from religious observance to the pleasures of shopping. What is the medium of geography in the making of human identity? How do places from nations to neighbourhoods reflect and in turn shape social developments? Are global flows of capital and culture contributing to new, perhaps liberating, forms of human identity and allegiance, or reaffirming older, perhaps more limiting ones? Human geographers are presently preoccupied with issues of cultural difference and determination, but is there in this a risk of underestimating the power of economic imperatives (Sayer, 1994) and environmental forces (Stoddart, 1987 and this volume), moreover of overlooking the common ground of human experience and awareness (Tuan, 1974)? Older definitions of human geography such as 'the earth as the home of man' may have glossed over the ideological implications of every noun in this phrase, but made it 'immediately clear that geography, for all the technical sophistication of its specialized subfields, is not remote or esoteric knowledge but rather a basic human concern' (Tuan, 1991, p. 99).

Many of the contributors to this volume see the role of the geographer as not just analysing the world but helping to change it for the better (D. Smith 1994). '[I]t is not enough to stand by and describe. We need to ask what can be done' (Stoddart, 1987, p. 332 and this volume); 'in order to engage in a changing world, we need a well-developed sense not only of what the world looks like now, but also of what it *should* look like for future generations' (S. Smith, 1993, p. 72 and this volume). Here is the moral imperative which attracts so many students to geography and is expressed in calls for geography more clearly to inform, and be informed by, a variety of extramural social practice from state planning to community activism.

Sometimes, in calls to go beyond the library and classroom, the importance of geographical education is overlooked, the humane education for an informed appreciation of the world. The call to relevance, to practical action, should never obscure the need for scholarly reflection on the world as it is or was, if only because geography has a history of complicity in socially destructive, if sometimes well intentioned, attempts to reshape the world. Human geography is an imaginative as well as a practical discipline; it matters as an aesthetic as well as a moral enterprise (Cosgrove, 1989; Bishop, 1994). For that reason we have chosen writings which are concerned to portray the richness and complexity of the worlds they describe and are, not least we hope, a pleasure to read.

Reading human geography

Reading human geography, as this Introduction implies, is a complex and critical act of interpretation. Each text in this volume is a particular and provisional reading of the landscape, of worlds which are already construed, or misconstrued, by meaning and imagery. Reading these readings is a further act of interpretation. This Introduction, and those to particular sections, offer a framework for interpreting the texts; here, in addition, we outline some basic procedures.

Each contribution to this volume had an original context which it may be helpful to reconstruct. Some were chapters in book-length studies, others articles in special issues of professional journals. Some started life as research papers, others as plenary lectures at international conferences. Each of the original occasions of the writings entailed particular kinds of community. The texts themselves imply a community, of readers and writers. The issue of authorship and authority is important here, but also the various genres of writing – manifesto, case study, literature review – sometimes within the same text. Such contextual considerations should help place these writings but they should not thereby confirm them. Issues of who these authors are, what stance they take, who they address and how they write, should not obscure what they say. Are their claims, however meaningful, valid, not least when tested against evidence available elsewhere?

Texts may be recontextualized in various ways. This edited volume is an example, with its selection, arrangements, abridgments, commentary and bibliography. The form of the book is the product of a lengthy process of negotiation, among a number of parties, but we would not claim to have fixed its structure, finalized the map of the territory it represents. We trust the volume's texture is sufficiently open to encourage the texts to be read in a variety of ways, to cut across the categorizations, reshuffle the texts, reassemble the further reading, challenge the commentary. This is perhaps to invite the inevitable, that any book entails worlds of reading beyond those in which it was written and produced.

References and further reading

Barnes, T.J. and Duncan, J. S. (eds) 1992: *Writing worlds: Discourse, text and metaphor in the representation of landscape*. London: Routledge.

Barrell, J. (ed.) 1992: *Painting and the politics of culture*. Oxford: Oxford University Press.

Bishop, P. 1994: Residence on earth: *anima mundi* and a sense of geographical 'belonging'. *Ecumene* 1(1) 51–64.

Carter, E., Donald, J. and Squires, J. (eds) 1993: *Space and place: Theories of identity and location*. London: Lawrence & Wishart.

Cosgrove, D. 1989: Geography is everywhere: culture and symbolism in human landscapes. In Gregory, D. and Walford, R. (eds) *Horizons in human geography*. Basingstoke: Macmillan, 118–35.

Gregory, D. 1994: *Geographical imaginations*. Oxford: Basil Blackwell.

Harris, C. 1978: The historical mind and the practice of geography. In Ley, D. and Samuels, M. S. (eds), *Humanistic geography: Prospects and problems*. London: Croom Helm.

Harvey, D. 1990: Between space and time: reflections on the geographical imagination. *Annals of the Association of American Geographers* 80(3), 418–34.

Jackson, P. 1993: Changing ourselves: a geography of position. In Johnston, R. J. (ed.), *The challenge for geography. A changing discipline: A changing world*. Oxford: Basil Blackwell, 198–214.

Johnston, R. J. 1991: *Geography and geographers: Anglo-American geography since 1945*, 4th edn. London: Edward Arnold.

Johnston, R. J. (ed.) 1993: *The challenge for geography. A changing discipline: A changing world*. Oxford: Basil Blackwell.

Lee, R. 1989: Social relations and the geography of material life. In Gregory, D. and Walford, R. (eds), *Horizons in human geography*. Basingstoke: Macmillan.

Livingstone, D. 1992: *The geographical tradition: Episodes in the history of a contested enterprise*. Oxford: Basil Blackwell.

Lowenthal, D. 1961: Geography, experience and imagination: towards a geographic epistemology. *Annals of the Association of American Geographers* 51(3), 241–60.

Mitchell, W. J. T. (ed.) 1993: *Landscape and power*. Chicago: University of Chicago Press.

Ó Tuathail, G. and Agnew, J. 1992: Geopolitics and discourse: practical geopolitical reasoning in American foreign policy. *Political Geography* 11(2), 19–204.

Peet, R. and Thrift, N. (eds) 1989: *New models in geography: The political-economy perspective*. London: Unwin Hyman.

Rose, G. 1992: *Feminism and geography: The limits of geographical knowledge*. Cambridge: Polity Press.

Said, E. 1978: *Orientalism*. Andover, Hants: Routledge, Chapman & Hall.

Sayer, A. 1994: Editorial: Cultural studies and 'the economy, stupid'. *Environment and Planning D: Society and Space* 12, 635–7.

Shields, R. 1991: *Places on the margin: Alternative geographies of modernity*. London: Routledge.

Shurmer-Smith, P. and Hannam, K. 1994: *Worlds of desire: Realms of power. A cultural geography*. London: Edward Arnold.

Smith, D. 1994: *Geography and social justice*. Oxford: Basil Blackwell.

Smith, S. 1993: Social landscapes: continuity and change. In Johnston, R. J. (ed.), *The challenge for geography. A changing world: A changing discipline*. Oxford: Basil Blackwell, 54–75.

Stoddart, D. 1987: To claim the high ground: geography for the end of the century. *Transactions of the Institute of British Geographers* NS 12, 327–36.

Taylor, P. J. 1993: Full circle, or new meaning for the global? In Johnston (ed.), *The challenge for geography. A changing world: A changing discipline*. Oxford: Basil Blackwell, 181–97.

Tuan, Y. F. 1991: *Space and place: The perspective of experience*. London: Edward Arnold.

Tuan, Y. F. 1990: A view of geography. *Geographical Review* 81, 99–107.

Zanetto, G. (ed.) 1987: *Les langages des représentations géographiques*. Venice: University of Venice, Department of Economic Science.

SECTION ONE
MAKING AND BREAKING GEOGRAPHIES

Editors' introduction

Perhaps the most important question to ask before studying any subject is why it is worth studying. So, why geography? One answer is that geography matters (Massey, 1984). In exploring why it matters in a little more detail, we can begin to chart a course through geography that both highlights its intellectual and practical significance and shows how it offers particular interpretations of the world, at the same time as it is shaped by the world that it tries to imagine and understand.

Why geography matters

A long-standing preoccupation of geography has been to examine the influence of location on social practice. Indeed, for Abler *et al.* (1971) a concern for what, in the title of their book, they call 'spatial organization' represents 'the geographer's view of the world'. Well-known examples of work in this genre include the concern of studies of industrial location for the profitability of production, or studies of central places for the effectiveness of markets in the distribution of goods and services. Such work assesses the significance of the spatial arrangement of phenomena for the ways in which they work. It demonstrates that in influential but largely instrumental ways the geographies of social processes condition the locational organization of our daily lives.

But geography matters in a deeper sense too: as well as shaping the spatial organization of our lives it forms a fundamental constituent of them. For one thing, human life is predicated on the dynamic and often conflict-ridden relationships between nature, culture and society. For another – and as many of the readings in this section demonstrate – the networks of social relationships through which we define an identity, find the means of emotional and material support and make our living (in the broadest sense of the term) *take place* in and through their often highly differentiated geographies. It is for such reasons that the geographical constitution of social life rarely takes place without a struggle over what kind of geography is acceptable. We focus more fully on this struggle in

Section Two. In this section, our concern is with the ways in which both the discipline of geography and the practice of geography on the ground are socially constructed and so form an integral part of social practice.

Human life is inherently social and so is shaped at particular times and particular places by the prevailing sets of social relations into which we are born. For Norbert Elias (1978) this sociability of human life is central to social understanding. Elias disputes the distinction between individuals and society – for him the one is constituted through the other – and speaks instead of people and relationships. He argues that people are necessarily caught up in a dynamic interweaving of relationships, what he calls 'figurations', and uses the example of games to illustrate the power of this idea. A game can have no independent existence beyond the relationships of the individuals participating in it but, at the same time, the game cannot be reduced to the mere summation of the individual players. It is rather a dynamic process driven by the constantly formed and re-formed relationships between players. It is structured by the changing balance of power between them, but this balance may be closely affected by the particular circumstances in which the game is played (as, for example, when an 'outsider' wins in a knock-out competition).

In such ways, then, people both shape and are shaped by the society into which they are born. And such relations do not just happen, they are the consequences (both intended and unintended) of the struggle to create a social environment amenable to a particular way of life. In such struggles, relations of power (expressed, for example, through gender relations such as patriarchy, or through racism or colonialism) may be dominant but they are not necessarily determinant as they may be challenged. Thus, although the contemporary world is dominated by the social relations of capitalism, it has, according to some historical geographers and economic historians (see, for example, Wallerstein, 1974; Braudel, 1982; Blaut, 1992), taken over five hundred years of world history to achieve this dominance, which is still not entirely secure and even less completely accepted. Furthermore, the emergence of capitalism has been beset by markedly uneven development in both time and space. Nevertheless, capitalism imposes a particularly unambiguous set of values (associated primarily with profitability and accumulation) upon the way in which social life may be constructed; it has also facilitated a tendency to globalization (the construction of geographies articulated at a global scale) held in check from time to time by the actions of nation states attempting to retain control over processes operating increasingly at a supranational level.

Thus the geographies of our own lives are both shaped and evaluated according to the requirements of a capitalism. And as a result of the global extent and operation of contemporary capitalist geographies, geographically distant places may be evaluated and compared in terms of their contribution to the maintenance and expansion of such geographies.

Western Europe and North America, for example, come to be evaluated against the productive capacity of South-East Asia. The survival and trajectory of particular places are, therefore, caught up in the dynamics of an expansionary but highly selective and discriminating geography of capitalist growth. It is in such a context of globally prevalent capitalist social relations that we engage in making the historical geographies of our own lives. The particular characteristics of these geographies – the nature and level of their development, and the economies, polities and cultures made through the practical and moral experiences of their construction – provide the conditions through which we engage with the prevailing social relations, to adapt to them and to try to make an accommodation with them, to reform them, or even to overthrow them.

What is especially important here is the tension between our ability to construct – albeit not without a struggle – a particular set of social relations through which we may choose to live our lives, and the prior existence of a previously constructed set of social relations which may be so powerfully established that the scope for change is extremely limited. This tension is caught particularly well in the immensely rich insistence of Karl Marx that people make their own histories but not necessarily under conditions of their own choosing. In stressing the struggle involved in making histories, this view rejects any notion of determinism and reflects a concern and respect for difference. However, Marx might have added that histories may be made only within and through the construction of geographies – as the work of David Harvey (1982, 1989) and others has sought to demonstrate – and so these geographies are themselves contested social constructs; our lives are constituted in part by our engagement with them or against them.

And here we can see that the distinction that we have made between the way in which geography both organizes and constitutes our lives becomes blurred. An example may help to make this point a little more clear. At the time of writing, a debate over the structure and location of shopping centres in and around European towns pits two very different kinds of geographical organization against each other with implications not merely for the geography of retailing but for the nature of social life. On the one hand, a geography based upon large-scale property investment offers high returns on green-field out-of-town sites but relies on the car for access and is destructive of long-established town centres as centres of retail trade and as supposed loci of democratic social interaction. And on the other, a geography based on the smaller-scale reshaping of the built environment of the town centres themselves reduces the scope for profitable investment and ease of provision for (motorized) access but supposedly enhances or preserves a notion and practice of the town centre or the high street as a place of public meeting and interaction. The outcome of this debate will clearly shape our lives in instrumental ways but it will also constitute them through the alternative notions of sociability and interaction implied in these different views of the built environment.

If geography matters in such ways, how do geographers go about studying it? Before introducing the individual readings in Section One – which offer specific answers to this question – we must briefly explore some of the ways in which geographers working in and on the socially constructed world have set about its study and outline some of the ideas that they have brought to bear upon it.

Imagining geographies

Geographers have long been concerned with what we might call the geographical 'logic' of human activity – the ways in which such activity may be understood and geographically ordered and constrained. But this concern has been prone to a kind of reductionism and naturalization: for example, both geographical space itself and the ways in which people relate to it have been regarded at various times in the development of the discipline as unproblematic and given. The region and regional geography, spatial science and the notion of geography as a passive container of powerful economic and social processes are examples of reductive approaches to geographical space, while environmental determinism, economic rationality, behaviouralism and structuralism are examples of ways in which geographers have simplified social practice.

The net effect of such reductive imaginings is that the notion of geography as a complex set of processes of formative differentiation – through which human beings construct their histories and geographies in places already distinguished and differentiated by a historical geography of social practice – becomes irrelevant. We thereby overlook the intimate, formative linkages between people, society, place and time and so may forget that 'spaces are extraordinarily complex' (Rose, 1993, p. 155). To take the cases of spatial science and economic rationality for example (see Gregory, 1994), we are sometimes asked to believe that all people ultimately conform (*must* conform) to a physically derived, universal logic of economic rationality which works itself out across a geometrical surface devoid of social meaning other than the pre-given notions of the economic and of social physics. In such ways, narrowly founded *formulations* of the world come to be translated into universal and abstract *constructions* of the world – an approach which is inherently a-geographical.

But if we contest such a view by insisting upon the recognition of social difference we open up the danger of an interpretation of others from the perspective only of the self; of assuming a self-centred normality and an abnormal 'other'. Such a danger is not only apparent but institutionally reinforced in certain curricula – for example, the National Curriculum in England and Wales for students up to the age of 16. Here self and home are placed at the centre of a geographical universe which is explored as if it revolves around the home location defined predominantly in terms of a centred family and nationality and a decentred other, rather than as one element in a global network of links which serve to sustain social life. And yet, as we have argued above, precisely because human life is social, the spatiality of our lives is clearly structured by prevailing relations of power stretched over space and associated notions of normality, progress and regress which we have to accept (willingly or unwillingly, consciously or unconsciously), reject or, in the process of constructing our own geographies, struggle to change. It is around this tension between individual creativity and identity and the social relations which are at one and the same time both vital to and a constraint upon human life that human geographies are made – both as a discipline in the mind and as social practice on the ground. And in studying geography we should recognize, therefore, that the way in which we and therefore it views the world is itself socially produced.

Over twenty years ago, David Harvey (1974) asked 'What kind of geography for what kind of public policy?'. He argued that the ways in which we make or break alternative disciplinary constructions of geography as a means of investigating the world and of recommending geographies of change is highly political; it cannot help but reflect particular kinds of social and scientific understanding or advocacy. As a discipline, geography is never innocent or value free, it is always loaded with political, social, moral and environmental significance. Our images and models of the world are made in part through the ways in which we look at it, and so particular constructions of the discipline of geography can be very powerful in pre-conditioning and shaping our understanding of the geographies in which social life is produced. The example of the contested geographies of retail investment shows how alternative views or models of the world shape the assessment and evaluation of – and the preferences for – alternative geographies on the ground.

But the flow of causality between geographies on the ground and in the mind is not one-way. The discipline of geography not only shapes but feeds off the practice of geography; we cannot study either aspect in isolation from the other. Certainly, this is very much the view taken by recent historians of the subject of geography. As David Livingstone (1992, p. 2), for example, has argued, 'accepting or rejecting any scientific theory is always and irreducibly a social act, by a specific social group, in particular cultural circumstances'. And, as we suggested above, those acts, groups and circumstances are themselves shaped and conditioned by the geographies in which they are located. Thus the way in which we think about geography as a discipline will be shaped in part by the kinds of geographies that constitute our lives in practice.

It follows from this that the geographies that we inhabit and continue to transform on the ground are multicentred; there is no grand central place or single, privileged vantage point (the English and Welsh National Curriculum in Geography notwithstanding) around which or from which all geographical landscapes and our experiences of them rotate and are defined. Thus Ron Martin (1994), for example, argues for an economic geography that is multidimensional (not privileging particular levels or scales of analysis, taking in the transnational and the global as well as the national, the local and the individual), multiperspectival (not privileging a single totalizing theory such as neoclassical economics) and multivocal (not privileging particular participants, such as individual WASP males) in the construction of geographies. He might have added that economic geography should be multilocational (not privileging a view of the world from particular places; see, for example, Blaut (1976, 1992, 1994)).

However, as we have argued above, although difference is an inherent feature of the geography of social life, we do not live in a free-floating world in which anything goes without social constraint: capitalist values and norms prevail and so both the practice and discipline of geography remain directed and structured by powerful social relations (see, for example, Harvey and Scott, 1989). Although our imaginations should not be foreclosed, neither can they run riot. The intimate connections between the practice and the study of geography constantly remind us that human creativity is forever released and constrained by human sociability.

So geography matters – both as discipline and as practice. As a discipline, it asks questions which are fundamental to our understanding of the world and such questions are inescapably soaked in social values. At the same time, the ways in which the geography of the world is constructed in practice have a fundamental effect on the ways in which we are constituted and able to live our lives. Sections One and Two of this book offer some examples of how such issues may be considered. In Section Two, attention is focused on how geographical space is both employed in and used by social activity: we ask 'what difference does space make?' (Sayer, 1985). As a complement to this, in Section One, we use the work of human geographers to show how geography is a fundamental constituent, far more than a mere setting, for social practice – a term which tries to encompass the diversity of ways in which all human beings live their lives.

The readings

What is apparent in all of the following readings is the constant tension between creativity and constraint in the making of geographies. What is more, it quickly becomes apparent that the nature of the human in human geography is itself not amenable to neat packaging (economic, social, cultural, political and so on). The multicentred nature of society and humanity (defined in terms such as gender, religion, class, race and level of development) cannot be broken down into manageable segments either by those wishing to know about the events narrated or by the participants in those narratives. Nevertheless, these essays also show that choices are always possible – there is always the possibility of constructing alternative geographies – although, as they make perfectly clear, the struggle to develop such alternatives is not only usually extremely costly in terms of human effort and life but the capacity to engage in such struggles is also unevenly developed. The two-thirds of the world's population who will never be able to aspire to minimally decent standards of living would be entirely justified in retorting that choice is a possibility merely for the already powerful.

These themes and more are addressed by **David Harvey**. Using a range of documentary sources, Harvey reveals the complex historical geographies of the basilica of Sacré-Coeur in Paris. The building was imagined as a symbol of the continuing power of a centralized religion, the links between this religion, its cults and a centralized, if contested, State; and a hierarchical but increasingly decrepit social order. Given the influence of these geographies, such a symbol had to take the form of a single dominant and overwhelming monument. However, this geographical expression of centralized power was contested by decentralized geographies of resistance – to Paris from the provinces, for example, and to the power of Church and State by the communards and republican movements within Paris – sometimes given institutional form in the shape of the local State. Harvey details the struggles to begin and to sustain the construction of the building and, once begun, the struggle of the State and its systematic use of merciless violence to retain political legitimacy in the face of passionate opposition. And he shows, above all, the contested meanings which may be inscribed in this particular geography. Apparently an attempt at re-establishing a religious reading of social change and political legitimacy, Sacré-Coeur represents a complex mosaic of motivation and meaning. Whatever it is, it cannot be read, simplistically, as monument to a singular social dynamic; rather it is the product of struggle – long-lived, physical and violent as well as cunning, quiet and rhetorical – and of the power of money to constrain politics. Here in a single building it is possible to explore the complexity of the social construction of human geographies.

Such complexity is the focus of the remarkably sensitive exploration by **Cindi Katz** of the social processes through which societies make ready to sustain their own reproduction. In an essay which reports the results of a piece of ethnographic research involving the close observation over an extended period of production and reproduction in the village of Howa in the Sudan, Katz focuses upon the socialization and education of children through the everyday practices of work, play and learning. A particular concern is the incorporation of the village into a State-sponsored agricultural development project and the consequent disruption of local social norms and agronomic practices by the enforced intrusion of capitalist social relations with consequently serious implications for the restructuring of village society and environmental degradation. Nevertheless, struggle on the basis of local knowledge helps to subvert and modify the excesses of capitalist intrusion, although the question then arises as to whether this local knowledge and resistance merely helps to make the local geography of capitalism that much more effective as it too gains from an education provided through struggle by the villagers. Such a question is similar to that concerning the effects of struggle of the working class in industrial Britain against the more exploitative features of capitalist development, so helping to sustain the extended reproduction of capitalism which might otherwise have collapsed under the weight of its own contradictions.

The making of geographical landscapes and the constraints imposed upon such social constructions – no matter how powerful the driving forces – are considered by **Jack Langton** in the context of the geographical shape of the Industrial Revolution in Britain. The Industrial Revolution cannot be reduced to a series of technical innovations with their consequent effect upon production nor even to a series of national transformations. It was much more complex and much more interesting than that because it was geographically and culturally constituted. And, once again, it was so in a double sense. The penetration of capitalism into more and more aspects of production drove the Industrial Revolution and, in turn, revolutionized the geography of social life – but not necessarily as rapidly as is often inferred (Gregory, 1990). As Sidney Pollard (1973, 1981) has argued, the Industrial Revolution was simultaneously an international and a regional process: international because its productive power quickly transcended localities but regional in that the geographical requirements for its manifestation were far from uniform and were found, in particular, on and around the coalfields of Europe. At the same time – and this is the second part of its doubly geographical constitution – the penetration of capitalism was resisted on a more local scale within the experience and reach of the people drawn into its ultimately extra-local scale of operation. Indeed, the argument here rests very much upon local circumstance rather than, for example, the driving force of capitalist expansion. The recognition of the Industrial Revolution as a doubly constituted geography and the two-way interactions between the regional and the international offer a powerful insight into the simultaneous autonomy and local power of industrial regions – especially of the industrial magnates within them – and their growing dependence upon access to the international economy of finance and trade provided through the increasingly global services offered through the financial centre of the City of London. The progressive closure of local stock exchanges during the latter part of the nineteenth and early twentieth century (see Kindleberger, 1974) in the regions is a manifestation of this geographical relationship.

The politically structured relationships between production and reproduction discussed by Katz are at the heart of **Ray Hudson**'s concern for one region – the north-east of England – produced and shaped by the dynamics of the Industrial Revolution. In outlining the changes in his own understanding of the region, Hudson illustrates the dynamism of the intersection of the two domains of geography discussed above. He points to the central role of the State in securing and shaping processes of reproduction appropriate for the extended reproduction of capitalism within the region – a role which reflects in turn the dependence of the State upon the productive economy for its own material legitimacy. At the same time, he argues that resistance to such programmes and policies was to be found within the operation of the State through the contestation of national party politics, for example, with its own highly distinctive and differentiated geographies. Resistance and support were also locally constituted, through involvements in agencies such as the Labour Party, but were far from unambiguous and remained contradictory and fragmented. One reason for this was the the nature of the North-East as a region – created by distinctive and integrated forms of industrial capitalism in the nineteenth century and then, during its phase of disintegration and locally uneven development during the twentieth century, reimposed as part of the apparatus of national State policies in the middle of the twentieth century.

For **Manuel Castells**, the reconstitution of the regions of the global economy in the late twentieth century is a process intimately bound up with the use and production of information. The processing of material objects remains an important feature of any economy – converting them from a less to a more useful form. However, two related trends are reducing the relative significance of control over physical production as a source of power in the contemporary world. On the one hand, production is itself increasingly informed by knowledge-based control systems requiring a high level of technical infrastructure and highly skilled labour. On the other, the effect of the satisfaction of material wants and needs among the minority but economically dominant section of the world's population found within the upper- and middle-income brackets of the developed world is having the effect of shifting effective demand – in relative terms at least – away from material goods towards non-material services (e.g. personal care) and information-based commodities (e.g. financial advice). The geographical construction of the 'informational economy' that Castells perceives as arising from such trends is having a number of dramatic manifestations, the most startling of which, perhaps, is the claim 'that today we can speak of *the end of the Third World as a relatively homogeneous economic region*'. The informational economy is creating a new international division of labour, fragmenting the old order of core and periphery and inserting each into the other. The uneven nature of this process is, according to Castells, creating a new geography: a Fourth World of marginalized and excluded economies whose societies respond by attempting to make a living via the criminal or sub-criminal economy, by a tendency to increasing intercommunal and international violence and by the rise of religious or ideological fundamentalism.

But this is a system-wide and top-down view of the contemporary expansion of the global economy. The global scale of the contemporary economy poses even more profound questions of local penetration, dependence, resistance and transformation. These are explored by **Michael Watts** in an extraordinary study of the complexity of response to the imposition on Nigeria of global capitalism primarily in the form of the black gold (referred to elsewhere by Watts as 'the devil's excrement') dominated by the international petroleum industry. This chapter creates a symmetry with that of Harvey. It shows up the violence of change imposed by the powerful, it stresses the strength, dynamism and coherence of resistance from beyond a narrow economic calculus framed within a particular set of social relations (capitalism), it points to the contested variety of driving forces of change and, more especially, of resistance to change and, above all, despite the violence and death of struggle, it insists on the possibility of a new form of social construction responsive to the needs of the people undertaking the construction. This account is remarkable not merely for the breadth of its understanding and the way in which it breaks down conventional divisions between global economic processes and profound local understandings and beliefs but because it is both brutally realistic and yet optimistic. It points above all to the power of humanity to see beyond the surface, to recognize the profound and to struggle to make new geographies which reflect such powers. It points, in short, to the remarkable ways in which people continue to make and to remake their own historical geographies – despite the conditions in which they have to do so.

References and further reading

Abler, R., Adams, J. S. and Gould, P. 1971: *Spatial organization: The geographer's view of the world.* Englewood Cliffs, NJ: Prentice-Hall.

Blaut, J. M. 1976: Where was capitalism born? *Antipode* 8(2), 1–11 (reprinted in Peet, R. (ed.) 1977: *Radical geography.* Chicago: Maaroufa Press, 95–110).

Blaut, J. M. 1992: Fourteen ninety-two. *Political Geography* 11, 335–86.

Blaut, J. M. 1994: Robert Brenner in the Tunnel of Time. *Antipode* 26, 351–74.

Braudel, F. 1982: *Civilization and capitalism 15th–18th century,* vols 1–3. London: Fontana.

Cloke, P., Philo, C. and Sadler, D. 1991: *Approaching human geography.* London: Paul Chapman.

Dear, M. J. 1988: The postmodern challenge: reconstructing human geography. *Transactions of the Institute of British Geographers* 13, 262–74.

Elias, N. 1978: *What is sociology?* London: Hutchinson.

Glacken, C. 1967: *Traces on the Rhodian shore: Nature and culture in Western thought from ancient times to the end of the eighteenth century.* Berkeley, CA: University of California Press.

Gregory, D. 1990: A new and differing face in many places: three geographies of industrialization. In Dodgshon, R. A. and Butlin, R. A. (eds), *An historical geography of England and Wales.* London: Academic Press, 351–99.

Gregory, D. 1994: *Geographical imaginations*: Oxford: Basil Blackwell.

Gregory, D., Martin, R. and Smith, G. (eds) 1994: *Human geography: Society, space and social science.* Basingstoke: Macmillan.

Harvey, D. 1973: *Social justice and the city*. London: Edward Arnold.

Harvey, D. 1974: What kind of geography for what kind of public policy? *Transactions of the Institute of British Geographers* 63, 18–24.

Harvey, D. 1982: *The limits to capital*. Oxford: Basil Blackwell.

Harvey, D. 1989: *The condition of postmodernity*. Oxford: Basil Blackwell.

Harvey, D. and Scott, A. 1989: The practice of human geography: theory and empirical specificity in the transition from Fordism to flexible accumulation. In Macmillan, B. (ed.), *Remodelling geography*. Oxford: Basil Blackwell, 217–29.

Johnston, R. J. (ed.) 1993: *The challenge for geography. A changing world: A changing discipline*. Oxford: Basil Blackwell.

Johnston, R. J. and Taylor, P. J. (eds) 1989: *A world in crisis? Geographical perspectives*, 2nd edn. Oxford: Basil Blackwell.

Kindleberger, C. P. 1974: *The formation of financial centres: A study in comparative economic history*. Princeton Studies in International Finance no. 36. International Finance Section, Department of Economics, Princeton University, NJ.

Livingstone, D. 1992: *The geographical tradition*. Oxford: Basil Blackwell.

Martin, R. 1994: Economic theory and human geography. In Gregory, D., Martin, R. and Smith, G. (eds), *Human geography: Society, space and social science*. Basingstoke: Macmillan, 21–53.

Massey, D. 1984: Geography matters. Introduction in Massey, D. and Allen, J. (eds), *Geography matters!* Cambridge: Cambridge University Press, 1–11.

Pollard, S. 1973: Industrialisation and the European economy. *Economic History Review* 26, 636–48.

Pollard, S. 1981: *Peaceful conquest*. Oxford: Oxford University Press.

Pred, A. and Watts, M. J. 1992: *Reworking modernity: Capitalisms and symbolic discontent*. New Brunswick, NJ: Rutgers University Press.

Rose, G. 1993: *Feminism and geography: The limits of geographical knowledge*. Cambridge: Polity Press.

Sayer, A. 1985: The difference that space makes. In Gregory, D. and Urry, J. (eds), *Social relations and spatial structures*. Basingstoke: Macmillan, 49–66.

Wallerstein, M. 1974: *The modern world system*. London: Academic Press.

Watts, M. 1994: Oil as money: The devil's excrement and the spectre of black gold. In Corbridge, S., Martin, R. and Thrift, N. (eds), *Money, power and space*. Oxford: Basil Blackwell, 406–45.

1 David Harvey,
'Monument and Myth'

Reprinted in full from: *Annals of the Association of American Geographers* 69, 362–81 (1979)

Strategically placed atop a hill known as the Butte Montmartre, the Basilica of Sacré-Coeur occupies a commanding position over Paris. Its five white marble domes and the campanile that rises beside them can be seen from every quarter of the city. Occasional glimpses of it can be caught from within the dense and cavernous network of streets which makes up old Paris. It stands out spectacular and grand to the young mothers parading their children in the Jardins de Luxembourg, to the tourists who painfully plod to the top of Notre Dame or who painlessly float up the escalators of the Centre Beaubourg, to the commuters crossing the Seine by metro at Grenelle or pouring into the Gare du Nord, to the Algerian immigrants who on Sunday afternoons wander to the top of the rock in the Parc des Buttes Chaumont. It can be seen clearly by the old men playing *boules* in the Place du Colonel Fabien, on the edge of the traditional working-class quarters of Belleville and La Villette – places that have an important role to play in our story.

On cold winter days when the wind whips the fallen leaves among the aging tombstones of the Père Lachaise cemetery, the Basilica can be seen from the steps of the tomb of Adolph Thiers, first President of the Third Republic of France. Though now almost hidden by the modern office complex of La Défense, it can be seen from more than 20 kilometers away in the Pavillion Henri IV in St Germain-en-Laye where Adolph Thiers died. But by a quirk of topography, it cannot be seen from the famous Mur des Fédérés in that same Père Lachaise cemetery, where on 27 May 1871 some of the last few remaining soldiers of the Commune were rounded up after a fierce fight among the tombstones and summarily shot. You cannot see Sacré-Coeur from that ivy-covered wall now shaded by an aging chestnut. That place of pilgrimage for socialists, workers, and their leaders is hidden from a place of pilgrimage for the Catholic faithful by the brow of the hill on which stands the grim tomb of Adolph Thiers.

Few would argue that the Basilica of Sacré-Coeur is beautiful or elegant (Figure 1.1). But most would concede that it is striking and distinctive, that its direct Byzantine style achieves a kind of haughty grandeur which demands respect from the city spread out at its feet. On sunny days it glistens from afar and even on the gloomiest of days its domes seem to capture the smallest particles of light and radiate them outwards in a white marble glow. Floodlit by night it appears suspended in space, sepulchral and ethereal. Thus does Sacré-Coeur project an image of saintly grandeur, of perpetual remembrance. But remembrance of what?

The visitor drawn to the Basilica in search of an answer to that question must

Fig. 1.1   The Basilica of Sacré-Coeur

first ascend the steep hillside of Montmartre. Those who pause to catch their breath will see spread out before them a marvellous vista of rooftops, chimneys, domes, towers, monuments – a vista of old Paris that has not changed so much since that dull and foggy October morning in 1872, when the Archbishop of Paris climbed those steep slopes only to have the sun miraculously chase both fog and cloud away to reveal the splendid panorama of Paris spread out before him. The Archbishop marveled for a moment before crying out loud: 'It is here, it is here where the martyrs are, it is here that the Sacred Heart must reign so that it can beckon all to it!'[1] So who are the martyrs commemorated here in the grandeur of this Basilica?

The visitor who enters into that hallowed place will most probably first be struck by the immense painting of Jesus which covers the dome of the apse. Portrayed with arms stretched wide, the figure of Christ wears an image of the Sacred Heart upon his breast. Beneath, two words stand out directly from the Latin motto: GALLIA POENITENS. And beneath that stands a large gold casket, containing the image of the Sacred Heart of Jesus, burning with passion, suffused with blood and surrounded with thorns. Illuminated day and night, it is here that pilgrims come to pray.

Opposite a life-size statue of Saint Marguerite-Marie Alacoque, words from a letter written by that saintly person – date, 1689, place, Paray-le-Monial – tell us more about the cult of the Sacred Heart:

THE ETERNAL FATHER WISHING REPARATION FOR THE BITTERNESS AND ANGUISH THAT THE ADORABLE HEART OF HIS DIVINE SON HAD EXPERIENCED AMONGST THE HUMILIATIONS AND OUTRAGES OF HIS PASSION DESIRES AN EDIFICE WHERE THE IMAGE OF THIS DIVINE HEART CAN RECEIVE VENERATION AND HOMAGE

Prayer to the Sacred Heart of Jesus which, according to the scriptures, had been exposed when a centurion thrust a lance through Jesus's side during his suffering upon the cross, was not unknown before the seventeenth century. But Marguerite-Marie, beset by visions, transformed the worship of the Sacred Heart into a distinctive cult within the Catholic Church. Although her life was full of trials and suffering, her manner severe and rigorous, the predominant image of Christ which the cult projected was warm and loving, full of repentance and suffused with a gentle kind of mysticism.[2]

Marguerite-Marie and her disciples set about propagating the cult with great zeal. She wrote to Louis XIV, for example, claiming to bring a message from Christ, in which the King was asked to repent, to save France by dedicating himself to the Sacred Heart, to place its image upon his standard and to build a chapel to its glorification. It is from that letter of 1689 that the words now etched in stone within the Basilica are taken.

The cult diffused slowly. It was not exactly in tune with eighteenth-century French rationalism, which strongly influenced modes of belief among Catholics and stood in direct opposition to the hard, rigorous, and self-disciplined image of Jesus projected by the Jansenists. But by the end of the eighteenth century it had some important and potentially influential adherents. Louis XVI privately took devotion to the Sacred Heart for himself and his family. Imprisoned during the French Revolution, he vowed that within three months of his deliverance he would publicly dedicate himself to the Sacred Heart and thereby save France (from what, exactly, he did not, nor did he need to, say). And he vowed to build a chapel to the worship of the Sacred Heart. The manner of Louis XVI's deliverance did not permit him to fulfill that vow. Marie-Antoinette did no better. The Queen delivered up her last prayers to the Sacred Heart before keeping her appointment with the guillotine.

These incidents are of interest because they presage an association, important for our story, between the cult of the Sacred Heart and the reactionary monarchism of the *ancien régime*. This put adherents to the cult in firm opposition to the principles of the French Revolution. Believers in the principles of liberty, equality and fraternity, who were in any case prone to awesome anticlerical sentiments and practices, were, in return, scarcely enamored of such a cult. Revolutionary France was no safe place to attempt to propagate it. Even the bones and other relics of Marguerite-Marie, now displayed in Paray-le-Monial, had to be carefully hidden during these years.

The restoration of the monarchy in 1815 changed all that. The Bourbon monarchs sought, under the watchful eye of the European powers, to restore whatever they could of the old social order. The theme of repentence for the excesses of the revolutionary era ran strong. Louis XVIII did not fulfill his dead brother's vow to the Sacred Heart, but he did build, with his own moneys, a Chapel of Expiation on the spot where his brother and his family had been so unceremoniously interred – GALLIA POENITENS. A society for the propagation of the cult of the Sacred Heart was founded, however, and proceedings for the glorification of Marguerite-Marie were transmitted to Rome in 1819. The link between conservative monarchism and the cult of the Sacred Heart was further consolidated.

The cult spread among conservative Catholics but was viewed with some suspicion by the liberal progressive wing of French Catholicism. But now another enemy was ravaging the land, disturbing the social order. France was undergoing the stress and tensions of capitalist industrialization. In fits and starts under the July Monarchy (installed in 1830 and just as summarily dispensed with in the revolution of 1848) and then in a great surge in the early years of the Second Empire of Napoleon III, France saw a radical transformation in certain sectors of its economy, in its institutional structures, and in its social order.[3] This transformation threatened much that was sacred in French life, since it brought within its train a crass and heartless materialism, an ostentatious and morally decadent bourgeois culture, and a sharpening of class tensions. The cult of the Sacred Heart now assembled under its banner not only those devotees drawn by temperament or circumstance to the image of a gentle and forgiving Christ, not only those who dreamed of a restoration of the political order of yesteryear, but also all those who felt threatened by the materialist values of the new social order.

To these general conditions, French Catholics could also add some more specific complaints in the 1860s. Napoleon III had finally come down on the side of Italian unification and committed himself politically and militarily to the liberation of the central Italian states from the temporal power of the Pope. The latter did not take kindly to such politics and under military pressure retired to the Vatican, refusing to come out until such time as his temporal power was restored. From that vantage point, the Pope delivered searing condemnations of French policy and the moral decadence which, he felt, was sweeping over France. In this manner he hoped to rally French Catholics in the active pursuit of his cause. The moment was propitious. Marguerite-Marie was beatified by Pius IX in 1864. The era of grand pilgrimages to Paray-le-Monial began. The pilgrims came to express repentence for both public and private transgressions. They repented for the materialism and decadent opulence of France. They repented for the restrictions placed upon the temporal power of the Pope. They repented for the passing of the traditional values embodied in an old and venerable social order. GALLIA POENITENS.

Just inside the main door of the Basilica of Sacré-Coeur in Paris, the visitor can read the following inscription:

THE YEAR OF OUR LORD 1875
THE 16TH JUNE
IN THE REIGN OF HIS HOLINESS POPE PIUS IX IN ACCOMPLISHMENT
OF A VOW FORMULATED DURING THE WAR OF 1870–71 BY ALEX-
ANDER LEGENTIL AND HUBERT ROHAULT DE FLEURY RATIFIED BY
HIS GRACE MGR. GUIBERT ARCHBISHOP OF PARIS; IN EXECUTION OF
THE VOTE OF THE NATIONAL ASSEMBLY OF THE 23RD JULY 1873
ACCORDING TO THE DESIGN OF THE ARCHITECT ABADIE; THE FIRST
STONE OF THIS BASILICA ERECTED TO THE SACRED HEART OF
JESUS WAS SOLEMNLY PUT IN PLACE BY HIS EMINENCE CARDINAL
GUIBERT . . .

Let us flesh out that capsule history and find out what lies behind it.

As Bismarck's battalions rolled to victory after victory over the French in the summer of 1870, an impending sense of doom swept over France. Many interpreted the defeats as righteous vengeance inflicted by divine will upon an errant and morally decadent France. It was in this spirit that the Empress Eugene was urged to walk with her family and court all dressed in mourning, from the Palace of the Tuilleries to Notre Dame, to publicly dedicate themselves to the Sacred Heart. Though the Empress received the suggestion favorably, it was, once more, too late. On 2 September, Napoleon III was defeated and captured at Sedan, on 4 September the Republic was proclaimed on the steps of the Hôtel-de-Ville and a Government of National Defense was formed. On that day also the Empress Eugene took flight from Paris, having prudently, and at the Emperor's urging, already packed her bags and sent her more valuable possessions on to England.

The defeat at Sedan ended the Empire but not the war. The Prussian armies rolled on and by 20 September they had encircled Paris and put that city under a seige that was to last until 28 January of the following year. Like many other respectable bourgeois citizens, Alexander Legentil fled Paris at the approach of the Prussian armies and took refuge in the provinces. Languishing in Poitiers and agonizing over the fate of Paris, he vowed in early December that 'if God saved Paris and France and delivered the sovereign pontiff, he would contribute according to his means to the construction in Paris of a sanctuary dedicated to the Sacred Heart'. He sought other adherents to this vow and soon had the ardent support of Hubert Rohault de Fleury.[4]

The terms of Legentil's vow did not, however, guarantee it a very warm reception, for, as he soon discovered, the provinces 'were then possessed of hateful sentiments towards Paris'. Such a state of affairs was not unusual and we can usefully divert for a moment to consider its basis.

Under the *ancien régime*, the French State apparatus had acquired a strongly centralized character which was consolidated under the French Revolution and Empire. This centralization thereafter became the basis of French political organization and gave Paris a peculiarly important role in relation to the rest of France. The administrative, economic, and cultural predominance of Paris was assured. But the events of 1789 also showed that Parisians had the power to make and break governments. They proved adept at using that power and were not loath, as a result, to regard themselves as privileged beings with a right and duty to foist all that they deemed 'progressive' upon a supposedly backward, conservative, and predominantly rural France. The Parisian bourgeois despised the narrowness of provincial life and found the peasant disgusting and incomprehensible.[5]

From the other end of the telescope, Paris was generally seen as a center of power, domination, and opportunity. It was both envied and hated. To the antagonism generated by the excessive centralization of power and authority in Paris were added all of the vaguer small-town and rural antagonisms towards any large city as a center of privilege, material success, moral decadence, vice, and social unrest. What was special in France was the way in which the tensions emanating from the 'urban–rural contradiction' were so intensely focused upon the relation between Paris and the rest of France.

Under the Second Empire these tensions sharpened considerably. Paris experienced a vast economic boom as the railways made it the hub of a process of national spatial integration. At the same time, falling transport costs and the free-trade policies signalled by the Anglo-French Treaties of Commerce in 1860 brought the city into a new relationship with an emerging global economy. Its share of an expanding French export trade increased dramatically, and its population grew rapidly, largely through a massive inmigration of rural laborers.[6] Concentration of wealth and power proceeded apace as Paris became the center of financial, speculative, and commercial operations. The contrasts between affluence and poverty became ever more startling and were increasingly expressed in terms of a geographical segregation between the 'bourgeois' quarters of the west and the working-class quarters of the north, east and south. Belleville became a foreign territory into which the bourgeois citizens of the west rarely dared to venture. The population of that place, which more than doubled between 1853 and 1870, was pictured in the bourgeois press as 'the dregs of the people' caught in 'the deepest depths of poverty and hatred' where 'ferments of envy, sloth and anger bubble without cease'.[7] The signs of social breakdown were everywhere. As the economic boom ran out of steam in the 1860s and as the authority of Empire began to fail, Paris became a cauldron of social unrest, a prey ripe for agitators of any stripe.

And to top it all, Haussmann, at the Emperor's urging, had set out to 'embellish Paris' with spacious boulevards, parks and gardens, monumental architecture of all sorts. The intent was to make Paris a truly imperial city, worthy not only of France but of Western civilization. Haussmann had done this at immense cost and by the slipperiest of financial means, a feat which scarcely recommended itself to the frugal provincial mind. The image of public opulence which Haussmann projected was only matched by the conspicuous consumption of a bourgeoisie, many of whom had grown rich speculating on the benefits of his improvements.[8]

Small wonder, then, that provincial and rural Catholics were in no frame of mind to dig into their pockets to embellish Paris with yet another monument, no matter how pious its purpose.

But there were even more specific objections which emerged in response to

Legentil's proposal. The Parisians had with their customary presumptuousness proclaimed a republic when provincial and rural sentiment was heavily infused with monarchism. Furthermore, those who had remained behind to face the rigors of the siege were showing themselves remarkably intransigent and bellicose, declaring they would favor a fight to the bitter end, when provincial sentiment showed a strong disposition to end the conflict with Prussia.

And then the rumors and hints of a new materialist politics among the working class in Paris, spiced with a variety of manifestations of revolutionary fervor, gave the impression that the city had, in the absence of its more respectable bourgeois citizenry, fallen prey to radical and even socialist philosophy. Since the only means of communication between a besieged Paris and the nonoccupied territories was pigeon or balloon, abundant opportunities arose for misunderstanding, which the rural foes of republicanism and the urban foes of monarchism were not beyond exploiting.

Legentil therefore found it politic to drop any specific mention of Paris in his vow. Even so, the vow gained adherents slowly. But towards the end of February, the Pope endorsed it and from then on the movement gathered some strength. And so on 19 March, a pamphlet appeared which set out the arguments for the vow at some length.[9] The spirit of the work had to be national, the authors urged, because the French people had to make national amend for what were national crimes. They confirmed their intention to build the monument in Paris. To the objection that the city should not be further 'embellished' they replied: 'were Paris reduced to cinders, we would still want to avow our national faults and to proclaim the justice of God on its ruins.'

The timing and phrasing of the pamphlet proved fortuitously prophetic. On 18 March, Parisians had taken their first irrevocable steps towards establishing self-government under the Commune. The real or imagined sins of the communards were subsequently to shock and outrage bourgeois opinion. And as much of Paris was indeed reduced to cinders in the course of a civil war of incredible ferocity, the notion of building a basilica of expiation upon these ashes became more and more appealing. As Rohault de Fleury noted, with evident satisfaction, 'in the months to come, the image of Paris reduced to cinders struck home many times'.[10] Let us rehearse a little of that history.

The origins of the Paris Commune lie in a whole series of events which ran into each other in complex ways. Precisely because of its political importance within the country, Paris had long been denied any representative form of municipal government and had been directly administered by the national government. For much of the nineteenth century, a predominantly republican Paris was chafing under the rule of monarchists (either Bourbon 'legitimists' or 'Orleanists') or authoritarian Bonapartists. The demand for a democratic form of municipal government was long-standing and commanded widespread support within the city.

The Government of National Defense set up on 4 September 1870 was neither radical nor revolutionary.[11] But it was republican. It also turned out to be timid and inept. It labored under certain difficulties, of course, but these were hardly sufficient to excuse its weak performance. It did not, for example, command the respect of the monarchists and lived in perpetual fear of the reactionaries of the right. When the Army of the East, under General Bazaine, capitulated to the Prussians at Metz on 27 October, the general left the impression that he did so because, being monarchist, he could not bring himself to fight for a republican government. Some of his officers who resisted the capitulation saw Bazaine putting his political preferences above the honor of France. This was a matter which was to dog French politics for several years. Rossel, who was later to command the armed forces of the Commune for a while, was one of the officers shocked to the core by Bazaine's evident lack of patriotism.[12]

But the tensions between the different factions of the ruling class were nothing compared to the real or imagined antagonisms between a traditional and remarkably obdurate bourgeoisie and a working class that was beginning to find its feet and assert itself. Rightly or wrongly, the bourgeoisie was greatly alarmed during the 1860s by the emergence of working-class organizations and political clubs, by the activities of the Paris branch of the International Working Men's Association, by the effervescence of thought within the working class and the spread of anarchist and socialist philosophies. And the working class – although by no means as well organized or as unified as their opponents feared – were certainly displaying abundant signs of an emergent class consciousness.

The Government of National Defense could not stem the tide of Prussian victories or break the siege of Paris without widespread working-class support. And the leaders of the left were only too willing to give it in spite of their initial opposition to the Emperor's war. Blanqui promised the Government 'energetic and absolute support' and even the International's leaders, having dutifully appealed to the German workers not to participate in a fratricidal struggle, plunged into organizing for the defense of Paris. Belleville, the center of working-class agitation, rallied spectacularly to the national cause, all in the name of the republic.[13]

The bourgeoisie sensed a trap. They saw themselves, wrote a contemporary commentator drawn from their ranks, caught between the Prussians and those whom they called 'the Reds'. 'I do not know,' he went on, 'which of these two evils terrified them most; they hated the foreigner but they feared the Bellevillois much more.'[14] No matter how much they wanted to defeat the foreigner, they could not bring themselves to do so with the batallions of the working class in the vanguard. For what was not to be the last time in French history, the bourgeoisie chose to capitulate to the Germans, leaving the left as the dominant force within a patriotic front. In 1871, fear of the 'enemy within' was to prevail over national pride.

The failure of the French to break the siege of Paris was first interpreted as the product of Prussian superiority and French military ineptitude. But as sortie after sortie promised victory only to be turned into disaster, honest patriots began to wonder if the powers that be were not playing tricks which bordered on betrayal and treason. The Government was increasingly viewed as a 'Government of National Defection'.[15]

The Government was equally reluctant to respond to the Parisian demand for municipal democracy. Since many of the respectable bourgeois had fled, it looked as if elections would deliver municipal power into the hands of the left. Given the suspicions of the monarchists of the right, the Government of National Defense felt it could not afford to concede what had long been demanded. And so it prevaricated endlessly.

As early as 31 October, these various threads came together to generate an insurrectionary movement in Paris. Shortly after Bazaine's ignominious surrender, word got out that the Government was negotiating the terms of an armistice with the Prussians. The population of Paris took to the streets and, as the feared Bellevillois descended *en masse*, took several members of the Government prisoner, agreeing to release them only on the verbal assurance that there would be municipal elections and no capitulation. This incident was guaranteed to raise the hackles of the right. It was the immediate cause of the 'hateful sentiments towards Paris' which Legentil encountered in December. The Government lived to fight another day. But, as events turned out, they were to fight much more effectively against the Bellevillois than they ever fought against the Prussians.

So the siege of Paris dragged on. Worsening conditions in the city now added their uncertain effects to a socially unstable situation. The Government proved inept and insensitive to the needs of the population and thereby added fuel to the smoldering fires of discontent.[16] The people lived off cats or dogs, while the more privileged partook of pieces of Pollux, the young elephant from the zoo (forty francs a pound for trunk). The price of rats – 'the taste is a cross between pork and partridge' – rose from sixty centimes to four francs a piece. The Government failed to take the elementary precaution of rationing bread until January, when it was much too late. Supplies dwindled and the adulteration of bread with bone meal became a chronic problem which was made even less palatable by the fact that it was human bones from the catacombs which were being dredged up for the occasion. While the common people were thus consuming their ancestors without knowing it, the luxuries of café life were kept going, supplied by hoarding merchants at exorbitant prices. The rich that stayed behind continued to indulge their pleasures according to their custom, although they paid much more dearly for it. The Government did nothing to curb profiteering or the continuation of conspicuous consumption by the rich in callous disregard for the feelings of the less privileged.

By the end of December, radical opposition to the Government of National Defense was growing. It led to the publication of the celebrated *affiche rouge* of 7 January. Signed by the central committee of the twenty Parisian *arrondissements*, it accused the Government of leading the country to the edge of an abyss by its indecision, inertia, and foot-dragging, suggested that the Government knew not how to administer or to fight, and insisted that the perpetuation of such a regime could end only in capitulation to the Prussians. It proclaimed a program for a general requisition of resources, rationing, and mass attack. It closed with the celebrated appeal: 'Make way for the people! Make way for the Commune!'[17]

Placarded all over Paris, the appeal had its effect. The military responded decisively and organized one last mass sortie which was spectacular for its military ineptitude and the carnage left behind. 'Everyone understood,' wrote Lissagaray, 'that they had been sent out to be sacrificed.'[18] The evidence of treason and betrayal was by now overwhelming for those close to the action. It pushed many an 'honest patriot' from the bourgeoisie, who put love of country above class interest, into an alliance with the dissident radicals and the working class.

Parisians accepted the inevitable armistice at the end of January with sullen passivity. It provided for national elections to a constituent assembly which would negotiate and ratify a peace agreement. It specified that the French Army lay down its arms but permitted the National Guard of Paris, which could not easily be disarmed, to remain a fighting force. Supplies came into a starving city under the watchful eye of the Prussian troops.

In the February elections, the city returned its quota of radical republicans. But rural and provincial France voted solidly for peace. Since the left was antagonistic to capitulation, the republicans from the Government of National Defense seriously compromised by their management of the war, and the Bonapartists discredited, the peace vote went to the monarchists. Republican Paris was appalled to find itself faced with a monarchist majority in the National Assembly. Thiers, by then seventy-three years old, was elected president in part because of his long experience in politics and in part because the monarchists did not want to be responsible for signing what was bound to be an ignoble peace agreement.

Thiers ceded Alsace and Lorraine to Germany and agreed to a huge war indemnity. He was enough of a patriot to resist Bismarck's suggestion that Prussian bankers float the loan required. Thiers reserved that privilege for the French and turned this year of troubles into one of the most profitable ones ever for the gentlemen of French high finance.[19] The latter informed Thiers that if he were to raise the money, he must first deal with 'those rascals in Paris'. This he was uniquely equipped to do. As Minister of the Interior under Louis Philippe, he had, in 1834, been responsible for the savage repression of one of the first genuine working-class movements in French history. Ever contemptuous of 'the vile multitude', he had long had a plan for dealing with them – a plan which he had proposed to Louis Philippe in 1848 and which he was now finally in a position to put into effect.[20] The plan was simple. He would use the conservativism of the country to smash the radicalism of the city.

On the morning of 18 March, the population of Paris awoke to find that the remnants of the French Army had been sent to Paris to relieve that city of its cannons in what was obviously a first step toward the disarmament of a populace which had, since 4 September, joined the National Guard in massive numbers (Figures 1.2 and 1.3). The populace of working-class Paris set out spontaneously to reclaim the cannon as their own. On the hill on Montmartre, weary French soldiers stood guard over the powerful battery of cannons assembled there, facing an increasingly restive and angry crowd. General Lecomte ordered his troops to fire. He ordered once, twice, thrice. The

Fig. 1.2 The hillside of Montmartre on the eve of 18 March 1871

Fig. 1.3 Members of the Parisian National Guard with one of the famous cannons of Montmartre

soldiers had not the heart to do it, raised their rifle butts in the air, and fraternized joyfully with the crowd. An infuriated mob took General Lecomte prisoner. They stumbled across General Thomas, remembered and hated for his role in the savage killings of the June days of 1848. The two generals were taken to the garden of No. 6, rue des Rosiers, and, amid considerable confusion and angry argument, put up against a wall and shot.

This incident is of crucial importance to our story. The conservatives now had their martyrs. Thiers could brand the insubordinate population of Paris as murderers and assassins. But the hilltop of Montmartre had been a place of martyrdom for Christian saints long before. To these could now be added the names of Lecomte and Clement Thomas. In the months and years to come, as the struggle to build the Basilica of Sacré-Coeur unfolded, frequent appeal was to be made to the need to commemorate these 'martyrs of yesterday who died in order to defend and save Christian society'.[21] On that 16th day of June in 1875 when the foundation stone was laid, Rohault de Fleury rejoiced that the Basilica was to be built on a site which, 'after having been such a saintly place had become, it would seem, the place chosen by Satan and where was accomplished the first act of that horrible saturnalia which caused so much ruination and which gave the Church two such glorious martyrs'. 'Yes,' he continued, 'it is here where Sacré-Coeur will be raised up that the Commune began, here where Generals Clement Thomas and Lecomte were assassinated.' He rejoiced in the 'multitude of good Christians who now stood adoring a God who knows only too well how to confound the evil-minded, cast down their designs and to place a cradle where they thought to dig a grave'. He contrasted this multitude of the faithful with a 'hillside, lined with intoxicated demons, inhabited by a population apparently hostile to all religious ideas and animated, above all, by a hatred of the Church'.[22] GALLIA POENITENS.

Thiers's response to the events of 18 March was to order a complete withdrawal of military and government personnel from Paris. From the safe distance of Versailles, he prepared methodically for the invasion and reduction of Paris. Bismarck proved not at all reluctant to allow the reconstitution of a French Army sufficient to the task of putting down the radicals in Paris, and released prisoners and material for that purpose.

Left to their own devices, and somewhat surprised by the turn of events, the Parisians, under the leadership of the Central Committee of the National Guard, arranged for elections on 26 March. The Commune was declared a political fact on 28 March. It was a day of joyous celebration for the common people of Paris and a day of consternation for the bourgeoisie.

The politics of the Commune were hardly coherent. While a substantial number of workers took their place as elected representatives of the people for the first time in French history, the Commune was still dominated by radical elements from the bourgeoisie. Comprising as it did diverse political currents shading from middle of the road republican, through the Jacobins, the Proudhonists, the socialists of the International, and the Blanquist revolutionaries, there was a good deal of factionalism and plenty of contentious argumentation as to what radical or socialist path to take. Much of this proved moot, however, since Thiers attacked in early April and the second siege of Paris began. Rural France was being put to work to destroy working-class Paris.

What followed was disastrous for the Commune. When the Versailles forces finally broke through the outer defenses of Paris – which Thiers had had constructed in the 1840s – they swept quickly through the bourgeois sections of western Paris and cut slowly and ruthlessly down the grand boulevards that Haussmann had constructed into the working-class quarters of the city. So began one of the most vicious bloodlettings in an often bloody French history. The Versailles forces gave no quarter. To the deaths in the street fighting, which were not, by most accounts, too extensive, were added an incredible number of arbitrary executions without judgement. The Luxembourg Gardens, the barracks at Lobau, the celebrated and still venerated wall in the cemetery of Père Lachaise, echoed ceaselessly to the sound of gunfire as the executioners went to work. Between twenty and thirty thousand communards died thus.[23] GALLIA POENITENS – with a vengeance (Figures 1.4 and 1.5).

Out of this sad history there is one incident which commands our attention. On the morning of 28 May, an exhausted Eugène Varlin – bookbinder, union and food cooperative organizer under the Second Empire, member of the National Guard, intelligent, respected and scrupulously honest, committed socialist, and brave soldier – was recognized and arrested. He was taken to that same house on rue des Rosiers where Lecomte and Clement Thomas died. Varlin's fate was worse. Paraded around the hillside of Montmartre, some say for 10 minutes and others for hours, abused, beaten, and humiliated by a fickle mob, he was finally propped up against a wall and shot. He was just thirty-two years old. They had to shoot twice to kill him. In between fusillades he cried, evidently unrepentant, 'Vive la Commune!' His biographer called it 'the calvary of Eugène Varlin'. The left can have its martyrs too. And it is on that spot that Sacré-Coeur is built.[24]

The 'bloody week', as it was called, also involved an enormous destruction of property. Paris burned. To the buildings set afire in the course of the bombardment were added those deliberately fired for strategic reasons by the retreating communards – from whence arose the myth of the 'incendiaries' of the Commune who recklessly took revenge, it was said, by burning everything they could. The communards, to be sure, were not enamored of the privileges of private property and were not averse to destroying hated symbols. The Vendôme Column – which Napoleon III had doted upon – was, after all, toppled in a grand ceremony to symbolize the end of authoritarian rule. The painter Courbet was later held responsible for this act and condemned to pay for the reconstruction of the monument out of his own pocket. The communards also decreed, but never carried out, the destruction of the Chapel of Expiation by which Louis XVIII had sought to impress upon Parisians their guilt in executing his brother. And when Thiers had shown his true colors, the communards took a certain delight in dismantling his Paris residence, stone by stone, in a symbolic gesture which de Goncourt

Fig. 1.4 Gouache by Alfred Darjon of the executions at the Mur des Fédérés in Père Lachaise cemetery (Musée Carnavelet)

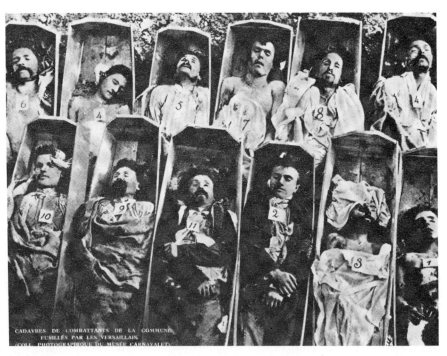

CADAVRES DE COMBATTANTS DE LA COMMUNE
FUSILLÉS PAR LES VERSAILLAIS.
(COLL. PHOTOGRAPHIQUE DU MUSÉE CARNAVALET)

Fig. 1.5 Bodies of communards shot by the Versailles troops, May 1871 (Musée Carnavelet)

felt had an 'excellent bad effect'.[25] But the wholesale burning of Paris was another matter entirely (Figures 1.6 and 1.7).

No matter what the truth of the matter, the myth of the incendiaries was strong. Within a year, the Pope himself was describing the communards as 'devils risen up from hell bringing the fires of the inferno to the streets of Paris'.[26]

The ashes of the city became a symbol of the Commune's crimes against the Church and were to fertilize the soil from which the energy to build Sacré-Coeur was to spring. No wonder that Rohault de Fleury congratulated himself upon that felicitous choice of words; 'were Paris to be reduced to cinders . . .'. That phrase could strike home with redoubled force, he noted, 'as the incendiaries of the Commune came to terrorize the world'.[27]

The aftermath of the Commune was anything but pleasant. The bloodletting began to turn the stomachs of the bourgeoisie until all but the most sadistic of them had to cry 'stop!' The celebrated diarist, Edmond de Goncourt, tried to convince himself of the justice of it all when he wrote:[28]

> It is good that there was neither conciliation nor bargain. The solution was brutal. It was by pure force. The solution has held people back from cowardly compromises . . . the bloodletting was a bleeding white; such a purge, by killing off the combative part of the population defers the next revolution by a whole generation. The old society has twenty years of quiet ahead of it, if the powers that be dare all that they may dare at this time.

These sentiments were exactly those of Thiers. But when de Goncourt passed through Belleville and saw the 'faces of ugly silence', he could not help but feel that here was a 'vanquished but unsubjugated district'. Was there no other way to purge the threat of revolution?

The experiences of 1870–71, when taken together with the confrontation between Napoleon III and the Pope and the decadent 'festive materialism' of the Second Empire, plunged Catholics into a phase of widespread soul-searching. The majority of them accepted the notion that France had sinned and this gave rise to manifestations of expiation and a movement of piety that was both mystical and spectacular.[29] The intransigent and ultramontane Catholics unquestionably favored a return to 'law and order' and a political solution founded on respect for authority. And it was the monarchists, generally themselves intransigent Catholics, who held out the promise for that law and order. Liberal Catholics found all of this disturbing and distasteful, but they were in no position to mobilize their forces – even the Pope described them as the 'veritable scourge' of France. There was little to stop the consolidation of the bond between monarchism and intransigent Catholicism. And it was such a powerful alliance that was to guarantee the building of Sacré-Coeur.

The immediate problem for the progenitors of the vow was, however, to operationalize a pious wish. This required official action. Legentil and Rohault de Fleury sought the support of the newly appointed Archbishop of Paris.

Mgr. Guibert, a compatriot of Thiers from Tours, had required some persuading to take the position in Paris. The three previous archbishops had

Fig. 1.6 View of Paris burning from above the Père Lachaise cemetery

Fig. 1.7 The toppling of the Vendôme Column by the communards

suffered violent deaths: the first during the insurrection of 1848, the second by the hand of an assassin in 1863, and the third during the Commune. The communards had early decided to take hostages in response to the butchery promised by Versailles. The Archbishop was held as a prime hostage for whom the communards sought the exchange of Blanqui. Thiers refused that negotiation, apparently having decided that a dead and martyred archbishop (who was a liberal Catholic in any case) was more valuable to him than a live one exchanged against a dynamic and aggressive Blanqui. During the 'bloody week,' the communards took whatever vengeance they could. On 24 May, the Archbishop was shot. In that final week, seventy-four hostages were shot, of whom twenty-four were priests. That awesome anticlericalism was as alive under the Commune as it had been in 1789. But with the massive purge which left more than twenty thousand communards dead, nearly forty thousand were held prisoner and countless others fled, Thiers could write reassuringly on 14 June to Mgr. Guibert: 'the "reds", totally vanquished, will not recommence their activities tomorrow; one does not engage twice in fifty years in such an immense fight as they have just lost'.[30] Reassured, Mgr. Guibert came to Paris.

The new archbishop was much impressed with the movement to build a monument to the Sacred Heart. On 18 January, 1872, he formally accepted responsibility for the undertaking. He wrote to Legentil and Rohault de Fleury thus:[31]

> You have considered from their true perspective the ills of our country . . . The conspiracy against God and Christ has prevailed in a multitude of hearts and in punishment for an almost universal apostasy, society has been subjected to all the horrors of war with a victorious foreigner and an even more horrible war amongst the children of the same country. Having become, by our prevarication, rebels against heaven, we have fallen during our troubles into the abyss of anarchy. The land of France presents the terrifying image of a place where no order prevails, while the future offers still more terrors to come . . . This temple, erected as a public act of contrition and reparation . . . will stand amongst us as a protest against other monuments and works of art erected for the glorification of vice and impiety.

By July 1872, an ultraconservative Pope Pius IX, still awaiting his deliverance from captivity in the Vatican, formally endorsed the vow. An immense propaganda campaign unfolded and the movement gathered momentum. By the end of the year, more than a million francs was promised and all that remained was to translate the vow into its material, physical representation.

The first step was to choose a site. Legentil wanted to use the foundations of the still-to-be-completed Opera, which he considered 'a scandalous monument of extravagance, indecency and bad taste'.[32] Rohault de Fleury's initial design of that building had, in 1860, been dropped at the insistence of Count Walewski ('who had the dubious distinction of being the illegitimate son of Napoleon I and the husband of Napoleon III's current favorite').[33] The design that replaced it (which exists today) most definitely qualified in the eyes of Legentil as a 'monument to vice and impiety' and nothing could be more appropriate than to efface the memory of Empire by constructing the Basilica on that spot. It probably escaped Legentil's attention that the communards had, in the same spirit, toppled the Vendôme column.

By late October 1872, however, the Archbishop had taken matters into his own hands and selected the heights of Montmartre because it was only from there that the symbolic domination of Paris could be assured. Since the land on that site was in part public property, the consent or active support of the Government was necessary if it was to be acquired. The Government was considering the construction of a military fortress on that spot. The Archbishop pointed out, however, that a military fortress could well be very unpopular while a fortification of the sort he was proposing might be less offensive and more sure. Thiers and his ministers, apparently persuaded that ideological protection might be preferable to military, encouraged the Archbishop to pursue the matter formally. This the latter did in a letter of 5 March 1873.[34] He requested that the Government pass a special law declaring the construction of the Basilica a work of public utility. This would permit the laws of expropriation to be used to procure the site.

Such a law ran counter to a long-standing sentiment in favor of the separation of Church and State. Yet conservative Catholic sentiment for the project was very strong. Thiers prevaricated. But his indecision was shortly rendered moot. The monarchists had decided that their time had come. On 24 May, they drove Thiers from power and replaced him with the archconservative royalist, Marshall Mac-Mahon, who, just two years before, had led the armed forces of Versailles in the bloody repression of the Commune. France was plunged, once more, into political ferment – a monarchist restoration seemed imminent.

The Mac-Mahon Government quickly reported out the law which then became part of its program to establish the rule of moral order in which those of wealth and privilege – who therefore had an active stake in the preservation of society – would, under the leadership of the King and in alliance with the authority of the Church, have both the right and duty to protect France from the social perils to which it had recently been exposed and thereby prevent the country falling into the abyss of anarchy. Large-scale demonstrations were mobilized by the Church as part of a campaign to reestablish some sense of moral order. The largest of these demonstrations took place on 29 June 1873 at Paray-le-Monial. Thirty thousand pilgrims, including fifty members of the National Assembly, journeyed there to dedicate themselves publicly to the Sacred Heart.[35]

It was in this atmosphere that the Committee formed to report on the law presented its findings on 11 July to the National Assembly, a quarter of whose members were adherents to the vow. The Committee found that the proposal to build a basilica of expiation was unquestionably a work of public utility. It was right and proper to build such a monument on the heights of Montmartre for all to see, because it was there that the blood of martyrs – including those of yesterday – had flowed. It was necessary 'to efface by this work of expiation, the crimes which have crowned our sorrows' and France, 'which has suffered so much', must 'call upon the protection and grace of Him who gives according to His will, defeat or victory'.[36]

The debate which followed on 22 and 23 July in part revolved around technical–legal questions and the implications of the legislation for State–Church relations. The intransigent Catholics recklessly proposed to go much further. They wanted the Assembly to commit itself formally to a national undertaking which 'was not solely a protestation against the taking up of arms by the Commune, but a sign of appeasement and concord'. That amendment was rejected. But the law passed with a handsome majority of 244 votes.

A loan dissenting voice in the debate came from a radical, republican deputy from Paris:[37]

> When you think to establish on the commanding heights of Paris – the fount of free thought and revolution – a Catholic monument, what is in your thoughts? To make of it the triumph of the Church over revolution. Yes, that is what you want to extinguish – what you call the pestilence of revolution. What you want to revive is the Catholic faith, for you are at war with the spirit of modern times. . . . Well, I who know the sentiments of the population of Paris, I who am tainted by the revolutionary pestilence like them, I tell you that the population will be more scandalized than edified by the ostentation of your faith. . . . Far from edifying us, you push us towards free thought, towards revolution. When people see these manifestations of the partisans of monarchy, of the enemies of the Revolution, they will say to themselves that Catholicism and monarchy are unified, and in rejecting one they will reject the other.

Armed with a law which yielded powers of expropriation, the Committee formed to push the project through to fruition acquired the site atop the Butte Montmartre. They collected up the moneys promised and set about soliciting more so that the building could be as grand as the thought that lay behind it. A competition for the design of the Basilica was set and judged. The building had to be imposing, consistent with Christian tradition, yet quite distinct from the 'monuments to vice and impiety' built in the course of the Second Empire. Out of the seventy-eight designs submitted and exhibited to the public, that of the architect Abadie was selected. The grandeur of its domes, the purity of the white marble, and the unadorned simplicity of its detail impressed the Committee – what, after all, could be more different from the flamboyance of that awful Opera House?

By the spring of 1875, all was ready for putting the first stone in place. But radical and republican Paris was not, apparently, repentant enough even yet. The Archbishop complained that the building of Sacré-Coeur was being treated as a provocative act, as an attempt to inter the principles of 1789. And while, he said, he would not pray to revive those principles if they happened to get dead and buried, this view of things was giving rise to a deplorable polemic in which the Archbishop found himself forced to participate. He issued a circular in which he expressed his astonishment at the hostility expressed towards the project on the part of 'the enemies of religion'. He found it intolerable that people dared to put a political interpretation upon thoughts derived only out of faith and piety. Politics, he assured his readers, 'had been far, far from our inspirations; the work had been inspired, on the contrary, by a profound conviction that politics was powerless to deal with the ills of the country. The causes of these ills are moral and religious and the remedies must be of the same order'. Besides, he went on, the work could not be construed as political because the aim of politics is to divide 'while our work has for its goal the union of all. . . . Social pacification is the end point of the work we are seeking to realize'.[38]

The Government, now clearly on the defensive, grew extremely nervous at the prospect of a grand opening ceremony which could be the occasion for an ugly confrontation. It counselled caution. The Committee had to find a way to lay the first stone without being too provocative. The Pope came to their aid and declared a day of dedication to the Sacred Heart for all Catholics everywhere. Behind that shelter, a much scaled-down ceremony to lay the first stone passed off without incident. The construction was now under way. GALLIA POENITENS was taking shape in material symbolic form.

The forty years between the laying of the foundation stone and the final consecration of the Basilica in 1919 were often troubled ones. Technical difficulties arose in the course of putting such a large structure on a hilltop rendered unstable by years of mining for gypsum. The cost of the structure increased dramatically and as enthusiasm for the cult of the Sacred Heart diminished somewhat, financial difficulties ensued. And the political controversy continued.

The Committee in charge of the project had early decided upon a variety of stratagems to encourage the flow of contributions. Individuals and families could purchase a stone, and the visitor to Sacré-Coeur will see the names of many such inscribed upon the stones there. Different regions and organizations were encouraged to subscribe towards the construction of particular chapels. Members of the National Assembly, the army, the clergy and the like all pooled their efforts in this way. Each particular chapel has its own significance.

Among the chapels in the crypt, for example, the visitor will find that of Jésus-Enseignant, which recalls, as Rohault de Fleury put it, 'that one of the chief sins of France was the foolish invention of schooling without God'.[39] Those who were on the losing side of the fierce battle to preserve the power of the Church over education after 1871 put their money here. And next to that chapel, at the far end of the crypt, close to the line where the rue des Rosiers used to run, stands the chapel to Jésus-Ouvrier.

That Catholic workers sought to contribute to the building of their own chapel was a matter for great rejoicing. It showed, wrote Legentil, the desire of workers 'to protest against the fearsome impiety into which a large part of the working class is falling' as well as their determination to resist 'the impious and truly infernal association which, in nearly all of Europe, makes of it its slave and victim'.[40] The reference to the International Working Men's Association is unmistakable and understandable since it was customary in bourgeois circles at that time to attribute the Commune, quite erroneously, to the nefarious influence of that 'infernal' association. Yet, by a strange quirk of fate, which so often gives an ironic twist to history, the chapel to Jésus-Ouvrier stands almost exactly at the spot where ran the course of the 'calvary of Eugène Varlin'. Thus it is that the Basilica, erected on high in part to commemorate the blood of two recent martyrs of the right, commemorates unwittingly in its subterranean depths a martyr of the left.

Legentil's interpretation of all of this was in fact somewhat awry. In the closing stages of the Commune, a young Catholic named Alfred de Munn watched in dismay as the communards were led away to slaughter. Shocked, he fell to wondering what 'legally constituted society had done for these people' and concluded that their ills had in large measure been visited upon them through the indifference of the affluent classes. In the spring of 1872, he went into the heart of hated Belleville and set up the first of his *Cercles-Ouvriers*.[41] This signaled the beginnings of a new kind of Catholicism in France – one which sought through social action to attend to the material as well as the spiritual needs of the workers. It was through organizations such as this, a far cry from the intransigent ultramontane Catholicism that ruled at the center of the movement for the Sacred Heart, that a small trickle of worker contributions began to flow towards the construction of a Basilica on the hilltop of Montmartre.

The political difficulties mounted, however. France, finally armed with a republican constitution (largely because of the intransigence of the monarchists) was now in the grip of a modernization process fostered by easier communications, mass education, and industrial development. The country moved to accept the moderate form of republicanism and became bitterly disillusioned with the backward-looking monarchism that had dominated the National Assembly elected in 1871. In Paris the 'unsubjugated' Bellevillois, and their neighbors in Montmartre and La Villette, began to reassert themselves rather more rapidly than Thiers had anticipated. As the demand for amnesty for the exiled communards became stronger in these quarters, so did the hatred of the Basilica rising in their midst. The agitation against the project mounted.

On 3 August 1880, the matter came before the city council in the form of a proposal: a 'colossal statue of *Liberty* will be placed on the summit of Montmartre, in front of the church of Sacré-Coeur, on land belonging to the city of Paris'. The French republicans at that time had adopted the United States as a model society which functioned perfectly well without monarchism and other feudal trappings. As part of a campaign to drive home the point of this example, as well as to symbolize their own deep attachment to the principles of liberty, republicanism and democracy, they were then raising funds to donate the Statue of Liberty that now stands in New York Harbor (Figure 1.8). Why not, said the authors of this proposition, efface the sight of the hated Sacré-Coeur by a monument of similar order?[42]

No matter what the claims to the contrary, they said, the Basilica symbolized the intolerance and fanaticism of the right – it was an insult to civilization, antagonistic to the principles of modern times, an evocation of the past, and a stigma upon France as a whole. Parisians, seemingly bent on demonstrating their unrepentant attachment to the principles of 1789, were determined to efface what they felt was an expression of 'Catholic fanaticism' by building exactly that kind of monument which the Archbishop had previously characterized as a 'glorification of vice and impiety'.

By 7 October the city council had changed its tactics. Calling the Basilica 'an

Fig. 1.8 The Statue of Liberty stands in its Paris workshop preparatory to its shipment to the United States. It was just such a statue that the Paris Council wished to erect in front of the Basilica of Sacré-Coeur

incessant provocation to civil war', the members decided by a majority of sixty-one to three to request the Government to 'rescind the law of public utility of 1873' and to use the land, which would revert to public ownership, for the construction of a work of truly national significance. Neatly sidestepping the problem of how those who had contributed to the construction of the Basilica – which had hardly yet risen above its foundations – were to be indemnified, it passed along its proposal to the Government. By the summer of 1882, the request was taken up in the Chamber of Deputies.

Archbishop Guibert had, once more, to take to the public defense of the work. He challenged what by now were familiar arguments against the Basilica with familiar responses. He insisted that the work was inspired not by politics but by Christian and patriotic sentiments. To those who objected to the expiatory character of the work he simply replied that no one can ever afford to regard their country as infallible. As to the appropriateness of the cult of the Sacred Heart, he felt only those within the Church had the right to judge. To those who portrayed the Basilica as a provocation to civil war he replied: 'Are civil wars and riots ever the product of our Christian temples? Are those who frequent our churches ever prone to excitations and revolts against the law? Do we find such people in the midst of disorders and violence which, from time to time, trouble the streets of our cities?' He went on to point out that while Napoleon I had sought to build a temple of peace at Montmartre, 'it is we who are building, at last, the true temple of peace'.[43]

He then considered the negative effects of stopping the construction. Such an action would profoundly wound Christian sentiment and prove divisive. It would surely be a bad precedent, he said (blithely ignoring the precedent set by the law of 1873 itself), if religious undertakings of this sort were to be subject to the political whims of the government of the day. And then there was the complex problem of compensation not only for the contributors but for the work already done. Finally, he appealed to the fact that the work was giving employment to six hundred families: to deprive 'that part of Paris of such a major source of employment would be inhuman indeed'.

The Parisian representatives in the Chamber of Deputies which, by 1882, was dominated by reformist republicans such as Gambetta (from Belleville) and Clemenceau (from Montmartre) were not impressed by these arguments. The debate was heated and passionate. The Government for its part declared itself unalterably opposed to the law of 1873, but was equally opposed to rescinding the law since this would entail paying out more than twelve million francs in indemnities to the Church. In an effort to defuse the evident anger from the left, the Minister went on to remark that by rescinding the law, the Archbishop would be relieved of the obligation to complete what was proving to be a most arduous undertaking at the same time as it would provide the Church with millions of francs to pursue works of propaganda which might be 'infinitely more efficacious than that to which the sponsors of the present motion are objecting'.

The radical republicans were not about to regard Sacré-Coeur in the shape of a white elephant, however. Nor were they inclined to pay compensation. They were determined to do away with what they felt was an 'odious' manifestation of pious clericalism and to put in its place a monument to liberty of thought. They put the blame for the civil war squarely on the shoulders of the monarchists and their intransigent Catholic allies.

Clemenceau rose to state the radical case. He declared the law of 1873 an insult, an act of a National Assembly which had sought to impose the cult of the Sacred Heart on France because 'we fought and still continue to fight for human rights, for having made the French Revolution'. The law was the product of clerical reaction, an attempt to stigmatize revolutionary France, 'to condemn us to ask pardon of the Church for our ceaseless struggle to prevail over it in order to establish the principles of liberty, equality and fraternity'. We must, he declared, respond to a political act by a political act. Not to do so would be to leave France under the intolerable invocation of the Sacred Heart.[44]

With impassioned oratory such as this, Clemenceau fanned the flames of anticlerical sentiment. The Chamber voted to rescind the law of 1873 by a majority of 261 votes to 199. It appeared that the Basilica, the walls of which were as yet hardly risen above their foundations, was to come tumbling down.

The Basilica was saved by a technicality. The law was passed too late in the session to meet all the formal requirements for promulgation. The Government, genuinely fearful of the costs and liabilities involved, quietly worked to prevent the reintroduction of the motion into a Chamber which, in the next session, moved on to consider matters of much greater weight and moment. The Parisian republicans had gained a symbolic but Pyrrhic parliamentary victory. A relieved Archbishop pressed on with the work.

Yet somehow the matter would not die. In February 1897, the motion was re-introduced.[45] Anticlerical republicanism had by then made great progress, as had the working-class movement in the form of a vigorous and growing socialist party. But the construction atop the hill had likewise progressed. The interior of the Basilica had been inaugurated and opened for worship in 1891 and the great dome was well on the way to completion (the cross which surmounts it was formally blessed in 1899). Although the church was still viewed as a 'provocation to civil war', the prospect for dismantling such a vast work was by now quite daunting. And this time it was none other than Albert de Mun who defended the Basilica in the name of a Catholicism that had, by then, seen the virtue of separating its fate from that of a fading monarchist cause. The Church was beginning to learn a lesson and the cult of the Sacred Heart began to acquire a new meaning in response to a changing social situation. By 1899, a more reform-minded Pope dedicated the cult to the ideal of harmony among the races, social justice, and conciliation.

But the socialist deputies were not impressed by what they saw as manoeuvers of co-optation. They pressed home their case which would bring down the hated symbol, even though almost complete, and even though such an act would entail indemnifying eight million subscribers to the tune of thirty million francs. But the majority in Chamber blanched at such a prospect. The motion was rejected by 322 to 196.

This was to be the last time the building was threatened by official action. With the dome completed in 1899, attention switched to the building of the campanile, which was finally finished in 1912. By the spring of 1914, all was ready and the official consecration set for 17 October. But war with Germany intervened. Only at the end of that bloody conflict was the Basilica finally consecrated. A victorious France – led by the fiery oratory of Clemenceau – joyfully celebrated the consecration of a monument conceived of in the course of a losing war with Germany a generation before. GALLIA POENITENS at last brought its rewards.

Muted echoes of this tortured history can still be heard. In February 1971, for example, demonstrators pursued by police took refuge in the Basilica. Firmly entrenched there, they called upon their radical comrades to join them in occupying a church 'built upon the bodies of communards in order to efface the memory of that red flag that had for too long floated over Paris'. The myth of the incendiaries immediately broke loose from its ancient moorings and an evidently panicked rector summoned the police into the Basilica to prevent the conflagration. The 'Reds' were chased from the church amid scenes of great brutality. Thus was the centennial of the Paris Commune celebrated on that spot.[46]

And as a coda to that incident, a bomb exploded in the Basilica in 1976, causing quite extensive damage to one of the domes. On that day, it was said, the visitor to the cemetery of Père Lachaise would have seen a single red rose on August Blanqui's grave.

Rohault de Fleury had desperately wanted to 'place a cradle where [others] had thought to dig a grave'. But the visitor who looks at that mausoleum-like structure that is Sacré-Coeur might well wonder what it is that is interred there. The spirit of 1789? The sins of France? The alliance between intransigent

Catholicism and reactionary monarchism? The blood of martyrs like Lecomte and Clement Thomas? Or that of Eugène Varlin and the twenty thousand or so communards mercilessly slaughtered along with him?

The building hides its secrets in sepulchral silence. Only the living, cognizant of this history, who understand the principles of those who struggled for and against the 'embellishment' of that spot, can truly disinter the mysteries that lie entombed there and thereby rescue that rich experience from the deathly silence of the tomb and transform it into the noisy beginnings of the cradle.

All history is, after all, the history of class struggle.

Notes

1 R. P. Jonquet, *Montmartre, autrefois et aujourd'hui* (Paris: Dumoulin, no date).
2 Jonquet, op. cit. (note 1), provides considerable background on the cult. See also Adrien Dansette, *Histoire religieuse de la France contemporaine* (Paris: Flammarion, 1965).
3 Roger Price, *The economic modernization of France* (London: Croom Helm, 1975) and Fernand Braudel and Ernest Labrousse (eds), *Histoire économique et sociale de la France, tome III* (Paris: Presse Universitaire de France, 1976).
4 Hubert Rohault de Fleury, *Historique de la Basilique du Sacré-Coeur*, 3 vols, printed but not published (Paris: Bibliothèque Nationale, 1903, 1905, 1907).
5 Theodore Zeldin, *France, 1848–1945*, 2 vols (London: Oxford University Press, 1973 and 1977).
6 Jeanne Gaillard, *Paris, la ville, 1852–70* (Paris: Honoré Champion, 1977).
7 C. Lepidis and E. Jacomin, *Belleville* (Paris: Veynier, 1975).
8 David Pinkney, *Napoleon III and the rebuilding of Paris* (Princeton, NJ: Princeton University Press, 1958).
9 Rohault de Fleury, op. cit. (note 4), vol. 1, pp. 10–13.
10 Rohault de Fleury, op. cit. (note 4), vol. 1, pp. 10–13.
11 Henri Guillemin, *Cette curieuse guerre de 1870* (Paris: Gallimard, 1956).
12 Edith Thomas, *Rossel (1844–1871)* (Paris: Gallimard, 1967).
13 Prosper-Olivier Lissagaray, *Histoire de la Commune de 1871* (Paris: Maspero, 1976 edition).
14 Quoted in Jean Bruhat, Jean Dautry and Emile Tersen, *La Commune de 1871* (Paris: Editions Sociales, 1971), p. 75.
15 Marx uses this phrase to telling effect in his passionate defense of the Commune; Karl Marx, *The civil war in France* (New York: International Publishers, 1968 edition). The idea was widespread throughout Paris at that time; see Marcel Cerf, *Edouard Moreau* (Paris: Denoel, 1971).
16 Louis Lazare, *La France et Paris* (Paris: Etudes Historiques et Municipales, 1872) and George Becker (ed.), *Paris under siege, 1870–71; From the Goncourt Journal* (Ithaca, NY: Cornell University Press, 1969).
17 There is a voluminous literature on the Commune and an extensive bibliography is provided by Bruhat, Dautry and Tersen, op. cit. (note 14). A recent work in English is Stewart Edwards, *The Paris Commune* (Chicago: Quadrangle Books, 1971).
18 Lissagaray, op. cit. (note 13), p. 75.
19 Henri Guillemin, *L'avènement de M. Thiers et réflexions sur la Commune* (Paris: Gallimard, 1971), pp. 308–11; Bruhat, Dautry and Tersen, op. cit. (note 14), pp. 104–5; and R. Dreyfus, *Monsieur Thiers contre l'Empire, la guerre, la Commune* (Paris: Grasset, 1928), p. 266.

20 John Allison, *Monsieur Thiers* (New York: Norton, 1932), Chapter 9; and Guelle-min, op. cit. (note 19).

21 This phrase was actually used by the Committee of the National Assembly appointed to report on the proposed law which would make the Basilica a work of public utility. See Rohault de Fleury, op. cit. (note 4), vol. 1, p. 88.

22 Rohault de Fleury, op. cit. (note 4), vol. 1, p. 264.

23 See Bruhat, Dautry and Tersen, op. cit. (note 14), and the works they cite for full accounts of the Commune.

24 M. Foulon, *Eugène Varlin* (Clermont Ferrand: Editions Mont-Louis, 1934).

25 Becker, op. cit. (note 16), p. 288.

26 Dansette, op. cit. (note 2), p. 343.

27 Rohault de Fleury, op. cit. (note 4), vol. 1, p. 13.

28 Becker, op. cit. (note 16), p. 312.

29 Dansette, op. cit. (note 2), pp. 340–5.

30 Guillemin, op. cit. (note 19), pp. 295–6; and Rohault de Fleury, op. cit. (note 4), vol. 2, p. 365.

31 Rohault de Fleury, op. cit. (note 4), vol 1, p. 27.

32 Jonquet, op. cit. (note 1), pp. 85–7.

33 Pinkney, op. cit. (note 8), pp. 85–7.

34 Rohault de Fleury, op. cit. (note 4), vol. 1, p. 75.

35 Dansette, op. cit. (note 2), pp. 340–5.

36 Rohault de Fleury, op. cit. (note 4), vol. 1, p. 88.

37 Rohault de Fleury, op. cit. (note 4), vol. 1, p. 88.

38 Rohault de Fleury, op. cit. (note 4), vol. 1, p. 244.

39 Rohault de Fleury, op. cit. (note 4), vol. 1, p. 269.

40 Rohault de Fleury, op. cit. (note 4), vol. 1, p. 165.

41 Dansette, op. cit. (note 2), pp. 356–8; and Lepidis and Jacomin, op. cit. (note 7), pp. 271–2.

42 Ville de Paris, Conseil Municipal, Procès-Verbal, 3 August, 7 October and 2 December 1880 (Paris: Hôtel de Ville).

43 Rohault de Fleury, op. cit. (note 4), vol. 2, pp. 71–3.

44 Rohault de Fleury, op. cit. (note 4), vol. 2, pp. 71 et seq., gives the text of the debate.

45 Paul Lesourd, *Montmartre* (Paris: Editions France Empire, 1973), pp. 224–5.

46 Lesourd's account, op. cit. (note 45), pp. 239–45, is rather one-sided as evidenced by his erroneous insistence that no communards died on Montmartre.

---

2   Cindi Katz,

'Sow What You Know: The Struggle for Social Reproduction in Rural Sudan'

Excerpts from: *Annals of the Association of American Geographers* 81, 488–514 (1991)

A child is perched precariously atop a donkey laden with a sack of sorghum seeds, a digging stick, and a couple of hoes. She steadies herself and rides surely along the canals as the sun rises. It takes nearly an hour to reach her family's field. She and her brother and sister will spend the morning planting part of their family's farm tenancy in sorghum while their father clears the irrigation ditches nearby. Punctuating their work at irregular – and to their father annoying – intervals, this girl and her brother will set up a home-made net trap in an unsuccessful attempt to ensnare some of the birds that descend on the area during the rainy season. On other days they may succeed in trapping a dozen or more small birds which the boy will kill, following Islamic practice, and the children's mother or older sisters will cook for a family meal. School is out during the rains, mainly to allow teachers to return home from rural areas which become inaccessible and difficult to live in during this time. Partly by design, but mostly by coincidence, this schedule also allows all children, including students, to assist their households with the heavy burdens of agricultural work. As the children make their way to the fields, they cross paths with a number of herdboys leading flocks of small animals out to pastures just turning green with the arrival of the rains.

The survival of agricultural production systems over time turns, at least in part, on what children learn about the natural environment, and how they use this knowledge and its attendant skills during their childhood and as they come of age. This narrative drawn from a year of geographic field research in rural Sudan suggests both the importance of and the variation in children's environmental interactions in an agrarian community. What children learn about the environment and how they use this knowledge in their work and play are fundamental cultural forms and practices, shared in a social matrix and bearing a specific relationship to the prevailing social relations of production and reproduction in the area. Inherent in them are the contradictory possibilities of replication, reformulation, and resistance. While this contradictory relationship is increasingly recognized in social theory, there have been few studies in any field and almost none in geography that examine its possibilities and practices on the ground.[1] This piece invokes one such investigation to argue that the cultural forms and practices of social reproduction, such as those which were its focus – the production, exchange, and use of environmental knowledge – have the potential to disrupt, subvert and even reconstitute the accumulation of capital and its attendant social relations of production.

In an agriculturally based economy, learning about the environment – about farming, animal husbandry, and the use of local resources – is an aspect of socialization essential to maintaining and reproducing society. Moreover . . . children's work often is fundamental to the daily maintenance of their households, and thus the community as a whole. My study approached the question of children's environmental interactions as central not only to the activities of production but as fundamental to the daily reproduction of their households, and their environmental learning and knowledge as crucial to the long-term maintenance of the socioeconomic system itself.

My research on these questions enabled me to examine the entwined processes of socioeconomic transition and cultural–ecological change from a perspective little addressed in the development literature in geography, sociology, anthropology, or economics, and to cast new light on the practical response of Third World populations experiencing pronounced shifts in the nature of their articulation with the relations of capitalist production. This study links the human-environment tradition in geography, and in particular its concern with how people come to know the environment and act to transform it, with the larger project of cultural studies which seeks to understand the connections between particular aspects of culture, such as art, ideology, consciousness, dreams and fantasies, literature, knowledge, and everyday life, and social and economic structures and practices (e.g. Thompson, 1963; Gramsci, 1971; Genovese, 1972; Aronowitz, 1973; Bourdieu, 1977; Williams, 1977; Willis, 1977; Said, 1978; Johnson, 1979; Samuel and Jones, 1982; de Certeau, 1984; Spivak, 1987). Its central argument is that under circumstances of socioeconomic transformation, what children learn about the environment and how they acquire and use that knowledge can have contradictory effects not only upon the children as they come of age but on the outcome of the social change itself.

In recent years geographers have addressed the complex relationships between human agency and the social and economic structures of society. Their work represents an admirable effort to enrich our understanding of the central problematics of human geography – spatial relationships, the making of place and human–environment relations – by articulating rigorous historical analyses of socioeconomic, spatial, and political structures, and the means by which people create, transform, and respond to them (e.g. Gregory, 1982; Christopherson, 1983; Thrift, 1983; Watts, 1983; Clark and Dear, 1984; Pred, 1984a, b; Smith, 1984; Gregory and Urry, 1985; Warf, 1988; Harvey, 1989, 1990; Soja, 1989). It is difficult, however, to move analytically between structure and substance, and most studies end up concentrating on socioeconomic and political structures without any real analysis or understanding of the practical activities of the people who create and are constituted by these structures. Alternatively, they focus on human behavior and consciousness without locating these in a mutually determining sociospatial and political–economic field. All too often, people are recognized as 'making their own history', but this history is rather thin and pale, a narrative of socioeconomic change that points to but glosses over the material social practices of everyday life to focus only on their temporal and spatial outcomes. Equally problematic, the fact is elided that people do not make their own history out of circumstances of their own choosing, and the material social practices of everyday life are presented as if unbounded by any social or economic structures. In this way, history and geography become voluntaristic free-for-alls.

These are political decisions and omissions. Part of the problem is that few of the analyses claiming to address structure and agency empirically are grounded in theory that can analyze or explain the mutual determinations between the two and their material outcomes over time and space. Moreover, few of these studies draw even partially on an ethnographic approach to address the multiplicity of forms and practices that constitute social activity. We are often left with only the traces of human action that are measurable and lose the texts and textures of that action.

Serious consideration of feminist theory and research over the past two decades would improve this work substantially. Although it is not clear from reading geographic work in what has come to be known as the structurationist school, much of the ground linking human agency to social and economic structure was broken by feminist theorists who turned to 'everyday life' to find subversive power in the voices that had been systematically excluded from history (e.g. Dalla Costa, 1972, 1977; Caulfield, 1974; Ehrenreich and English, 1975; James, 1975; Conference of Socialist Economists, 1977; 'Development and the sexual division of labor', 1981; Moraga and Anzaldua, 1981; Sargent, 1981).[2] In addition to its influence on the direction of research in social science, feminist theory is at the root of much poststructuralist literary theory which analyzes texts as, *inter alia*, expressions of socioeconomic and political struggle (e.g. de Lauretis, 1982; Haraway, 1984; Spivak, 1987). In broadly defining the 'text' and analyzing it against the grain of sociocultural and political–economic structuring, this work, though rarely acknowledged by geographers, is at the root of the social science project linking agency and structure.

As a geographer, I sought as part of my project in Sudan to address a single place – the village of Howa – at a particular historical moment – ten years after its incorporation in a state-sponsored capitalist agricultural project – as one such 'text', constituting at once the ground (literally) for a particular set of material social practices and a repository which expressed in material form the outcomes of these practices. These were understood as mutually constituting. The scale was local, the historical subjects small, but the material social practices associated with their acquisition and use of environmental knowledge are articulated fundamentally with the profound socioeconomic and cultural–ecological changes under way there and in the rest of Sudan. In addressing these, my intent was to analyze theoretically and practically the relationship between the social relations of production and social reproduction under conditions of socioeconomic transformation.

Background

During 1980–81 I conducted a year-long ethnographic study in a farming village I call Howa in central eastern Sudan. My study focused primarily upon the environmental learning, knowledge, and interactions of ten-year-old children addressed in relation to household production and the reproduction of the social relations of production. I chose to undertake this study in an area undergoing profound socioeconomic change in an attempt to locate instances of contestation between the reproduction of what Bernstein (1982, after Marx, 1967, vol. 3) calls the natural economy and the reproduction of capitalist relations of production.[3] The latter had been imposed on the area most decisively by incorporation in the government-sponsored Suki Agricultural

Development Project in 1971, ten years prior to my study and the year the children who are its focus were born.

Study site

Howa, a village on the banks of the ephemeral Dinder River east of Sennar in central eastern Sudan (Figure 2.1), was settled in the late nineteenth century by pastoralists. Until 1971, its people cultivated sorghum on a subsistence basis, supplemented by sesame which they sold to passing traders in order to meet their limited needs for cash. Animals were an important source of subsistence and savings for the population. According to local residents and historical accounts of the area, most families kept at least a few goats and sheep for milk and occasional meat, and many households kept some cattle or camels along with flocks of ten to fifty small animals (Tothill, 1948; al Tayib, 1970; Ahmad, 1974; O'Brien, 1978; Gruenbaum, 1979; Duffield, 1981). Many families maintained close ties with relatives who remained exclusively pastoralist, not only having their herds travel with the pastoralists for part of the year, but renewing and maintaining familial relations by intermarriage.

During the 1950s the village was further integrated with the national cash economy through the private cotton schemes along the Blue Nile approximately fifty kilometers away. Men from the village worked as agricultural wage laborers and a few managed to become tenants in these private pump schemes. These tenants apparently began to accumulate capital when cotton fetched record prices during the 1950s and early 1960s. Apart from involvement in these schemes, most of the population of Howa remained subsistence cultivators until 1971.

That year, Howa was incorporated in the State-sponsored Suki Agricultural Development Project. Not only was the basis of the socioeconomic formation

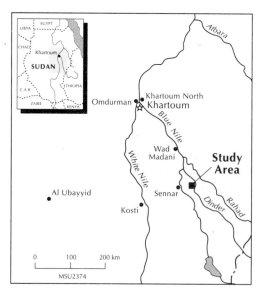

Fig. 2.1   Sudan, showing provincial boundaries, main rivers and location of study site (courtesy of the author)

of Howa altered from the subsistence production of food crops to the irrigated cultivation of cotton and groundnuts as cash crops, but, more importantly, local control over production and reproduction was undermined and the relation between them interrupted (cf. Barnett, 1975, 1977; Duffield, 1981 for other examples in Sudan). Under the Project, agents of State capitalism – the project authorities – determined not only which crops would be grown by tenants, but also the production schedules and acceptable agricultural tools and practices for their cultivation. The peasant farmers of Howa actively resisted each of these externally imposed changes on their farming practices.

At the root of this disruption in the rhythm of daily and annual work cycles was an altered relationship between the local population and productive resources, primarily the land. Land in the vicinity of Howa historically had been held in common and allocated through customary right by local sheikhs to villagers for dryland cultivation. The local economy was geared primarily to the production or extraction of use-values, i.e. goods to satisfy its own subsistence needs, from a combination of agriculture, animal husbandry and forestry. Under these socioeconomic conditions, constraints on production were determined more by the physical and economic limits of available labor and other resources than by external political–economic relations such as those associated with the Suki Project. It not only circumscribed the land available for cultivation, but determined who had access to it under what conditions.

It would be erroneous to assume that State intervention and economic penetration by merchant capital are the sole sources of transformation in this or any socioeconomic formation. Indeed, my conceptualization of the problematic was one of active negotiation between social, economic, cultural, political, and ecological relations and practices. This study addresses some of its manifestations on the premise that people are not dupes, but rather are active subjects making their own histories and geographies within and against the determinations of historically and geographically specific structures. In Howa these practices were a nexus of struggle between and among the local population and fractions therein, including agents of State capitalism such as schoolteachers and Project authorities, and local religious leaders, particularly of mystical and fundamentalist orders of Islam (cf. el Hassan, 1980). It is noteworthy that these struggles, which are fundamentally over capitalist hegemony, were carried out between, and even within, real people. They are trivialized if they are constructed as roles played out in a structuralist drama that pits the agents of state capitalism against the poor peasants (cf. Thrift, 1983, p. 35).

Many of the changes brought about by inclusion in the agricultural project were welcomed by the local population. For years, many had sought increased incomes as agricultural laborers and, when possible, tenants in the private cotton schemes along the Blue Nile. They saw the Suki Project as offering the opportunity for increased income at home. But under the Project the local community lost much autonomous control over production, and it was over these relations that much of the ensuing struggle turned. This shift in the social relations of production and reproduction – what Watts (1987) calls the 'multidirectional and episodic' nature of capitalist development – marks the larger context for my study of children's acquisition and use of local environmental knowledge.

Methodology

This study was primarily ethnographic. I worked intensively with a small number of children and their families with constant reference to the sociocultural and political–economic dynamic of the village as a whole. The children were from households of tenants and non-tenants of each socioeconomic status. They themselves were a diverse group: boys and girls, students and non-students, of each birth-order position. This population was selected based on a full enumeration and survey of the entire village. This, along with the diversity of the methodology I developed, the standards I maintained in working with the children, and comparisons of my results with those of the few existing relevant studies, gave me confidence in the validity of the information produced. Nevertherless, it was not my intent to produce findings that could be analyzed statistically with any reliability; the complexity of the information and the small sample size raise questions about even the simplest of statistical analyses. Rather, my agenda was to discover, document, and describe the range of children's environmental interactions and the forms and content of their environmental knowledge in all their complexity; and to analyze these in relation to the larger context in which they occurred.

The experience of living in the area for a year and working closely with the children and their families produced extremely rich data. These data were discovered and grounded in a particular temporal and geographic context which I shared. It is important to remember that in this sort of research, distantiation is impossible (cf. Koptiuch, 1985; Probyn, 1990). Unlike most positivist approaches to empirical research, ethnographic research does not claim to be objective. Indeed, its essence is that it is not. Its goal, cultural description, is reached in a wholly subjective manner even though a range of scientific methods are employed. This text is the result of my experiences during a particular year in Howa. Not only my research interests, but my background and personality framed my experience and filtered both what I saw and the way I interpreted it. I do not claim, then, to speak for 'the other' (cf. Clifford and Marcus, 1986; Marcus and Fischer, 1986; Spivak, 1988), the children and adults who participated in this study, but only for myself. To claim otherwise would be dishonest intellectually.

The changing roles of children during socioeconomic and cultural–ecological transformation

The general hypothesis that guided this work from the outset was that a change in the production system, such as was caused by incorporation in the Suki Agricultural Project, would alter the settings and activities for reproducing that production system. My interest in this question was rooted in the perspective that these settings and activities were not simply the outcome of economic factors, but rather were themselves constructed by the material social practices of living historical subjects. My goal was to examine the articulation between the two, for in it lie the multitudinous possibilities of reproduction, reaction, resistance, and reformulation. The household, the peer group and the school or other sites of formal training were the settings of particular concern, and children's work, play, and formal learning were the activities of particular interest. Following Marx (1967), reproduction was understood as physical – encompassing both biological reproduction and the appropriation and/or production of means of subsistence adequate to ensure the daily maintenance of the population – and sociocultural – reproducing the conditions of life and labor in which the skills and knowledge associated with social production figure prominently. My research addressed children's roles in production and the provision of the means of existence, *and* their acquisition of the knowledge and skills necessary to maintain the system of production and reproduction over time. These were examined as lived experiences and contested practices.

Although there is a generally recursive nature to these material social practices addressed analytically in the literature on everyday life (e.g. Lefebvre, 1984), these practices and their relationships to the social relations of production and reproduction are always and everywhere in flux. Everyday life is significant as a critical concept, not as a descriptive notion for the mundane and unspectacular practices by which we construct ourselves and reproduce society, but because inherent in these is the potential for rupture, breakdown and transformation (cf. Kaplan and Ross, 1987; Katz, 1989). At particular historical junctures, the potential for these is heightened. The altered relations of production imposed by inclusion in the Suki Agricultural Project created such a moment in Howa. The acquisition, deployment, content and organization of children's environmental knowledge were addressed to examine the means by which the social formation of Howa was being reproduced and to locate discontinuities in these cultural forms and practices.

By the time of my research in 1981, the Suki Agricultural Development Project, established in 1971, had already had a significant effect in transforming not only the social relations of production and reproduction in Howa, but the local ecology as well. These transformations had led to conditions which altered, among other things, the nature of children's interactions with the environment as well as the means and content of their environmental learning. My initial hypothesis was that as a result of the socioeconomic changes under way, more children would attend school and thus participate less in the work of their households. By extension, I thought that the decline in children's work would begin to erode the traditional relationship between work and play, and, in turn, the experience of the two as means of environmental learning. While a year of field research did not allow sufficient time to analyze definitely how these activities were changing either in themselves or in relation to one another, analysis of the sample population of children and return trips to Howa in 1983 and 1984 made clear that this hypothesis was off the mark.

One of the contradictory effects of incorporation in the agricultural project was that rather than increasing school enrolment and children's play time as I had hypothesized originally, it appeared that the changes wrought by inclusion in the Project demanded more labor from children. According to teachers in the village school, enrolment had not increased in the years since Howa was included in the Suki Project. Moreover, it was their impression, although they did not keep figures, that a greater proportion of children in the village primary school left before completion than had done so prior to inclusion in the Project. The reasons for this were threefold: (1) the higher labor demands associated with the irrigated cultivation of cotton and groundnuts compared with the rainfed cultivation of sorghum and sesame; (2) the environmental changes brought about by the irrigation project; and (3) the increased need for cash engendered by incorporation in the agricultural development project and the global cash economy which it represented. These are discussed in turn.

In interviews concerning the changes taking place in Howa, adults frequently indicated that the demands of cultivating cotton and groundnuts as cash crops exceed those associated with the rainfed cultivation of sorghum and sesame that had prevailed before 1971. In addition to the labor demands of irrigation and the use of imported fertilizers, pesticides, and herbicides, Project authorities required four weedings of each crop with a short-handled hoe that was more difficult and tiresome to use than the customary long-handled or very short-handled variety.[4] In most households, these labor demands were met with the increased use of family labor, especially children. Many tenant households, particularly those of lower socioeconomic status, reported that children were kept from school enrolment or forced to withdraw after a couple of years because they were needed to help with the full range of agricultural tasks, many of which took place during the school year. Some studies that address children's contribution to household labor suggest that when children are needed for labor-intensive agricultural or other tasks, they are kept home from school (e.g. Landy, 1959; Tienda, 1979). My experience suggests that when this was the case for specific seasonal tasks, households managed without the inputs of their children. But when children's labor was important to a range of tasks such as agriculture, or for an essential year-round activity such as herding, either they were never enrolled or they left school prematurely.

Another reason that children's work in Howa appeared to have increased was the deforestation that had resulted from the shifts in land-use associated with the irrigation project. The traditional system of mixed land-use, combining subsistence dryland agriculture and the raising of small animals, left wooded areas adequate to meet local needs. With the establishment of the Project in 1970–71, the amount of woodland in the vicinity of the village was severely curtailed. By 1981 there were few trees apart from ornamentals within a half-hour's walk from the settlement, and most of the remaining trees within an hour's walk were less than five centimeters in diameter. Adults in the village noted that this situation had increased the time required to procure adequate household fuel supplies. In Howa, where many aspects of fuel provision were the responsibility of children, these changes led to substantial increases in children's work time. Not only did they have to go further afield to collect or cut fuelwood, but the poor quality and small size of most of what was available increased the number of trips per week necessary to provide sufficient wood for domestic consumption.

Finally, children's environmental and other work had increased because of the larger economic changes associated with the introduction of the agricultural project. Not only did the Project bring about enormous changes in the relations of production in Howa, but it heightened the integration of the village into the national cash economy. With the establishment of the Project, access to many goods that had been commonly held or freely available was restricted, for example, wood products. The issue of forestry resources again provides an example of particular relevance to the question of children's labor. As wood products became more difficult to procure, some wealthier households began to purchase them rather than increase the demands on children or other household members. Members of poorer households in the village, including children, began to provide wood for sale. In this way a freely held good gradually becomes a commodity. As more freely held goods become commodities, the need for cash increases. By 1981 this process was well under way, compounded by an explosion in the number of merchants and traders in the village since 1971. Their presence introduced an increasingly wide array of consumer goods to the village.

Commoditization is tied to socioeconomic differentiation. In Howa, the ascendance of the cash economy led to increases in children's workload, because in many households they were needed to earn money to help meet the growing needs for cash. Twelve of the seventeen children in the sample group earned cash that helped provide household subsistence. The twinned processes of commoditization and differentiation particularly affected two resources that children were significant in procuring: wood and water. When marginalized families sought new means to earn cash, it often fell to children to fetch water or cut wood for sale. Ten-year-old children also helped to produce and scavenge charcoal for sale in nearby towns, harvested vegetables from family garden plots and hawked these in the village, and worked as hired help in the tenancies of other village households. In these ways, the increased need for cash, created by the agricultural project and fanned by the exigencies of the monetized economy of which it was a part, increased the work of children in Howa.

These shifts in children's work had consequences for the relationship between work and play, and the nature of these as means for the acquisition and use of environmental knowledge (cf. Katz 1986a, b), as well as for school attendance. The gains in school enrolment I expected may have been limited, at least in part, by the increased demand for children's labor in Howa. In 1981, 42 per cent of the boys and 4 per cent of the girls aged seven to twelve years old were enrolled in the village school. During 1979 in the largely rural Blue Nile Province as a whole, 53 per cent of the boys and 25 per cent of the girls between these ages were enrolled in primary school (Sudan, Ministry of Education and Guidance, 1981). Whatever the cause, the implications of low school enrolment are serious both for the children as they come of age and for the socioeconomic formation of Sudan as a whole.

My research indicated that most ten-year-old children in Howa were learning the knowledge, skills, and values necessary to reproduce the social relations and practices of production that characterized their community in 1981. In their work and play, children learned the environmental knowledge and practices associated with maintaining a farming community. But for a combination of reasons, it was apparent that relatively few of those ten years old in 1981 would have access to a farm tenancy when they come of age in the 1990s. Displacement of the farming population results from three interrelated phenomena: (1) the static land tenure relationships associated with the agricultural project – with 250 tenancies allocated to the village in 1970, there were from the outset fewer tenancies than the number of households (335 by 1981); (2) the size of the average household in Howa – with the fixed number of tenancies, and an average household size of 5.7, most children do not stand to inherit access to their family's tenancy; and (3) the frequent proximity in age between children and their parents, i.e., the parents of many ten-year-old children were still in their twenties or early thirties and thus unlikely to turn over their tenancies until well after their children reached adulthood. In the absence of further agricultural development (and none was planned for the area), much of what children played and worked at during their childhoods will not exist for them in the world of their adulthood. This eventuality points to a serious disjuncture in the course of social reproduction which could lead to profound shifts in the children's lives as they reach adulthood.

The outcomes differ for boys and girls. My research suggests that while most of the boys were learning to be farmers, they will not be. Rather they will be marginalized as agricultural wage laborers or forced to seek nonagricultural work in the Project headquarters nearby, in regional towns, or in urban centers further away. By contrast, girls were being socialized largely to assume their mothers' social and work roles. While women's roles were likely to be stable for a longer period than men's, it appeared likely that as men increasingly migrate from the area in search of labor, women would assume a large role in agricultural production. While girls participated extensively in agricultural tasks such as planting and harvesting, unlike boys they were not taught to organize the full range of agricultural operations, had little practical experience in some of these, including clearing and weeding, and had not mastered the use of most tools. Moreover, their participation in all agricultural tasks except harvesting tapered off as they reached puberty. When these girls come of age, they are likely to need knowledge they will not have acquired fully in their childhoods.

This discontinuity between childhood learning and adult opportunities is part of a process that, in effect, results in the wholesale deskilling and marginalization of rural populations such as those in the area of Howa. Given the general lack of formal schooling which might offer the chance for 'reskilling,' there was little likelihood of most children finding employment in their adulthoods except at the lowest skill requirements. These discontinuities were not the same for all children. The dramatic differences in the rates of school enrolment between girls and boys in Howa (4 per cent and 42 per cent respectively) suggest that girls will be even less capable than boys of undertaking non-farm or non-domestic work. Just as girls lacked experience with the full range of agricultural tasks and were not instructed in their overall organization, many boys in Howa did not have the opportunity to acquire particular agricultural skills and knowledge because their households lacked land in the agricultural project. Children from non-tenant households lost much of the opportunity shared by tenants' children to acquire and use agricultural knowledge in the course of their everyday lives. Thus, certain children, by virtue of their parents' socioeconomic or occupational status, will be less skilled in agriculture than many of their contemporaries, and possibly at a disadvantage in obtaining and holding positions as agricultural wage laborers. Under prevailing socioeconomic conditions, these were among the only viable jobs available. In this way, the process of socioeconomic differentiation engenders further differentiation. My research revealed some of the mechanisms of this process in children's experience.

For the socioeconomic formation of Howa, the intertwined processes of deskilling and differentiation may lead in the short run to declines in rural productivity and, in the long run, to an adult population unable or unwilling to carry out the tasks of production associated with the Suki Project. Rural productivity may decline as the changing relations of production and the ensuing redefinition of vocational skill dislocate the household as the center of production and reproduction (cf. Dalla Costa, 1977). These dual dislocations have resulted historically in the depopulation of the household, first as waged work is found outside of the home and ultimately as children leave in growing numbers to attend school. As a result, less labor is available to the rural household to maintain previous levels of agricultural productivity. The process of labor migration was just beginning in Howa in 1981.

Finally, the increases in children's work in Howa had begun to alter the traditional relationship between work and play, the balance between the two as means for the acquisition and use of environmental knowledge. This process appeared likely to continue whether the work responsibilities of the children continued to increase or greater numbers began to attend school. When play and work are separated, play becomes trivialized as 'childish' activity in the eyes of adults. Severed from work, play remains a central means by which children are socialized in terms of both mastering particular kinds of knowledge or skills and internalizing cultural values and other principles. However important its socializing role may be, play divorced from work is less grounded in the general experience of the community as a whole and thus comes to be viewed as inconsequential. When play becomes isolated and trivialized as an activity *only* for children or as something adults do *only* in their time off from work, the peer group becomes less integral to the larger society because it is no longer a social setting in which work and play are united. This represents the loss of an important aspect of autonomous traditional culture and is thus a means by which capitalism 'colonizes' experience.

Conclusion

This study has examined some of the ways that capitalism is articulated on the landscape of everyday life. Its central logic, the accumulation of capital, at once

engenders and is achieved in the colonization of experience and the transformation of time, space, place, and nature. In Howa it was possible to witness
these entwined processes taking place. My research on the practices of social
reproduction, and in particular children's learning, their use of knowledge, and
the organization and content of their knowledge concerning the environment,
was spurred, in part, by the desire to find spaces that will not be colonized or to
locate instances of experiential decolonization, glimmers of oppositional practice. These ends and those of the children are connected. Engaged myself in the
production of knowledge that opposes received notions about the relationship
between production and reproduction, I have written this piece at once to point
to the subversive power that inheres in the everyday practices by which
knowledge is produced, deployed and exchanged, and to reformulate or
subvert that knowledge in a way that recognizes the oppositional potential of
these very practices of social reproduction.

What I have shown – that children shared a rich and intricate knowledge of a
resource use complex under erasure; that their autonomous practices of work
and play were being transformed and sundered as unified means for the
acquisition and use of particular kinds of knowledge; and that in the wake of
capitalism's local impress, children were not being prepared for the world they
are likely to face as adults – does not occasion optimism about the potential for
opposition. But in examining the acquisition and use of local knowledge as
practices of social reproduction in articulation with the political–economic
relationships that at once structure and are structured by them, this piece not
only has demonstrated the breadth and intensity of children's environmental
interactions, but, in constituting these within the critical construction of everyday life, has pointed to their contradictory potential to alter the trajectory of
socioeconomic change.

Most of the evidence presented indicates signs of rupture in the means by
which children acquired and used environmental knowledge, and breakdown
in the relationship between production and social reproduction. These
disjunctures appeared to serve the advance of capitalism in Howa. The transformation of the local production system and its attendant processes of socioeconomic differentiation, environmental degradation, commoditization and
deskilling are emblematic of the erosion of the countryside as a viable arena of
noncapitalist relations of production and reproduction. Capitalist hegemony is
neither achieved nor maintained without struggle, and the community as a
whole was responding to the changes imposed upon it in a range of ways. The
State regulation of production practices, for example, was successfully limited
by the tenants' union when they gained the right to grow sorghum on Project
land. The shifting contents of what constitutes adequate socialization for
adulthood was recognized by the villagers, and met in the mid-1980s with a
village self-help project to construct a girls' school. While the extension of
formal schooling *may* further capitalist hegemony in the area, inherent in the
nature of education is the possibility that it may not, but, in fact, may enable a
population to become conscious of their position in the larger society and resist
such changes actively rather than reactively (Freire, 1970). These are but two

examples of the local response to the socioeconomic and structural changes imposed in Howa since 1970. The great vitality and variation I discovered in the children's work, play, and learning, and the contradictions that inhere in them as material social practices of production and reproduction, suggest another possible arena by which these changes might be opposed, resisted or subverted. In order for this to be accomplished, children and their elders would have to consciously appropriate and link to political struggle the strength inherent in the production and exchange of knowledge, returning it to their own interests – to steady themselves and ride surely along the canals as the sun rises.

Acknowledgments

The research upon which this paper is based was supported by a Predoctoral Research Grant from the National Science Foundation and a Dissertation Fellowship from the American Association of University Women. I remain grateful to them and to the people of Howa for their generous support of my work. Thanks to Andrew Kirby, Sallie Marston, Susan Saegert and Neil Smith as well as several anonymous reviewers for helping me to better sow what I know.

Notes

1 Notable exceptions include Willis (1977) in sociology, Taussig (1980) and Scott (1985) in anthropology, and Johnson (1977) in geography.
2 The literature on everyday life associated with the French social theorist Henri Lefebvre (1984) is germane here as well. In recent years it has been getting increasing attention in North American geography and social science in general. In geography it has been drawn on largely by those interested in the articulation between social and spatial relations (e.g. Soja, 1989; Harvey, 1989), rather than in the reproduction of particular human-environment relations. Its crucial insight is its construction of everyday life as a critical concept, that is, one in which the possibilities of its own transformation are immanent to the very practices of reproduction that constitute it (cf. Kaplan and Ross, 1987). However, this formulation, with the associated litera- ture, is one that I came upon after completing the present project. In tracing my path to it, feminist theory has been most influential and offers emancipatory insights that geographers interested in social change frequently ignore.
3 According to Marx, the natural economy is based in agriculture complemented by domestic handicraft and manufacturing. Its central characteristic is that 'a very insignificant portion' of the product enters into the process of circulation (1967, vol. 3, pp. 786–7). In other words, 'the conditions of the economy are either wholly or for the overwhelming part produced by the economy itself, directly replaced and reproduced out of its gross product' (p. 795). The abstraction natural economy describes a particular relationship to the production of the means of existence and the relative lack of surplus and thus circulation. It should not invoke notions of classlessness; indeed, socioeconomic differentiation is often a characteristic of so-called natural economies. I follow Bernstein (1982) in using Marx's category of natural economy as an abstraction to suggest a social formation in which the production of use-values predominates, although there is an exchange of surpluses at a basic level. This is an

apt characterization of the socioeconomic formation of Howa prior to 1971. Since my purpose is an analysis of the relationship between production and reproduction as material social practices in Howa, and not one of the historical transformation of the village as a socioeconomic system, an abstraction such as natural economy is useful as a means to locate the village theoretically.

4 This information was provided in the course of open-ended interviews I conducted with nine couples, eight of whom were parents of children participating in the research. The remaining couple were the grandparents of two children in the sample population. More significantly, a similar perspective was revealed in the open-ended discussions I had with adults in most village households while I was completing the village-wide census at the start of my project. Also, it was reinforced consistently during the informal discussions with a range of adults in Howa throughout the study period.

Selected references

Ahmad, Abd al Ghaffar M. 1974: *Shaykhs and followers: Political struggle in the Rufa'a al-Hoi Nazirate in the Sudan*. Khartoum: Khartoum University Press.

Aronowitz, S. 1973: *False promises: The shaping of American working class consciousness*. New York: McGraw-Hill.

Barnett, T. 1975: The Gezira scheme: production of cotton and the reproduction of underdevelopment. In Okaal, I., Barnett, T. and Booth, D. (eds), *Beyond the sociology of development: Economy and society in Latin America and Africa*. London: Routledge & Kegan Paul, 183–207.

Barnett, T. 1977: *The Gezira scheme: An illusion of development*. London: Frank Cass.

Bernstein, H. 1982: Notes on capital and the peasantry. In Harriss, J. (ed.), *Rural development*. London: Hutchinson University Library, 160–77.

Bourdieu, P. 1977: *Outline of a theory of practice*. Cambridge: Cambridge University Press.

Caulfield, M. D. 1974: Imperialism, the family and cultures of resistance. *Socialist Revolution* 20.

Christopherson, S. 1983: The household and class formation: determinants of residential location in Ciudad Juárez. *Environment and Planning D: Society and Space* 1, 323–38.

Clark, G. and Dear, M. 1984: *State apparatus: Structures and language of legitimacy*. Boston: Allen & Unwin.

Clifford, J. and Marcus, G. E. 1986: *Writing culture: The poetics and politics of ethnography*. Berkeley: University of California Press.

Conference of Socialist Economists. 1977: *On the political economy of women*. CSE Pamphlet 2. London: CSE.

Dalla Costa, M. 1972: Women and the subversion of the community. In Dalla Costa, M. and James, S. (eds), *The power of women and the subversion of the community*. Bristol: Falling Wall Press, 19–54.

Dalla Costa, M. 1977: Riproduzione e emigrazione. In Serafini, A. *et al.* (eds), *L'operaio multinazionale in Europa*, 2nd edn. Milan: Feltrinelli, 207–41.

de Certeau, M. 1984: *The practice of everyday life*. Berkeley: University of California Press.

de Lauretis, T. 1982: *Alice doesn't: Feminism, semiotics, cinema*. Bloomington: Indiana University Press.

Development and the sexual division of labor. 1981: *Signs: Journal of Women in Culture and Society* Special Issue 7(2); 265–512.

Duffield, M. R. 1981. *Maiurno: Capitalism and rural life in Sudan*. London: Ithaca Press.

Ehrenreich, B. and English, D. 1975: The manufacture of housework. *Socialist Revolution* 26.

Freire, P. 1970: *Pedagogy of the oppressed*. New York: Seabury Press.

Genovese, E. 1972: *Roll, Jordan, roll: The world the slaves made*. New York: Pantheon Books.

Gramsci, A. 1971: *Selections from the prison notebooks*, ed. and trans. by Hoare, Q. and Smith, G. N. New York: International Publishers.

Gregory, D. 1982: *Regional transformation and industrial revolution: A geography of the Yorkshire woollen industry*. Minneapolis: University of Minnesota Press.

Gregory, D., and Urry, J. (eds) 1985: *Social relations and spatial structures*. New York: St Martin's Press.

Gruenbaum, E. 1979: *Patterns of family living: A case study of two villages on the Rahad river*. Monograph 12. Khartoum: Khartoum University, Development Studies and Research Centre.

Haraway, D. 1984: Teddy bear patriarchy: taxidermy in the Garden of Eden, New York City, 1908–1936. *Social Text* 11, 20–64.

Harvey, D. 1989: *The condition of postmodernity*. Oxford: Basil Blackwell.

Harvey, D. 1990: Between space and time: reflections on the geographical imagination. *Annals of the Association of American Geographers* 80, 418–34.

el Hassan, I. S. 1980: On ideology: the case of religion in northern Sudan. PhD dissertation, University of Connecticut.

James, S. 1975: Sex, race and working class power. In James, S. (ed.), *Sex, race and class*. London: Falling Wall Press and Race Today Publications, 9–19.

Johnson, K. 1977: 'Do as the land bids': A study of Otomi resource use on the eve of irrigation. PhD dissertation, Graduate School of Geography, Clark University.

Johnson, R. 1979. Three problematics: elements of a theory of working class culture. In Clarke, J., Crichter, C. and Johnson, R. (eds), *Working class culture, studies in history and theory*. London: Routledge & Kegan Paul, 201–37.

Kaplan, A. and Ross, K. 1987: Introduction. *Yale French Studies* 73, 1–4. Special issue: Everyday life.

Katz, C. 1986a: Children and the environment: work, play and learning in rural Sudan. *Children's Environments Quarterly* 3(4), 43–51.

Katz, C. 1986b: 'If there weren't kids, there wouldn't be fields': children's environmental learning, knowledge and interactions in a changing socioeconomic context in rural Sudan. PhD dissertation, Graduate School of Geography, Clark University.

Katz, C. 1989. 'You can't drive a Chevy through post-Fordist landscape': everyday cultural practices of resistance and reproduction among youth in New York City. Paper presented at the Marxism Now: Traditions and Differences Conference, Amherst, MA.

Koptiuch, K. 1985: Fieldwork in the postmodern world: notes on ethnography in an expanded field. Paper presented at the 84th annual meeting of the American Anthropological Association, Washington, DC.

Landy, D. 1959: *Tropical childhood*. Chapel Hill: NC: University of North Carolina Press.

Lefebvre, H. 1984: *Everyday life in the modern world*. New Brunswick, NJ: Transaction Books.

Marcus, G. E. and Fischer, M. J. 1986: *Anthropology as cultural critique: An experimental moment in the human sciences*. Chicago: University of Chicago Press.

Marx, K. 1967: *Capital*, 3 vols, ed. Engels, F. Trans. Moore, S. and Aveling, E. New York: International Publishers.

Moraga, C. and Anzaldua, G. 1981: *This bridge called my back: Writings by radical women of color*. Watertown, MA: Persephone Press.

O'Brien, J. 1978: How traditional is traditional agriculture? *Sudan Journal of Economic and Social Studies* 2, 1–10.

Pred, A. 1984a: Structuration, biography formation and knowledge: observations on port growth during the late mercantile period. *Environment and Planning D: Society and Space* 2, 251–75.

Pred, A. 1984b: Space as historically contingent process: structuration and the time-geography of becoming places. *Annals of the Association of American Geographers* 74, 279–97.

Probyn, E. 1990: Travels in the postmodern: making sense of the local. In Nicholson, L. J. (ed.), *Feminism/postmodernism*. New York: Routledge, 176–89.

Said, E. 1978: *Orientalism*. New York: Pantheon.

Samuel, R. and Jones, G. S. 1982: *Culture, ideology and politics*. London: Routledge & Kegan Paul.

Sargent, L. (ed.) 1981: *Women and revolution: A discussion of the unhappy marriage of Marxism and feminism*. Boston, MA: South End Press.

Schildkrout, E. 1981: The employment of children in Kano (Nigeria). In Rodgers, G. and Standing, G. (eds) *Child work, poverty and underdevelopment*. Geneva: International Labour Office, 81–112.

Scott, J. C. 1985: *Weapons of the weak: Everyday forms of peasant resistance*. New Haven, CT: Yale University Press.

Smith, N. 1984: *Uneven development*. Oxford: Basil Blackwell.

Soja, E. W. 1989: *Postmodern geographies*. London: Verso.

Spivak, G. C. 1987: *In other worlds: Essays in cultural politics*. New York: Methuen.

Spivak, G. C. 1988: Can the subaltern speak? In Nelson, C. and Grossberg, L. (eds), *Marxism and the interpretation of culture*. Urbana: University of Illinois Press, 271–313.

Sudan, Democratic Republic. Ministry of Education and Guidance. 1981: Education in the Sudan: Sector review paper. Prepared for UNICEF Preview Meeting, 22 October 1980.

Taussig, M. 1980: *The devil and commodity fetishism in South America*. Chapel Hill, NC: University of North Carolina Press.

al Tayib, G. el D. 1970: The southeastern Funj area: a geographical survey. Khartoum: University of Khartoum, Sudan Research Unit. Funj Project Paper 1.

Thompson, E. P. 1963: *The making of the English working class*. New York: Vintage Books.

Thrift, N. 1983. On the determination of social action in space and time. *Environment and Planning D: Society and Space* 1, 23–57.

Tienda, M. 1979: Economic activity of children in Peru: labor force behavior in rural and urban contexts. *Rural Sociology* 44, 370–91.

Tothill, J. D. (ed.) 1948: *Agriculture in the Sudan*. London: Oxford University Press.

Warf, B. 1988: Regional transformation, everyday life, and Pacific Northwest lumber production. *Annals of the Association of American Geographers* 78, 326–46.

Watts, M. 1983: *Silent violence*. Berkeley: University of California Press.

Watts, M. 1987: Powers of production – geographers among the peasants. *Environment and Planning D: Society and Space* 5, 215–30.

Williams, R. 1977: *Marxism and literature*. Oxford: Oxford University Press.
Willis, P. 1977: *Learning to labor: How working class kids get working class jobs*. New York: Columbia University Press.

---

3 John Langton,
'The Industrial Revolution and the Regional Geography of England'

Reprinted in full from *Transactions of the Institute of British Geographers* NS 9, 145–67 (1984)

'There is no idea, however ancient and absurd, that is not capable of improving our knowledge'.[1]

The industrial revolution and regional geography

Although English geographers have often joined vigorously in theoretical debates about the regional concept, relatively little regional geography has been written about England. The theoretical literature tells us why. England ceased to be a patchwork of regionally distinctive environments, economies and societies owing to the nationally pervasive effects of industrialization. The industrial revolution destroyed England's regional geography. The regional method of inquiry

> is admirably suited to the historical geography of Europe before the Industrial Revolution, or indeed to the limited and shrinking areas of the world today whose economies are still based on peasant agriculture and local self-sufficiency in most of the material things of life, but it is not applicable to a country which has undergone industrial revolution.[2]

It is perhaps not surprising that the most virulent and colourful attack on the validity of the regional concept came from an Englishman, Kimble, who claimed that 'the region is an eighteenth-century concept . . . The world that fathered it now lies "mouldering in the grave". . . . [It] was sired by feudalism and raised in the cultural seclusion of a self-sufficient environment'.[3] Modern Marxist geographical theory has concurred in this judgement, generalized it further and added its own explanatory gloss. Of the 'two principal bases of social integration, functional and territorial', the former is based upon rational calculation, the latter upon historical associations and sentiment, 'transcending interests of class'.[4] With industrialization, class conflict replaces territorially based rivalries, and regional coherence and consciousness are destroyed.

Given these geographers' views, it is predictable that work within the various analytical branches of history should imply and even sometimes state the same thing. Their recent reinvigoration through the incorporation of ideas and methods from cognate social sciences has been marked by a further relegation of regional differences to the very lowest level of concern. Modern approaches, like modern societies, have no place for regions.[5] The most up-to-date textbook on English economic history deliberately sets out to display the benefits that come from the application of economic theory to the subject. Its two volumes contain few hints that there were any regional variations within the country. All of significance is conceived of in terms of national sectors, trends and interest groups.[6] When this kind of work was just beginning, Hartwell observed that it had not yet been demonstrated that 'there was an English economy rather than a collection of self-contained or trading regions within England' at the time of the industrial revolution.[7] The new methods of economic history require that what has still not been demonstrated is simply assumed.

There is a similar deliberate neglect of regional differences, underlain by unease about them, in modern historical demography and social history. The magnificent work of the Cambridge Group contains no acknowledgement that regional differences might in any way jeopardize the usefulness of their national average vital rates, even those calculated for pre-industrial times.[8] The characteristic stance in the equally vigorous new field of radical social history, where concern with the lives of ordinary people and with culture in the round might lead one to expect a sensitivity to regional differences, is that profound regional variations in social structure, behaviour and attitudes would severely inutilize formulations about national classes, cultures and their interactions if they had existed, but that in fact they happily did not do so. Neale, from a similar Marxist standpoint, echoes Friedmann: regionalism had been important in the seventeenth century and earlier, but 'in the course of the eighteenth century regional loyalties declined in strength'. Although 'regionalism continued as a divisive force into the modern period', his complete silence about it thenceforth suggests that he does not consider it to have had much potency in modifying the class-based affiliations with which he deals, notwithstanding his intriguing but unelaborated claim that 'in the eighteenth century it helped to inhibit the growth of class consciousness within many strata'.[9] He has the authority of the most influential modern social historian behind him. E. P. Thompson was concerned to show in *The making of the English working class* that there was nationwide cohesion amongst labour movements, an emerging national class-consciousness, at least at various critical times, in the late eighteenth and early nineteenth centuries. Like Sidmouth and *Sybil*, he concluded that it was the growth of manufacturing industry that produced the Two Nations.[10] Neither the carefulness of Thompson's own reconstruction of the nature and timing of this process, nor the considerable amount of subsequent work in which the number of classes and the timing of their formation are hotly debated, have deterred social historians of earlier periods from ignoring his chronology. The conclusion of a recent text on the seventeenth century, for example, is entitled 'Nation and locality' and asserts that the period 'witnessed the increasingly close involvement of provincial Englishmen of upper and middling rank in national affairs. Indeed, one of its most striking features . . . is the emergence of the people'.[11]

Even books informed by the perspectives of social anthropology treat peasant behaviour patterns and customs in pre-industrial times as self-evidently capable of firm national generalization,[12] and so do those which evaluate the social and economic contexts of literature and art.[13] Regional distinctions thus disappear altogether, preparing the ground for the conceptions of 'class struggle without class' and 'patrician society and plebeian culture' which Thompson developed, after he wrote about the industrial revolution, to depict English society in the early eighteenth century.[14] The clear impression conveyed by the 'new' social historians of England is that a multitude of numerous inchoate localisms gradually coalesced into coherent and unitary national social groups, ready to be reformed in conflict during the industrial revolution.[15]

This is neat and theoretically satisfying, and it might be considered that the studied neglect of regional distinctions in English history is simply one of those convenient fictions which are necessary if history is to be written at all. Indeed, such is its allure that a prominent English historical geographer has recently advocated that we, too, adopt it so that we can use neoclassical and Marxist economic models which require that geographical differences, and therefore geography itself, are forgotten.[16] The purpose of what follows is simply to emphasize that this is a fiction; that there were important regional as well as local differences in pre-industrial England, and that it is at least arguable that, far from eradicating them, the process of industrialization both intensified them and heightened people's consciousness of their existence.

The regional structure of pre-industrial England

Although the period before the industrial revolution is not the main concern, it is necessary to make some observations about the regional structure of England at that time, in order to provide a context for and a contrast with the regional patterns and forms produced by industrialization.

The counties

Whilst specialist economic and social historians customarily neglect it, the importance of regional subdivision within pre-industrial England currently lies at the very centre of one of the most active debates in the synthetic tradition of historiography. A lively revisionist movement has recently questioned all teleological explanations of the Civil War, whether in Whiggish or Marxist terms of the rise of Parliament, the fall of absolutism or class conflict.[17] Much of this debate has concerned the significance of the so-called 'county communities'. Was England at that time an entity that split into parts defined nationally according to religious, class or political affiliations, or was it an amalgam of 'county commonwealths', 'a union of partially independent county-states'?[18] If the latter, the conflict can most properly be construed as a revolt of these self-consciously separate communities as their customary prerogatives to decide their own affairs (particularly the apportionment of taxation and the dispensation of law within their boundaries) were infringed by an increasingly interventionist central government.

Perhaps for the first time, the degree and nature of regional fragmentation in England has become a major historiographical issue. The inevitable tendency in synopses starkly to polarize the positions into 'county commonwealth' and 'teleological' schools, and to focus argument on the strengths and weaknesses of county social groupings, should not be allowed to obscure observations made across the whole spectrum of the argument about the existence of allegiances to and differences between regions on a smaller spatial scale. Even so, it is appropriate to stress the importance of the county in English social and cultural life at the time, which had no near equivalent elsewhere in Europe.

It is symbolized by the prominent emphasis given, in colour, to the county divisions of England and Wales on the maps which were increasingly bought and used by government agents and county gentry after their introduction in the late sixteenth century.[19] For a century and a half, these were the only spatial classifications invariably depicted and named on English maps; the famous portrait of the aged Queen Elizabeth I by Marcus Gheeraerts shows her standing on a map of a realm split into counties. Of course, such maps demonstrate the singularity of the kingdom as well as its subdivision, and it would be foolish to imply that Englishmen of the time had the same expectations as Huckleberry Finn about the correspondence between differences in colour on a map and differences on the ground. None the less, the pervasiveness of this image of England subdivided starkly into counties must, to some extent, have both reflected and reinforced the perceived realities of the time.

The county was an important unit of administration, headed by the sheriff as royal agent and the Lord Lieutenant as the apex of county society itself. It was

> conceived as more than a merely geographical area; it had a corporate capacity, with its own officials, its own finances, and the legal capacity to be punished by a fine if it failed to perform its proper functions.[20]

National taxes were imposed through the county administrations, which organized collection through constituent hundreds and parishes before drawing up accounts and forwarding the proceeds to London. Some taxes, such as the Land Tax which so much exercised the feelings of the gentry after it was introduced in 1692, were levied on a quota system in which county liabilities were set by central government (according to invariant anachronistic criteria), and the county authorities then decided how this total was to be split between hundreds and their constituent parishes before actually collecting it.[21]

Tudor legal reforms made the county an important agency in the administration of justice, too. The Lord Lieutenant selected the panel of Justices of the Peace, who were responsible for the dispensation of law in the localities where they lived and for the operation of the courts of Quarter, General and Petty Sessions. This system gave considerable flexibility for legal interpretation to vary from place to place but ensured that within each county there would be some degree of uniformity. Many Members of Parliament – the officers of the highest court in the land – were, too, Knights of the Shire until the Reform Act of 1832. They did not, like the borough members, represent particular small constituencies, but a number were elected on the franchise of all the freeholders in each county. Elections and hustings were held for the whole county in the county town; so were special commissions, meetings to decide on the contents of petitions to Parliament by newly elected members and county court assemblies, which lost their judicial function and were used more and more to formulate county opinion on matters of county concern and, less often, issues of national political debate. Thousands of freeholders might be brought together at these meetings from all over the shire, demonstrating both the unity and the power of the county communities in national life.

The county town thus acted as a focus for the fiscal, judicial and political concerns of the whole shire. The regular coming and going of Justices of the Peace and litigants and their representatives, and the irregular assembly of the constituency of freeholders made the county towns important agencies of synthesis in shire society, places where new and old wealth were combined through alliances, where coherent opinions were crystallized and where gentry and lesser freeholders articulated their concerns. Indeed, many of the gentry, who must stay regularly in their county town for the purposes of justice and administration, had houses there, and so did the pseudo-gentry whose wealth came from sources independent of broad acres. The social seasons, based on Assize week, aping those of London, emphasized in a local 'court' the unity of county society around the Lord Lieutenant who presided over it.[22] With the wealthy came their wealth, and slowly but surely during the sixteenth, seventeenth and eighteenth centuries the county towns assumed a functional dominance over other central places for the provision of high-order goods and services, creating a coherence in the urban economic structure of the shire no less marked than that developing in their social formations.

Arguments such as these are readily countered by derogators of the significance of the county communities. Clearly, they are appropriate largely to the gentry – although not exclusively so because county meetings were open to all freeholders, and many humble men and women must have attended the political meetings, come to watch the social events and use the shops and services that were in origin expressions of gentry power and wealth. None the less, it may well be that spatially structured concerns on a smaller scale than the county were important in shaping the attitudes, perceptions and behaviour of most people. The local community of the parish must, of course, have exerted a considerable influence in these respects. In addition, some degree of uniformity of experience and life-style, an economic and social coherence of which people were aware and by which their preoccupations would to some extent be determined, was present in the *pays* and urban hinterlands of pre-industrial England.

Pays *or 'farming countries'*

In the seventeenth century the direct translation 'country' of the French word *pays* was widely current, and agricultural historians frequently refer to the 'farming countries' of pre-industrial England. Both usages carry the same meaning as the French word: a tract of land over which similar natural environmental conditions and resources had given rise to a uniformity of economic activity, social structure, attitudes and beliefs. As Kerridge put it, 'man found natural regions, but . . . made the farming countries'.[23] Self-sufficiency and isolation are not necessary to sustain such regions. Indeed, the growing trade between reciprocating regional agricultural economies and between them all and London in the seventeenth century must have accentuated their outlines by encouraging specialization.

Because of the intricacy of England's physical geography, these regions were small and numerous. Everitt, characterized as the most influential progenitor of the 'county community' school of thought by its opponents, has, in fact, been at least as concerned to portray the realities of distinctions between these smaller areas.[24] Present knowledge about and interest in them are largely due to his inspiration. Despite their kaleidoscopic variegations, certain broad generalizations can be made about their nature. Everitt himself suggested that 'for elementary purposes' eight types of *pays* can be defined: fielden or champion, forest, fell and moorland, marshland, heathland, fenland, downland and wold. It is customary, too, to recognize at a higher level of generalization the major human ecological divide between fielden and wood pasture regions, between chalk and cheese in Underdown's phrase.[25] This division, common to the whole of Western Europe, has been examined elsewhere.[26] It would be superfluous to duplicate that account here, where it is appropriate simply to stress the depth of the contrast between the arable farming, communal behaviour, increasingly polarized societies of yeomen and their labourers, dominated by squirearchy and established Church in the former, and the looser social structures based on kin, pastoral preoccupations increasingly combined with industrial pursuits, the importance of commons for resources and colonization, and the anti-authoritarian attitudes, expressed most clearly in religious non-conformity, in the latter.

The urban regions

The role of the county town in cementing a 'consciousness of belonging together'[27] within the shire has already been stressed. Towns lower in the hierarchy acted in a similar if lesser way. Market towns frequently sat at the junctions of farming countries to mediate their exchanges and must have caused some fusion across their boundaries. But not all towns were primarily market towns. By the seventeenth century, and increasingly as it passed, certain towns and the areas around them had come to specialize in the production of particular craft goods for regional and national markets. Again in Everitt's words, there was a marked tendency

> for certain staple crafts, once practised widely, to become concentrated in a gradually narrowing circuit of countryside . . . until a distinct *craft-region* emerged, with its own character, its own traditions, its own sense of identity and its own distinctive culture . . . and in every case an 'entrepreneurial town' of some kind played a crucial role in this development.[28]

This has been a very abbreviated treatment of regional structures in pre-industrial England, but it should be clear that regions – areas of economic and social cohesion and cultural identity – existed then. This is what anyone with even a slight acquaintance with literature about regional geography would expect, of course. But those regions were by no means as simple as the normal preoccupation of theoretical discussions with the concept of *pays* would suggest. There were different degrees of regional cohesion, even different kinds at different spatial scales. Regional differences were complex and presented different patterns according to different criteria, in terms of different aspects of life and for different people. Like chronological rhythms, spatial structures are compounded of many wavelengths, some of which do and some of which do not mesh together.[29] The upshot of this complex aggregation over England outside London might well have been best represented by a singular term – the country; the lack of clear geographical divides, the dissonance of spatial wavelengths, prevented any neat categorizations.

In consequence, although the concrete noun 'region' was applicable, perhaps the abstract noun 'regionalism' – which does convey a sense of coherence over many aspects of life amongst different sectors of society within a single mesh of areas and a conscious identification of people with these territories – was not. Perhaps there were regions but not regionalism in seventeenth-century England. Perhaps regionalism only developed as the singular 'country' became the plural 'provinces' during the industrial revolution.[30]

The effects of industrial development

The justification of these surmises will comprise three parts. First, the considerable regional fragmentation of various social and political movements in the late eighteenth and early nineteenth centuries will be demonstrated. Then it will be shown that people in the country at large, and especially in newly industrializing areas, were becoming conscious of these regional distinctions and identifying with them. Third, both of these tendencies will be related to the essentially regional structure of the emerging manufacturing economy of the time.

Regional differences

The dissolution of national associations   With rapid industrialization in the late eighteenth century came the development of pressure groups and lobbies organized on a nationwide basis to represent the new manufacturing and commercial interests to both Parliament and people. Given the argument outlined above, it is not surprising that the first – to press for economic and political reforms to remove the causes of failure in the American War and prevent a change in taxation to the disadvantage of manufacturing areas – was based in county associations, particularly the Yorkshire Association founded by Christopher Wyvill in 1779.[31] In further accord with pre-industrial traditions, a petition was drawn up (denouncing corruption in government) and signed by nearly nine thousand freeholders. In 1780 a further forty-one petitions were presented to Parliament, twenty-six of them from counties. Eight more county associations were formed to support the petitions, and a central committee was organized in London for delegates from the nine county associations, five other counties and four boroughs.

What had begun as a pressure group based in a single county thus rapidly became a nationally organized movement for political and economic reform. National meetings of delegates were held in London in 1780 and 1781. But, after coming together, the movement quickly split apart. The Lancashire manufacturers refused to become involved because of their overriding concern to promote conditions of internal order, in which they considered that their particular interest would thrive best; the West Midlands was indifferent because manufacturers there were pressing for more comprehensive reforms; differences in political objectives between the Yorkshire and Middlesex associations caused splits within the group that did combine; and the Gloucester Association refused to accept that any general view should outweigh the 'deliberations and self-formed opinions of each county respectively'. Very quickly, the different interests of different counties and districts broke up what had for a short time appeared to be a nationally coherent pressure group. Wyvill himself ruefully recognized this. In connection with the failure to concert pressure from the associations with respect to Pitt's reform proposals of 1785 he observed that

> in London, from various motives, the measures announced met with a faint and languid assistance; in Manchester, and other great unrepresented towns, it received none. Of the counties, those of Nottingham and York petitioned for reform; but the rest . . . were silent.[32]

As this national movement collapsed, another began to form, constituted specifically to represent the interests of manufacturers generally. The General Chamber of Manufacturers was set up in 1785 as a national institution above party politics, and its Midlands instigators, Garbett and Wedgwood, intended that it should play a permanent role as a national pressure group.[33] It was successful in concerting opinions from many diverse manufacturing districts against a new excise on undyed fustian cloths in 1784 and the Irish Resolutions of 1785. Unanimity shattered when an attempt was made to organize opinion on the proposed commercial treaty with France in 1786 and to put the General Chamber on to a permanent and regular footing. The newer manufactures of cotton, iron and pottery supported the freer trade that the treaty would have encouraged, but delegates from the traditional handicrafts were opposed to it. Based largely in London and the South, they flooded the assembly in the capital in 1787 and passed a petition on behalf of the General Chamber pleading for a postponement of the application of the treaty. The Midland and Northern delegates were enraged as 'a fatal split . . . more or less on regional lines' developed to cause the collapse of the General Chamber.[34]

A new organization was proposed to represent only the interests of the modern provincial manufactures, meeting by rotation in Birmingham, Manchester and the Potteries, but it was not formed. Their interests were too diverse: even the West Midlands instigators themselves were, in fact, suspected of 'sacrificing the independence of the General Chamber to secure special concessions for the iron trades'.[35]

> The new industrialists had learned an important lesson. It was to be over seventy years before they again began to think of a permanent national organization, with headquarters in London. They had withdrawn to their separate strongholds in the North and Midlands, and they centred their organizations and agitations during the next two generations in the provinces.[36]

As late as 1842, the first attempt to co-ordinate the successful but separate regional associations of proprietors in the single industry of coal-mining failed because of 'this country's geographical . . . peculiarities'.[37]

This was the common pattern in the first half of the nineteenth century. Pressure groups were narrowly regionally based. Signs of national cohesion might develop in response to particularly acute concern, such as in connection with the Commission on the Woollen Manufactures, opposition to the Orders in Council or to the reform of the Poor Laws (or, in the case of colliery proprietors, the threat of a national strike on the one hand and government regulation on the other). But incipient co-ordination always fragmented or collapsed into one or more regionally based pressure groups or associations, and the most successful movements, such as those directed towards factory reform and the repeal of the Corn Laws, were narrowly based in particular regions from the start. Quite evidently, there were deep divisions of interest between the 'separate strongholds of the North and Midlands'. 'The General Chamber was . . . important precisely because it collapsed. Behind its particular objectives lay a more general awareness that the manufacturing regions now had distinct concerns of their own'.[38]

The disunity of social protests Substantially the same theme runs through the now vast literature concerning pressure exerted from the other end of the social spectrum, despite the overt objective of most of it to demonstrate the emergence of a unitary national class structure. Notwithstanding the eloquence of Thompson's plea, it seems from other research that Luddism was never, in fact, more than a conglomeration of disjointed regionally based disturbances. The pressures of rising prices, falling wages, rising unemployment, rising poor rates and falling levels of poor relief varied considerably in their timing and effects from one region to another. As Gregory has recently stressed,

> it is clear that the depression of 1811–12 was expressed through a series of *regional* crises. Popular reactions were thus to some degree the product of *regional* experiences and *regional* expectations rather than national evaluation.. . . There was certainly little effective inter-regional co-ordination in practical terms . . . there was nothing to compare with the violent struggles in the West Riding during which the protests in Lancashire had reverted to more constitutional forms.[39]

In Lancashire, complaint was mainly against overcrowding in the handloom weaving trade rather than against machines, and Luddism there was much more closely linked to aspirations for political reform than it was elsewhere.[40] Wells has recently emphasized that although mass protest can certainly be related to general infringements of the conventions of the 'moral economy' in the early nineteenth century, 'other factors demand analysis. Regional economic and social structures are two of the most important'.[41]

The same can even be said of Chartism.[42] Indeed, Disraeli's *Sybil*, written in 1845 and commonly considered to be a powerful statement of the thesis that there were 'Two Nations' at the time, actually depicts the degree and nature of regional fragmentation within the Chartist movement more clearly than its unity. In fact, the subtitle of 'The Two Nations' might well have been intended as an irony. The phrase is used by the extreme Chartist agitator Stephen Morley, not by the hero Egremont or Sybil herself, except in his remark that he had been *told* that things were so and in her declamation, at the end of the book, that things were *not* so. It is uttered by Morley in the same spirit as his animadversions about the barbarity of the family – and there can be little doubt about what Disraeli meant his readers to make of that. Much of the book represents a tour through numerous manufacturing districts in which it is emphasized that each has its own brand of economy, social structure and causes of unrest. Agricultural areas, rural industrial districts, northern factory settlements and Midland towns and villages of small manufacturing workshops are all displayed. The following exchange amongst workers in Wodgate (Wednesbury) typifies Disraeli's recognition of their particularities:

> 'I should like to hear the top sawyer from London,' said Juggins. 'We had a Chartist here the other day, but he did not understand our case at all.'
> 'I heard him,' said Master Nixon, 'but what's his Five Points to us? Why, he ayn't even got tommy among them.'
> 'Nor long stints,' said Waghorn.
> 'Nor butties,' said Juggins.

Morley and the other Chartists continually lament the fragmentation of workers' experiences between different industrial areas. As the moderate Chartist, Gerard, remarked to Morley: 'I wish the woollen and cotton districts were as bad to do as the iron, and we should need no holiday [i.e. symbolic pan-national cause] as you say.'[43]

What was clear to Disraeli has become even clearer since, notwithstanding – even in consequence of – the attempts of Thompson and those who have followed him in seeking evidence of national unity amongst the Chartists. In the South, predominantly in London, the movement was radical in political orientation, aimed mainly at political reform through the implementation of the Five Points, and its artisan leaders had considerable middle-class support. But although the ideas of the London Working Men's Association and leaders like William Lovett were endorsed by Midland reformers, they were not shared in the North, where the movement was anti-Whig middle class. Chartism failed conspicuously to impress the factory workers of northern textile towns, who were more preoccupied with immediate issues of living conditions, wages, hours of work and factory reform, concerns which were shared by the factory-owning Whig reformers of Lancashire.

It was the increasingly marginalized handloom weavers who took to Chartism in the North and in the textiles areas of the Midlands, but theirs was not the Chartism of Lovett and London. Led by Feargus O'Connor, it was a Tory movement there, nostalgic rather than reformist, concerned with the restoration of paternalist responsibilities and customary rights. O'Connor's rhetoric, larded with boasts about his landed connections, suited their cast of mind, not the manifestos of London artisan and middle-class reformers who 'thought and spoke in metaphors of industrial progress not credible to unskilled workers who continued to think with a peasant's mentality'.[44] The failure of the Complete Suffrage Unions in the North was due to the indifference of those guided by what Lovett saw as 'the abuses of the *Northern Star*', O'Connor's newspaper. What succeeded were the land banks set up by O'Connor to settle surplus industrial labour in ideal rural communities. These schemes, conversely, held no attraction for Chartist farmworkers, skilled urban artisans or factory workers.

> The 70,000 subscribers who seized the opportunity to escape into the past came mostly from the small Northern towns with declining industries, which filled the Chartist movement.[45]

The co-operative movement, inspired by a combination of Chartism and Owenism in the 1830s, was deeply divided along the same lines.[46] *Tout court* it involved the establishment of independent communities of property owners and artisans, who would exchange goods according to the hours of labour expended on them. Retail stores were initially intended to make profits to help finance the communities; indeed, they were frowned on by more rigorous devotees. The northern Chartists, as we have seen, took to the notion of utopian communities. So eventually did their southern brethren, amongst whom the incursion of Owenite objectives and the leadership of clergymen and other professional people with the growth of Christian Socialism after 1848 gave the movement an identical paternalistic tinge. The co-operative retail store mainly preoccupied people who had been unconcerned with Chartism, northern factory workers and miners who divorced it from the idea of labour exchanges and utopian communities. The purpose of co-operativism as they construed it was to provide, through the stores, wholesome food at a reasonable price combined with a means of saving. The movement was to serve the needs of consumers, not producers, and the starkly realistic ethos that informed their version was in heavy contrast to the idealism of the advocates of co-operative utopian communities. The co-operative 'movement' was thus fragmented from its beginnings:

> To say that co-operation in England in the 1850s lacked definition is to understand the situation. While it is true that the work of the Equitable Pioneers had gained considerable attention, Rochdale was not viewed as the centre of a co-operative movement – indeed, no such centre existed, nor for that matter was there much of anything to be called a Movement.[47]

This regional division in aims and philosophy was marked. The first attempt to organize co-operative wholesale societies to supply the retail stores was launched in 1831 in the North-West. In 1863 the successful North of England Co-operative Wholesale Agency (which became the CWS) was founded in Manchester. Only five of the forty-three members came from outside Lancashire and the West Riding; overtures from retail societies in the South were rebuffed, whilst societies in the North-East refused to have anything to do with the Agency unless it opened a depot in Newcastle.

The fragmentation of trade unions   Attempts to concert working-class pressure in trade unions were torn apart in the same way. Unions which did achieve national prominence and are sometimes in consequence taken to represent the worries and aspirations of all members of particular occupational groups were, nevertheless, regionally based organizations mainly concerned (especially when successful) with regional issues. The coal-miners, in advance of other workers in the effectiveness of their organization, were the first to attempt a national union.[48] The North-East was in the vanguard of militancy amongst the miners until the 1850s and the drive for national unity came from there. But militancy and solidarity were based upon the issue of the annual bonds through which, uniquely in England, hiring was organized in the Great Northern Coalfield. Bonded hiring had been common in other coalfields, but elsewhere it disappeared in the late eighteenth century. Not only was the negotiation of the bond each year an issue around which all miners in the North-East could rally, but the system binding men to contractual work after the bond was signed prevented labour stoppages at any other times and focused discontent powerfully on the meetings between the parties and their lawyers to fix next year's contracts. Labour relations were considerably different in the North-East in consequence.

Similarly, the preoccupations ascribed by Disraeli to Juggins, Nixon and Waghorn in the West Midlands would have been almost unintelligible to miners elsewhere. The butty or subcontracting system and the tommy shops that went with it had, like the bond, deep and widespread roots in the mining industry. 'By the late eighteenth century the system was operating in districts as far apart as western Scotland and South Wales, but in many areas it was already a declining force. In South Staffordshire, however, sub-contracting on an extensive scale persisted in full vigour', and was still employed at every colliery as late as the 1870s.[49] Bonded labour and the piece rates that went with it were appropriate to the large, deep, highly capitalized collieries of the North-East where men operated individually at pillar and stall workings; the butty system was suited to the numerous small collieries of the Black Country where men worked either very thick or very thin coal in gangs at longwall faces.

The North-East and Black Country did not simply define a spectrum, with all other coalfields settling somewhere in between, differing only in degree. In the part of the Lancashire coalfield between Wigan and Worsley (and in parts of South Wales, where the butty system was also retained, and eastern Scotland) the tradition of women working underground went back to the seventeenth century and was still strong in the early nineteenth. There, untroubled by the issues which exercised the miners of the North-East and Staffordshire, violence and subversion occurred during and after 1842 when women and children were deprived of the right to work underground with their husbands and fathers. This legislation was considered disruptive of family life and economically punitive in the Wigan coalfield. It was applauded elsewhere and strongly supported by both the Chartists and the Miners' Association of Great Britain and Ireland; a Wigan miner who moved to Oldham, where 1062 colliers signed a petition in 1842 deprecating the employment of women underground, was forced to return when he obdurately continued to take his wife to work with him.[50]

Thus, although miners were the first to react nationally against threats to wages and working hours, any move towards national action almost inevitably foundered on these regional particularities. In 1831, representatives of miners' unions in North Wales, Staffordshire, Lancashire, Cheshire and the West Riding came together with a delegate from South Wales at Bolton, at a time of great unrest in the coalfields.[51] There was no other sign of national co-ordination until 1842, when the Miners' Association of Great Britain and Ireland was founded. It lasted until 1848. Since the Bolton meeting, the union in the North-East had been crushed by opposition (though it regrouped briefly in the acrimonious bond negotiations of 1836–7), and that in the North-West had crumbled in satisfied lassitude after success. The Association was formed during the severe troubles of 1842 to aid strikes by providing funds and stopping blacklegs on a national scale. After initially resolving to combine with coal-owners against the public to force up prices, profits and wages, the Association was faced with a call for a national strike at its third meeting, at Glasgow, in 1844. Over 50,000 miners were represented at the meeting, and the strike call emanating from the North-East narrowly failed to get a majority vote. 'There could clearly be no general strike; but the North-East was too deeply committed in act and, perhaps more important, in feeling to accept a general verdict'.[52] The conference therefore gave licence to a general strike across the Great Northern Coalfield but refused permission to the Nottinghamshire and Yorkshire unions. Only token support was given to the North-East elsewhere and the flow of blacklegs was not staunched.

The strike failed, but unsanctioned wildcat action at particular collieries elsewhere succeeded in forcing up wages, and the Miners' Union of Lancashire, for example, organized strong concerted action within its region whilst the national movement was falling apart: money collected from the twenty-seven sub-districts into which the Lancashire branch of the national association was organized was channelled to men at the single collieries which were being picked off in sequence in a series of successful strikes. No money or help of other kind came into Lancashire from outside throughout this effective campaign. The precocious miners were like all other workers in this: national co-ordination was inappropriate and ineffectual in the early nineteenth century, but although inter-regional bonds were weak intra-regional solidarity was strong.

Regional identities

It was not just that national unity was fragile while it lasted and continually shattered quickly. The lines along which it shattered became more definite and consistent as industrialization unrolled. Artisanal London lined up against newer manufacturing areas elsewhere on a range of issues; south-east Lancashire around Manchester, south-west Lancashire around Liverpool, the Potteries around nascent Stoke, the West Midlands around Birmingham, south Yorkshire around Sheffield, west Yorkshire around Leeds, and Northumbria around Newcastle were often ranged for or against each other on particular issues, and broad arable acres still defined a coherent interest group that allied sometimes with and sometimes against shifting combinations of the rest.

Region coherence The growing cohesion and unity of character in the different industrial regions came to be generally recognized in the early nineteenth century. Not only did particular regions become identified with particular issues of national political reform, which was increasingly the case from the factory reform of the West Riding of Yorkshire, the anti-Poor Law reform and anti-Corn Law League of Manchester, to the currency reform of Birmingham.[53] These regional differences of preoccupation, generalized beyond particular issues, entered popular consciousness – 'the very name Manchester became synonymous with the new liberalism, even with a particular cultural style'[54] – and became one of the major currencies of English literature when the regional novel emerged as an important genre in the 1840s. This subject has received considerable attention from geographers and it would be superfluous to dwell on it here beyond emphasizing that regional novels were not concerned to distinguish London from the rest of England but to convey the peculiarities of particular provincial regions, adding vivid cultural accoutrements to Disraeli's economic and social analysis.

As will already be clear, economic differences lay at the roots of this comprehensive fragmentation. Alexis de Tocqueville recognized this on his visit to England in 1835, when he was particularly struck by the contrast between Manchester and Birmingham:

> At Birmingham almost all the houses are inhabited by one family only; at Manchester a part of the population lives in damp cellars, hot, stinking and unhealthy; thirteen to fifteen individuals in one. At Birmingham this is rare. At Manchester, stagnant puddles, roads paved badly or not at all. Insufficient public lavatories. All that is almost unknown in Birmingham. At Manchester a few great capitalists, thousands of poor workmen and little middle class. At Birmingham few large industries, many small industrialists. At Manchester workmen are counted by the thousand, two or three thousand in the factories. At Birmingham the workers work in their own houses or in little workshops in company with the master himself. At Manchester there is above all need for women and children. At Birmingham, particularly men, few women . . . the working people of Birmingham seem more healthy, better off, more orderly and more moral than those of Manchester.[55]

In Birmingham, as in Sheffield, there was usually widespread support for one particular cause in politics, whereas in Manchester, Leeds and Newcastle pressure was often divided as the employers sought one set of reforms and the workers another. In regions of small workshop production, radicalism had a degree of coherence that was absent from factory textiles and heavily capitalized mining areas, where society and social pressures were much more nearly split between capitalists and proletariat.

Thus, alongside the forces of fragmentation between regions there developed a growing uniformity of character within them, forged in the single great provincial cities around which the economies of each were becoming integrated. Faucher observed in 1844 that

> Manchester, like a diligent spider, is placed in the centre of the web, and sends forth roads and railways towards its auxiliaries, formerly villages but now towns, which serve as outposts to the grand centre of industry.. . . An order sent from Liverpool in the morning is discussed by the merchants in the Manchester Exchange at noon, and in the evening is distributed amongst the manufacturers in the environs. In less than eight days, the cotton spun at Manchester, Bolton, Oldham or Ashton, is woven in the sheds of Bolton, Stalybridge or Stockport; dyed and printed at Blackburn, Chorley or Preston and finished, measured and packed at Manchester.[56]

As economic activities in the same place became more interdependent and as sub-regional economic specializations made the interlinkages of different places within the same region more and more obvious (even though at the same time it made these places in some ways more and more different),[57] these tendencies towards regionwide integration were further encouraged; the liberalism of Manchester, for example, bound together numerous people from other south Lancashire towns.[58]

Migration patterns to the new industrial areas acted to the same end. Although sometimes across long distances between regions, they were overwhelmingly short-distance and intra-regional in character.[59] Changes of occupation were much less common than mobility between places to maintain the same kind of job, also, so that local customs of work practice were synthesized regionally as the industrial revolution proceeded.[60] The integration and expansion of the south-west Lancashire mining industry through competition in Liverpool was marked by the migration of colliers between Wigan, Prescot and St Helens but few miners came into the coalfield from outside Lancashire – indeed, few came even from the eastern part of the county. Bonded hiring in the North-East must have greatly cemented such tendencies towards uniformity in myriads of short-distance shifts of workplace after the annual renegotiations; certainly the similar shifting around of farm labourers in the South caused by bonded hiring had a powerful integrating effect on a regional scale in the nineteenth century.[61] Long-distance movements of any importance were often associated with the deliberate bringing in by employers of blacklegs, novel work practices or cheap labour and would be resented and resisted rather than accepted and encouraged amongst industrial labour forces. Short-distance movements were necessary to maintain the kinship and other bonds with home – and even more to permit the continual oscillation between old home and new place of work and develop the family networks across different industrial towns and villages – that seem to have been so important to successful integration into newly proletarianized industrial society.[62]

The potent localisms of pre-industrial England were thus gaining, through processes set in motion by industrialization, at least partial synthesis on the regional scale, and powerful new agencies came into being to define and emphasize these incipient but at first perhaps inchoate tendencies towards regional unity of outlook and purpose. The regional distinctions revealed in imaginative literature and expressed in national politics were to a significant extent consciously created by the people who were being distinguished; they were not simply precipitated automatically by general economic and social forces.

Regional consciousness　In the fullest examination of this creation of consciousness made to date, Money fixed its beginnings in the 1760s:

> from the whole experience of the West Midlanders during the thirty years which preceded the Revolutionary Wars in 1793, both with regard to the major events of national history and to their own local preoccupations, there emerges a growing sense, not only of the region's own special identity, but also of the contribution which it had to make to the wider development of society.[63]

Many of the elements that combined to produce this effect were local instances of the general tendencies already described, refracted through the particular needs and circumstances of the West Midlands. Leaders of commerce and industry in the region quickly realized that a fully roused and completely orchestrated public concern, encompassing landowners, farmers and artisans as well as captains of industry and commerce, formed the surest redoubt from which to launch sallies at central government. Garbett, Wedgwood and Boulton succeeded splendidly in their mobilization of regional opinion behind their initiative of the 1780s. It was on this firm platform that they tried to build the General Chamber of Manufacturers.

Before that, other issues affecting the whole region, transcending purely local concerns and requiring the intercession of Parliament, had provided similar and perhaps even more potent catalysts. The administration of the Poor Law, the formulation of building regulations, organizing the provision of a hospital, dispensary, asylum and workhouse in Birmingham itself, which was growing rapidly near a county boundary and without parliamentary representation, patently required the co-ordination of activity over a wide area to be effective.

> Examples of the reciprocal relationship which existed between Birmingham and its surroundings, and of the ways in which the different parts of the region were becoming aware of what they had in common are not hard to find, [but it was the building of canals in particular] that made the interdependence of different parts of the region impossible to ignore. It made the region as a whole increasingly aware of its relations with other parts of England. It produced a continuous exchange of views on a subject both indigenous to the region and important to the nation at large, an exchange which reflected not merely the rise of one centre but rather the need for particular interests in different places to learn to co-operate with each other, and with more distant areas for the sake of mutual advantage. Quite apart from the material benefits conferred by the canals themselves, the various activities connected with their construction thus exerted considerable influence on the emerging self-consciousness of the West Midlands.[64]

The need for the acquiescence of local landowners, capitalization and parliamentary legislation (and therefore a strong lobby) forged a powerful region-wide pressure group, as the same stimulus did in the same decades in south-west Lancashire.

In both these regions, newspapers were important in this process. Their customary blend of partisanship on national questions and neutrality on local issues gave a clear expression of regional cohesion in apposition to national concerns. In Birmingham, a regular column of canal news reflected and reinforced unitary local feeling. Numerous clubs and societies were also of inestimable importance in blending and articulating a coherent regional consciousness. From the various working men's drinking, insurance, debating and reading clubs (repositories of the proliferating broadsheets as well as newspapers) to the brilliantly intellectual Lunar Society of Matthew Boulton and his friends, these associations, which often recruited over wide areas and were overlapped and interleaved in a tangle of complexity, ensured both that people were able to 'ask questions and give answers of *our own* making',[65] and that the blueprints according to which this was done were not too dissimilar. The Lunar Society was, in its patrician attitudes and free-thinking radicalism, atypical of the generally Tory ethos of these societies in the West Midlands. It never had many more than a dozen members and did not outlast the eighteenth century.[66] The Bean Club was much more central in tying together the conservatism of landowners, craftsmen and professional people, a middle-class version of the 'Church and King' mentality which animated the mobs that pilloried Priestley and other 'Lunaticks' for suspected Jacobinism in the 1790s.

In Manchester, in contrast, the radical liberalism of a Whig Unitarian clique came completely to dominate the tone of politics and social concern. By the 1820s an uneasy alliance of free-thinking utilitarianism with a love of high culture and acute concern for social problems and responsibilities had been created in the two Unitarian congregations of the city. 'If we focus on the cultural and political formation of a liberal culture in the 1820s and 1830s we find individuals from these two chapels playing a strategic role: the same names recur again and again', comments Seed, in the foundation and running of the Literary and Philosophical Society, the Institution for the Encouragement of the Fine Arts, the Mechanics' Institute, the *Manchester Guardian*, the Society for the Diffusion of Useful Knowledge, the Chamber of Commerce, the Athenaeum, the Complete Suffrage Union, the Anti-Corn Law League and the Domestic Missions.[67] The Unitarian liberal philosophy maintained a hegemony in Manchester which was utterly different from the Toryism that was equally deeply entrenched in Birmingham. It may well be true that a consciousness of common interests was developing among the English upper class,[68] but none the less it was fractured by deep regional differences in the early nineteenth century.

Regional cultures It is no exaggeration to claim that regional cultures or *mentalités* were in process of formation amongst the distinctive economic structures, social associations, conflicts and appropriately shaped reactions to national parliamentary policies in the different regions of early industrial England. Workers and entrepreneurs alike, factory hands and miners as well as handloom weavers and artisans, were all to some extent consciously under the sway of impersonal forces outside the remit of their local communities and the strictures that could be applied there. Regional as well as class formation and solidarity was a response to these incursions into people's lives. As Kimble observed,

> It is not without interest to note . . . that wherever men are sensible of the permeation of society by a monotype culture, they are busy organizing associations for the encouragement of old regional ways. In France, where the differentiation of the country into *pays* . . . is probably stronger than in any other part of the world, staunch endeavours are being made to resuscitate dying folk-habits, local dialect and traditional arts and crafts. The French know (who better?) that it is the 'silent backward tracings', the feelings of cultural identity and group experiences surrounding place and home that compose the stuff by which regional consciousness is sustained and fostered.[69]

The cultural threat in England was the insecurity to both means of sustenance and home itself that industrialization brought; the industrial revolution did not destroy regional identities, as Kimble went on to assert, but, in a similar way to that which he recognized in modern France, it led to a considerable and deliberate revival. Nostalgia became a potent source of identity and security in the new industrial world. The richness of the pre-industrial cultural variants to which workers and their employers looked back combined with identifications forged for more immediately material purposes to make the regional consciousness of the time particularly acute.

Sustained interest in the dying folk customs, proverbs, pastimes, games and modes of speech of ordinary people dates back in England to the work of John Ray in the late seventeenth century.[70] It gradually increased through the eighteenth century, with articles on local dialects appearing in the *Gentleman's Magazine* from the 1740s, to reach a peak in the early nineteenth century.[71] Intense interest was maintained until the end of the century, which saw the publication of authoritative and scholarly bibliographies, glossaries and dictionaries of English dialects.[72] Weber has recently emphasized the importance for regional distinctiveness in France of the fact that a large proportion of Frenchmen spoke a local patois rather than the French language until the last quarter of the nineteenth century.[73] English dialect speech must have had the same effect.

True to Kimble's prediction, interest in and use of dialect became much more intense and self-conscious in the late eighteenth and nineteenth centuries in all industrial areas, but most particularly in those where a large and distinct proletariat was being formed. The beginnings of both were in south-east Lancashire, where *The View of the Lancashire Dialect; by way of a dialogue between Tummus o' William's o' Margit o' Roaph's and Meary o' Dick's o' Tummy o' Peggy's. Showing in that speech the comical adventures and misfortunes of a Lancashire clown* was published in 1746. Complete with a glossary, this first written encouragement to sustain dialect speech in the region was enormously successful amongst the ordinary people at whom it was aimed by its author, John Collier (a Milnrow schoolmaster) alias Tim Bobbin, 'an Opp'n speyker o' th' dialect' and 'Fellow of the Syssyphean Society of Dutch Loom Weavers'. The gentle lampoon of folkways, hilarity at misfortune, mockery of pretentiousness and firm identification with ordinary workers expressed in the title and the pseudonymic attributions of Collier's book were to remain typical of the genre. Twenty-six editions and numerous pirated versions of Tim Bobbin's work were produced in Lancashire before 1820.[74]

The antiquarian interest in dialect and other expressions of folk culture was nationwide, and national literature contained carefully worked versions of regional modes of speech; but apart from William Barnes, all purely dialect writers of note came from the proletariat of newly industrialized areas. Their writings were the true literature of the new working class.[75] Nostalgic in mode of expression, imagery and subject matter, dialect literature gave a powerful impetus to conservatism. It was also rigidly and deliberately exclusive. George Eliot might, in her rendering of dialect, have been 'constantly checked by the duty of being generally intelligible',[76] but dialect writers gloried in their general unintelligibility, giving the most powerful possible expression to introverted regional consciousness. Dialect literature was meant to be read aloud in public, making full use of regional phonetic characteristics which are difficult to express in writing. It sounds much more distinctive and opaque to the outsider than it appears in print.[77]

Whilst dialect literature came from the working class, its exclusiveness was more to region than to class. As Vicinus has stressed, this prevented the development of a national working-class literature; but, 'although the use of dialect meant speaking to a limited audience, it had the advantage of building up local feeling – *my* region and culture against the rest of the country. . . . The most successful writing was integral to a particular locality and could not be translated without loss'.[78] Moreover, the easy facility in different modes of speech (which amounted almost to bilingualism) possessed by most Englishmen of the time[79] meant that all classes could share in the proud if self-mocking displays of local chauvinism that the highly popular dialect readings, if not normal dialect conversation, provided. Certainly, the antiquarian interest in dialect and its philology was an exclusively upper- and middle-class concern, and poets such as Edwin Waugh and Ben Brearley were as at home in the salons of the Manchester Literary Club as they were at the annual celebrations of village co-operative and temperance societies.[80]

It is difficult to generalize about dialect literature because its form, subject matter and context changed through time and varied from region to region.[81] However, there does seem to have been a general progression from nostalgic concern with a disappearing past during most of the second half of the eighteenth century to expressions in ordinary people's language of more general issues – or rather with the reaction of ordinary people to interests suggested to or foisted upon them by their betters or from 'outside'. Broadsheets of this kind became very common at the end of the eighteenth century and remained so until the time of Chartism, and newspaper columns of the same style became features of the local press in most industrial areas. Both these preoccupations continued to be widespread, and so did the comic, satirical or pathetic tone of most dialect writing, gently parodying insiders, mocking outsiders distinguished by their standard speech, or evoking wistful sadness at the vulnerability of workers and their families in the industrial world. By the middle of the nineteenth century a new dimension was added as dialect poetry reached its peak of artistic achievement in the lyrics of Edwin Waugh, Ben Brearley and Samuel Laycock in Lancashire and John Hartley in the West Riding. Their verse might seem to stray too far into sentimentality for modern taste, but their accomplished use of the lengthened vowels and elided, clipped or extended consonants which give such marked rhythms to dialect speech produced effects of exquisite, haunting beauty.

It is important to stress the very great popularity of this literature and that dialect was the *lingua franca* of ordinary people: there was a lively debate in Rochdale over whether the free school teaching under the Act of 1870 should be in dialect or standard English. It is also important to stress the generally stoical tenor of the idiom. Outside north-east England, where dialect songs, verses and dialogues commonly expressed social protest and radical sentiments,[82] dialect was most frequently directed against new-fangled notions brought in from outside and against the conceptualization in abstract terms of the economic and social contexts in which people lived.[83] It was an existentialist literature, one that proselytized native shrewdness, self-help, community support and, above all, the strength of the bulwark provided by the family against the harsh pressures that dependence on industrial employment brought. It is surely not difficult to imagine the effectiveness of the attacks in dialect on Priestley and Jacobinism in general in Birmingham in the 1790s;[84] or the corrosiveness to Chartism of lampoons of O'Connor and O'Connell in heavy dialect conversations distributed as broadsheets, and the ridicule heaped upon the labour theory of value in such writings as Sally Bobbinwinder's *Conversations between Harry Pickenpeg, Jack Shuttle and Henry Emptybobbin*, written in 1838, the year of the Charter.[85]

Then, at about mid-century, when dialect entertainment was moving from bawdy pub gatherings towards the music hall in the North-East, it elided with middle-class concerns in the North-West and West Riding. The respectable factory operatives of the textiles towns and many of those below them in the social order were fully able to express 'in their own way' the values of temperance, co-operativism, moderation and family life. It would be a cardinal error to neglect the impact of poems such as Waugh's 'Come whoam to thy childer an' me' (which sold 20,000 copies within days of its publication in Manchester in 1856) on beliefs in the virtues of temperance and domestic devotion; or of Laycock's 'Welcome bonny brid' on confidence in family consolation and a rejection of political reaction to the effects of the Cotton Famine.[86] Modern Marxist historians emphasize that language was of inestimable importance in the development of consciousness in the nineteenth century.[87] But the language of the working class was not that of the political speeches, broadsheets and texts with which they concern themselves. Dialect speech and literature, in their subject matter, imagery and values as much as their phonetics, united in bonds that were regionally specific what political economy in theory divided, and divided what in theory it united.

Even though Lancashire and the West Riding were the regions where a confrontation between capitalists and proletariat had promised to be most stark in the early nineteenth century, it is surely not entirely satisfactory to conceive of this as something of marginal significance in the development of English society, a series of 'hegemonic' impositions of 'false consciousness' on working people in those regions where dialect traditions were strongest. Family solidarity, community support, self-help and independence of spirit had always been as important in the domestic industrial economies of the North, which were subject to intense cyclical disruption long before the industrial revolution, as they were, for other reasons, in Barnes's and Hardy's Wessex. So, too, one can presume, had a predisposition towards hilarity or pathos rather than gentler sentiments or cool reason and abstract argument. The crystallization of these values and attitudes in the dialects of south-east Lancashire and the West Riding, no less than in Wessex, was as much a tenacious espousal of what was valued in the old as it was a false evaluation of the new; stoicism is neither without intellectual pedigree nor indefensible as a philosophy of life, and extremities of mood and tone are not without cathartic value. Their vivid expression in dialect speech generally, and in its literature in particular, gave both a justification for and a means of displaying a hotter pride in regional identity – in being Lanky, Tyke, Geordie or Brummy – than in membership of some nationwide category defined in the abstractions of political economy. The very use of dialect actually repudiated such notions; it was a message as well as a medium.

The economic basis of regionalism

Consciousness of regional identity was deeply rooted in fertile soil. The intense local peculiarities of pre-industrial England were blended in the mainly short distance migrations that peopled the new industrial towns. In one way a reaction to threats posed to old values and life styles by industrial urbanization, in another it was moulded by the institutions and practices that were created by industrial life, then intensified in opposition to economic and political pressures that came from 'outside'. To explain it would require an account of why economic development was so diverse between regions, so markedly variable in relation to national commercial policies from region to region, and so cohesive within the different regions themselves.

Canals and regional economic development   Such an explanation cannot be attempted here. Neither the space nor the necessary information on England's economic geography are available. It is, none the less, worthy of remark that one of the most striking peculiarities of English industrialization was that it was based for over a generation upon haulage along a waterway network. The expense of canal construction per mile and topographical constraints ensured a sparse density.[88] But the reduction of haulage costs by canals was greater by far, on average to 25 per cent of prior costs, than that resulting from any other transport innovation. Thus, relatively few places, particularly the nodes and termini, were given enormous advantages for mass production when the canal system was built. Reciprocal connections between these places were intense, and by the end of the eighteenth century the spatial rationalization of production through competition and the development of efficient economic linkages along the canals was beginning to produce regularly patterned and highly integrated structures of production.[89]

This arterial network of the industrial revolution was not a single unitary system of sparse but high-capacity channels. Because of topography and the disposition of the coalfields which alone could guarantee a return on investment, it was very patchy and disjointed. Through traffic was difficult on the canals too, because of variations in width, depth and lock sizes and the frequent trans-shipments required by the general absence of firms in the long-distance carriage business. Places on the canals were the equivalent of twenty-five times further apart in terms of journey times than places at equal distances apart on the surfaced roads of today. The vast majority of shipments were, for these various reasons, over short distances or to and from the main coastal ports. Dense patches on the network thus developed highly integrated economies largely separate from each other. It was the realization of the intra-regional nature of the huge benefits that canal transport brought which generated such strongly regionalized pressures for canal construction.

As they developed on the basis of their comparative advantages and the external economies of scale available to particular industries within them, the canal-based economies became more specialized, more differentiated from each other and more internally unified. Each emergent regional system had its own economic dynamic, produced by the interplay of local resource endowments, traditional skills and the character of the markets it served. Each, too, contained a large proportion of the multiplier effects generated by manufacturing, simply because it was so separate from the others and from London. In particular, tertiary functions were contained within each region and became, like all other aspects of production, more clearly sorted spatially within them as growth proceeded.[90] Manchester, Liverpool, Leeds, Birmingham and the other great regional capitals were, by the end of the eighteenth century and increasingly so as the nineteenth century passed, the places where provincial manufacturers made their contacts with each other and with overseas suppliers and buyers. With this regional economic integrity came full regional containment of the whole social spectrum that was produced by manufacturing and commerce. This is why the provincial capitals were so different from each other and why the political lobbies that could be assembled within them were so formidable and so separate.

Command of the overseas markets upon which these industrial regions depended was heavily dependent upon policies pursued by national government.[91] The necessary oppositional element in the growth of regional consciousness was provided by the interaction of all the industrial (and agricultural) regions with Parliament in London. It was a threat to overseas markets – or rather a series of them – that set off the intense lobbying from manufacturing interests in the 1780s, and it was in that coming together that the manufacturers of different regions realized the depth of the differences between them.

The early effects of railways This delicate balance between regional separation and national integration was, it has often been remarked, tilted sharply in favour of the latter by the building of the dense, rapid transit and nationally integrated railway network. As Samuel Smiles observed, 'the locomotive . . . virtually reduced England to a sixth of its size'. (The fraction would in fact have been much larger for the haulage of goods and smaller for the movement of people and information.) Long-term processes of integration were set in motion. The difficulties of communication which had bedevilled effective national co-ordination between social groups and organizations of all kinds, and especially, perhaps, those of working-class protest and self-help, were removed. In his authoritative history of the English trade union movement, Pelling emphasized that 'the freer movement of men and materials had to wait for the coming of the railways in the 1830s and 1840s, and it was not until thereafter that national unions of particular industries became practicable'.[92] Raw materials and products for the home market quickly began to flow over long distances and burst through the old regional barriers. This was one of the causes of the formation of the national coal proprietors' association of the 1840s.

Inexorably, as part of this process of national social and economic integration, London again began to exert the sway over national commerce that it had lost to the canal-based regional capitals.[93] With this commercial activity came those whose business it was. The role of London changed from that of an external irritant suffered by all provincial regions to that of a truly national economic and social metropolis to which all regions were more and more closely bound by functionally necessary ties.[94] This shift of economic reality is clearly evident in the economic indices calculated by Lee.[95] By the third quarter of the nineteenth century, London and the South-East were growing faster than any other region, with a much higher commercial component in a more diverse economy than those of the provincial regions. Regional cultures, like regional economies, began to suffer the same metropolitan threat: the railways

> made it possible for a single entertainer to visit all major working class centres in a matter of months.. . . The dominant movement in the music halls was away from the particular and towards the general. National fads and national stars could not help but alter the nature of class culture which had received its life and vitality from the concrete, the familiar and the local.[96]

The centre of this popular entertainment was, of course, London.

The railways thus inevitably set in motion, both directly through more rapid communication of people and ideas, and indirectly through the economic forces they released, powerful currents of national integration. And yet the middle forty years of the nineteenth century, during which the railway network was built was the very period when regional cultural consciousness and cohesion reached its zenith: the regional novel, no less than the national unions and employers' associations, came with the railway. Moreover, the national unions and associations of the middle nineteenth century split apart no less comprehensively than the General Chamber of Manufacturers of the 1780s. This is neither contradictory nor paradoxical. Greater national integration in all aspects of life would at first throw into sharp relief the differences between the regional economies and cultures that had been evolving for nearly a century in relative isolation.[97] Moreover, national economic cohesion brought greater regional specialization in the short and medium terms. The process that would eventually extinguish regionalism at first necessarily intensified it.

Conclusion

It has only been possible in this paper to sketch crude outlines in bold strokes. Examples and references to relevant literature have been sparsely illustrative rather than exhaustive and I am acutely aware that many of my baldly formulated assertions would require much finer detail and more careful colouring to make them readily convincing. Even so, it should be apparent that when the wide range of subjects which have been included are brought together it is possible to discern a coherent pattern amongst them: one of increasingly integrated and differentiated regions. This is not simply to say that each separate aspect was regionally varied, but that the differences manifested by each of them co-varied to a striking extent. The implication of this is not that we require more regional studies of individual historical elements, but some examination of how far differences in all these elements hung together geographically. Modern historians are increasingly becoming specialist in particular analytically defined fields of study. As the references provided show, they are more and more thoroughly revealing the spatial variance that existed within particular aspects of life in early industrial England; but they rarely seem to notice the relationships between these differences. And why should they? Their analytical terms do not allow this kind of conceptualization. 'The identification of inter-relationships between apparently disparate phenomena is the very essence of . . . regional geography'[98] and it is our job, not theirs, to write the regional geography of early industrial England.

I am not, of course, arguing that doing so would solve many currently pressing problems of historical explanation. It would simply add another dimension to those problems. Regionalism was no more important than the other identifications of which people were becoming conscious – indeed, creating – in order to exert some control over the effects of industrialization upon their lives. Awareness of class, nationalism, heightened community consciousness, nonconformist religion and utilitarian agencies such as unions, co-operatives, insurance clubs and temperance societies, and even more the philosophy that underlay them, all provided other sources of identity and influence. The relationships between them were as contradictory as they were coherent, and regionalism does not offer a privileged point of synthesis amongst them. None the less, it did grow, interact with and influence the rest; the failure of national co-ordination in social and political movements of all kinds, the economic surge of the middle nineteenth century and the lack of national class formation must all have been related to the evolving regional structure of English economy and society. Changes in the economic, social and political systems of the time cannot be fully comprehended, nor can the accommodations made by ordinary people to the effects of industrialization on their lives, without some exploration of England's regional geography.

At the very least, it is incontestably true that a regional geography worthy of exploration did actually exist during and after the industrial revolution; that territorial identifications grew rather than withered away, and that recognition of this might lead us to discover something that is important for understanding the history of that period and all that has flowed from it. The regional concept deserves to be treated as something more than an absurd stalking horse, of use only to those who wish to sneak into the modish closets of epistemology; perhaps it still provides the only terms in which important problems in the empirical study of industrial as well as pre-industrial societies can be expressed.

Notes

1 Feyerabend, P. 1978: *Against method: outline of an anarchistic theory of knowledge* (London), p. 47.

2 Wrigley, E. A. 1965: Changes in the philosophy of geography. In Chorley, R. J. and Haggett, P. (eds), *Frontiers in geographical teaching* (London), pp. 9–10.

3 Kimble, G. H. T. 1951: The inadequacy of the regional concept, in Stamp, L. D. and Wooldridge, S. W. (eds), *London essays in geography* (London), p. 151.

4 Friedmann, J. 1979: On the contradictions between city and countryside. In Folmer, H. and Oosterhaven, J. (eds), *Spatial inequalities and regional development* (The Hague), p. 29.

5 It is perhaps not entirely paradoxical that there seems recently to have been renewed interest in regional studies in history of a more old-fashioned kind. For example, Pollard, S. 1981: *Peaceful conquest: The industrialisation of Europe 1760–1970* (London); Marshall, J. D. 1981: The study of local and regional communities, *Northern Hist.* 17, 203–30; Thompson, F. M. L. 1981: review article on regional histories, *History* 66, 436–69.

6 Floud, R. and McCloskey, D. (eds) 1981: *The economic history of Britain since 1750* (Cambridge); see also Crouzet, F. 1982: *The Victorian economy* (London).

7 Hartwell, R. M. 1969: Economic growth in England before the industrial revolution: some methodological issues. *J. Econ. Hist.* 29, 30.

8 Wrigley, E. A. and Schofield, R. 1980: *The population history of England 1547–1871* (London).

9 Neale, R. S. 1981: *Class in English history 1680–1850* (Oxford), p. 77.

10 Thompson, E. P. 1968: *The making of the English working class* (Harmondsworth).

11 Wrightson, K. 1982: *English society 1580–1688* (London), p. 225. This view is elaborated in Wrightson, K. 1977: 'Aspects of social differentiation in rural England c. 1580–1660'. *J. Peasant Stud.* 5, 32–47.

12 See, notably, MacFarlane, A. 1978: *The origins of English individualism* (Oxford); Bushaway, B. 1982: *By rite: Custom, ceremony and community in England 1700–1880* (London).

13 For example, Barrell, J. 1972: *The idea of landscape and the sense of place 1730–1840: An approach to the poetry of John Clare* (Cambridge) and Barrell, J. 1980: *The dark side of the landscape: the rural poor in English painting 1730–1840* (Cambridge).

14 Thompson, E. P. 1974: Patrician society, plebeian culture. *J. social Hist.* 7, 382–405 and Thompson, E. P. 1979: Eighteenth century society: class struggle without class. *Social Hist.* 4, 133–66.

15 The importance of village culture in mediating working-class responses to political pressure and economic changes had been thoroughly explored by Calhoun, C. 1982: *The question of class struggle: Social foundations of popular radicalism during the industrial revolution* (Oxford).

16 Butlin, R. A. 1981: *The transformation of rural England c. 1580–1800: A study in historical geography* (Oxford), pp. 9–22.

17 For some recent synopses see Fulbrook, M. 1982: The English revolution and the revisionist revolt, *Social Hist.* 7, 249–64; Holmes, C. 1979–80: The county community in Stuart historiography, *J. Br. Stud.* 19, 54–73; Herrup, C. 1983: The counties and the country: some thoughts on seventeenth century historiography, *Social Hist.* 8, 169–81.

18 The phrases are from Morrill, J. S. 1976: *The revolt of the provinces* (London), p. 22.

19 Morgan, V. 1979: The cartographic image of 'the country' in early modern England. *Trans. R. Hist. Soc.* 5th Ser. 29, 129–54.

20 Keith-Lucas, B. 1980: *The unreformed local government system* (London), p. 42. Much of the information in this and the next paragraph has been taken from this source.

21 Ward, W. R. 1953: *The English land tax in the eighteenth century* (London).

22 Borsay, P. 1977: The English urban renaissance: the development of provincial urban culture *c.* 1680–*c.* 1760. *Social Hist.* 5, 581–603.

23 Kerridge, E. 1973: *The farmers of old England* (London), p. 73.

24 For a summary of his views see Everitt, A. 1979: Country, county and town: patterns of regional evolution in England. *Trans. R. Hist. Soc.* 5th Ser. 29, 79–108.

25 Underdown, D. 1979: The chalk and the cheese: contrasts among the English clubmen. *Past and Present* 85, 25–48. This distinction, long used by agrarian historians, is now becoming commonplace in social history. For example, Wrightson 1977: op. cit (note 11); Bushaway, B. 1981: Custom, crime and conflict in the English woodlands. *Hist. Today* 31, 37–43.

26 Langton, J. and Hoppe, G. 1983: Town and country in the development of early modern Western Europe. *Hist. Geogr. Res. Ser.* 11.

27 The phrase is from Everitt 1979: op. cit., p. 106 (note 24).

28 Everitt 1979: op. cit., p. 94 (note 24).

29 Hart, J. F. 1982: The highest form of the geographer's art. *Ann. Ass. Am. Geogr.* 7, 1–29 draws a sensible comparison between the conceptualization and definition of periods in history and regions in geography.

30 On the supression of the term 'the country' by 'the provinces' in the late eighteenth century see Everitt 1979: op. cit. (note 24); Read, D. 1964: *The rise of the provinces: A study in political influence* (London), pp. 1–4.

31 Material on the County Associations has been taken from Read 1964: op. cit., pp. 10–17.

32 Read 1964: op. cit., pp. 23–4 (note 30).

33 The section on the General Chamber is based on Read 1964: op. cit., pp. 23–4 (note 30); Bowden, W. 1925: *Industrial society in England towards the end of the eighteenth century* (New York), pp. 169–93; Money, J. 1971: Birmingham and the West Midlands, 1760–1793: Politics and regional identity in the English provinces in the later eighteenth century. *Midland History* 1, 1–19; Money, J. 1977: *Experience and identity: Birmingham and the West Midlands 1760–1800* (Manchester), pp. 35–47.

34 Read 1964: op. cit., p. 34 (note 30).

35 Money 1977: op. cit., p. 39 (note 33).

36 Read 1964: op. cit., p. 13 (note 30).

37 Taylor, A. J. 1953: Combination in the mid-nineteenth century coal industry. *Trans. R. Hist. Soc.* 5th Ser. 3, 39.

38 Money 1977: op. cit., p. 46 (note 33).

39 Gregory, D. 1982: *Regional transformation and the industrial revolution: A geography of the Yorkshire woollen industry* (London), p. 152.

40 Dinwiddy, J. 1979: Luddism and party politics in the Northern Counties. *Social Hist.* 33–63.

41 Wells, R. 1977: The revolt of the South-West, 1800–01: A study in English popular protest. *Social Hist.* 6, 714.

42 Chartism is at present the subject of lively debate and it is impossible to offer uncontroversial generalizations. Thompson 1968: op. cit. (note 10) stressed the national cohesiveness of the movement, in contradiction to the view presented in Briggs, A. 1959: *Charist studies* (London). There now seems to be a swing back towards Briggs's view. See Gregory 1982: op. cit. (note 39); Epstein, J. and Thompson, D. (eds) 1982: *The Chartist experience: Studies in working class radicalism and culture, 1830–1860* (London); Thomis, M. J. and Holt, P. 1977: *Threats of revolution in Britain 1788–1848* (London).

43 Disraeli, B. 1845: *Sybil, or the two nations* (1980 edn, Harmondsworth), quotations from pp. 440 and 388.

44 Soffer, R. N. 1965: Attitudes and allegiances in the unskilled North, 1830–1850. *Int. J. Social Hist.* 10, 439. The appropriateness of this interpretation has been splendidly restated by Calhoun 1982: op. cit. (note 15).

45 Soffer 1965: op. cit., p. 453 (note 44).

46 I am indebted to Martin Purvis of St John's College, Oxford, for the following information about the co-operative movement, which is the subject of his DPhil research.

47 Backstrom, P. 1964: *Christian socialism and cooperation in Victorian England* (London), p. 41.

48 Taylor, A. J. 1955: The Miners' Association of Great Britain and Ireland, 1842–48: a study in the problem of integration. *Economica* NS 22, 45–60.

49 Taylor, A. J. 1960: The sub-contract system in the British coal industry in Pressnell, L. S. (ed.), *Studies in the industrial revolution* (London), pp. 215–35.

50 John, A. V. 1978: Colliery legislation and its consequences: 1842 and the women miners of Lancashire. *Bull. John Rylands Univ. Lib. of Manchester* 61, 78–114; John, A. V. 1980: *By the sweat of their brows: Women workers at Victorian coalmines* (London); Langton, J. 1979: *Geographical change and industrial revolution: Coalmining in South-West Lancashire, 1590–1799* (Cambridge).

51 The following account is based on Taylor 1955: op. cit. (note 48).

52 Taylor 1955: op. cit., pp. 54–5 (note 48).

53 Read 1964: op. cit. (note 30).

54 Seed, J. 1982: Unitarianism, political economy and the antinomies of liberal culture in Manchester. *Social Hist.* 7, 1–26.

55 Quoted in Read 1964: op. cit., p. 36 (note 30).

56 Quoted in Gregory, D. (1984) Contours of crisis? Sketches for geography of class struggle in the early industrial revolution. In Gregory, D. and Baker, A. R. H. *Explorations in historical geography* (London).

57 This is emphasized both by Gregory (1984) and in Hudson, P. (1983) in a review of Gregory 1982: op. cit. (note 39) in *J. Hist. Geogr.* 9, 313–15.

58 Seed 1982: op. cit. (note 54).

59 Redford, A. 1964: *Labour migration in England 1800–1850* (Manchester); Anderson, M. 1971: *Family structure in nineteenth century Lancashire* (Cambridge).

60 For example, Langton 1979: op. cit. (note 50).

61 Barrell, J. 1982: Geographies of Hardy's Wessex. *J. Hist. Geogr.* 8, 347–61; Anderson 1971: op. cit. (note 59); Hochstadt, S. 1982: Social history and politics: a materialised view. *Social Hist.* 7, 75–83; Rose, M. E. 1981: Social change and the industrial revolution. In Floud and McCloskey (eds) op. cit., pp. 253–78 (note 6).

63 Money 1971: op. cit., p. 1 (note 33).

64 Money 1971: op. cit., p. 2 (note 33).

65 Money 1977: op. cit., p. 99 (note 33).

66 Gill, C. 1952: *History of Birmingham* (Oxford), vol. 1, pp. 145–6.

67 Seed 1982: op. cit., p. 4 (note 54).

68 Mantoux, P. 1961: *The industrial revolution in the eighteenth century* (London), p. 388; Billinge, M. Reconstructing societies in the past: the collective biography of local communities. In Baker, A. R. H. and Billinge, M. (eds), *Period and place: research methods in historical geography* (Cambridge), pp. 19–32.

69 Kimble 1952: op. cit., p. 168 (note 3).

70 Ray, J. 1674: *A collection of English words not generally used . . .* (London).

71 Skeat, W. W. 1873: *English dialect society: bibliographical list*, Part I (London).
72 Notably, Wright, J. (ed.) 1898–1905: *The English dialect dictionary*, 6 vols (London) based on the work of the English Dialect Society, founded in 1873, which also published numerous bibliographies under the editorship of W. W. Skeat and J. H. Nodal.
73 Weber, E. 1977: *Peasants into Frenchmen: The modernisation of rural France, 1870–1914* (London).
74 Brook, G. L. 1963: *English dialects* (London).
75 Brook 1963: op. cit.; Vicinus, M. 1974: *The industrial muse: A study of nineteenth century British working class literature* (London).
76 Skeat 1873: op. cit., p. viii, quoting a letter from Eliot.
77 Brook 1963: op. cit. (note 74).
78 Vicinus 1974: op. cit. p. 190 (note 75).
79 Bodleian Library/English Dialect Society/Miscellaneous Circulars &c/Soc 30205 C²⁄₀₁ contains some interesting observations on people's use of different modes of speech. For example, a cutting from the *Saturday Review*, 12 May 1888, suggests that 'farmers talk to their labourers in one tongue and to their equals in another . . . to their superiors yet another, [a person] only unbending himself to his equals . . . in his own tongue'.
80 Vicinus 1974: op. cit. (note 75).
81 The following account is based mainly on Vicinus 1974: op. cit. (note 75), although it should be pointed out that she does not comment upon the regional differences she describes and treats dialect literature nationally as a species of false class consciousness unless it expressed sentiments of social protest.
82 Colls, R. 1977: *The collier's rant: Song and culture in the industrial village* (London).
83 Indeed, 'the vocabulary of dialects is extraordinarily rich and vigorous in certain fields, but it is usually confined to the affairs of everyday life and is inadequate for the expression of many of the abstract ideas that need to be expressed in literature'. Barnes's use of dialect 'enabled him to elude in his verse those dreams and speculations which cannot leave alone the mystery of things . . . and helped him to fall back on dramatic truth by making his personages express the notions of life prevalent in their sphere'. Brook 1963: op. cit., pp. 190–1 (note 74); Hardy, T. 1908: 'Preface' in *Selected poems of William Barnes* (London), pp. xi–xii.
84 Money 1977: op. cit. (note 33).
85 Vicinus 1974: op. cit. (note 75).
86 'Like Edwin Waugh and many other dialect authors, Laycock is at his best when portraying strong family affection against a background of poverty' and William Barnes's 'favourite theme is married happiness'. Brook 1963: p. 193 (note 75).
87 For example, Seed 1982: op. cit. (note 54); Jones, G. S. 1982: The language of Chartism. In Epstein and Thompson 1982, pp. 3–58 (note 42).
88 Information on canals has been taken from Jackman, W. T. 1916: *The development of transportation in modern England* (London); Dyos, J. and Aldcroft, D. 1969: *British transport: An economic survey from the seventeenth century to the twentieth* (Leicester). Theoretical ideas have been drawn from Lachene, R. 1965: Networks and the location of economic activity. *Pap. Reg. Sci. Ass.* (Ghent Meeting), 183–96; Wrigley, E. A. 1962: The supply of raw materials in the industrial revolution: *Econ. Hist. Rev.* 2nd Ser. 15: 1–16.
89 For example, Langton, J. 1983: 'Liverpool and its hinterland in the late eighteenth century'. In Anderson, B. L. and Stoney, P. J. M. (eds), *Commerce, industry and transport: Studies in economic change on Merseyside* (Liverpool), pp. 1–25.

90 For example Wise, M. W. 1949: Birmingham and its trade relations in the early
    eighteenth century. *Univ. of Birmingham Hist. J.* 2, 53–68; Rowlands, M. B. 1975:
    Masters and men in the West Midland metal trades in the industrial revolution
    (Manchester); Gregory (forthcoming) op. cit. (note 56).

91 Although it is now customary to play down the importance of overseas trade in English
    economic growth generally in the early nineteenth century, it is still conceded that
    overseas markets and raw materials were of massive importance to the rapidly growing
    manufacturing industries. Crouzet 1982: op. cit. (note 6); Thomas, R. P. 1981: Over-
    seas trade and Empire. In Floud and McCloskey (eds), op. cit. (note 6), pp. 87–102.

92 Pelling, H. 1963: *A history of British trade unionism* (London), p. 4.

93 Dyos, H. J. 1971: Greater and greater London: metropolis and provinces in the
    nineteenth and twentieth centuries. In Bromley, J. S. and Kossman, E. H. (eds),
    Britain and the Netherlands (The Hague), vol. 4, pp. 89–102.

94 It should be remembered too, that this was the time when central government took
    upon itself the control through legislation of large sectors of life which had previously
    been subject to local authority. Hennock, E. P. 1982: Central/local government
    relations in England: an outline 1800–1950. *Urban Hist. Yb* (Leicester), pp. 38–49.

95 Lee C. H. 1981: Regional growth and structural change in Victorian Britain. *Econ.
    Hist. Rev.* 2nd Ser. 34, 438–52.

96 Vicinus 1974: op. cit., p. 257 (note 75).

97 Lee 1981: op. cit. (note 95); Jewkes, J. 1930: The localisation of the cotton industry:
    Econ. Hist. 2, 91–110; Taylor, A. J. 1949: Concentration and specialisation in the
    Lancashire cotton industry, 1825–1850. *Econ. Hist. Rev.* 2nd Ser. 1, 114–22.

98 Hart 1982: op. cit., p. 22 (note 29).

4   Ray Hudson,
Preface to 'Wrecking a Region'

Excerpts from: R. Hudson, *Wrecking a Region: State Policies, Party
Politics and Regional Charge in North East England.* London: Pion
(1989)

I was born and brought up in Alnwick, a small market town just off the
northern tip of the north-east coalfield in rural mid-Northumberland. The town
is located at a sort of cultural divide, between mining areas to the south,
agricultural ones to the north. The northernmost deep mine, Shilbottle, is (or,
more accurately, was) located some three miles south of Alnwick and provided
employment for many men in the town, my father amongst them. In the latter
half of the 1960s I went off to university in Bristol. As I returned periodically
for holidays I become conscious of the changes that were increasingly apparent
in the region: collieries closed while new factories opened, railways were shut
down while new roads opened, town centres were pulled apart and put together
again in a very different style – all around there was evidence of change. In
1972, more by an accident of the labour market for recent doctoral research

students than through any design of mine to become a return migrant, I took up a job at Durham University and returned to the North-East (albeit on the 'wrong' side of another critical cultural divide within the North-East, the River Tyne). I was curious to discover more about the character of and the reasons for the changes that were, in various ways, transforming the North-East and affecting the lives of people that I had known for many years. Even the most cursory examination soon revealed the enormous significance of state policies as the proximate causes of these changes. Thus began a series of research projects, centred on trying to unravel the relationships between State policies and different aspects of such changes that have provided the basis for this book.

There are probably very few books that do not alter in conception between the initial proposals and the end product. This one is no exception for the reasons outlined below.

For many years one of the main concerns of human geography – indeed, its main preoccupation – was the understanding of regions, with the main emphasis on the description of their unique characteristics. In so far as there was an attempt to explain these, it drew upon the internal characteristics of regions without relating them to wider social processes. This emphasis upon the unique helped trigger a counter-revolution which focused upon the search for general laws of spatial structure, deploying the positivistic approaches of mainstream physical science and turning the emphasis from the uniqueness of place to the generality of space, typically reduced to transport costs. In the past decade or so there has been a considerable re-evaluation of the relationships between society and space emerging from an engagement between human geography and modern social theory which emphasises the interrelationship between the uniqueness of places and more general social processes. Geographers such as Massey (1978) have stressed the need for regions to emerge from, rather than be presupposed by, analyses of uneven development, and have gone on (Massey, 1984), following the lead given by Lipietz (1977), to develop the links between social relations and the geography of production. Harvey, in *The limits to capital* (1982), has produced an unrivalled restatement of Marxian political economy which situates regional differentiation within a general value theory analysis of capitalist uneven development. Harvey convincingly demonstrates that capitalist development is inherently uneven, both between sectors and spatially; in that sense, 'problem regions' such as the North-East are inscribed into the inner logic of the capitalist mode of production. This is undeniable, but it is also necessary to go beyond it. As the title of his book implies, there are limits as to how far one can proceed in terms of value analysis alone, though let me stress that I am not advocating a rejection of Harvey's rigorous exposition; quite the contrary. For it allows us to focus precisely on those issues that require a somewhat different approach and an analysis at a lower level of abstraction of actual capitalist societies than that of the capitalist mode of production. Although Harvey's analysis shows that there will inevitably be 'problem regions', such as the north-east of England, because of causal mechanisms that are an integral part of the process of uneven development, it does not and cannot reveal *which* regions will become 'problematic'. This is a contingent matter, as the switch in the position of the North-East from 'core' to 'periphery' in the world economy and the emergence of this aspect of uneven development as a *political* question exemplifies. To put the point another way, there are important questions concerning how the structural relationships of and the limits to capitalist societies – as opposed to those of the more abstract concept of the capitalist mode of production – are socially produced and reproduced. For example, the issue of *how* the antagonistic class structural relationship between capital and labour, around which hinges surplus value production, is reproduced is clearly a crucial one and one that needs to be explained rather than assumed away; likewise, there is the question of *how* competition between capitals over realised surplus value is resolved. It is precisely these sorts of issues that began to command greater attention as part of a more generalized critique of structuralist Marxism (for example, Althusser and Balibar, 1970; Althusser, 1977) that emerged in structurationist approaches during the 1970s (for example, see Giddens, 1978). Moreover, given the centrality of place in analyses of the 'regional problem', the convergent emphasis in the work of social theorists such as Giddens (1981, 1984) and Urry (1981a, b) and geographers such as Gregory (1978, 1981, 1982), Thrift (1983) and Soja (1980, 1983) in seeking to demonstrate the importance of place – alongside dimensions such as class, race and gender – in the constitution of society has provided important theoretical insights. Although there are differences between them, these authors share a commitment to the importance of the relationships between agency, structure and place in the reproduction of capitalist societies which I accept and have tried to use theoretically to inform my analyses both of changes within north-east England and of its socially produced change from 'core' to 'peripheral' status.

A concern to unravel the links between social reproduction and the constitution of society in places in turn leads to a concern with theories of the capitalist state, especially in regions such as north-east England. Much of the impetus for new forms of State involvement in the North-East in the inter-war years sprang from the major capitalist combines, which saw in this a way to protect and further their own interests. After initial suspicion and hostility, trade unions and the Labour Party, as the main institutional forms of political representation of working-class interests, also came to favour such involvement in the belief that they too could shape State policies in the direction that they desired. Implicit in this was a belief that the interests of capital and labour were compatible, or at least could be made so through the medium of State involvement, and a belief that the State was a neutral instrument to be captured and put to social democratic reformist purposes rather than a mere tool of the capitalist class (or its monopoly fraction). There are theories of the State that would support both these viewpoints, but they are inadequate in capturing the nuances of the varying forms of State involvement in a region such as the North-East. In the final analysis there are limits to the policies of a capitalist State which are structurally prescribed by its relation to capitalist property relations, but within these limits considerable scope exists for political struggle over the form and content of State policies. In this sense, the State itself is an arena for struggle. One expression of this is in terms of party politics, the areas of agreement and disagreement between political parties as to what constitute the legitimate boundaries to State activities and how policies are to be shaped within them. Furthermore, differentiation within the State itself (for example, between central government departments or between central and local government) in terms of aims and objectives can lead to competition and conflict within the State as different classes, fractions of classes, or non-class-based interest groups seek to establish priority for their interests through struggles to influence State policies. Thus, rather than the State being an internally undifferentiated monolith which non-problematically promotes the capitalist interest, it is the locus of a variety of struggles, structured both between and within classes and on non-class or cross-class territorial bases. The latter aspect is particularly important in the context of regional change in relation to the formation of cross-class agreements to promote 'regional interests'. The shifting form and content of State policies must be understood within this context as well as in terms of the demands for legitimation which tend to channel State policies in the direction of *attainable* goals within the broad confines of capitalist social relations. This is important in defining what is excluded from, as well as included on, the various agendas for State policies.

The various theories of the State have been extensively reviewed (for example, Jessop, 1982; Clark and Dear, 1984), but generally they take little account of the spatial patterning of societies and its effects upon both the internal organization of the State and State policy formation. Of the many variants of Marxian theories of the capitalist State, the most useful in analysing change in regions such as the North-East are what might be termed 'neo-Gramscian' and class theories (Urry, 1981b) and 'crisis theories' (Offe, 1974, 1975a, b, 1984; Habermas, 1975). A national State attempts to secure conditions for profitable accumulation within its territory but in doing so necessarily manoeuvres within and seeks to orchestrate the heterogeneous relationships that constitute civil society and are located *between* the State and the economy. It is important to stress that these boundaries are both changing and permeable; and that this is perhaps especially so in regions like the North-East. Considerable emphasis is placed on the maintenance of hegemony, on the generalized acceptance of the relationships of capitalist production in general, and on the legitimacy of the position of the dominant power bloc in particular. Maintaining hegemony involves helping organize the dominant classes and disorganize subordinate classes and other social groups that might challenge the existing order and securing their acceptance of that order, but this is not without problems. Challenges to the prevailing order *can* (but do not necessarily) arise at a variety of levels, including the emergence of a concern with 'regional problems' as part of the unacceptable face of capitalist societies. The generation of challenges to the existing order in the form of various crises (regional crises, for example) links to the concerns of 'crisis theorists' such as Habermas and Offe. They have suggested that crisis tendencies that are inherent to capitalist production are displaced from the economic to the ideological and political spheres, emphasizing the links between economic and political changes as mediated through the changing forms and content of State policies. Given that capitalist societies are necessarily constituted in places, the expression of these crisis tendencies can often assume a spatial dimension – most obviously when they enter a wider discourse as 'urban' or 'regional' crises which may (but do not inevitably) produce demands for new forms of State policies, or even a reorganization of responsibilities within the State on a 'new' territorial basis – re-emphasizing the importance of the spatiality of social reproduction.

At this point, where heavy emphasis is being placed upon acknowledging the importance of the spatiality of capitalist societies in understanding change in and through north-east England as an exemplar of a 'problem region', a few words about the ambivalence that surrounds the use of the term 'region' may be helpful. I pointed out above that Massey (1978) argues that 'regions' should emerge from an analysis of uneven development rather than be presupposed by it. Although I accept this as far as it goes, I would argue that it is necessary to go beyond this. Sayer (1984) makes a useful point in this context, which links both to broader epistemological issues and to the role of the State *vis-à-vis* the regional problem. Although not denying the validity of Massey's claims that regions ought to emerge from, rather than be presupposed by, analysis, Sayer (p. 227) points out that regions are 'chaotic' groupings, cutting across structures and causal groupings. Nevertheless, they must be analysed as such, not least because they become objects of State (regional) policies. Although there may seem to be an incompatibility between the views of Massey and Sayer on this point, it is important to take both on board in analysing the regional problem. It is crucial to show how the North-East was first constituted as a region as an integral part of the process of capitalist development. Equally, it is crucial to show how the changing currents of the accumulation process increasingly marginalized the North-East as a location relative to the demands of capitalist production, and how political pressures were constructed in an attempt to protect interests tied within it. In the course of this, a new 'chaotically conceived' definition of the North-East as an object of emergent State regional policies was produced and subsequently modified.

My purpose in the preceding paragraphs has been to sketch out some of the theoretical debates which have influenced how I have attempted to analyse the particular case of north-east England. However, one obvious but important point does need to be made at this stage about the relationship between these theoretical debates and empirical investigation of change in the North-East. The latter was conducted over a period of a decade or so; theoretical positions themselves have evolved over that period, and so has my own (hopefully for the better, as a comparison between, say, Carney *et al.* (1976) and Hudson and Sadler (1986) would reveal). Inevitably, there has been no simple relationship between theoretical and empirical investigation; it would certainly be untrue to claim that the analysis of the North-East has been systematically informed by a single coherent theoretical position consistently held over a decade, but equally untrue to suggest that it has been wholly theoretically uninformed. In reality, the guiding theoretical positions have altered.

But, to return to a point I made earlier, there was more to the change of plan for the book than just developments internal to the social sciences, and this relates back to the delay between conception and execution of the book. My involvement in campaigns to preserve capacity and employment in nationalised industries in the North-East from the late 1970s and, in particular, the experiences of the 1984–85 miners' strike led me to the conclusion that a rather different sort of book needed to be written from the one I originally had in mind; not least, this savagely re-emphasized the significance of State policies for regions such as the North-East, and the ways in which they could be used to destroy the fabric of social and economic life there.

One element in this change of plan is the period covered. Initially my intention was to compare and contrast the periods 1942–62 and 1962–75 in terms of the priorities of State policies and the effects of implementing these in the North-East. The early 1960s marked a watershed in central government economic policies, with consequent effects on those of nationalized industries and local authorities in the North-East. Likewise, 1974–75 marked an equally significant turning point but, since the research on the pre-1975 period was being carried out in the second half of the 1970s, there then seemed insufficient time to consider in any depth the effects of these changes, which were just beginning to be worked through. However, by the early 1980s, and especially after the effects of the 1979 General Election had become evident, it seemed both possible and necessary to consider this post-1975 period in order to give a tripartite comparison. Much of the research on nationalized industry policies was carried out as background in relation to my involvement in campaigns to preserve jobs and capacity in the North-East and this was then complemented by consideration of central and local government policies in the post-1975 period. But the type of book that I wanted to write also changed somewhat as a consequence of the changed political terrain within the United Kingdom. What I felt was needed was as detailed an account as it was possible to give of why and how State policies were formulated as they were, why and how they were implemented as they were; a book that, as it were, offered a more politicized account of State policies. Although focused on the North-East, such an interpretation would by no means be confined to the North-East in terms of the sorts of relationships it explored or in its implications. Rather than setting out with the almost obligatory theoretical review chapters – and so, however much I denied it as the intention, opening the door to the possibility that others would interpret the descriptive empirical account that followed these chapters as in some sense a 'test' of competing theories – what seemed to be needed was an interpretative account which set out the complexities involved in formulating and implementing State policies, and which also explicated the links – or lack of them – between policies articulated and implemented within different parts of the overall State apparatus. It seemed, and still seems, important to go beyond the sorts of accounts of State policies, for example regional policy or nationalized industry policy, which do little more than describe the legislation. Although there is an extensive literature on nationalized industries (for example, Thornhill, 1968; Reid and Allen, 1970) and on spatial policies (for example, McCrone, 1969; McClennan and Parr, 1977), it is usually divorced from broader theoretical debates about the State and uneven development. Equally, it seemed important to go beyond an account of their impacts which presumed that a 'policy effect' could be abstracted from all the other complex changes occurring in the political–economic environment. Indeed, the claim that one can identify a 'policy effect' itself has considerable significance in making legitimate the case for particular types of State policy. In contrast to such approaches, what I want to do here is to try to disentangle *why* policies were formulated and implemented in the way they were, to establish *how* they were implemented and with *what effects*, intentional and unintentional, and to politicise the discussion of policy both in terms of party political agreements and differences, local and central government agreements and differences, *and* in terms of specifying *whose* interests were served by the formulation and implementation of State policies.

The focus is very much on the 'logic' of policy formulation and implementation as seen from within various State organizations and political parties rather than, say, from the perspective of those members of the working class within the region who predominantly experienced these changes. This account 'from below' must await another book. In seeking to reconstruct and interpret why and how central government and nationalized industry policies were formulated and implemented, I have drawn on and used widely available sources such as *Hansard*, various House of Commons Committee Reports, government publications and political biographies to help reconstruct the sequence of events and the 'flavour' of the contemporary debates. At the level of local government policies, however, such an approach is much less feasible and I have made considerable use of unpublished documentary sources (such as local authority minutes and reports) as well as interviews with key actors. Some of these were 'formal' interviews, others were more in the nature of ongoing discussions in the course of collaborative work with and for various local authorities within the North-East. Consequently, I have made considerable use of often lengthy quotations from sources such as minutes (for, although full references to sources are given in the text, these are generally only to be found in one location within the North-East, such as a county record office). The style is – deliberately – descriptive, attempting to reveal the way in which policies were conceived, what sorts of issues and interests were seen to be at stake, which came out on top. Put another way, the approach is empirical – though hopefully not empiricist – with the theoretical concerns in the background as a guiding hand rather than in the foreground as a constraining framework.

References

Althusser, L. 1977: *For Marx*. London: New Left Books.

Althusser, L. and Balibar, E. 1970: *Reading capital*. London: New Left Books.

Carney, J. Hudson, R. Ive G. and Lewis J. 1976: Regional underdevelopment in late capitalism: a study of North East England. In Masser, I. (ed.), *London Papers in Regional Science 6. Theory and Practice in Regional Science*. London: Pion, 11–29.

Clark, G.L. and Dear, M. 1984: *State apparatus*. London: Allen & Unwin.

Giddens, A. 1978: *Central problems in social theory*. London: Macmillan.

Giddens, A. 1981: *A contemporary critique of historical materialization*. London: Macmillan.

Giddens, A. 1984: *The constitution of society*. Cambridge: Polity Press.

Gregory, D. 1978: *Science ideology and human geography*. London: Hutchinson.

Gregory, D. 1981: Human agency and human geography. *Transactions of the Institute of British Geographers* 6, 1–18.

Gregory, D. 1982: *Regional transformation and Industrial revolution*. London: Macmillan.

Habermas, J. 1975: *Legitimation crisis*. London: Heinemann Educational Books.

Harvey, D. 1982: *The limits to capital*. Oxford: Basil Blackwell.

Hudson, R. and Sadler, D. 1986: Contesting works closures in Western Europe's old industrial regions: defending place or betraying class? In Scott, A. J. and Storper, M. (eds), *Production, work, territory*. Winchester, MA Allen & Unwin 172–94.

Jessop, B. 1982. *The capitalist State*. Oxford: Martin Robertson.

Lipietz, A. 1977: *Le capital et son espace*. Paris: Maspéro.

McClennan, D. and Parr, J. (eds) 1979: *Regional policy: Past experience and new directions*. Oxford: Martin Robertson.

McCrone, G, 1969: *Regional policy in Britain*. London: Allen & Unwin.

Massey, D. 1978: Regionalism: some current issues. *Capital and Class*, 6, 106–25.

Massey, D. 1984: *Spatial divisions of labour*. London: Macmillan.

Offe, C. 1974: Structural problems of the capitalist state. In Beyme, K. (ed.) *German political studies*. London: Sage, 31–57.

Offe, C. 1975a: The theory of the capitalist state and the problem of policy formation. In Lindberg, L. N., Alford, R., Crouch, C. and Offe, C. (eds), *Stress and contradiction in modern capitalism*. Lexington, MA: D.C. Heath, 125–44.

Offe, C. 1975b: Introduction to Part II. In Lindberg, L. N., Alford, R., Crouch, C. and Offe, C. (eds), *Stress and contradiction in modern capitalism*. Lexington, MA: D. C. Heath, 245–59.

Offe, C. 1984: *Contradictions of the Welfare State*. London: Hutchinson.

Reid, G. L. and Allen, K. 1970: *Nationalized industries*. Harmondsworth: Penguin Books.

Sayer, A. 1984: *Method in social science*. London: Hutchinson.

Soja, E. 1980: The socio-spatial dialectic. *Annals of the Association of American Geographers* 70, 207–25.

Soja, E. 1983: *The spatiality of social life: towards a transformable retheorization*. Mimeo available from the Department of Geography, University of California at Los Angeles, CA, USA.

Thornhill, W. 1968: *The nationalized industries*. Walton-on-Thames: Nelson.

Thrift, N. 1983: On the determination of social action in space and time. *Society and Space* 1, 23–57.

Urry, J. 1981a: Localities, regions and social class. *International Journal of Urban and Regional Research* 5, 455–73.

Urry, J. 1981b: *The anatomy of capitalist societies*. London: Macmillan.

5   Manuel Castells,
'The Informational Economy and the New International Division of Labor'

Reprinted in full from: M. Carnoy, M. Castells, S. S. Cohen and F. H. Cardoso (eds), *The New Global Economy in the Information Age: Reflections on our Changing World*, Chapter 2. University Park: Pennsylvania State University Press (1989)

The informational economy

We live in a new economy, gradually formed over the past half century and characterized by five fundamental features which are systemically interrelated. The first such feature is that sources of productivity – and therefore of economic growth in real terms – are increasingly dependent upon the application of science and technology, as well as upon the quality of information and management, in the processes of production, consumption, distribution, and trade.

The pathbreaking work of Robert Solow in 1957,[1] followed by the aggregate-production-function studies on the sources of economic productivity by Denison, Malinvaud, Jorgenson, and Kendrick, among others,[2] has shown that advanced economies increased their productivity not so much as a result of the amount of capital or labor added to the production process, as was the case in the early stages of industrialization, but as the outcome of a more efficient combination of the factors of production. Although econometric equations are obscure in identifying the precise sources of the new productivity pattern, the 'statistical residual' found to be critical in the new production function has often been assimilated to the new inputs represented by the deeper penetration of science, technology, labor skills, and managerial know-how in the production process.[3]

A similar finding was reported on the evolution of the Soviet economy by Abel Aganbegyan, Gorbachev's first economic adviser. According to Aganbegyan's calculations, the Soviet economy grew at a robust rate until 1971, or as long as the State could rely on purely quantitative expansion by injecting more capital and labor and by pumping more and more natural resources into a rather primitive industrial structure. Once the Soviet economy became more complex, as a result of industrialization, it needed to introduce more sophisticated know-how into the production process in order to sustain growth. Because of the difficulty of developing and applying science and technology within a command economy, growth rates plummeted from 1971 onward, until reaching zero growth in the mid-1980s,[4] thus prompting the need for *perestroika* and precipitating the demise of Soviet communism.

Thus, it seems that the increasingly important role of applied knowledge and information is a characteristic of advanced economic systems, transcending the historical characteristics of their modes of production. It would also seem that the salient role of knowledge and technology is not exclusive to the late-twentieth-century economy, nor has this economy resulted simply from a sudden change of production techniques. We are observing in fact a secular trend. Knowledge has always been important in organizing and fostering economic growth.[5] But the greater the complexity and productivity of an economy, the greater its informational component and the greater the role played by new knowledge and new applications of knowledge (as compared with the mere addition of such production factors as capital or labor) in the growth of productivity.[6]

The second feature of the new world economy – and another secular trend that has accelerated in recent years – is the shift, in advanced capitalist societies, from material production to information-processing activities, both in terms of proportion of GNP and in the proportion of the population employed in such activities.[7] This seems to be a more fundamental change than the one proposed by the notion of the transition from industry to services, for today's 'service sector' is so diverse that it becomes a residual category, mixing fundamentally different activities (from computer-software writing to cleaning floors) to the point that any analysis of economic structure must now start with a typological differentiation of the so-called service activities.[8] Furthermore, as Cohen and Zysman have forcefully argued,[9] there is a systemic linkage between manufacturing and the service sector, so that many such activities are in fact an integral part of the industrial production process.

Thus, the real transformation of the economic structure of advanced societies is the emergence of what Marc Porat in his seminal 1977 study labeled 'the information economy,' wherein an ever-growing role is played by the manipulation of symbols in the organization of production and in the enhancement of productivity.[10] In 1990, 47.4 per cent of the employed population in the United States, 45.8 per cent in the United Kingdom, 45.1 per cent in France, and 40.0 per cent in West Germany were engaged in information-processing activities, whether in the production of goods or in the provision of services,[11] and the proportion continues to rise over time.[12] Moreover, the quality of the information and one's efficiency in acquiring and processing it now constitute the strategic factor in both competitiveness and productivity for firms, regions, and countries.[13]

Along with the fundamental changes taking place in the production process itself is a third feature of the new economy: a profound transformation in the *organization* of production and of economic activity in general. This change can be described as a shift from standardized mass production to flexible customized production and from vertically integrated, large-scale organizations to vertical disintegration and horizontal networks between economic units.[14] This trend has sometimes been assimilated to the dynamic role played by small and medium-size businesses (expressions of the new flexibility) in opposition to bureaucratized large corporations, as in the formulation of Piore and Sabel,[15] and has been discussed in the context of the so-called Third Italy model of industrial development.[16] The organizational transformation of the economy, however, goes beyond the size of the firm and does not contradict the fundamental trend toward the concentration of economic power in a few major conglomerates. While it is true that small businesses have shown great resilience, becoming dynamic units in an advanced economy, the organizational pattern of decentralization and flexibility is also characteristic of large corporations, both in their internal structure and in their relationship to a network of ancillary firms, as is illustrated by the 'just in time' supply technique introduced by the large Japanese automobile firms. Thus, the matter at hand is not so much the decline of the large corporation (still the dominant agent of the world economy) as it is the organizational transformation of all economic activity, emphasizing flexibility and adaptability in response to a changing, diversified market.

Fourth, the new economy is a global economy, in which capital, production, management, markets, labor, information, and technology are organized across national boundaries. Although nation-states are still fundamental realities to be reckoned with in thinking about economic structures and processes, what is significant is that the unit of economic accounting, as well as the frame of reference for economic strategies, can no longer be the national economy. Competition is played out globally,[17] not only by the multinational corporations, but also by small and medium-size enterprises that connect directly or indirectly to the world market through their linkages in the networks that relate them to the large firms.[18] What is new, then, is not that international trade is an important component of the economy (in this sense, we can speak of a world economy since the seventeenth century), but that the national economy now works as a unit at the world level in real time. In this sense, we are seeing not only a process of internationalization of the economy, but a process of globalization – that is, the interpenetration of economic activities and national economies at the global level. The coming integration into the world economy of Eastern Europe, the former Soviet Union, and China – probably over the course of the next decade – will complete this process of globalization which, while not ignoring national boundaries, simply includes national characteristics as important features within a unified, global system.

Finally, these economic and organizational transformations in the world economy take place (and not by accident) in the midst of one of the most significant technological revolutions of human history.[19] The core of that revolution is in information technologies (microelectronics, informatics, and telecommunications), around which a constellation of major scientific discoveries and applications (in biotechnology, new materials, lasers, renewable energy, etc.) is transforming the material basis of our world in less than twenty years. This technological revolution has been stimulated in its applications by a demand generated by the economic and organizational transformations discussed above. In turn, the new technologies constitute the indispensable material base for such transformations.[20] Thus, the enhancement of telecommunications has created the material infrastructure needed for the formation of a global economy,[21] in a movement similar to that which lay behind the construction of the railways and the formation of national markets during the nineteenth century. The fact that new information technologies are available at the very moment when the organization of economic activity relies increasingly on the processing of a vast amount of information, moreover, contributes to removing the fundamental obstacle to labor-productivity growth as economies evolve from material production to information processing as the source of employment for most workers. In the United States, the differential of productivity growth between information jobs and non-information jobs increased until 1980; thereafter, however, the trend was projected to turn around as new information technologies diffused throughout the economy.[22] Furthermore, these information technologies are also the critical factor allowing for flexibility and decentralization in production and management: production and trade units can function autonomously yet be reintegrated functionally through information networks, constituting in fact a new type of economic space, which I have called 'the space of flows'.[23]

Thus, with the revolution in information technology as the material basis of the emerging system, the various features of structural economic transformation that we have identified relate closely to each other. In fact, they join together to form a new type of economy that I, along with a growing number of economists and sociologists,[24] propose to call the 'informational economy'[25] because, at its core, the fundamental source of wealth generation lies in an ability to create new knowledge and apply it to every realm of human activity by means of enhanced technological and organizational procedures of information processing.[26] The informational economy tends to be, in its essence, a global economy; and its structure and logic define, within the emerging world order, a new international division of labor.

The new international division of labor, the end of the Third World, and the rise of the Fourth World

The informational economy develops on a planetary scale. But its expansion is uneven, thus originating a new international division of labor between countries and economic macroregions, one that will shape the evolution of the world economy in the coming decade. Analysis of the new international division of labor, however, has often been cast in extremely simplistic terms, leading to serious mistakes in international and national economic policies. Thus we must take a hard, analytical look at the recent dynamics of the international economy, paying special attention to those factors which account for the differential competitiveness of nations in an increasingly interdependent world market.

The experience of the past twenty-five years seems to indicate that, beyond the variations of business cycles, four principal factors are responsible for the success of nations and/or economic regions in winning market share and fostering economic growth.[27] First of all, there is the technological capacity of the productive structure of a given economy, in line with the overall transformation of the economic system toward the new logic of the information economy. Thus, econometric studies by Dosi and Soete[28] have provided evidence of the correlation between the technological level of industrial sectors and their competitiveness in international trade for all member countries of the OECD (Organisation for Economic Co-operation and Development). Using the same data, they have also shown that there is no correlation between labor costs and competitiveness. Castells and Tyson[29] have reviewed comparative evidence on the differential competitiveness of Third World countries in the international economy, showing both the extremely uneven distribution of science and technology throughout the world and the importance of techno-logical modernization in explaining differentials of competitiveness for developing countries in the open world economy.

Second, access to a large, integrated, expanding market, such as the United States, the European Economic Area (EEA),[30] or Japan, seems to be a fun-damental factor in determining competitiveness.[31] This must be interpreted both as the capacity to operate in a somewhat protected domestic (or intraregional) market and as the possibility of having access to other large markets. Thus, the larger and deeper the economic integration of a given economic zone, the greater the chances of spurring productivity and profitability for the firms locating in that zone. But it is important also to underscore that the best possible combination for competitiveness for a given area is to be domestically protected from competition while having access to other large, integrated zones.[32]

Third, another important factor in explaining competitive performance in the world market is the differential between production costs at the production site and prices in the market of destination – a calculation that is more appropriate than a simplistic formula relying on labor costs, since other very important cost factors are involved (e.g. land costs, taxes, and environmental regulation).[33] However, this factor is critical only in relation to the two preceding factors. That is, the potential profit involved in the differential can be realized only if there is access to a large, rich market. Also, cost/price differentials are specific to a given technological level for the traded good: for a computer to be cheap, for example, it must first of all be a reliable computer. Since higher-value-added commodities have become increasingly important in the overall trade structure, it would seem that comparative advantages linked to differential technological capacity pre-cede and frame the specific effect of cost/price differentials.[34]

Finally, competitiveness in the new informational, global economy seems to be be highly dependent on the political capacity of national and supranational institutions to steer the growth strategy of those countries or areas under their jurisdiction, including the creation of comparative advantages in the world market for those firms which are considered to represent the interests of the national and supranational collectivities underlying such political institutions. To use Chalmers Johnson's terminology, the 'developmental state'[35] has played a fundamental role in affecting the transformation of the world economic struc-ture in recent years.

These four factors, working together in close interaction, seem to account for much of the transformation of the international economy. Let us first outline the main characteristics of such transformation, leaving it for later to concentrate on the elements that may determine its future dynamics.

To examine empirically the transformation of the world economy over the past twenty-five years I will use a source that, although its data are limited to the period from 1967 to 1986, organizes those data in a way permitting comparison on a homogenous basis at the level of the world's economic regions. Also, the dependability of the source assures us of a reasonably solid foundation. Our source is a study conducted by the Paris-based Centre d'Etudes Prospectives et d'Informations Internationales (CEPII) and making use of that organization's data bank, known as 'CHELEM' (from the French 'Comptes Harmonisés sur les Echanges et l'Economie Mondiale').[36]

I have considered it more rigorous to rely on this single source, despite the obvious risks, than to refer to various data sources that are not necessarily comparable for different variables and different countries. The reader should, however, keep in mind that in the past six years (1987–92) – not included in this data base – several important transformations have taken place in the structure of the world economy: the increasing integration of the EEC and the signing of a common market agreement with EFTA to form the European Economic Area; the disintegration of the Soviet Union and the end of the Comecon; the new commercial treaties between the United States on the one hand and Canada and Mexico on the other, preparing for a future North American integration; and the growing economic interdependence between Japan and the Asian Pacific economies. Yet, careful observation of the structural evolution of the world economy during the critical years 1967–86 seems to yield clues for understanding its transformation at the end of the present century.

(1) The first major transformation concerns the growing interdependency of the global economy, albeit within the limits of the preservation of substantial, distinctive cleavages between major economic areas which operate as trading blocs. In fact, if we distinguish major economic zones in the world, following the CEPII's calculations, intrazone trade increased from 37.6 per cent of total world trade in 1967 to 40.5 per cent of the world total in 1986. Thus, we have, at the same time, the marking out of macroregions in the world economy and a growing cross-regional pattern of investment, location of firms, exports, and imports, with substantial differences in the degree of penetration of each region by capital, goods, and services from other regions.

(2) At the core of the world economy, North America, Japan, and the EEC–EEA constitute the three fundamental economic regions,[37] to the extent that the rest of the world seems to be increasingly dependent upon its ability to link up with these centers of capital, technology, and market potential. One basic trend has been an evolution, in the relationship among these three macroregions, from US hegemony toward multipolarity. Table 5.1 shows the decreasing contribution of the US economy to world production and the increasing contribution from Japan. The EEC's share of world production also declined during that period, although the process of European market integration has lent more meaning to its presence in the world economy: an integrated 22.9 per cent of the world's production in 1986 carries more weight than a simple statistical addition amounting to 26.3 per cent in 1967. It cannot go without notice that the truly spectacular growth as a share of world production – greater even than that of Japan – is in 'Developing Asia', which

Table 5.1 Share of world economic regions and countries in world output

GDP at international equivalence prices and of purchasing power in 1980	Billions of US$	Structure (%)			
	1986	1967	1973	1980	1986
USA	3,215.2	25.8	23.1	21.3	21.4
France	517.3	3.8	3.8	3.7	3.4
Belgium–Luxembourg	94.6	0.7	0.7	0.7	0.6
Western Germany	628.4	5.0	4.9	4.6	4.2
Italy	525.1	3.9	3.9	3.7	3.5
Netherlands	136.8	1.1	1.1	1.0	0.9
UK	530.1	4.8	4.3	3.7	3.5
Scandinavia	247.9	1.9	1.8	1.7	1.6
Alpine countries	139.6	1.2	1.1	1.0	0.9
Southern Europe	616.3	3.8	4.1	4.2	4.1
Western Europe	**3,436.1**	**26.3**	**25.7**	**24.4**	**22.9**
Canada	330.6	2.1	2.1	2.2	2.2
Australia and New Zealand	176.6	1.2	1.3	1.2	1.2
South Africa	96.5	0.8	0.7	0.7	0.6
CANZAS	**603.7**	**4.1**	**4.1**	**4.1**	**4.0**
Japan	**1,160.6**	**5.8**	**7.2**	**7.4**	**7.7**
Indonesia	192.5	0.7	0.9	1.2	1.3
India	488.3	3.0	2.7	2.8	3.2
Newly industrializing countries of Asia	322.7	0.9	1.2	1.6	2.1
Other Asian countries	451.3	2.4	2.4	2.8	3.0
China	1,167.2	3.8	4.6	5.4	7.8
Developing Asia	**2,622.0**	**10.8**	**11.8**	**13.8**	**17.4**
Venezuela–Ecuador	94.8	0.7	0.7	0.7	0.6
Mexico	273.2	1.5	1.7	2.1	1.8
Brazil	426.5	1.6	2.2	2.9	2.8
Other Latin American countries	401.6	3.1	3.0	3.1	2.7
Latin America	**1,196.1**	**6.9**	**7.6**	**8.8**	**7.9**
Persian Gulf region	**315.1**	**1.8**	**2.4**	**2.5**	**2.1**
Algeria–Libya	73.4	0.4	0.4	0.5	0.5
Non-OPEC North Africa	117.7	0.6	0.6	0.8	0.8
Non-OPEC Middle East	58	0.3	0.3	0.4	0.4
Nigeria–Gabon	62.3	0.4	0.6	0.6	0.4
Other African Countries	147.2	1.2	1.1	1.0	1.0
Developing Africa	**458.6**	**2.9**	**3.0**	**3.3**	**3.1**
Soviet Union	1,475.0	11.0	10.8	10.3	9.8
Central Europe	553.3	4.6	4.3	4.1	3.7
All Eastern Europe	**2,028.3**	**15.6**	**15.1**	**14.4**	**13.5**
World total	15,035.7	100	100	100	100

Bold text represents the Subtotal for each region.

includes the Pacific Basin's newly industrialized countries (NICs) but also China (which, owing to its sheer size, is in fact statistically responsible for most of the region's growth). The 'Developing Asia' region, according to the CEPII data, represented 17.4 per cent of world production in 1986, compared to 7.7 per cent for Japan. This is a crucial point to which we shall return.

Factors that have been proposed as crucial in this changing dynamics of competition among the core economies are measured by the export performance of manufacturing industries (Table 5.2) and by relative position in electronics production and in high-technology production across countries and economic zones, largely explaining the growing differential in the current balance between Japan and Western Europe, on the one hand, and the United States and most of the Third World, on the other. By all possible measures, we can indeed speak of a dramatic decline in the US position along with a seemingly irresistible ascent by Japan and the Asian Pacific region, with Europe improving its position relative both to itself and to the United States (but clearly lagging in the pace of growth *vis-à-vis* its Pacific competition, probably because of a combination of technological dependency, imperfect market integration, and indecisive political decision-making institutions at the supranational level). The center of the world economy, then, is gradually shifting toward the Pacific Basin, although the new impulse of European integration in 1993 could reverse the trend.

Table 5.2 Classification of world regions and countries according to their performance in manufacturing exports in 1967–86 (in 1/1000 parts of world trade)

	1973/67	1980/73	1986/80
Japan	15.6	9.0	10.4
Newly industrializing countries of Asia	14.7	17.0	9.4
Western Germany	9.0	−17.4	6.6
Southern Europe	6.1	4.0	5.5
Italy	−8.7	4.9	4.4
China	−0.6	0.5	4.2
Alpine countries	−1.8	0.7	2.8
Brazil	5.0	3.3	2.0
Netherlands	0.7	−4.0	1.5
Algeria–Libya	−0.6	—	0.9
Indonesia	0.4	0.5	0.8
Scandinavia	−1.5	−3.1	0.5
Mexico	1.8	−0.2	0.2
Non-OPEC Middle East	0.2	−0.7	0.2
Non-OPEC North Africa	−1.2	−0.4	0.1
Persian Gulf region	0.9	0.7	—
Nigeria–Gabon	−0.2	−0.1	—
Other Asian countries	−0.4	4.0	−0.1
Venezuela–Ecuador	0.1	0.5	−0.2
All Eastern Europe	4.1	0.8	−0.4
Other African countries	−1.9	−1.9	−0.7
India	−0.9	−0.9	−0.8
Other Latin American countries	−2.7	0.6	−1.5
Belgium–Luxembourg	2.7	−6.7	−1.6
South Africa	−1.8	1.5	−1.9
Australia–New Zealand	3.8	−4.2	−2.2
Canada	−5.4	−4.3	−3.4
France	2.5	−3.0	−4.4
UK	−17.8	2.0	−13.1
USA	−22.9	1.5	−21.1

Source: CEPII, CHELEM data base on international trade, 1989.
Note: For each subperiod, variation in gains or losses in markets for commodities of the industries studied in the CHELEM data base.

(3) The informational economy is also affecting North–South economic relations in a fundamental way and through very different processes, depending upon the country and region, to the point that today we can speak of *the end of the Third World as a relatively homogeneous economic region.*[38] At the root of this increasing differentiation lie the emergence of a new international division of labor, the shift to a new model of economic growth (characterized by the critical role of technology and the outward orientation of dependent economies as factors favoring growth), and the varying capacity of countries to engage themselves in this new growth model by linking up with world economic processes. Let us examine the evolution of the so-called Third World.

Three development strategies

The developing world in the post-World War II period has relied on three basic development strategies, often combined within the same country:[39] (a) traditional international trade, accepting the old international division of labor, whereby raw materials and agricultural commodities were traded for manufactures and know-how in a classic pattern of unequal exchange;[40] (b) import-substitution industrialization, according to the model associated with the policies articulated by CEPAL (the Spanish acronym for the UN Commission for Latin America) and designed and theorized by such leading economists as Raúl Prebisch and Aníbal Pinto;[41] and (c) an outward-oriented development strategy, taking advantage of cost/price differentials and focusing either on exports from domestic manufacturing firms (e.g. South Korea, Hong Kong, Taiwan, and Brazil) or, less often, on exports from offshore manufacturing facilities of multinational corporations (e.g. northern Mexico, Malaysia, and Singapore).[42] I argue, for the sake of simplicity, that the first development model collapsed in the 1960s, the second in the 1970s, and the third in the 1980s (with all due acknowledgment to the exceptions of individual countries and regions).[43] It does not follow that only those countries and regions which have been able and/or will be able to adapt to the new conditions of a worldwide informational economy will improve their situation and will be able to transform the current international economy. Let us briefly examine the empirical basis of our hypothesis.

Concerning the traditional international division of labor (primary commodities versus manufactured goods), the critical element is the transformation of the structure of world trade and production. As shown in Table 5.3, agriculture and mining have both lagged substantially in relation to the expansion of manufacturing. Thus, with some exceptions (most notably in countries with energy resources), specialization outside manufacturing leads to a growing deterioration of the terms of trade. In addition, the general deterioration of primary commodity prices (see Table 5.4), likely to worsen by the end of the century, destroys the economic foundation for a simple survival strategy.

Import-substitution strategy and models for economic growth based on the domestic market have been the cornerstone of left-wing development theory.[44] Indeed, such thinking has played a major role in successful industrialization

Table 5.3 Volume growth of world merchandise trade and production by major product group, 1960–1986 (average annual per cent change)

	1960–70	1970–80	1980–86	1985	1986
Exports					
Agriculture	4.0	4.5	1.0	0	−1.0
Mining	7.0	1.5	−1.5	−2.0	7.5
Manufacturing	10.5	7.0	4.5	5.0	3.0
All merchandise	8.5	5.0	3.0	3.5	3.5
Production					
Agriculture	2.5	2.0	2.5	2.0	1.0
Mining	5.5	2.5	−1.5	1.0	6.0
Manufacturing	7.5	4.5	2.5	3.5	3.5
All merchandise	6.0	4.0	2.0	3.0	3.0

Source: GATT, *Report on International Trade, 1980–1987* (Geneva: GATT, 1987).

programs throughout Latin America (most notably in Mexico, Brazil, and Argentina)[45] and in Asia (China and India). Thus, it is not true, as neoconservative economists argue, that only an outward-looking economy can foster economic growth. Even South Korea had a very strong import-substitution policy in the 1960s, and it held on to substantial protectionist measures all along the development process.[46] However, the import-substitution model that was relatively successful in the 1950s and 1960s, particularly in Latin America, faced a crisis in the 1970s, owing to the 'oil shocks', rampant inflation, and a weakening of domestic demand when the primary export sectors could not generate enough revenue to fuel the government machine and redistribute export earnings (or royalties) throughout the economy.[47]

Extravagant military expenditures and the economic disruption caused by political unrest (however justified) certainly made things worse. By 1980, in Latin America, only those countries which had emphasized an export-oriented strategy – particularly Brazil, Mexico, and Chile – were able to sustain high rates of economic growth.[48]

In fact, a new model of development had emerged in East Asia, spreading to South and Southeast Asia and then to Latin America. Now, by taking advantage of cost/price differentials *vis-à-vis* the developed economies, the export of manufactures would be made competitive.[49] Certainly this was the experience of Asia's 'four tigers' at the beginning of their development process, but it also extended to India (where, in the 1980s, manufactured goods exceeded 60 per cent of total exports), the Philippines (81 per cent), Pakistan (78 per cent), Thailand (64 per cent), and, after the 'open door' policy was initiated in 1979, China.[50] This is the model associated with the so-called theory of the new international division of labor, which, in its most dogmatic manifestation, erroneously attributes such international division of labor to the decentralization of multinational corporations throughout the Third World.[51] (This is only one element of the model, and not the dominant one.)

It is important to realize that this model was based *not* on a sectoral specialization between developed and developing economies, but on a division of

Table 5.4 World consumption and prices of major raw materials, 1969/71–2000

	Average annual rates of growth in consumption[a] (%)			Unit	Price[b] $US (constant)			
	1969/71–1979/81	1979/81–1984/86	Projected 1984/86–2000		1969/71	1979/81	1985	Projected 2000
Agricultural non-food[c]	1.99	0.66	1.42					
Cotton	1.81	1.78	1.52	lb.	1.72	1.51	1.56	1.38
Jute	1.06	-0.74	1.43	m.t.	7.76	3.21	5.83	3.00
Natural rubber	2.31	2.07	2.22	lb.	0.61	0.64	0.42	0.50
Tobacco	2.15	1.96	1.68	lb.	1.21	1.01	0.86	0.79
Timber	2.04	-0.62	1.13					
Metals and minerals[c]	2.75	0.61	1.32					
Copper	2.49	0.86	1.44	lb.	1.66	0.88	0.64	0.73
Iron ore	2.01	-0.43	0.68	m.t.	37.00	24.00	23.00	14.00
Tin	0.22	-3.21	-1.05	lb.	4.33	6.75	5.41	3.34
Nickel	2.83	0.97	1.06	lb.	3.38	2.75	2.23	1.69
Bauxite	4.21	0.14	1.95	m.t.	33.00	39.00	30.00	26.00
Lead	1.52	0.21	0.42	lb.	0.35	0.43	0.18	0.17
Zinc	1.31	1.84	1.27	lb.	0.37	0.35	0.36	0.36

Source: World Bank, *Price Prospects for Major Primary Commodities* (Washington, DC: World Bank, October 1986), vols 1, 3, and 4, annex tables.
Note: Foods, beverages, and fuels are excluded.
[a] Evaluated in 1979/81 average prices.
[b] Average price. Current dollars deflated by manufacturing unit value index: 1985 = 100.
[c] Weighted average.

labor between high-level and low-level technological components within each product group. Thus, as Table 5.5 shows, most manufacturing trade between developed and developing countries takes place within product groups, and the importance of intra-product group trade has substantially increased over time. To understand this is critical for the purpose of our analysis because therein lies the key to understanding the crisis associated with the model.

Indeed, during the 1980s, while some regions of some countries did thrive on the basis of the model of low production costs at the low end of the manufacturing world assembly line (e.g. the Bangkok area or the *maquiladora* industries in northern Mexico), most other industrializing countries, particularly in Latin America, suffered a severe crisis and seemed to lose ground in their race to connect productively with the world economy. Two factors combined to create a major obstacle to development in a decisive moment of

Table 5.5 The growing importance of trade within product groups in the trade of the developing areas with the developed countries, 1970–1986

	1970	*1980*	*1986*
Textiles	66	85	94
Household appliances	35	68	92
Raw materials	52	71	91
Non-ferrous metals	35	71	84
Office and telecommunication equipment	22	68	84
Other semi-manufactures	55	61	84
Food	63	97	79
Other consumer goods	95	99	68
Ores and minerals	24	39	57
Iron and steel	19	21	49
Other machinery and transport equipment	12	22	45
Chemicals	17	28	35
Road vehicles	2	5	29
Clothing	47	30	17
Machinery for specialized industries	2	6	17
Fuels	8	5	13

Source: GATT, *Report on International Trade, 1980–1987* (Geneva: GATT, 1987).
Note: For all product groups except food, clothing, and other consumer goods, the dollar values of exports and imports in the trade of the developing areas with the developed countries have become more balanced over time. This development is evident from the indexes presented. For each of the sixteen product groups shown in this table, the figures are calculated by taking the absolute amount of net trade of the developing areas with the developed countries (i.e. exports minus imports, ignoring the question of whether it is a trade surplus or a trade deficit) as a percentage of gross trade (i.e. exports plus imports), and adjusting it so that it becomes 100 if the dollar value of imports of an individual category precisely matches the dollar value of exports of that category (all figures are calculated on a free on board [f.o.b.] basis which represents the valuation of goods in trade up to the point of embarkation). It becomes zero if there are only exports or only imports.
For example, in 1986 the developing areas exported chemicals worth $6.9 billion to the developed countries and imported chemicals worth $32.9 billion from them. The amount of net trade in chemicals was thus $26 billion, and gross trade was $39.8 billion. Net trade as a percentage of gross trade was 65 per cent. The index represents the difference between that percentage and 100: namely, 35. Thus, an increase over time in the percentage in the table indicates that trade in the particular product category is becoming more balanced (i.e. net trade is becoming proportionately smaller) – a sign that countries are specializing more within the particular product category.

the development process: one a conjunctural circumstance and one a structural impediment.

Structurally, the continuous upgrading of the technological component of manufacturing products and processes required a leap forward in order to keep up with international competition. Cheap labor was not a sufficient comparative advantage when automation could easily replace unskilled labor while also improving quality.[52] Relatively low-cost labor combined with automation and with a higher technological component was the winning formula. This was particularly so for those Pacific Asian NICs which made the technological transition, actually becoming competitive worldwide in the low to middle range of electronic products and rapidly winning market share in high-technology international trade.[53] Other countries, such as Argentina, did not even try, and saw their exports substantially decline (in the case of Argentina, from an average annual rate of growth of 4.7 per cent in 1966–80 to −0.3 per cent in 1980–87).

Other countries did try conversion into higher-value-added manufacturing exports, and failed. Partly they failed because the technological leap forward was far beyond their reach – not only in terms of their ability to license new technologies, but in terms of the required overall revamping of industrial structure and productive infrastructure, including education and training, tele-communications, and communications. Partly they failed because of the con-junctural element of the foreign debt burden, which had a critical impact on the inability of many developing nations to restructure their economies at the historical moment when it was most needed. Service of the debt, together with the austerity policies imposed by lenders or international institutions, deprived many countries of substantial resources needed to modernize their econ-omies.[54] Thus, GDP growth of the seventeen most highly indebted countries with middle- and low-income economies fell from an average annual rate of 6.1 per cent in 1965–80 to 1.1 per cent in 1980–87. To be sure, responsibility for the debt problem lies both in irresponsible lending by private banks during the petrodollar euphoria of the 1970s and in often wasteful use of those loans by borrowing countries. Also, within the limits of these financial constraints, many countries in the 1980s could have pursued more courageous, deliberate policies: for instance, Peru's economic catastrophe has something to do (but not everything) with the demagogy of Alan García's administration. Overall, though, it would seem that the structural effort of adaptation to the new competitive environment was so demanding that only a handful of economies and societies were able to make it by themselves. Here, the case of Brazil is much to the point.[55]

In spite of all the social inequality and political inequity involved in the process, Brazil's GDP grew at an astounding average annual rate of 9 per cent in 1965–80, falling to a moderate 2.7 per cent annual growth in 1980–86. Particularly important in this slowdown of economic growth was the decreasing rate of export growth (from 9.4 per cent to 4.3 per cent annually for the corresponding periods), not to mention the drop in the investment rate: as a proportion of GDP, it fell from 22.5 per cent in 1980 to 15.9 per cent in 1988, thus slowing down substantially the process of industrial modernization that underlay Brazilian competitiveness. The austerity measures introduced by President Fernando Collor de Mello halted the dynamism of the Brazilian economy, which fell into negative growth in 1990 (-4.6 per cent). Thus, while Brazil remains competitive in some intermediate commodities (e.g. petrochemicals, iron and steel, aluminum), its manufacturing industry is losing competitiveness in all high-value-added sectors. Given the current movement toward privatization of the national companies and the gradual phasing out of the market reserve policy in strategic sectors, Brazil's inability to modernize the industrial structure could lead to its partial demise. The wrecking of the Brazilian economy, the only one in Latin America that had become a world-class manufacturing exporter, would signal a dramatic decline of Latin America in the world economy, underscoring the inability of a substantial part of the Third World to integrate into the new economy in the making.

On the other hand, several Latin American economies showed signs of restructuring and growth during the 1990–91 period. According to the Inter-American Development Bank, Mexico was on a path of steady growth (3.1 per cent in 1989, 3.9 per cent in 1990, 5.3 per cent in 1991); Chile continued to grow (above 10 per cent in 1989, 2.1 per cent in 1990, 4.1 per cent in 1991); and Argentina seemed to have recovered in 1991 (3 per cent) after negative growth rates in 1989 and 1990. But Peru is literally disintegrating, with growth rates of -11.2 per cent in 1989, -3.9 per cent in 1990, and -4.8 per cent in 1991. Overall, Latin America seems to be in a state of economic uncertainty in the early 1990s. On the one hand, austerity policies have restructured the economy in some countries, albeit at a very high social cost. On the other hand, the stability of new-found growth depends largely on the ability of these more stable economies to link up with the new markets and the new production processes of the dominant economic areas. That is why Mexico, increasingly integrated into the North American economic area, and Chile, a small economy focused entirely outward, are the bright spots of the new Latin American economy. Yet only if the region integrates internally, expanding its domestic markets, and only if the productive infrastructure undergoes a substantial process of modernization can Latin American–based firms compete and grow in the new world economy.

The foregoing analysis should afford us a better reading of the global economic evolution of the South over the past twenty-five years. In that regard, let us now examine the data provided by the World Bank in its *World Development Report, 1991*.

An uneven process

The story that statistics and specialized literature seem to suggest is both complex and highly varied with respect to countries, geographic regions, and time periods. Certainly it has nothing to do with the traditional left-wing imagery of a Third World that never develops. There are substantial differences in development performance between the 1965–80 period and the 1980s (the World

Bank data presented here concern the period 1980–89). From 1965 to 1980, the GDP of low-income economies grew at an average annual rate of 4.8 per cent, that of middle-income economies at 6.2 per cent. Demographic growth substantially reduced the benefits of such economic growth, though still maintaining it at a moderately positive pace (an annual average of 2.9 per cent growth for the 1965–89 period for the low-income economies). Indeed, up to 1980, the performance of Latin America as a whole was not far behind that of East Asia (7.3 per cent annual growth for East Asia, 6.1 per cent for Latin America); and Brazil's performance (9 per cent annual growth in GDP, 9.3 per cent annual growth in exports) or even Mexico's (6.5 per cent and 7.6 per cent, respectively) is comparable to that of the Asian role models. Albert Fishlow has provided detailed statistical evidence of comparable development paths for Latin America and East/Southeast Asia until the 1980s.[56] The big change came during the 1980s: sub-Saharan Africa and Latin America plummeted, falling from an annual GDP growth of 4.2 per cent and 6.1 per cent, respectively, to 2.4 per cent and 1.6 per cent in 1980–89 (which, in per capita terms, meant negative growth).

But even in the 1980s we must establish fundamental differences within the so-called Third World. Asia, overall, maintained healthy growth during the 1980s.[57] Indeed, East Asia increased its pace from 7.2 per cent annual growth to 7.9 per cent in the 1980–89 period; and South Asia (mainly India) improved its growth rate from 3.7 per cent to 5.1 per cent. Some of this Asian growth is linked to the development phenomenon known as the 'saga of four tigers';[58] statistically speaking, though, the main actor of Asian development is China, which shot from a 6.9 per cent average annual growth rate in real GDP (1965–80) to an astonishing 9.7 per cent (1980–87). Even when we include demographic growth in our accounting, given the relative success of birth-control policies in China, per capita average annual growth for the entire 1965–89 period amounts to 5.7 per cent for China, compared with 4.3 per cent for Japan. (Admittedly, China's starting point was abysmally lower.) A major force in the surge of Chinese economic growth in the 1980s has been the increase in exports (10.4 per cent per year in 1980–87) as the Chinese began to imitate their neighbors, following Deng Xiaoping's declaration that 'it is glorious to be rich'.[59] However, doubts arise about the political capacity of the Chinese regime to accomplish economic modernization without political change. Moreover, the technological and managerial upgrading of the Chinese economy, indispensable for its future competitiveness in the world market, still has a long way to go.[60]

Nevertheless, the fact that Asia as a whole has been very much on the road to development, even in the transitional 1980s, invalidates the catastrophic vision of a starving Third World, particularly when one remembers that Asia accounts for about two-thirds of the world's population. Obviously, there is widespread poverty, hunger, and sickness throughout Asia, and the process of economic growth is extremely uneven, both territorially and socially (though no more than during the European industrialization in the nineteenth century). But the basic fact remains that Asia has begun a process of economic growth that, though fragile, could really alter the fate of this planet if that process were to be supported and consolidated at the critical moment of passage into the informational economy.

Yet, at the same time, most of Africa, the non-oil producers in the Middle East, and most of Latin America entered a structural economic crisis in the 1980s – one that could have damaging, lasting consequences for the economies and peoples of those areas, if not for all humankind. What is at issue here is not only that national economies are heavily indebted, that economic growth is sluggish or even negative, and that a substantial proportion of the population is fighting for survival every day. The critical point is that the current dramatic transformation of the world economy into a dynamic, highly integrated system could bypass entire countries or the majority of their population. The more economic growth depends on high-value-added inputs and expansion in the core markets, then the less relevant become those economies which offer limited, difficult markets and primary commodities that are either being replaced by new materials or devalued with respect to their overall contribution to the production process. With the absolute costs of labor becoming less and less important as a competitive factor (versus low labor costs relative to a certain level of technological sophistication and economic integration in the world economy), many countries and regions face a process of rapid deterioration that could lead to destructive reactions.[61] Within the framework of the new informational economy, a significant part of the world population is shifting from a structural position of exploitation to a structural position of irrelevance.

The Third World is no more – rendered meaningless by the ascendance of the newly industrialized countries (mainly in East Asia), by the development process of large continental economies on their way toward integration in the world economy (such as China and, to a lesser extent, India), and by the rise of a Fourth World, made up of marginalized economies in the retarded rural areas of three continents and in the sprawling shantytowns of African, Asian, and Latin American cities. Most of Africa has already been engulfed in this downward spiral. Latin America still struggles, with Mexico, Brazil, Argentina, Chile, Venezuela, Colombia, and Bolivia in the midst of a restructuring process that could pave the way for their articulation into the new world economy while other countries seem to be trapped in the fatal oscillation between hyperinflation and economic stagnation. Furthermore, a way out via self-sustaining policies seems to be excluded in a world where the sources of capital and technology are increasingly concentrated in the centers of an integrated worldwide economic system. This structural crisis, fundamentally linked to the incapacity of a number of countries (either for geographic, historical, or institutional reasons) to adapt to the new conditions of economic growth, leads to a plurality of collective reactions, all of them having high destructive potential. The first, and most straightforward, is to establish new linkages with the world economy via the criminal economy: drug production and trafficking, illegal arms deals, smuggling, and commerce in human beings (women and children in particular), or even in human organs for transplants in the private clinics of the North. We know all too well that entire societies have been entirely penetrated and restructured by criminal economic activity, prompted by high demand in the core countries and having dire consequences at both ends of the exchange.

A second reaction is the expression of utter desperation through that widespread violence, either individual or collective, which has transformed major cities in the Fourth World (and entire regions in some countries) into savage, self-destructive battlegrounds. In Africa, the collective frustration over disintegrating economies and societies often expresses itself through ancestral ethnic struggles, with the inevitable massacres and mad spirals of genocidal revenge that the rest of the world generally views with indifference.

A third reaction, rapidly developing in the Fourth World (and in some areas of the First World that could be assimilated to the special conditions of the Fourth World) is the rise of ideological/religious fundamentalism, easily associated with terrorism and/or semi-religious war. The logic of exclusion embedded in the current dominant system is met with reciprocal appeals for exclusion of the dominants by the excluded. The shift from exploitation to irrelevance in some areas of the world, in relation to the dominant dynamics of the system, leads to the breakdown of any relationship and, therefore, to the alienation of entire groups, cultures, or countries from the dominant structure of the new world order. Not to be excessively mechanistic, I suggest, based on comparative observations of social dynamics over the past decade,[62] that there is a thread within the diversity of fundamentalist movements that have mushroomed around the world: namely, opposition to an overall model of development that threatens cultural identity as it expands across the planet while only partially reintegrating the fragments of the societies shattered by technoeconomic modernization. That is to say, there is a commonality between Islamic fundamentalism, Sendero Luminoso's special brand of Maoism, and Pol Pot's Marxism–Leninism: cut all bridges with 'the Other' (i.e. the developed world and its logic in the developing world), since there is little chance that the excluded can ever become true partners in a system that is so extraordinarily inclusive of economies and somewhat exclusive of societies. The instrument for cutting off such ties is the ferocious defense of territorial and cultural boundaries through unrestricted violence: jihad against all infidels.

If the rise of the Fourth World is not counterveiled by a deliberate reform of the current world development model, the informational economy of the twenty-first century will have to reckon not only with the depressing image of starving children, but with the proliferation of powerful worldwide criminal mafias, dramatic interethnic violence, and a profound fundamentalist groundswell that will shake our tolerance and shatter our newly found peace.

The place of the transitional command economies in the new international division of labor

The end of communism as a system[63] and the rapid conversion of former command economies to market economies is a new, fundamental trend that forces us to rethink the foreseeable evolution of the international economy. The conditions of that evolution now include the gradual incorporation of the economies of Eastern Europe and the republics of the former Soviet Union.

Indeed, the Khrushchevian dream of peaceful coexistence and gradual convergence of the two systems on the basis of economic competition[64] was fulfilled, albeit in the opposite direction from his vision. Soviet production as a share of total world production declined from 11 per cent in 1967 to 9.8 per cent in 1986, with Eastern Europe following a parallel course from 4.6 per cent to 3.7 per cent.[65] The inability of the Soviet system to adapt to the conditions of the informational economy, together with the growing economic and technological differential between an integrated market economy and a stagnant pool of command economies, led to piecemeal economic reforms, then to a full-fledged *perestroika*, then to the de-Sovietization of Eastern Europe and, finally, to the disintegration of the Soviet Union and the rise of a new, democratic Russia in an uncertain and unstable geopolitical era.[66]

Whatever the final outcome of such dramatic processes, the world market economy will certainly be deeply modified. The former command economies will eventually be transformed into market economies; and, in our world, this implies their full economic integration into the international system. Their sheer size and productive potential means that their incorporation will transform the current pattern of the international division of labor. Thus, our analysis would not be complete without my at least suggesting some potential future developments, notions drawn mainly from my current research on the process of technological modernization and social transformation under way in Russia.[67]

First of all, the short-term future will be dominated by a gigantic effort to revamp the productive infrastructure and to adapt existing institutions to the logic of the market economy and an open society. Such an effort is already well under way in Eastern Europe, with the possible exception of Romania, but is still in the preliminary stage in the former Soviet Union. Acute political and social instability in coming years is likely to prevent any large-scale integration effort of the former Soviet economies in the short term. Thus, for the first half of the 1990s, the most likely role to be played by the command economies in the international economy is to be net recipients of Northern (i.e. Western and Japanese) capital and technology and, potentially, exporters of cheap, semi-skilled labor. The border between the EEC and East European countries could well become the 'Rio Grande' of Europe, as Europe's demographic decline may lead to the need for additional labor in order to sustain economic growth, and cultural barriers with the Muslim world will most likely prevent further immigration from the Southern Mediterranean region.

In a different version of the same strategy of exporting labor, strikingly reminiscent of the *maquiladora* arrangement in Mexico, European companies could set up factories on the borderline in order to lower production costs. However, preliminary assessments of the situation in Poland, as well as assessments of the conversion of East German plants, do not seem optimistic about the success of such scenarios, particularly because low-cost labor areas with much better infrastructure and more favorable institutional features still exist in the EEC, Andalusia being the most notable case in point. Still, the 'Polish *maquiladoras*' option could be a reasonable scenario by the year 2000.

Second, the strongest, most likely, and most immediate connection with the world economy will be the export and joint-processing of natural resources, particularly energy resources (oil, gas, coal, and hydroelectric power – via superconductive powerlines in the not too distant future), rare metals, gold, diamonds, timber, and fish. Siberia, with its vast and only partly explored resources, is probably the critical region in this potential linkup between West and East. The rational exploitation and transport of energy resources from Siberia to Europe and Japan could provide the crucial energy source the world needs while waiting for the transition to nuclear fusion and other renewable energy sources, eliminating dependence on the always unpredictable Middle East (remember that the former Soviet Union was, in the mid-1980s, the largest producer of oil in the world). This resource-extraction development program will require a massive influx of capital, technology, machinery, and expertise and could well be the first stage of the eventual integration of the former command economies into the world economy.

A third possibility, for some East European economies around the year 2000, would be the mobilization of the scientific and technical human potential that now exists, vastly underutilized, in many areas (in Hungary and the Baltic republics, for instance). Joint ventures between Western and local firms to tap into the highly skilled labor market existing in such societies could represent a new frontier of decentralized production for Western companies. The recent development of an active software industry in Hungary, catering to Western firms, and the spontaneous growth of a high-technology complex around the old, distinguished Tartu University in Estonia are examples of how market economies can make use of scientific potential that was being wasted under the command system.

In the mid-term, between ten and twenty years from now, the critical role that such economies (particularly the economies of the various former Soviet republics) can play in the world system is to provide the expanded markets needed to match the fast-growing productive capacities of the information economy. This, however, requires that Western firms gradually infuse capital and technology into the productive fabric of Eastern Europe and the former Soviet republics, so that these economies themselves become sources of dynamism. The full incorporation of a market of 400 million consumers in the Western economy – with particular emphasis on the West European economy – will ensure the necessary outlet for an increasingly productive system as we move full speed into the informational economy over the coming two decades.

One contribution that the collapse of the Soviet system has already made to the world economy is the 'peace dividend' that we can perhaps now afford. It would, of course, be utopian to pretend that we have reached the point where we can proceed with general disarmament, as the Gulf War dramatically showed. The historic transition that we are experiencing in so many dimensions of our social and economic systems is full of opportunities, but also full of dangers. Thus, democracies must be ready to resort to military force, whenever and wherever necessary: the notion of a unified, civilized world depends for its fulfillment on the determination of the civilized world to defend itself, on behalf of the whole of humankind. Therefore, leaner, smaller, more effective, high-tech-equipped, *and information-oriented* military forces must be at the disposal of all major nations, perhaps increasingly co-ordinated through international peacekeeping institutions. Yet, the dismantlement of the enormous military apparatus that sustained the balance of nuclear terror during the Cold War represents a fantastic saving not just of capital and equipment, but also of human, technological, and scientific resources that can now be put to use in a full-scale, globally oriented development program.

The challenges represented by the disintegration of the Second World, the end of the Third World, and the rise of the Fourth World must be taken up in the current process of restructuring our world. The opportunities and the dangers arising in such a process constitute the raw material from which are made the new social conflicts and political strategies that together will shape the world of the twenty-first century.

Notes

1 Robert Solow, Technical change and the aggregate production function. *Review of Economics and Statistics* 39 (1957): 312–20.
2 For a thorough discussion of the literature on the question of productivity sources, see Richard R. Nelson, Research of productivity growth and productivity differences: dead ends and new departures. *Journal of Economic Literature* 19 (September 1981), 1029–64.
3 See Christian Sautter, L'Efficacité et la rentabilité de l'économie française de 1954 à 1974. *Economie et Statistique* 68 1976; Edward Denison, *Trends in American economic growth 1929–1982* (Washington, DC: Brookings, 1985).
4 Abel Aganbegyan, *The economic challenge of perestroika* (Bloomington: Indiana University Press, 1988), pp. 10–11.
5 See Nathan Rosenberg and L. E. Birdzell, *How the West grew rich: The economic transformation of the industrial world* (New York: Basic Books, 1986).
6 Jerome A. Mark and William H. Waldorf, Multifactor productivity: a new BLS measure, in *Monthly Labor Review* 106 (December 1983), 3–15.
7 Tom Stonier, *The wealth of information: A profile of the postindustrial economy* (London: Thames Methuen, 1983).
8 See Pascal Petit, *Slow growth and the service economy* (London: Pinter, 1986).
9 Stephen S. Cohen and John Zysman, *Manufacturing matters: The myth of the postindustrial economy* (New York: Basic Books, 1987).
10 See Marc Porat, *The information economy: Definition and measurement*, Special Publication 77–12(1) (Washington, DC: US Department of Commerce, Office of Telecommunications, 1977).
11 Research in progress: data elaborated by Manuel Castells and Yuko Aoyama, University of California–Berkeley, 1992.
12 See Mark Hepworth, *Geography of the information economy* (London: Belhaven Press, 1989).
13 See Bruce R. Guile and Harvey Brooks (eds), *Technology and global industry:*

Companies and nations in the world economy (Washington, DC: National Academy Press, 1987).

14 See Robert Boyer, *Technical change and the theory of regulation* (Paris: CEPRE-MAP, 1987).

15 Michael Piore and Charles Sabel, *The second industrial divide* (New York: Basic Books, 1984).

16 See Vittorio Capecchi, The informal economy and the development of flexible specialization in Emilia-Romagna. In A. Portes, M. Castells and L. Benton (eds), *The informal economy: Studies in advanced and less developed countries* (Baltimore: Johns Hopkins University Press, 1989).

17 See A. Michael Spence and Heather A. Hazard (eds), *International competitiveness* (Cambridge, MA: Ballinger, 1988).

18 See Manuel Castells, Lee Goh and R. W. Y. Kwok, *The Shek Kip Mei syndrome: Economic Development and public policy in Hong Kong and Singapore* (London: Pion, 1990).

19 See Tom Forester, *High Tech Society* (Oxford: Basil Blackwell, 1987).

20 See Manuel Castells *et al.*, *Nuevas tecnologías, economía y sociedad en España* (Madrid: Alianza Editorial, 1986).

21 See François Bar, Configuring the telecommunications infrastructure for the computer age: the economics of network control, PhD dissertation, University of California–Berkeley, 1990.

22 See C. Jonscher, Information resources and economic productivity, *Information Economics and Policy* 2(1) (1983), 13–35.

23 See Manuel Castells, *The informational city: Information technology, economic restructuring, and the urban-regional process* (Oxford: Basil Blackwell, 1989).

24 See J. Beniger, *The control revolution: Technological and economic origins of the information society* (Cambridge, MA: Harvard University Press, 1986); and Prospettive sociologiche per la società postindustriale. Lo scenario internazionale, *Sociologia* (Rome), no. 1 (1989).

25 I prefer 'informational economy' to Daniel Bell's 'postindustrial society' because it gives substantive content to an otherwise purely descriptive notion.

26 See Ralph Landau and Nathan Rosenberg (eds), *The positive sum strategy: Harnessing technology for economic growth* (Washington, DC: National Academy Press, 1986).

27 See Gerard Lafay and Colette Herzog, *Commerce international: La fin des avantages acquis* (Paris: Economica, for Centre d'Etudes Prospectives et d'Informations Internationales, 1989); Stephen Cohen, David Teece, Laura D'Andrea Tyson and John Zysman, *Competitiveness*, vol. 3: *Global competition: The new reality*, the Report of the President's Commission of Industrial Competitiveness (Washington, DC: GPO, 1985); John Dunning (ed.), *Multinational enterprises, economic structure, and economic competitiveness* (Chichester: John Wiley, 1988); and Robert B. Reich, *The work of nations* (New York: Random House, 1991).

28 Giovanni Dosi and Luc Soete, Technology, competitiveness, and international trade. *Econometrica* (1983), 3.

29 Manuel Castells and Laura D'Andrea Tyson, High technology choices ahead: Restructuring interdependence. In John Sewell and Stuart Tucker (eds), *Growth, exports, and jobs in a changing world economy* (Washington, DC: Transaction Books, for Overseas Development Council, 1988).

30 The EEA combines the European Economic Community (EEC) and the European Free-Trade Association (EFTA).

31 See Laura D'Andrea Tyson, William T. Dickens and John Zysman (eds), *The dynamics of trade and employment* (Cambridge, MA: Ballinger, 1988).

32 See Cohen *et al.*, *Global competition* (note 27).

33 See Edward K. Y. Chen, *The newly industrializing countries in Asia. Growth experience and prospects* (Hong Kong: University of Hong Kong, Center for Asian Studies, 1985); and Bela Belassa *et al.*, *Toward renewed economic growth in Latin America* (Washington, DC: Institute for International Economics, 1986).

34 See Giovanni Dosi *et al.*, *Technical change and economic theory* (London: Pinter, 1988).

35 See Chalmers Johnson, *MITI and the Japanese miracle* (Stanford, CA: Stanford University Press, 1982).

36 Lafay and Herzog, *Commerce international* (note 27).

37 See Kenichi Ohmae, *Triad power: The coming shape of global competition* (New York: Free Press, 1985).

38 See Nigel Harris, *The end of the Third World* (London: Penguin Books, 1986).

39 See Gary Gereffi, Rethinking development theory: insights from East Asia and Latin America. *Sociological Forum* 4 (1989), 505–35.

40 See Arghiri Emmanuel, *L'échange inégal* (Paris: Maspero, 1973).

41 See Alain Touraine, *La parole et le sang: Politique et société en Amérique Latine* (Paris: Odile Jacob, 1988).

42 See Frederic Deyo (ed.) *The political economy of New Asian industrialism* (Ithaca, NY: Cornell University Press, 1987).

43 For a general discussion of new issues in development theory and practice, see Alejandro Portes and A. Douglas Kincaid, Sociology and development in the 1990s: critical challenges and empirical trends, Gary Gereffi, Rethinking development theory: insight from East Asia and Latin America; and Peter Evans, Predatory, developmental, and other apparatus: a comparative political economy perspective on the Third World state – all in *Sociological Forum* 4(4)(1989), a special issue.

44 See Fernando Calderón, *Los movimientos sociales ante las crisis* (Buenos Aires: CLACSO, 1986).

45 See Fernando H. Cardoso and Enzo Faletto, *Dependencia y desarrollo en América Latina.* (Mexico: Siglo XXI, 1969), which was also published in expanded translation by the University of California Press 1979.

46 See Hyun-Chin Lim, *Dependent development in Korea, 1963–1979* (Seoul: Seoul University Press, 1985).

47 See Fernando Fajnzylber, *La industrialización truncada de América Latina* (Mexico: Nueva Imagen, 1983).

48 See Celso Furtado, *A nova dependência* (Rio de Janeiro: Paz e Terra, 1983).

49 Fernando Fajnzylber, Las economías neoindustriales en el sistema centro–periferia de los ochenta. *Pensamiento Iberoamericano* 9 (1986), 125–72.

50 See Manuel Castells, High technology and the new international division of labour. *International Labour Review* (October 1989).

51 See Folker Frobel, Jürgen Heinrichs and Otto Kreye, *The new international division of labor* (New York: Cambridge University Press, 1981).

52 Manuel Castells and Laura D'Andrea Tyson, High technology and the changing international division of production: implications for the US economy. In Randall B. Purcell (ed.), *The newly industrializing countries in the world economy: Challenges for US policy* (Boulder, CO: Lynne Rienner, 1989), pp. 13–50.

53 See Dieter Ernst and David O'Connor, *Technological capabilities, new technologies, and newcomer industrialization: An agenda for the 1990s* (Paris: OECD Development Centre, 1990).

54 See Jacobo Schatan, *World debt: Who is to pay?* (London: Zed Books, 1987).
55 See Claudio R. Frischtak, Structural change and trade in Brazil and in the newly industrializing Latin American economies in Purcell (ed.), *The newly industrializing countries* (note 52).
56 Albert Fishlow, 'Economic growth in Asia and Latin America: a comparative analysis (research paper, University of California–Berkeley, 1987).
57 See Carl J. Dahlman, Structural change and trade in East Asia newly industrial economies and emerging industrial economies. In Purcell (ed.), *The newly industrializing Countries* (note 55), pp. 51–94.
58 See Manuel Castells, Four Asian tigers with a dragon head: a comparative analysis of the State, economy, and society in the Asian Pacific rim. In Richard Appelbaum and Jeff Henderson (eds), *State and society in the Pacific rim* (London: Sage Publications, 1992).
59 See Lynn Pan, *The new Chinese revolution* (London: Hamish Hamilton, 1987).
60 See Patrizio Bianchi, Martin Carnoy and Manuel Castells, *Economic modernization and technology transfer in the People's Republic of China* (Stanford, CA: CERAS, Stanford University, 1988).
61 Manuel Castells and Roberto Laserna, The new dependency: technological change and socio-economic restructuring in Latin America. *Sociological Forum* 4(4) (1989), 535–60.
62 Fernando Calderón and Mario R. Dos Santos (eds), *¿Hacia un nuevo órden estatal en América Latina?* (Buenos Aires: Biblioteca de Ciencias Sociales, 1988).
63 See Manuel Castells, 'El fin del comunismo'. *Claves* (Madrid), 1 (April 1990).
64 See *Khrushchev remembers: The glasnost tapes* (Boston: Little, Brown, 1990).
65 'CHELEM' data bank, Centre d'Etudes Prospectives et d'Informations Internationales (Paris).
66 See Padma Desai, *Perestroika in perspective* (Princeton, NJ: Princeton University Press, 1989); Bernard Gwertzman and Michael T. Kaufman (eds), *The collapse of communism* (New York: Times Books, 1990); Boris Kagarlitsky, *Farewell perestroika: A Soviet chronicle* (London: Verso, 1990); and Manuel Castells, *La nueva revolución rusa* (Madrid: Sistema, 1992).
67 Fieldwork in 1989, 1990, 1991, and 1992 in Moscow, St Petersburg, and Siberia; under the auspices of the Autonomous University of Madrid, the Soviet Sociological Association, the Russian Sociological Association, the USSR Academy of Sciences, and the Russian Academy of Sciences. For preliminary results of this research project, see Manuel Castells, *La nueva revolución rusa* (note 67).

---

6 Michael Watts,
'The Shock of Modernity: Petroleum, Protest, and Fast Capitalism in an Industrializing Society'

Excerpts from: A. Pred and M. J. Watts, *Reworking Modernity: Capitalisms and Symbolic Discontent*, Chapter 2. New Brunswick, NJ: Rutgers University Press (1992)

His face is turned toward the past. Where we perceive a chain of events, he sees one single catatrophe which keeps piling wreckage upon wreckage and hurls it in front of his feet. The angel would like to stay, to awaken the dead, and make whole what has been smashed. But a storm is blowing from Paradise; it has got caught in his wings with such violence that the angel can no longer close them. The storm irresistibly propels him into the future to which his back is turned, while the debris before him grows skyward. This storm is what we call progress.

Walter Benjamin, *Illuminations*

Introduction

Born into rural poverty in 1927 in northern Cameroon, Mohammedu Marwa (alias Mallam Maitatsine, alias Muhammedu Marwa, alias Muhammedu Mai tabsiri) left his birthplace when he was about sixteen years old. He attached himself to a local Muslim cleric and apparently displayed exceptional brilliance in the Qur'anic science of exegesis (*tafsir*). His exegetical skills were acquired as an a student (*almajirai*) in local Muslim networks and non-formal schools (*makarantar allo*). Settling in the city of Kano, the mercantile capital of Nigeria, around 1945, he was a regular visitor at the preaching sessions around the Shahauci and Fagge grounds in the old quarters of the city, providing unorthodox interpretations of Qur'anic verses read by his associate, Mallam Aminu Umar, recently returned from learning 'in the East'. Marwa insisted that the Qur'an was the *only* valid guide to behavior and belief, and thus rejected both the Sunna and the shari'a. The basis of his inflammatory reading of the Qur'an involved stripping away the hidden meanings within the sacred text by rooting his analyses of verse in local West African conditions. In particular, by playing on the meanings and phonetic associations of certain Arabic and Hausa words, Marwa, or Maitatsine, as he became known locally, provided a powerful antimaterialist thrust to the Qur'an. His vehement denunciation of bicycles, apparel, cigarettes, buttons, cars, and so on brought him his name, Maitatsine, derived from the Hausa adage *Allah ta tsine* (God will curse). By 1962, Marwa had gained some local notoriety as a troublesome, charismatic, and unorthodox preacher, and Emir Sanusi of Kano actually brought him to trial. He was imprisoned for three months and promptly deported. Marwa's local stature grew substantially, however, following his prediction that Emir Sanusi would fall from power; he was, in fact, ousted several years later in the wake of the military coup.

Marwa returned to Kano shortly after his deportation – sustaining the popular belief that reactionary forces in high places supported his variety of militant Islam – and continued to live and preach in the city. He was arrested and imprisoned again in 1966–67 and also in 1973–75 but was not deported. In the period following Marwa's return to Kano, the open spaces of 'Yan Awaki and Kofar Wombai provided a sort of beachhead, a sanctuary in which his students could be housed in makeshift dwellings and which by the late 1970s included urban gardens to sustain the growing numbers of followers. By 1979 there was something like a community (*tsangaya*) in place; Maitatsine's compound in 'Yan Awaki housed at least three thousand persons.[1] At the suggestion of Maitatsine, the followers carried little or no money – to sleep with more than one naira (equivalent to about seventy-five cents) was to exhibit a lack of trust in Allah – and dressed simply, characteristically begging for alms or working as transient laborers in occupations typically reserved for dry season migrants (*'yan cin-rani*), such as cart pushing, tea selling, and petty trade.

Maitatsine's followers (*'Yan Tatsine*) became increasingly visible around the old city, operating in small groups of three to five people, preaching at major junctions near the Sabon Gari mosque, around Koki, and at Kofar Wombai (see Figure 6.1). Through recitations and unorthodox interpretations of the Qur'an, the students vigorously attacked materialism, modernity, unjust leaders, corrupt clerics (*ulema*), and all brotherhood followers.[2] Unorthodox behavior fueled rumor on a grand scale. Kano's wealthiest contractors and one of the most powerful voices of the northern oligarchy, popular opinion had it,

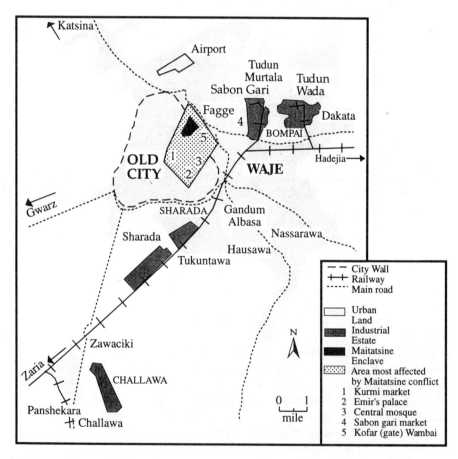

Fig. 6.1 The geography of the Maitatsine movement, Kano City, 18–28 December 1980 (courtesy of the author)

materially supported the Maitatsine movement. In addition, hearsay had it that Maitatsine was lent support, and financial sustenance, both from luminaries within the ruling Nigerian federal party, the conservative and northern Muslim-dominated National Party of Nigeria (NPN), and from the incumbent Kano State administration, the populist People's Redemption Party (PRP). Rumor also fed the mystique of Maitatsine's magical powers. The government tribunal on the 'Yan Tatsine movement reported grotesque (but largely unsubstantiated) tales of cannibalism, human slaughter (a 'human spare parts department', as the northern press referred to it), mass graves, drugged students, and brainwashed women. At the same time, there were reports of extraordinary bravery – Marwa certainly felt himself to be invulnerable – and impressive self-discipline by the 'Yan Tatsine. There was, in short, something like a moral economy within the *tsangaya*. Sometime in 1979, according to testimony by one of his wives, Marwa apparently declared his own prophethood.

On 26 November 1979, the governor of Kano State wrote to Marwa demanding that the quarter be vacated within two weeks. Originally intending to vacate 'Yan Awaki, Marwa apparently changed his mind, and promptly sent out a letter to his diaspora communities calling in reinforcements to fight the 'infidels.' The 'Yan Tatsine planned to overrun and take control of the Friday Mosques in Kano, NEPA (the national electricity utility), and the emir's palace; in their denunciation of the government and appropriation of 'all land in the name of Allah', there was an allusion at least to some sort of seizure of power. On 18 December 1980, four police units were sent to the Shahauci playground, near the emir's palace, to arrest some of Maitatsine's preachers. Disorganized police forces were ambushed by 'fanatics' – the language is taken from the popular press – armed with bows and arrows, daggers, and machetes. Arms were seized and police vehicles burned; by late afternoon, a huge plume of smoke hung over the city. Over the next few days, in a climate of growing chaos and popular fear, fighting spread and casualties were mounting. By 21 December, with the police effectively unable to control the situation, vigilante groups ('Yan Tauri) entered the scene, and complex negotiations ensued between the Kano State governor, Abubakar Rimi (who feared the imposition of martial law by the federal government and hence for his own political survival), and local authorities concerning whether the army should be invited to intervene. On 22 December, 'Yan Tatsine supporters were reportedly entering Kano to join the insurrection (six busloads of supporters from Sokoto were diverted *en route*), and trucks full of corpses were seen leaving the city.

After five days of stalemate, confusion, and escalating violence, the army intervened on 29 December, with ten hours of mortar barrage, supported by air force bombardment. Incurring major losses, the 'Yan Tatsine escaped and marched out of the city into the western districts along the Gwarzo Road. Maitatsine led the exit from the 'Yan Awaki quarter after the ferocious bombardment by state security and military forces but was injured and died in the western districts outside the city walls. His body was later removed from a shallow grave, kept at a local mortuary for several days, and then cremated at the request of local authorities to obviate possible martyrdom among his converts and followers. Photographs of Maitatsine's body were hot-selling items in the aftermath of the insurrection, peddled by young boys at busy intersections in the city (Christelow, 1985).

According to the official tribunal figures, 4177 people died (excluding police and military), but the human toll was clearly much greater. Some quite reliable estimates range as high as 10,000 dead; 15,000 were injured and 100,000 rendered homeless. The physical damage was enormous. In Fagge, 82 houses and 249 shops were destroyed; in 'Yan Awaki 165 houses were destroyed and heavily scarred. Of the 917 people arrested, 12 per cent were juveniles, and 185 were non-Nigerian. Many thousands of Maitatsine's supporters avoided arrest and scattered to various states in the North.[3] Between 1981 and 1985, four more incidents occurred between Maitatsine's followers and state authorities in urban and quasi-urban locations across northern Nigeria; perhaps four thousand to five thousand persons died in these conflagrations.

Oil, Islam, and capitalism have, on occasion, made for an explosive mixture. Muhammed Reza, Iran's late Shah of Shahs, is simply the most notorious casualty – and Ayatollah Khomeini only the most vilified product – of just such an inflammable concoction of petrolic accumulation and Muslim sensibilities. There are, of course, other stories to tell of life on the petroleum roller-coaster, stories at once more prosaic and less radical in character than Iran's Shi'ite revolution, but equally capable of throwing into dramatic relief the complex relations among culture, class, and community; indeed, of capturing what Robert Hughes (1980) calls 'the shock of the new'. This case study analyzes a Muslim millenarian movement in Kano City, in northern Nigeria, the so-called Maitatsine insurrection whose broad contours were described at the beginning of this chapter. A bustling, energetic city forged in the crucible of seventeenth- and eighteenth-century trans-Saharan trade, Kano has become the economic fulcrum of Nigeria's most populous state, a densely settled agricultural heartland of perhaps well over ten million people. In the course of sixty years of British colonial rule, Kano developed as West Africa's pre-eminent entrepôt, a city whose fortunes were organically linked to the vicissitudes of the world market in one commodity: peanut oil. But it was oil of an altogether different sort – petroleum – that ushered in the revolutionary changes of the past two decades.

Awash in petrodollars, urban Kano was transformed, seemingly overnight, from a traditional Muslim mercantile center of 400,000 at the end of the Civil War (*c.* 1970) into a sprawling, anarchic metropolis of over 1.5 million, equipped with an industrial workforce of over 50,000. From its mercantile cocoon, Kano emerged as a full-fledged metropolitan industrial periphery, propelled by a radical deepening of capitalist social relations. At the zenith of the petroleum boom, new industrial estates sprang up at Challawa and Sharada in the city periphery (Figure 6.1), armies of migrants poured into the city, and the icons of modernity, the massive State-sponsored building projects, dotted the city. Kano became, on the one hand, an enormous construction site and, on the other, a theatre of orgiastic consumption.

The reconfigurations of urban life, community relations, and styles of consumption in urban Kano were, of course, part of an overarching transformation of Nigerian society wrought by OPEC and the oil boom. The Nigerian State banked $140 billion between 1970 and 1983 from its federally controlled petroleum industry. Government revenue grew at close to 40 per cent per annum during the 1970s. Oil price hikes in 1973–74 and in 1978–79, the symbols of a restructuring of the world petroleum industry, unleashed a spasm of State-led investment and industrial development in Nigeria, reflected in the national index of manufacturing output, which almost tripled between 1972 and 1980. The absolute number of manufacturing establishments and of industrial wage workers, the Nigerianization of management, the scale of direct investment by multinationals, and the shares of federal and regional State capital in industrial output all witnessed positive growth rates throughout a halcyon boom period presided over by a succession of military governments (1972–79). The luster of black gold promised, for the chosen few, the 'dawn of prosperity and progress for the petroleum rich' (Amuzegar, 1982, p. 814).

Fifteen years after the euphoria of the first oil boom, Nigeria's economic future – and, indeed, the prospects for other oil producers, such as Mexico and Venezuela – appears by contrast to be quite bleak, if not austere. Spiraling debt, fueled by a seemingly infinite appetite for imports, the collapse of oil prices in the early 1980s, and the onslaught of Draconian IMF programs have prompted massive retrenchment and economic hardship. They are, in fact, the hallmarks of a roller-coaster economy, which has fundamentally shaped the everyday life of all sectors of Nigerian society. In this sense, Sayre Schatz (1984) is quite mistaken to emphasize what he refers to as an 'inert' Nigerian economy – the transition under oil from an economy with a weak engine of growth to one with no engine at all – since the scale of public-sector activity and the growing commodification of many aspects of everyday life represented an important source of social change, however limited was self-sustaining capitalist growth.[4] These perturbations – what I, following Walter Benjamin, shall call the shock of modernity – were triggered by the frenzied consumption, investment, and construction of the oil boom era, and it is this world awash with money that provides the environment within which the Muslim insurrectional activity of the 1980s was incubated.

The ferocious Muslim-inspired revolts that surfaced between 1980 and 1985 in several cities of northern Nigeria represent a particular political and cultural expression of the changing economic geography of Nigerian capitalism. Social protest in a newly industrializing state, such as Nigeria, must be rooted in the particular trajectory, the actually existing local configuration, of capitalist development (cf. Trotsky, 1969, 1977). In this regard, the impact of oil on Nigeria, and its capacity to generate huge rents for the State throughout the 1970s, lent industrial development, and urban social processes more generally, a particularly intense, speedy, and yet, as I hope to show, quite anarchic quality. This phenomenon approximates in the abstract what Paul Virilio (1986, p. 3) calls the 'production of speed'. It is this fast capitalism amidst Islam – an articulation of precapitalist and capitalist institutions, and of new material practices with deeply sedimented cultural forms – that provides the material and symbolic raw material upon which Maitatsine and his followers drew. In light of what David Harvey calls the 'progressive monetization of relations in social life [which] transforms the qualities of time and space' (1989, p. 228), the oil boom fashioned a period of 'space–time compression', but in the Nigerian case it represented a specific articulation of two world-systemic processes: Islam and capitalism. It is the experience of this quite singular form of space–time compression that provides the context of the millenarian movements of northern Nigeria in the 1980s.

And what of the Muslim insurrections themselves? To what extent were they significant features of the social and political landscape of Nigeria's oil boom? Were these so-called 'fanatics' and 'disturbances', to use the official lexicon, structurally significant? What sort of meaning can they be given? Not surprisingly, in a context of fragile civilian government, debates over the role of sharī'a in a purportedly secular state, and deep-seated regional antagonisms animated by the 1979 Nigerian elections, the Maitatsine disturbances were invested with wildly different interpretations. Throughout the 1980s, *Maitatsine* was employed as a term of abuse and delegitimation; in the popular press, the 'Yan Tatsine were described as 'fanatics' – and as 'cult followers' by the *New York Times* (12 January 1981, p. 4) – particularly in the pages of the influential northern newspapers, whose strong connections to the powerful brotherhoods and to the northern aristocracy predisposed them to conservative interpretations. For many Christians in Nigeria, Maitatsine represented a terrifying drift toward Muslim fundamentalism, of which the ongoing debate over sharī'a law was part, while for the northern clerics, Maitatsine was a heretic and as such denied any Muslim status whatsoever. Ahmed Beita Yusuf (1988), a member of the northern Muslim intelligentsia, describes Marwa as evil incarnate, 'witchcraft married to cannibalism', a devil who indoctrinated 'coconut skulls and scuttle brains'. Conversely, for Western critics, such as Daniel Pipes (1980), the insurrection, like the Shi'ite revolution in Iran, was the unrefined by-product of oil, a commodity 'primarily responsible for the surge in Islamic political activities.' The official federal inquiry, the Aniagolu tribunal (Nigerian Federal Government, 1981), blamed Maitatsine's fanatical control of Qur'anic students and a wider environment of religious intolerance, weakening of traditional authority, and acts of negligence by Kano State officials and the security forces.

The Maitatsine followers, I shall argue, constituted a certain disenfranchized segment of the northern popular classes (the *talakawa* in Hausa) who experienced, handled, and resisted a particular form of capitalism through a particular reading of – a counterhegemonic discourse within – Islamic tradition. It is a truism that Islam is a text-based religion, but we need to grasp the relationships between texts and the meanings they are purported to provide, what Lambek (1990, pp. 23–4) calls local hermeneutics:

> The specific problems raised by the translation of objective meaning of written language into the personal act of speaking . . . [is an act of] appropriation. . . . The

nature of texts and the knowledge to be drawn from them in any given historical
context are shaped by a sociology or political economy of knowledge: how textual
knowledge is reproduced . . . what social factors mediate access to texts, who is able
to read and in what manner, who has the authority to represent . . . and how
challenges to such authority are manifested.

Islam is a text-based religion that is made socially relevant through citation,
reading, enunciation, and interpretation, and to this extent Islam does not
prescribe wholly unambiguous action for its adherents (Fischer and Abedi,
1990). Indeed, as Fischer and Abedi have brilliantly shown in their book,
Debating Muslims, there is a dialogic and hermeneutical tradition within Islam
rooted in the enigmatic, oral, performative, and esoteric qualities of the Qur'an.
The same religious symbols can therefore be infused with radically different
meanings (Gilsenan, 1980). Tradition itself is constantly negotiated, contested,
and reinvented in the context of efforts by rulers and ulema to enforce other
meanings in a world turned upside down by 'modern' oil monies. Just as Gramsci
once observed that every religion is in reality a multiplicity of distinct and
contradictory religions (cited in Billings, 1990, p. 21), so there is a multiplicity of
Muslim voices, and this multivocality can be fueled by the heteronomy,
difference, and fragmentation propagated by commodity booms. That is to say,
capitalism of a particular sort threw these religious multiplicities into bold relief,
generating struggles over meanings.[5] Such symbolic contests escalated, for
conjunctural reasons that I shall describe, into violent insurrection.

This chapter also speaks to a second matter, namely, the construction of a
collectivity, or, more properly, the imagination of a community and the
capacity of its members to act – in short, the common identity shared by a
self-consciously Muslim community, the nature of belief associated with its
insurrectional activities, and the historical conditions of modernity within
which the community is forged (Cooke, 1990). Here, I take note of William
Roseberry's prescient observation that proletarianization is an uneven process,
creating a heterogeneous, fractioned popular class; hence the question is 'How
is the feeling of community or homogeneity created within social relations that
are neither communal nor homogeneous'? (1989, p. 224). The Maitatsine
movement in Nigeria was creative in at least two senses. First, the community
was an act of imagination distinguished, as Ben Anderson (1983) has observed
more generally, by the style in which it was imagined. And second, within a
historical context of more embracing communities of class and nation, the
Maitatsine community built a local alternative, a counterhegemonic image of
community imagined from within Islam itself. Central to this process were the
cultural and symbolic forms – the selected tradition, as Raymond Williams
(1977) calls it – by which an alternative image and a counter-discourse were
built, fought for, and struggled over. These images are both products of, and
responses to, particular forces, events, and structures in Nigerian society, but
they also involve a particular reading of the past to shape the present. Walter
Benjamin, in his great study of Baudelaire, spoke directly to this tradition of
the oppressed:

To the form of the means of production, which to begin with is still dominated by the old (Marx), there correspond images in the collective consciousness in which the new and the old are intermingled. These images are ideals, and in them the collective seeks not only to transfigure, but also to transcend, the immaturity of the social product and the deficiencies of the social order of production. In these ideals there also emerges a vigorous aspiration to break with what is outdated – which means, however, with the most recent past. These tendencies turn the fantasy, which gains its initial stimulus from the new, back upon a primal past. In the dream in which every epoch sees in images the epoch which is to succeed it, the latter appears coupled with elements of prehistory – that is to say of a classless society. The experiences of this society, which have their store-place in the collective unconscious, interact with the new to give birth to the Utopias which leave their traces in a thousand configurations. . . .[6]

The fantastic intermingling of the old and new is central to the Maitatsine insurrection and to its utopian vision (cf. Marx, 1963). These utopias are often contradictory, of course, reflecting the contradictory experience of past and present and a contradictory consciousness among the agents – peasants, workers, and so on – themselves. But as the case of Maitatsine reveals, these contradictions need not inhibit the capacity of subaltern classes to act in strategically significant ways, and rework in unorthodox ways a modernity of their own.

On the roller coaster: black gold and fast capitalism

Oil creates the illusion of a completely changed life, life without work, life for free. Oil is a resource that anesthetizes thought, blurs visions, corrupts. . . . In this sense oil is a fairy tale, and, like every fairy tale, is a bit of a lie. . . . Oil, though powerful, has its defects.

Ryszard Kapuscinski, *Shah of Shahs*

A bubble of oil flows through the arteries which converge into the electoral heart.

Pablo Neruda, 'Venezuela'

The 1970s was the decade of oil and of bristling petrolic nationalism. Twenty-eight Third World states were exporters of petroleum; each experienced, in varying measure, a huge influx of oil rents leveraged from a petroleum-dependent world by OPEC's successful cartelization.[7] Oil producers are, of course, a heterogeneous lot; lilliputian city-states, such as Qatar, with limited absorptive capacity[8] stand in sharp contrast to populous high absorbers, such as Indonesia, Venezuela, and Mexico. They also differ in their dependence on – and hence in the transformative power of – petroleum. Among OPEC members, for example, petroleum represented on average a whopping 78 per cent of national export earnings in 1980. Nigeria stands, in this regard, as an archetypical high absorber since its domestic petroleum output in the 1970s – roughly 1.3 million barrels per day – was sufficient to sustain growth rates in State revenue of over 100 per cent per annum. By 1980 Nigeria was, in fact, a monoculture, more so than it had ever been in the colonial era; 95.3 per cent of total export revenues derived from oil, and over 55 per cent of government revenue derived from the petroleum sector. Average annual growth rates for credit, money supply, and State expenditures were, respectively, 45 per cent, 66 per cent, and 91 per cent between 1973 and 1980.[9]

How, then, can we begin to grasp, to use the language of the French regulationists (Lipietz, 1987), the social character of the oil-based regime of accumulation? Let us note two rather obvious points at the outset. The first is that oil, as a global, highly internationalized commodity, necessarily projects oil producers into international circuits of capital. To this extent, one might talk of an *internationalization* of the State (Watts, 1984). The second is that the enclave character of the oil industry, combined with the fact that oil revenues typically flow directly into national treasuries, has profound implications for state centralization and autonomy, and for what Albert Hirschmann (1976) calls fiscal linkages.[10] In this sense, the disposition of oil acts as a powerful centralizing force at the level of the State, which is accordingly projected into civil society (that is, '*domesticated*') via expanded forms of public ownership and investment. The oil boom initiated (1) an ostensibly new relationship with the world economy; (2) a new strategy of capital accumulation, as oil earnings overwhelmed previous sources of state surplus; and (3) a process of State centralization, growth, and enhanced autonomy, which generated the 'problem of [the State] simultaneously managing capital accumulation and legitimizing itself and the accumulation process in civil society' (Moghadam, 1988, p. 229).

The rise of a centralized, bureaucratic petrostate, with earnings in 1980 in excess of twenty-five billion US dollars, transformed the material basis, if not the political character, of class rule in Nigeria. The regional elites no longer depended on access to surpluses generated by peasant producers but on oil rents redistributed through the State apparatuses.[11] Indeed, while the military–civil servant alliance maintained its precarious northern political hegemony, the vastly expanded oil revenues bankrolled a huge rent-seeking edifice, what Bardhan (1988, p. 82) in describing India has referred to as a 'flabby and heterogeneous dominant coalition preoccupied with a grabbing of public resources . . . through an elaborate network of patronage and subsidies'. Not only did the State embark upon a massive program of infrastructural and industrial investment – attempting to lay the groundwork for systematic capitalist accumulation – but these expenditures became the means by which petrodollars were diverted to create pacts and coalitions within a divided national polity. Patronage, contracting, and subsidies were part of what Claude Ake (1981) describes as the desperate struggle to win control of the State. The State was privatized in unprecedented ways. Public office became, to employ Max Weber's language, a prebend.[12] Corruption on a gargantuan scale, hugely inflated contracts, and large State-sector subsidies abounded at all levels of the political hierarchy. The bureaucratic environment was characterized by astonishing indiscipline, chaos, and venality.[13]

In the wake of the return to civilian rule in 1979 these pathologies of the State reached new levels of venality. Government was more than ever, as Chinua

Achebe (1988) observed in his novel, *Anthills of the savannas*, a 'crummy family business'. Corruption contributed to a degeneration of State authority. According to Nolutshungu (1990, p. 96), effective control of every tier of government became impossible; sporadic efforts to impose bureaucratic discipline 'resulted in farce (for example, government buildings being set alight . . . with total impunity . . . to destroy incriminating documents)'. To the extent that the bureacracy generally expanded – by 1980, the State wage bill was US$1.5 billion, 35 per cent of recurrent expenditures – the State siphoned off oil revenues to irrigate civil society, by fair means or foul, creating what Chatelus and Schemeil (1985) call a 'circulation economy'.

I have concentrated here on the growth and centralization of a State whose relative autonomy was cross-cut by the social-structural preconditions, by the inherited struggles, of the [federal and democratic] First Republic. A sort of spoils politics developed at the same moment that the State redistributed petrodollars to manufacture some sort of political consensus and simultaneously endeavored to assume the mantle of a developmental state. What transpired was a classic *rentier* State, crippled not simply by virtue of its rapid, and largely unplanned, growth but by endemic corruption and bureaucratic indiscipline.[14] A culture of corruption and extreme privatization of the State (an administrative crisis, in James O'Connor's (1984) language) was, of course, incompatible with an ambitious State capitalist program (that is, the accumulation functions of the State). In sum, a petrostate, in its efforts to perform enterpreneurial functions and simultaneously negotiate political alliances, had become both *the instrument for, and obstacle to, systematic capitalist accumulation*. In so far as petroleum-based accumulation in Nigeria encouraged administrative failure (less generously, absolute chaos and a total lack of political accountability) and a flabby sort of industrial growth, it was inevitable that the State manufactured little in the way of popular legitimacy in civil society.

Four related facets of the oil boom fundamentally shaped the environment in which Maitatsine emerged. The first was the extraordinary commodity boom unleashed by the State. Nigerian merchandise imports increased from N1.1 billion in 1973 to N14.6 billion in 1981. Fueled by the explosion of federal and State bureaucracies and the infusion of money ushered in by the Udoji Commission salary increases in 1975, the oil boom wrought a spending frenzy. The proliferation of everything from stallions to stereos, a world apparently awash in money, produced a sort of commodity fetishism, what one commentator called Nigerian cargo cultism (Freund, 1978).[15] The second was an urban construction boom of Stalinist proportions, spawned by public investment. The construction industry (roads, office construction, industrial plant) grew at 20 per cent in the 1970s, sucking rural labor into mushrooming and hopelessly unplanned cities.[16] Third, the boom in oil led to the so-called Dutch disease, producing a lagged sector, notably in agriculture. Labor drawn from the rural sector, combined with escalating input costs, created a profit squeeze for many peasant producers and hence a sluggish agrarian economy (Roemer, 1983; Watts, 1987). Nigeria's classic agrarian exports (cocoa, groundnuts, palm oil) collapsed completely. Food imports exploded –

wheat in particular – prompting a series of expensive State schemes (large-scale irrigation perimeters in the north) to import-substitute.[17] Expensive, badly planned, and socially disruptive, these agrarian interventions contributed to the growth of land speculation and quite dramatic social differentiation in some rural communities associated with the rise of so-called overnight farmers and large farmer–traders.[18] All of this contributed to rural–urban drift, to social dislocation in the countryside, and to the growing sense of state corruption and violence. And fourth, the appreciation of the exchange rate in a period of intractable inflation produced a classic 'overshooting'. A relatively rigid and inflexible growth of public-sector imports (especially the expensive capital goods sector required to sustain the industrial sector) accounted for substantial balance-of-payments deficits by the mid-1970s and an escalation of external debt underwritten by chaotic and unregulated federal and local-state borrowing (see Table 6.1).[19] The good ship oil prosperity was, as a consequence, already heading for the reefs of austerity even in the halcyon period. The ship ran aground completely, however, in the early 1980s with the 'discovery' of a massive external debt and the downturn in oil prices.[20]

Table 6.1   Public debt service charges in Nigeria, 1951–86

Period	Average per year	% of GDP	Debt service ratio (%)
1951–60	N3.2 million	0.2	n.a.
1961–70	N53.3 million	1.8	n.a.
1971–75	N75.6 million	3.0	0.9
1976–80	N274.0 million	1.2	1.6
1981–86	N1.9 billion	3.0	18.0

Sources: Ihimodu (1983); World Bank (1988); Economist Intelligence Unit (1981–88).

Even with the second oil price hike in 1979, Nigeria's petro-euphoria and spending spree was already turning to pessimism and disillusion. At best the oil revenues had lubricated the return to civilan rule. Less generously, the oil roller-coaster also permitted substantial political continuity within the hegemonic bloc. On balance, the oil windfall proved to be an unmitigated disaster. By the early 1980s the civilian Government was publicly talking of the 'end of the boom' and of impending Draconian measures (Awojobi, 1982; Othman, 1984). The terrible vulnerability of an extreme dependence on one commodity had materialized with a vengeance. In this regard the comments of Dudley Seers over a twenty-year period are especially prescient. In 1964 he noted that petroleum economies, by virtue of the boom-and-bust cycle, possessed a 'potentially explosive character'. As head of the ILO mission to Nigeria in 1981, he concluded that the oil boom had almost certainly produced a deterioration in income distribution and, in the face of copious evidence of growing absolute rural and urban poverty, the conspicuous failure to meet 'the basic needs of the people'.[21]

Experiencing petrolic modernization: poverty and morality, and culture and class among the Kano poor (*Talakawa*)

> At the gates of the city, dispossessed of his land, deprived of his cultural identity and social framework, subject to uncertainty and harassment for the whole of his life, he arrived, demoralised and exhausted looking for streets paved with oil. And he was turned into a disguised beggar.
>
> Hamza Katouzian, *The Political Economy of Modern Iran*

> I call petroleum the devil's excrement. It brings trouble . . . Look at this *locura* – waste, corruption, consumption, our services falling apart . . . and debt we shall have for years. . . . We are drowning in the devil's excrement.
>
> Juan Pablo Alfonzo, Venezeulan diplomat, founder of OPEC

How was the peculiar conflation of surplus money, commodification, industrialization, and rapid material change 'experienced', and quite specifically experienced by the urban poor (the *talakawa*) – the social basis of the 'Yan Tatsine recruits – in Kano?[22] I want to suggest that the question of experience contains two dimensions. The first is that the oil boom was experienced in class terms but that the social character of this class in Kano was, to use Marx's language, inherited from the past – this is the second aspect, the lived traditions, of Hall's (1980) definition. The central concept here is the self-conscious popular strata in Hausa-Fulani society identified locally as *talakawa*. The second is that the roller-coaster of fast capitalism was experienced explicitly in terms of what Hall calls 'meanings and values' (1980, p. 26), and the central frame of reference here is, of course, Islam.

To begin with the question of class experience, according to a World Bank study in the early 1980s (cited in Lubeck, 1985, p. 379), 52–67 per cent of Kano's urban population existed at the 'absolute poverty level'. This amorphous subaltern class, embracing small traders, workers, informal sector workers, the unemployed, and so on, had a social unity, however, in terms of a popular self-identity in Hausa society as commoners, or talakawa. According to Bargery's Hausa dictionary (1934, p. 983), a *talaka* is 'a person who holds no official position . . . a man in the street . . . a poor person'. As an indigenous social category, it is of considerable antiquity, emerging from the social division of labor between town and countryside associated with the genesis of political kingdoms (the *sarauta* system) in the fifteenth century, and subsequently the emirate system under the Sokoto caliphate (1806–1902), in which a lineage-based office-holding class (*masu sarauta*) exercized political authority over subject populations (see Lubeck, 1981; Watts, 1983). *Talakawa* refers, then, to a class relationship of a precapitalist sort but also a political relationship among status honor-groups with distinctive cultural identities and lifestyles. Naturally, the *talakawa* have been differentiated in all sorts of complex ways through the unevenness of proletarianization – the industrial working class (*leburori*), for example, constituting an important social segment of the *talakawa* as such (Lubeck, 1986).

While there is a generic sort of subalternity embodied in the notion of the *talaka*, I wish to identify two distinctive social segments from it, which represent the building blocks of the Maitatsine movement. Both are of some antiquity and were fashioned by locally distinctive social and cultural processes. The first are dry-season migrants (*'Yan cin-rani*), who circulate through the urban economy during the long dry season, relieving pressures on domestic grain reserves in the countryside; they may generate limited savings, which are typically of great value to dependent sons preparing for marriage. I would include in this category migrants who are, strictly speaking, not participants in seasonal circulatory networks but as a consequence of the urban construction boom and the collapse of agriculture were drawn into the urban labor market in huge numbers. Almost wholly male, single, and young, and typically drawn from the densely settled and land-scarce northern provinces, they became semipermanent city residents, characteristically working in the construction sector, and as cart pushers, refuse collectors, itinerant laborers, and so on.[23] This floating population expanded dramatically in the 1970s, not only because of the construction boom, but because of the devastating impact of drought and food shortages in the early 1970s, and because of the dispossession of peasants associated with land speculation, fraudulent land claims, and inadequate state compensations in the periurban areas and in the vicinity of the huge State irrigation schemes.[24] In any event, the *'Yan cin-rani* were shuttled into the northern cities, such as Kano, during the oil boom, filling niches in the secondary labor market, constituting a sort of lumpenproletariat.

The second *talakawa* social stratum is rooted in the informal Muslim schooling system (*makarantar allo*), what Lubeck (1985) calls 'koranic networks'. These networks long predate the jihad and refer to a peripatetic tradition, rooted in the human ecology of the Sahel, in which students study with lay clerics (*mallams*) during the dry season. Students (*almajirai*) migrated to centers of Muslim learning and typically studied the Qur'anic science of exegesis at the feet of notable scholars, often living in the entryways (*zaure*) of influential merchants and notables. Maitatsine was himself a product of this system. These networks were sustained by a sort of urban moral economy – begging and almsgiving as part of a normative set of relations between rich and poor – which served both to extend Islam into the countryside and to provide a measure of social and ideological integration for Hausa society as a whole. The students themselves often worked and they acquired important commercial and craft skills. In Kano these students are referred to as *gardawa*, although, as Hiskett (1987) points out, this is a semantically dense term and also refers to adult Muslim students, aspirant *mallams* of sorts, who are not seasonal migrants as such, but longer-term urban residents.[25] As an ancient center of learning, of vigorous brotherhood activity, and of enormous mercantile wealth, Kano was quite naturally a major center of gardawa activity in spite of the fact that the colonial state had endeavored to systematically regulate Qur'anic education, in the course of which the *gardawa* were increasing marginalized from, and became aggressively hostile to, Nigerian society.

If the *talakawa* as a class category (and the *'Yan cin-rani* and *gardawa* as segments of it) represent the structural preconditions through which the oil boom was experienced by Maitatsine followers, then what are the immediate, proximate qualities of that experience in urban Kano? I shall focus on three sets of social relations: state mediation in the form of corruption and violent but undisciplined security forces, urban social processes (cf. Lubeck, 1986), and the return to civilian party politics in 1979.

The State mediated the oil boom in terms of corruption, chaos, and bureaucratic indiscipline. The *talakawa* were systematically excluded from access to the State, which they experienced as morally bankrupt, illegitimate, and incompetent. The police, who had been placed under federal jurisdiction, and the internal security forces were widely held to be particularly corrupt, disorganized, and violent; they embodied the moral and political decay of State authority and legitimacy (Usman, 1982). In the context of rising urban crime, it was the police who appeared to be the trigger for all sorts of community violence; they were uniformly feared and loathed by Kano's urban poor. Indeed, it was the antiriot police who perpetrated the hideous slaughter of at least fourteen peasants at the Bakalori irrigation project, in a conflict over land compensation, six months prior to the Maitatsine insurrection. In the popular imagination, the police were feared and were explicitly refered to as *daggal* – literally, 'the devil'.

The second experience has been refered to by Paul Lubeck (1986) as 'urban social processes', which operate at the level of the community in a manner analogous to the labor process for the individual worker at the point of production. The central issue here is not simply the anarchic and chaotic growth of Kano itself – how so much wealth could engender so much chaos, as the London *Economist* put it in 1982 – but the changing material basis of *talakawa* reproduction and the assault on the community itself. First, urban land became a source of speculation for Kano merchants and civil merchants, reflected in the fact that the price of urban plots in the working-class Tudun Wada neighborhood increased twenty times between 1970 and 1978. Land records invariably disappeared (usually through mysterious fires), and compensation for land appropriated by the State was extremely corrupt and a source of recurrent conflict. Second, the escalation of food prices, typically in the context of price rigging, hoarding, and licensing scandals, far outstripped the growth of urban wages (see Table 6.2).[26] The inflationary spiral in wages and goods went hand in hand, of course, with an extraordinary internationalization of consumption by Kano's elites – car ownership grew by 700 per cent in six years – and with the erosion of many of the traditional occupations within the secondary labor market taken by *gardawa* and *'Yan cin-rani*. Nigerian novelist Chinua Achebe put it acutely: '[T]he peasant scratching out a living . . . the petty trader with all his wares on his head, the beggar under the fly over. . . . Twenty of these would be glad any day to be able to share *one* minimum wage packet' (1984, pp. 22–4).

And third, the State-funded Universal Primary Education (UPE) program represented both an ideological attack by proponents of 'Western education' on its Qur'anic counterpart and a practical assault on the *mallams* and the *almajirai* system. In Kano State, enrollment increased by 491 per cent between

Table 6.2   Food prices and wages in Kano during the oil boom, 1972–80

Year	Minimum urban wages in Kano City (N per year)	Rural wages in Kano State (N per day)	Food prices in Kano City market (N per measure)		Composite CPI (1975 = 100)	Rate of inflation (%)
			Rice	Millet		
1972	276	80K–N1	83K	17K	n.a.	n.a.
1973	276	—	—	—	66.3	6.1
1974	276	60K	—	—	75.2	13.4
1975	720	N1–2	N1.60	50K	100.0	33.0
1976	720	N1.20–1.60	—	—	123.9	23.9
1977	768	—	—	—	143.0	15.4
1978	768	N2	N2.50	N1.10	166.7	16.5
1979	846	N3	—	—	186.3	11.8
1980	1,200	N4	N5.50	N1.20	204.8	9.9
Per cent increase (1972–80)	435%	444%	662%	705%	309%	Average = 13.3% (1973–80)

Sources: World Bank (1979, 1981, 1985); Williams (1980); Bienen (1983); Berry (1985); Lubeck (1987); Watts (1987).
Notes: One naira (N) or 100 Kobo (K) up until 1986 was equivalent to US $1.34. As of 1989, the exchange rate was N1 = US $6.70. The composite CPI (Consumer Price Index) is an aggregate of rural and urban prices for all items of consumption.

1973 and 1977; in the emirate of Hadejia, for example, the number of primary schools leapt from 36 in 1970 to 392 in 1980 (Stock, 1985). With the return to civilian rule in 1979 and the subsequent fiscal crisis, primary education has, in fact, collapsed but the general point holds that in the 1970s the *mallams* in particular were vigorous critics of UPE and this is suggestive of a broader crisis in the *gardawa* system itself, which, as I suggested earlier, had been systematically marginalized by colonial rule.

The last aspect of the experience of modernity in Kano is explicitly political, namely, the return to civilian rule in 1979. In spite of the fact that the NPN – the party of the conservative northern oligarchy – was victorious at the federal level and dominated several state legislatures, a populist/socialist party – the PRP – swept to power in Kano State. The local government reforms of the 1970s had virtually eliminated the once-powerful Native Authority officials, who were replaced by university-educated administrators, but the triumph of PRP on a strong anti-aristocratic platform marked a qualitatively new political environment for the *talakawa*.[27] Much could be said about the PRP – not least its political split between 'radical' and 'conservative' factions – but in essence the assertion of a populist, procommoner administration provided a political space in which the Maitatsine movement could operate and indeed flourish. A militantly populist rhetoric by the PRP certainly spoke to all *talakawa* in a way that previous political discourses had not, and there is some evidence . . . that the Maitatsine movement, as a *déclassé* segment of northern Muslim society, was tolerated by virtue of its antielitism, and perhaps actually coddled by the governor's office.[28]

The moral economy of Islam and struggles over meaning

> I, too, like all migrants am a fantacist. I build imaginary countries and try to impose them on the ones that exist. I, too, face, the problem of history: what to retain, what to dump, how to hold onto what memory insists on relinquishing, how to deal with change.
>
> Salman Rushdie, *Shame*

> Every religion is in reality a multiplicity of distinct and contradictory religions.
>
> Antonio Gramsci, *Prison notebooks*

Let me, then, turn to the other aspect of the experience of modernity, which starts from the presumption that culture, in this instance Islam, is a field of material and symbolic struggle. One can only assess the particular meanings rendered to certain intellectual traditions and religious texts by Marwa and his drift toward violence and militancy against this broader canvas.

The . . . extraordinary ferment throughout the Muslim world in the 1970s and 1980s must be seen as part of a much longer reformist debate over Muslim interpretations of modernization and European dominance, dating back to the eighteenth century (Lapidus, 1983; Christelow, 1985; Roff, 1987; Burke and Lapidus, 1988). The context for these debates is, of course, the transformation of everyday life wrought by the incorporation of the Muslim world into a growing capitalist economy as well as the experience of European hegemony. How, in other words, would the intersection of two world processes, Islam and capitalism, be decoded through a shared symbolic matrix: the blueprint provided by the early Islamic *umma* (religious community) that flourished at Medina in the Prophet's lifetime and during the reign of the first four Rashidun caliphs that followed? Burke (1986) has traced these movements of ferment in the Arab world in the record of social protest between 1750 and the fundamentalism of the 1980s, but one might as readily examine the revivalist ferment at the end of the eighteenth century and in the nineteenth century as an example of these longer-term cycles of renewal. The resurgence of Muslim politics in the era of petroleum should, in this sense, be seen as part and parcel of long-standing tensions within Islam itself.

[L]ike other great traditions, Islam is paradigmatic in a cultural sense, and its origins provide the normative basis of Muslim governance (Fischer and Abedi, 1990). At the heart of this paradigm, in so far as it shapes attitudes toward State, society, wealth, and poverty, is the concept of justice. As Burke and Lubeck note, 'popular Islamic ideas of justice . . . inhibit the flaunting of wealth and the taking of interest, and encourage charity. The scripturalist tradition . . . thus constrain[s] the choices open to Muslim actors . . . and also provide[s] repertoires of popular action and cultural vocabularies for their expression' (1987, p. 649). Of course, these abstractions derived from texts and scripturalist discourses are filtered through local experiences and through quite contrary models of the Islamic polity. One might say that despite the distinctions and historical differences in political practice within the Sunni tradition, there is a thread – a patrimonial thread, embedded in a morally grounded social compact – that runs through the great tradition. The search for justice in an unjust world in the Muslim diaspora is, as Burke (1986) notes, analogous to the Western European notion of a moral economy. One could by way of an illustration point, for example, to the widely held belief that the Muslim State ensured the supply of grain at reasonable prices. As E. P. Thompson (1968) shows in his elaboration of the moral economy, these obligations are part of a patrimonial order, which was manipulated by the plebs and gentry alike.[29] Like its European counterpart, the Islamic moral economy was a configuration of symbols and traditions to be interpreted, struggled over, and fought for. Whatever its historical veracity, the moral economy is invoked to debate the present; if it is historical, the moral economy is also an ideological product of the present (Roseberry, 1989, p. 223).

[T]he advent of petrodollars and fast capitalism was directly experienced and reworked through the symbolic matrix of Islam. But Islam is not a monolithic lens through which the lived world is unproblematically filtered. The radical populist or Jacobin interpretation of social change – the Muslim moral economy – is central here, but . . . debate over Islam and modernity long predated the oil boom and was part of a serious and deep reformist debate within an ideologically fragmented Muslim population.

Maitatsine was, in this regard, legitimately part of a wide-ranging struggle among Muslims and that debate provided a social space, and in a sense tacit support and legitimacy, for Marwa's admittedly unconventional preaching. While the language of Muslim reformism resonated with some sections of northern Nigerian society – Marwa was not, in other words, simply an 'isolated fanatic' – the struggles over the meanings of central Muslim symbols (the centrality of the Qur'an, the role of the Sunna and the Hadith) conducted by sects, brotherhood, *mallams*, alkalis, and state officials increasingly marginalized the gardawa and the Maitatsine movement. There was, as Christelow (1984, p. 384) observes, a breakdown in the traditional mechanisms of assimilation. But this dissolution is more complex and recondite than he infers. It was the fragmentation of the social world of Islam, the marginalization of the *almajirai/gardawa* system, and the exploitation of the Maitatsine followers by political forces that at once enabled and constrained the movement, and that ultimately propelled Marwa to establish an independent religious community, to provide the grist for a particularly radical interpretation of the moral economy (a literal interpretation of the Qur'an), and finally to defend his beliefs militantly against a state presence (the police) explicitly seen as the embodiment of the devil.

Idioms of accumulation: money, commodification, and Muslim identity

There's a peculiar thing about money. . . . In large quantities it tends to have a life of its own. . . . The power of money becomes very difficult to control.

Philip Marlowe, *The long goodbye*

Kudi cinye gaskiya (Money corrupts truth).

Popular Hausa adage

The Maitatsine insurrection sprang up in the interstices of Nigeria's oil-based modernization, within what I have referred to in shorthand as fast capitalism. More precisely, the appeal of Marwa must be located in a series of complex articulations: between Islam and capitalism, between precapitalist and capitalist institutions, and between class and culture. It would be much too facile to see the millenarian qualities of the movement as a lumpen insurrection plain and simple. The 'Yan Tatsine were, according to Maruf (1986), uniformly poor; 80 per cent had income well below the minimum wage. But the 'fanatical' qualities of the social explosions that occurred between 1980 and 1985 can be fully comprehended only in terms of the material and status deprivation of 'Yan Tatsine recruits scrambling to survive in an increasingly chaotic and Hobbesian urban environment and the unprecedented ill-gotten wealth and corruption of the dominant classes in urban Kano. In theoretical terms, this requires an analysis of 'class relations . . . as they are experienced in terms of both everyday and canonical texts by producers and reproducers of the hegemonized transactions of the ruling bloc's socially extended and pervasive alliance systems with all the latter's split loyalties . . . feuds and betrayals . . . and their ambivalent awards of social success or failure' (Rebel, 1989, p. 130).

Marwa was, first of all, a long-time resident of Kano and was witness to the extraordinary transformation in the political and cultural economy of urban Kano during the oil years. As a charismatic preacher with a compelling, if idiosyncratic, reading of the Qur'an, Marwa recruited followers from the influx of migrants and students into the city and from the marginal underclass of Kano. His disciples recruited at the truck stops and railway stations in Kano, where they typically sustained themselves by selling tea and bread (Nigerian Federal Government, 1981). The *'Yan cin-rani* and *gardawa* more generally were products of the same Qur'anic system as was Marwa (the *makarantar allo*); a survey by Maruf (1986) established that 80 per cent of the Kano followers were educated in this system. Furthermore, Marwa's use of syncretist and pre-Islamic powers resonated strongly with migrants from the rural areas, where the *bori* cult and other vestiges of ancient Hausa metaphysical belief remained quite influential. Slowly Marwa was able to build up an enclave in 'Yan Awaki (see Figure 6.2) fashioned around a disciplined and self-consciously austere, egalitarian community of Muslim brothers (*'yan'uwa*), who supported themselves largely through alms. A survey conducted by Saad (1988, p. 118) among the arrested 'Yan Tatsine revealed that 95 per cent believed themselves to be unequivocally Muslim. As Marwa's following grew, land and urban gardens were appropriated to support the devotees.[30] Marwa's unorthodox and literalist interpretation of the Qur'an focused specifically on the icons of modernity: bicycles, watches, cars, money, and so on. By the same token, Marwa addressed not only commodities *per se* but, of course, the means by which they were acquired. Indeed, the two were inseparable. Consequently, many Kano merchants, bureaucrats, and elites were implicated. The State emerged in Marwa's analysis as the most illegitimate and morally bankrupt part of the Muslim *umma*, and the police as its quintessential embodiment. By the same token, any Muslim affiliation with the State naturally contaminated Islamic practice.

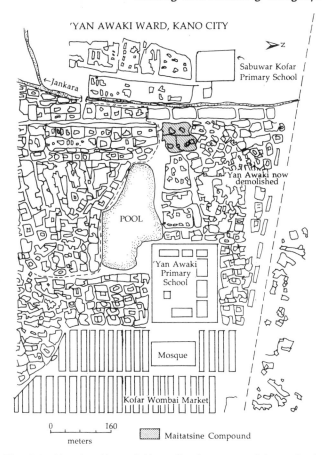

'YAN AWAKI WARD, KANO CITY

Sabuwar Kofar Primary School

←Jankara

'Yan Awaki now demolished

POOL

'Yan Awaki Primary School

Mosque

Kofar Wombai Market

0 160
meters

Maitatsine Compound

Fig. 6.2 Yan Awaki ward, Kano City (courtesy of the author)

The 'Yan Tatsine did not necessarily stand in opposition to the popular classes among whom they lived.[31] In the 1980 conflicts for example, 'Yan Tatsine who had ocupied a cinema on the Kofar Mata Road told local residents that their fight was strictly with the police, while young immigrant workers living in Fagge 'appeared to be just as fearful of the police and of the vigilantes as they were of 'Yan Tatsine' (Christelow, 1984, p. 377). Marwa himself scrupulously returned property to its rightful owner if it was unlawfully appropriated by his followers. And it is to be recalled that Marwa was held in high esteem by certain extremely influential sections of Kano society. Among large sections of the *talakawa* there is reason to presume that Marwa's own discourse was anything but marginal or irrelevant. The geography of the violent conflict that broke out in December 1980 in the wards around 'Yan Awaki is especially interesting: specifically, it was the mercantile and petty bougeois quarters (the purveyors of modernity) that felt the brunt of the attack. In Koki and Yan Awaki wards, the heart of the struggle, five times as many kiosks, shops, and market stalls as residences were destroyed (Nigerian Federal Government,

1981, p. 154). Similarly, Marwa appropriated land as he needed it, and stole food as his followers grew in number, but this popular appropriation was directed at the State and the market.

We have already alluded to the fact that any social protest must contain 'molecular processes of contrasting speed' (Stinchcombe, 1978; Burawoy, 1989) that explain the conjunctural forces and processes generating the insurrectional momentum. The Kano disturbances occurred during the dry season as many young male migrants poured into the city, drawn by the second oil boom. Further, the wider Muslim environment was animated by both the onset of the new century and the debates surrounding the role of sharī'a in the constitution. But it was the return to civilian rule and its attendant corruption, combined with the rise of the PRP in Kano, that explain the significance of 1980 and the timing of the final insurrection. The PRP was, on ideological grounds, certainly loath to intercede in the 'Yan Awaki Ward among a large constituency of 'commoners', while the tensions between the left-leaning Kano State administration and the conservative federal oligarchy created a critical two-week hiatus between the ultimatum sent to Marwa on 26 November 1980 and the first efforts to arrest his followers.[32] During this critical time, Marwa drew in new recruits, armed his followers, and developed a siege mentality. The appearance of the police on 18 December elicited cries of 'infidels!' from the well-organized 'Yan Tatsine and promptly initiated ten days of bloodshed and slaughter.

While there are structural conditions that account for the experience of modernity among the Kano popular classes, commodification and money are clearly central to understanding the ideology of Maitatsine. Harvey (1989) has suggested that capitalist restructuring in the core countries produces a type of time–space compression in which money is central. The same argument may be made, I think, for those periods of transformation of peripheral capitalism. There is a long line of thinking, of course, on the erosive, glacial qualities of money and on money as a form of domination (Simmel, 1978; Harvey, 1985; Shipton, 1989). Suffice it to say, however, that the social relations of money strike to the core of Maitatsine and his ideological appeal. The *gardawa mallams* were conspicuously non-salaried, and the 'Yan Tatsine carried little or no money on their persons. Further, there was a strong sentiment among the *gardawa* that wealth, especially in the 1970s, was ill-gotten (*haram*); in the popular imagination, behind every instance of wealth there is a crime. Indeed, this builds upon an important cultural distinction embedded in Hausa society between fruitful and barren capital. Money capital (literally, 'mother of money', *uwa*) may be fertile (*uwa mai amfani*) or ominous (*jarin tsiya*), a distinction rooted in cultural notions of work and proper conduct. Certain money is bitter and illegitimate (for example, interest for Muslims), and this is powerfully expressed in popular reactions to the petronaira in Nigeria.[33] Karen Barber (1982, 1986) has documented, for example, the recurrent theme of good and bad money in Nigerian popular plays and literature, and it is clear that the notion of the 'benevolent rich man' was culturally transgressed in the robbery and venality that flourished around a corrupt state during the oil boom.[34]

There is a cultural economy of money in Islam, which requires serious intellectual exploration, and this is necessarily the case in northern Nigeria, where the consequence of the oil boom was to produce wealth on a hitherto unimaginable scale; in oil economies money seems literally to appear out of thin air and without the expenditure of effort. Money was, however, experienced as a form of domination and social power, and this was expressed in symbolic and metaphorical terms.[35] There is good reason to presume that the sentiments of the Venezuelan diplomat who in lamenting his own country's predicament referred to petroleum as 'the devil's excrement' might have found much support among Maitatsine and his followers (Watts, 1994).

In so far as money constitutes one aspect of the oil-based transformation in Nigeria, commodification – and specifically the profusion of Western 'things' – provides another. Commodities, in fact, loom large in Marwa's preaching. The basis of his provocative reading of the Qur'an as the *only* valid guide to human conduct (thereby excluding the Sunna and the Hadith) rested on the revelation of hidden meanings within the sacred text, and in his rooting of verse in local conditions. Marwa's vehement denunciation of cigarettes, motor vehicles, buttons, apparel, and so on was revealed within the text through his careful textual analysis. Marwa deconstructed Qur'anic texts in part by playing on the meanings and phonetic associations of certain Hausa and Arabic words. Furthermore, he played creatively with the relations between signs and their referents. In his public preaching, he pointed to the physical similarity between the Arabic character for Allah and a simple graphical depiction of a bicycle. This homology not only validated his accusation that all persons who rode bicycles were by definition pagan but also confirmed his far-reaching attack on the corruption of Islam at the highest levels by virtue of its association with Western modernity. Perhaps more than anything else, Marwa's preaching vividly illustrates how a 'sign becomes an arena of class struggle' (Volosinov, [1929] 1979, p. 23), how symbolic struggles over the definition of 'legitimate culture' strike to the heart of political economy.

Making sense of Maitatsine

> To theorize hegemonized social experience we need to theorize not only 'experience' as such but, in addition, the textual limits of determined social relations.
>
> Hermann Rebel, *Cultural hegemony and class experience*

> The history of subaltern groups is necessarily fragmented and episodic.
>
> Antonio Gramsci, *Prison notebooks*

The Maitatsine insurrection represented a powerful, counterhegemonic reading and critique of the Nigerian oil boom and of the Nigerian ruling classes. To this extent one should not be diverted by the syncretist character of Marwa, by the use of juju and other magic, by the possible Mahdist overtones, and by accusations of cannibalism. Marwa's self-identity, including his prophethood, are perhaps of less relevance than the antimaterialist, class-based reading of the moral superiority of the Qur'an that led him to attack decadence, profligacy, and corruption. His antimaterialism was in one sense an effort to fashion a sort of Muslim modernity, yet it also contained an explicit class antagonism: specifically against corrupt ulema, the wealthy merchants, an illegitimate State, evil police, and private property more generally. Maitatsine's recruits typically were young men – unskilled migrants, Qur'anic scholars and rural destitutes – products of shifting relations between town and countryside during the 1970s. Like the Kano insurrection, the subsequent Maitatsine conflicts in the North were led by low-status workers and craftsmen schooled in the Qur'anic networks. It was the presence of the police that invariably triggered outright conflict.

The Maitatsine insurrection speaks directly to the question of hegemony and counterhegemony. Like any Marxist concept, hegemony is susceptible to what Raymond Williams (1977, p. 112) calls 'epochal' as opposed to 'historical' definition, and 'categorical' as opposed to 'substantive' description. I have tried to situate the symbolic and interpretive struggles within Islam in northern Nigeria in terms of such historical and substantive specificities – in terms of the details of oil-based capitalism, the changing social organization of Islam, and the historical legacy of certain local class identifications. In this way one can come to appreciate the necessary preconditions for counterdiscursive assertions to be made, the space and modalities for discursive contestation, and the place of discursive engagement (Terdiman, 1987, p. 65). Hegemony can accordingly be seen less as a bundle of techniques to orchestrate consent than as a moment when 'socially engaged selves, already split and de-centered . . ., in addition have to act in order to hold together *within themselves* a society that has split and turned against itself in irreconcilable and mutually inconstruable social relations' (Rebel, 1989, p. 129). At a certain point, these hegemonic processes could no longer occur, and one has, from within the belly of the beast, counterhegemonic movements as a response to these irreconcilable social relations. The Maitatsine movement as a form of resistance was finally choked off, of course, through, in Gramsci's language, repressive rule rather than hegemonic consent.

Two final matters are striking in the case of Maitatsine. First, struggles of a class nature are also fundamentally cultural; in this sense Islam and the other cultural traditions fought over provide an *active* part of social change. As Paul Willis (1977, p. 124) put it, the cultural does not simply mark or in some simple sense live out wider social contradictions; 'it works upon them with its own resources to achieve partial resolutions, recombinations, limited transformations to be sure but concrete . . . and the basis for actions and decisions that are vitally important to that wider social order'. My second point, however, is precisely the limited nature of the transformations and of the cultural vision of this specific form of Muslim populism. Maitatsine represented a serious challenge to the Nigerian ruling class and to its fragile hegemony. Indeed, one can only understand the ferocity of state coercion, and the bloodbath that ensued, in relation to the fact that Maitatsine had exploded the myth of what Rebel (1989, p. 129) calls 'hegemonized social experience'. The

movement revealed the serious fractures *within* the dominant northern regional ruling bloc and jeopardized the fragile political unity *among* the regions in
what was interpreted in the southern regions as a drift toward Islamic fundamentalism. It was also, of course, a self-consciously Muslim movement,
speaking directly to the then Muslim President of Nigeria, employing a revolutionary rhetoric of Islam. Unlike the Shi'ite revolution in Iran, however, it was
not transformative. And I would suggest that the contrast resides in the fact
that Maitatsine had a limited social base outside the *gardawa* and *'Yan cin-rani*,
especially among the middle classes. To this extent Muslim populism was
hampered by its incapacity to generate an alternate social vision, and in
particular an alternative economic vision, to mobilize segments of Nigerian
society.

The question of the social basis of recruitment resonates strongly with the
present nevertheless, because the period since the Maitatsine insurrections has
seen a further deterioration in living conditions for the Nigerian industrial
working and middle classes (see Table 6.3). The oil bust, a gargantuan debt
service, and a Draconian structural adjustment program (SAP) have collectively imposed a terrifying burden on labor and state functionaries in particular (see Usman, 1986; Biersteeker *et al.*, 1987; IBRD, 1988; Main, 1989;
Bangura and Beckman, 1989). Several industries slashed their workforces by
60 per cent between 1982 and 1988; industrial capacity utilization fell to 27 per
cent; and real wages fell by at least 25 per cent. Staple food prices rose by close
to 300 per cent between 1981 and 1987, and public sector layoffs were widespread. Negotiating the bust in the immediate wake of the halcyon years of the
boom deepened the legitimation crisis of the Nigerian military and the ruling
coalition more generally. The conflation of legitimation and accumulation
crises produced a quite ferocious sort of authoritarianism. Three laws – the
Constitution Decree no. 1 (1984), the State Security Decree no. 2 (1984), and
the Robbery and Firearms Decree no. 5 (1984) – deny the most basic civil
liberties. One might venture to say that organized labor, students, and many
professional associations have felt the State violence that Maitatsine so vividly
captured in his condemnation of the police as 'devils'. In May and June of 1989
the police and State security forces surfaced as central actors in a wave of
massive detentions, arrests, and murders.[36] In 1990 President Babangida
decreed that the anticipated return to civilian rule in 1992 (including the
process of party formation) must accept structural adjustment as a precon-
dition for political debate.[37]

Oil and Islam no more determine revolutionary, or, indeed, insurrectional, outcomes than does a mixture of copper and Christianity. But Muslim populism,
which possesses a great capacity to resist co-optation and to provide a culturally
convincing critique of 'oil prosperity', constitutes a powerful ideology in weak
Islamic States experiencing the petroleum boom (Burke and Lubeck, 1987).
Maitatsine revealed in a fantastic way that the efforts by the Nigerian State to
form a stable class coalition by redistributing oil rents were morally bankrupt.
The fantastic intermingling of the old and new that Maitatsine wove from

Table 6.3   Economic structure of the 'bust' in Nigeria, 1981–88

Macroeconomic indicator	1981	1982	1983	1984	1985	1986	1987	1988
GDP at market prices (billions of N)	52.2	54.5	54.0	70.1	80.3	82.9	107.6	135.0[a]
Real GDP growth (%)[b]	−2.9	−1.9	−6.4	−5.5	1.2	−2.1	1.8	4.1[c]
Consumer price inflation (%)	22.3	6.4	23.2	39.6	5.5	5.4	10.2	25.0[c]
Population (millions)[d]	83.3	86.1	89.0	92.0	95.2	98.5	101.9	n.a.
Exports (billions of $ f.o.b.)[i]	17.94	13.66	10.70	11.90	12.57	6.80	7.60	6.90[a]
Imports (billions of $ c.i.f.)[j]	20.53	15.00	9.06	9.40	8.89	4.44	4.46	4.60[a]
Current account (billions of $)	−6.2	−7.2	−4.1	0.1	2.6	0.4	1.6	−0.5
Reserves, excl. gold (millions of $)	3,895	1,613	990	1,462	1,667	1,081	1,165	686[e]
Total external debt disbursed (billions of $)	5.90	8.49	11.76	18.66	19.52	24.47	28.71	29.50[a]
Debt service ratio (%)	4.6	10.3	18.6	25.5	30.7	17.9	10.0	n.a.
Crude oil production (millions of barrels per day)	1.44	1.29	1.24	1.37	1.48	1.46	1.28	1.38[a]
Exchange rate (average N per $)[g]	0.614	0.673	0.724	0.764	0.892	1.347	4.006	4.429[h]

Source: Economist Intelligence Unit 1981–89.
[a] EIU estimate.
[b] At 1984 factor cost.
[c] Provisional official figures.
[d] IMF estimates; no reliable census data.
[e] September 1988.
[f] Including private and short-term debt.
[g] The two-tier rates were unified as of 2 July, 1987.
[h] January–November 1988. As of 30 January, 1989, N6.77 per $.
[i] f.o.b. is the valuation of goods in trade including all costs of movement.
[j] c.i.f., cost insurance freight or charged in full.

certain Muslim texts and the experience of oil-based capitalism also shaped, I would argue, new personal and collective identities, and in so doing fashioned a curious and ambiguous sort of Muslim modernity.

My reading of the Maitatsine movement and the preachings of Marwa himself suggest that it is less about 'fanatics and heretics' than about the compelling need for a radically new class coalition and social compact. But manufacturing political consent and consensus in an era of petroleum bust and structural adjustment is a different story altogether. At the very least, as Nobel Laureate Wole Soyinka observed, this demands a national debate and dialogue. At this historic juncture in Nigeria, it is precisely this debate and dialogue that, as the Nigerian Civil Liberties Organization has made perfectly clear, is wholly absent in the face of state repression.[38] In these circumstances, to return to the motif of the Maitatsine movement, a charismatic leader with a coherent ideology and capable of speaking to the uprooted, excluded, and oppressed, could generate oppositional energies capable of a quite different outcome than the brutal oppression that transpired in a dusty, impoverished quarter of Kano in December 1980.

Notes

1 Maitatsine's diaspora extended across much of northern Nigeria and into southern Niger Republic, a region sharing a cultural kinship with the Hausa heartland in Nigeria. These networks provided fertile recruiting grounds for *almajirai* and *gardawa*. Witness no. 49 before the official tribunal (Nigerian Federal Government, 1981, p. 58), one Uzairu Abdullahi, was one such Hausa disciple, recruited from Niger eleven months prior to the insurrection.

2 The Aniagolu Report (Nigerian Federal Government, 1981) notes, however, that while there were a number of complaints over Marwa's activities and clashes with police throughout the period 1974–79, there was a marked escalation of complaints in 1980. Eleven in all, these complaints pertained to heretical preaching, violent personal attacks on local residents, the popular appropriation of a public bathroom, and the unlawful expansion of Marwa's compound on to other private lots, including the blockage of a major drain. The brotherhoods are social organizations with West African Islam, which emerged as institutions of refuge, but now serve as the religious and political vehicles for particular interpretations of Islam and for the promotion of specific Muslim practices.

3 This section is drawn from the following works: Lubeck (1981, 1984, 1985, 1987); Nicolas (1981); Nigerian Federal Government (1981); Lavers (1982); Christelow (1984, 1985); Na-Ayuba (1986); NIPSS (1986); Omomiwa and Abu (1986); Clarke (1987); Hiskett (1987); Yusuf (1988); 'Maitarsine had 10,000 men,' *New Nigerian*, 5 February, 1981, p. 7; ibid., 23 December, 1980, p. 1.

4 Total manufacturing output, in any case, increased at 13 per cent per annum during 1972–80, even though the industrial sector accounted for only 6.7 per cent of GDP in 1979–80. The marginal propensity to import was extremely high (67.7 per cent); consumer durables and nondurables increased by over 700 per cent between 1973 and 1980.

5 For similar arguments within Muslim discourse in relation to capitalism, see Ong (1990) and Lambek (1990).

6 Benjamin (1973, p. 159). I am especially indebted to the brilliant work of Susan Buck-Morss (1989), whose study of Benjamin's Arcades Project is enormously helpful in clarifying his thinking.

7 There is a huge literature on the so-called oil syndrome. For a representative literature, see Seers (1964), Gelb (1981), Hausmann (1981), Pesaran (1982), Commander and Peek (1983), Petras and Morley (1983), Roemer (1983), Crystal (1985), Imam-Jomeh (1985), and Pollard (1985).

8 Absorptive capacity is the capacity to absorb oil revenues locally as productive capital (as distinct from the capacity to import). See Gelb (1981) for a discussion.

9　The relevant literature for Nigeria, which provides statistical estimates of these aggregate growth trends as a function of oil revenues is as follows: Usman (1980); Kirk-Greene and Rimmer (1981); Bienen (1983); Onoh (1983); *The Economist* (1984); Watts (1984); IBRD (1985a, b); *Oil, debts, and democracy in Nigeria* (1986); Wright (1986).

10　This has been explicitly addressed by a scholar of Iran, Hamza Katouzian: '[O]il revenues accrue directly to the state . . . [which] does not have to depend on the domestic means of production. . . . Once these revenues rise to a high level . . . they afford the state an unusual degree of economic and political autonomy. . . . [Therefore] the entire system . . . depends on the size and strategy of state expenditure' (1981, p. 34). See also Evans and Reutschmeyer (1985) on the relative autonomy of the state.

11　By 1980 agricultural exports constituted only 2.4 per cent of GDP by value.

12　Novelist Chinua Achebe observed that Nigeria is 'without shadow of a doubt one of the most corrupt nations in the world' (1984, p. 42). For example, the National Petroleum Company lost twenty-five billion US dollars over a four-year period as a result of smuggling and contract malfeasance. Records in State ministries were regulary torched in 'accidental fires,' and the culture of not 'being on seat' was the lodestar of Nigerian bureaucratic machinery.

13　Nigerian contracts (for example, for house, road, or office construction) were typically 200–400 per cent higher than in comparable African states (*The Economist* 1984, p. 17).

14　In his monumental study, *Global rift*, Stavrianos cites a UN survey that estimated that a civil servant in oil-rich Kuwait worked an average of sixteen minutes per day (1981, p. 664). My suspicion is that many Nigerian civil servants, for ostensibly similar reasons, logged in a similar 'work-day'.

15　One of my most vivid impressions of the commodity boom in Nigeria was of a child trader standing in a traffic jam on Lagos Island, selling Father Christmas paperweights containing snow-filled wintry scenes, reindeers and all.

16　Port Harcourt, for example, increased by 400 per cent between 1969 and 1977.

17　By 1981 the staple food import bill stood at three billion US dollars, roughly 17 per cent of total domestic consumption. Nigeria was self-sufficient in the mid-1960s. The major change here was, of course, in taste, specifically the emergence of white bread, what Andrae and Beckman (1985) call the 'wheat trap', as a staple of the urban poor. Interestingly, many of the 'Yan Tatsine supported themselves as sellers of tea and bread to the Kano *talakawa*.

18　The northern irrigation schemes (1.5 million hectares at N0.5 billion per year) were sources of lucrative contracting in their own right; in addition to their cost (and hence political attractiveness) and inefficiency, the largest project at Bakalori was associated with bloody strife and conflicts over land accumulation and compensation. For discussion of these and other agrarian transformations, including the impact of World Bank-funded Green Revolution programs see the following sources: Agbonifo (1980); Kaduna State (1981); Ukpolo (1983); Watts (1983, 1987); Alkali (1985); IBRD (1985a, b); Jega (1985); Andrae and Beckman (1987, 1985); Iliya (1988); Adams (1988); Williams (1988); Kimmage (1989.)

19　In 1982 the Central Bank of Nigeria could not provide estimates of income, expenditure and external debt. To this day there is still a debate over the exact magnitude of Nigeria's external debt.

20　Oil production fell by two-thirds between January and August of 1981; oil revenues slumped from US \$27.4 billion in 1980 to US \$11 billion the following year. The

Economic Stabilisation Act of 1982 substantially reduced state expenditures, capital investment, and imports. The boom had finally bust.

21 See Seers (1964, p. 236); ILO (1981). In 1978, four million households were below the poverty line, an increase of over 25 per cent since 1973. For other discussions of the income and equity issue, see Jamal (1981), Sanusi (1982), and Collier (1983).

22 I follow the lead of Raymond Williams, E. P. Thompson, Paul Willis, and others who posit culture as interwoven with all social practices. As Stuart Hall (1980, p. 26) put it, culture is '*both* the meanings and values which arise amongst distinctive social groups and classes on the basis of their given historical conditions and relationships, through which they handle and respond to the conditions of existence; *and* as they are lived traditions and practices through which those understandings are expressed and in which they are embodied'.

23 Hiskett (1987) is quite mistaken to refer to the '*Yan cin-rani* simply as 'opportunists and Dick Whittingtons'. Many were the casualties of land grabs, of the failure of the State to compensate for land appropriation (cf. the Bakalori scheme), and the victims of generalized rural poverty. Many fled the rural areas under a cloud of shame as destitutes (*yawon dendi*).

24 An extraordinary series of documents – the twelve-volume Kaduna State Lands Commission study – produced by the PRP provides endless examples of how peasants lost access to land through nefarious land scams, fraud, and state corruption (Kaduna State, 1981). See also Swindell (1986).

25 Hiskett (1987, p. 213) is also wide of the mark, however, when he links the gardawa to an urban subculture of magicians (yan tauri). It should be pointed out, however, that syncretic (pre-Islamic) beliefs have always been a central part of Hausa society at all levels, and Maitatsine clearly had a reputation for magical powers which he successfully welded on to his Qur'anic exegetical skills.

26 The notorious Ricegate scandal, in which a cabinet official was directly implicated in rice smuggling and hoarding, is, of course, well known to scholars of Nigeria.

27 The PRP's ticket proclaimed that it promoted 'the freedom and dignity' of the 'common people' against 'retrograde northern feudalists' and the 'hard core of the NPN made up of a tiny oligarchy' (PRP, 1982, p. 215). The PRP abolished local rural taxes as semifeudal hangovers.

28 The governor's aides apparently met (and dined?) with the Maitatsine leadership, and the governor himself visited 'Yan Awaki Ward prior to the insurrection.

29 I have discussed the moral economy at length in my book *Silent violence* (Watts, 1983, esp. ch. 3).

30 By 1980 the residential compound occupied close to 3000 square meters.

31 Herbst's (1990, p. 197) hopelessly oversimplified explanation argues that the Maitatsine were 'outsiders' and that the insurrection was simply a function of the disappearance of 'exit options', that they had 'nowhere else to go'. Because of their heretical ideas and their limited mobility (but the the Maitatsine did flee!), Herbst believes that violent confrontation was inevitable (p. 198).

32 The Kano State Government 1981: response to the Aniagolu Report reveals the extreme tension between the NPN-dominated federal government and the PRP State administration. The former, at one level, did not wish to assist its political protagonists; on the other hand, the political sensitivity of a 'Muslim' revolt in the North during a sensitive period of debate over Sharī'a created some concern among the NPN, which was dominated by the conservative northern oligarchy.

33 Sunni Islam demands that ill-gotten wealth must be distributed to the needy, a sentiment conspicuously absent among the Kano notables.

34 In Nigerian society, wealth is not *per se* bad or unworthy; rather, it must be acquired according to a cultural blueprint. As Barber (1982) shows, the rise of the petronaira was associated with the notion of 'magic-money' – wealth without any evidence of work or dutiful effort. This is a popular theme in Nigerian literature (see Emechera, 1982). I have explored this in depth in Watts (1994).

35 There is a substantial literature, of course, on money in Africa and its relationship to witchcraft and the supernatural, and on rules pertaining to the disposition of illegitimate wealth. See Shipton (1989).

36 One of the most important prominent national figures under detention is Balarabe Musa of the PRP.

37 In April 1990 there was an attempted coup against the Babangida regime by disgruntled officers who complained of northern dominance in the federation.

38 Several public conferences on SAP and its alternatives, featuring such speakers as Soyinka and the prizewinning novelist Festus Iyayi, have been banned by the government, and many participants arrested. See *Bulletin of Concerned Africanist Scholars* no. 28 (Fall 1989).

References

Achebe, C. 1984: *The trouble with Nigeria*. London: Heinemann.

Achebe, C. 1988: *Anthills of the savannas*. New York: Vintage.

Adams, W. 1988: Rural protest, land policy and the planning process on the Bakalori Project, Nigeria. *Africa* 58(3), 315–35.

Agbonifo, P. 1980: State farms and rural development. PhD dissertation, University of Wisconsin, Madison.

Ake, C. 1981: *A political economy of Africa*. Harlow: Longman.

Alkali, A. R. 1985: US agribusiness and the proleterianization of the peasantry in Kaduna State. Paper presented to the Seminar on Nigerian Economy and Society, Zaria, Ahmadu Bello University.

Amuzegar, J. 1982: Oil wealth: a very mixed blessing. *Foreign Affairs*, Spring, 814–35.

Anderson, B. 1983: *Imagined communities*. London: Verso.

Andrae, G. and Beckman, B. 1987: *Industry goes farming*. Uppsala: Scandinavian Institute of African Studies.

Andrae, G. and Beckman, B. 1985: *The wheat trap*. London: Zed Press.

Awojobi, A. 1982: *Where our oil money has gone?*, Lagos: Nigerian Press. Lecture delivered at the University of Ile-Ife, 11 May, 1982.

Bangura, Y. and Beckman, B. 1989: African workers and structural adjustment: a Nigerian case study. Paper prepared for UNRISD/ISER Conference on Economic Crisis and Third World Countries, Jamaica, April.

Barber, K. 1982: Popular reactions to the Petro-Naira. *Journal of Modern African Studies* 20(3), 431–50.

Barber, K. (1986): Radical conservatism in Yoruba popular plays. *Bayreuth African Studies Series* 7, 5–32.

Bardhan, P. 1988: Dominant proprietory classes and India's democracy. In A. Kuli (ed.), *India's democracy*.. Princeton NJ: Princeton University Press 76–83.

Bargery, G. P. 1934. Bargery's Hausa – English Dictionary.

Benjamin, W. 1973: *Charles Baudelaire: A lyric poet in the era of high capitalism*. London: New Left Books.

Berry, S. 1985: *From fathers to their sons*. Berkeley: University of California Press.

Bienen, H. 1983: Oil revenues and public choice in Nigeria. Working Paper no. 592. Washington, DC: World Bank.

Bierstecker, T. 1988: *Multinationals, the State, and control of the Nigerian economy.* Princeton NJ: Princeton University Press.

Bierstecker, T., Diamond, L., Callaghy T. and Lewis, P. 1987: The prospects for structural adjustment in Nigeria. Manuscript prepared for the Annual Meetings of African Studies, Denver, CO.

Billings, D. 1990: Religion as opposition. *American Journal of Sociology* 96(1), 1–31.

Buck-Morss, S. 1989: *The dialectics of seeing: Walter Benjamin and the arcades project.* Cambridge, MA: MIT Press.

Burawoy, M. 1989: Two methods in search of science: Skocpol versus Trotsky. *Theory and Society* 18, 759–805.

Burke, E. 1986: Understanding Arab protest movements. *Arab Studies Quarterly* 8(4), 333–45.

Burke, E. and Lapidus, I. (eds) 1988: *Islam, politics and social movements.* Berkeley: University of California Press.

Burke, E. and Lubeck, P. 1987: Explaining social movements in two oil-exporting states. *Comparative Studies in Society and History* 29(4), 643–65.

Chatelus, M. and Schemeil, Y. 1985: Towards a new political economy of state industrialization in the Arab Midle East. *International Journal of Middle Eastern Studies* 16(2), 145–68.

Christelow, A. 1984: Religious protest and dissent in northern Nigeria: from Mahdism to Qur'anic integralism. *Journal of the Institute of Muslim Minority Affairs* 6(2), 375–91.

Christelow, A. 1985: The 'Yan Tatsine disturbances in Kano: a search for perspective. *Muslim World* 75(2), 69–84.

Clarke, P. 1987: The Maitatsine movement in northern Nigerian in historical and current perspective. In Hackett, R. (ed.), *New religious movements in Nigeria*, vol. 5. Lewiston: Edwin Mellen, 93–115.

Collier, P. 1983: Oil and inequality in Nigeria. In Ghai, D. and Radwan, S. (eds), *Agrarian policies and rural poverty in Africa.* Geneva: ILO, 191–248.

Commander, S. and Peek, P. 1983: Oil exports, agrarian change and the rural labor process. Working Paper no. 63. Geneva: ILO.

Cooke, P. 1990: *Back to the future: Modernity, postmodernity, and locality.* London: Allen & Unwin.

Crystal, J. 1985: Coalitions in oil monarchies: patterns of state building in the Gulf. Unpublished manuscript, Department of Government, Harvard University.

The Economist. 1984: *The political economy of Nigeria.* Cambridge: Cambridge University Press.

Economist Intelligence Unit. 1981–89: *Quarterly Economic Report for Nigeria.* London: The Economist.

Emecheta, Buchi. 1982: *Naira power.* London: Macmillan.

Evans, P. and Reutschmeyer, D. 1985: The state and economic transformation. In Evans, P. *et al.*, (eds), *Bringing the State back in.* Cambridge: Cambridge University Press, 44–7.

Fischer, M. and Abedi, M. 1990: *Debating Muslims.* Madison: University of Wisconsin Press.

Freund, W. 1978: Oil boom and crisis in contemporary Nigeria. *Review of African Political Economy* 13, 91–101.

Gelb, A. 1981: Capital importing oil-exporters. Working Paper no. 375. Washington, DC: World Bank.

Gilsenan, M. 1980: *Recognizing Islam*. London: Pantheon.

Hall, S. 1980: Cultural studies in two paradigms. In Bennett, T. *et al.*, (eds), *Culture, ideology and social process*. London: Batsford, 19–37.

Harvey, D. 1985: *Consciousness and the urban experience*. Oxford: Basil Blackwell.

Harvey, D. 1989: *The condition of postmodernity: An enquiry into the origins of cultural change*. Oxford: Basil Blackwell.

Hausmann, R. 1981: State landed property, oil rent and accumulation in Venezuela. PhD dissertation, Cornell University, Ithaca, NY.

Herbst, J. 1990: Migration, the politics of protest and state consolidation in Africa. *African Affairs* 89(355), 183–203.

Hirschmann, A. 1976: A generalised linkage approach to economic development with special reference to staples. *Economic Development and Cultural Change* 56, 134–59.

Hiskett, M. 1987: The Maitatsine riots in Kano, 1980. *Journal of Religion in Africa* 17, 209–23.

Hughes, R. 1980: *The shock of the new*. London: BBC Publications.

IBRD. 1988: *The Nigerian structural adjustment program*. Washington, DC: World Bank.

IBRD. 1985a: *Nigeria: Agricultural pricing policy*. Washington, DC: World Bank.

IBRD. 1985b. *Nigeria: Agricultural sector memorandum*. Washington, DC: World Bank.

Ihimodu, A. 1983: External loans and debt servicing problems in the Nigerian economy. Unpublished manuscript, Nigerian Institute for Social and Economic Research, Ibadan.

Iliya, M. 1988: Induced agricultural change in northwest Nigeria. PhD dissertation, University of Birmingham.

ILO. 1981: *First things first*. Geneva: ILO.

Imam-Jomeh, I. 1985. Petroleum-based accumulation and state form. PhD dissertation, University of California, Los Angeles.

Jamal, V. 1981: Rural–urban gap and inequality in Nigeria. Working Paper JASPA/ILO, Addis Ababa.

Jega, A. 1985: The state, peasants and rural transformation in Nigeria: a case study of the Bakalori irrigation project, Sokoto State. PhD dissertation, Northwestern University, Evanston, Ill.

Kaduna State. 1981: *Report of the Land Investigation Committee*. 12 vols and General Findings and Recommendations. Kaduna: Government Printer.

Kano State Government. 1981: *The views and comments of the Kano State Government on the report of the Kano disturbances tribunal of inquiry*. Kano: Kano State Government.

Katouzian, H. 1981: *The political economy of modern Iran*. New York: New York University Press.

Kimmage, K. 1989: The evolution of the wheat trap: the great Nigerian wheat rush. Unpublished manuscript, Department of Geography, Cambridge University.

Kirk-Greene, A. and Rimmer, D. 1981: *Nigeria since 1970*. London: Hodder & Stoughton.

Lambek, M. 1990: Certain knowledge, contestable authority. *American Ethnologist* 17(1), 23–40.

Lapidus, I. 1983: *Contemporary Islamic movements in historical perspective*. Berkeley: Institute of International Studies.

Lavers, J. 1982: Popular Islam and unpopular dissent: religious disturbances in northern Nigeria. Paper delivered to the African Studies Conference, University of Illinois, Urbana-Champaign.

Lubeck, P. 1981: Conscience de classe et nationalisme islamique à Kano. *Politique Africaine* 1(4), 31–68.

Lubeck, P. 1984: Islamic networks and urban capitalism: an instance of articulation from northern Nigeria. *Cahiers d'études africaines*, nos 81–82, 67–78.

Lubeck, P. 1985: Islamic protest under semi-industrial capitalism. *Africa* 55(4), 369–89.

Lubeck, P. 1986: *Islam and urban labor in northern Nigeria*. Cambridge: Cambridge University Press.

Lubeck, P. 1987: Islamic protest and oil-based capitalism. In Watts, M. (ed.), *State, oil and agriculture*. Berkeley: Institute of International Studies, 268–90.

Main, H. 1989: Workers, retrenchment and urban–rural linkages in Kano, Nigeria. In Swindell, K. *et al.* (eds), *Inequality and development*. London: Macmillan, 223–42.

Maruf, B. 1986: Yan Awaki redevelopment scheme Kano. MSc thesis, Architecture, Ahmadu Bello University.

Marx, K. [1852] 1963. *The eighteenth brumaire of Louis Bonaparte*. Reprint. New York: International Publishers.

Moghadam, V. 1988: Oil, the state and limits to autonomy. *Arab Studies Quarterly* 10(2), 225–38.

Na-Ayuba, A. 1986: Yantatsine: an analysis of the Gardawa uprising in Kano, Nigeria 1980–1985. MSc dissertation, Bayero University, Kano.

Nicolas, G. 1981: Guerre sainte à Kano. *Politique Africaine* 1(4), 73–81.

Nigerian Federal Government. 1981: *Report of tribunal of inquiry on Kano disturbances* (Aniagolu Report). Lagos: Federal Government Press.

NIPSS, 1986: *Religious disturbances in Nigeria*. Kuru: Research Department, National Institute for Policy and Strategic Studies.

Nolutshungu, S. 1990: Fragments of a democracy. *Third World Quarterly* 12(1), 86–115.

O'Connor, J. 1984: *The accumulation crisis*. Oxford: Basil Blackwell.

Omoniwa, M. and Abu, J. 1986: *The Maitatsine riots in Nigeria 1980–1984*. Zaria: Kashim Ibrahim Library.

Ong, A. 1990: State versus Islam. *American Ethnologist* 17(2), 258–76.

Onoh, J. 1983: *The Nigerian oil economy*. New York: St Martin's Press.

Othman, S. 1984: Classes, crises and coup. *African Affairs* 27, 441–61.

Pesaran, M. 1982: The system of dependent capitalism in pre- and post-revolutionary Iran. *International Journal of Middle Eastern Studies* 14, 501–22.

Petras, J. and Morley, M. 1983: Petro-dollars and the state. *Third World Quarterly* 5, 8–27.

Pipes, D. 1980: *In the path of God*. New York: Basic Books.

Pollard, H. 1985: The erosion of agriculture in an oil economy. *World Development* 13(7), 819–35.

PRP, 1982: *The struggle for a new social order*. Kaduna: People's Redemption Party.

Rebel, H. 1989: Cultural hegemony and class experience. *American Ethnologist* 16(1), 117–36.

Roemer, M. 1983: The Dutch disease in developing countries. Working Paper no. 156, Harvard Institute of International Studies.

Roff, W. (ed.) 1987: *Islam and the political economy of meaning*. London: Croom Helm.

Roseberry, W. 1989: *Anthropologies and histories*. New Brunswick, NJ: Rutgers University Press.

Saad, H. 1988: Urban blight and religious uprising in northern Nigeria. *Habitat International* 12(2), 111–28.

Sanusi, H. 1982: State and capitalist development in Nigeria. PhD dissertation, Northwestern University, Evanston, IL.

Schatz, S. P. 1984: The inert economy. *Journal of Modern African Studies* 22(1), 45–57.

152 *Exploring Human Geography*

Seers, D. 1964: The mechanism of an open petroleum economy. *Social and Economic Studies* 13(2), 233–42.

Shipton, P. 1989: *Bitter money: Cultural economy and some African meanings of forbidden commodities*. American Ethnological Society Monograph Series, no. 1. Washington, DC.

Simmel, G. 1978. *The philosophy of money*. London: Routledge & Kegan Paul.

Stavrianos, G. 1981: *Global rift*. New York: William Morrow.

Stinchcombe, A. 1978: *Theoretical methods in social history*. New York: Academic.

Stock, R. 1985: The rise and fall of universal primary education in northern Nigeria. *TESG* 71, 274–87.

Swindell, K. 1986. Urban peripheries in Africa. Unpubl. manuscript, University of Birmingham.

Terdiman, R. 1987: *Discourse/counter discourse*. Baltimore: Johns Hopkins University Press.

Thompson, E. P. 1968: *The making of the English working class*, 2nd edn. Harmondsworth: Penguin.

Trotsky, 1969 [rpt]: *The permanent revolution*. Reprint. New York: Pathfinder.

Trotsky, L. [1932] 1977: *The history of the Russian Revolution*. Reprint. New York: Pathfinder.

Ukpolo, V. 1983. An economic evaluation of the Yobe River Irrigation Project in Nigeria. PhD dissertation, The American University, Washington, DC.

Usman, Y. B. 1980: *For the liberation of Nigeria: essays and lectures 1969–1978*. London: New Beacon Books.

Usman, Y. B. (ed.) 1982: *Political repression in Nigeria*. Zaria: Gaskiya.

Usman, Y. B. 1986: *Nigeria against the IMF*. Kaduna: Vanguard Press.

Virilio, P. 1986: *Speed and politics*. New York: Semiotexte.

Volosinov, V. [1929] 1986: *Marxism and the philosophy of language*. Reprint. Cambridge: Harvard University Press.

Watts, M. 1983. *Silent violence: Food, famine and peasantry in northern Nigeria*. Berkeley: University of California Press.

Watts, M. 1984. State, oil and accumulation: from boom to crisis. *Society and Space* 2 403–28.

Watts, M. (ed.) 1987: *State, oil and agriculture in Nigeria*. Berkeley: Institute of International Studies.

Watts, M. 1994: The devil's excrement: oil money and the spectacle of black gold. In Thrift, N. (ed.), *Money, power and space*. Oxford: Basil Blackwell.

Williams, G. 1988: Why is there no agrarian capitalism in Nigeria? *Journal of Historical Sociology* 1(4), 345–98.

Williams, R. 1977: *Marxism and literature*. Oxford: Oxford University Press.

Willis, P. 1977: *Learning to Labour*. Farnborough: Saxon House.

World Bank. 1979: *World development report*. Oxford and New York: Oxford University Press and World Bank.

World Bank. 1981: *World development report*. Oxford and New York: Oxford University Press and World Bank.

World Bank. 1985: *World development report*. Oxford and New York: Oxford University Press and World Bank.

World Bank. 1988: *World development report*. Oxford and New York: Oxford University Press and World Bank.

Wright, S. 1986: *Nigeria: The dilemmas ahead*. Economist Intelligence Unit Special Report no. 1072. London.

Yusuf, A. 1988: *Maitatsine: Peddler of epidemics*. Syneco: Kano.

SECTION TWO
WHAT DIFFERENCE DOES GEOGRAPHY MAKE?

Editors' introduction

The readings in Section One of this book demonstrate that the making and breaking of geographies is a socially informed process, subject to contestation and struggle. They emphasize the two-way flow of influence between the geographies in which we participate on the ground and the geographies that we construct in our minds. In Section Two the argument is extended by looking in more detail at the complex ways in which geography makes a difference. Here our concern goes beyond the ways in which geography shapes our locational behaviour to explore the ways in which socially constructed geographies on the ground are perceived, used, represented, struggled over and transformed, and so constitute social practice.

Geography as a fundamental but contested influence

Geography makes a difference; it shapes and constitutes social action rather than being a mere manifestation of it. But, as we have seen, geographies on the ground are informed by understanding and contested through their production and consumption in social practice. If this is the case, the particular ways in which geographies are constructed and the understandings and usages of those spaces become central to social understanding. The same space may mean very different things to different people and may be constructed, controlled and contested so as to achieve very different objectives. The readings in this section of the book explore the intersections between socially constructed geographies and the social action which takes place in and through – and so transforms – them. As we shall see, these intersections are also sites of struggle.

An essential feature of the ways in which geographies shape as well as are shaped by social practice is the struggle over how to evaluate them; how to sort out 'good' from 'bad', 'better' from 'worse'. Once again, however, what we consider to be 'good' or 'bad', 'better' or 'worse' is a product of our own understandings of the world in which we live. For some, for example, what is 'good' may be profitability; for others social justice or environmental sustainability; while yet others may see no difference between these criteria. But the essential point is that the nature and direction of evaluation reflect a set of socially constructed norms. In one sense debate about such norms and the meanings they engender is the stuff of politics. But it is also more profound than the institutional politics under which most of us live. Rather it reflects alternative views of the good life: what kinds of social relations and material circumstances – what kinds of geographies – combine to create an acceptable or even desirable set of conditions in which to live (see Smith, 1995).

Once again, therefore, we are faced not merely with arguments which assert that geography matters but with the much deeper geographical argument that the ways in which geography matters are themselves contested. We have, therefore, to think simultaneously of geography *and* difference: geography matters but in a variety of ways.

The readings

A common theme in the readings in this section of the book is the struggle over acceptable geographies and their significance for social practice. The first reading considers the acceptability of alternative analyses within geography and related disciplines of the nature and operation of emergent spaces of production and the significance of alternative economic geographies for the efficacy of production. The other three are concerned more with the contestation between alternative meanings of geographical spaces as expressed through the social practices which take place in and through them.

As a bridge between thinking of geography as being an inherent feature of – and created through – social practice in Section One of this book and the closely related notion of geography as constitutive of social action in Section Two, **Ash Amin** and **Nigel Thrift** review the arguments advanced by some theorists of production. Most notable here is the work of Allen Scott and Michael Storper (see Storper and Scott (1989) for a summary). They argue for a 'return to place': a tendency to geographical agglomeration and the creation of 'new industrial spaces' (Scott, 1988) which allows a whole host of influences to work through place on the business of production (see, for example, Thrift, 1994). What is so compelling about the work of Scott and Storper is its spatiality. They insist in novel and convincing ways on the geographical foundations of economic activity and so place geographical space at the centre of their analyses. In assessing this work, Amin and Thrift accept that place certainly constitutes social practice but that the way in which this constitution takes place is shaped by the geographical requirements of social practice itself. The return to place or localization of economies is not an autonomous influence of geography on production but is itself shaped by the geographical demands of an increasingly globally integrated economic geography. One of the conditions of existence of such a global system is the presence of centres to act as places of representation (centres of authority), interaction (centres of sociability) and as a means of tracking innovations (centres of discourse). These centres need to be geographically formed, place-bound communities if they are to perform such tasks effectively. Places are, in short, doubly geographical: they are required for social practice and they help to constitute that social practice. Both of these formative features of place interact in a two-way fashion; neither may be reduced to the other.

This theme is echoed in the other contributions to this section. But there is a further qualification to add to the notion that geographies are created through social practice: social practice is not divisible into separate fragments – economic, cultural, political, etc. – each driven by a separate 'logic'. On the contrary, the attempt is frequently made to assert a singular view (e.g. the economic) over the inherently more complex view of human beings. And yet the nature of the economic not only may be conceived and understood differently in different times and places – it is itself cultural and political – but also may be endowed with different levels of significance relative to other dimensions of human being.

It is in such a complex context of understanding and action that the meaning and significance of geographical space for social practice becomes influential. As **John Allen** and **Michael Pryke** argue in their analysis of the work of Henri Lefebvre (most notably Lefebvre, 1991), the meanings of space inscribed by representatives of the powerful (what Lefebvre refers to as *representations of space*) frequently come into conflict with the meanings of space held and practised in everyday usage of space (referred to as *representational space*).

A good example of this difference and the significance of it is the struggle between, on the one hand, those who control the conditions under which professional association football is played and sold as a spectacle in England and those, on the other, who wish to witness the spectacle represented by the game. The representation of space of the former is shaped by the desire for order, control and profitability. The physical space emerging from such representations is that of the all-seater stadium – with the implication that clubs unable to meet the required standards of accommodation may be excluded from the national football league. The representational space of the latter reflects the wish to participate actively as a crowd in a gladiatorial and place-based contest between geographically identified if not locally constituted teams with (local) heroes and (distant) villains, winners and losers. The implication here is that substantial sections of stadiums should be reserved for standing in order to allow the most effective form of participation.

As Allen and Pryke point out in their study of the City of London, these different forms of space may contradict or come into tension with one another, a contradiction articulated by relations of power but not necessarily without subversions from those (in this case, the contract cleaners of the spaces through which the abstract spaces of finance in the City are represented) with apparently very little power in the system. In the case of the footballing analogy, the crowd may subvert the representational space of an all-seater stadium by standing on newly installed seats (and occasionally detaching them for use as weapons), so increasing the likeli-hood of disorder beyond that which was immanent when, formerly, they stood pressed together on the relatively firm foundation of the terraces.

This representational shaping of space is apparent in the study by **Jon Goss** of the geographically induced magic of the mall. The micro-geography of the layout of malls is driven by (incomplete, contested and constantly changing) understandings of human motivation with the intention of maximizing the return on the investment in the space of the mall. The mall becomes a place in which spending is seen not merely as a natural but as a highly desirable social practice justified and to be encour-aged and supported because it takes human experience way beyond the mere acquisition of goods or services. Anything which challenges such an experience (like reminders of the real world outside the mall: the acres of dreary and eternally fallow parking lot; the inequality and exclusion from the joys of consumption as represented by those who subvert the the mall as a space of consumption and use it as a space of shelter and warmth) or disrupts the most appropriate (i.e. profitable) flow of con-sumers through the mall through inappropriate social behaviour is excluded or designed away. The mall becomes a privately controlled 'public' space. As such, it is not a development of or replacement for the public high street in the area of the automobile but its very opposite. Furthermore, the mall becomes a geographical essay – redolent of 'new industrial spaces' – in the social construction of external economies whereby the relative location of different types of activity is designed in the attempt to maximize the profitability of each.

Nevertheless, despite the intervention of gurus in the attempt to condi-tion human behaviour, its bricks and mortar (more frequently, concrete) cannot, ultimately, subdue resistance to its intended influence. There is a massive irony in this which may be revealed by considering the wider significance of the representation of space of the mall. It represents not merely a shopping machine tuned to the peak of efficiency but, more fundamentally (and grossly inaccurately), an image of the economy as existing simply to satisfy its subjects' wants and needs. Consumption is seen as the object of production whereas – and perhaps more insistently in capitalism than any other social form of economy – consumption is merely one moment in social reproduction, the driving force of which within capitalist society is accumulation. To ensure that this objective is constantly met, consumers are the object of detailed social control in order not merely that they engage in maximum consumption, so ena-bling the producers and retailers to realize – in the form of profit – the surplus value contained within the commodities they sell, but, and pre-cisely because consumption is not the end of production, to transmit the idea to its practitioners that it is.

Of course, as long as it is represented as the climax of production, pleasurable consumption contributes to the widespread acceptance of the prevailing mode of social reproduction: it offers a seductive legitimacy. Such legitimation is enhanced at the same time as profitability is increased via control of the labour process in the delivery of products and services. Drawing on the research of Philip Crang (1994) amongst others, **Scott Lash** and **John Urry** show how the design and control of the 'representational' micro-spaces of a restaurant are critical to such service delivery. The quality of design and, more particularly, the performance of service delivery conducted in and through the spaces of service production, construct an experience of the service. They must, therefore, be controlled and regulated in the most detailed manner. As in the case of the mall, such control is exerted not only through the regulation of the producers of the service but by the behaviour of its consumers. Once again, this control offers a double-edged sword and some space for subversion. The notion of consumer sovereignty may be taken seriously by framing demands in ways which do not conform to the production-orientated ethos of fast food in which choice is illusory and pre-arranged to satisfy the requirements of production.

References and further reading

Crang, P. 1994: It's showtime: on the workplace geographies of display in a restaurant in southeast England. *Environment and Planning D: Society and Space* 12, 675–704.

Gregory, D. and Urry, J. (eds) 1985: *Social relations and spatial structures.* Basingstoke: Macmillan.

Harvey, D. 1985: The geopolitics of capitalism. In Gregory, D. and Urry, J. (eds), *Social relations and spatial structures.* Basingstoke: Macmillan, 128–63.

Johnston, R. J. 1991: *A question of place: Exploring the practice of human geography.* Oxford: Basil Blackwell.

Lefebvre, H. 1991: *The production of space.* Oxford: Basil Blackwell; first published in France in 1974; English translation by Donald Nicholson-Smith.

Scott, A. J. 1988: *New industrial spaces: Flexible production organization and regional development in North America and Western Europe.* London: Pion.

Smith, D. M. 1995: Back to the good life: towards an enlarged conception of social justice. Paper read at the Annual Conference of the Institute of British Geographers, University of Northumbria, January; forthcoming in *Society and Space.*

Smith, S. J. 1993: Bounding the borders: claiming space and making place in rural Scotland. *Transactions of the Institute of British Geographers* 18, 291–308.

Soja, E. 1989: *Postmodern geographies.* London and New York: Verso.

Storper, M. and Scott, A. J. 1989: The geographical foundations and social regulation of flexible production complexes. In Wolch, J. and Dear, M. (eds), *The power of geography: How territory shapes social life.* Winchester, MA: Unwin Hyman, 19–40.

Thrift, N. 1994: On the social and cultural determinants of international financial centres: the case of the City of London. In Corbridge, S., Martin, R. and Thrift, N. (eds), *Money, power and space.* Oxford: Basil Blackwell, 327–55.

7   Ash Amin and Nigel Thrift,
'Neo-Marshallian Nodes in Global Networks'

Reprinted from: *International Journal of Urban and Regional Research* 16, 571–87 (1992)

Introduction

The literature on industrial districts seems to have reached something of an impasse. On one side the proponents of industrial districts sit around their camp-fires, supposedly wild-eyed with enthusiasm, talking flexible specialization and post-Fordism. On the other side are a series of supposedly grim-faced critics, shouting destructive comments about globalization and corporate networks from out of the mist. This paper is an attempt to break out of this often acrimonious impasse. We want to take the emergence of new localized industrial complexes seriously, but we want to set them firmly within a context of expanding global corporate networks.

Accordingly, the paper is in four parts. In the first part of the paper, we summarize the key arguments of the localization thesis which predicts a return to industrial districts, and some of the major criticisms that have been made of the claim that there is a resurgence of the regional economy on a pervasive scale. In the second part of the paper, we attempt to reformulate the localization and globalization theses so as to provide a space for local agglomeration within growing global production filieres. In particular, we want to focus on Marshall's idea of industrial atmosphere, indicating a set of socio-cultural characteristics which are still crucial in global production filieres and which can lead to a degree of localization. The third part of the paper attempts to illustrate these and other contentions via a consideration of the history of two industrial districts. The first, Santa Croce in Tuscany, has become a Marshallian industrial district of the old kind over the past twenty years. The second, the City of London in London, finally stopped being a conventional Marshallian industrial district at the same time that Santa Croce was becoming one. But the City did not, therefore, cease to be a localized complex. Rather, we argue, it heralds a new form of localization. Finally, in the fourth part, we address some of the local economic development policy implications of the previous parts of the paper.

The localization thesis

The most powerful case for the possibility of a major return to the regional economy comes from a group of writers speculating on the rise of locally agglomerated production systems out of the crisis of mass production. What is envisaged, to put it somewhat reductively, is a return to a division of labour between self-contained, product specialist regional economies as first conceived by Adam Smith at a national level. This is a thesis which draws upon the work of Michael Piore and Charles Sabel (Piore and Sabel, 1984; Sabel 1989), Allen Scott and Michael Storper (Scott, 1988; Storper and Scott, 1989; Storper, 1989), Paul Hirst and Jonathan Zeitlin (1989, 1991) and others borrowing the concepts of 'flexible specilization' or 'flexible accumulation'[1] to describe the transition to a new era of vertically disintegrated and locationally fixed production.

The key argument is that the irreversible growth in recent decades of consumer sovereignty, market volatility and shortened product life-cycles requires production to be organized on an extremely flexible basis. Size, scale, hierarcy, vertical integration and task dedication on the part of machinery and employees are deemed to be too inflexible to turn out short runs of better quality and differentiated goods with the minimum of time and effort. Instead, the market is said to require decentralized co-ordination and control; the 'deverticalization' of the division of labour between independent but inter-linked units; numerical and task flexibility among the workforce; greater reliance on innovation, ingenuity and skills; the deployment of multi-purpose and flexible tools and machinery; and the elimination of time and wastage in supply and delivery.

Such a change is said to be particularly evident in industries which face pronounced volatility and product innovation in their niche markets. Examples include electronics, designer clothing, craft products and other light industrial consumer products. In organizational terms, the new market circumstances are said to require a radical transformation of the production system towards flexible intra-firm and inter-firm arrangements which can simultaneously combine the economies of scale, scope and versatility.

This change, it is argued, implies a return to place – a dependence on locational proximity between different agents involved in any production filiere. Agglomeration is said to offer a series of advantages upon which a system of vertically disintegrated production can draw. Echoing the factors first identified by Alfred Marshall in his work on small-firm districts in Lancashire and Yorkshire during the nineteenth century, these advantages are said to include the build-up of a local pool of expertise and know-how and a culture of labour flexibility and co-operation resulting from dense social interation and trust; lowered transport and transaction costs; and the growth of a local infrastructure of specialized services, distribution networks and supply structures. Via the consolidation of particular product specialisms in different regions a federation of self-contained regional economies is anticipated, each with its own cumulative causation effects drawing upon strong external economies of agglomeration.

Empirical verification of this thesis comes from the claim that over the past few decades the most dynamic and competitive examples of industrial restructuring have been 'Marshallian' in their spatial dynamics. The examples which are quoted have now become almost too familiar. They include high-tech, R & D and innovation-intensive areas such as Silicon Valley, Boston, the M4 corridor in England, Grenoble and other successful technopoles. They also include industrial districts in both semi-rural contexts such as those in the Third Italy regions and those in inner-city environments (e.g. motion pictures in Los Angeles, the furniture industry in inner London), in which networks of specialist small firms produce craft or quality consumer goods. Finally, also cited is the example of areas such as Baden-Württemburg in Germany, where leading-edge large companies such as Bosch are said to rely on local sub-contracting and supply networks for their flexibility and innovative excellence.

The significance of this thesis should not be underestimated, equating, as it does, industrial renovation with territorial development. The cited examples are very real cases of success, and their experiences could inform policy measures in other areas. The novel conceptual aspect of the thesis is the (re)discovery of the locational importance of patterns of linkages and the formation of inter-firm relationships, notably in relation to the exchange of information and goods between buyer and seller and its influence on linkage costs. The new literature makes the interesting proposition that negotiations involved in producing and exchanging certain types of commodity are less conveniently carried out at a distance. Customer-specific supplies, for instance, are often based on extensive technical cooperation between the seller and the buyer. Therefore such co-operation requires reliable and rapid communication, usually best conveyed through personal contacts. Production of customized goods and services under conditions of 'dynamic' competition, the hallmark of the post-mass-production economy, will therefore tend to bring with it agglomeration and local networking.

To anticipate a pervasive perhaps even total, return to local production complexes in the post-Fordist economy is nonsensical, for a number of reasons.[2] First, it is inaccurate to refer to the conditions and areas cited by the localization thesis as the only examples of success. Others must surely include the reconsolidation of the major metropolitan areas such as London, Milan, Frankfurt and Paris as centres of growth through their magnet-like pull on finance, management, innovation, business services and infrastructure. Reasons related to their status as core metropolitan areas and size as centres of consumption have far more to do with their economic success than the redis-covery of Marshallian tendencies. Should any citation of success not also include the resurgence of major provincial cities such as Birmingham, Turin and Grenoble, which have managed to carve out a niche as intermediate centres of agglomeration within global financial, corporate and service net-works? Indeed, why not also include, as an example, the growing concentra-tion of wealth in certain rural areas characterized by an odd combination of capital intensification in agriculture, the decentralization of offices and service industries and in-migration by commuters looking for a pleasant lifestyle? These additions to the geography of 'post-Fordist' success have little in common with the logic of flexible specialization.

Second, in proposing local agglomeration as the symbol of a future regime of capital accumulation, the localization thesis effectively rules out the possibility of transformation and change within the very areas cited as examples of post-Fordist growth. These areas, too are likely to evolve, and perhaps fragment internally, in much the same way as did, for example, Alfred Marshall's cutlery district in Sheffield in the course of the twentieth century. Evidence of such change is already apparent in 'mature' production complexes such as Silicon Valley, now being drawn into a wider spatial division of labour as a result of intense inward investment by overseas multinational corporations, and the export of assembly and intermediate production functions respectively to areas of cheap labour and growing market demand. Some Italian industrial districts, too, are undergoing change, as local linkages begin to replace external ones, owing to either the threat of takeover of local banks by foreign financial institutions, or the increase in international rather than local intra-firm and inter-firm linkages (see the section on Santa Croce below, and Amin, 1989; Bianchini, 1990; Harrison, 1990).

Third, taking the ingredients for local success identified by the localization thesis seriously, it has to be concluded that the proliferation of localized production complexes is likely to be restricted in so far as these ingredients are not readily transferable to other areas. Local containment of the division of labour requires a gradual build-up of know-how and skills, co-operative traditions, institutional support, specialist services and infrastructure. These not only take time to consolidate, but also escape the traditional instruments of spatial policy owing to their ephemeral and composite nature (Amin and Robins, 1990). In addition, there remains the problem that 'new' growth cannot, as on a *tabula rasa*, sweep aside local traditions which might resist such change (Glasmeier, 1991). The dismal failure of strategies to promote technopoles in different European less favoured regions (LFRs), as well as efforts to encourage greater local networking among and between small and large firms within the depressed industrial regions, bears witness to this difficulty.

A final problem with the notion of a pervasive spread of local production complexes is related to the observation made by a number of critics that there is no conclusive evidence of the demise of Fordist principles of mass production and consumption and of the multitude of labour processes which co-existed under Fordism (e.g. customization, batch production, mass assembly, continuous flow). The idea of a clean break between one macrosystem dominated by one way of doing things and another regime with its own distinctive organizational structure is too simple a caricature of historical change and a denial of the ebb and flow, the continuity and discontinuity and the diversity and contradiction that such change normally suggests (see Gertler, 1988; Sayer, 1989; Thrift, 1989). Sensitivity to diversity is particularly essential when it comes to the analysis of the geography of production. Depending on the labour process in an industry, the organizational cultures of the players involved, the nature of the areas in which activity is located and the market or macroeconomic circumstances surrounding individual sectors, a diversity of industrial geographies can be produced, with each offering different options of the spectrum between locational fixity and global mobility.

The emergence of new localized production complexes, to conclude this section, should be noted seriously. But this cannot become a basis for assuming, as two observers have done, that 'the mode of production, has in a sense, gone back to the future', with 'local economies . . . already on the march' (Cooke and Imrie, 1989, p. 326). If localities are on the march, it is, if anything, as argued in the next section, to the tune of globalizing forces in the organization of production – a process in which local territorial integrity is far from guaranteed.

A reformulation: global networks

So far we have followed a fairly standard critique of the current literature on the resurgence of local economies. The literature has rather limited analytical power, most particularly because of a tendency to cling to a model which is locally based and which does not therefore recognize the importance of emerging global corporate networks. In this paper we still want to retain the notion of 'localization', but we want to relocate the account in two ways. First, we want to consider industrial districts and local complexes as the outgrowths of a world economy which is still rapidly internationalizing and which is still a world of global corporate power. Second, against an incipient economism in explaining the strengths of localized production, in order to provide a reformulation of the significance of local networking, we want to build on Marshall's work on 'industrial atmosphere', trying to analyse why such an atmosphere might still prove central in a world economy where transactions are increasingly indirect. In other words, we want to cross the new international political economy with the new economic sociology.

We take it that an important shift has occurred in the 1970s and 1980s, namely a move from an international to a global economy. This global economy has many characteristics, of which four are particularly important. First, industries increasingly function on an integrated world scale, through the medium of global corporate networks. As a consequence, the control that multinational corporations (whether foreign or domestically owned) exert over employment, investment and trade has continued to grow in most developed economies through the 1980s and into the 1990s. Second, corporate power has continued to advance, so that the new global industries are increasingly oligopolistic, progressively cartelized. This intensifying concentration is best seen in the various merger booms around the world in the 1980s. For example, the EC saw a massive 25 per cent increase in the number of industrial mergers across a wide range of sectors (Jacquemin *et al.*, 1989), leading to a growth in seller concentration levels, increasingly on an international rather than only national scale.

But, third, and importantly, today's global corporations have themselves become more decentralized through increased 'hollowing out', new forms of subcontracting, new types of joint ventures, strategic alliances and other new 'networked' forms of corporate organization. Thus corporations increasingly resemble 'flattened hierarchies'. However, there is little evidence to suggest that operational and organizational decentralization has resulted in a similar degree of devolution of power and control. 'Hollowing out', for example, has led to forward vertical integration by market leaders in order to secure strategic control over markets and distribution networks. Also, new developments in subcontracting have often led to preferred status being bestowed on fewer suppliers, linking them more tightly into corporate hierarchies and threatening the survival and growth of other suppliers. Strategic alliances, too, appear to be global partnerships between major oligopolies seeking to share markets and R & D costs. In other words, some form of centred control still exists, and in the hands of global corporations, thus suggesting that new developments like those noted above may well represent simply an extension and sharing of power beyond the boundaries of the individual firm, among key actors in a value-added network, rather than a genuine spread of authority to smaller or local players in corporate networks (Amin and Dietrich, 1991).

Further, it is by no means clear that these new developments are local phenomena or even have inevitable localized consequences. Increasing corporate integration may well be accompanied by increasing *geographical* integration, as more and more places are drawn into, or excluded from, the web of global corporate networks. Thus, against the benefit that the operational status of sites within these networks might be more complex and more autonomous than that of sites trapped in rigid (Fordist) intra-corporate hierarchies, the fact remains that they are still locked into a global corporate web and therefore not restricted to local ties. In other words, the sites might be relatively autonomous but they are not free agents.

Fourth, and finally, there is a new, more volatile balance of power between nation-states and corporations, which we might call 'short-run corporatism'. Nation-states' ability to intervene in the world economy has been weakened because states have been 'hollowed out' (Held, 1991), and because states are often internally divided. But corporations also find it difficult to impose a strategic direction on the world economy for reasons such as the unstable nature of business alliances and the contradictory interests embedded in individual industries (and even, sometimes, individual firms). The result is the increasing prominence of cross-national issue coalitions 'uniting fragments of the state, fragments of particular industries and even fragments of particular firms in a worldwide network' (Moran, 1991, p. 133).

The net result of these four developments has been the growth of increasingly integrated global production filieres orchestrated and co-ordinated by large corporations. But, because these filieres are more decentralized and less hierarchically governed, there are in fact a number of very considerable problems of integration and co-ordination. Three of these, each related to the other, stand out. The first problem is one of *representation*. Information has to be gathered and analysed about what is happening in these filieres. But the benefit of advances in global communications and information-processing capacity to the growth of a globally oriented business press (Kynaston, 1985) and a whole industry of industrial research and analysis is a two-edged one. It has produced a massive increase in the quantity and even the quality of information, but the problem of how that information is interpreted and who has access to the interpretation remains; indeed, it is probably more pressing. There is *a growing interpretive task*. What can be said is that the 'stories' that are circulated about a global production filiere, and how they are scripted, constitute that filiere's understanding of itself. Indeed, new work in 'economic sociology' (e.g. Adler and Adler, 1984; Block, 1990; Zukin and Dimaggio, 1990) suggests that the only way of making sense of large and complex economic systems is through the formation of social cliques within which these stories circulate. This point relates to those of Giddens (1990, 1991) and Strange (1988, 1991), who have pointed out that what they call 'expert systems' or 'knowledge structures' have become a critical part of the global economy, and that these systems or structures are increasingly asymmetric.

The second problem is one of social *interaction*. Global production filieres are not just social structures, they are sociable structures. There is constant social interaction within them. Indeed, this is one of the ways in which they are able to be understood. Interaction promotes particular discourses and taps into particular knowledge structures. Perhaps one of the most misleading articles of the early 1980s was Offe and Wiesenthal's (1979), where they suggested that the capitalist class is a monological entity. Of course, capitalists have many advantages, but they are still dialogical beings. In particular, social interaction is still needed to gather information and to tap into particular knowledge structures, to make agreements and coalitions, and continually to cement relations of *trust*, of implicit contract (Marceau, 1989). New or heightened forms of corporate interaction, like joint ventures and strategic alliances, have made social interaction more rather than less central to many aspects of corporate life.

The third problem is one of tracking *innovation*. The problem is how to keep up levels of product and process innovation in a decentralized system (especially when the pressure to produce more products has increased) and, perhaps more importantly still, how to successfully market products in the early customized stages when they can succeed or fall and when a small critical mass of customers is needed. In turn, success depends critically on representation and interaction, since the stories that are told and who they are recounted to influence a product's chance of success.

Thus the world economy may have become more decentralized, but it is not necessarily becoming decentred. Centres are still needed, even in a world of indirect communication, for three reasons related to the problems above regarding representation, interaction and innovation.

Centres, in the first place, are needed to represent, that is, to generate and disseminate discourses, collective beliefs, stories about what world production filieres are like. These discourses are constitutive of the direction in which industries and corporations can go – whether we are talking about new fashions in design or products or new management trends (like strategic alliances). They are the understandings industries make of themselves. Centres are also needed as points at which knowledge structures, many of which carry considerable social barriers to entry, can be tapped into. Often such centres can constitute a local knowledge structure which has 'gone global'. In other words, these are centres of *authority*.

Second, centres are needed to interact, that is, to act as centres of sociability, so gathering information, establishing or maintaining coalitions and monitoring trust and implicit contracts. Third, they are needed in order to develop, test and track innovations. Centres produce a discursive mass sufficient to help generate innovations; contact with numerous knowledgeable people identifies gaps in the market, new uses for technologies and so on. In the case of certain products (e.g. financial products), development occurs in close liaison with most who are the potential sources of reward. Centres are associated to provide sufficient mass in the early stages of innovation. Their social networks provide rapid reactions and an initial market. The success or failure of products, especially in the early stage, can depend upon the stories told about them. Finally, centres are still needed, to some at extent at least, to keep track of innovations; that is, as judges of their success.

These have to be *geographical* centres; that is, place-bound communities in which the agglomeration and interaction between firms, institutions and social groups act to generate and reinforce that 'industrial atmosphere' which nurtures the knowledge, communication and innovation structures required for retaining competitive advantage in a given global production filiere. In other words, the localization of the functions of the 'head' contributes towards resolving problems outlined earlier facing global corporate networks.

To be sure, this form of localization is quite different from the older and more familiar habit of the vertically integrated, hierarchical firm of concentrating its strategic functions, its 'head', in headquarters located in major metropolitan cities. In contrast to this latter example of 'tight encasement' of the 'head' within a closed corporate structure, neo-Marshallian nodes in global networks act, as it were, as a collective 'brain', as centres of excellence in a given industry, offering for collective consumption local contact networks, knowledge structures and a plethora of institutions underwriting individual entrepreneurship (see Peck, 1991; Todling, 1991; Tornqvist, 1991).

Such 'socialization' of the functions of the head, amounting to the 'valorization' of a local community, itself as an active factor serving to help local industry to maintain industrial supremacy, appears to be of particular relevance in industries characterized by knowledge-based competition, rapidly changing technological standards and volatile markets. All three are conditions of a greater spread of costs and risks between individual agents, as long as continuity in the flow of information, goods and services between firms, institutions and social groups is maintained. This is precisely the advantage which Marshallian nodes are able to offer: an industrial atmosphere and infrastructure which firms, small and large, isolated or interconnected, can dip into as and when required.

Two examples

Two examples follow to illustrate the significance of centred places in a global system. In the case of Santa Croce, a vertically disintegrated small-firm industrial district of the classical Marshallian type has evolved within the past twenty years, but is now experiencing a further change. In the case of the City of London, what was a Marshallian industrial district of considerable local integrity has evolved into an industrial complex which still has some Marshallian features but which now relies on global networking to cement these features in place.

These districts may appear dissimilar at first sight. For example, the City has a much larger employment base than Santa Croce. But we would argue that such dissimilarities are outweighed by some notable similarities. In particular, five similarities can be noted. First, they are in global industries with similar market conditions (product volatility, reduced product life-cycles, design intensity, flexibility of volume, etc.). Second, in both districts, despite intensifying external linkage formation, many needs can be met locally. In Santa Croce this is the result of cumulative historical circumstance. In the City it is essentially the result of sheer scale. Third, both districts rely on strong knowledge structures. Fourth, both districts have strong traditions of 'thick' social interaction and 'collective consciousness', the result of distinctive institutional mixes. Fifth and finally, both districts are under threat. In the case of Santa Croce there is the threat of its incorporation back into global networks through vertical reintegration. In the case of the City, that threat is no longer relevant. The real threat now comes from an American-forced change from implicit to explicit contracts as the financial system becomes increasingly rule-based. In turn, this shift might increase transaction costs and reduce the need for specialized knowledge to the point where many crucial intermediaries are no longer necessary or viable. (However, increasing automation may well bring transaction costs down, thereby countering this tendency.)

Marshall in Tuscany: leather tanning in Santa Croce sull'Arno

Santa Croce is a small town in the lower Arno Valley, forty kilometres east of Pisa, which specializes in the production of medium- to high-quality cured bovine leather for predominantly the 'fashion' end of the shoe and bag industries. There are only two other major leather tanning areas in Italy: Arzignano in the Veneto, which is dominated by a small number of large, vertically integrated and highly mechanized tanneries, orientated towards the furnishing and upholstery industry; and Solofra in the South (Campania), which specializes in less refined, non-bovine, cured leather for the clothing industry. The lower Arno Valley accounts for about 25 per cent of the national employment in the leather and hide tanning industry.

In Santa Croce, an area no larger than ten square kilometres, are clustered 300 artisan firms employing 4500 workers and 200 subcontractors employing 1700 workers. The real figures are probably much higher, as the latter capture only those firms officially registered with the Santa Croce Association of Leather Tanners and the Association of Subcontractors respectively. In 1986, the combined turnover of these 500 firms was £860 million (one-tenth of which was that of the subcontractors). On average, the area derives 15 per cent of its sales revenue from exports, almost 80 per cent of which are destined for the

EC. Although the share of exports has been growing, the industry is still heavily dependent on the Italian market, particularly upon buyers in Tuscany, who account for over 40 per cent of the domestic market.

Twenty years ago, Santa Croce was not a Marshallian industrial district. There were many fewer firms, production was more vertically integrated, the product was more standardized (albeit artisanal) and the balance of power was very much in favour of the older and larger tanneries. Today, Santa Croce is a highly successful 'flexibly specialized' small-firm industrial district, which derives its competitive strength from specializing in the seasonally based fashionwear niche of the industry. Typically, market conditions in this sector – e.g. product volatility, a very short product life-cycle, design intensity, flexibility of volume – demand an innovative excellence and organizational flexibility which Santa Croce has been able to develop and consolidate over the last two decades by building upon its early artisan strengths.

The boom in demand for Italian leather fashionwear in the 1970s and 1980s provided the occasion for area-wide specialization and growth in the output of cured leather. That such growth was to occur through a multiplication of independent small firms supported by a myriad of task-specialist subcontractors was perhaps more a result of specific local peculiarities than an outcome of the new market conditions. Opposed to the highly polluting effects of the tanning process – Santa Croce is one of those places in which you can recognize the Marshallian 'industrial atmosphere' by its smell – the local Communist administration was unsympathetic to factory expansion applications and also refused, until very recently, to redraw the Structure Plan to allow for more and better factory space. This, together with the strong tradition of self-employment and small-scale entrepreneurship in rural Tuscany, effectively led to a proliferation of independently owned firms scattered in small units all over Santa Croce. Two further encouragements to this process of fragmented entrepreneurship were, first, the preference of local rural savings banks to spread their portfolio of loans widely but thinly to a large number of applicants as a risk-minimization strategy, and second, the variety of fiscal and other incentives offered by the Italian state to firms with fewer than fifteen employees.

This initial, and somewhat 'accidental', response to a situation of rapidly expanding demand was gradually turned into an organizational strength capable of responding with the minimum of effort and cost to new and rapidly changing market signals. The tanners – many of whom call themselves 'artists' – became more and more specialized, combining their innate 'designer' skills with the latest in chemical and organic treatment techniques to turn out leathers of different thickness, composition, coloration and design for a wide variety of markets. The advantage for buyers, of course, was the knowledge that any manner of product could be made at the drop of a hat in Santa Croce.

The small firms were also able to keep costs down without any loss of productive efficiency, via different mechanisms of co-operation. One example is the joint purchase of raw materials in order to minimize on price. Another is the pooling of resources to employ export consultants. The main device for cost flexibility, however, has been the consolidation of an elaborate system of putting-out between tanners and independent subcontractors (often ex-workers). The production cycle in leather tanning is composed of 15–20 phases, of which at least half are subcontracted to task-specialist firms (e.g. removal of hair and fat from the uncured skins, splitting the hide, flattening and drying). Constantly at work, and specializing in operations which are most easily mechanized, the subcontractors have been able to reduce drastically the cost of individual tasks at the same time as providing the tanners with the numerical flexibility demanded by their market. This articulate division of labour among and between locally based tanners and subcontractors, combining simultaneously the advantages of complementarity between specialists and competition between the numerous firms operating in identical market niches, is perhaps the key factor of success.

But other factors have also played their part. One is area specialization. Santa Croce, like other industrial districts past and present, is a one-product town which offers the full range of agglomeration and external economies involved in local excellence along the entire filiere of activities associated with leather tanning. In the area there are the warehouses of major international traders of raw and semi-finished leather as well as the offices of independent import agents, brokers and customs specialists. There are the depots of the major multinational chemical giants as well as locally owned companies selling paints, dyes, chemicals and customer-specific treatment formulae to the tanners. There are at least three savings banks which have consistently provided easy and informal access to finance. There are several manufacturers of plant and machinery, tailor-made for the leather tanning industry, and there is a ready supply base for second-hand equipment and maintenance services. There are several scores of independent sales representatives, export agents and buyers of finished leather in the area. The local Association of Leather Tanners, the mayor's office, the bigger local entrepreneurs and the Pisa offices of the Ministry of Industry and Trade also act as collective agents to further local interests at national and international trade fairs. There are several international haulage companies and shipping agents capable of rapidly transporting goods to any part of the world. There is, at the end of the value-added chain, a company which makes glue from the fat extracted from the hides and skins. Finally, there is a water purification depot collectively funded by the leather tanners, the effluence of which is sold to a company which converts the non-toxic solids into fertilizer. All in an area of ten square kilometres!

The entire community in Santa Croce, in one way or another, is associated with leather tanning. This provides new opportunities, through spin-off, along the value-added chain, which in deepening and refining the social division of labour guarantees the local supply of virtually all the ingredients necessary for entrepreneurial success in quality-based and volatile markets. To use the language of neoclassical economics, over and above firm-specific and asset-specific advantages, there exists an area-wide asset which individual entrepreneurship draws upon. This 'valorization' of the milieu is a product of the progressive deepening of the social division of labour (vertical disintegration) at the local level. The area produces not only specialized skills and artisan capability, but also powerful external economies of agglomeration and a constant supply of industry-specific information, ideas, inputs, machinery and services – Marshall's 'industrial atmosphere'.

Thus far, the success of Santa Croce as a Marshallian industrial district has been ascribed to two broad sets of factors. One is the 'fortuitous' combination, since the early 1970s, of new market opportunities (the fashionwear sector) and a minimum set of inherited local capabilities (leather-tanning skills, a craft culture and so on). The second is the progressive vertical disintegration of the division of labour and its local containment. But there is also a third factor which has come to play a key role in safeguarding the success of the area. This is the institutionalization, at the local level, of individual sectional interests (e.g. the Association of Leather Tanners, the Association of Subcontractors, savings banks, the mayor's office, trade union branches, etc.), as well as a sense of common purpose which draws upon Santa Croce's specialization in one industry and the intricate interdependences of a vertically disintegrated production system. Not only has this prevented the growth of rogue forms of individual profiteering which may destabilize the system of mutual interdependence, but it has also created a mechanism for collectivizing opportunities and costs as well as ensuring the rapid transmission of information and knowledge across the industrial district.

The 'collectivization of governance' has been of particular importance for the industrial district in recent years, as it has tried to cope with new pressures. By the mid-1980s, a honeymoon period of spectacular success for virtually all enterprises was coming to an end. This was the result of growing competition in international markets from fashionwear-oriented tanneries in Southeast Asia, a decline in demand from the Italian footwear industry, big price increases coupled with shortages in the availability of uncured skins and hides, and new costs attached to the introduction of environmental controls on effluence discharge. These are problems which have affected the entire community, problems which different interest groups have not been able to resolve individually. Resulting collective responses have ranged from joint funding by the tanners of an effluence treatment plant and multi-source funding (involving tanners, subcontractors, a local bank and the regional authorities) of an information service centre which offers advice on market trends, management skills and information technology, through to frequent and heated debates in the bar of the central piazza on new trends affecting the industry. How successful these efforts will be is not to be known. What matters, however, is that Santa Croce continues to possess a local institutional capability to respond collectively and swiftly to new market pressures and to steer the evolution of the industrial district in a particular direction.

This said, however, there is already some evidence to suggest that, into the 1990s, the organization of industry in Santa Croce will be 'post-Marshallian'; that is, less locally confined and less vertically disintegrated. Increasingly, the trend is for tanners to import semi-finished leather, owing to difficulties in obtaining uncured hides and skins. If this practice becomes the norm, more than half of the production cycle will be eliminated from the area, to the detriment of locally based hide importers, subcontractors and chemical treatment firms. There is also a threat of 'forward' internationalization of the division of labour. A handful of companies – the oldest and the most powerful – have begun to open distribution outlets overseas as well as tanneries, usually through joint ventures, in countries either producing hides and skins or promising growth in the leather goods industries. They have also gone into the business of selling turnkey tanneries[3] for the East European countries – a development which stands to threaten Italian tanneries, including those in Santa Croce, if the finished leather ends up being imported by the domestic leather goods industry.

The risk, then, is that Santa Croce will come to perform only specific tasks in an internationally integrated value-added chain, thus threatening a shakeout of firms dependent upon tasks no longer performed locally. Through a narrowing of functional competencies, the area's industrial system will become less vertically disintegrated. Such a narrowing runs the risk of threatening the institutional synergy and richness of activity which hitherto have secured the area's success as an industrial district. It is also possible that, with functional simplification and the offer of larger and better premises more recently by the local authority in its new Structure Plan, the larger tanners will seek to internalize individual production tasks more than before. Initial signals of such a development include the recommendation by the Associations of Leather Tanners and Subcontractors that transfers to the new industrial zone involve horizontal mergers, stricter loan scrutiny by banks of applications for business start-ups and the grouping of firms into business consortia in order to maximize on firm-level scale economies in such activities as purchasing and marketing.

If the twin processes of internationalization of the division of labour and vertical integration at the local level become the dominant trend, Santa Croce will lose its current integrity as a self-contained 'regional' economy. But, and this is the point, it will continue to remain a central node within the leather-tanning industry. Twenty years of Marshallian growth have made Santa Croce into a nerve centre of artisan ability, product and design innovation and commercial acumen within the international fashion-oriented leather goods filiere. This unrivalled expertise will guarantee its survival as a centre of design and commercial excellence, even if the activities of the 'hand' are reduced or internalized. The open question is whether, without the hand, the head will lose its might or successfully engineer a transition into other industrial ventures.

Marshall in London: the City and global financial services

Throughout much of the nineteenth century, and well into the twentieth century, the City of London[4] could have been characterized as a classical Marshallian industrial district. During this period it consisted of a network of small financial service firms, and a set of markets and market-clearing mechanisms, in close contact with and close proximity to one another, employing as many as 200,000 people. These firms and markets consistently minimized transaction costs through social and spatial propinquity, creating an industrial 'soup' rather than an industrial atmosphere, an upper-middle-class craft community of quite extraordinary contact intensity (Thrift and Leyshon, 1992).

This 'old City' was dynamized by the dictates of mercantile capital accumulation as described by Marx in the *Grundrisse*; that is, on the one hand its members strove towards endless expansion in the search for new products for old markets or new markets for old products so as to gain comparative advantage over rivals and, on the other, they tried to enlist non-economic power to regulate the system and to give monopolistic advantages to its members (usually relating to price competition). This regime of accumulation could survive precisely because of its mode of social regulation. Indeed, in a sense, it was the mode of regulation that generated the regime of accumulation. This statement is borne out by the following observations.

First, the City was run on 'mesocorporatist' (Cawson, 1985; Moran, 1991) lines: that is, it was a largely self-regulating system of collective governance with the Bank of England acting to protect it from pluralist regulatory systems and politics. 'Representation and regulation were fused: the associations and institutions in City markets had authority because this was recognized by the Bank and because of this they were able to operate restrictive practices benefiting their members' (Moran, 1991, 63). Second, the City was tightly socially integrated. All its key workers were drawn from highly specific social backgrounds based on clearly drawn divides of class, gender and ethnicity, and this social specificity was reinforced throughout the workers' lives by various socializing processes at work and after work (the firms themselves, often partnerships, the markets, the livery companies, the Masonic lodges, the clubs and so on). This commonality of background maximized face-to-face communication in a small area, generated a 'collective consciousness' or common 'gentlemanly' discourses, and also afforded quick assessments of character and, effectively, economic viability. Thus the old City was a trust-maximizing system and the knowledge structure was, in effect, the social structure. (That said, much of the City's economic dynamism and innovative capacity came from members of the City excluded from its mainstream – refugees, Jews, etc. – who were Weberian pariah capitalists in the strongest sense. It was those who were outside the system and therefore able to 'see' it who were most able to innovate (Chapman, 1984).)

Third, the City's markets were large and liquid, although in comparison with the later period they were based on comparatively few products and relatively slow rates of innovation. Again, to participate in these markets it was often important to know the right people; the right gentlemanly discourses and the right occupational languages. And fourth, the City was tightly concentrated in space, the result of the ability of the key mesocorporatist institutions such as the Bank of England and the various markets to demand propinquity, the existence of various market-clearing mechanisms with quite restricted spatial ranges, and the peculiar importance of face-to-face transactions, an importance which can be interpreted as both a cause and a result of the dense spatial arrangement (Pryke, 1991). (Indirect systems of communication such as the telegraph and the telephone were a feature of the City from an early period, but these probably had the effect of strengthening rather than weakening social interaction.)

Thus, the old City of London was a protected, self-regulating, socially and culturally specific enclave able to wield very considerable social power (Ingham, 1984). It was, of course, tied in, in the strongest possible way, to the world economy of the time, but here was a case of the 'the local going global' (Thrift, 1987a, 1990b; Thrift and Leyshon, 1991; Pryke, 1991).

Since the late 1950s or early 1960s there has been a sea change in the way that the City of London has been able to go about its business, sufficient to be able to write of the emergence of a 'new City'. In particular, at least five major changes have threatened the City's integrity as an industrial district. The first change has been the emergence, through successive rounds of corporate restructuring, of larger and larger oligopolistic financial service firms, whether in the form of institutional investors (such as pension funds and insurance companies), securities houses or banks. Many of these firms are substantial multinational corporations that span the globe. The second change has been in the nature of international financial markets, which have altered in a number of ways. To begin with, they have become increasingly international in both space and time, often operating around the clock. They have also become, through a massive investment in telecommunications capacity, increasingly electronic, which means that more and more communication is taking place at a distance, with some markets becoming almost entirely decentralized. Most importantly, perhaps, many new fictitious capital markets are increasingly based on securitized products – not only bonds and securities but also various derivatives which demand new 'disintermediated' relationships between financial service firms.

The third change has been in the mode of regulation of the City. As Moran (1991) points out, neither the word 'deregulation' nor 'reregulation' adequately describes what has occurred. What has occurred has been the progressive accretion[5] of a more carefully codified, institutionalized and legalistic mesocorporatism, forced on the City by specific market circumstances, by a State succumbing to American pressure for change and by the diffusion of an American ideology of correct and incorrect practice. As Moran puts it, 'The story of the financial services revolution is the story of the rapid creation of new institutions struggling for regulatory jurisdiction, the development of increasingly complex and unclear rules and the creation of growing numbers of regulators inside and outside firms, all quarrelling over the meaning of an expanding, contradictory and unclear body of jurisprudence' (Moran, 1991, p. 134). In other words, formal contracts have replaced implicit contracts.

A fourth change has occurred in the City's social structure. It has become more open in terms of class, gender and ethnicity – although no doubt it is still not as open as might be wished for (Rajan, 1988, 1991; Thrift and Leyshon, 1991). Socially specific selection of personnel of the old style has certainly been retained by a few small parts of the City, but these are increasingly sidelined. The City's social structure is now more mixed and more keyed into the knowledge structure in financial services. The fifth change has been in the

City's rate of product innovation (which in turn has been facilitated by the investment in telecommunications technologies). Innovation in products is now much more rapid than before, but they are also more likely to fail (de Cecco, 1987). For example, of the nineteen futures contracts launched by the London International Financial Futures Exchange, eight have failed. Failure of products is a particular problem in financial services because liquidity and success are very tightly connected and because products and markets are so tightly interconnected.

In this process of multiple economic and social change, the City, like the financial services industry as a whole, has moved from a mercantile capitalist model to something more closely resembling an industrial model of production or, at least, an industrialized mercantile model of production. But, given the scope of the changes that have taken place and the undoubted loss of social power that they describe, one might well ask why the City of London has persisted at all. Why has something very like an industrial district, still relatively socially and spatially concentrated, persisted in and near to the confines of the old City of London, especially in the face of competition from other European financial centres?

The answer to this question can be related to the imperatives of the new global financial services production filiere. In its old incarnation, the City was the result of the local going global. In its new incarnation, the City is a result of the global going local. In particular, the City survives for three related reasons. First, it is a centre of representation. The City has become one of the chief points of surveillance and scripting of the global financial services filiere; London is where the stories are. Thus, much of the *world's* financial press (which has also rapidly globalized) operates from or near to the City; so does much research analysis, information processing and so on (Kynaston, 1985; Driver and Gillespie, 1991). The concentration of this activity in one place has the advantage that the City can watch and script the global financial services filiere industry by watching itself. Equally important, the City represents an important part of the knowledge structure of world financial services. Although in principle these collective assets could be decentralized, the fact is that it is still more convenient to have this massive body of knowledge, much of which is highly specialized, easily accessible in one place.

This point relates to the second reason for the City's persistence as an industrial district: its role as a centre of interaction. The City is a social centre of the global corporate networks of the financial service industry, with a large throughflow of workers from other countries, and people simply meeting. It is accepted in this role partly because of the concentration of headquarters and regional headquarters of financial services corporations in and around the City, partly because of a symbolic value which it explicitly plays up through 'trappings of trust' such as 'traditional' oak-lined meeting rooms (the City is still symbolically equated with financial services in a powerful way throughout the world), partly because of its accessibility in real and electronic space to markets and firms, and partly because of its knowledge base (which means that the wherewithal is always at hand to watch and script, buy and sell, borrow and lend). Thus the City is still a vital meeting place in which important deals can be made, issues marketed, coalitions formed, syndicates established and trust/ implicit contracts cemented.

The third reason for the city's persistence is as a proving ground for product innovation. An important characteristic of financial service products is that product innovation and marketing are very closely tied together. A product survives only if a primary market can be established, and usually a secondary market too (not even counting the derivatives markets which are now so important). Thus a product cannot take off unless it is aggressively marketed, usually to a quite specific set of people in large investment institutions and companies. A place like the City allows new products to be evolved and tested quickly and efficiently, since there is always sufficient liquidity on tap and sufficient placement power available to assess an innovation's worth. More than this, the availability in one place of representatives of many investment institutions and companies means that products can be easily socialized and customized. Many derivatives products first started life as quite specific products for quite specific customers.[6]

Clearly these three reasons are closely interrelated. For example, product innovation depends on a 'thick' discursive atmosphere, on requisite knowledge structures and on availability of custom.

To conclude, the City is still an industrial district, but it is an industrial district which depends on fewer, larger firms, which still need a place from which and with which they can represent and analyse their world, a place where they can meet in order to add flesh and trust to electronically mediated personae, and a place which can be counted on to continue to invent new products and markets. Clearly, the City faces, and will continue to face, challenges from other financial centres, especially European financial centres such as Frankfurt and Paris (see Leyshon and Thrift, 1992). In part, this will depend on the social power it can still muster in what has become a complex geopolitical game, but in part it will also clearly continue to depend on its constitution as a local and global social space.

Conclusion

The argument of the first half of this paper is that there does not appear to be any inexorable trend towards the localization of production. This is not to deny that the trend towards vertical disintegration may have become more pronounced than in the past, nor is it to play down the significance that 'networking' may have in encouraging the resurgence along Marshallian lines of some regions as self-contained units of economic development. Against this, however, it has to be stressed that networking is also a global phenomenon, one which has come to coexist with, rather than replace, more orthodox forms of internationalization. Contemporary organizational change is very much a process of layering of new global corporate networks upon old international production hierarchies.

In this age of intensifying global hierarchies and global corporate networks, with both, as proposed in this paper, representing a reworked centralization of corporate command and control, it can only be a truism to propose that local economic prospects are becoming more dependent upon global corporate organizational forces. In such a context, it is difficult to think of localities as independent regional economies which participate freely, as the Marshallians would have it, in a global system integrated only by trade. But, then, what of the argument that an integral component of globalization is more localization of corporate activity, as companies turn decentralization and locational proximity into key conditions for flexibility and innovation? It cannot be denied that the growth of networking could lead to greater functional and operational decentralization down the corporate hierarchy as well as greater reliance on local external linkages for profitable production. However, and this is the point, the rediscovery of place is occurring only in a quite restricted set of localities, and efforts to encourage Marshallian growth in other areas through the formation of highly localized production systems are likely to fail. The examples of Santa Croce and the City of London illustrate only too clearly that the conditions for such growth are difficult to capture through even the most innovative policy measures, *unless certain basic structures are already in place*. These include a critical mass of know-how, skills and finance in rapidly evolving growth markets, a socio-cultural and institutional infrastructure capable of scripting and funding a common industrial agenda, and entrepreneurial traditions encouraging growth through vertical disintegration of the division of labour.

Collective intervention, both private and public, may be able to build upon and manipulate these basic structures, but it cannot generate them. Such an awareness of the limits of policy intervention is, in our view, important. Otherwise, typically Marshallian efforts to regenerate local economies through locally regulated ventures such as efforts to strengthen links between firms and between business and other local institutions (e.g. training colleges, development authorities, etc.) run the risk of doing little more than legitimizing a false belief in the possibility of achieving solutions for what are global problems beyond local control.

Somewhat bleakly, then, we are forced to conclude that the majority of localities may need to abandon the illusion of the possibility of self-sustaining 'growth' and accept the constraints laid down by the process of increasingly globally integrated industrial development and growth. Concretely, this may simply amount to pursuing those interregional and international linkages (trade, technology transfer, production, etc.) which will be of most benefit to the locality in question. It may also involve – and on this point, the literature on industrial districts is helpful – upgrading the position of the locality within international corporate hierarchies and networks by improvements to a locality's skill, research, supply and infrastructure base in order to attract 'better-quality' branch investments.

This, of course, is not much of a solution. On the other hand, it has to be stressed that as things are today even the neo-Marshallian nodes of global corporate networks are finding it difficult to retain their status. Furthermore, it has to be noted that the stakes for achieving the status of a node at the apex of an international filiere are truly high, and must be discounted for the vast majority of local areas which either lack or have lost the social and cultural infrastructure for innovation and transaction-rich competition. *Plus ça change* in the post-Fordist economy?

Notes

1 These two concepts, it should be noted, are not interchangeable. Flexible speciali-zation is a concept deployed to describe transformations in the production process stimulated by new technological, skill and market developments. In contrast, the term flexible accumulation, drawing upon the Regulation Approach developed in France as well as a recent essay of David Harvey (Harvey, 1989), refers to a broader macroeconomic design for the twenty-first century, transcending the 'Fordist' regime of accumulation which was built upon the pillars of mass consumption, mass pro-duction and Keynesian regulation of the economy.

2 Some of the exponents of the localization thesis, for example Allen Scott and Michael Storper (Scott, 1991; Storper, 1991), have begun in their more recent work to talk of the future as a complex juxtaposition of local and global production networks. However, this development still does not draw them sufficiently far away from the localization thesis to warrant a reformulation of their position in the debate on the geography of flexible accumulation.

3 These are factories in which all aspects of the plant, including technology and support services, are supplied by the seller, thus allowing the purchaser to produce the commodity at the 'turn of a key'.

4 Clearly, over time, the City of London has consisted of a heterogeneous set of markets and firms. In this necessarily abbreviated account we have had to treat these markets and firms as rather more homogeneous than they actually were, but the contact intensity between all these markets and firms is not in doubt (see, for example, Dunning and Morgan, 1971).

5 Thus, the City's banking sector underwent its main period of deregulation in the 1960s, while the securities markets were not deregulated until the 1980s in the process known as 'Big Bang'. One of the chief reasons for taking the late 1950s or early 1960s as the dividing line between an old and a new City is, of course, that it was in this period that deregulation first started to bite, and with it came a progressive loss of social power.

6 This is not, of course, to suggest that financial products always need to be provided locally, and it is certainly not to suggest that they will continue in localized fashion if they are successful.

References

Adler, P. and Adler, P. (eds) 1984: *The social dynamics of financial markets*. Green-wich, CT: JAI Press.

Amin, A. 1989: Flexible specialisation and small firms in Italy: myths and realities. *Antipode* 21(1), 13–34.

Amin, A. and Dietrich, M. 1991: From hierarchy to 'hierarchy': the dynamics of contemporary corporate restructuring in Europe. In Amin, A. and Dietrich M. (eds), *Towards a new Europe?* Aldershot: Edward Elgar.

Amin, A. and Robins, K. 1990: The re-emergence of regional economies? The mythical geography of flexible accumulation. *Environment and Planning D: Society and Space* 8(1), 7–34.

Bianchini, F. 1990: The 'Third Italy': model or myth? Mimeo. Centre for Urban Studies, University of Liverpool.

Block, F. 1990: *Post industrial possibilities*. Berkeley, CA: University of California Press.

Cawson, A. 1985: Varieties of corporatism: the importance of the meso-level of interest intermediation. In Cawson, A. (ed.), *Organised interests and the state*, London: Sage.

Chapman, S. 1984: *The rise of merchant banking*. London: Allen & Unwin.

Cooke, P. and Imrie, R. 1989: Little victories: local economic development in European regions. *Entrepreneurship and Regional Development* 1(4), 313–27.

de Cecco, M. 1987: *Money and innovation*. Basil Blackwell, Oxford.

Driver, S. and Gillespie, A. 1991: Spreading the word? Communications technologies and the geography of magazine print publishing. Newcastle PICT Working Paper I, Centre for Urban and Regional Development Studies, University of Newcastle.

Dunning, J. H. and Morgan, K. 1971: *An economic study of the City of London*. Allen & Unwin, London.

Gertler, M. 1988: The limits to flexibility: comments on the post-Fordist vision of production and its geography. *Transactions of the Institute of British Geographers* 13, 419–32.

Giddens, A. 1990: *Consequences of modernity*. Polity Press, Cambridge.

Giddens, A. 1991: *Modernity and self-identity*. Polity Press, Cambridge.

Glasmeier, A. 1991: Technological discontinuities and flexible production networks: the case of Switzerland and the world watch industry. Mimeo. Department of Geography, University of Texas at Austin.

Harrison, B. 1990: Industrial districts: old wine in new bottles? Working Paper 90–35, School of Urban and Public Affairs, Carnegie Mellon University, Pittsburgh.

Harvey, D. 1989: *The condition of postmodernity: An inquiry into the origins of cultural change*. Basil Blackwell, Oxford.

Held, D. 1991: Democracy, the nation state and the global system. *Economy and Society* 20(12), 138–72.

Hirst, P. and Zeitlin, J. 1989: Flexible specialisation and the competitive failure of UK manufacturing. *Political Quarterly* 60(3), 164–78.

Hirst, P. and Zeitlin, J. 1991: Flexible specialisation vs. post-Fordism: theory, evidence and policy implications. *Economy and Society* 20(1), 1–56.

Ingham, G. 1984: *Capitalism divided*. Macmillan, London.

Jacquemin, A., Buiges, P. and Ilzkovitz, F. 1989: Horizontal mergers and competition policy in the European Community. *European Economy* 40 (May), CEC Directorate-General for Economic and Financial Affairs.

Kynaston, D. 1985: *The 'Financial Times'. A centenary history*. Viking, London.

Leyshon, A. and Thrift, N. J. 1992: European integration and the international financial system. *Environment and Planning A* 24, 49–81.

Marceau, J. 1989: *A family business? The making of an international business elite*. Cambridge University Press, Cambridge.

Moran, M. 1991: *The politics of the financial services revolution*. Macmillan, London.

Offe, K. and Wiesenthal, J. 1979: Two logics of collective action. In Zeitlin, M. (ed.), *Power and social theory*, Greenwich, CT: JAI Press.

Peck, J. 1991: Labour and agglomeration: vertical disintegration, skill formation and flexibility in local labour markets. Mimeo. School of Geography, University of Manchester.

Piore, M. and Sabel, C. F. 1984: *The second industrial divide*. Basic Books, New York.

Pryke, M. 1991: An international city going global. *Environment and Planning D: Society and Space* 9, 197–222.

Rajan, A. 1988: *Create or abdicate?* London: Witherley Press.

Rajan, A. 1991: *Capital people*. London: Industrial Society.

Sabel, C. F. 1989: Flexible specialisation and the re-emergence of regional economies. In Hirst, P. and Zeitlin, J. (eds), *Reversing industrial decline? Industrial structure and policies in Britain and her competitors*. Oxford: Berg.

Sayer, A. 1989: Post-Fordism in question. *International Journal of Urban and Regional Research* 13(4), 666–95.

Scott, A. J. 1988: *New industrial spaces: Flexible production organisation and regional development in North America and Western Europe*. London: Pion.

Scott, A. J. 1991: The role of large producers in industrial districts: a case study of high-technology systems houses in southern California. UCLA Research Paper in Economic and Urban Geography, No. 2 (February).

Storper, M. 1989: The transition to flexible specialisation in the US film industry: the division of labour, external economies and the crossing of industrial divides. *Cambridge Journal of Economics* 13(2), 273–305.

Storper, M. 1991: Technology districts and international trade: the limits to globalisation in an age of flexible production. Mimeo. Graduate School of Urban Planning, University of California, Los Angeles.

Storper, M. and A. J. Scott 1989: The geographical foundations and social regulation of flexible production complexes. In Wolch, J. and Dear M. (eds), *The power of geography: How territory shapes social life*. Winchester, MA: Unwin Hyman.

Strange, S. 1988: *States and markets*. London: Pinter.

Strange, S. 1991: An eclectic approach. In Murphy, C. N. and Tooze, R. (eds), *The new international political economy*. Boulder, CO: Lynne Rienner.

Thrift, N. J. 1987: The fixers: the urban geography of international commercial capital. In J. Henderson and M. Castells (eds), *Global restructuring and territorial development*. London: Sage.

Thrift, N. 1989: The perils of transition models. *Environment and Planning D: Society and Space* 7, 127–9.

Thrift, N. 1990a: The perils of the international financial system. *Environment and Planning A* 22, 1135–7.

Thrift, N. 1990b: Doing global regional geography. In R. J. Johnston and J. A. Hoekveld (eds), *Regional geography*. London: Routledge.

Thrift, N. and Leyshon, A. 1991: In the wake of money. In Budd, L. and Whinnster, C. S. (eds), *Global finance and urban living*. London: Routledge.

Thrift, N. and Leyshon, A. 1992: *Making money*. London: Routledge.

Todling, F. 1991: The geography of innovation: transformation from Fordism towards post-Fordism? Mimeo. Institute for Urban and Regional Studies, University of Economics and Business Administration, Vienna.

Tornqvist, G. 1991: Swedish contact routes in the European urban landshape. Mimeo. Department of Social and Economic Geography, University of Lund.

Zukin, S. and Dimaggio, P. (eds) 1990: *Structures of capital: The social organisation of the economy*. Cambridge: Cambridge University Press.

8   John Allen and Michael Pryke,
'The Production of Service Space'

Excerpts from: *Environment and Planning D: Society and Space* 12, 453–75 (1994)

Introduction

As the dust jacket to the English translation of *The production of space*[1] points out, Henri Lefebvre's work 'spans some sixty years and includes original work on a diverse range of subjects, from dialectical materialism to architecture, urbanism and the experience of everyday life'. *The production of space* connects with each of these subjects and, according to some, it would be deplorable to interpret Lefebvre's insights on space outside of his wider interests and philosophical preoccupations. It is not our intention, however, to convey the full, meandering range of Lefebvre's thought, nor to catalogue his works. Others have done that: within the discipline of human geography, Ed Soja in particular has drawn attention to the breadth of Lefebvre's writing. Rather, our aim is more modest, in that we wish to convey something of the richness of Lefebvre's analysis of social space, as well as its limitations (to be found mainly in the notes), and to illustrate both aspects through the abstract space of finance. In this case, it is the abstract space of the City of London which provides the illustrative context.

In our view, there are three related insights in *The production of space* which can extend and deepen our understanding of social space. The first is the attention that Lefebvre pays to the *relations* between two forms of social space – representations of space and representational spaces – and the spatial practices which circumscribe them.[2] According to Lefebvre, representations of space are the dominant spaces in any society and today are perhaps best exemplified by the more formal, abstract representations that find their true expression in the rationality of the planned urban location or the meticulous design of an architectural project. In contrast, representational spaces are regarded as 'lived' spaces. By this, we understand Lefebvre to mean spaces that take their shape literally through the daily routine of 'users'. Thus, the very way in which spaces are imagined represents a means of living in those spaces. Such spaces may be public or private, they may overlay or disrupt the dominant spaces, or indeed they may take shape alongside them. Above all, representational spaces should be understood in *relation* to the well-defined representations of space.

Spatial practices give shape to both forms of social space in a multitude of ways, from the routine walks which endow a place with meaning to the global networks which bind and code places on opposite sides of the world. The sheer variety of spatial practices is perhaps less important to note, however, than the degree of competence and ability with which people produce social space through their spatial practice. There is an element of *performance* involved, whereby specific practices attempt to construct and maintain a particular sense of place, and in so doing limit alternative interpretations. We will elaborate both on this aspect and on the different forms of social space in the second and third sections of the paper.

The second insight of Lefebvre which deserves closer examination is the notion that the two forms of social space and their associated spatial practices may *contradict* or be in tension with one another. The idea of spatial contradictions may strike some as a rather alien notion, yet it does convey the possibility of certain spaces embodying a clash of social interests. Contradictions *of* space, in Lefebvre's terms, for example, may entail a challenge to or a subversion of a particular dominant coding of space by a less powerful 'user' of that space or indeed a challenge from outside by an equally powerful potential 'user'.[3]

This leads directly to the third insight of Lefebvre, which is the stress that he places upon *power* in his analyses of space and, in particular, to the notions of *dominated* and *appropriated spaces*. As a brief aside, it is perhaps important at the outset to acknowledge that his account of power is itself unexceptional; what is particularly fruitful about the analysis is that it draws attention to the ways in which spatial practices produce and secure a dominant space – although never with utter success. More specifically, it draws attention to how a dominant space is achieved and maintained through adaptation and manoeuvre: the modes of power involved, the sites of power, and the social relationships through which power is secured. On the basis of his analysis of power alone, Lefebvre's account of the production of social space merits further discussion.

In the remainder of the paper, we wish to show how Lefebvre's approach to social space may help us to disentangle the social spaces which constitute the City of London. In the next section, we look at how the City of London achieved and maintained a dominant representation of itself as an abstract space of finance, in the first instance through a coding based upon the spatial practices of a 'gentlemanly capitalism' rooted in an imperial past and, latterly, through the trading practices and networks of global finance. Following that, we look at how 'other' spaces have developed *within* the abstract space of finance whose codes have the *potential* to disrupt the dominant form rather than simply rest alongside. These are the representational spaces of a contract workforce; that is, those spaces which draw their meaning and symbolism from the everyday practices of those who clean, cater within, and secure the abstract space of finance.

The abstract space of finance

As noted above, modern social space according to Lefebvre is characterized by its abstract quality. Abstract here refers to a social abstraction; that is, a representation of space as uniform, coherent, devoid of difference.[4] As a *representation* of space it is an expression of certain social relations or, more pointedly, the impression of sameness is something that is produced and secured rather than simply given. Thus, in the case of finance, the abstract space of the City of London has secured its dominance over time through its ability continually to mould the space around it in its own image. The City *is* finance, and the traces of other uses and routine practices which give meaning to particular spaces within the buildings of the Square Mile have historically been sidelined or pushed out of the frame, so to speak. Indeed, this is even more striking if one looks at the City's latest built form – which at first sight presents a formidable representation of the homogeneity of global finance. This is the goal as it were of any abstract space, which, if we are to take Lefebvre literally, attempts to repress the diversity of space in order to convey a singular image.[5]

Abstract space, therefore, and the abstract space of finance in particular, are bound up with *practices* of power. The emphasis here is intentional as it is not the possession of power in itself which is critical, but rather the strategies through which a dominant coding of space is achieved and the mode in which it is secured. Within the City, the mode of power is not simply economic as expressed in the speed and magnitude of monetary flows, but also representational – through the abolition of meanings, the manipulation of codings, the translation of tradition and the seduction of the built form. As a *representation of space*, the City may be understood through its spatial codes, as something which may be read formally and deciphered, as well as apprehended through the ear (the near silence of the old finance 'cathedrals' and the hectic noise of the dealing floors, for example) or the gaze (the visual gestures of the City's built form, for instance).[6]

The production of a dominant coding, however, and the ability to secure it through the smothering of difference are attributable to the spatial practices of the City's institutions. The ability to endow a site with meaning is an expression of power, but it is the spatial practices of the City, their repetition (or rhythm, as Lefebvre emphasizes[7]) and variety, which signify what may and may not take place in and around the various institutions that make up the City and who is 'out of place' and indeed time.

Monumental space

Since its inception, from the late seventeenth century through to the present day, the City of London has shaped and been shaped by the world's financial system. Up to the middle of the present century, the City occupied a critical position within the networks of international finance and owed much of its formative role and prestige to the days when it controlled the lines of finance and trade which lay behind the British Empire (Michie, 1992) (see Figure 8.1) From the City's collective roots in the Royal Exchange and the coffee houses of the seventeenth century, such as Lloyd's and Jonathan's, come certain embryonic spatial practices: its inward-looking character, its cohesive 'clubbiness', the dress codes, the web of gentlemen's agreements. Together these practices made it possible, until comparatively recently, to recognize the insider – 'the

Fig. 8.1 Abstract space of finance: Sterling days (courtesy of the authors)

right sort of person to be around and doing business in the City' – as well as spot the outsider (not only in class terms, but gender too).[8] Indeed, until the 1980s and the onset of global financial practices in the City, the legacy of past spatial practices weighed heavily on the daily routines of City space, encouraging change and innovation only if they met a system of oblique references that signified the continuation of best practice and tradition. Fostered by legislation, the extraordinarily large measure of self-regulation practised by City institutions enabled a kind of 'gentlemanly capitalism' to operate at the more leisurely pace of sterling and to resist the rhythms of external change (Cain and Hopkins, 1986, 1987). Control over the pace and tempo of financial activity was the key, not just to the stability of spatial practice in the City, but also to keep out those who were clearly not part of the upper-class social network. Despite changes in its composition, especially after 1850 with the rise of the new moneyed class and the decline of landed wealth, the City's social network was effective in maintaining its social space. As an international centre of finance (as opposed to a global centre), the City for much of that time, in the spirit of Lefebvre, may be referred to as a *monumental space*; that is, a space which offered its members 'an image of that membership'.[9]

For Lefebvre, the defining characteristic of monumental space is not the chain of signs and symbols which may be read from the appearance of certain buildings or sites, important as they are, but rather the ability to prescribe a certain use for a space, and the manner and style in which it is used.[10] Prior to the City of London's transition from an international to a global space, the City was notably a collection of prohibited spaces, with social as well as physical barriers limiting membership.[11] At the heart of the old spatial matrix, the Bank of England, as the 'magical power' of this central space,[12] imposed a series of expectations upon successive generations as to how different spaces may be used and indeed who was 'fit and proper' to use them. In so doing, it defused the threat of alternative practices posed by such institutions as foreign banks that wished to enter the City's space in growing numbers in the early post-war period.

For example, between 1694 and 1974, the Bank of England supervised change in the banking sector through the practices of the Discount Office. In terms of style, the supervision was informal, with an emphasis upon a code of gentlemanly conduct: a system of professional ethics and practices which ostensibly had evolved over two centuries in line with changing circumstances. On the presentation of their annual reports to the Discount Office, for instance, the banks in the City would outline the business they had been doing that year, eliciting comment from the Bank of England's representative. 'There was not much talking about figures at all. And that in itself was not necessarily to be despised because, what it was, was the opportunity, very often to say things that were worrying them in the City – ranging from ethics to types of business that was about, to who was next door, to people who turned up in the City whom they didn't think were really the right people to be about' (Pryke, 1991, pp. 207–8). In this informal way, the Bank of England was able to monitor and shape the practices and, indeed, the location of banks coming into the Square Mile. As a *site* of power, the Square Mile accorded a certain legitimacy to the representation of financial space produced by City institutions.

Individual buildings within the old spatial matrix, such as the Stock Exchange, the Baltic Exchange, and the old Lloyd's of London building, also expressed a form of social exclusion, in this instance, as Lefebvre would have it, through their 'acoustic, gestural and ritual movements'.[13] The Baltic Exchange, for example, which dates back formally to the establishment of the Baltic Club in 1823 and before that to the City's coffee houses, was (and is to be once again on reopening) characterized by a set of spatial practices which were inextricably bound up with its own monumental space. The animated space of the Baltic, which was designed to define both membership and practice, had a trading floor of some 20,000 ft^2 which was overlooked by a large central dome supported by marble columns. At the edge of the floor were raised rostrums, from which 'waiters', figures from an interpreted past, could summon individual members to the floor. Trading on the floor could be 'measured by the ear': the sounds and voices recording the level of bid and counter-bid, although rarely rising above that of a gentlemanly babble.[14]

Similarly, at the old Lloyd's building, a sense of membership was offered by its monumental space. Anthony Sampson, writing about the Lloyd's building, captured that blend of symbolic practices which enabled the City's insurance markets to change, yet remain exclusive, through time (Sampson, 1969, pp. 450–1):

The Room contains a typical mixture of old and new devices. In the middle is a raised rostrum containing a man known as a 'caller', in a big red robe with a wide black collar looking like a town-crier, reciting the names of brokers through a microphone . . . when a broker is wanted, one of the 'waiters' (who stand around the Room in scarlet uniform) writes on a 'telewriter' and the name is reproduced by an electronic hand in front of the 'caller', who then calls for the broker. There are no typewriters, computers, dictaphones, teleprinters or girls in the Room. . . . Round the Room are anterooms, dining rooms and committee rooms, all built since the war in a heavy style which emphasises the country-gentleman image of Lloyd's. . . . The names form a proud club. . . . Old school ties dominate the names: people working at Lloyd's who are not members – known as substitutes – are kept severely separate, and they even have their own 'substitutes' lavatory.

Alongside many of the City's commercial banks, these old finance 'cathedrals' generated an atmosphere of power which, even when empty, excluded others by their very silence.[15] Indeed, they exhibited a will to power in a direct and transparent fashion; one that was both seductive and restrictive. With the coming of global finance, however, the ability of this form of gentlemanly power to meet change has diminished somewhat. To be precise, it is not change in and of itself which is at issue, but rather the pace of change which has accompanied the City's transition from an international to a global centre of finance. The new (Richard Rogers-designed) Lloyd's building, for example, still requires that business be carried out in the Room by accredited Lloyd's brokers, yet the ability of Lloyd's as a set of regulatory practices to adapt to global change *within its own time* is decidedly uncertain.[16] In one sense, the old buildings of the City have been robbed of much of their monumentality by the City's latest built form and its associated practices: the 'Big Bang' buildings of global finance.

Global space

The dividing line between the old, traditional City and the new, globally geared space of finance is marked in popular terms by the 'Big Bang', an event which stemmed from the belief that the City was losing its competitive edge and market share to continental and US brokers. The City's move from international to global status, prompted by the deregulation of the equities markets in 1986, did indeed represent a dilution of the power of the once dominant institutions in the City such as the Bank of England and the Stock Exchange. The shift to global finance, however, did not amount to a decrease of local control, nor to an increase in the geographical scope of market trading for that matter; rather it represented a *qualitative* shift in both the way that many of the financial markets operate and the built form of the City. Not all the exchanges in the City have experienced this shift in the way that they conduct business, but the changes are all around and, in representational terms, the City is not what it used to be.

In comparison with the old monumental space, the global financial space of the City is altogether more successful in masking the traces of other social spaces in and around the Square Mile. Much of the City's new built form, characterized by its steel and glass towers and its faceless structures, represents a *more* formal, abstract representation of space than that conveyed by the old monuments (see Figure 8.2). In Lefebvre's terms, such buildings effect 'a brutal condensation of social relationships' which attempts to reduce a variety of past social relationships to the marvels of modern technology and electronic information.[17] The representation of homogeneity around the singular image of high-technology trading, however, is one that masks many things, including the tiny courtyards and alleyways that dot the City, the mahogany-fronted shops which serve a traditional culture of finance within the City and the lingering power of one type of financial space over another. As with the symbolism of the old built form, there are certain ways of doing business, certain spatial practices, through which this power is secured.

The exterior design of the new developments in the City, such as those around the City's northern boundary at Broadgate, the internal layouts of the buildings, and the way in which they are 'fitted out', though built primarily to house the high-tech traders and their support systems, are none the less also shaped by the practices of corporate finance. The screen traders, those who deal in equities, gilts, and the money markets, may well be regarded as the City's income earners within the new global networks of finance, but it is the conversational dealers, those involved in investment banking and corporate finance, who occupy the most powerful spaces within the finance houses. Within these spaces, the pace of business is still largely 'British' and the cultivation of relationships still the major activity (Pryke, 1994; Thrift, 1994).

Fig. 8.2 Abstract space of finance: global days (courtesy of the authors)

For example, at the top of some of the new City buildings, oak-panelled executive dining rooms, heavy patterned curtains, Victorian wall coverings, and recessed bookshelves are to be found, purposefully replicating the old City and its class traditions. In contrast to the clocks found on the walls of the trading floors below which show the time in New York, Los Angeles, Tokyo, and Hong Kong, the walls of the executive suites are adorned by fine art. This recreation of symbolic space, with its ritualized ways of doing business, draws upon the legacy of past practices performed in monumental space to effect a new form of social exclusion. On entering such a building, a bank's corporate customers are likely to be swept by lift from the ground floor reception and security area, past the equity and debt trading floors, up to the client contact rooms located on the top floors. The lift in this instance acts as a sort of suggestive 'time machine', transporting clients from the abstract global space of finance to the purported rhythms and detail of the 'old City'.[18]

Screen-based trading most clearly represents the 'global' culture of finance. When Lefebvre refers to finance capital as the 'supreme abstraction' it is in the context of the dominance of abstract space in the current global era.[19] It is the global space of finance, the pace and tempo of its trading practices, which valorize certain relationships between people and the new City space. Within the new buildings, the trading floors take their meaning from the global flows of finance which serve to legitimize both the practice of electronic trading and a spatial code which suggests uniformity and coherence. As before, it is the spatial practice of the traders which formally signifies the spaces of 'Big Bang', although now the codes are different and so too are many of the people who live by them (Thrift and Leyshon, 1992).

The stereotypical contrast between players and gentlemen does fail, however, to capture the shifts that have taken place on both sides. Traders are also involved in the cultivation of client relationships, the management of trust, and the maintenance of goodwill; they do not spend all their time on the dealing floors. Likewise conversational dealers are not divorced from the brash space of electronic trading, and among the new recruits not all mesh with the 'gentlemanly capitalism' image. Yet the tension between the two does reveal the presence of social spaces which interpenetrate one another.

For example, the traders are able to reinforce their own space through a series of gestures. A verbal curtain, as it were, seals off the trading area during trading time. To be *in* the space is to be familiar with the shorthand specialized trading language employed by the traders and to feel comfortable with it. To approach a trader at the wrong moment or to use the language in an unskilful manner is to be 'out of place' and likely to be subject to a sharp and colourful rebuke. Trading in 'global stock' is instantaneous and the ability to process rapid flows of information both from screens and from colleagues is an essential characteristic. Each trader is in telephone contact with all the others in the trading space, but the need to interpret information and obtain supplementary detail from colleagues requires that traders communicate at eye level over high-tech trading desks. In that sense they mirror the practices of the old Exchanges, but the bank of screens strewn out across rooms signifies the speed and presence of global finance, even when trading is over for the day and the floors are silent.

It is important to stress the coexistence of two cultures of finance within the new spaces of finance: they neither contradict one another, nor does a situation arise whereby one subsumes the other. The power of the conversational dealers over screen traders is *not* one of domination, whereby the former group in virtue of its structural power directs the practices of the traders. Rather the relationship is one of authority, whereby conversational dealers secure the assent of traders to buy and sell in the marketplace. The functional relationship is thus one of mutual dependence, which, while allowing for a degree of manoeuvre between them, enables the space of the City to be represented as an *abstract* space of finance.

It should be recalled, however, that this image of homogeneity is something that has been *accomplished* through the spatial practices of dealers and traders rather than simply given in virtue of the institutional power of finance capital. The achievement, therefore, as with all outcomes of power, may be contradicted or undermined.

Contradictions of space

Contradictions of space arise through the inability of a dominant space to suppress entirely the diversity and difference within its bounds. The power of the City, therefore, to present itself as a space of finance may be gauged by its ability to mask the traces of alternative representations, be they of a formal nature or of a more imaginary design – as is the case with the representational spaces of the contract service workers who labour within the City's finance spaces. As noted in the introduction, representational spaces, according to Lefebrve, take their shape through the everyday routine of the 'users'. Indeed, the key feature of representational spaces is that they are directly lived, although not in the simple sense that abstract spaces are also lived and produced through spatial practices. In contrast to modern abstract space, the ways in which representational spaces are *imagined* provide the informal tactics for living in those spaces.[20] Representational spaces are *dominated spaces* and the spatial practices which produce them are defined by the absence of power.[21] It is the absence of power which, in turn, leads Lefebvre to stress the creative and often unprompted use of the trappings of formal social space by groups, such as the City's contract workforce, which are merely tolerated by the demands of the division of labour. Largely unseen and rarely acknowledged, the spatial practices of those who clean, secure, and cater within the City on a contract basis overlay the abstract space of finance; yet the two are worlds apart.

Dominated spaces

The spatial practices of cleaning, for example, are concerned with surface space. Different kinds of surfaces are cleaned in different ways with varying combinations of skills, machinery, and chemicals. The floors of finance within the new buildings may take their meaning from the coding of the old City and the more recent sense of globalization that pervades the markets, but they are lived by cleaners as a variety of desk tops, terminals, chrome panels, and floor coverings – whether marble, wood, tile, non-slip, or a particular type of carpet. Each surface requires a technique of cleaning: computer screens and their casings can be dusted down but keyboards require an intricate clean using small wipes; computer rooms may require high-quality buffing or burnishing; whereas kitchens require 'deep cleaning' with specialist equipment and acid preparations; dust-free computer rooms may be adjacent to areas complete with antique furnishings redolent of a previous era; and so forth. In this way, the pre-existing space of finance is coded as bundles of surfaces, with each bundle allotted a specific cleaning time or shift. (Or in the vernacular of contract cleaning, the place has been 'eyeballed'.) Rooms may contain a various assortment of bundles, although each assortment will possess a clear boundary line which is etched on the cleaner's imagination – one that remains imperceptible to the abstract eye of those who work in finance. Cleaning space, in this sense, is lived as *sections* and *surfaces*, unaffected by the global networks which give formal meaning to the floors and buildings.

Interestingly, the employers of contract labour, the cleaning companies themselves, may be as multinational as the finance houses at which they hold a contract. In recent years, for example, UK multinationals as well as foreign-owned cleaning firms have won an increasing share of the contracts coming on the market in the City.[22] Moreover, it is not only the companies which are global in character, but also the parts of their workforce that are drawn from a migrant background. Where, for example, screen traders define their use of City space in terms of the pace and intensity of global finance, a group of migrant cleaners from Colombia or Nigeria or Portugal will mark their City space in their own translated terms. Traders and migrant cleaners are both part of overlapping networks of global relations, but the latter are distinguished by their informal networks which disperse ethnic minorities into distinct job concentrations in London (Cross and Waldinger, 1992). Where the two workforces differ is in how they *live* the wider sets of global relations in their daily spatial practice. For the employees of a cleaning multinational, the global character of the firm is not especially relevant to their daily routine, whereas the ethnic composition of a cleaning team is something that is keenly experienced in their daily spatial practice.

The spatial practice of cleaners, the organized routine of cleaning particular sections, exhibits a competence that, in part, stems from the absence of the dominant users of that space. Their absence, however, does not imply that the workplace is an empty space. On the contrary, it is merely that a different space is being worked, the cleaning space of surfaces. Whether day or night cleaners, they remain largely out of sight, and the traces of this predominantly migrant workforce remain unacknowledged unless the work is either not performed or not performed to a standard that reveals their past presence. Even in the daytime, cleaners will often be requested to take their lunch break at a different time from that of the 'core staff'. Indeed, their existence as a workforce within the dominant space becomes apparent only through their non-work; that is, by what they have not cleaned (especially if it is a 'high-profile area' such as the staff toilets). Moreover, it is often on such occasions that the interplay of two forms of social space – with different gestures, routes, and distances – becomes visible.

The spaces occupied by the contract catering workforce are more diverse in both their coding and spatial practice than that of cleaning space. There is the more familiar divide between 'back' and 'front' regions, where the former is marked off by the noise and smells of the kitchens and the latter is bounded by the display of consumption in the serving and eating areas.[23] Yet different occupations within catering – chefs, catering assistants, kitchen porters, waiters, butlers – have their own distinctive routes through these areas, as well as their own distinctive places within a region. This complexity of codes, however, each with its own prescribed relationships and pathways, does not amount to a 'produced' social space in Lefebvre's sense of the word.

The spaces of catering are not produced spaces in the sense that they are able to escape the dominant coding of space laid down by finance. Rather, they are 'induced' spaces; the kitchens and the serving areas are spaces internal to the dominant form and brought into being in accordance with the demands of the division of labour and needs.[24] (Bankers, clients, dealers, traders, and the like need sustenance as much as the next 'master of the universe'.) There is thus no conflict or contradiction between the different uses of space, between catering and finance. The representational spaces of the catering work force are *absorbed* by the dominant space. After all, when you look up at the Barclays de Zoete Wedd building or Midland Montagu's building in the City of London and point out the dealing floors, who also points to the kitchens on the upper floors? The spaces of catering disappear into the abstract space of finance.

Much the same may be said for various members of the catering workforce. It is interesting to contrast, for example, the physical co-presence between waiters or butlers and directors in the latter's exclusive dining rooms in many of the top finance houses, with the mediated co-presence of financial dealers who buy and sell from one another half-way across the globe. Where the former setting may be characterized, according to Goffman (1972), as one of unfocused interaction in which the butler is rarely 'seen' unless something is wrong (a dirty glass, a chipped plate, poorly presented food, for instance), in which case a signal or gesture will communicate the 'error', the latter setting may represent a more intimate form of co-presence despite the considerable distance involved and the technologies which mediate the interaction. Where one relationship is characterized by physical proximity, yet social absence, the other is characterized by physical distance, yet social presence.[25]

The social presence of the catering workforce is also called into question by the practice of the client removing the traces of their contract identity in the staff restaurants. In the serving areas within the finance houses, the counter staff often bear no signs, literally, of their employer – either on their uniforms or on their equipment – only the anonymity that enables them to disappear into the dominant space. As one catering contractor commented wryly of their client, 'they want us to feel that we're part of them, though obviously my staff know that they aren't. I know that if they were, they would be paid a lot more. . . .' It is not only their employment identity which is at issue, therefore; their suppressed contract status also hides an impoverished set of employment relations around pay, job security, and fringe benefits.[26]

The spaces of security in the City are different again, in so far as they are a straightforward *extension* of dominated space. Security guards produce controlled spaces through their spatial practice, yet they do not occupy those spaces. They secure the formal spaces of finance through their own rhythms and rituals, yet the pace and movement is dictated by events and routines beyond their control. For much of the time, the spatial practice of guards is shaped by the comings and goings of others. Their task is reactive. They monitor arrivals and departures through a bank of technologies, waiting for the flicker of the screen which denotes movement, with an explicit brief to sanction or forbid entry into the spaces of finance. In so far as such spaces offer an 'image of membership', security guards formally recognize who may be a member from their code of behaviour.

In the day, in contrast to both cleaning and catering staff, a highly visible presence is demanded of the security guards; that is, a uniformed presence which, in many cases, is as remote as that of a night guard or cleaner. The comings and goings of the finance workforce take place at regular intervals at the start and end of the 'working day' in numbers sufficiently large to minimize social contact with the security staff. Contact, however, is not part of the product of security; rather it is the performance of the guard as a standardized body which signifies the controlled nature of a formal space. Being male, uniformed, and preferably tall is itself only an ideal gesture; it becomes an organized gesture through the (reactive) performance of the guard within the entrance and exit spaces of the finance houses.[27]

Much of the work of security, however, is performed at night outside the working day of the dominant users. In common with night cleaners, the absence of the finance workforce does not imply that the buildings represent an empty work space. What is different, though, in this instance is that the space of security at night is worked, literally, through codes. In a twelve- or thirteen-hour shift, it is the regularity of the 'walks' through a building, the isolation, and the near silence that define the spatial practice of the guards.[28] It is the formal coding (often in bar-code form), placed by the contractor on the walls, door openings, landings, and such at regular intervals on the walks, that dictates the routes through a building, however. (The codes may be 'read' by a type of 'gun' carried by the guard and automatically logged on computer at a distant control centre as the guard moves through a building opening and closing doors.) In this way, the spatial practice of guards may be both monitored and surveyed at a distance to ensure that the practice is actually performed.

At such moments, it is doubtful whether it is adequate to describe such an extension of the dominant space as a representational space. In many ways, the spatial practices of the night guards reproduce the formal representations of space laid down by the finance houses. Indeed, the objectification of their work in the form of computer printouts lends itself to this interpretation (the printouts, incidentally, form part of the 'product' of security). Of the three forms of contract space, therefore, the space of security is the least negotiated, the least occupied.

All three spaces of the contract workforce are, none the less, effectively smothered by the dominant, abstract space of finance (see Figure 8.3). The

Fig. 8.3 Abstract space of finance: smothered days and nights (courtesy of the authors)

work of cleaning, catering, and security is *abstracted out*, in so far as the daily routines and practices of this workforce are excluded from the formal representations of space. In Lefebvre's terms, their different spaces are 'internal' to the dominant form of financial space, especially the space of security.[29] That, however, does not imply that the different forms of representation simply coexist, with one form of social space subordinate to the other. According to Lefebvre, the *power* of abstract space to exclude or reduce differences is never completely effective; opportunities are afforded by attempts to minimize differences which, in turn, produce social spaces that 'escape the system's rule'.[30]

Appropriated spaces

Appropriated spaces are forged out of different spatial practices from those noted above and may take a variety of forms. The most effectively appropriated spaces are those that make symbolic use of what is around them and turn it to their advantage, either by subverting the codes of the dominant space or by representing an alternative form of social space alongside them.[31] Such spaces, according to Lefebvre, may be 'fixed, semi-fixed, movable or vacant', but above all they are lived spaces.[32] Through the routine practices and tactics of 'users' they may undermine or challenge the representational mode of power exercised by the finance houses. It is in this sense that they may *contradict* the formal representations of space through a spatial code which is neither simply read nor interpreted, but *used* as a means of living in that space.[33]

Within the old and new buildings of finance, for example, there are often concealed spaces; spaces in the interstices of buildings that are occupied by cleaners, yet which have no formal presence or recognition. In the daytime, such areas may form appropriated spaces, often of a semi-fixed nature. These are not Lefebvre's 'counter-spaces'; that is, spaces which in a specific way represent a rejection of all that is signified by a particular dominant space.[34] Rather, they are spaces manipulated by cleaners to meet their own needs and not those laid down by the dominant coding (a place to put up posters, read newspapers, listen to the radio, and the like). Such spaces often fall outside the gaze of finance, although rarely that of their employer, the contractor. If they are visible to the contractor, their toleration will often carry the compromise of having to store the machinery and materials of cleaning alongside their own personal effects.

Beyond the working day of finance, when most cleaning work is performed, the use of concealed spaces is less frequent. As noted earlier, the pre-existing space of finance is recoded as sections and surfaces and the space 'lived' through the rhythms and practices of cleaning, rather than those of finance. Although this overlay does not represent a challenge to the dominant coding of space, as with concealed spaces, it tends to deflect the power of the formal coding and weaken its claims to a singular identity.

Within the practice of catering, opportunities for the production of concealed spaces are less available, in part because the work itself is performed alongside or in front of the dominant users. Even the 'back space' of the kitchens is part of the formal space and readily accessible to the client. Waiters and butlers, however, usually do have their semi-private spaces (for the polishing of cutlery, general preparation, and so forth), although in general it is their *way of using* the dominant spaces which may subvert the latter. Submissive in their conduct, their code of presentation is a code that is forged between waiters and butlers themselves. It has less to do with the formal presentation of food or serving to please and rather more to do with meeting the standards set by their peers in respect of professional practices. This may involve the general presentation of the table: for example, the arrangement of the cutlery and napkins, and the polished shine on the glasses. Each detail is suggestive to other waiters and butlers, but not necessarily to those seated at the table. Thus the lack of focused co-presence that characterizes much of their work and which, in this instance, is designed to reveal their subordinate relationship to the directors, may be used to meet a set of needs that are essentially alien to the system. According to Michel De Certeau, it is possible to argue that this group of workers escape the dominant space *without leaving it* (1988, p. xiii). Although they lack the formal means to negotiate the dominant coding, they are able to deflect its power through their spatial practice.

The space of security is altogether different and affords few opportunities for appropriation to occur. In Lefebvre's discourse, it would not be inapt to describe the space of security as an example of *alienated space*.[35] For much of the time, security guards 'live' someone else's space as a superimposed space; that is, as one coded, literally, by their employers which leaves little room for manoeuvre or manipulation. Unlike cleaning and catering staff, security guards rarely have the opportunity to use space; as noted earlier, they react to events that occur within the space of finance. However, as guards 'always think that something is going to happen, but it never does', the nature of this work is one of relentless tedium, broken occasionally by events outside their control and by tactics to overcome the monotony of empty time. At night, for example, playing cards, reading, or listening to the radio only ever partially fill the stretches of empty time.

Of the three forms of contract space, therefore, the space of security is least able to resist the pressure towards the homogenization of finance space and thus least effective at appropriating space. Interestingly, one possible reason for this inability to make use of abstract space, to reorientate it to meet their own ends and references, is the symbolic power exercised by the employer, the contract guarding company. In one sense, the spatial grid laid down by the employer acts both to reify the dominant space and to disarm the guards symbolically. Hence the appropriateness of the term 'alienated space' to describe the remoteness of everyday life within contract security.

Concluding comments

In drawing upon the coded spaces of the City of London to explore and embellish Lefebvre's ideas on social space, we have intentionally focused on those aspects that we consider to be the most fruitful, rather than dwelling upon the limitations of his thought. (As indicated, some of our criticisms and reservations are to be found in the footnotes.) In a paper of this length, it is not possible to engage with all aspects of a large work such as *The production of space* and, as stated in the introduction, we have identified three related insights which, in our view, extend our understanding of social space. The first refers to the importance attached by Lefebvre to the relationship between two forms of social space – representations of space and representational spaces – and the spatial practices which underpin them. The second refers to the potential contradictions between the two forms of social space, and the third insight draws attention to the practices of power which produce, secure, challenge, or negotiate spatial codes.

Of the three insights, it is the stress on power which, in our view, is the most significant in Lefebvre's analysis of social space. If social space is 'over-inscribed',[36] the ability to produce and maintain a dominant coding, to suppress alternatives, or to create the impression of a coherent space is one of power. Power, however, is not simply one kind of social activity; there are different modes, sites, and relations through which power is effective. To suggest, for example, that the identity of the City is taken from finance is to invoke a representational mode of power. However, there is nothing inscribed in the social relations of finance which will secure that representation, only particular *spatial practices* – verbal and non-verbal, rhythmic and routine – which signify what kind of activity is appropriate to a particular place and who is 'out of place' in the City. At issue then is not so much who has power, but rather how it is practised to achieve certain ends.

Spatial practices are the key to the production of City space, or indeed any social space, for it is only through their reproduction in people's everyday experience that the meaning of a place is secured. Indeed, one of Lefebvre's considerable achievements was to connect everyday life to the wider, even global relationships that make up places like the City as a series of inter-penetrating spaces, without reducing daily experience to trivia.[37]

In drawing attention to the different workforces which occupy the same place of finance, yet live those spaces in markedly different ways, our intention was to show how the power of an abstract space seeks to strip all meaning from other 'users', although never with complete success. On Lefebvre's view, the meaning of social space is frequently contested, but the *production* of a domi-nant coding is something that is achieved, maintained through adaptation and alteration, and secured through spatial practice. Once secured, however, a coding is open to challenge and subversion, although in ways that are not always overt or dismissive. The City of London is only one such social space for which this analysis holds true.

Notes

1 First published in 1974 as *La production de l'espace* and translated into English in 1991. In what follows, references to the book are abbreviated to PS and the page numbers refer to the English translation.

2 In the extended introduction to *The production of space*, Lefebvre stresses the intercon-nections between spatial practices, representations of space and representational spaces. Indeed, he refers to the three moments of social space as a conceptual triad: the perceived, the conceived, and the lived (pp. 33–46). This is a product of Lefebvre's particular 'take' on Hegel's dialectical logic, which in contrast to formal logic wishes to achieve a synthesis of thought and being (see Lefebvre, 1939). The emphasis placed by Lefebvre, following Marx, upon practical activity led him to the view that a more libertarian organization of urban space should be sought on the basis of lived experi-ence. The difficulty that this poses for an understanding of social space, however, is that it strips the formal representations of space (conceived space) of the 'everyday' spatial practices which produce and secure a dominant coding of place. Relatedly, the categori-cal attachment of perception to spatial practices distorts our view of such practices as unmediated by concepts or at one remove from lived experience. In our view, the categorical scaffolding imposed upon the three moments of space should be understood in a nominal, descriptive sense, rather than as part of a broader 'logical' system.

3 It is only *in* space that a clash of social interests can come about, but it is only a spatial contradiction if the clash is over the meaning *of* space (PS, p. 358, also p. 365). There is a tendency within Hegelian discourse to talk about the resolution of contradictions through practice, the progressive overcoming of difference. It is better to consider contradiction, however, as the *inability* of the whole (in Lefebvre's case, the representation of a dominant space as a singular, homogeneous image) to suppress diversity and difference – that is, the representational spaces which the dominant space seeks to mask (PS, pp. 306–11). The failure of totalizing projects is an insight that is rarely accorded to Hegel, although Slavoj Žižek (1989) is among those who recognize this aspect of his logic.

4 Lefebvre compares the category of abstract space to Marx's notion of abstract labour; that is, as an abstraction which has a social existence. In so far as it is possible to talk of the exchange value of labour *in general*, so too is it possible to talk of space *in general* as opposed to this or that particular space. Thus to refer to the space of finance is to abstract out the specific spaces of accountancy, law, merchant banking, restaurants, leisure, and so forth which constitute the City of London (PS, pp. 306–12).

5 'Thus to look upon abstract space as homogeneous is to embrace a representation that takes the effect for the cause, and the goal for the reasons why that goal is pursued' (PS, p. 287).

6 PS, pp. 47–8.

7 'A rhythm invests places, but it is not itself a place; it is not a thing, nor an aggregation of things, nor yet a simple flow. It embodies its own, its own regularity, which it derives from space – from its own space – and from a relationship between space and time. . . . What we *live* are rhythms – rhythms experienced subjectively' (PS, p. 206).

8 See Pryke (1991).

9 PS, p. 220.

10 PS, p. 223–4.

11 See Pryke (1991) for an account of the City of London's transition from an international centre to a global centre of finance. Prior to globalization, the City's institutions, in particular the Bank of England, acted collectively as a 'financial synchromesh', adjusting the pace of distinct elements of international finance to the 'gentlemanly' tempo of the City. Globalization, however, brought with it a series of technical practices and financial instruments which, notwithstanding the greater volume of transactions, served to integrate capital and money markets in such a way that the very rhythms of the City were challenged.

12 PS, p. 234.

13 'Acoustic, gestural and ritual movements, elements grouped into vast ceremonial unities, breaches opening onto limitless perspectives, chains of meanings – all are organized into a monumental whole' (PS, p. 224).

14 PS, p. 225.

15 PS, p. 226.

16 One of the defining characteristics of membership at Lloyd's to date has been that of unlimited liability. Until recently, this served effectively to exclude corporate capital (which operates with limited liability) from the insurance market and reinforce the inward-looking nature of the institution, together with its confidence in self-regulation to meet change. Insurance losses on a global scale in the late 1980s, however, severely knocked this confidence and in October 1993 members of Lloyd's voted in favour of corporate interests entering the market.

17 PS, p. 227. By the end of 1986, for example, there were over two hundred information services available in the City of London (*The Banker*, 1986), with continuous flows of specialist information on US Treasury Bonds, UK gilts, FOREX, US fixed-rate investments, and the like feeding supply brokers, market makers, analysts, and so forth (*Banking World*, 1986).

18 Such strategies are not restricted to the corporate banking sector. On the eleventh floor of the new Lloyd's insurance building, the two hundred-year-old Adam's room from the old building has been re-erected, complete with original Adam ceiling. As in the old building, it is the meeting place for the Council of Lloyd's. Other attempts to translate tradition include the requirement of a single underwriting room and the housing of the latest information technology in traditional modular-style underwriting boxes.

19 PS, p. 308.

20 This point tends to be misunderstood if one adopts too rigid an interpretation of representational spaces as the only form of social space that is lived and experienced directly. Clearly all social space is shaped through everyday spatial practices, but *modern* social space for Lefebvre is lived as a formal representation of space – in the abstract and with little room for the play of imagination.

21 PS, pp. 164–6.

22 See Allen and Henry (1994a).

23 See Goffman (1959), and also Giddens (1984), for a critique and extension of Goffman's dramaturgical model.

24 PS, pp. 396–7. Likewise, the activities which support the central role of financial dealers and traders, such as those workers involved in communications, programming, operations, personnel, and the like, occupy 'induced' spaces. Unlike the contract cleaning and catering workforce, however, their spatial practices reinforce the abstract space of finance and its prescribed uses. To suggest otherwise, that financial support staff produce their own representational spaces, is to miss the fact that their lived experience at work is directly helping to secure a homogeneous representation of the City as finance.

25 See Shields (1992), for a review of the 'worlds of near and far', and the remoteness of the everyday in (post)modernity.

26 See Allen and Henry (1994b).

27 '"Organized gestures" which is to say ritualized and codified gestures, are not simply performed in "physical" space, in the space of bodies. Bodies themselves generate spaces, which are produced by and for their gestures' (PS, p. 216).

28 It is common for walks to take place every hour, with the first walk taking longer than the rest in order to secure the space.

29 PS, p. 387.

30 PS, p. 382.

31 PS, pp. 164–8; also pp. 373–4.

32 PS, p. 363.

33 PS, pp. 362–5.

34 PS, pp. 381–5.

35 PS, p. 308.

36 PS, p. 142.

37 See Lefebvre's *Critique of everyday life* (1947, English translation 1991) for an evaluation of everyday life that mirrors the double-sided character of modernity. On the one side, the impoverishment of daily life that stems from an increasingly abstract, commodified existence and, on the other side, the creative possibilities held

out by modernity that promise to enrich everyday life. The neatness of the dualism may no longer hold the attraction once credited to such oppositions, but the assertion that the everyday should not be taken for granted or assumed familiar is one that has increased resonance at a time when the categories of presence and absence are coming under continued scrutiny in spatial terms.

References

Allen, J. and Henry, N. 1994a: Growth at the margins: contract labour in a core region. In Hadjimichalis, C. and Sadler, D. (eds), *Europe at the margins*. Chichester: John Wiley.

Allen, J. and Henry, N. 1994b: Divisions in Labour: contract services and the emergence of a new employment regime. South East Occasional Paper Series 11, The Open University, Milton Keynes.

The Banker. 1986: Banking tomorrow: dealing rooms. September, pp. 93–109.

Banking World. 1986: Dealing rooms, April, pp. 41–51.

Cain, P. J. and Hopkin, A. G. 1986: Gentlemanly capitalism and British expansion overseas I. The old colonial system, 1688–1850. *Economic History Review* NS 39, 501–25.

Cain, P. J. and Hopkins, A. G. 1987: Gentlemanly capitalism and British expansion overseas II. New Imperialism, 1850–1945. *Economic History Review* NS 40, 1–26.

Cross, M. and Waldinger, R. 1992: Migrants, minorities and the ethnic division of labour. In Fainstein, S. S., Gordon, I. and Harloe, M. (eds), *Divided cities*. Oxford: Basil Blackwell, 151–74.

De Certeau, M. 1988: *The practice of everyday life*. Berkeley, CA: University of California Press.

Giddens, A. 1984: *The constitution of society*. Cambridge: Polity Press.

Goffman, E. 1959: *The presentation of self in everyday life*. New York: Doubleday.

Goffman, E. 1972: *Interaction ritual*. London: Allen Lane.

Lefebvre, H. 1939: *Le matérialisme dialectique*. Paris: Editions Sociales; English translation, 1968: *Dialectical materialism*. London: Jonathan Cape.

Lefebvre, H. 1947: *Critique de la vie quotidienne I: Introduction*. Paris: Grasset; English translation, 1991. *Critique of everyday life*. London: Verso.

Lefebvre, H. 1974: *La production de l'espace*. Paris: Anthropos; English translation, 1991: *The production of space*. Oxford: Basil Blackwell.

Michie, R. C. 1992: *The City of London: Continuity and change, 1850–1990*. Basingstoke: Macmillan Education.

Pryke, M. 1991: An international city going 'global': spatial change in the City of London. *Environment and Planning D: Society and Space* 9, 197–222.

Pryke, M. 1994: Looking back on the space of a boom: (re)developing spatial matrices in the City of London. *Environment and Planning A* 26, 235–64.

Sampson, A. 1969: *Anatomy of Britain today*. Oxford: Oxford University Press.

Shields, R. 1992: A truant proximity: presence and absence in the space of modernity. *Environment and Planning D: Society and Space* 10, 181–98.

Thrift, N. 1994: On the social and cultural determinants of international financial centres: the case of the City of London. In Corbridge, S., Martin, R. and Thrift, N. (eds), *Money, space and power*. Oxford: Basil Blackwell.

Thrift, N. and Leyshon, A. 1992: In the wake of money: the City of London and the accumulation of value. In Budd, L. and Whimster, S. (eds), *Global finance and urban living*. Andover: Routledge, Chapman & Hall, 282–311.

Žižek, S. 1989: *The sublime object of ideology*. London: Verso.

9   Jon Goss,

'The "Magic of the Mall": An Analysis of Form, Function, and Meaning in the Contemporary Retail Built Environment'

Excerpts from: *Annals of the Association of American Geographers* 83, 18–47 (1993)

> And the truth-sayers of the shopping mall, as the death of the social, are all those lonely people, caught like whirling flotsam in a force field which they don't understand, but which fascinates with the coldness of its brilliance
>
> (Kroker *et al.*, 1989, p. 210).

Shopping is the second most important leisure activity in North America, and although watching television is indisputably the first, much of its programming actually promotes shopping, through both advertising and the depiction of model consumer lifestyles. The existential significance of shopping is proclaimed in popular slogans such as: 'Born to shop', 'Shop till you drop', and 'I shop therefore I am'. An advertisement for Tyson's Corner, Virginia, asks: 'The joy of cooking? The joy of sex? What's left?' and the answer provided is, of course, 'The joy of shopping'! As Tyson's obviously knows, recent market research shows that many Americans prefer shopping to sex (Levine, 1990, p. 187).

Despite increases in catalog sales, shopping remains essentially a spatial activity – we still 'go' shopping – and the shopping center is its chosen place. By 1990, there were 36,650 shopping centers in the USA, providing 4.2 billion square feet (151 square miles!) of gross leasable area and accounting for more than $725 billion of sales, or 55 per cent of retail sales excluding automobile sales ('Retail uses', 1991, p. 23). The time spent in shopping centers by North Americans follows only that spent at home and at work/school. Centers have already become tourist destinations, complete with tour guides and souvenirs, and some include hotels so that vacationers and conferees need not leave the premises during their stay. Downtown retail complexes often include condominia, and residential development above the suburban mall is predicted to be an inevitable new trend ('The PUD market guarantee', 1991, p. 32). Their residents can literally shop without leaving home (or be at home without leaving the shops?). Moreover, planned retail space is colonizing other privately owned public spaces such as hotels, railway stations, airports, office buildings and hospitals, as shopping has become the dominant mode of contemporary public life.

Nevertheless, there persists a high-cultural disdain for conspicuous mass consumption resulting from the legacy of a puritanical fear of the moral corruption inherent in commercialism and materialism, and sustained by a modern intellectual contempt for consumer society. This latter critique condemns the system of correspondences between material possesions and social worth (Veblen, 1953; Boorstin, 1973), the homogenization of culture and alienation of the individual (Marcuse, 1964; Adorno and Horkheimer, 1969) and the distortion of human needs through the manipulation of desire (Haug, 1986). The contemporary shopper, while taking pleasure in consumption, cannot but be aware of this authoritative censure, and is therefore, like the tourist (Frow, 1991, p. 127), driven by a simultaneous desire and self-contempt, constantly alternating between assertion and denial of identity. This ambivalence is, I think, precisely expressed in the play of the slogans cited above, which cock a snook at the dominant order of values, but in so doing also acknowledge its inevitable authority.

This paper argues that developers have sought to assuage this collective guilt over conspicuous consumption by designing into the retail built environment the means for a fantasized dissociation from the act of shopping. That is, in recognition of the culturally perceived emptiness of the activity for which they provide the main social space, designers manufacture the illusion that something else other than mere shopping is going on, while also mediating the materialist relations of mass consumption and disguising the identity and rootedness of the shopping center in the contemporary capitalist social order. The product is effectively a *pseudoplace* which works through spatial strategies of dissemblance and duplicity.[1]

This account is necessarily limited to the workings of the design; that is, the assumptions made about the retail built environment and its users, and the intent of the developers as inferred from a reading of their professional literature and of the landscape itself. This requires some care lest we fall into the same trap that compromises the modernist critique of consumption, a critique which holds much intellectual force but little political potential. This is to conceive of the consumer as cultural dupe and helpless object of technical control, exactly as the (mostly) male middle-class designers imagine them. Consumers are constructed as passive, sensual, and vulnerable victims of the 'force field which they don't understand', just as the designers' discourse is both manifestly elitist and gendered – from 'market penetration analysis' to the persistent tropes of seduction, stimulation, and physical manipulation.

The key point is that the shopper is not merely the object of a technical and patriarchal discourse and design, but is also a subject who may interpret the design aberrantly or intentionally appropriate meaning for her/his own purposes. The manner in which the shopping center is read by consumers, both as individuals and social subjects, is a complex and politically vital question in dire need of [ethnographic] research. With this latter project barely begun, I will confine my conclusions to an outline of strategies by which consumers might, armed with the conception of shopping centers sketched here, consciously challenge the purpose and operation of the planned retail built environment.

The commodification of reality

Advertizing does not have to directly instruct its audience, but need only highlight latent correspondences (Sahlins, 1976, p. 217) or homologies (Bourdieu, 1984,

p. 137) between the commodity and common cultural symbols, for contemporary consumers are expected to have accumulated a considerable store of cultural knowledge and acquired the skills necessary to interpret complex texts and subtle rhetorical devices used to elicit cultural meaning (Bourdieu, 1984, p. 66). And if the audience is predisposed to believe, the real magic of advertizing is to mask the materiality of the commodity – fetishism in the Marxist sense – that is, to sever it from the social and spatial relations that structure its productions and the human labor it embodies. This is especially so for mass-produced commodities, which threaten to invalidate the conditions required for rightful and righteous possession, so advertizing necessarily divorces the commodity from the labor process that produced it. Whether it is high fashion sewn in immigrant sweatshops or electronic gadgets assembled in Third World factories, few consumers, therefore, know or can afford to give thought to what the commodity is composed of, or where, how and by whom it was made (Jhally, 1987, p. 49).

Critical to the processes by which the commodity is simultaneously severed from its origins and associated with desirable sociocultural attributes is its context – the real or imagined landscape in which it is presented (Sack, 1988, pp. 643–4). Advertizers draw upon knowledge of places, and upon the structuration of social space, to create an imaginary setting that elicits from us an appropriate social disposition or action. With the collapse of time–space produced by global electronic media and tourism (Meyrowitz, 1985), the stock of place imagery in the consumer's *musée imaginaire* (Jencks, 1987, p. 95) has expanded dramatically, and we are able to read with facility a vast array of clichéd signs of real and fictitious elsewheres.

At the same time, there has been a marked decline in the textual content of advertizing (Leiss *et al.*, 1986), so that appeal to price and utility has been displaced by a system of commodity aesthetics in which appearance has become more important than function, and sign value has subordinated use value, or rather *has become* use value (Haug, 1986). In Debord's (1983) 'society of the spectacle', individuals live in a world that is fabricated for them, and what was once directly lived is now experienced as a commodified or bureaucratically administered representation, preferable (cleaner, safer, and sexier) to reality. In Baudrillard's (1983) society of the simulacrum, the real has been irrevocably replaced by the illusion, and the world is not merely *represented in* commodified images, but *consists of* such images. The image has more substantive effect than reality – it is 'hyperreal'.

This brief examination is critical to an understanding of the contemporary shopping center, for there is a close connection between the means of the 'consciousness industry' (Enzenberger, 1974) and environmental design: they are both media of mass communication, employing rhetorical devices to effect hidden persuasions; both may be experienced passively; they both belong unobtrusively to everyday life; and they are both motivated by profit (Eco, 1986, p. 77). Developers, therefore, readily employ the glitz and showcraft of entertainment – literally 'learning from Las Vegas' (Venturi *et al.*, 1972); the iconography of advertizing (Frampton, 1983, p. 19) – 'learning from Madison

Avenue'; and the 'imagineering' of North American theme parks (Relph, 1987) – 'learning from Disney'. Sophisticated techniques of illusion and allusion enable them to create an appropriate and convincing context where the relationship of the individual to mass consumption and of the commodity to its context is mystified. This technical capacity, the predispositions of contemporary consumers (increasingly well understood owing to market research), and the economic and political capacity of speculative capital combine to manufacture a total retail built environment and a total cultural experience.

The making of the mall

> Of course, it must be kept in mind that architects do not design malls for architects; they design them for developers and retailers that are interested in creating malls and other shopping centers to attract consumers and keep them coming back
>
> (Richards, 1990, p. 23).

The developer's profit accrues from the construction and sale of shopping centers, lease rent, and deductions from retail revenues. Unlike other forms of real estate, where markets have been rapidly saturated and are dependent upon urban and regional economic fortunes, shopping center construction has been a relatively secure investment, whether in the suburbs, always provided a big-name department store could be enticed to sign an agreement (Frieden and Sagalyn, 1989, p. 79), or downtown, provided subsidies could be negotiated from co-operative municipal governments. Recently, however, there has been a marked slowdown in the speculative development observed in the 1970s and early 1980s . . . many regions are effectively saturated and intercenter competition is intense. Profit increasingly depends, therefore, upon image making and the creative management of shopping centers.

It is important at the outset to realize the scale and detail of the conception. Shopping centers are typically produced by huge corporations or *ad hoc* coalitions of finance, construction, and commercial capital (typically pension funds, developers, and department stores), and are meticulously planned. They usually involve state agencies and teams of market researchers, geo-demographers, accountants, asset managers, lawyers, engineers, architects, landscape artists, interior designers, traffic analysts, security consultants, and leasing agents. Development, therefore, involves the co-ordination of a complex of concerns, although always overdetermined by the goals of retail profit . . . The measure of success of the center is 'operating balance per square foot of Gross Leasable Area [GLA]' ('Retail uses', 1991) and in the professional literature the figure for 'sales per square foot of GLA' is ascribed a special mystique.

The shopping centers profit from an internalization of externalities; that is, by ensuring strict complementarity of retail and service functions through an appropriate tenant mix (Goss, 1992, p. 167). Leasing agents plan the mix of tenants and their locations within the center, inevitably excluding repair shops, laundromats, or thrift stores that might remind the consumer of the materiality of the commodity and attract those whose presence might challenge the normality of consumption. Where resale shops are found, they conventionally indicate difficulty in attracting more desirable tenants (Ricks, 1991, p. 56). Similarly, vacant stores are hidden behind gaily painted hoardings, and we are assured that a store will be 'opening soon', in case we might suspect that this, like downtown, is not the thriving place where everyone wants to be. Detailed lease agreements create the appropriate atmosphere by insuring uniform store opening hours; regulating signage, sightlines, lighting, store front design, and window display; and stipulating advertizing minima for each store (see Frieden and Sagelyn, 1989, p. 66).

While individual retailers may pursue their own strategies for profit within limited bounds, the center operates as a whole to maximize 'foot traffic' by attracting the target consumers and keeping them on the premises for as long as possible. The logic is apparently simple:

> Our surveys show [that] the amount of spending is related *directly* to the amount of time spent at centers. . . . *Anything* that can prolong shoppers' visits are [*sic*] in our best interests overall.
> (a senior vice-president of leasing and marketing cited in
> Reynolds, 1990a, p. 52, emphasis added).

The task begins with the manufacture and marketing of an appropriate sense of place (Richards, 1990, p. 24), an attractive place image that will entice people from their suburban homes and downtown offices, keep them contentedly on the premises, and encourage them to return. This occurs in an increasingly competitive retail market resulting from the 'overmalling of America' and, in response to consumer loyalties shifting from name retailers to specific shopping centers, the personality of the center is critical (McDermott, 1990, pp. 2–3).

Imag(in)ing the mall

> The sense of place is also a political fact. What can be done to the look of a locality depends on who controls it. . . . People can be excluded, awed, confused, made acquiescent, or kept ignorant by what they see and hear. So the sense of the environment has always been a matter of moment to any ruling class.
> (Lynch, 1976, pp. 72–3).

In constructing an attractive place image for the shopping center, developers have, with remarkable persistence, exploited a modernist nostalgia for authentic community, perceived to exist only in past and distant places, and have promoted the conceit of the shopping center as an alternative focus for modern community life. Shopping districts of the early years of this century, for example, were based on traditional market towns and villages, and a strong sense of place was evoked using stylized historical architecture and landscaping (typically evoking the village green). They were built on a modest scale, functionally and spatially integrated into local communities, in order to provide an idyllic context for consumption by the new gentry (Rowe, 1991, p. 141).

The picturesque Country Club Plaza in Kansas City, Missouri, built in 1922, is a prototypic example. With the contemporary postmodernist penchant for the vernacular, this original form is undergoing a renaissance in the specialty center, a collection of high-end outlets that pursue a particular retail and architectural theme. Typically these are also idealizations of villages and small towns, chock-full of historical and regional details to convince the consumer of their authenticity (Goss, 1992, p. 172). Examples include Pickering Wharf in Salem, Massachusetts (a New England village), the Borgata in Scottsdale, Arizona (a thirteenth-century Italian village), the Pruneyard in San Jose, California (a Spanish–American hacienda), the Mercado in Phoenix, Arizona (a Mexican hillside village).

In contrast, the modern regional shopping center was built on a large scale with regular, unified architecture. Its harsh exterior modernism and automobile-focused landscaping refused any compromise with the rustic aesthetic. As Relph (1987, p. 215) notes, however, 'modernism . . . never wholly succeeded in the landscape of retailing', and the interior contained pedestrian walkways, courts, fountains and statuary that referred reassuringly to the traditional urbanism of southern Europe (Gruen, 1973; Rowe, 1991, p. 126), Victorian Britain or New England. According to Victor Gruen, the acknowledged pioneer of the modern mall, his 'shopping towns' would be not only pleasant places to shop, but also centers of cultural enrichment, education, and relaxation, a suburban alternative to the decaying downtown (Gruen and Smith, 1960).

Gruen's shopping centers proved phenomenally successful, and he later argued that by applying the lessons of environmental design learned in the suburbs to downtown, 'we can restore the lost sense of commitment and belonging; we can counteract the phenomenon of alienation, isolation and loneliness and achieve a sense of identity' (Gruen, 1973, p. 11). James Rouse, effectively heir to Gruen and heralded as 'the savior of downtown America' (Sawicki, 1989, p. 347), similarly argued that shopping centers 'will help dignify and uplift the families who use them. . . . promote friendly contact among the people of the community, . . . [and] expose the community to art, music, crafts and culture' (1962, p. 105). Thus, if the developers could create the illusion of urban community in the suburbs, they could also create this illusion in the city itself. The key, Rouse argues, is not so much the design features of the shopping mall, but centralized retail management (CRM) and leasing strategies (cited in Stokvis and Cloar, 1991, p. 7), which would include levels of security and maintenance well beyond that provided by municipal authorities, market research, co-operative advertizing, common business hours, common covenants, and a regulated tenant mix (Cloar, 1990). Downtown is now 'learning from the mall': as the director of the National Mainstreet Center, an organization established by the National Trust for Historic Preservation, argues, 'shopping centers . . . are well-planned, well-funded, and well-organized. . . . Main streets need management like that' (Huffman, 1989, p. 95).

The new downtown retail built environment has taken two essential forms, which in practice may be mixed. First is the commercial gentrification of decaying historical business and waterfront districts, pioneered by James Rouse with Quincy Market in Boston. Its opening in 1979 supposedly marked 'the day the urban renaissance began' (Rouse, cited in Teaford, 1990, p. 253), and subsequently no self-respecting city seems complete without its own festival marketplace, replicating more or less the original formula.[2] Historical landmarks and 'water exposure' (Scott, 1989, p. 185) are critical features, as this retail environment is consciously reminiscent of the commercial world city, with its quaysides and urban produce markets replete with open stalls, colorful awnings, costermonger barrows, and nautical paraphernalia liberally scattered around.

A second form is the galleria, the historic referent of which is the Victorian shopping arcade and especially the famous Galleria Vittorio Emanuele II in Milan. After Cesar Pelli pioneered the galleried arcade in the early 1970s (at The Commons in Columbus, Ohio and the Winter Gardens in Niagara Falls, New York), glazed gallery and atria became standard features in downtown mixed-use developments, their huge vaulted spaces suggesting a sacred–liturgical or secular–civic function. They have since been retrofitted to suburban malls and natural daylight has enabled support of softscapes – interiorized palms, trees, and shrubs – reminiscent of the street in the model garden city, the courts of Babylon, and, most especially, the tropical vacation setting (Figure 9.1A and B). Enclosed streetscapes refer to the idealized, historic middle-American main street or to exotic streets of faraway cities, including Parisian boulevards, Mexican paseos, and Arabic souks or casbahs, if only because the contemporary North American street invokes fear and loathing in the middle classes. They reclaim, for the middle-class imagination, 'The Street' – an idealized social space free, by virtue of private property, planning, and strict control, from the inconvenience of the weather and the danger and pollution of the automobile, but, most important, from the terror of crime associated with today's urban environment.

The malling of downtown could not work, however, without the legislative and financial support of the local state. These developments exploit historic preservation laws and federal and municipal funds to subsidize commercial development. Newport Center in Jersey City, for example, is the recipient of the largest-ever Urban Development Action Grant (Osborne, 1988).

In creating these spaces, developers and public officials articulate an ideology of nostalgia, a reactionary modernism that expresses the 'dis-ease' of the present (see Stewart, 1984, p. 23), a lament on the perceived loss of the moral conviction, authenticity, spontaneity, and community of the past; a profound disillusionment with contemporary society and fear of the future. More specifically, we collectively miss a public space organized on a pedestrian scale; that is, a setting for free personal expression and association, for collective cultural expression and transgression, and for unencumbered human interaction and material transaction. Such spaces no longer exist in the city, where open spaces are windswept tunnels between towering buildings, abandoned in fear to marginal populations; nor were they found after all in the suburb, which is

Fig. 9.1 Interior of Miller Hill Mall in Duluth as constructed in 1973 (*above*) and after renovation and 'interior landscaping' in 1988 (*below*, courtesy of the author). Source: Retail Reporting Corporation.

subdivided and segregated, dominated by the automobile, and repressively predictable and safe. Such spaces only exist intact in our *musées imaginaire*, but their forms can now be expertly reproduced for us in the retail built environment. Below, I discuss the form and the contradictions inherent in the reproduction of such spaces as conceived in their idealized civic, liminal and transactional forms.

The shopping center as civic space

By virtue of their scale, design, and function, shopping centers appear to be public spaces, more or less open to anyone and relatively sanitary and safe. This appearance is important to their success for they aim to offer to middle Americans a third place beyond home and work/school, a venue where people, old and young, can congregate, commune, and 'see and be seen' (Oldenburg, 1989, p. 17). Several strategies enhance the appearance of vital public space, and foremost is the metaphor of the urban street sustained by street signs, street-lamps, benches, shrubbery, and statuary – all well kept and protected from vandalism. Also like the ideal, benign civic government, shopping centers are extremely sensitive to the needs of the shopper, providing a range of 'inconspicuous artifacts of consideration' (Tuan, 1988, p. 316), such as rest areas and special facilities for the handicapped, elderly, and shoppers with young children (recently including diaper-changing stations). For a fee they may provide other conveniences such as gift wrapping and shipping, coat checking, valet parking, strollers, electric shopping carts, lockers, customer service centers, and videotext information kiosks. They may house post offices, satellite municipal halls, automated government services, and public libraries; space is sometimes provided for public meetings or religious services. They stage events not only to directly promote consumption (fashion and car shows), but also for public edification (educational exhibits and musical recitals). Many open their doors early to provide a safe, sheltered space for morning constitutionals – mall-walking – and some have public exercise stations with health and fitness programs sponsored by the American Heart Association and YMCAs (Jacobs, 1988, p. 12). Some even offer adult literacy classes and university courses.

Such services obviously address the needs of the public and attest to the responsiveness of management. Many facilities, however, are not so much civic gestures as political maneuvers to persuade local government to permit construction on the desired scale. This is particularly the case with day care facilities, now featured in many shopping centers (Reynolds, 1990b, p. 30).[3] It is also clear from the professional literature that many concessions are made in order to enhance the atmosphere of public concern precisely because it significantly, increases retail traffic (McCloud, 1991, p. 25). Public services not consistent with the context of consumption are omitted or only reluctantly provided, often inadequate to actual needs and relegated to the periphery. This includes, for example: drinking fountains, which would reduce soft drink sales; restrooms, which are costly to maintain and which attract activities such as drug dealing and sex that are offensive to the legitimate patrons of the mall (Hazel,

1992, p. 28); and public telephones, which may be monopolized by teenagers or drug dealers. As a result, telephones in some malls allow only outgoing calls (Hazel, 1992, p. 29).

The idealized public street is a relatively democratic space with all citizens enjoying access, with participatory entertainment and opportunities for social mixing, and the shopping center represents a similarly liberal vision of consumption, in which credit-card citizenship allows all to buy an identity and vicariously experience preferred lifestyles, without principles of exclusion based on accumulated wealth or cultural capital (Zukin, 1990, p. 41). It is, however, a strongly bounded or purified social space (Sibley, 1988, p. 409) that excludes a significant minority of the population and so protects patrons from the moral confusion that a confrontation with social difference might provoke (see also Lewis, 1990). Suburban malls, in particular, are essentially spaces for *white* middle classes.[4] There have been several court cases claiming that shopping centers actively discriminate against potential minority tenants, employees, and mall users. Copley Place in Boston, for example, has been charged with excluding minority tenants ('Race is not the Issue', 1990, p. 32); a Columbia, South Carolina mall was accused of discriminatory hiring practices ('NAACP in hiring pact . . .', 1991, p. A20); and security personnel have been widely suspected of harassing minority teenagers. Security personnel target those who, despite implicit signs and posted notices that this is not the place for them, seek to hang out, to take shelter or to solicit alms. Rowdy teenagers may spill out of the amusement arcades designed purposefully to keep them on the periphery, or use the parking lot for cruising, disrupting the comfortable shopping process of adults and particularly the elderly. Consequently, some managers have even tried to regulate hours during which teenagers can shop without adult supervision ('Retailers use bans . . .', 1990, p. B1), and passed ordinances and erected barricades in parking lots to prevent 'unnecessary and repetitive driving' ('Suburbs rain on teens' . . .', 1990, p. 2C1). 'Street people' are harassed because their appearance, panhandling, and inappropriate use of bathrooms (Pawlak *et al.*, 1985) offend the sensibility of shoppers, their presence subverting the normality of conspicuous consumption and perverting the pleasure of consumption by challenging our righteous possession of commodities. Even the Salvation Army may be excluded from making its traditional Christmas collections, perhaps because they remind the consumer of the existence of less privileged populations and so diminish the joy of buying.

Developers must of course protect their property and guard themselves against liability (Hazel, 1992, p. 29), but the key to successful security apparently lies more in an overt security presence that reassures preferred customers that the unseemly and seamy side of the real public world will be excluded from the mall. It is argued that the image of security is more important than its substance:

> Perception is perhaps even more important than reality. In a business that is as dependent as film or theater on appearances, the illusion of safety is as vital, or even more so, than its reality.

> (Hazel, 1992, p. 28)

In extreme cases, however, overt and pervasive security may itself be part of the attraction, and this applies particularly to the 'defensible commercial zones' (Titus, 1990, p. 3) which reclaim part of the decaying inner city for the display of cultural capital and lifestyles of the middle classes. For example, the trademark of Alexander Haagen Development Co., a pioneering inner-city developer much celebrated in the professional literature, is an 8-ft ornamental security fence with remote-controlled gates (Bond, 1989). Such pan-optical presence has been enhanced in some cases by donating mall space for local police.

Finally, the politics of exclusion involves the exclusion of politics, and there is an ongoing struggle by political and civil liberties organizations to require shopping centers to permit handbilling, picketing, and demonstrations on their premises, on the grounds that they cannot pretend to be public spaces without assuming the responsibility of such, including recognition of freedom of expression and assembly. Courts have generally found in favor of free speech in shopping centers by virtue of their scale and similarity to public places, provided that the activities do not seriously impair their commercial function (Peterson, 1985). The Supreme Court, however, has ruled that it is up to individual states to decide (Kowinski, 1985, p. 357), and in a recent case, an anti-war group was successfully banned from leafletting in New Jersey malls ('Judge bars group . . .', 1991, p. 31).

The shopping center as liminal space

The market, standing between the sacred and secular, the mundane and exotic, and the local and global, has always been a place of liminality; that is, according to Turner (1982), a state between social stations, a transitional moment in which established rules and norms are temporarily suspended (see also Shields, 1989; Zukin, 1991). The marketplace is a liminoid zone, a place where potentiality and transgression is engendered by the exciting diversity of humanity, the mystique of exotic objects, the intoxicating energy of the crowd channeled within the confined public space, the prospects of fortunes to be made and lost in trade, the possibility of unplanned meetings and spontaneous adventures, and the continuous assertion of collective rights and freedoms or *communitas* (Bahktin, 1984, pp. 8–9). The market thrives on the possibility of 'letting yourself go', 'treating yourself', and of 'trying it on' without risk of moral censure, and free from institutional surveillance.

Places traditionally associated with liminoid experiences are liberally quoted in the contemporary retail built environment, including most notably seaports and exotic tropical tourist destinations, and Greek agora, Italian piazzas, and other traditional marketplaces. Colorful banners, balloons and flags, clowns and street theater, games and fun rides, are evocative of a permanent carnival or festival. Lavish expenditure on state-of-the-art entertainment and historic reconstruction, and the explosion of apparent liminality is perfectly consistent with the logic of the shopping center, for it is designed explicitly to attract shoppers and keep them on the premises for as long as possible:

The entertainment at Franklin Mills keeps shoppers at the center for 3–4 hours, or twice as long as a regular mall [and] the more you give shoppers to do, the longer they stay and the more they buy.

> (marketing executive, cited in 'Entertainment anchors: . . ., 1989, p. 54).

This strategy reaches its contemporary apotheosis in the monster malls that contrive to combine with retailing the experiences of carnival, festival, and tourism in a single, total environment. The shopping center has become hedonopolis (Sommer, 1975). Shopping centers have become tourist resorts in their own right, recreating the archetypical modern liminal zone by providing the multiple attractions, accommodations, guided tours, and souvenirs essential to the mass touristic experience, *all* under a single roof.[5] The West Edmonton Mall (WEM) in Canada, which receives 15 million visitors a year (and is responsible for more than 1 per cent of all retail sales in Canada (Jones and Simmons, 1987, p. 77)), claims that:

> Tourists will no longer have to travel to Disneyland, Miami Beach, the Epcot Park . . . New Orleans . . . California Sea World, the San Diego Zoo, the Grand Canyon . . . It's all here at the WEM. Everything you've wanted in a lifetime and more.
> (Winter City Showcase, cited in Hopkins, 1990, p. 13).

There are necessarily strict limits to any experience of liminality in these environments. Developers are well aware of the 'more unsavory trappings of carnival life' (McCloud, 1989b, p. 35), and order must be preserved. . . . Liminality is thus experienced in the nostalgic mode, without the inherent danger of the real thing: the fairground is recreated without the threat to the social order that the itinerant, marginal population and the libidinal temptations that traveling shows might bring, while the revitalized waterfronts lack the itinerant sailors, the red lights, the threatening presence of foreign travelers and shiphands. The contrived retail carnival denies the potentiality for disorder and collective social transgression of the liminal zone at the same time that it celebrates its form. It is ironic, therefore, that WEM is struggling to cope with the liminality it has unintentionally unleashed, including accidental deaths on fairground rides, terroristic activity, drug trading, and prostitution (Hopkins, 1990, p. 14).

The shopping center as transactional space

Regardless of the location and scale of the development, a constant theme in contemporary retail space is a nostalgia for the traditional public marketplace, or what we might call *agoraphilia*. In the idealized traditional market place, there is an immediate relationship between producer and consumer, and both apply knowledge and skill to judge quality and negotiate price. Vendors ideally sell their own product and have direct responsibility for its quality. They are also in competition with other traders, so presentation and service are important, and they acquire considerable interpersonal skill and extensive knowledge of their customers. Such commitment and initiative are not to be expected among the retail staff of the increasingly large, centralized retail corporations, but in response to the perceived deterioration of service, mall management may organize training sessions to improve sales techniques.

To further solve the problem of indolent and insolent attendants, contemporary retailing has learned from the theater, and particularly the total theater of North American theme parks (Aronson, 1977; Davis, 1991). For example, as if the management had read Goffman (or did Goffman read Disney?), sales staff in a Fred Meyer megastore in appropriately named Hollywood West in Portland, Oregon, enter through the Stage Door and are admonished to 'get into character' ('Fred Meyer megastore . . .', 1990, p. 76). The Disney Store sales staff are 'cast members' and customers are 'guests'. . . . Personal service and craft quality of the product are also suggested by reproduction accoutrements of the traditional marketplace. Costermongers' barrows, for example, are increasingly ubiquitous in conventional shopping centers, quoting the traditional marketplace and the virtues of petty trade even when they are franchised and display mass-produced T-shirts.

The modern consumer, like the modern worker, has been threatened by deskilling and loss of identity in the impersonal, abstract relationships of the mass market. Contemporary retailing, however, under the postmodern impulse, seeks to reskill the consumer, and there has arisen an expanded 'class' of cultural intermediaries who through TV shows and consumer magazines help the busy consumer process the enormous volume of product information required to interpret correctly the latest advertized commodity and style (Zukin, 1990, p. 45). Perhaps the equivalent in this context is the regional and urban shopping guides produced by tourist bureaus, chambers of commerce, or other promotional organizations, and guides published for specific shopping centers.

The shopping center is *instrumental space*

> Areas in Tyson's Corner used by the public are not public ways, but are for the use of the tenants and the public transacting business with them. Permission to use said areas may be revoked at any time.
> (text of notice at entrance of Tyson's Corner, cited in Kowinski, 1985, p. 355)

Most shoppers know that the shopping center is a contrived and highly controlled space, and we all probably complain about design features such as the escalators that alternate in order to prevent the shopper moving quickly between floors without maximum exposure to shopfronts, or the difficulty of finding restrooms. Some of us are also disquieted by the constant reminders of surveillance in the sweep of the cameras and the patrols of security personnel. Yet those of us for whom it is designed are willing to suspend the privileges of public urban space to its relatively benevolent authority, for our desire is such that we will readily accept nostalgia as a substitute for experience, absence for presence, and representation for authenticity. We overlook the fact that the shopping center is a contrived, dominated space that seeks only to resemble a spontaneous, social space. Perhaps also, we are simply ignorant of the extent to which there is a will to deceive us. The professional literature is revealing. In this literature, the consumer is characterized as an object to be mechanistically manipulated – to be drawn, pulled, pushed, and led to flow magnets, anchors, generators, and attractions; or as a naive dupe to be deceived, persuaded, induced, tempted, and seduced by ploys, ruses, tricks, strategies, and games of the design. Adopting a relatively vulgar psychogeography, designers seek to environmentally condition emotional and behavioral response from those whom they see as their *mall*eable customers.

The ultimate conceit of the developers, however, lies in their attempt to recapture the essence of tradition through modern technology, to harness abstract space and exchange value in order to retrieve the essence of use value of social space (Lefebvre, 1971). The original intention may have been more noble, but the contradiction soon became apparent, and the dream of community and public place was subordinated to the logic of private profit. Victor Gruen himself returned to his home city of Vienna disillusioned and disgusted at the greed of developers (Gillette, 1985), while James Rouse formed a non-profit organization engaged in urban renewal.[6] The contemporary generation of developers may still express the modernist faith in the capacity of environmental design to realize social goals, but one somehow doubts that Nader Ghermezian, one of the developers of the monstrous WEM, is genuine when he claims their goal is 'to serve as a community, social, entertainment, and recreation center' (cited in Davis, 1991, p. 4).

The shopping center as a spatial system

The built environment forms a spatial system in which, through principles of separation and containment, spatial practices are routinized and sedimented (Giddens, 1985, p. 272) and social relations are reproduced. First, the locale provides the context in which particular roles are habitually played and actions predictably occur, establishing spatiotemporal fields of absence and presence, and affecting the potentialities for social interaction. The association of regions with particular group membership, activities, and dispositions allows the individual to orient to the context and infer the appropriate social role to play – one literally comes to know one's place. The built environment is, therefore, socially and psychologically persuasive (Eco, 1986, p. 77). Second, the configuration of spatial forms determines the relative permeability of structures, physically limiting the possibility of movement and interaction. The relative connectivity, transitivity, and commutativity of spaces serves to segregate individuals and practices, and to (re)inforce the differential capacities of agents for social action. Social relations are realized in homolgous geometrical relations. For example, the dialectic of inside–outside (Bachelard, 1964, p. 215) realizes priciples of inclusion–exclusion, while that of open and closed realizes distinctions between public and private realms. The built environment is then also physically persuasive or coercive.

Within the shopping center, social segregation is reproduced through separation of specific functions and of class-based retail districts. Bridgewater

Commons in Bridgewater, New Jersey, for example, has three distinct leasing districts designed to appeal to specific market segments and, by implication, not to appeal to others: The Commons Collection contains upscale boutiques and includes marble floors, gold leaf signage, brass accents, individual wooden seating, and extensive foliage; The Promenade contains stores catering to home and family needs, storefronts have a more conservative look, and aluminum and steel features and seating are predominant; The Campus contains stores catering to a 'contemporary clientele' with dynamic window displays, plastic laminate, ceramic tiling, bright colors, and neon signage (see Rathbun, 1990, pp. 19–21). Almost every shopping center marks the distinction between high-end and low-end retail by such environmental cues.

The shopping center is designed to persuade the targeted users to move through the retail space and to adopt certain physical and social dispositions conducive to shopping. Let us begin with the entrance to the regional mall. The approved mode of approach is obviously the automobile, and the shopper proceeds across the bleak desert of the parking lot towards the beckoning entrance, usually the only break in the harsh, uniform exterior and typically announced with canopies, columns, and glass atria, surrounded by lush vegetation, all suggestive of an oasis or sanctuary inside. Here external reality is immediately displaced: the temperature is kept at a scientifically determined optimum for human comfort, typically a pleasant 68°F in winter and a refreshing 72°F degrees in summer. Shophouse-style storefronts are often reduced to 5/8 scale (as in Disney's theme parks) to give shoppers an exaggerated sense of importance, transporting them into a looking-glass world.

Indoor lighting is soft to prevent glare on shopfronts and to highlight the natural colors of the commodities on display. Lights act as 'silent salesmen . . . [which] showcase the most pricey merchandise to stellar advantage and transform the most pedestrian goods into must-haves' (Connor, 1989, p. 191). . . . Muzak has been replaced by customized foreground music, which research shows may increase retail sales by up to 40 per cent (Pyle, 1990, p. 23). Mirrors and reflective glass add to the decorative multiplication of images and colors, double the space and the shopping crowd (Fiske *et al.*, 1987, p. 101), and reflect shoppers, asking them to compare themselves with the manikins and magical commodities on display in the fantasy world of the shop window. Even in glasshouse malls, there are no windows that look out on the world except up at the sky; there are no means but the seasonal promotional activities to determine the time of year, no clock to tell the time of day, and no means but the identity of retail chains to determine regional location. The modern shopping center is literally a utopia, an idealized nowhere (*ou* = no; *topos* = place), and thus on a Saturday afternoon at about 2 p.m., the terror of time and space evaporates for the millions of Americans at the mall.

This utopia is kept scrupulously clean and orderly, without any material contamination nor hint of the gradual obsolescence that characterizes material objects. It is kept perfect and ageless by personnel who may be employed to do nothing else but constantly polish or touch up the spotless shiny surfaces. The backstage areas, where commodities are delivered, prepared and serviced, are concealed by landscaping, painted panels, and underground construction to protect the customers from knowledge of the activities that take place there, so preserving the myth of the pure, abstract commodity for sale. Access to these areas is impossible for those who do not know the plan.

The floorplan exerts strong centripetal tendencies, and the shopper is drawn further into the fantasy by tantalizing glimpses of attractive central features, past the relatively drab marginal tenants (mostly services) into the colorful and well-lit wonderland of consumption. This experience disorients the shopper and, just as in the fantasy worlds of popular literature and film, it is then notoriously difficult to find one's way out. According to one designer, 'a too direct and obvious a route between the entrance and exits must be avoided' (Beddington, 1982, p. 16), and exits must be carefully designed because 'if too prominent and inviting as seen from within they may sweep the unsuspected [*sic*] shopper from the centre' (Beddington, 1982, p. 27). Even fire exits are disguised as shopfronts or hidden behind mirrors almost to the point of invisibility (Scott, 1989, pp. 192–3). The mall is thus designed as a non-commutative space, and the goal is to trap the consumer in the world of consumption.

The shopping center is a machine for shopping: it employs crude, but very effective, behaviorist principles to move patrons efficiently through the retail built environment. The developer's first law of shopper behavior says that the American shopper will not willingly walk more than 600 ft (Garreau, 1991, pp. 117–18, 464). Mall length is conventionally limited to this distance lest shoppers be disinclined to walk to the next department store (or be tempted to get into their cars to drive to it!). There are a number of generic designs depending on the number of anchors: a wheelspoke layout draws customers to a single anchor from surrounding car parks; the classic dumbbell design (developed by Gruen) channels consumers along a corridor between two anchors; and a T or L shape is used for three and a cruciform for four anchors. If mall distances are longer, this fact must be concealed from the consumer, typically by breaking the space with strong focal points and attractions, or by obscuring the view with pop-out shopfronts. One developer, for example, explains:

> throughout the mall, towers, fountains and dramatic shop fronts are partially revealed to shoppers as they pass a bend. . . . Sensing the promise of another reward 100 ft ahead, shoppers are encouraged to head towards this next destination.
>
> ('Fitting a shopping center . . .', 1991, p. 28)

Another strategy designed to keep shoppers circulating while reducing the friction of distance is the construction of a narrative which unfolds around the center, such as numbered plants with botanical descriptions, or 'historic' markers. Pier 39 in San Francisco, for example, uses numbered plaques narrating the story of the construction of the shopping center in appropriately heroic terms and directing the shopper further into the center to read the next installment (Figure 9.2).

Mall widths are conventionally restricted to about 6 m in order to allow shoppers to take in shopfronts on both sides, and to maintain the sense of

Fig. 9.2 Constructing a narrative and directing the shopper through the mall: Pier 39 in San Francisco (courtesy of the author)

intimate, human scale. Wider malls allow for placement of seating, softscape, and kiosks in the center, obstacles that might draw shoppers along while also deflecting them towards intervening stores (Gottdiener, 1986). Pop-out displays and open storefronts are designed to coax shoppers into the interior to make the impulse purchase. More subtle is the use of floor patterns to suggest pathways through the mall and towards open storefronts, a strategy employed, for example, in Pearlridge Shopping Center in Pearl City, Hawaii.

In multistory shopping centers, the design must also encourage vertical movement so that pedestrian traffic is exposed to shop displays on all floors. Maitland (1990, pp. 49–50), in a design manual, suggests 'devices' to 'persuade' and 'invite' people to move upward; these include 'glass-bubble' elevators, stacked escalator banks (as in the Trump Tower), overhanging platforms and aerial walkways (as at Pier 39 and Horton Plaza respectively), towering waterfalls and fountains, and mobiles of birds, manikins, balloons and aircraft. Such design features celebrate the drama and aesthetics of motion, drawing the eye and the person to upper levels.

Shoppers cannot be kept moving all the time, of course; they must be allowed to rest from the arduous tasks of shopping, particularly as the average trip to the shopping center has reportedly increased from only twenty minutes in 1960 to nearly three hours today (Crawford, 1992, p. 14). However,

Pause points for shoppers to rest, review their programmes and re-arrange their purchases etc. also need planning with care. Seating, while offering a convenient stopping point, must not be too luxurious or comfortable. Shoppers must move on and allow re-occupation of seating and the danger of attracting the 'down and outs'of various categories must be avoided.

(Beddington, 1982, p. 36)

The need to rest for longer periods is recognized mainly in the food court, where, of course, shoppers will be consuming at the same time. Food courts have become an absolute necessity, in part because of the increased role of food as a marker of social taste, in part also because the presentation of diverse culinary experiences enhances the sense of elsewhere (food courts now typically present a range of 'ethnic' cuisines), and because it provides a vantage point for watching others display their commodified lifestyles (Goss, 1992, 174). Although development costs are greater than for other outlets, food courts are significant determinants of the shoppers' choice of shopping center, and are the main attraction for downtown office workers during lunch hour. Located in the interior or on upper floors they can also, like department stores, draw customers past the specialty stores. Research finds that food courts can prolong a visitors stay by an average of ten to fifteen minutes (Reynolds, 1990b, p. 51).

The space created by the developer – pedestrian malls and mock street cafes – and the activity it is designed to sustain – relaxed strolling, window-shopping, and people-watching – seem reminiscent of *flanerie*, the progress of the voyeuristic dandy who strolled the streets and arcades of Paris in the nineteenth century. Several authors have drawn on the work of Benjamin (1973) in making this observation, and, with appropriate gender neutralization of the term, have been predisposed to see in it a recovery of a lost form of public behavior and personal expression (see, for example, Shields, 1989; Hopkins, 1990; Friedberg, 1991). But while the 'mallies' (Jacobs, 1988) seek pleasure in the display, the commercialization of the context has radically altered meaning, and what we witness, I suspect, is not the recovery of *flanerie* but a nostalgia for its form which only marks its effective absence. The contemporary flaneur cannot escape the imperative to consume: she or he cannot loiter in the mall unless implicitly invited to do so, and this generally applies only to the respectable elderly;[7] those without shopping bags and other suspicious individuals (teenagers, single men, the unkempt, and social science researchers) will draw the attention of security, who use the charge of loitering as grounds for eviction. Moreover, shoppers do not independently pick their way like the leisurely flaneur, but follow the meticulously conceived plan which has plotted paths, set lures, and planted decoys for its purpose. There is little chance of taking a route or occupying a position unforeseen by this plan (Bukatman 1991, p. 69).

The shopping center is, therefore, a *strategic* space, owned and controlled by an institutional power, which, by its nature, depends upon the definition, appropriation and control of territory (De Certeau, 1984). Its designers seek to deny the possibility of *tactics*, an oppositional occupation by everyday practices; that is, activities which do not require a specific localization or spatially but which may temporarily use, occupy or take possession of strategic space

(De Certeau, 1984). There are no spaces that might be claimed by uninvited gestures or unprescribed 'pedestrian utterances' (De Certeau, 1985, p. 129) since potential microspaces are pre-emptively filled: whether dignified by static features (such as sculptures or potted plants), 'animated' by active, permanent features (such as mobiles, mechanical displays, or fountains), or 'programmed' with a performance by musicians, mimes, or street artist (see Garreau, 1991, p. 443, 456). In case anyone should be inspired to spontaneous performance, the stages and gazebos provided for programs are inevitably roped off and sign-posted to discourage them. When activated, these installations nevertheless provide a sense of public space and help draw shoppers through the mall. Graphics and murals are also used to enliven routes, dramatize motion, and avoid 'the depressing effects of dead areas' (Beddington, 1982, p. 82). Spaces and surfaces should be filled because, if everywhere in this environment there is a sign, the absence of a sign becomes a sign of absence: perhaps signifying a lack of anticipation and consideration on behalf of the developer, or more seriously, the perceived emptiness of consumption itself, but inevitably inviting a motion to fill the void.

The shopping center and signification

Elements of the built environment are signifiers which refer, through culturally determined systems of association, to abstract concepts, social relations, or ideologies. In combination, they constitute texts which communicate social meaning to acculturated readers. The built environment first denotes its function, informing the user of its practical purpose. Thus, for example, the shopping center announces itself through its location and its conventional form as a p(a)lace of consumption. A wide range of styles is practicable, however, in realizing this basic function, and even the most technologically constrained architectural solutions give symbolic expression (Winner, 1980, p. 127). The built environment is also always, therefore, connotative of meaning, consistent with, but extending beyond its immediate function. As Barthes (1979, p. 6) expresses it: 'architecture is always dream and function, [an] expression of a utopia and instrument of a convenience.

[T]he presence of nature, albeit tamed in a garden setting, naturalizes consumption, and mitigates the alienation inherent in commodity production and consumption. Hence the recent proliferation of natural-products stores and the extraordinary lengths developers may go to in order to capture and display commodified nature for this premium.[8]

Water seems to be particularly important. Fountains signify civilized urban space, while, on a larger scale, the importance of the waterfront to retail environments is due to their association with sport and recreation, historic trade, and the potential for a new life of adventure. . . .

Similarly pervasive is the signification of the past in the retail built environment, as the 'heritage industry' (Hewison, 1989) exploits our collective nostalgia for real places and historic roots. This is best illustrated in the festival marketplaces, which reproduce historical landscapes in the city with restored architectural details, antique material artifacts strewn almost casually on the landscape, and professional actors in period costume portraying historical characters. Needless to say, this historical vernacular effects an idealization of the past and mystifies its relationship with the present. Although extreme attention is paid to minor details, the reconstruction is fitted with modern facilities, and no reference is made to exploitative social relations that may have actually structured life at the time.

If the sense of history is violated in the shopping center, so is time itself. A symptomatic and almost universal new feature of the postmodern retail environment is the clock (Goss, 1992, p. 174). Previously banished because of its reminder of the precious value of time and the power of its regime over the modern individual, it is now often set prominently in a plaza or court, where it quotes public places of the past, or is mounted on towers and bracketed to façades, quoting the respectable historical institutions of the church and main street business.

The combination of the prominent clock and atria or gallery bears a resemblance to the nineteenth-century railway station (see Figure 9.3), a place that marks liminality, with its prospects for romance and mystery extolled in countless popular novels and movies.

Fig. 9.3 A clock as a focal point, reminiscent of a Victorian railway station. The Galleria, San Francisco (courtesy of the author)

One of the most dramatic innovations, a part of the carnivalization of the retail built environment, is the carousel. These oxymoronic conceits represent the fairgrounds of an imagined childhood, and play upon a collective nostalgia for the lost innocence of youth and for *old-fashioned* fun – hence the carousel must be a restored antique or exact reproduction. The 49th Street Galleria, part of Franklin Mills in Philadelphia, even advertizes a 'turn of the century family outing' and indoor Family Fun Centers are now replacing the banks of video games with more wholesome 'old-fashioned modes of fun' (Sicard, 1991, p. 26).

Art, on the other hand, has always had a place in the retail built environment because it symbolizes a non-commercialized aesthetic, and because it is a form of object display sanctioned by high culture (Harris, 1990). Its auratic content is also meant to spill over into the commodities on sale and to sanctify shopping by association with the legitimate activity of aesthetic appreciation. Hence shopping centers host symphonies (Southland hosted the Minneapolis Symphony Orchestra), operas (the Bel Canto competition is held in shopping centers across the country), and Shakespearean plays (staged, for example, at Lakeforest Mall in Gaithersburg, Maryland) (see Goss, 1992, p. 174). Considerable sums are invested in fixed art displays. . . . This art rarely demands to be interpreted, so one suspects that its purpose is merely to be recognized as a sign of what it is – that is, Art, a mystified quality of high culture. At the same time, of course, it does allow those with cultivated tastes to exercise and display their cultural capital and so mark their distinction from the mass consumer (see Bourdieu, 1984). Art exhibits also act as focal features drawing customers along the mall, filling empty spaces, and enhancing the sense of public space ('City's love of art . . .', 1991, p. 103). Like other corporate art, shopping center displays signify a commitment to public edification expected of a benevolent authority and are a means to express and legitimate the power of the owner.

Art has, of course, long been deployed in marketing, and the separation of the commercial and aesthetic was always problematical, yet the distinction has definitively ruptured under the assault of contemporary commodification. The ultimate collapse of the categorical distinction is presaged by the fact that art and cultural museums are now sited in mixed-use retail centers. . . . Moreover, museums have opened retail outlets in shopping centers where 'authentic reproductions' and souvenirs of artifacts are sold (for example, satellite stores of the Museum of Modern Art sell high-quality reproductions of art and souvenir merchandise). Most telling, however, is that the first funds ever awarded to a private corporation by the National Endowment for the Arts went to Rouse and Co. to develop art projects in shopping malls ('NEA funds art . . .' 1990, p. C1).

More recent too is continuous reference to the television and the emulation of televisual experience within the retail built environment. The shopper strolls through experiences as he or she might scan through TV channels (see Kowinkski, 1985, 71–3; Kroker *et al.*, 1989, p. 109; Davis, 1991, p. 5) and is bombarded by simultaneous images of multiple places and times; spatial narratives dissolve and individual pedestrian trajectories or narratives are constantly broken by contrived obstacles. Developers recognize that their customers expect drama, excitement, and constant visual stimulation thanks to the effect of television, and they seek to provide a surrogate televisual experience (O'Connor, 1989, p. 290).

The connection with TV goes further. As noted earlier, both the retail built environment and the TV function primarily to display and sell commodities and the lifestyles associated with them; both are escapes from suburban every-day life, a means of transport from reality; and both are highly controlled media that play to the cultural bottom line, presuming a passive, psychologi-cally manipulatable public. There has been recently a phenomenal televisuali-zation of the retailing concept that is, the direct lifting of retail concepts from television shows in stores such as Cartoon Junction, the Disney Store, Hanna Barbera Shop, NFL for Kids, Circle Gallery of Animation and Cartoon Art, Sanrio Co., and the Sesame Street General Store). Thus it can truly be said that 'shopping malls are liquid TVs for the end of the twentieth century' (Kroker *et al.*, 1989, p. 208).

Also analogous to the TV, in its capacity to allow viewers to be simultaneously in multiple times and places even while sitting at home, the shopping center creates a diverse range of temporal and spatial experiences within a comfortable landscape for consumption. Hopkins (1990), for example, has described the metonymical strategies by which shopping centers exploit 'myths of elsewhere' to elicit specific behavioral responses. First, they employ semantic metonyms or place names. Typically, early centers favored names redolent of Arcadia or pas-toral scenes (Country Club, Highland Park, Farmers Market, etc.), while modern suburban malls employ utopian, placeless names (Northland, Southland, etc.), and contemporary centers may imply tourist and other liminal destinations (Harborfront, Seaport Village, Forest Fair, etc.). Garreau (1991, p. 471) suggests facetiously that such evocative names are used in direct propor-tion to their distance from the reality they describe. More effective perhaps is the use of iconic metonyms, or objects which function as signs of other places and times, to evoke stereotypical associations. Standing synecdochally for other places, such icons are also metaphors for the spatial experience of other places, in the manner by which, say, the Eiffel Tower, which first stands for Paris, then evokes *haute cuisine*, cosmopolitan sophistication, and relaxed elegance. Gen-eric icons such as fountains, benches, statuary, and clocks signify traditional urban public space, and evoke notions of community and civic pride. More elaborate reconstructions of other places, whether generic . . . or specific . . . quote well-worn clichés of place from our collective *musée imaginaire*. These simulated places exude an 'aura of familiarity' (Davis, 1991, p. 2) and provoke predictable associations and dispositions facilitating consumption.

Moving on the mall: reclaiming the shopping center

Fer sure, we have the wolfpacks and kyotes comin down from the hills, and the freewaymen robbin us, but we are lucky because we live in the Great Mall, where the Wall portect us, and we have the Warmth and Stuff inside. After the fal de rol, isn't the Mall the winner of our disconnect?

(Kowinski, 1985, p. 394).

The shopping center appears to be everything that it is not. It contrives to be a public civic place even though it is private and run for profit; it offers a place to commune and recreate, while it seeks retail dollars; and it borrows signs of other places and times to obscure its rootedness in contemporary capitalism. The shopping center sells paradoxical experiences to its customers, who can safely experience danger, confront the Other as a familiar, be tourists without going on vacation, go to the beach in the depths of winter, and be outside when in. It is quite literally a fantastic place. It is a representation of space masquerading as a representational space (Lefebvre, 1991, pp. 38–9); that is, a space conceptualized, planned scientifically and realized through strict technical control, pretending to be a space imaginatively created by its inhabitants. The shopping center is conceived by the elitist science of planning, which operates under the calculus of retail profit and applies behavioral theories of human action for purposes of social control, and yet part of that conception is its disguise as a popular space which has been created by the spontaneous, individual tactics of everyday life.

While it is an insult to the shopper to suggest that she or he is totally duped by the spatial strategies described above (Shields, 1989, p. 157; Hopkins, 1991, p. 270), the postmodernist celebration of the *jouissance* experienced by the knowledgeable consumer and of the *flanerie* of the new dandy involves an equally problematical elitist position. The 'captains of consciousness' perhaps understand as well as the academic culture theorists the class structuration of consumption, and they have exploited this in the design of a multiply coded retail built environment that communicates particular meanings to different audiences, as in the conceit of postmodernism, which nods condescendingly to the majority and winks knowingly at the cognoscenti (see Jencks, 1986, p. 373). The shopping center apparently caters to all, with circuses for the masses and fine art for the elite, consciously providing those 'in the know' with the means to mark their distinction. More seriously, this optimistic assessment underestimates the capacity of the organizational intelligence behind the spatial strategies of control. A sophisticated apparatus researches consumers' personal profiles, their insecurities and desires, and produces a space that comfortably satisfies both individual and mass consumers and manipulates the behavior of both to not-so-different degrees.

The question then is how to retrieve these spaces from such calculated control, and there are a number of possible tactics directed at each of the conceptions of the retail built environment developed above. First is the exposure of the fetishism of the commodity and the re-problematization of the relations of consumption. Consumer activists, for example, have exposed the materialism of the commodity by organizing information campaigns and consumer boycotts undermining the magic of commodities such as Coors beer, Burger King fast foods, and Ratners jewelry (see also Smith, 1990). Advertizers have been forced by the increasing environmental consciousness and social awareness of consumers to make some progressive changes in their campaigns, but they have also countered effectively by further mystifying the connections, exploiting the magic of advertizing to associate even the most environmentally culpable products, such as nuclear power and oil, with nature, cleanliness, and justice, as a browse through any liberal magazine will attest.

Consumers may also infer meanings unintended by the captains of consciousness, or appropriate meanings to which they are not socially entitled, such as the manner in which surplus military clothing becomes a skinhead's uniform. There are, however, inherent limits to this form of subversion of commodity symbolism, in that while temporarily challenging the established order of the image, it still employs the object code and is thus relatively easily co-opted – radical soon becomes radical chic.

Second is the attempt to resist the economic and spatial logic of the shopping center. As noted, the struggle of community groups against large-scale retail development in their neighborhoods has had some limited success in some parts of the USA, particularly the North-West, through delaying construction and negotiating environmental concessions from developers ('Building despite the obstacles . . .', 1990). In most places, however, these strategies are more limited owing to what is generally perceived by localities and states to be the need for capital investment in their communities. Most urban communities, in particular, are only too happy, if financially capable, to provide developers with incentives, and in this context development offers an undoubted improvement in environmental quality. Moreover, environmental and community-based resistance is effective only against new development, while renovation of existing centers is fast becoming the dominant trend.

Third is the struggle to open the shopping center to all activities consistent with public space, even those that may affront the sensibilities of the consumer or disrupt the smooth process of consumption. This requires sustaining and broadening the pressure upon management already being exerted by civil rights groups in courts of law, and by teenagers and others in petty, everyday skirmishes with security. While ideologically interpreted as assaults upon the rights of private property, such political and tactical actions must be supported as a struggle for public space and at least minimal rights of citizenship for all in the consumer society. By confronting the rights of exclusion, encouraging the presence of undesirable activities, and challenging the legality of such rights in court, we can expose the ersatz and profoundly undemocratic nature of public space and the controlled carnival manufactured in the contemporary retail environment.

Fourth is the tactical occupation of spaces, particularly by actions that would be excluded by the signs and security guards of private property. No architectural form is entirely effective, and all spaces must open up some possibilities as they shut others down. As Eco (1986, p. 77) notes, architecture fluctuates between being coercive, forcing one to live and behave in a particular way, and indifferent, allowing one freedom to move, express oneself, and dream. Users of the shopping center may pursue such freedoms and exploit the opportunities that shopping centers present. It is only the overwhelming normalcy of everyone and everything in the shopping center that allows the will of the plan to remain unquestioned. The unpredictabilities of the world are constantly penetrating the mall, of course, and designers and managers must keep up a constant rate of architectonic innovation to keep it at bay. Petty vandalism, such as graffiti, packets of detergent thrown into mall fountains (Scott, 1989, p. 74), and increasing occurrences of interpersonal violence (Hazel, 1992, p. 27) are examples of some of the more overt and male-dominated tactics, while increasing theft is an example of a covert, female-dominated tactic.

Finally there is the attempt to subvert the systems of signification operating in the retail built environment. This involves recognizing the intention behind the sign – which I have attempted – and a far more creative appropriation, or reassignment of meaning. The built environment is always complexly and multiply coded, and the assignation of specific meaning depends upon the predisposition of the reader. There is always the potential for consciously perverted interpretation, a challenge to the meaning of sign and to the class structuration of the signification system.

More significant then will be attempts by the users themselves to subvert meaning through strategies of social parody and 'detournement of pre-existing aesthetic elements' (Knabb, 1981, p. 45; see also Bonnett, 1989, p. 135). [E]ffective tactics can only employ the means of the strategy against itself, by taking it at its word and taking its word to extremes. Users already do this to a limited extent, treating the mall as the social space it pretends to be, 25 per cent freely enjoying its facilities without making a purchase ('Who shops in shopping malls?', 1989, p. 43). What I have in mind, however, is the construction of situations; that is, the collective staging of games and farcical events, by artists, activists, and the shopping center patrons themselves, that can temporarily bring carnival into the shopping center, upsetting the conventional play of signification, subverting the cultural codes that are strategically deployed. The psychogeographers of the retail environment are perhaps pushing the limits of their spatial and representational strategies, and the shopping center may become too successful, as users take what is contrived as merely a *realistic* experience of public place as *really real*.

Ultimately, however, we must realize that the nostalgia we experience for authenticity, commerce, and carnival lies precisely in the loss of our ability collectively to create meaning by occupying and using social spaces for ourselves. While developers may design the retail built environment in order to satisfy this nostalgia, our real desire, as Frow (1991, p. 129) notes, is for community and social space free from instrumental calculus of design.

Notes

1 The term is borrowed from Wood (1985, p. 81), who uses it to describe 'places made over to be something they never were'.
2 Rouse's other schemes include Harborplace in Baltimore, South Street Seaport in New York, Santa Monica Place in Santa Monica, California; the Tivoli Brewery in Denver, the Grand Avenue in Milwaukee, St Louis Union Station in St Louis, Portside in Toledo, and Waterside in Norfolk. Other festival marketplaces based on this model include, for example, Harbour Island in Tampa, Trapper's Alley in Detroit, Rainbow Center in Niagara Falls, New York, Marina Marketplace in Buffalo, Pier 39 in San Francisco, and Charleston Place in Charleston, South Carolina.

Less publicized failures include 6th St Marketplace in Richmond and Water St Pavilion in Flint (Sawicki, 1989, p. 348).

3 Although required by some local governments, day care is not proving very successful because of the difficulty and cost of obtaining liability insurance and of parental distrust of strangers (Reynolds, 1990a, p. 29). More in keeping with the commodified setting is a novel enterprise, part day care, part entertainment for children, pioneered in Evergreen Plaza in Rolling Meadows, Illinois. Children may be deposited at 'kids only cartoon theaters', where they are 'barcoded' with identification tags and constantly monitored by video while they watch continuous cartoons. The parent is given a pager in case problems arise or they fail to return within the prescribed time. Electronic doors prevent children leaving, and the same adult must collect them with the barcode on the pager also matched with that on the child.

4 Note, however, that downtown developers have recently discovered the 'positive demographics' of minorities and have designed centers and tenant mix explicitly to capture these underserved markets. This applies especially to Hispanics; centers directed explicitly at Hispanic markets include, for example, the Mercado in Phoenix, Fiesta Marketplace in Santa Ana, California, Galleria of the Americas in New York, and Palm Plaza in Hialeah, Florida.

5 Hotels and conference centers act as anchor tenants, drawing tourists and conventioneers to shopping centers. Examples include Central Coast Plaza in San Luis Obispo, California; Pickwell Center in Pickwell, Ohio; Carnation Mall, Alliance, Ohio; Greenbrier Mall, Chesapeake, Virginia; and Harbour Island. The Riverchase Galleria, Birmingham, Alabama, for example, markets weekend shoppers' specials that keep its hotel full with busloads of people from neighboring states (McCloud, 1989a, p. 23).

6 Gruen claimed that 'the inventiveness which expressed itself so clearly in the first pioneering centers has given way to repetition and routine' (1973, p. 42), and that 'financial greed has debased . . . the idea . . . [The] environmental and humane ideas underlying, though not perfectly expressed, in the original centres . . . were completely forgotten' (1978, pp. 350–1).

7 The elderly are specifically encouraged to the shopping center by free transport and 'specials' because they impart a sense of safe public space and enhance the reputation of the management as civic-minded. Also, the 'mature market' (over fifty years old) is expanding rapidly as 'yuppies' become 'grumpies' (grown-up mature professionals), has the highest disposable income and greatest assets, and spends more on grandchildren's clothes than do the parents ('Sixty something', 1991, p. 31).

8 The developer personally chose the twenty-nine 30-ft palms that grace Tyson's Corner in Fairfax County, Virginia. Trees were dug up in Florida and kept for 18 months in shade houses to gradually acclimatize them to indoors before being taken in temperature-controlled trucks to their new home.

References

Adorno, T. and Horkheimer, M. 1969: *The dialectic of enlightenment*. New York: Continuum.

Aronson, A. 1977: The total theatrical environment: impression management in the parks. *Theatre Crafts* September, 35–76.

Bakhtin, M. M. 1984: *Rabelais and his world*. Bloomington: Indiana University Press.

Barthes, R. 1979: *The Eiffel Tower and other mythologies*. New York: Hill & Wang.

Baudrillard, J. 1983: *Simulations*. New York: Semiotexte.

Beddington, N. 1982: *Design for shopping centres*. London: Butterworth Scientific.

Benjamin, W. 1973: *Charles Baudelaire: A lyric poet in the era of high capitalism*. London: New Left Books.

Bond, R. 1989: Feeling safe again. *Shopping Center World*, November, 181–4.

Bonnett, A. 1989: Situationism, geography, and poststructuralism. *Environment and Planning D: Society and Space* 7, 131–46.

Boorstin, D. J. 1973: *The Americans: The democratic experience*. New York: Vintage Books.

Bourdieu, P. 1984: *Distinction: A social critique of the judgment of taste*. Cambridge, MA: Harvard University Press.

Building despite the obstacle: anti-growth sentiment, local restrictions slow retail development. 1990: *Chain Store Age Executive*, June, 27–32.

Bukatman, S. 1991: There's always tomorrowland: the Disney and hypercinematic experience. October 57, 55–78.

City's love of art expressed in mall. 1991: *Shopping Center World*, November, 103.

Cloar, J. A. 1990: Centralized retail management: New strategies for downtown. Washington, Urban Land Institute.

Connor, P. 1989: 'Silent salesmen' at work inside and out. *Chain Store Age Executive*, November, 191–5.

Crawford, M. 1992: The world in a shopping mall. In: Sorkin, M. (ed.), *Variations on a theme park: The new American city and the end of public space*. New York: Hill & Wang, 3–30.

Davis, T. C. 1991: Theatrical antecedents of the mall that ate downtown. *Journal of Popular Culture* 24(4), 1–15.

Debord, G. 1983: *Society of the spectacle*. Detroit: Red and Black.

De Certeau, M. 1984: The practice of everyday life. Berkeley: University of California Press.

De Certeau, M. 1985: Practices of space. In: Blonsky, M. (ed.), *On signs*, Cambridge, MA: Blackwell, 122–45.

Eco, U. 1986: Function and sign: the semiotics of architecture. In Gottdiener, M. and Lagopoulos, A. Ph. (eds), *The city and the sign*. New York: Columbia University Press, 55–86.

Entertainment anchors: new mall headliners. 1989: *Chain Store Age Executive*, August, 54, 63, 65.

Enzenberger, H-M. 1974: *The consciousness industry*. New York: Seabury.

Fiske, J., Hodge, R. and Turner, G. 1987: *Myths of Oz: Readings in Australian popular culture*. Boston: Unwin Hyman.

Fitting a shopping center to downtown. 1991: *Urban Land*, July, 28–9.

Fred Meyer megastore goes Hollywood. 1990: *Chain Store Age Executive*, March, 76–8.

Friedberg, A. 1991: Les flaneurs du mal(l): cinema and the postmodern condition. *Publications of the Modern Language Association* 106, 419–31.

Frieden, B. J. and Sagalyn, L. B. 1989: *Downtown, Inc.: How America rebuilds cities*. Cambridge, MA: MIT Press.

Frow, J. 1991: Tourism and the semiotics of nostalgia. *October* 57, 123–51.

Garreau, J. 1991: *Edge city: Life on the new frontier*. New York: Doubleday.

Giddens, A. 1985: Time, space and regionalization. In Gregory, D. and Urry, J. (eds), *Social relations and spatial structures*. New York: St Martin's, 265–95.

Gillette, H. 1985: The evolution of the planned shopping center in suburb and city. *Journal of the American Planning Association* 51(4), 449–60.

Goss, J. D. 1992: Modernity and postmodernity in the retail built environment. In Gayle, F. and Anderson, K. (eds), *Ways of seeing the world*. London: Unwin Hyman.

Gottdiener, M. 1986: Recapturing the center: a semiotic analysis of shopping malls. In *The city and the sign*, ed. M. Gottdiener and A. Ph. Lagopoulos, pp. 288–302. New York: Columbia University Press.

Gruen, V. 1973: *Centers for the urban environment: Survival of the cities*. New York: Van Nostrand Reinhold.

Gruen, V. 1978: The sad story of shopping centers. *Town and Country Planning* 46(7/8), 350–2.

Gruen, V. and Smith, L. 1960: *Shopping towns USA: The planning of shopping centers*. New York: Van Nostrand Reinhold.

Harris, N. 1990: *Cultural excursions: Marketing appetites and cultural tastes in modern America*. Chicago: University of Chicago Press.

Haug, W. F. 1986: *Critique of commodity aesthetics*. Minneapolis: University of Minnesota Press.

Hazel, D. 1992: Crime in the malls: a new and growing concern. *Chain Store Age Executive*, 27–29 February.

Hewison, S. 1989: *The heritage industry*. London: Methuen.

Hopkins, J. S. P. 1990: West Edmonton Mall: Landscape of myths and elsewhereness. *Canadian Geographer* 34(1), 2–17.

Hopkins, J. S. P. 1991: West Edmonton Mall as a centre for social interaction. *Canadian Geographer* 35(3), 268–79.

Huffman, F. 1989: Mall Street, USA. *Entrepreneur*, August, 95–9.

Jacobs, J. 1988: *The mall: An attempted escape from everyday life*. Prospect Heights, IL: Waveland Press.

Jencks, C. 1987: *The language of post-modern architecture*. Harmondsworth: Penguin Books.

Jencks, C. 1986: *Modern movements in architecture*. London: Academy Editions.

Jhally, S. 1987: *The codes of advertising*. London: Frances Pinter.

Jones, K. and Simmons, J. 1987: *Location, location, location: Analyzing the retail environment*. London: Methuen.

Judge bars group from leafletting in malls. 1991: *New York Times*, July 28, Sec. 1, p. 31.

Knabb, K. 1981: *Situationist international anthology*. Berkeley, CA: Bureau of Public Secrets.

Kowinski, W. S. 1985: *The malling of America: An inside look at the great consumer paradise*. New York: William Morrow.

Kroker, A., Kroker, M. and Cooke, D. 1989: *Panic encyclopedia: The definitive guide to the post-modern scene*. New York: St Martin's.

Lefebvre, H. 1971: *Everyday life in the modern world*. New York: Harper & Row.

Lefebvre, H. 1991: *The production of space*. Cambridge, MA: Blackwell.

Leiss, W., Kline, S. and Jhally, S. 1986: *Social communication in advertising: Persons, products and images of well-being*. London: Methuen.

Lewis, G. H. 1990: Community through exclusion and illusion: the creation of social worlds in an American shopping center. *Journal of Popular Culture* 24, 121–36.

Lynch, K. 1976: *Managing the sense of region*. Cambridge: MIT Press.

McCloud, J. 1989a: Hotels check in to stay. *Shopping Center World*, April, 22–32.

McCloud, J. 1989b: Fun and games is serious business. *Shopping Center World*, July, 28–35.

McCloud, J. 1991: Today's high-tech amenities can increase owners' profits. *Shopping Center World*, July, 25–8.

McDermott, M. J. 1990: Too many malls are chasing a shrinking supply of customers. *Adweek's Marketing Week*, February 5, 2–3.

Maitland, B. 1990: *The new architecture of the retail mall*. New York: Van Nostrand Reinhold.

Marcuse, H. 1964: *One-dimensional man*. Boston: Beacon Press.

Meyrowitz, J. 1985: *No sense of place: The impact of the electronic media on social behavior*. New York: Oxford University Press.

NAACP in hiring pact with South Carolina Mall. 1991: *New York Times*, March 7, Sec. A, p. 20.

NEA funds art in shopping malls. 1990: *Washington Post*, November 9, Sec. C, p. 1.

O'Connor, K. M. 1989: Focus on change: responding to changing consumer trends and remaining flexible are vital for retailers facing the future. *Shopping Center World*, August, 290–302.

Oldenburg, R. 1989: *The great good life*. New York: Paragon House.

Osborne, T. 1988: Revolutionizing the retail landscape. *Marketing Communications*, October, 17–25.

Pawlak, E. J., *et al*. 1985: A view of the mall. *Social Service Review*, June, 305–17.

Peterson, E. C. 1985: Diverse special interest groups may have access to center property. *Shopping Center World*, May, 85.

The PUD market guarantee. 1991: *Chain Store Age Executive*, April, 31–2.

Pyle, D. C. 1990: Music makes sales sing. *Shopping Center World*, December, 23.

Race is not the issue, Copley Place says. 1990: *Boston Globe*, 16 August, 32.

Rathbun, R. D. 1990: *Shopping centers and malls 3*. New York: Retail Reporting Corporation.

Retail uses. 1991: *Urban Land*, March, 22–6.

Retailers use bans, guards and ploys to curb teen sport of mall-mauling. 1990: *Wall Street Journal*, 7 August, Sec. B, p. 1.

Relph, E. 1987: *The modern urban landscape*. Baltimore: Johns Hopkins University Press.

Reynolds, M. 1990a: Food courts: tasty! *Stores*, August, 52–4.

Reynolds, M. 1990b: Day care in malls. *Stores*, November, 29–31.

Richards, G. 1990: Atmosphere key to mall design. *Shopping Center World*, August, 23–9.

Ricks, R. B. 1991: Shopping center rules misapplied to older adults. *Shopping Center World*, May, 52, 56.

Rouse, J. W. 1962: Must shopping centers be inhuman? *Architectural Forum*, June, 105–7, 196.

Rowe, P. G. 1991: *Making a middle landscape*. Cambridge: MIT Press.

Sack, R. 1988: The consumer's world: place as context. *Annals of the Association of American Geographers* 78, 642–64.

Sahlins, M. 1976: *Culture and practical reason*. Chicago: University of Chicago Press.

Sawicki, D. S. 1989: The festival marketplace as public policy: guidelines for future policy decisions. *American Planning Association Journal*, Summer, 347–61.

Scott, N. K. 1989: *Shopping centre design*. London: Van Nostrand Reinhold.

Shields, R. 1989: Social spatialization and the built environment: West Edmonton Mall. *Environment and Planning D: Society and Space* 7, 147–64.

Sibley, D. 1988: Survey 13: The purification of space. *Environment and Planning D: Society and Space* 6, 409–21.

Sicard, A. H. 1991: It's time for fun and gains. *Shopping Center World*, October, 26–9.

Sixty something. 1991: *Chain Store Age Executive*, July, 30–2.

Smith, N. C. 1990: *Morality and the market: Consumer pressure for corporate accountability*. London: Routledge.

Sommer, J. W. 1975: Fat city and hedonopolis: The American urban future. In Abler, K. *et al.* (eds), *Human geography in a shrinking world*. North Scituate, MA: Duxbury Press, 132–48.

Stallings, P. 1990: *Essay – the call of the mall*. MacNeil/Lehrer Newshour, 27 November. Transcript. New York: WNET.

Stewart, S. 1984: *On longing: Narratives of the miniature, the gigantic, the souvenir, the collection*. Baltimore: Johns Hopkins University Press.

Stokvis, J. R. and Cloar, J, A. 1991: CRM: applying shopping center techniques to downtown retailing. *Urban Land* April, 7–11.

Suburbs rain on teens' '1 Big Hormone' parade. 1990. *Chicago Tribune*, 5 August, sec. 2C, p. 1.

Teaford, J. C. 1990: *The rough road to renaissance: Urban revitalization in America, 1940–1985*. Baltimore: Johns Hopkins University Press.

Titus, R. M. 1990: Security works. *Urban Land, January*, 2–3.

Tuan, Y.- F. 1988: The city as a moral universe. *Geographical Review* 78(3), 316–24.

Turner, V. 1982: *From ritual to theater*. New York: Performing Arts Publications.

Veblen, T. 1953: *The theory of the leisure class*. New York: Mentor Books.

Venturi, R., Scott-Brown, D. and Izenour, S. 1972: *Learning from Las Vegas*. Cambridge: MIT Press.

Who shops in shopping malls? 1989: *Stores*, November, 43.

Winner, L. 1980: Do artifacts have politics? *Daedalus* 109, 121–35.

Wood, J. S. 1985: Nothing should stand for something that never existed. *Places* 2(2), 81–7.

Zukin, S. 1991: *Landscapes of power: From Detroit to Disney World*. Berkeley: University of California Press.

Zukin, S. 1990: Socio-spatial prototypes of a new organization of consumption: the role of real cultural capital. *Sociology* 24(1), 37–56.

10 Scott Lash and John Urry, 'Economies of Signs and Space'

Excerpts from: S. Lash and J. Urry, *Economies of Signs and Space*, pp. 198–203. London: Sage (1994)

Is it possible to take over the form of explanation found useful in manufacturing industry to explain the location of service industry? In the classic restructuring theses of Massey (1984) and Massey and Meegan (1982), it is the differential availability, price and organization of 'labour' which are central to explaining the character of the restructuring found within a given industrial sector. Can this thesis be applied to the location of service employment within a given economy (for more detail, see Bagguley *et al.*, 1990, ch. 3)?

[I]t does seem difficult to argue that the relative *organizational* strength of labour in different plants and places is a likely determinant of the emerging spatial structure of service employment. Industrial disputes, and hence the threat of such disputes, reflecting the strength of labour are fairly rare in most service industries, at least in the private sector. In Britain in the 1980s there were only two service industries where industrial disputes were common: transport and public administration. Elsewhere in services industrial disputes were uncommon and this is true even where fairly large employers are to be found (as in the case of hotels, see Johnson and Mignot, 1982; *Employment Gazette*, July 1990, tables 4.1 and 4.2).

An interesting example of the industrial relations practices of a service industry is Marshall's analysis of the workplace culture of a large licensed restaurant (1986; and see the classic Whyte, 1948). Marshall had expected that the combination of 'paternalism' and the opportunities for fiddles and pilferage would be sufficient to explain why most staff did not appear to resent either the long and demanding hours of work or the considerable wealth of the owner (on fiddles in waiting see Mars, 1984). However, Marshall argued that in fact such resentment failed to develop because most staff did not experience their work *as* work. Much of what they did consisted of activities that elsewhere would be classified as leisure. There was an erosion of the symbolic boundaries between what was work and what was play, what was work time and what was non-work time. This was reinforced by the fact that work rhythms were more like those outside paid work. Even poorly paid staff were 'free' to organize their activities according to their own designs. Indeed, much of the 'work' of the staff consisted of socializing with customers who were often friends from outside. The staff did not even use phrases such as 'going to work'. For most of them it was a 'way of life' resulting from the physical proximity of employee and consumer, of work and leisure.

To the extent to which other service establishments take on similar characteristics then this is likely to prevent the emergence of widespread labour organization, even where the companies themselves are large, as in the case of multinational hotel groups. Nor, since most service plants are fairly small, will the availability of large pools of labour be a likely factor that could generate widespread labour organization.

There are, however, some other important respects in which the analysis of 'labour' is indeed central to explaining the character of the social relations found within different service industries. First, in many service enterprises labour costs represent a very high proportion of total costs, often between two-thirds and three-quarters, and so employers will certainly seek to monitor and where possible minimize such costs. Current examples would be in British universities where staff costs are around 75 per cent of the total. However, most service establishments will not be able to lower costs in the manner achieved by McDonalds – to an extraordinary 15 per cent of the value of sales (Percy and Lamb, 1987; and more generally see Ritzer, 1992). Some of the techniques used to lower costs include the relocation of 'back offices' or sometimes the whole office (as in parts of the British insurance industry), or the early-retirement programmes in British banks or universities.

Second, since much service work is design intensive, adequate supplies of highly qualified labour will be crucial to geographical location. For example, the availability of particular kinds of skilled labour has been central to the development of the M4 corridor and to other parts of the south-east of England. In such cases, the provision of adequate supplies of appropriate houses (right price, size, style and location especially in rural areas) is important in ensuring an adequate pool of qualified labour (see Bassett *et al.*, 1989 on how much of the Swindon service class lives outside the town). In the USA, Noyelle notes how most of the large insurance companies have reorganized their systems divisions so that they are located in university towns or technology centres where there are adequate supplies of college graduates. He sees this as illustrating a general trend, that 'spatial reorganization is driven by the need for skilled labour' (1986, p. 20). There has been a shift from 'vertical mobility' within a firm (often over a lifetime), to 'lateral mobility' within a profession/occupation and hence the need for *places* to provide the appropriate range of attractions and services.

Third, labour is to varying degrees implicated in the service delivery. This occurs as the intended outcome of a necessarily social process in which some interaction occurs between one or more producers and one or more consumers, and in which the quality of the interaction is itself part of the service being offered. This is particularly important in the case of high-contact systems, where there is considerable involvement of the consumer in the production of the service (see Pine, 1987). The producers whom the consumers come most into contact with may or may not be those primarily responsible for the production of the service in question (lecturer on the one hand, waiter/waitress on the other). Nevertheless, because the production of most services is social there has to be some spatial proximity between one or more of the producers (but not necessarily all) and of the consumers. This is one important constraint upon location. Important exceptions to this occur where where the service can be 'materialized', such as a distance learning package rather than a directly given lecture, or the securitization of loans which can then be traded on secondary markets (see Sassen, 1991, pp. 92, 111). Indeed, many culture industries are services which take a tradable, storable and exportable form, but which are protected by copyright and not patent law (see Lury, 1993).

Fourth, the social composition of the producers, or at least those who are in the first line, is often part of what is 'sold' to customers. In other words, the 'service' consists in part of a process of production which is infused with particular social characteristics, of gender, age, race, educational background and so on. When the individual buys a given service, what is purchased is a certain social composition of the service producers (see Hochschild, 1983 on how this applies in the case of flight attendants; but see Wouters, 1989). This is particularly the case where the service is wholly or in part semiotic. In addition, it should be noted that what is also sometimes bought is a particular social composition of the other service consumers. Examples of this are to be found in tourism/travel services where differences of social tone between places develop on the basis of the social characteristics of the other visitors with whom people travel (see Urry, 1990).

Finally, since labour is in many cases part of the service product, this poses particular difficulties for management. These difficulties are more significant, the longer, the more intimate and the greater the importance of 'quality' for the consumer of the particular service. It means that employees' speech, appearance and personality may all be treated as legitimate areas of employer intervention and control, where part of the product is the person. Indeed, many services require 'emotional labour', particularly to smile in a pleasant, friendly and involved way to the consumers (Hochschild, 1983). In the case of flight attendants, Hochschild, however, notes that this emotional work has been made much more difficult with the intensification of work on the airlines since the mid-1970s: 'The workers respond to the speed-up with a slow-down: they smile less broadly, with a quick release and no sparkle in the eyes, thus dimming the company's message to the people. It is a war of smiles' (1983, p. 127).

Such a decline in quality is exceptionally hard for management to monitor and control, even if they are well aware that the attendants are no longer providing the service that the consumers expect and which supports the 'image' of the enterprise desired by senior management. It should also be noted that the nature of this emotional labour has probably changed in recent years as air travel has become more common, more democratized. Wouters suggests that the emotional labour has become more flexible and less standardized: 'Behaviour in contacts between flight attendants and passengers correspondingly had to become less uniform or standardized and more varied and flexible . . . in each contact there is a need to attune one's behaviour to the style of emotion management of the individual passenger' (1989, p. 113). Such modification of behaviour necessitates employees being reflexive cultural analysts, who in a more or less self-conscious way are able to interpret and modify their interactions with customers.

The paradox of this is of course that the actual delivery of many services is in fact provided by relatively poorly paid employees, who may have little involvement or engagement with the overall enterprise, and who may be subject to 'functional flexibility'. They are often female except in older forms of transport or in societies where occupations such as 'waiting' have high status. Overlaying the interaction, the 'service', are particular assumptions and notions of gender-specific forms of behaviour, often in part involving a dominant 'male gaze' of both the customers and other staff. And yet for many consumers what is actually consumed as a service *is* the particular moment of delivery or interaction by the relatively low level and often temporary or part-time service deliverers: the smile on the flight attendant's face, the pleasantness of the manner of the waiter, the sympathy in the eyes of the nurse, and so on. The problem for management is how to ensure that these moments do work out appropriately, while minimizing the cost and an undesirably intrusive (and hence resented) system of management/supervision, as well as minimizing friction with other, more highly paid workers backstage (see Whyte, 1948).

Jan Carlzon, the president of the Scandinavian airline SAS, terms these 'moments of truth' (1987). There are for SAS something like fifty million moments of truth each year, each of which lasts perhaps fifteen seconds, when a customer comes into contact with an employee. It is, he says, these moments of truth that determine whether or not SAS will succeed or fail.

The importance of such moments means that organizations may have to be reorganized, towards service to the customer as the primary objective. As a consequence, the actual service deliverers, the company's 'foot soldiers' who know most about the 'front-line' operations, have to be given much more responsibility to respond more effectively, quickly and courteously to the particular needs of the customer.

Recent research on a 'fun' 'southern-style' restaurant in Cambridge suggests some further elaboration of this argument (see Crang, 1993). What is shown is that the work of waiting in such a restaurant does not simply involve low skill and all-embracing managerial control. Intervening between the two are the geographies of skilled display to customers. Such service encounters are shown to have a performative character and thus one can think of this kind of workplace as a stage, as a dramatic setting for certain kinds of performance, involving a mix of mental, manual *and* emotional labour.

Crang considers what the implications of this kind of work are for the self. First, the staff themselves 'buy into' the restaurant and its location in the local cultural hierarchy. It is a fashionable place to work because of its image. Second, staff are chosen in terms of their possession of the right sort of cultural capital: they have to be informal, young, friendly, with the appropriate skills of emotional control, and with the right sort of body and skills in presenting it in their performances. Third, staff have to make cultural judgments when interacting with customers. They have to locate their customers socially in terms of a range of cultural categories and then to adjust their performances accordingly, even in those cases where the whole imaginary geography of such a 'southern-style' restaurant is rejected. Fourth, the self is crucial to the restaurant because in many ways the staff have become the product – and the product involved being oneself, assuming that one's self is fun-loving, informal and sociable. Such selves are the product. And the place is one of emotions. Staff talk of the need to 'get in the mood' at the beginning of the evening, to allow the emotions to flow. Finally, such 'work' is very different for waiters as opposed to waitresses. In waiting work women predominate, as opposed to kitchen and bar work where men are statistically much more common. And since the work of waiting in this restaurant is intrinsically emotional, emotional work is central. Thus there is a sense in which the job of waiting is different for men and women, and this is because different selves are involved, engaged in contrasting social encounters.

Broadly speaking, there are, then, two kinds of design-intensive service organizations. First, there are many services similar to fast food operations. The design is embodied into the management of each outlet. As an executive in the industry said of fast food: it is 'not a chef system, but a food management system' (quoted in Gabriel, 1988, p. 92). Such developments have dissolved the tyranny of fixed meal-times and the rigid timetabling of each day. In order to provide fresh, hot, cheap food at any moment, complex systems have been designed to manage the service delivery. Such outlets typically employ young, very cheap staff, so much so in Britain that working in fast food is now the commonest first job (Gabriel, 1988; Urry, 1990, ch. 4). The design even extends to the programming of the conversation between customers and the staff, whose script may be printed on the back of the menu.

And second, there are those service organizations, such as SAS, in which design has been pushed downwards to the 'foot soldiers'. It is argued by Hirschhorn, for example, that this becomes ever more necessary as markets become 'post-industrial', (that is, segmented or targeted), strategy making is decentralized, information is local or subjective, and there is direct feedback via communication rather than indirectly simply through services that may or may not be purchased (1985). Many service organizations, especially in the USA, extensively use self-administered questionnaires/surveys (including of course 'deliverers of higher education services'). As markets become more complex so organizations can no longer plan for the 'average' case, but must allow their staff to respond much more variably, flexibly and responsibly than under a mass consumption pattern (see Reynolds, 1989 on some of the resulting changes occurring in British Airways, as well as Crang, 1993 above).

References

Bagguley, P., Mark Lawson, J., Shapiro, D., Urry, J., Walby, S. and Warde, A. 1990: *Restructuring: Place, class and gender*. London: Sage.

Bassett, K., Boddy, M., Harloe, M. and Lovering, J. 1989: Living in the fast lane: economic and social change in Swindon. In Cooke, P. (ed.), *Localities*. London: Unwin Hyman, 45–85.

Carlzon, J. 1987: *Moments of truth*. Cambridge, MA: Ballinger.

Crang, P. 1993: A new service society: on the geographies of service employment. PhD dissertation, Department of Geography, University of Cambridge.

Gabriel, Y. 1988: *Working lives in catering*. London: Routledge.

Hirschhorn, L. 1985: Information technology and the new services game. In Castells, M. (ed.), *High technology*. London: Sage, 172–89.

Hochschild, A. 1983: *The managed heart*. Berkeley, CA: University of California Press.

Johnson, K. and Mignot, K. 1982: Marketing trade unionism to service industries: an historical analysis of the hotel industry. *Services Industries Journal* 2, 5–23.

Lury, C. 1993: *Cultural rights*. London: Routledge.

Mars, G. 1984: *The world of waiters*. London: Allen & Unwin.

Marshall, G. 1986: The workplace culture of a licensed restaurant. *Theory, culture and society* 3, 33–48.

Massey, D. 1984: *Spatial divisions of labour*. London: Macmillan.

Massey, D. and Meegan, R. 1982: *The anatomy of job loss*. London: Methuen.

Noyelle, T. 1986: Services and the world economy: towards a new international division of labour. ESRC Workshop on Localities in an International Economy, Cardiff, September.

Percy, S. and Lamb, H. 1987: The squalor behind the bright fast food lights. *Guardian*, 22 August.

Pine, R. 1987: *Management of technical change in the catering industry*. Aldershot: Avebury.

Reynolds, B. 1989: *The hundred best companies to work for in the UK*. London: Fontana/Collins.

Ritzer, G. 1992: *The McDonaldization of society*. London: Sage.

Sassen, S. 1991: *The global city*. Princeton, NJ: Princeton University Press.

Urry, J. 1990: *The tourist gaze*. London: Sage.

Whyte, W. 1948: *Human relations in the restaurant industry*. New York: McGraw.

Wouters, C. 1989: The sociology of emotions and flight attendants: Hochschild's *Managed Heart, Theory, Culture and Society* 6, 95–124.

SECTION THREE

GEOGRAPHICAL IDENTITIES

Editors' introduction

This section examines the medium of geography in the making of human identities. A variety of human identities − of class, ethnicity, gender, generation − are articulated in spatial patterns at a variety of scales. Social territories from the neighbourhood to the nation incorporate some identities and exclude others, sometimes strategically so. Their very integrity may be negatively defined by those 'others' beyond their borders. The notion of borders, of frontiers, implies strategies of categorization, policing and control. **Doreen Massey** recalls the studies of regions she was required to do as a student as too concerned to inscribe borders, to overlook the complex, overlapping movements, networks, activities and mythologies which make up the cultural character of places. No less than people, places have multiple identities. This is not just evidently multicultural places like some inner-city neighbourhoods but apparently unicultural places such as English villages or Greek islands with their complex horizons of social history visibly inscribed in the landscape.

The first two contributions enquire whether the 'new times' of flexible accumulation in the economy and post-modernity in culture are producing new forms of social−geographical identity. There is a tendency among some scholars of the new times, especially highly paid jet-setting academics, to offer reeling visions of cyberspace, of new global orders and virtual realities, when life for many people consists of waiting with your shopping for the bus that never comes (Moore, 1994). The contributors here take a sceptical, down-to-earth view. In 'A global sense of place' Doreen Massey examines the concept of 'time−space compression' (Harvey, 1989) with reference to the geographies of her local shopping street, Kilburn High Road in north London. She asks how various social groups are positioned in respect to global flows and connections, the 'power geometry' of these processses. Rather than go with the flow, many people seek to forge a stable sense of place, a 'secure mooring in a shifting world' (Harvey, 1989, p. 302). The current acceleration of social life may be strongly determined by economic forces but it is not the economy alone which determines the experience of place and space: 'women's mobility, for instance is restricted . . . not by "capital", but by men'.

In 'Social landscapes: continuity and change', **Susan Smith** raises the question of whether the dynamic world of 'new times' has in fact entailed a new openness and flexibility in social life, with opportunities for creatively restructuring of human identities. Variety and plurality have not displaced persistent inequalities. She points to the continuities in the social landscape, and the role of expert policy in fixing oppressive categories. Material needs of housing and health are mediated by moral discourses rooted in Victorian views of the deserving and undeserving poor. The naturalization of gender and racial differences continues, as does the 'medicalization' of such groups as the 'elderly', 'disabled' and 'mentally ill', with direct consequences for living and working arrangements.

Leonore Davidoff, Jean L'Esperance and **Howard Newby** look back to the nineteenth century for an understanding of persistent patterns of role ascription for middle-class women. Their essay 'Landscape with figures: home and community in English society' is strongly influenced by Raymond Williams's book *The country and the city* (Williams, 1973), and brings out the gender implications of Williams's analysis of rural and urban myths. Addressing a variety of discourses, from poetry to town planning, the authors examine the patriarchal power of the 'Beau Ideal'. A blend of domestic and rustic imagery, the Beau Ideal fixed physical and social horizons for middle-class women, notably in the landscape of the suburban home and garden. It was defined by its antithesis, a chaotic world of destitution and deviance which made up the image of the slum. The Beau Ideal was a model, a way of composing reality, which helped create reality in a very concrete way, and continued to do so in post-war Britain. This article was first published in 1977, since when new working structures and cultural mythologies for middle-class women have come to the fore. The cosy, domestic world of *Woman's Realm* has been joined by the sexy, careerist world of *Cosmopolitan*.

In 'Outsiders in society and space', **David Sibley** considers a living space strategically excluded from respectable places, the Gypsy encampment. Gypsies have been treated as beyond the pale of respectability, beyond even the boundaries of society itself. Like many semi-nomadic groups, from some native American tribes to New Age travellers, they have been subject to a double stereotyping, as colourful romantics freed from the constraints of settled society and as dirty deviants who threaten civilized life. In efforts to clear modern encampments – with their modern chrome trimmed trailers and piles of scrap metal – the romantic image is often defined as the real one, and actual Gypsies accused of not being real ones. But how do Gypsies themselves regard their world, its patterns of work and leisure, and how do they regard the dominant *gauje* (non-Gypsy) culture which confronts them? Moreover, what are the interactions between these worlds, the intermarriage and the economic transactions?

The work of Birmingham University's Centre for Contemporary Cultural Studies, especially during the stewardship of Stuart Hall in the 1970s, has been influential in configuring a new cultural geography in Britain (Jackson, 1989). In 'Street life: the politics of Carnival', **Peter Jackson** considers the conflict between media and participatory images of Afro-Caribbean identity. Sensational press coverage of the 1976 Notting Hill Carnival, with its outbreaks of violence and looting, is the occasion for examining the role of Carnival in the politics of 'race' relations. The identity issues extend to the question of young male delinquency (this period saw in Britain a high tide of 'soccer hooliganism') and urban policing. The meanings of Carnival differ in Trinidad and Notting Hill but transgressive conventions of role reversal, masquerade and street freedom are a persistent feature. Such conventions can be traced back to the saturnalia of medieval Europe. For centuries English cities had their occasions of popular ritual. Revel and riot at Tyburn or Bartholomew Fair rivalled that at the Notting Hill Carnival. Jackson's paper makes a larger point about urban geography. Cities are structured and animated by ritual and symbol, by bodily performance. Cities are theatres of social life (Cosgrove, 1992).

Certain cities, in certain times, are seen as world stages, as places where the new dynamics of modern life are being played out: Venice in the sixteenth century, London in the eighteenth, Manchester in the 1840s, Paris in the 1870s, New York in the 1910s, Chicago in the 1930s. The mantle seems to have passed at present to Los Angeles. Teams of scholars, including a self-styled 'LA School' of human geography (see the special issue of *Society and Space*, 1986), observe the scene. In 1990 urban sociologist and native Angeleno **Mike Davis** published a highly influential book on the city, entitled *City of quartz: Excavating the future in Los Angeles*. This looks critically at the structure and images of the Los Angeles, not least the city's double mythology of glamour and gloom, 'sunshine' and '*noir*'. The extract published here examines a landscape which has been luridly reported but poorly understood, the young black gangland of south-central Los Angeles. This extract was written before the 1992 riots occasioned by the police beating of Rodney King. But it is strangely prophetic. Davis examines the roots and dynamics of territorial gang culture. He connects its lethal violence to circumstances well beyond the streets of the ghetto, to the 'rewiring' of the Los Angeles economy to East Asia, and with it the catastrophic decline in black blue-collar employment, and to the extension of the international drug traffic in 'crack' cocaine. Peddling high-profit drugs, a gang like the Crips 'have become as much lumpen capitalists as outlaw proletarians'. With an overburdened school system, and the curtailing of job creation programmes, 'a whole generation is being shunted toward some impossible Armageddon'.

References and further reading

Anderson, K.J. 1987: The idea of Chinatown: the power of place and the institutional practice of the making of a racial category. *Annals of the Association of American Geographers* 77, 580–98.

Anderson, K. and Gale, F. 1992: *Inventing places: Studies in cultural geography Melbourne*: Longman Cheshire.

Bird, J. *et al.* (eds) 1992: *Mapping the futures: Local cultures, global change.* London: Routledge.

Cosgrove, D. 1992: *The Palladian landscape.* Leicester: Leicester University Press.

Daniels, S. 1992: Place and the geographical imagination. *Geography* 77(2), 310–22.

Environment and Planning D: Society and Space, 1986: 4(3). Special issue on Los Angeles.

Harvey, O. 1989: *The condition of postmodernity.* Oxford: Basil Blackwell.

Hooson, D. (ed.) *Geography and national identity.* Oxford: Basil Blackwell.

Jackson, P. 1989: *Maps of meaning.* London: Unwin Hyman.

Keith, M. and Pile, S. (eds) 1993: *Place and the politics of identity.* London: Routledge.

Moore, S. 1994: Watch this space: it's the community. *Guardian*, 1 December, p. 7.

Philo, C. (ed.) 1991: *New words, new worlds: Reconceptualising social and cultural geography.* Department of Geography, St David's University College, Lampeter.

Smith, S. J. 1993: Bounding the Borders: claiming space and making space in rural Scotland. *Transactions of the Institute of British Geographers* NS 18(3), 291–308.

Ward, D. 1976: The Victorian slum: an enduring myth? *Annals of the Association of American Geographers* 66, 323–36.

Williams, R. 1973: *The country and the city.* London: Chatto & Windus.

11 Doreen Massey,
'A Global Sense of Place'

Reprinted in full from: *Marxism Today* (June 1991)

This is an era – it is often said – when things are speeding up, and spreading out. Capital is going through a new phase of internationalization, especially in its financial parts. More people travel more frequently and for longer distances. Your clothes have probably been made in a range of countries from Latin America to South-East Asia. Dinner consists of food shipped in from all over the world. And if you have a screen in your office, instead of opening a letter which – care of Her Majesty's Post Office – has taken some days to wend its way across the country, you now get interrupted by e-mail.

This view of the current age is one now frequently found in a wide range of books and journals. Much of what is written about space, place and postmodern times emphasizes a new phase in what Marx once called 'the annihilation of space by time'. The process is argued, or – more usually – asserted, to have gained a new momentum, to have reached a new stage. It is a phenomenon which has been called 'time–space compression'. And the general acceptance that something of the sort is going on is marked by the almost obligatory use in the literature of terms and phrases such as speed-up, global village, overcoming spatial barriers, the disruption of horizons, and so forth.

One of the results of this is an increasing uncertainty about what we mean by 'places' and how we relate to them. How, in the face of all this movement and intermixing, can we retain any sense of a local place and its particularity? An (idealized) notion of an era when places were (supposedly) inhabited by coherent and homogeneous communities is set against the current fragmentation and disruption. The counterposition is anyway dubious, of course; 'place' and 'community' have only rarely been coterminous. But the occasional longing for such coherence is none the less a sign of the geographical fragmentation, the spatial disruption, of our times. And occasionally, too, it has been part of what has given rise to defensive and reactionary responses: certain forms of nationalism, sentimentalized recovering of sanitized 'heritages', and outright antagonism to newcomers and 'outsiders'. One of the effects of such responses is that place itself, the seeking after a sense of place, has come to be seen by some as necessarily reactionary.

But is that necessarily so? Can't we rethink our sense of place? Is it not possible for a sense of place to be progressive; not self-enclosing and defensive, but outward-looking? A sense of place which is adequate to this era of time–space compression? To begin with, there are some questions to be asked about time–space compression itself. Who is it that experiences it, and how? Do we all benefit and suffer from it in the same way?

For instance, to what extent does the currently popular characterization of time–space compression represent very much a Western, colonizer's, view? The sense of dislocation which some feel at the sight of a once well-known local street now lined with a succession of cultural imports – the pizzeria, the kebab house, the branch of the Middle Eastern bank – must have been felt for centuries, though from a very different point of view, by colonized peoples all over the world as they watched the importation, maybe even used the products, of, first, European colonization, maybe British (from new forms of transport to liver salts and custard powder), later US, as they learned to eat wheat instead of rice or corn, to drink Coca-Cola, just as today we try out enchiladas.

Moreover, as well as querying the ethnocentricity of the idea of time–space compression and its current acceleration, we also need to ask about its causes: what is it that determines our degrees of mobility, that influences the sense we have of space and place? Time–space compression refers to movement and communication across space, to the geographical stretching-out of social relations, and to our experience of all this. The usual interpretation is that it results overwhelmingly from the actions of capital, and from its currently increasing internationalization. On this interpretation, then, it is time, space and money which make the world go round, and us go round (or not) the world. It is capitalism and its developments which are argued to determine our understanding and our experience of space.

But surely this is insufficient. Among the many other things which clearly influence that experience, there are, for instance, race and gender. The degree to which we can move between countries, or walk about the streets at night, or venture out of hotels in foreign cities, is not just influenced by 'capital'. Survey after survey has shown how women's mobility, for instance, is restricted – in a thousand different ways, from physical violence to being ogled at or made to feel quite simply 'out of place' – not by 'capital', but by men. Or, to take a more complicated example, Birkett, reviewing books on women adventurers and travellers in the nineteenth and twentieth centuries, suggests that 'it is far, far more demanding for a woman to wander now than ever before'.[1] The reasons she gives for this argument are a complex mix of colonialism, ex-colonialism, racism, changing gender relations, and relative wealth. A simple resort to explanation in terms of 'money' or 'capital' alone could not begin to get to grips with the issue. The current speed-up may be strongly determined by economic forces, but it is not the economy alone which determines our experience of space and place. In other words, and put simply, there is a lot more determining how we experience space than what 'capital' gets up to.

What is more, of course, that last example indicated that 'time–space compression' has not been happening for everyone in all spheres of activity. Birkett again, this time writing of the Pacific Ocean:

> Jumbos have enabled Korean computer consultants to fly to Silicon Valley as if popping next door, and Singaporean entrepreneurs to reach Seattle in a day. The borders of the world's greatest ocean have been joined as never before. And Boeing has brought these people together. But what about those they fly over, on their islands five miles below? How has the mighty 747 brought them greater communion with those whose shores are washed by the same water? It hasn't, of course. Air travel

might enable businessmen to buzz across the ocean, but the concurrent decline in shipping has only increased the isolation of many island communities . . . Pitcairn, like many other Pacific islands, has never felt so far from its neighbours.[2]

In other words, and most broadly, time–space compression needs differentiating socially. This is not just a moral or political point about inequality, although that would be sufficient reason to mention it; it is also a conceptual point.

Imagine for a moment that you are on a satellite, further out and beyond all actual satellites; you can see 'planet Earth' from a distance and, rarely for someone with only peaceful intentions, you are equipped with the kind of technology which allows you to see the colours of people's eyes and the numbers on their numberplates. You can see all the movement and tune in to all the communication that is going on. Furthest out are the satellites, then aeroplanes, the long haul between London and Tokyo and the hop from San Salvador to Guatemala City. Some of this is people moving, some of it is physical trade, some is media broadcasting. There are faxes, e-mail, film distribution networks, financial flows and transactions. Look in closer and there are ships and trains, steam trains slogging laboriously up hills somewhere in Asia. Look in closer still and there are lorries and cars and buses, and on down further, somewhere in sub-Saharan Africa, there's a woman on foot who still spends hours a day collecting water.

Now, I want to make one simple point here, and that is about what one might call the *power geometry* of it all; the power geometry of time–space compression. For different social groups, and different individuals, are placed in very distinct ways in relation to these flows and interconnections. This point concerns not merely the issue of who moves and who doesn't, although that is an important element of it; it is also about power in relation *to* the flows and the movement. Different social groups have distinct relationships to this anyway differentiated mobility: some people are more in charge of it than others; some initiate flows and movement, others don't; some are more on the receiving end of it than others; some are effectively imprisoned by it.

In a sense, at the end of all the spectra are those who are both doing the moving and the communicating, and in some way in a position of control in relation to it: the jet-setters, the ones sending and receiving the faxes and the e-mail, holding the international conference calls, the ones distributing the films, controlling the news, organizing the investments and the international currency transactions. These are the groups who are really in a sense in charge of time–space compression, who can really use it and turn it to advantage, whose power and influence it very definitely increases. On its more prosaic fringes this group probably includes a fair number of Western academics and journalists – those, in other words, who write most about it.

But there are also groups who are also doing a lot of physical moving, but who are not 'in charge' of the process in the same way at all. The refugees from El Salvador or Guatemala and the undocumented migrant workers from Michoacan in Mexico, crowding into Tijuana to make a perhaps fatal dash for it across the border into the USA to grab a chance of a new life. Here the experience of movement, and indeed of a confusing plurality of cultures, is very different. And there are those from India, Pakistan, Bangladesh, the Caribbean, who come half-way round the world only to get held up in an interrogation room at Heathrow.

Or – a different case again – there are those who are simply on the receiving end of time–space compression. The pensioner in a bed-sit in any inner city in the UK, eating British working-class-style fish and chips from a Chinese take-away, watching a US film on a Japanese television; and not daring to go out after dark. And anyway, the public transport's been cut.

Or – one final example to illustrate a different kind of complexity – there are the people who live in the *favelas* of Rio, who know global football like the back of their hand, and have produced some of its players; who have contributed massively to global music, who gave us the samba and produced the lambada that everyone was dancing to last year in the clubs of Paris and London; and who have never, or hardly ever, been to downtown Rio. At one level they have been tremendous contributors to what we call time–space compression; and at another level they are imprisoned in it.

This is, in other words, a highly complex social differentiation. There are differences in the degree of movement and communication, but also in the degree of control and of initiation. The ways in which people are placed within 'time–space compression' are highly complicated and extremely varied.

But this in turn immediately raises questions of politics. If time–space compression can be imagined in that more socially formed, socially evaluative and differentiated way, then there may be here the possibility of developing a politics of mobility and access. For it does seem that mobility and control over mobility both reflects and reinforces power. It is not simply a question of unequal distribution, that some people move more than others, and that some have more control than others. It is that the mobility and control of some groups can actively weaken other people. Differential mobility can weaken the leverage of the already weak. The time–space compression of some groups can undermine the power of others.

This is well established and often noted in the relationship between capital and labour. Capital's ability to roam the world further strengthens it in relation to relatively immobile workers, enables it to play off the plant at Genk against the plant at Dagenham. It also strengthens its hand against struggling local economies the world over as they compete for the favour of some investment. The 747s that fly computer scientists across the Pacific are part of the reason for the greater isolation today of the island of Pitcairn. But also, every time someone uses a car, and thereby increases their personal mobility, they reduce both the social rationale and the financial viability of the public transport system – and thereby also potentially reduce the mobility of those who rely on that system. Every time you drive to that out-of-town shopping centre you contribute to the rising prices, even hasten the demise, of the corner shop. And the 'time–space compression' which is involved in producing and reproducing the daily lives of the comfortably off in First World societies – not just their own travel but the resources they draw on, from all over the world, to feed their lives – may entail environmental consequences, or hit constraints, which will limit the lives of others before their own. We need to ask, in other words, whether our relative mobility and power over mobility and communication entrenches the spatial imprisonment of other groups.

But this way of thinking about time–space compression also returns us to the question of place and a sense of place. How, in the context of all these socially varied time–space changes do we think about 'places'? In an era when, it is argued, 'local communities' seem to be increasingly broken up, when you can go abroad and find the same shops, the same music as at home, or eat your favourite foreign-holiday food at a restaurant down the road – and when everyone has a different experience of all this – how then do we think about 'locality'?

Many of those who write about time–space compression emphasize the insecurity and unsettling impact of its effects, the feelings of vulnerability which it can produce. Some therefore go on from this to argue that, in the middle of all this flux, people desperately need a bit of peace and quiet – and that a strong sense of place, of locality, can form one kind of refuge from the hubbub. So the search after the 'real' meanings of places, the unearthing of heritages and so forth, is interpreted as being, in part, a response to desire for fixity and for security of identity in the middle of all the movement and change. A 'sense of place', of rootedness, can provide – in this form and on this interpretation – stability and a source of unproblematical identity. In that guise, however, place and the spatially local are then rejected by many progressive people as almost necessarily reactionary. They are interpreted as an evasion; as a retreat from the (actually unavoidable) dynamic and change of 'real life', which is what we must seize if we are to change things for the better. On this reading, place and locality are foci for a form of romanticized escapism from the real business of the world. While 'time' is equated with movement and progress, 'space'/'place' is equated with stasis and reaction.

There are some serious inadequacies in this argument. There is the question of why it is assumed that time–space compression will produce insecurity. There is the need to face up to – rather than simply deny – people's need for attachment of some sort, whether through place or anything else. None the less, it is certainly the case that there is indeed at the moment a recrudescence of some very problematical senses of place, from reactionary nationalisms, to competitive localisms, to introverted obsessions with 'heritage'. We need, therefore, to think through what might be an adequately progressive sense of place, one which would fit in with the current global–local times and the feelings and relations they give rise to, *and* which would be useful in what are, after all, political struggles often inevitably based on place. The question is how to hold on to that notion of geographical difference, of uniqueness, even of rootedness if people want that, without it being reactionary.

There are a number of distinct ways in which the 'reactionary' notion of place described above is problematical. One is the idea that places have single, essential, identities. Another is the idea that identity of place – the sense of place – is constructed out of an introverted, inward-looking history based on delving into the past for internalized origins, translating the name from the Domesday Book. Thus Wright recounts the construction and appropriation of Stoke Newington and its past by the arriving middle class (the Domesday Book registers the place as 'Newtowne': 'There is land for two ploughs and a half. . . . There are four villanes and thirty-seven cottagers with ten acres', pp. 227 and 231), and contrasts this version with that of other groups: the white working class and the large number of important minority communities.[3] A particular problem with this conception of place is that it seems to require the drawing of boundaries. Geographers have long been exercised by the problem of defining regions, and this question of 'definition' has almost always been reduced to the issue of drawing lines around a place. I remember some of my most painful times as a geographer have been spent unwillingly struggling to think how one could draw a boundary around somewhere like the 'East Midlands'. But that kind of boundary around an area precisely distinguishes between an inside and an outside. It can so easily be yet another way of constructing a counterposition between 'us' and 'them'.

And yet, if one considers almost any real place, and certainly one not defined primarily by administrative or political boundaries, these supposed characteristics have little real purchase.

Take, for instance, a walk down Kilburn High Road, my local shopping centre. It is a pretty ordinary place, north-west of the centre of London. Under the railway bridge the newspaper stand sells papers from every county of what my neighbours, many of whom come from there, still often call the Irish Free State. The postboxes down the High Road, and many an empty space on a wall, are adorned with the letters IRA. Other available spaces are plastered this week with posters for a special meeting in remembrance: 'Ten Years after the Hunger Strike'. At the local theatre Eamon Morrissey has a one-man show; the National Club has the Wolfe Tones on, and at the Black Lion there's *Finnegans Wake*. In two shops I noted this week's lottery ticket winners: in one the name is Teresa Gleeson, in the other, Chouman Hassan.

Thread your way through the often almost stationary traffic diagonally across the road from the newsstand and there's a shop which as long as I can remember has displayed saris in the window. Four life-sized models of Indian women, and reams of cloth. On the door a notice announces a forthcoming concert at Wembley Arena: Anand Miland presents Rekha, live, with Aamir Khan, Salman Khan, Jahi Chawla and Raveena Tandon. On another ad, for the end of the month, is written 'All Hindus are cordially invited'. In another newsagent's I chat with the man who keeps it, a Muslim unutterably depressed by events in the Gulf, silently chafing at having to sell the *Sun*. Overhead there is always at least one aeroplane; we seem to be on a flight-path to Heathrow and by the time they're over Kilburn you can see them clearly enough to tell the airline and wonder as you struggle with your shopping where they're coming from. Below, the reason the traffic is snarled up (another odd effect of time–space compression!) is in part because this is one of the main entrances to and escape routes from London, the road to Staples Corner and the beginning of the M1 to the North.

This is just the beginnings of a sketch from immediate impressions – but a proper analysis could be done – of the links between Kilburn and the world. And so it could for almost any place.

Kilburn is a place for which I have a great affection; I have lived there many years. It certainly has 'a character of its own'. But it is possible to feel all this without subscribing to any of the static and defensive – and in that sense reactionary – notions of 'place' which were referred to above. First, while Kilburn may have a character of its own, it is absolutely not a seamless, coherent identity, a single sense of place which everyone shares. It could hardly be less so. People's routes through the place, their favourite haunts within it, the connections they make (physically, or by phone or post, or in memory and imagination) between here and the rest of the world vary enormously. If it is now recognized that people have multiple identities then the same point can be made in relation to places. Moreover, such multiple identities can either be a source of richness or a source of conflict, or both.

One of the problems here has been a persistent identification of place with 'community'. Yet this is a misidentification. On the one hand communities can exist without being in the same place – from networks of friends with like interests, to major religious, ethnic or political communities. On the other hand, the instances of places housing single 'communities' in the sense of coherent social groups are probably – and, I would argue, have for long been – quite rare. Moreover, even where they do exist this in no way implies a single sense of place. For people occupy different positions within any community. We could counterpose to the chaotic mix of Kilburn the relatively stable and homogeneous community (at least in popular imagery) of a small mining village. Homogeneous? 'Communities' too have internal structures. To take the most obvious example, I'm sure a woman's sense of place in a mining village – the spaces through which she normally moves, the meeting places, the connections outside – are different from a man's. Their 'senses of the place' will be different.

Moreover, not only does 'Kilburn', then, have many identities (or its full identity is a complex mix of all these) it is also, looked at in this way, absolutely *not* introverted. It is (or ought to be) impossible even to begin thinking about Kilburn High Road without bringing into play half the world and a considerable amount of British imperialist history (and this certainly goes for mining villages too). Imagining it this way provokes in you (or at least in me) a really global sense of place.

And finally, in contrasting this way of looking at places with the defensive reactionary view, I certainly could not begin to, nor would I want to, define 'Kilburn' by drawing its enclosing boundaries.

So, at this point in the argument, get back in your mind's eye on a satellite; go right out again and look back at the globe. This time, however, imagine not just all the physical movement, nor even all the often invisible communications, but also and especially all the social relations, all the links between people. Fill it in with all those different experiences of time–space compression. For what is happening is that the geography of social relations is changing. In many cases such relations are increasingly stretched out over space: economic, political and cultural social relations, each full of power and with internal structures of domination and subordination, stretched out over the planet at every different level, from the household to the local area to the international.

It is from this perspective that it is possible to envisage an alternative interpretation of place. In this interpretation, what gives a place its specificity is not some long internalized history but the fact that it is constructed out of a particular constellation of social relations, meeting and weaving together at a particular locus. If one moves in from the satellite towards the globe, holding all those networks of social relations and movements and communications in one's head, then each 'place' can be seen as a particular, unique, point of their intersection. It is, indeed, a *meeting* place. Instead, then, of thinking of places as areas with boundaries around, they can be imagined as articulated movements in networks of social relations and understandings, but where a large proportion of those relations, experiences and understandings are con-structed on a far larger scale than what we happen to define for that moment as the place itself, whether that be a street, or a region or even a continent. And this in turn allows a sense of place which is extroverted, which includes a consciousness of its links with the wider world, which integrates in a positive way the global and the local.

This is not a question of making the ritualistic connections to 'the wider system' – the people in the local meeting who bring up international capitalism every time you try to have a discussion about rubbish collection – the point is that there are real relations with real content – economic, political, cultural – between any local place and the wider world in which it is set. In economic geography the argument has long been accepted that it is not possible to understand the 'inner city', for instance its loss of jobs, the decline of manufac-turing employment there, by looking only at the inner city. Any adequate explanation has to set the inner city in its wider geographical context. Perhaps it is appropriate to think how that kind of understanding could be extended to the notion of a sense of place.

These arguments, then, highlight a number of ways in which a progressive concept of place might be developed. First of all, it is absolutely not static. If places can be conceptualized in terms of the social interactions which they tie together, then it is also the case that these interactions themselves are not motionless things, frozen in time. They are processes. One of the great one-liners in Marxist exchanges has for long been 'ah, but capital is not a thing, it's a process'. Perhaps this should be said also about places; that places are pro-cesses, too.

Second, places do not have to have boundaries in the sense of divisions which frame simple enclosures. 'Boundaries' may of course be necessary, for the purposes of certain types of studies for instance, but they are not necessary for the conceptualization of a place itself. Definition in this sense does not have to be through simple counterposition to the outside; it can come, in part, precisely through the particularity of linkage to that 'outside' which is therefore itself part of what constitutes the place. This helps get away from the common association between penetrability and vulnerability. For it is this kind of association which makes invasion by newcomers so threatening.

Third, clearly places do not have single, unique 'identities'; they are full of internal conflicts. Just think, for instance, about London's Docklands, a place which is at the moment quite clearly *defined* by conflict: a conflict over what its past has been (the nature of its 'heritage'), conflict over what should be its present development, conflict over what could be its future.

Fourth, and finally, none of this denies place nor the importance of the uniqueness of place. The specificity of place is continually reproduced, but it is not a specificity which results from some long, internalized history. There are a number of sources of this specificity – the uniqueness of place.[4] There is the fact that the wider social relations in which places are set are themselves geographically differentiated. Globalization (in the economy, or in culture, or in anything else) does not entail simply homogenization. On the contrary, the globalization of social relations is yet another source of (the reproduction of) geographical uneven development, and thus of the uniqueness of place. There is the specificity of place which derives from the fact that each place is the focus of a distinct *mixture* of wider and more local social relations. There is the fact that this very mixture together in one place may produce effects which would not have happened otherwise. And finally, all these relations interact with and take a further element of specificity from the accumulated history of a place, with that history itself imagined as the product of layer upon layer of different sets of linkages, both local and to the wider world.

In her portrait of Corsica, *Granite island*, Dorothy Carrington travels the island seeking out the roots of its character.[5] All the different layers of peoples and cultures are explored; the long and tumultuous relationship with France, with Genoa and Aragon in the thirteenth, fourteenth and fifteenth centuries, back through the much earlier incorporation into the Byzantine Empire, and before that domination by the Vandals, before that being part of the Roman Empire, before that the colonization and settlements of the Carthaginians and the Greeks . . . until we find that even the megalith builders had come to Corsica from somewhere else.

It is a sense of place, an understanding of 'its character', which can only be constructed by linking that place to places beyond. A progressive sense of place would recognize that, without being threatened by it. What we need, it seems to me, is a global sense of the local, a global sense of place.

Notes

1 D. Birkett, *New Statesman and Society*, 13 June 1990, pp. 41–2.
2 D. Birkett, *New Statesman and Society*, 15 March 1991, p. 38.
3 D. Wright, *On living in an old country*. London: Verso, 1985.
4 D. Massey, *Spatial divisions of labour: Social structures and the geography of production*. Basingstoke: Macmillan, 1984.
5 D. Carrington, *Granite island: A portrait of Corsica*. Harmondsworth: Penguin Books, 1971.

12 Susan J. Smith,
'Social Landscapes: Continuity and Change'

Reprinted in full from: R. J. Johnston (ed.), *The Challenge for Geography*, pp. 54–75. Oxford: Basil Blackwell (1993)

In so far as it is possible to isolate a distinctively social world, the starting point for discussion must be anchored in the cultural significance of postmodernism. The term 'postmodern' has become synonymous with a new fluidity and flexibility for social life as it engages with the dynamism of the so-called 'new times'. Although interpretations of postmodernism and of its relationship with capitalism, sexism and racism vary (Harvey, 1989; Bondi, 1990; Cooke, 1990), the term is widely associated with the dissolution – at least at the level of experience – of old social categories (especially 'classes') and with the creation of new opportunities for the restructuring (or destructuring) of society.

It is often argued, and it may be true, that the postmodern world, with its ostensible classlessness and its mosaic of 'three-minute' cultures, offers real possibilities for marginalized groups. It may herald new political opportunities for racialized minorities (Hall, 1988); it could promise a (for some) welcome transition from feminism to feminisms; it allows us to expose and examine in their own right the multitude of social causes once collapsed into categories like 'disadvantage' and 'deprivation' (Smith, 1989a). Certainly, one of postmodernism's attractions is its promise of 'greater democracy through its recognition of the reality of a variety of viewpoints, a plurality of cultures' (Massey, 1991, p. 32).

Nevertheless, it can equally be argued that in order to exploit what is new about the postmodern world, it is necessary not only to document what is fluid and flexible in the accompanying social arena, but also to explain why and how certain other themes endure. Accordingly, a key concern of this chapter revolves around the possibility that while postmodernism may have added some colour to the construction of everyday life, it has not adequately challenged the basic social categories with which politicians, the public and perhaps even the majority of scholars still work. As a consequence, the thrust of my argument will not be that there is an inexorably changing world which, *ipso facto*, needs a changing discipline to study it. Rather, I will argue that precisely because there are persistencies, consistencies and continuities in the social world, because there are inequalities and injustices that we have so far failed to address adequately, and because these things are so far largely *unchanging* – despite the advent of numerous value-committed, radical, moral and applied geographies – only a radically changed discipline can hope to tackle them.

For the purposes of this chapter, therefore, the crucial leap is not from a restructured world to a changing discipline, but rather from a restructured discipline to a changing world. The difference between these is important. The first formula implicitly limits geography to an analytical role (which is not, of course, unimportant), whereas the second advocates more explicit engagement with a traditionally neglected realm of normative theory: the first approach implies detachment and impartiality in mapping the world as it is today, while the second demands a renewed commitment actively to shape the world as it *ought* to be according to some basic assumptions about human rights and social entitlements.

Structuring the social

My starting point – that there are continuities linking the old and new times – is shared by many authors. Harvey (1989) makes a powerful and persuasive argument that there are profound continuities in the relations of production which link 'old' industrial capitalism with the project of flexible accumulation. And Massey (1991, p. 34), albeit in a footnote, points out that 'All those lists of dualist differences between modernism and postmodernism . . . obscure the fact that an awful lot remains tediously the same'. Yet, although the broad thrust of these arguments for continuity in the sphere of political economy is widely accepted, much less attention has been paid to the possibility that continuity rather than change might also be a hallmark of the socio-cultural world. Indeed, analysts like Harvey (whose most quotable of quotes insists that postmodernism is simply the 'cultural clothing' of flexible accumulation) often imply that the very flux and variety of cultural life are required to mask the injustices of capitalism's route to a more flexible regime. A newly fluid social world – a mosaic of consumer cultures – is, effectively, cast as a prerequisite of the transition to post-Fordism. The cultural kaleidoscope of postmodernism is not, from this perspective, an illusion (as some have suggested), but rather a 'real' and necessary smoke-screen for 'more of the same' in the spheres of production, investment and accumulation.

Yet ordinary people, steeped as they are in the ephemera of consumerism, seem more interested in stability than change as the twentieth century lurches to a close. Some years ago, Mary Douglas (1966) referred to that 'yearning for rigidity' which characterizes so many societies. Harvey himself admits that this has not changed. He argues that, as far as the general public is concerned, 'The greater the ephemerality, the more pressing the need to discover or manufacture some kind of eternal truth that might lie therein' (1989, p. 292); and the greater the social fragmentation, the more potent 'the search for personal or collective identity, the search for secure moorings in a shifting world' (p. 302) – a world where localism and nationalism gain strength 'precisely because of the quest for the security that place always offers in the midst of all the shifting that flexible accumulation implies' (p. 306). In short, it seems that in the haste to reject meta-theory as a means of connecting and representing the world, social science is in danger of ignoring the extent to which people want and need to make ordered sense of their lives against a background of fragmentation and ephemera. Whether or not the world actually possesses structure and regularity, whether or not there are real ordering principles which dictate identity and shape behaviour, much of social life is acted out *as if* these principles exist. Yet our grasp on how collective ideas about a social order are developed and sustained is the first to loosen amid the excitement of analysing and conceptualizing the dynamic contours of the postmodern landscape.

In this chapter there is no space to demonstrate further what I shall take for granted; that the search for anchorage and stability continues to pervade social life. My aim is not to address the question of whether there are social continuities: there is every evidence that some fundamental divides and inequalities persist, however much they may be repositioned and renegotiated from time to time. My concern is rather to ask how it is that ordinary people (including politicians and other decision-makers) construct and experience those continuities, at a time when ideas about the class structure, consumption sector cleavages and the provisioning divide are so decidedly peripheral to the public imagination.

By way of an answer, I shall reconsider the power of metaphor – particularly of natural science metaphors – to mould perceptions and influence or justify behaviour. Metaphor is a powerful device for shaping and sharing common-sense understandings of the social world (Mills, 1982). Because of their role in establishing the 'customary vision' of a society, shaping social needs and aspirations, metaphors become vehicles for assessing what people can and, crucially, should do. Metaphors are therefore normative as well as descriptive devices, and natural science metaphors have offered a particularly powerful and enduring framework on which to construct and rationalize the emerging social order. As Bell (1990) illustrates, ideas about nature and the natural origins of the human character and behaviour are especially enduring. Historically, this natural science metaphor has been rivalled in importance in accounting for human activity only by other weighty concepts like progress and freedom.

My point here is that, despite the advent in the modern period of a wide range of powerful and persuasive social and political theories of society, despite the supposed rationality that came with modernism, and despite the advance of science itself, which has exploded so many social myths, the tenacity of natural science metaphors as an 'explanation' of, and as a source of legitimacy for, some fundamental social inequalities has been sustained, if not enhanced, by the shift to the 'new times'. I shall argue that these 'new times', which are themselves a product of technological change and innovation – a testimony to what science can achieve – encourage rather than, as we often expect, undermine our long-standing (and misplaced) tendency to justify social difference by appeal to the logic of natural science.

My argument, then, is that social and spatial boundary building is as much a feature of the postmodern world as is boundary breaking. This boundary building is not reducible to the division of labour, but neither is it a wholly welcome blossoming of cultural variety. The social bounding of the postmodern world works to legitimize, and even drive, political and economic change, but it also has a momentum of its own. And one source of this momentum is the appeal of natural science as a store of enduring 'truths' against which to measure the vagaries of human existence. My concern, then, is with the ultimate irony of a flight from progressivism: the extent to which it throws us back on those certainty-seeking models of science which, as Gould (1981, p. 217) so often shows, are only too ready to provide an 'objectivity' for what society at large wants to hear.

Social relations, spatial structures and the metaphors of natural science

Few dispute the extent to which, historically, the ideas of natural science have been used – with and without the sanction of natural scientists – to legitimize and reproduce inequalities and injustices in the social world. Nature, Cope argues (1985, p. 7), has become a form of unscientific rationalization which 'projects historically specific activities, demeanours and thoughts as "natural" to all past and possible human social arrangements and relationships'. We are, nevertheless, only beginning to understand the extent to which geography itself is implicated in that process. Perhaps the best account is given by Livingtone (1991), who shows how geographers drew scientific climatology into the process of race categorization, domination and exploitation which underpinned the colonial project of nineteenth-century Europe. He shows that 'the idea that climate had stamped its indelible mark on racial constitution not just physiologically, but psychologically and morally, was a motif that was both deep and lasting in English-speaking geography' (p. 10). This motif informed a naturalization of human values which allowed human potential, morals and social worth to be gauged in climatic terms. This 'language of climate's moral imperatives' was used as a legitimizing discourse for the colonists as they sought to erect 'crucial boundaries between civilisation and barbarism, between the white and black races, and of course, between virtue and vice' (p. 24).

The problem for social science today, however, is that the use of natural science metaphors as legitimizing discourses is not restricted to the past. It is part of a continuing process of renegotiation required as the social world is jostled by the exigencies of politics and economy. Some consequences are itemized by Cope (1985, p. 7):

> in response to a women's movement wanting the creation of new gender relations, present family structures are characterised as natural and to be found across all history. In response to struggles to change the unequal relation of human groups of different geographic origin and with different physical features, there arise theories about the natural superiority of 'race'. . . . In response to bitterness about the unequal results of schooling for industrialism emerge arguments that intelligence . . . is biologically inheritable, a gift or penalty of nature. In response to calls for the end of the arms race, it is argued that aggression is natural. Even our co-operative activity can be put down to the functioning of a selfish 'gene'.

Postmodern life remains shot through with such discourses, and they continue to oppress. Indeed, it can be argued that they have gained new life through the industrial, political and welfare restructurings that comprise the 'new times'.

The examples of the sustained naturalization of gender and 'race' differences well illustrate this point.

Women and work

Ideas about women's inherent suitability for certain kinds of work have always informed, and been informed by, the naturalization of gender differences (the process by which socially constructed differences between men and women are accounted for in biological terms, thus emphasizing their inevitability rather than their openness to change). These differences are enshrined in the social contract of most countries of the developed world (Pateman, 1988). Nevertheless, times are changing: equal pay legislation has been enacted to challenge the practices that devalue women's work, and anti-discrimination legislation demands a more open set of employment policies. These have not succeeded in eradicating the inequalities that flow from occupational segregation and gender discrimination (Fincher, 1989), but symbolically, and in practice, their existence might be expected to undermine the natural science metaphor which has traditionally so readily legitimized income differentials.

Today, the work that women do is recognized as playing an important part in the economic restructurings of the 'new times' on a global as well a national scale. Yet in examining this restructuring, we find that ideas about women's supposedly 'natural' suitability for work in different parts of the production process have been reworked rather than discarded. These assumptions continue effectively to legitimize women's unequal opportunities, pay and conditions, even though the economic context has changed (Wekerle and Rutherford, 1989).

Ironically, at a time when female labour is widely required to bolster the casualized periphery of the post-Fordist economy, it is becoming hard to overstate the extent to which supposedly natural differences between men and women in their ability or suitability to perform certain tasks are still drawn on by employers to 'explain' the gender division of labour in the paid workforce. Elson and Pearson (1981), for instance, show how themes related to 'nimble fingers', 'natural manual dexterity' and 'patience' are constructed as female skills, and are inserted into a 'natural' hierarchy beneath male skills in order to sustain, and account for, women's secondary status in the Third World labour force (a labour pool which now drives the production process). In the same vein, Metter (1986) discusses the feminization of the British electronics industry – an industry in which women are valued for their 'natural manual dexterity' and 'patience'. Metter shows how these 'feminine' skills are constructed in an ideologically biased way to legitimize ideas about a 'natural' hierarchical distinction between the value (and therefore pay and conditions) of men's and women's work.

It is a short step from this type of analysis to argue that, in a country such as Britain, ideas about the natural location of women's work – the home – have legitimized, if not facilitated, a shift in women's work patterns from the regulated to the unregulated sectors of the labour market, or from the open to the hidden economy (McDowell and Massey, 1984). This same discourse has often helped drive women out of the workforce altogether in a political climate which favours a return to 'Victorian values' in the wake of rising unemployment. Bleir (1984) takes up this point by tracing the flexible yet persistent role of scientific metaphor in developing a myth of female inferiority, which has been consistently drawn upon to 'explain' and legitimate women's subordinate economic position in the Western world.

In short, it seems that with the advent of flexible accumulation, and the restructuring of the labour market that goes with this, the naturalization of gender differences, which secures at least some social legitimacy for a particular division of labour, is not a relic of the modern world. Rather, it plays a crucial part in both the geography and sociology of those economic restructurings which we associate with a shift to the 'new times'.

'Race' and politics

A similar set of examples can be drawn on to illustrate the sustained salience of 'race' in a period where a traditional appeal to the ordering principles dictated by the physical and biological sciences has no demonstrable foundation. Racialization is generally recognized as a process whereby somatic traits are overlaid with presumptions of natural origin, and infused with social significance. It refers to the social construction of human races, and to the naturalization of these categorizations. I have argued elsewhere that, in Britain in the past fifty years, the process of racialization – the assumption that human races are real – has informed the construction of selective immigration laws and has legitimized the unequal division of residential space between 'black' and 'white' Britons (Smith, 1989b). I have shown, too, how these themes of exclusion and segregation map on to a geography of racism, and I have argued that this geography helped mask the inequalities that flowed from, and indeed fuelled, Britain's post-war economic reconstruction. The naturalization of racial differences certainly has a role alongside the naturalization of gender difference in the regulation of industrial capitalism.

But there is more to it than this. For changing ideas about 'race' (and gender too) have also been at the heart of the political reorderings which have been as prominent in the transition to the 'new times' as has economic upheaval. As Barker (1981) ably shows, the shift towards neoconservatism which has characterized so much of the Western world in the 1980s has been accompanied by the tendency for 'respectable' politicians to retreat from the crude language and imagery of 'race'. They employ instead the postmodern language of pluralism, diversity and apparent tolerance of difference. This is a world where the dichotomy 'black/white' gives way to a deliberate cultural and ethnic pluralism. But it is also a backcloth for what might be called the racialization of culture: 'the conflation of "race" with culture, leading to the categorization and subjugation of individuals on the basis of how they are presumed to act, what they are presumed to think, and where their religious, linguistic and national loyalties are presumed to lie' (Smith, 1992, p. 137).

The presumption that lies at the heart of this line of thinking is that cultural difference is nature's product. Underlying the new veneer of cosmopolitanism there is, accordingly, a strong adherence to ideas about the essentially natural origins of cultural differences. It is significant, therefore, that these 'natural' cultural boundaries are not drawn round just any set of shared meanings. Rather, new debates on ethnicity and culture are shot through with euphemistic references to old 'race' categories. This is recognized by Cope (1985, p. 18), who points out that 'naturalising culture, culturalising structure, and thus making it seem that the world is the way it is in part because of primordial immutable traditions or ethnicities, is a polite new form of racism'.

Once defined, these 'natural' differences, whether they are described in terms of 'race', 'ethnicity' or 'culture', ensure that judgements of superiority and inferiority are expressed through the reasonable concept of difference, so that a friendly face conceals the uncomfortable facts of inequality. But today, no less than in the past, these ideas of difference are drawn on to define and strengthen distinctive forms of nationalism in the face of a reordering of world politics (Gilroy, 1987; Miles, 1987). The case of the UK is just one example of how, by packaging social categorizations based on skin colour or imputed national origins as a celebration of multiculturalism, politicians, the public and many analysts deflect attention from the racisms which bolster the force of nationalism. Today's implicit appeal to natural science as the source of social differentiation cloaks assertions of power in benign expressions of identity, but it legitimizes the geography of inequality every bit as effectively as older, more explicit references to a natural racial hierarchy.

The medicalization of social life

Having briefly used the examples of an entrenched naturalization of gender and 'race' differences to illustrate the sustained salience of a natural science model of social order throughout the processes of economic transition and political reordering, I shall now dwell in a little more detail on a third natural science metaphor. My aim is to illustrate how the medicalization of social life informs and is informed by a restructuring of welfare – a third integral element of the postmodern 'new times'.

Medicalization refers to the drawing of boundaries around social groups on the basis of presumed health, illness or susceptibility to disease. Such boundaries are overlaid with attitudinal, behavioural and territorial markers, and may be used as criteria in determining the differential apportionment of goods and services. Crucially, medicalization is about a process of social categorization for the purposes of *rationing* resources and *controlling* personal and public space. The history of this incorporation of medical metaphors into the project of domination and control is increasingly well documented. An explicit appeal to medical knowledge has, in particular, been used to control the life-spaces of women and racialized minorities throughout the modern period.

The essays collected by MacLeod and Lewis (1988), for instance, show how medicine was used as an agency of cultural domination in the colonial period: it was offered as proof of imperial superiority and used as a vehicle for the exercise of social control over colonized peoples. The spectre of uncontrolled infectious disease among 'native' populations was also used by colonizers to justify the segregation and subjugation of colonial populations. This is well illustrated in Frenkel and Western's (1988) account of the development of segregationism in Sierra Leone. An entrenched image of 'racial' outsiders as the harbingers of not only physical but also moral contamination was also influential in shaping the policies and institutions of segregation in South Africa (Swanson, 1977).

In a similar vein, Proctor's (1988) powerful account of 'racial hygiene' in Nazi Germany shows how potent a role medical science played in shaping a racial ideology. Proctor shows how medicine interacted with the project of national socialism to exemplify the broader generalization that 'if people can be convinced that the social order is a natural order, and that the misery (or abundance) they find around them derives from the will of God or Nature or both, then attention can be diverted from those parts of the social order that are the true source of that misery (or abundance)' (p. 2). The historical interlinking of medicine and racism is further explored by Littlewood and Lipsedge (1989), who show how psychiatry, by medicalizing the mental health problems of racialized minorities, has helped translate the outsider status associated with ideas about 'race' into the marginal status of people labelled 'mentally ill'.

The moral environmentalism so instrumental to early ideas of racial difference and spatial segregation in the public sphere has also been central to the control of women's life-space, especially in the private sphere. Mort (1987) attributes some of our most enduring constructions of gender difference to the social hygiene movement of the early twentieth century. This movement rolled together ideas about health, morality, sexual behaviour and passion, and produced new representations of sex difference organized around the themes of (male) normality and (female) abnormality.

The progressive medicalization of women's lives is taken up elsewhere. Ehrenreich and English (1979, 1981) show how early myths of female frailty have limited women's social opportunities, and they go on to illustrate that the medicalization of this syndrome not only debarred women from practising as doctors, but also qualified them as patients and so boosted the coffers of a newly developing male-dominated medical profession in the late nineteenth century. Cayleff (1988) traces this gender bias in the medical conceptualization, diagnosis and treatment (and associated common-sense understandings) of nervous disorders across the whole time–space spectrum from medieval Europe to twentieth-century North America. She points to the remarkable consistency with which a 'view of women's predisposed susceptibility to nervous debility transcended medical and scientific knowledge to include assertions that stemmed from deeply held beliefs about female and male "natures" and the acceptable parameters of women's behaviour and influence' (p. 1205). Exploring a related area, Clarke (1983) shows how the medicalization of childbirth which gave rise to its own branch of medicine – obstetrics and gynaecology, which is still dominated by men – has been harnessed to the social control of women. This theme is taken up by Abel and Kearns (1990), who show how the appropriation of maternity services into hospital settings has extended control into the most intimate spaces of women's lives and deprived them of autonomy and security in some key areas of family life.

The power of medicalization as an ordering principle for social life is not, then, in dispute. Neither, in any serious way, is its tenacity. Cayleff (1988) concludes her review with the sobering observation that 'gender ideologies still largely inform the illness labeling, medical diagnosis and management of woman's physiology' (p. 1205). Spallone (1989) argues in the same vein that the new reproductive technologies compromise women's integrity, rights and freedom every bit as much as the earlier population promotion and regulation policies. My own view is that medicalization may be one of the most powerful and persuasive natural science metaphors contributing to the ordering and reordering of society. From the perspective of this chapter, it is important because it is implicated not only in defining and controlling gender and 'race' difference, but also in positioning and discriminating among the many other social groupings – the 'elderly', the 'physically disabled' and so on – emerging through the process of postmodernization.

The medical metaphor currently informs many areas of policy and practice. For instance, it controls access to certain forms of employment: and as science itself advances, the potency of presumed health status as a barrier to access to the core sectors of the post-Fordist labour market seems set to increase. In the USA, for example, where black Americans with sickle-cell trait used to be debarred from the air force, tests for AAT deficiency (a genetically controlled shortage of an enzyme that detoxifies tar, and which may arguably predispose its incumbents to emphysema) are now commercially available to employers. Likewise, the medical metaphor is increasing rather than decreasing in importance as a means of regulating political frontiers and other territorial boundaries. Gordon (1983) shows how, during the late nineteenth and early twentieth centuries, health checks were used as immigration controls by the developed countries, ostensibly to stop the import of infectious disease but in reality to limit non-white immigration. Taking the example of the UK, Gordon makes the further claim that such controls are still used: not to protect public health but to discriminate among those British citizens who are, and those who are not, eligible to live with their families in the UK. An appeal to medical knowledge is made to determine, for instance, whether immigrant 'fiancées' are virgins, whether immigrant children are the 'natural' offspring of sponsoring parents, and whether such children are young enough to qualify as dependants. Gordon's point has more general relevance: 'medical controls have a special significance in that they appear to be based on the scientific judgement of objective facts, and therefore not tainted by more political considerations' (p. 17).

It is in this light that we can begin to understand the relevance and potency of the medical metaphor in the process of rationing resources and regulating deviance in a restructured welfare state. The potential extent and consequences of the medicalization of public policy are documented by Binney *et al.* (1990) in their study of community-based services for older people in the USA. This research shows how community-based service provision has been steadily restructured to favour medical intervention over social support. This has occurred to such an extent that the possibilities for providing comprehensive care are often frustrated, and socially oriented services – for many, a prerequisite for independent living – are frequently under threat. This example indicates that medicalization is not about implementing the welfare ideal of providing for individuals according to their own distinctive needs (medical or otherwise). Rather, it can be argued that the consequences of medicalization may fundamentally compromise (or may be used to legitimize policies which fundamentally compromise) this welfare ideal, as cutbacks in public expenditure are traded for tax concessions in a bid to roll back the State and free up the marketplace. In documenting this, I am concerned not with the crude medical metaphors of the colonial period but with a more subtle intrusion of quasi-medical categories into the process of welfare restructuring in the late twentieth century. In particular, I consider how medicalization impinges on social policy in a way that helps define and separate the 'deserving' and 'undeserving' poor in order to accommodate the residual model of welfare now embedded in our thinking about welfare transfers.

Housing and health: medicine and the urban order

To illustrate the point, I take the example of British housing policy, both because housing has been at the leading edge of welfare restructuring in the UK (Clapham *et al.*, 1990) and because the reorganization of living space this has entailed is of particular relevance to the project of geography and can be directly linked to some of the processes of medicalization with which I am concerned (Smith, 1990a).

The British housing system was, for many years, a cornerstone of the country's welfare state. It epitomized the widely accepted principle that a civilized society collectively provides for those disadvantaged in a market system by factors, like illness, which are beyond individuals' control. Thus from as early as the 1930s, but especially from the 1950s, public housing has acted as a safety net for people whose incomes are depressed by ill-health. Systems of housing allocation therefore include mechanisms for giving people with medical needs priority in access to, and transfer within, the subsidized rented stock. Housing provision is therefore theoretically health selective in favour of sick people: people with health problems traditionally have the pick of public housing space. And, if anything, the legislative impetus for this health selectivity has been enhanced in recent years (Smith, 1989c, 1990b), so that the principle of awarding priority access to mainstream housing on medical grounds is now firmly embedded in the housing management practices of most local authorities.

However, the public sector is changing. Britain, like North America (Wolch, 1989) and Australia (Fincher, 1989), has undergone a period of welfare restructuring. In the UK, this shift from the State to the market has been spearheaded by the reorganization of housing provision. Until very recently, therefore, housing has borne the brunt of policies aiming to reduce public expenditure in return for cuts in taxation. As Forrest and Murie (1988) show, it is in the sphere of housing provision and management that Britain has most effectively relinquished a model of provisioning based on direct State intervention (through the provision of subsidized rented dwellings) to a model based on market principles (through the encouragement of owner-occupation). Irrespective of whether this is a good or a bad thing, it has consequences which are relevant to the theme of this chapter.

The transition from State to market in housing provision has been achieved primarily through the sale of public rented homes to sitting tenants, at discounted prices and with advantageous mortgage arrangements. New capital investment has not kept pace with sales: indeed, councils have not usually been allowed to use receipts from sales to build replacement stock. Because the pattern of purchase has been uneven (suburban houses have sold more readily than inner-city flats; dry homes in good repair have proved a more attractive investment than damp homes in poor condition), the council rented stock which remains after a decade of the 'right to buy' has decreased in size, diminished in quality and become more restricted in its geography.

Observers link this residualization of council housing with an associated marginalization of council tenants (Forrest and Murie, 1987), since those tenants most able to buy are the better-off, middle-aged, securely employed families. Those who remain as renters tend to be very young or old, and, for the most part, benefit-dependent (for a variety of reasons, including unemployment and poor health). This marginalization is evident in the increasing sociotenurial polarization of the housing system as a whole (Bentham, 1986; Robinson, 1986). Council housing has become more explicitly the welfare arm of the housing system, so attracting more applications from people with medical needs, even as medical priority is forced to compete with a growing range of other priority claims (Smith, 1990b; Connelly and Roderick, 1992). The system is therefore under pressure and the ability of the mainstream housing stock to accommodate people with a range of general health problems is increasingly questionable (Parsons, 1987). Even those who do secure access to this part of the housing system have no guarantee of a healthy home (though certain adapted dwellings are exempt from the sales policy). It is at this point that our attention must shift from the welfare ideal (of matching housing accommodation to needs) to the process of medicalization (using ideas of health and disease to determine who does and does not deserve public subsidy).

The restructuring of housing provision is implicated in the medicalization of residential space in at least three ways. First, it encourages the incorporation of medical criteria into housing needs assessments, bringing clinical judgements to bear on the managerial problem of matching housing applicants to the available stock of dwellings. Second, it has underpinned the development of 'special' housing – separate living space – for people with certain health problems. Finally, it has a bearing on the health profile of homeless people, who, by virtue of their exclusion from mainstream housing services, occupy a quite different niche in the medicalized landscape.

1 Health problems and housing management   Many local authorities delegate the assessment of all applications for housing priority on medical grounds to a health professional (usually a public health physician, but sometimes an occupational therapist or local general practitioner). In a recent survey of one in three English local authorities, 68 per cent of housing departments claimed always to consult a medical adviser (and a further 16 per cent sometimes consult). In half the authorities concerned, the advice of the medical adviser is regarded as binding, and in a further 40 per cent of authorities the advice is 'usually followed' (Smith *et al.*, 1991).

This appeal to medical expertise is not intrinsically problematic. It may, for instance, provide a means of ensuring confidentiality to applicants with health problems. But it is a hallmark of institutional medicalization – a process usually deemed to occur 'when the physician is elevated to the position of "gate-keeper" to authorize eligibility for services' (Binney *et al.*, 1990, p. 762). In the field of housing provision, this kind of procedure has been criticized for translating housing management issues into questions of clinical judgement – a judgement which may be unnecessary or inappropriate given that the majority of housing outcomes are stock-led rather than needs-related (Parsons, 1987). The problems are only compounded when the health professionals concerned have relatively little knowledge of the housing system they are dealing with (Kohli, 1986).

Whatever the merits or otherwise of incorporating clinical judgements into housing needs assessments, the consequences of the medicalization of housing management decisions may be far-reaching. Although this system allows housing priority to be determined on the basis of health problems, it is not clear to what extent the health problems most likely to secure housing priority are actually housing-related, and it is not known to what extent rehousing is an appropriate health intervention in the majority of cases. Moreover, at a time when people with medical priority are competing with a range of other legitimate priority claims on the public housing system, there may be little justification for separating health from other welfare needs in the allocation of a limited quantity of living space (and some local authorities have recognized this by replacing their medical needs categories with a broader special needs list). On the other hand, as councils' better-quality properties need to be more stringently rationed in the face of increasing demand and decreasing supply, it is possible that definitions of health and illness – and their association with different levels of housing priority – will be increasingly important as measures of more or less eligibility for public housing services (and for the better-quality parts of public sector housing space). Those least eligible may slip through the welfare net altogether (see section 3 below); those most eligible are likely to be directed toward the 'special' housing spaces considered in the next section.

2 'Special' housing space   The difficulties the public sector now has in providing for general medical needs through mainstream housing allocations has produced an alternative model of housing provision. This has resulted in the development of a form of 'medicalized space' geared to the needs of the unambiguously 'deserving' poor. The production of 'special' medical space is epitomized in the advent of the special housing movement, which demands the standardization of illness for management purposes in ways which Turner (1987) finds at the heart of the medicalization of society.

'Special' housing is designed for people who need special home adaptations or special forms of care if they are to live independent lives in the community. It is ideal for people with certain medical or social support needs, and it has developed at least partly in response to policies of deinstitutionalization. Special housing includes: sheltered/amenity housing for older people; supported accommodation for people with learning difficulties or mental illness; and wheelchair or mobility standard housing for people with walking, stretching and reaching difficulties.

This model of provision has secured excellent homes for relatively small groups of 'elderly', 'mentally ill', 'mentally handicapped' and 'disabled' people. In practice, however, the current enthusiasm for special housing marks the end of the use of the public sector to meet general housing needs. It is a product of welfare restructuring and it is concerned not merely with targeting resources but also, and crucially, with rationing them (Clapham and Smith, 1990). Special housing is significant, then, not because of the amount of shelter supplied (which is relatively small) but because it is one of the few areas of public housing still receiving capital investment. In fact, we know that many people, even with supposedly legitimate special needs, never get homes in special schemes, and by comparing the geography and sociology of mainstream and special provision the social costs of the residual model of welfare from which the 'special' model flows can readily be appreciated.

First, the 'special' model tends to segregate client groups into 'special' space. Special housing is often segregated and has been criticized for providing mini-institutions in community settings. By packaging certain buildings with certain forms of care, this model of provision can also limit the locational options of those who only require the care or dwelling element of the package. Second, the cost of gaining access to special housing may be the sacrifice of individual identity to collective stigma. By catering in a standardized way to grouped needs, special accommodation may reinforce labels such as 'elderly', 'mentally handicapped' and so on, even though many older people are fit and well, and many learning difficulties are slight. Finally, it is necessary to acknowledge that housing provision has often been bound up with two opposing models of health care: that concerned with control and containment and that oriented towards disease prevention and health promotion (Smith, 1990a). There has always been a tension between these models, and there is a danger that special housing, which began in the spirit of prevention and promotion, is – as it becomes infused with medical metaphor – sliding towards the control/containment end of the spectrum.

The dilemma this raises is epitomized in the tensions running through the AIDS and housing movement. Because local authorities have few policies for admitting people with HIV/AIDS to mainstream housing systems, such people find they have to bargain for extra – new – resources to secure adequate and properly serviced accommodation. The current model for levering such resources from the closely guarded public purse is the 'special' one – but this runs the risk of isolating/stigmatizing an already persecuted group (at the same time as it deflects attention away from the inadequacies of provision via the mainstream housing services). The dangers of this model are heightened because the theme of quarantine, which Altman (1986, p. 18) identifies as 'probably the oldest public health measure', is ever-present in the current hysteria over the management of AIDS and HIV; and the social reactions evoked by this disease are strikingly similar to those that motivated past quarantine efforts (Musto, 1988).

This theme of the control and containment of people with HIV is evident on a variety of spatial scales. On the macro-scale there are immigration restrictions to prevent the entry of people who are HIV-positive to the USA, and in Australia calls have been made to confine gay men to particular islands (Altman, 1986). The same sentiments have appeared in regional policy: in 1983 the then-chief of infectious diseases in California is alleged to have invoked the idea of segregation as a means of dealing with 'recalcitrant' AIDS patients; in Britain, legislation passed in 1985 allows local authorities to keep people with AIDS in hospital if they are deemed a risk to others. The dangers of this line of thinking when extended to the micro-scale – into policies concerned with the apportionment of living space – can be seen in Sweden, where certain HIV-positive people (those classed as promiscuous) live, are cared for and are contained within special dwellings. What we see epitomized in the experiences of people with HIV/AIDS is the more general logic of the special housing model which, for all its positive achievements, leans towards a medical division of residential space, and lends weight to a growing social divide between those who are deemed fit, healthy and productive, and those known as sick, frail or benefit-dependent.

3 Homelessness and health   Homelessness is increasing rapidly in Britain, and this – like the advent of special housing – can be linked directly to the reorganization of housing provision (Murie, 1988). Homeless people have a distinctive health profile, which is readily related to their harsh and hazardous living space and to their demonstrably limited access to primary medical care (Smith, 1989c). This profile is increasingly prompting homelessness to be thought of in medical terms, just as it was once thought of as an index of criminality or a consequence of individual pathology (Shanks and Smith, 1991). Homelessness, which was in the past criminalized, is increasingly medicalized. Homeless people can thus be said to occupy a second kind of medicalized space: that available to the so-called 'undeserving poor', who have not been able to exercise their statutory right to shelter. (Usually, in the British example, homeless people who do not qualify as unintentionally homeless, in priority need and having a local connection, are excluded from the public sector: Clapham *et al.*, 1990.)

The image of poor health as a corollary of homelessness is, from the perspective of public policy, deflecting attention away from the causes of homelessness (in the housing system) and towards its effects (here, its consequences for public health). It is, of course, important that inequalities in access to primary medical care between housed and homeless populations are addressed, and to this end an emphasis on the role of the health services in tackling the health of homeless people is welcome. On the other hand, there is a very real possibility that many people with health problems are routinely excluded from public-sector housing (because of the way the bureaucratic rules defining eligibility admit some kinds of health problem and exclude others in order to ration a diminishing pool of suitable accommodation) at a time when there is an affordability crisis in the private sector. This in itself has a bearing on the problematic health profile of homeless people today. The irony, then, is that if the rules by which the housing system operates are interrogated, there is every indication that a growing segment of the health profile of homeless people is accounted for by the process of health selection out of housing and into the street (Smith, 1989c; Shanks and Smith, 1991). In short, the restructured housing system has an active role in shaping the health profile of homeless people, even as public responses to that profile – by constituting the problem in terms of health care rather than housing services – are effectively protecting the housing system from fundamental reform by diverting attention towards the gaps in health service provision.

The 'new times' are signalled by a process of welfare restructuring as well as by economic transition and political reordering. In Britain, the shift from State to market provisioning has changed the face of public-sector housing space, and the process has been both informed and legitimized by the medical metaphor. By drawing clinical boundaries around social groupings, it has been possible to reconstitute the distinction between a deserving and an undeserving poor, and shed the light of scientific certainty – of natural inevitability – around a new urban order which is, nevertheless, shot through by old inequalities.

Conclusion

The world I have looked at – and it has been a partial view – is undoubtedly changing. But my theme has been that, despite the cultural fluidity of these postmodern times, the processes of social categorization go on, and the basic axes of social inequality remain (notwithstanding some rescaling of their dimensions). The question at the heart of my discussion is therefore this: how and why do we, reasonable people, tolerate enduring inequality?

We do so, I have suggested, because the sources of the inequalities, and the social boundaries concerned, are acceptable at the level of common sense. One of several metaphors that make them seem plausible is the continued naturalization of social life. An appeal to that most rational of certainty-seeking human endeavours, natural science, wins legitimacy for the reproduction of inequality, and for the control and oppression of marginal groups. The point here is that for all our sophisticated social and cultural theory, for all our understanding of economic change and the processes of legitimation, the appeal of a scientific logic to social differences has not gone away. On the contrary, the very technical advances that gave the 'new times' their economic impetus also inform the naturalization of gender differences in a restructured workforce, the racialization of culture in a reorganized political world, and the medicalization of social needs in a restructured welfare state.

What can be done? That is the topic of another essay. I conclude, nevertheless, with the observation that in order to engage in a changing world, we need a well-developed sense not only of what that world looks like now, but also of what it *should* look like for future generations. Without a better sense of the value of normative theory, without more willingness to enter the politics of prescription, geography is powerless to challenge the subtle ideologies that legitimize enduring social inequalities. It is not enough simply to know how and why the world is changing; if geography has any relevance in the postmodern world, it must have something new to say about how and why the world *should* change.

References

Abel, S. and Kearns, R. 1990: Birth places: a geographical perspective on planned home birth in New Zealand. Unpublished paper, University of Auckland, Departments of Anthropology and Geography.

Altman, D. 1986: *AIDS and the new puritanism*. London: Pluto.

Barker, M. 1981: *The new racism*. London: Junction Books.

Bell, M. 1990: Class, community and nature in an English village. Draft of a PhD dissertation, Yale University.

Bentham, G. 1986: Socio-tenurial polarization in the United Kingdom 1953–83: the income evidence. *Urban Studies* 23, 157–62.

Binney, E. A., Estes, C. L. and Ingman, S. R. 1990: Medicalization, public policy and the elderly: social services in jeopardy? *Social Science and Medicine* 30, 761–71.

Bleir, R. 1984: *Science and gender*. Oxford: Pergamon Press.

Bondi, L. 1990: Feminism, postmodernism and geography: space for women? *Antipode* 22, 156–67.

Cayleff, S. E. 1988: Prisoners of their own feebleness? Women, nerves and Western medicine – a historical overview. *Social Science and Medicine* 26, 1199–208.

Clapham, D. and Smith, S. J. 1990: Housing policy and 'special needs'. *Policy and Politics* 18, 193–205.

Clapham, D., Kemp, P. and Smith, S. J. 1990: *Housing and social policy*. Basingstoke: Macmillan.

Clarke, J. 1983: Sexism, feminism and medicalism: a decade review of literature on gender and illness. *Sociology of Health and Illness* 5, 62–82.

Connelly, J. and Roderick, P. 1992: Medical priority for rehousing: an audit. In Smith, S. J., McGuckin, A. and Knill-Jones, R. (eds), *Housing for health*. London: Longman, 73–91.

Cooke, P. 1990: Modern urban theory in question. *Transactions of the Institute of British Geographers* NS 15, 331–43.

Cope, B. 1985: Racism and naturalness. *Social Literacy Monograph 14*, Centre for Multicultural Studies, University of Wollongong.

Douglas, M. 1966: *Purity and danger: An analysis of the concepts of pollution and taboo*. London: Routledge & Kegan Paul.

Ehrenreich, B. and English, D. 1979: *For her own good: 150 years of the experts' advice to women*. New York: Anchor Press/Doubleday.

Ehrenreich, B. and English, D. 1981: The sexual politics of sickness. In Conrad, P. and Kern, R. (eds), *The sociology of health and illness*. New York: St Martin's.

Elson, D. and Pearson, R. 1981: 'Nimble fingers make cheap workers': an analysis of women's employment in Third World export manufacturing. *Feminist Review* 7, 87–107.

Fincher, R. 1989: Class and gender relations in the local labor market and the local state. In J. Wolch and M. Dear (eds), *The power of geography*. Boston, MA: Unwin Hyman, 91–117.

Forrest, R. and Murie, A. 1987: The pauperization of council housing. *Roof*, Jan.–Feb., 20–3.

Forrest, R. and Murie, A. 1988: *Selling the Welfare State: The privatisation of public housing*. London: Routledge & Kegan Paul.

Frenkel, S. and Western, J. 1988: Pretext or prophylaxis? The malarial mosquito and racial segregation in a British tropical colony. *Annals of the Association of American Geographers* 78, 211–28.

Gilman, S. L. 1988: *Disease and representation*. Ithaca, NY: Cornell University Press.

Gilroy, P. 1987: *There ain't no black in the Union Jack*. London: Heinemann.

Gordon, P. 1983: Medicine, racism and immigration control. *Critical Social Policy* 3, 6–20.

Gould, S. J. 1981: *The mismeasure of man*. New York: Norton.

Hall, S. 1988: Brave new world? *Marxism Today* 32, 24–9.

Harvey, D. 1989: *The condition of postmodernity*. Oxford: Basil Blackwell.

Kohli, H. 1986: Medical housing 'lines'. *British Medical Journal* 293, 370–2.

Littlewood, R. and Lipsedge, M. 1989: *Aliens and alienists*, 2nd edn. London: Unwin Hyman.

Livingstone, D. N. 1991: Climate's moral economy: science, race and place in post-Darwinian British and American geography. Paper presented to the conference on Geography and Empire: Critical Studies in the History of Geography, Queen's University, Kingston, Ontario.

McDowell, L. and Massey, D. 1984: A woman's place? In Massey, D. and Allen, J. (eds), *Geography matters!* Cambridge: Cambridge University Press, 128–47.

MacLeod, R. and Lewis, M. (eds) 1988: *Disease, medicine and Empire: Perspectives on Western medicine and the experience of European expansion*. London: Routledge.

Massey, D. 1991: Flexible sexism. *Environment and Planning D: Society and Space* 9, 31–58.

Metter, S. 1986: *Common fate, common bond*. London: Pluto.

Miles, R. 1987: Recent Marxist theories of nationalism and the issue of racism. *British Journal of Sociology* 38, 24–41.

Mills, W. J. 1982: Metaphorical vision: changes in Western attitudes to the environment. *Annals of the Association of American Geographers* 72, 237–53.

Mort, F. 1987: *Dangerous sexualities: Medico–moral politics since 1830*. London: Routledge & Kegan Paul.

Murie, A. 1988: The new homeless in Britain. In Bramley, G., Doogan, K. Leather, P., Murie, A. and Watson, E. (eds), *Homeless and the London housing market*, Occasional Paper 32, Brown: School for Advanced Urban Studies. Providence, RI.

Musto, D. F. 1988: Quarantine and the problem of AIDS. In Fee, E. and Fox, D. M. (eds), *AIDS: The burdens of history*. Berkeley, CA: University of California Press, 67–85.

Parsons, L. 1987: Medical priority for rehousing. *Public Health* 101, 435–41.

Pateman, C. 1988: *The sexual contract*. Cambridge: Policy Press.

Proctor, R. N. 1988: *Racial hygiene: Medicine under the Nazis*. Cambridge, MA: Harvard University Press.

Robinson, R. 1986: Restructuring the Welfare State: an analysis of public expenditure, 1979/80–1984/85. *Journal of Social Policy* 15s, 1–21.

Shanks, N. and Smith, S. J. 1991: Public policy and the health of homeless people. *Policy and Politics* 20, 35–46.

Smith, S. J. 1989a: Social geography: social policy and the restructuring of welfare. *Progress in Human Geography* 13, 118–28.

Smith, S. J. 1989b: *The politics of 'race' and residence*. Cambridge: Polity Press.

Smith, S. J. 1989c: Housing and health: a review and research agenda. Discussion paper 27. Glasgow: Centre for Housing Research.

Smith, S. J. 1990a: AIDS, housing and health. *British Medical Journal* 300, 243–4.

Smith, S. J. 1990b: Health status and the housing system. *Social Science and Medicine* 31, 753–62.

Smith, S. J. 1992: Residential segregation and the politics of racialisation. In Cross, M. and Keith M. (eds), *Racism and the postmodern city*. London: Unwin Hyman.

Smith, S. J., McGuckin, A. and Walker, C. 1991: Housing provision for people with medical needs. Paper for the conference on Unhealthy Housing: The public health response, December.

Smith, S. J., McGuckin, A. and Knill-Jones, R. (eds) 1992: *Housing for health*. London: Longman.

Spallone, P. 1989: *Beyond conception: The new politics of reproduction*. Basingstoke: Macmillan Education.

Swanson, M. W. 1977: The sanitation syndrome: bubonic plague and urban native policy in the Cape Colony, 1990–1901. *Journal of African History* 18, 387–410.

Taylor, S. M. 1989: Community exclusion of the mentally ill. In Wolch, J. and Dear, M. (eds), *The power of geography*. Boston: Unwin Hyman, 316–30.

Turner, B. S. 1987: *Medical power and social knowledge*. London: Sage.

Wekerle, G. R. and Rutherford, B. 1989: The mobility of capital and the immobility of female labour: responses to economic restructuring. In Wolch, J. and Dear, M. (eds), *The power of geography*. Boston: Unwin Hyman, 139–72.

Wolch, J. R. 1989: The shadow state: transformations in the voluntary sector. Wolch, J. and Dear, M. (eds), *The power of geography*. Boston: Unwin Hyman, 197–221.

---

13   Leonore Davidoff, Jean L'Esperance and Howard Newby,

'Landscape with Figures: Home and Community in English Society'

Excerpts from: J. Mitchell and A. Oakley (eds), *The Rights and Wrongs of Women*, Chapter 4. Harmondsworth: Penguin Books (1977)

Home

Two birds within one nest;
Two hearts within one breast;
Two souls within one fair

Firm league of love and prayer,
Together bound for aye, together blest.

An ear that waits to catch
A hand upon the latch;
A step that hastens its sweet rest to win;
A world of care without
A world of strife shut out,
A world of love shut in.

Dora Greenwell, *Cornhill Magazine*, September 1863

The house constitutes the realm and, as it were, the body of kinship. Here people live together under one protecting roof. Here they share their possessions and their pleasures; they feed from the same supply, they sit at the same table. The dead are venerated here as invisible spirits, as if they were still powerful and held a protecting hand over their family. Thus, common fear and common honour ensure peaceful living and cooperation with greater certainty.

Ferdinand Tonnies, *Community and society*, 1887
(trans, Charles P. Loomis, 1957)

In the current renewed discussion of 'woman's place' it is of primary importance to examine how such ideas fit in with other aspects of the society. Little is gained and much is lost in analysing women as a 'problem' separate from what goes on in the economic, political and social structure. In order to make this analysis more explicit we have looked at some of the uses made of sexual differences by our society historically.

We have chosen to do this, first, because it is marginally easier to stand back and try to see what was going on in a situation a little removed from the present by time, but also because we feel that the period from the end of the eighteenth century was crucial in setting the stage, both in structural and intellectual terms, for the present situation. Girls are still socialized into an ongoing role by their female elders, which despite many superficial changes makes the young woman of the 1970s born about 1950 not basically so very different from her grandmother born in 1900 or even her great-grandmother born in 1875.

The ideal setting of women's lives in the home is a constant theme of the whole period. Analogous to it is the theme of the village community as the ideal setting for relationships in the wider society. These ideas had been present in Western thought for a very long time but during the period of which we are speaking they took on a special saliency: they were seen as an important controlling mechanism in the face of unprecedented changes in social relationships. It is our purpose in this paper to make these themes, *homes* and *village community*, manifest, to draw out the similar ways in which they were used to contain similar kinds of power relationships. Not only were these concepts analogous, however, they were interconnected. The very core of the ideal was home *in* a rural village community. Despite the close parallels between the two themes, however, there were two important differences in the two sets of ideal relationships. The home but not the community included legitimate sexual relations between the superordinate and one of his subordinates, i.e. husband and wife. Secondly, although the home, like the village, was ideally sheltered and separated from the public life of power – political economic, educational, scientific – this separation was doubly enforced by the physical walls of the house, by the physical boundaries extending to hedges, fences and walls surrounding its garden setting. The intensity of privacy was, of course, related to the core sexual relationship in marriage. The home, even more than the village, represented an extreme of the privacy in which individualism could flourish. On first sight this individualism might seem the antithesis of the 'community' which our two themes represent. If we look more closely, however, we will see that the individualism refers *only* to the orientation of the master/husband; the privacy was used by him when he cared to invoke it.

We are concerned in this paper with the home and community as *ideals*. The domestic and rural idyll provided a 'cognitive and moral map of the universe, as a response to the need for imposing order'[1] in an increasingly troublesome, impersonal and alienating real world. As such they contained a number of related dimensions. *First*, the home and the village community represented two of the small units of territoriality upon which deference to traditional authority depended; each was, so to speak, the spatial framework within which deference operated. However, the home and the village community were not merely geographical expressions, since the physical boundaries were also cognitive boundaries, limiting aspirations and ideas about what was possible and desirable. In this sense 'horizons' were both visually and socially limited.[2] The ideology of the home increased the traditional authority of the household head, emphasizing a solidarity of place while identifying the husband's personal authority over wife, children and servants. Similar ideologies of community were, consciously or unconsciously, put forward to promote integration between the various classes and status groups which made up a particular locality. In each case symbolic – and often substantive – boundaries could be maintained, within which those in the dominant positions could provide compatible definitions of subordinate roles. Within the home and within the community, subordinates 'know their place' because their self-contained situation allows them only limited access to alternative conceptions of their 'place' from outside.

One of the important 'feedback' effects of such a model was that the head of the household, just as the resident gentry in the village, felt that he had the legitimate right to make decisions which affected not only the everyday life but the total future of their subordinates, without consulting them. The resulting ignorance of the outside world was then used as a reason for not giving them responsibility, and their misuse of language and slow responses made them objects of derision. They could be ridiculed as country bumpkins, the 'little woman', or cute children. If they were young and sexually attractive, ridicule took the form of gentle teasing and amusement, or it could become coarse and brutal mockery in the case of, say, agricultural labourers. Such ridicule is particularly devastating within the authoritarian situation we have described above.

The more cut-off, the more 'total' this situation, the greater the likelihood that the definition will remain coherent and thus order and stability maintained; 'outside agitators' were not welcome in either home or village community.

Both settings were also seen as idealized 'organic' communities, hierarchical in structure, with a head, a heart and hands to maintain the life of the organism. For this reason both the home and the village community were incomplete without a full set of characters: 'The family as we understand it, is a small community formed by the union of one man with one woman, by the increase of children born to them and of domestic helpers who are associated with them'.[3] The ideal village, also, had its resident squire or aristocrat, its prosperous farmers and contented labourers. In each case the individuals fulfilling these roles were seen in stereotyped form; their basic relationship was one of deference and service on the one hand and kindly, protective patronage on the other.

This double-yoked model we have called the Beau Ideal ('that type of beauty or excellence, in which one's idea is realized, the perfect type or model', 1820, *OED*). In the domestic architecture, model villages (in both pasteboard and real bricks or stone), suburban development and new towns of the nineteenth century, the upper and middle classes briskly undertook the task of creating the necessary infrastructure to approximate the Beau Ideal, and, in a circular process, this social image in turn contributed to the physical landscape. Thus was laid the groundplan of retreat from the unwanted and threatening by-products of capitalism (and progress): destitution, urban squalor, materialism, prostitution, crime and class conflict.

The rural idyll

During the nineteenth century it was taken for granted that real communities could only be found in the English countryside. It was in rural England that the sense of community reigned and where the apparently automatic acceptance of the 'natural order' of things ensured that the norms of deference and paternalism remained at their strongest. One of us has noted elsewhere the easy assumption that community was *par excellence* a rural phenomenon,[4] where the Good Life prevailed amid the placid and the harmonious – 'a beautiful and profitable contrivance', fashioned and kept in smooth working order by that happily undoubting class to whom the way of life it made possible seemed the best the world could offer', as Best has described it.[5] As if to emphasize its rural roots, the term community was often provided with the adjective 'organic'. It was a neat conjunction of the connotations with agriculture and fertility and those with mutual and reciprocal co-operation for the good of all. The organic community was the epitome of the stable social hierarchy which the Victorian upper and middle class wished to preserve, or, where it had been disrupted by the intrusion of industrial and urban growth, recreate. This view of English rural life became such a literary convention that it is now one of our most ingrained cultural characteristics, commonly viewed as man's 'natural' abode, what Ruth Glass has summarized as 'a lengthy, thorough course of indoctrination, to which all of us, everywhere, have at some time or other been subjected'.[6] As it was succictly summarized in 1806:

> Such is the superiority of rural occupations and pleasures, that commerce, large societies or crowded cities may justly be reckoned as unnatural.[7]

This idiom has been impressed on the mind's eye through the years by vivid visual images. One such is village and great house joining harmoniously to play cricket on the village green, bathed of course in the magic golden/green light of an English summer afternoon. Another is the thatched cottage with heavily scented bowers of honeysuckle and roses climbing round its porch.

The reality, however, was that the aggrandizement of the landowning class, which had resulted from enclosure, created a rigid and arbitrarily controlled hierarchy in most rural areas of England. The cohesion of the traditional English landowing class rendered their power extensive. They were in ultimate control of all local institutions in many rural villages – economic, political, legal, educational, domiciliary, religious, etc. – and almost by definition in rural areas they held, either individually or as a class, a virtual monopoly over employment opportunities. Their power was, therefore, virtually total, tempered only by their gentlemanly ethic of obligation to their inferiors – just as the subordination of the agricultural labourer was equally extensive. By the end of the eighteenth century enclosure had reduced large numbers of the independent rural population to this position of total subordination, a proletarianization of the rural labour force which occurred only a short space of time before industrialism wrought a similar change in relationships in the towns.

It must be emphasized, then, that the view of the village community as man's natural habitation, the repository of all that is ancient and immemorial in life, *is* a convention. The reality of rural experience was *not* laid down on paper by the vast majority of the rural population – instead, they gave their verdict on the supposedly idyllic qualities of rural life by voting with their feet and moving to the towns. Perhaps one brief counter-example will highlight the partiality of the conventional view. George Crabbe was able to write from centuries of inherited experience of the Suffolk countryside and, in *The village*, was not above a little sarcastic humour at the expense of literary custom:

> I grant indeed that fields and flocks have charms
> For him that grazes or for him that farms;
> But when amid such pleasing scenes I trace
> The poor laborious natives of the place,
> Then shall I dare these real ills to hide
> In tinsel trappings of poetic pride?
> No . . .
> By such examples taught, I paint the Cot,
> As truth will paint it, and as Bards will not . . .

> O'ercome by labour, and bow'd down by time,
> Feel you the barren flattery of the rhyme?
> Can poets sooth you when you pine for bread,
> By winding myrtles round your ruin'd head?
> Can their light tales your weighty griefs o'empower,
> Or glad with any mirth the toilsome hour?

The originality of Crabbe lies in what he includes in his portrait of the rural world: the oppressive nature of rural society poverty, *work*. Crabbe's rural way of life consists not of 'natural order' but of a very real social hierarchy whose effect on those at its base was little different from the effect of industrialization on the urban working class:

> Here joyless roam a wild amphibious race;
> With sullen woe display'd in every face;
> Who far from civil arts and social fly,
> And scowl at strangers with suspicious eye.

Of course, Crabbe stood apart from the mainstream of the English literary tradition (*The village*, written in 1783, was in fact Crabbe's counterblast to Godsmith's *The deserted village*), where the rural idyll and the organic community remained an all-encompassing theme. From the middle of the eighteenth century it had become conventional to use the antithetical device or comparing the rural way of life – and its ecological derivative – with the city. It is a tribute to the endurance of this convention that, even today, to many of us the adjective 'rural' has pleasant, reassuring connotations: beauty, order, simplicity, rest, grass-roots democracy, peacefulness, *Gemeinschaft*. 'Urban' spells the opposite: ugliness, disorder, confusion, fatigue, compulsion, strife, *Gesellschaft*.[8] It was summed up by Cowper, writing only two years after Crabbe, in his damning verdict that

> God made the country, and man made the town,
> What wonder then, that health and virtue . . .
> . . . should most abound.
> And least be threatened in the fields and groves?

The characteristics of this literary tradition have been extensively analysed in all their randifications by Raymond Williams in his book, *The country and the city*. As Williams points out, the idyllic view of rural life, though possessing lengthy antecedents, became dominant during the eighteenth century, when agrarian capitalist triumphed: 'you might almost believe – you are often enough told – that the eighteenth-century landlord, through the agency of his hired landscapers, and with poets and painters in support, invented natural beauty'.[9] The idealization of the rural world and its associated social order was taken up by the nature poets in their use of nature as a retreat, as a principle of order and control. Life in the countryside was viewed as one of harmony and virtue as static and settled. It consisted in Gray's words, of 'peace, rusticity and happy poverty'. It was this idealized version of rural continuity and virtue that was increasingly used as a yardstick by which to measure the degradation of urban society.

In the early reaction to urbanization, however, another image overlay this: the view of the organic community as the life of the past – John Clare's 'far-fled pasture, long vanish'd scene'. The organic community, in other words, was always slipping away. This was partly due to the problem that many rural writers had of incorporating the manifest changes of rural life into an over-riding image of it which eliminated any dimension of change. Change could thus only be considered by placing it against an unchanging institution instilled with tradition and antiquity. Hence the rural community was particularly susceptible to the 'Golden Age' syndrome, the nostalgia for a half-remembered past, especially as migration was occurring *from* the countryside *to* the towns. The largest share of the responsibility for idealizing and popularizing a mythical merrie England in the countryside belongs to Cobbett. A host of nineteenth-century writers repeated Cobbett's vision of an ideal rural society, a society which consisted, in the words of his biographer, of 'a bene-ficent landowner a sturdy peasantry, a village community, self-supporting and static'.[10] They were also to repeat his idealization of the Middle Ages which was to become so prevalent in nineteenth-century social criticism, and which Chandler has summarized as 'a dream of order'.[11] Cobbett in an argument with a contemporary wrote: 'You are reducing the community to two classes: *Masters* and *Slaves* . . . when *master* and *man* were the terms, everyone was in his place and all were free.[12] Cobbett's arcadian vision of a happy peasantry and a sturdy beef-eating yeomanry was a picture repeated by Coleridge – 'a healthful, callous-handed, but high and warm-hearted tenantry'[13] – by Carlyle, Kingsley, Engels, Ruskin and many others. Indeed, to trace in detail the scope and pervasiveness of this deeply rooted cultural trait would be to construct an inventory of virtually all nineteenth-century British social thinkers as well as myriads of poets, writers, artists, intellectuals, etc. This view of countryside and village society as natural – 'the proper place for the proper Englishman to dwell in'[14] – continues in often subtle and unconscious ways to affect English literature and art, aesthetic ideas, politics, physical planning – and indeed its social science.[15]

It was, then, to the village community that the Victorian middle class looked as a haven from the industrial world. This was not simply a matter of the aesthetic qualities of green fields as opposed to city streets, but of the kind of society into which the individual fitted. The whole concept of community was invested with an emotional power which made it much more than merely locality; it had a greater sense of integration and meaningfulness, a sense of being more attuned to the realities of living, simply of 'belonging'. As one nineteenth-century American visitor pointed out, a country house meant much more than a house in the country:

> They have *houses* in London, in which they stay while Parliament sits, and occa-sionally at other seasons; but their *homes* are in the country. Their turretted mansions are there, pictures, tombs. . . . The permanent interests and affections of the most opulent classes centre almost universally in the country.[16]

Ensconced in this pastoral world the 'opulent classes' could indulge their recreational tastes – hunting, shooting, picnics, parties, balls – secure in the knowledge that the rural working class would remain quiescent and obliging – except in the hidden and, therefore, publicly unacknowledged class warfare of poaching. For as long as the village community remained a largely isolated and remote social world, the influences and judgements of the traditional élite members remained paramount within it. There was no opportunity to question the justice of *which* rights were being exchanged for *which* obligations. As Lord Percy was later to point out, 'any landowner, great or small, could manage men with whom he could talk'.[17] By their ideological alchemy they were able to convert the exercise of their power into 'service' to those over whom they ruled and a rigid and arbitrarily controlled hierarchy became the 'organic community' of mutual dependency. It was not, therefore, surprising that their leadership should be widely regarded as natural.

The domestic idyll

As the nineteenth century progressed and England became more urbanized, the real countryside became less accessible to the urban middle class. The custom of holidays in the country which had begun in the 1840s meant that most children grew up knowing only the superficial sun-filled pleasures of the country in summer; the thatched-cottage ideal of family life was thus annually reinforced. This ideal was, of course, deeply interwoven with the same quest for harmony. The home was to a house, what community was to a locality.[18]

Although from the seventeenth century onwards there had been an emphasis within the middle class on the home as a moral force, these arguments became more widespread, closely allied to the reform in temperance and the religious revival of the late eighteenth and early nineteenth centuries. They were part, too, of the great moral transformation of that time. The intensity of concern can be traced through the spate of literature from the early part of the century: advice manuals, tracts, poems, etc.[19] In a direct comparison with events in France, a writer in 1841 said: 'Household authority is the natural source of much national peace: its decline is one of the causes of the reckless turbulence of the people'.[20]

Cobbett illustrates the fusion of the two ideals. Again acting as the radical with a nostalgia for a golden past, he sighed for the self-sufficient household, in an heroic effort to stem the intrusion of wage work into family economy. He idolized cottage life where each is busy with his allotted task, the women never so attractive as when busy in the dairy making their own butter, kneading their own bread. Nostalgia was here too for a past when servants knew their place, children obediently followed parental directions and wives were untouched by siren calls from the great world and misguided prattlings about independence.

The underlying theme of 'home' was also the quest for an organic community: small, self-sufficient and sharply differentiated from the outside world. Like the village community it was seen as a living entity, inevitably compared to the functional organs of a body, harmoniously related parts of a mutually beneficial division of labour. The male head of this natural hierarchy, like the country squire, took care of and protected his dependants.

> The Master: the Husband, the Father, the Head of the House, the Bread-Winner is the responsible individual whose name and power upholds the household. . . . He holds the place of highest honour; he is the supporter and sustainer of the estab-lishment. He is also legally and politically responsible for all the other members of the family . . . such are the duties of a master, a husband and a father.[21]

It was he, therefore, and he alone who could be joined to the wider society as an individual and a citizen. His dependants, in turn, responded to him with love, obedience, service and loyalty. Ideally no taint of market forces should corrupt the love–service relationships within the domestic citadel.

In keeping with the functional analogy, members of the household were to be sharply differentiated by task, sex and age. Legitimate relationships were seen as vertical only. Subordinates' whole lives were to be spent within the community, thus ensuring total loyalty, privacy and trust. Wives, servants and children, the major subordinate constituents of the household, were never to leave the precincts of the 'domestic domain' except under the closest scrutiny and control.

In the construction of this 'country of the mind', the idea of domesticity as a general good was intimately tied to the powerful symbol of the home as a physical place. The house became both setting and symbol of the domestic community. In the upper-income ranges, the house's carefully guarded entran-ces with drives, gates and hedges, its attended portals and elaborate rituals of entrance, created a sense of security as well as preserving its inmates' rank from pollution by inferiors. Throughout the middle class and in respectable working-class homes, the front privet or iron fence, whitened doorsteps, clean curtains and shining brass door furniture presented the household to 'the World'.[22] The 'temple of the hearth' became a powerfully evocative image, not only in literature but in house design, and in spending resources of servants, labour and income in the lavish use of open coal fires in a deliberately wasteful manner.

> Then as the dusk of evening sets in, and you see in the squares and crescents the crimson flickering of the flames from the cosy sea-coal fires in the parlours, lighting up the windows like flashes of sheet lightning, the cold cheerless aspect of the streets without sets you thinking of the exquisite comfort of our English homes.[23]

If the husband (grown-up sons or brothers) looked for action, adventure, amusement away from home, then it was a fault of the domestic atmosphere, and wives (daughters, sisters) must strive to win them back by making home more attractive, warmer, better organized, more comfortable, more sprightly to counteract the weaknesses of male human nature. For the domestic organic community was the upholder of moral order in a chaotic external world. Women created this order by 'being good' themselves. There was, in fact, very little they could do actively to change their men; it was rather their general example and passive influence which ultimately alone could save men from their baser selves, through their redeeming power 'to love, to serve, to save'.

In the early part of the nineteenth century, this moral redemption was stated in religious terms, the 'sanctity' of home was described in a religious idiom. Family worship symbolized this fusion. The basic concepts of domestic peace and salvation, however, remained deeply part of a secular morality well into the twentieth century.

The essence of domesticity in the daily round, the weekly and seasonal rituals within the home, emphasized the cyclical and hence timeless quality of family life in opposition to the sharp disjunctive growth and collapse of commerce and industry. The stability and timelessness were often enhanced by nostalgic memories of one's own childhood home and the attempt to recreate it for one's children. These qualities were seen as part of the naturalness of domestic life: the family was felt to be part of nature (ideally of course, located in its rural, natural setting) in opposition to the unnaturalness of factory or counting house.

However, as we have seen within the rural idyll, it was natural in selected aspects only. Mothering and nurturing in a general way were important elements in domestic symbolism. The mother–wife was the protector, guide and example of morality. Women's sexuality, on the other hand, was denied, as well as the sexuality of children and servants. This was one of the reasons for the 'no followers' rule and for trying to oversee servants and children's activities day and night. Since it was obviously an impossible task, indications of sexual activity by household subordinates had to be denied or ignored whenever possible.

Sexual passion was cast out of the domestic ideal partly because it could be used to found the basis of an alliance among subordinates which would run counter to the legitimate bonds of authority and deference within the hierarchy. In any case what was called natural was a carefully selected, trimmed, even distorted view as only a very limited form of sexual behaviour could be formally admitted. The problem was to contain sexuality for procreation only within married love. The elevation of the home to mystical levels of sanctification, the sacredness of 'the walled garden', demanded an intensification of the double standard despite marriage on the basis of personal choice and love, not on that of parental arrangements.[24] The carefully cosseted married woman (and her forerunner, the even more carefully guarded pure, innocent, unmarried daughter) living at home never going into public places except under escort and then only on the way to another private home, surrounded by orderly rooms, orderly gardens, orderly rituals of etiquette and social precedent was in stark contrast to the woman of the streets, the outcast, the one who had 'fallen' out of the respectable society which could be based only on a community of homes, to the *ultima Thule* of prostitution.

If purity was the prime female virtue it was particularly endangered by the promiscuous life of the city. The multifarious pleasures of eighteenth-century London could represent only the road to damnation for the virtuous woman; it is significant that Richardson's Clarissa finally 'falls' because of her unfamiliarity with wicked city ways. The life of the streets, of inns and public gardens, once commonly enjoyed by men and women of the classes, became more and more restricted to poor women, or to the appropriately named 'women of the town' who could no longer have any pretence to respectability or decency.[25] By about 1820 prostitution had become '*the* sin of the great cities' and the opposition of pure country girls and abandoned town women was well established. The city streets were the downfall of many virtuous men who 'would have escaped the sin altogether, had they not been exposed to the incessant temptations thrown in their way by the women who infest the streets'.[26]

To the nineteenth-century thinker, man's sexual needs were so overwhelming there could be little hope of changing masculine behaviour; control of the women was the way to ensure that young men escaped the supposedly debilitating effects of fornication. Medical opinion especially campaigned vigorously from the 1840s for police control and medical inspection of the 'women of the town', ostensibly in the interest of public health, but revealing in their language a close approximation in the minds of the writers between the refuse of the streets and the women.[27] 'We object *in toto* to Ladies Committees,' wrote the *Quarterly Review* in 1848 in an article on Penitentiaries. 'We cannot think a board of ladies well suited to deal with this class of objects . . . we may express a doubt whether it is advisable for pure-minded women to put themselves in the way of such a knowledge of evil as must be learnt in dealing with the fallen members of their sex.' But during the next twenty years women themselves protested against their isolation from their sisters and contested with the many middle-class men who, like Charles Dickens, had become passionately involved in rescue work, their suitability for this task. 'It's a woman's mission,' wrote Mrs Sheppard who ran a home for the fallen in Frome, 'a woman's hand in its gentle tenderness can alone reach those whom *men* have taught to distrust them.'[28]

The Beau Ideal

We have seen that the rural and domestic idylls had many features in common. Territorially, these two areas merged together in the symbolism of the garden where nature could be enjoyed but was also tamed and controlled. About 1800 there was a move to unite the great house with its surroundings. Terraces were reintroduced, often balustraded with urns and other 'garden-furniture' which helped link the house with the garden, which became another bounded space for social interaction.[29]

Throughout the nineteenth century the art of landscape gardening expanded rapidly. In 1851, these were 4540 domestic gardeners; by 1911 they had increased to 118,739. While women were urged to take their share in this interest, there was still a basic division between indoor and outdoor activity being appropriate to females and males respectively. As an instrument of education, however, the garden was considered ideal for both sexes, and, indeed, the metaphorical equation of gardens, growth, fruition through tender care was a strong one in literature about children of this period; childhood as part of the organic community.

It was in the 1820s, 1830s and 1840s too, that the Scottish *émigré* landscape gardener John Claudius Loudon edited his very successful *Gardener's Magazine and Register of Rural and Domestic Improvements*. His primary audience was the newly wealthy middle class who were investing in large suburban villas with gardens rather than grand parks, as his own model semidetached house and garden in Bayswater indicated. This emulation went down the social scale:

> that this was a matter of class is very clear from one rather curious phenomenon: the man who, although he lived in the country, say upon the outskirts of a county town, but felt himself to be, in income and social habits, a member of the urban small burgers class, had not a cottage garden but a garden which in style and plant material was a suburban garden.[30]

Loudon's goals for the middle-class house and garden were suffused with the longing to approximate the orderliness and functions of the great country house. Robert Kerr, another very influential ex-Scotsman and architect, succinctly summarized this aspiration in his well-known book *The gentleman's house* (1864), in which he set out the fundamentals of England's 'peculiar model of domestic plan, the *Country-Seat*'. 'Let it be again remarked that the character of a gentleman-like Residence is not a matter of magnitude or of costliness, but of design – and chiefly of plan; and that, a very modest establishment may possess this character without a fault'.[31]

In 1833, Loudon published what was, in effect, a Utopian fantasy which the anonymous author – an architect – admitted was no longer really feasible in times when great disparity of wealth was no longer so acceptable (*sic*), yet he calls it 'The Beau Ideal' of an English villa, a picture of a modern English villa as it ought to be, and follows this with a thirty-page description of an imaginary country house, its gardens, its farm, its village.[32] This was to be, in fact, 'the true home epitomizing social, historical and cosmic community'.[33] Twenty-five years later, in the heyday of country-house building, architects were no longer so reticent.

> Providence has ordained the different orders and gradations into which the human family is divided, and it is right and necessary that it should be maintained. . . . The position of a landed proprietor, be he squire or nobleman, is one of dignity. Wealth must always bring its responsibilities, but a landed proprietor is especially in a responsible position. He is the natural head of his parish or district – in which he should be looked up to as the bond of union between the classes. To him the poor man should look up for protection; those in doubt or difficulty for advice; the ill disposed for reproof or punishment; the deserving, of all classes, for consideration and hospitality; and *all* for a dignified, honourable and Christian example. He has been blessed with wealth, and he need not shirk from using it in its proper degree. He has been placed by Providence in a position of authority and dignity, and no false modesty should deter him from expressing this, quietly and gravely, in the character of his house.[34]

The English country house, seen in this way, was 'the great good place' and embodied in its social relationships to its attendant village, its setting in gracious gardens, the 'unity of past, present and future; unity with nature . . . .'. In an era of travellers, wanderers and seekers the country house remains a 'still point' in an ever turning world, 'the sense of home, of place'.[35]

The large-scale English country house of the Beau Ideal could in fact, be achieved only by a small minority. A true estate employed everyone in the area as labourers and ideally recruited all servants, both indoor and outdoor, from the children of estate workers. But even in the early part of the nineteenth century middle-class bankers, professional men and merchants, divorcing their source of income from their personal living, started developing suburbs in imitation of this ideal.

Suburban life is the ultimate experience in the *separation* of classes. From the time of its origins in the eighteenth century the very rich and the very poor were excluded, and the middle-class pattern could develop unmolested, safe both from the glittering immorality of the fashionable world and from the equally affronting misery and shiftlessness of the poor.

The growth of professional landscape gardening and the increasing popularity of suburban homes were the enduring physical expressions of the Beau Ideal. The harmonious community of village and home, however, appeared in every guise. It was the unmistakable message of sermons, hymns, poems, popular songs, wall texts, household manuals, annuals, tracts, magazines and novels. The written word, an important new medium for a mass audience, was supplemented by illustrations in periodicals, advertisements and calendars. (This has continued to the present day in colour photographs and posters such as the 'Come to Britain' campaign of the British Tourist Board.) And the whole genre of nineteenth-century children's literature is full of paeans to family and village life.[36]

The Beau Ideal in action

As with the rural idyll, discussions of conflict or constraint were avoided in descriptions of domestic community. In fact, of course, the household could be not only an 'earthly paradise' but its opposite, a 'hell on earth', a prison.

The fact that no other external relationships were sanctioned for its inmates, at least below the rank of master, could make men tyrants over their wives, mothers over their daughters and both over their younger children and servants. The home could be not only a walled garden but also a stifling menagerie of evil forces unchecked by interference from any higher authority.[37] Even if such depths were not reached, middle-class homes not 'in' the fascinating social game of upper-middle or upper-class Society could be the incarnation of routinized boredom. Men and boys had alternative living places in, first, boarding schools, then college halls, barracks, clubs and chambers where they could be 'serviced' and find companionship. They might, indeed, feel guilty about such escapes but nevertheless they could legitimately flee to them. Without nunneries and with the suspicions cast on sisterhoods of any kind, the lack of openings overseas, girls and women had *no* alternative unless it be the homes of other relatives or friends.

Because one of the goals of family life was in keeping up a front, if not to rise in the ranks of society, at least to keep up respectability, the impetus always was to aim at the highest standard of living possible. This meant a constant urge to live beyond the means of the household and to make up the difference by exploiting the labour of the most subordinate members, i.e., young servants, children, unmarried daughters and, in lesser households, wives. The cash worth of such labour was played down; the ideal was the old family retainer, whose love and loyalty to the family was reward enough, no matter how hard the work. The spiritualized dwelling-place often bore little resemblance to the realities of half-cooked mutton, egg-stained table cloths, recalcitrant boilers and wailing, puking babies of real life. But the fact that the ideal, if it was even attempted, depended on hard, unremitting drudgery performed by often lonely, tired out, young maidservants secreted away in underground basements, sleeping in freezing attics, carrying hods of coal and heavy toddlers from early morning to late at night was not allowed to intrude on the dream; no one ever asked subordinates how they viewed the household.

Into the twentieth century

The direct continuity between the nineteenth-century Beau Ideal of the rural organic community and the twentieth-century approach to town and country planning has been traced in detail by Peterson, Thorns and many others.[38] The desire for an ordered social world which prompted the construction of model villages and towns like New Lanark, Saltaire, Port Sunlight and Bournville also stimulated Ebenezer Howard's 'Garden City' movement in the first decade of the twentieth century. The Garden Cities – a wonderfully felicitous Edwardian phrase which captured exactly the desired balance of rusticity and propinquity – were planned experiments in utopian living outside London, at Letchworth and Welwyn. They were the precursors of the British New Towns, which were to be similarly inspired by a utopian zeal. The Garden Cities conveyed a uniformly suburban appearance which has since spread to estate design in both Britain and the United States.

Suburbia became the last refuge of the Beau Ideal for architects and planners. Here they attempted to create the conditions for an arcadian existence – 'city homes in country lanes' – what one critic has summarized as lying 'somewhere on the urban fringe, easily accessible and mildly wild, the goal of a "nature movement" led by teachers and preachers, bird-watchers socialities, scout-leaders, city-planners and inarticulate commuters'.[39] To many dwellers (but not as often to their isolated wives) suburbia meant the sylvan, the natural, the romantic, the lofty and the serene, the distant but not withdrawn, neither in nor of the city, or the countryside, but at its border. 'Living in the country', as one commuter announced to *Harper's Weekly* in 1911, meant 'allowing the charms of nature to gratify and illumine, but not to disturb one's cosmopolitan sense'.[40] Here one was offered 'the cream of the country and the cream of the city, leaving the skim-milk for those who like that sort of thing'.[41] The Garden City Movement became a focus for such sentiments in Edwardian England. Here, in Howard's own words:

The town is the symbol of society – of mutual help and friendly cooperation, of . . . wide relations between man and man. . . . The country is the symbol of God's love and care for man. All that we are and all that we have comes from it. . . . It is the source of all health, all wealth, all knowledge. But its fulness of joy and wisdom has not revealed itself to man. Nor can it ever, so long as this unholy, unnatural separation of society and nature endures. Town and country *must be married*, and out of this joyous union will spring a new hope, a new life, a new civilisation . . .[42]

After the First World War, the basis of middle-class housing shifted to ownership rather than rental in the new outer-suburban developments. For the first time, too, there was a chance for the expanding white-collar sector and even upper-working-class families to own the by now ubiquitous semi-detached house with the possibility of having a 'tradesman's' entrance at the back, the illusion of privacy, gardens to give an air of rural surroundings.

Many of the Londoners dreaming of a new house in the suburbs were seeking to renew contact with the rural environment . . . they looked for at least a suggestion of the country cottage in their new suburban home . . . assiduously, often clumsily they strove to evoke at least a suggestion of that rural-romantic make-believe which was the very spirit of suburbia.[43]

They were seeking very much the same qualities that their grandfathers had sought, 'the subtly mixed aromas of Pears soap, Mansion Polish and toast. . . . The ambience of peace and stability'.[44]

At the heart of the suburban dream was the housewife. The immediate post-war unease, the signs of many women wanting to pursue a new social consciousness and a reluctance to return to the old domestic confines were stifled and forgotten. In terms of one of the most powerful cultural reflections of women's position, 'the new periodicals [for women] dedicated themselves almost without exception to upholding the traditional sphere of feminine interests and were united in recommending a purely domestic role for women'.[45] The celebration of domesticity had obvious connections with the need to sell consumer durables, connections made evident in the model mock-ups of homes in the annual *Daily Mail* Ideal Home Exhibitions which began in the 1920s. Ironically, one of the greatest pressures to renew the domestic idyll at this time was the increased work-load on middle-class wives because of the exodus of domestic servants from middle as well as lower-middle-class homes after the First World War. Servants had few illusions about the domestic idyll, as we have seen, and few hesitated to leave when alternative work was available.

The depression atmosphere of the 1930s also favoured the saving and protecting aspects of home life. The rhetoric of home continued to be a powerful rallying point throughout the Second World War, despite the mobility of all family members and especially the wider opportunities war offered to women.

I believe the value of a comfortably run home and family to be of immense moral and civic importance . . . that Woman not only has, but should confidently wield a special influence over Man. The feminine spiritual vision sees, or rather senses, further than man's.[46]

This was written in nineteen, not eighteen, forty-five.

In the course of the twentieth century, however, middle-class girls, as opposed to older women, were increasingly able to shun some of the demands of home discipline and obligation. They gained a degree of economic independence through the growth of the clerical sector for jobs and even social independence in bedsitters and flats. As the 'daughter-at-home' expectation waned, the married woman and mother became more than ever the identifiable constituent of the home. Increased educational opportunities for girls widened this generation gap.

The more that the wider society grows in centralized corporate and State power, in size of institutions and in alienating work environment, the more that the home becomes fantasized as a countering haven.[47] Home-baked bread, French farmhouse cookery, wine-making, organic gardening – the whole gamut of 'creative homemaking' – have become the suburban substitutes for the fully fledged return to the self-sufficient smallholding, made real only by a tiny minority.

When the rosy spectacles are laid aside, however, it is clear that what to the husband and children can be a refreshing hobby – after all, they are more often than not the consumers, not the producers, of the home-made jam – to the wife can be another variant of the natural mother image and in everyday terms can mean longer than ever hours at the chopping board. Moral and nutritional reactions to packaged foods now are as inextricably confused as the same reactions to tinned foods three generations ago.

The point has been made that the Beau Ideal was a model, a way of composing reality that helped to create that reality in a very concrete way, often embalmed in the bricks and mortar of houses, the layout of roads and services with which we are still living. Both the village and home sectors of this ideal represented a defence against various attacks on the social structure which made, particularly members of the middle class, fearful of disorder in every sphere of social life. The model was seen to stress consensus and affective ties. It thus shifted attention away from exploitation of groups and emphasized individual relationships.[48] It denied the reality of, and thus made less viable, the existence of households with other structures, namely without male heads, with working wives and mothers.

Much of the idiom of the model we have been discussing has been at a subliminal level in the form of visual images, and a social map where sex and class divisions are confined to certain specified physical areas. This means that it takes a special effort to see the model from the outside. It also has made the rebellion against the barren segregating categories of the hierarchy, against the ritualized narrow and stereotyped behaviour demanded by the model, a particularly disturbing one aimed primarily at an equally idealized search for life-giving self-fulfilment through unfettered sexuality.[49]

At the same time, women, especially married women, have been still left with the task of defending the remnants of the Beau Ideal, at least in its bare essentials of socializing young children into civilized behaviour and in nurturing and watching over their men.[50] In their suburban homes, wives are still expected to create a miniature version of the domestic idyll, set in subtopian pseudo-rural estate surroundings while their male counterparts swarm into central city offices and factories. Wives remain protectors of the true community, the 'still point'; a basic moral force to which the workers, travellers and seekers can return. In the archetypal portrayal of everyday life they still wait, albeit with less resignation as well as less hope, for the hand upon the latch.

Notes

1 'Ideology'. In *International encyclopedia of the social sciences*, vol. 7. New York, 1968, p. 69.
2 For the way such 'maps' can be built up from childhood, see P. Gould and R. White, *Mental maps*, Pelican, 1974.
3 Cassell's *Book of the household: A work of reference on domestic economy*, vol. 1, 1869, p. 27.
4 See the introduction to section one of C. Bell and H. Newby (eds) *The sociology of community*. Allen & Unwin, 1974; also H. Newby, 'The dangers of reminiscence'. *Local Historian II* (3) 334–9 (1973).
5 G. Best, *Mid-Victorian Britain, 1851–75*. Panther, 1973, p. 85.
6 R. Glass, 'Conflict in cities' in CIBA Foundation Symposium; *Conflict in society*, London, 1966, p. 142.
7 J. C. Loudon. *A treatise on forming, improving and managing country residences*, 1806, p. 5.
8 R. Glass, op. cit. (note 5), p. 142.
9 R. Williams, *The country and the city*, Chatto & Windus, 1973, p. 120.
10 W. B. Pemberton, *William Cobbett*, Penguin, 1949, p. 139.
11 A. Chandler, *A dream of order: The medieval ideal in nineteenth-century English literature*. Routledge & Kegan Paul, 1971.
12 *Political Register*, 14 April 1821.
13 Cited by R. Williams, *Culture and society, 1780–1850*. Penguin, 1961, p. 34.
14 P. Laslett, *The world we have lost*, Methuen, 1965, p. 25.
15 The chief importer into the sociological tradition is Ferdinand Tonnies. This has been well exemplified by J. C. McKinney and C. P. Loomis in their introduction to *Gemeinschaft und Gesellschaft*, Harper & Row, 1955, pp. 12–29. See also R. Glass, op. cit. (note 5); R. E. Pahl, 'The rural–urban continuum'. In R. E. Pahl (ed.), *Readings in urban sociology*. Pergamon Press, 1969; R. J. Green. *Country planning; The future of the rural regions*. Manchester University Press, 1971.
16 Cited by R. Gill, *Happy rural seat*, New Haven, 1972, p. 4.
17 E. Percy, *Some memories*. Eyre & Spottiswoode, 1958, cited by D. Spring, Some reflections on social history in the nineteenth century. *Victorian Studies*, 4, 58 (1960–61). Also H. Newby, The deferential dialectic. *Comparative Studies in Society and History* 17(2), 139–64 (1975).
18 W. Peck, *Home for the holidays*. Faber, 1955. Many middle-class memoirs speak of the custom of renting vicarages or even school houses in the country for family holidays.
19 Mrs Sarah Stickney Ellis is one of the best known writers of these advice books. For a fuller list see J. A. and O. Banks, The perfect wife. In *Feminism and family planning in Victorian England*. Liverpool University Press, 1964, pp. 58–70.
20 A mother and mistress of A. Family, *Home discipline – or thoughts on the origin and exercise of domestic authority*, 1841, p. 106.

21 Cassell's *Book of the household*, op. cit. (note 3), p. 31.

22 'The front fence . . . gives no real visual or acoustic privacy but symbolizes a frontier and a barrier'. Amos Rappoport, *House form and culture*, Princeton, NJ, 1969, p. 133.

23 Augustus Mayhew, *Paved with gold*, 1858, p. 8, quoted in Myron Brightfield, *Victorian England in its novels*, vol. 4. Los Angeles, 1968, p. 349.

24 Keith Thomas, The double standard. *Journal of the History of Ideas*, April 1959.

25 R. P. Utter and G. Needham, *Pamela's daughter*. New York, 1972.

26 *Meliora*, vol. 7, 1858, p. 75. Patrick Colquoun in his treatise *Police of the metropolis* (1797) refers to prostitutes as brazen lower-class hussies who should be kept from the sight of respectable women by the police. The classification of 'good' and 'bad' women is, of course, made by men in the masculine interest.

27 'The details of a control over prostitution need not form the subject of a separate bill,' argued the *British and Foreign Medical Chirurgical Review* in January 1854, 'any more than the Commissioners of sewers require a new clause for each clearage. The object would be completely accomplished by its being enacted that prostitution, meaning the demanding or receiving money for sexual intercourse, is a criminal act; and that as a punishment, the individual shall be placed under the control and surveillance of a commission, and that the commission be authorized to make such arrangements as may be considered necessary for the public safety.'

28 *The magdalen's friend and female homes intelligences*, June 1860, p. 93.

29 Elizabeth Burton, Gardens. *The early Victorians at home, 1837–1861*. Longman, 1972.

30 Edward Hyams, *The English garden*. Thames & Hudson, 1966, p. 273.

31 Robert Kerr, *The gentleman's house or how to plan English residences from the parsonage to the palace*, 3rd edn, 1871, p. 66. The most influential builder of country houses of the period was also a Scotsman, William Burn. The influence of Scotsmen in architecture and landscape gardening was part of the growth of these pursuits; a separation of the expert and the consumer. M. Girouard, *The Victorian country house*, Oxford University Press, 1971.

32 J. C. Loudon, *An encyclopaedia of cottage, farm and villa architecture and furniture, containing designs for dwellings from the cottage to the villa*, 1833, ch. 2, pp. 780–82.

33 R. Gill, op. cit. (note 16), p. 112.

34 Sir Gilbert Scott, *Secular and domestic architecture*, 1857, quoted in M. Girouard, op. cit. (note 31), p. 2.

35 R. Gill, op. cit. (note 16), p. 15.

36 One of the most famous and enduring was Mrs Sherwood's *The Fairchild family*, which was first published in 1818, ran to fourteen editions before 1847, and was still in print in 1913. The book begins: 'Mr and Mrs Fairchild lived very far from any town; their house stood in the midst of a garden . . .'. The Fairchild rural paradise is inhabited by the family of parents and children, the devoted servants and assorted loyal villagers.

37 A few well-known examples from the nineteenth century are Samuel Butler, *The way of all flesh*. Penguin, 1947; Florence Nightingale, Cassandra. In Ray Strachey, *The cause*, London, 1928; Betty Askwith, *Two Victorian families*, Chatto & Windus, 1971; Ruth Borchard, *John Stuart Mill*, London, 1957; Cynthia White cites the year-long correspondence in the *Englishwoman's Domestic Magazine* in the 1850s on the subject of corporal punishment of children 'in the course of which the corrective measures employed were fully described, throwing a new and sadistic light on the concept of the "pious" Victorian mother'. *Women's magazines: 1693–1968*, Michael Joseph, 1970, p. 46.

38 W. Peterson, The ideological origins of British new towns, *American Institute of Planners Journal* 34, 1968. D. Thorns, *Suburbia*, MacGibbon & Kee, 1972; and Planned and unplanned communities. *University of Auckland Papers in Comparative Sociology* no. 1, 1973.

39 P. J. Schmitt, *Back to nature: An Arcadian myth in urban America*. Oxford University Press, New York, 1969, p. xvii; and see John Betjeman's poem on Letchworth.

40 Eugene A. Clancy, The car and the country home. *Harper's Weekly*, 4, 6 May 1911, p. 30; cited by P. J. Schmitt, op. cit. (note 39), p. 17.

41 William Smythe, *City homes on country lanes*. New York, 1972 p. 60.

42 E. Howard, *Garden cities of tomorrow*, quoted in B. I. Coleman, *The idea of the city in nineteenth-century Britain*. Routledge & Kegan Paul, 1973, pp. 197–8.

43 A. Jackson, *Semi-detached London: Suburban development, life and transport, 1900–1939*. Allen & Unwin, 1973, p. 136.

44 Ibid., p. 143; L. Hanson, *Shining morning face: The childhood of Lance*. Allen & Unwin, 1949.

45 C. White, op. cit. (note 37), pp. 99–100.

46 D. Paterson, *The family woman and the feminist: A challenge*. Heinemann, 1945, p. 37.

47 P. Berger and H. Kellner, Marriage and the construction of Reality. In H. P. Dreitzel (ed.), *Recent sociology*. Patterns of Communicative Behaviour no. 2. Collier-Macmillan, 1970.

48 Domestic servants, agricultural labourers and married women were the last categories (bar children) to gain citizenship rights in the twentieth century. Married women are not quite full citizens to this day; see L. Davidoff, Mastered for life: Servant and wife in Victorian England. *Journal of Social History*, Summer 1974.

49 For example, in a writer like Dylan Thomas, middle-class and middle-aged women are seen as life *denyers*: men are perpetual boys, escaping their moral strictures, glorying in sexual and alcoholic adventures. See *Under Milk Wood*. This is simply a variation of the 'woman as saviour' theme; whichever is emphasized, women embody in themselves the moral order.

50 'It should be noted that the particular and peculiar pairing of "passivity" and "responsibility" may account for many aspects of the behaviour of adult women'. Harriet Holter, *Sex roles and social structure*, University of Oslo Press, 1970, p. 60.

14   David Sibley,
'Outsiders in Society and Space'

Reprinted in full from: K. Anderson and F. Gale (eds), *Inventing Places: Studies in Cultural Geography*, Chapter 7. Melbourne: Longman Cheshire (1992)

Introduction

Dirt, as Mary Douglas (1966) has noted, is matter out of place. Similarly, the boundaries of society are continually redrawn to distinguish between those who belong and those who, because of some perceived cultural difference, are deemed to be out of place. The analogy with dirt goes beyond this, however. In order to legitimate their exclusion, people who are defined as 'other' or residual, beyond the boundaries of the acceptable, are commonly represented as less than human. In the imagery of rejection, they merge with the non-human world. Thus, indigenous minorities like the Inuit (Eskimo) and other native North Americans have been portrayed 'at one with nature', as a part of the natural world rather than civilization. Similarly, in racist propaganda, social groups have been dehumanized by associating them with, or representing them as, animals which are widely considered to be unclean or polluting, like rats or pigs. As Frederick Douglass, an American slave, observed in his biography, the slaves of an estate were valued together with 'horses, sheep, and swine. There were horses and men, cattle and women, pigs and children, all holding the same rank in the scale of being, and were all subjected to the same narrow examination' (Boime, 1990, p. 211). Such associations effectively put the group outside society and, although mythical, the images become a part of common knowledge.

In this chapter, I will be concerned with the social construction of the outsider, examining both the stereotyped images which have entered popular consciousness and have confirmed marginal or residual status in advanced capitalist societies, and the nature of the spaces to which outsiders have been relegated. The perception of minority cultures as being beyond the boundary of 'society' is associated not only with characterizations of the group but also with images of particular places, the landscapes of exclusion which express the marginal status of the outsider group. I will illustrate my argument with reference to Gypsy communities in Britain, other European countries and North America, but the ideas could also be applied to groups other than racialised minorities. There are some similarities in the response to minority cultures, like Gypsies, and to groups who are inappropriately lumped together as 'deviant', particularly the mentally ill and mentally handicapped (Wolch and Dear, 1987; Philo, 1989). Here, we have a similar problem of misrepresentation and a desire to exclude in a social and spatial sense, expressed, for example, in the construction of isolated asylums in the nineteenth century. As Philo (1989, p. 284) observes: 'In the long term the practical consequence of having a network of "closed spaces" devoted specifically to mad people was to produce and then continually to reproduce a population designated as different, deviant, and dangerous by "mainstream" society'.

In order to understand how socio-spatial constructions of the minority have been shaped in the case of Gypsy communities, I will first look at the question of conflicting world views, the difference between the perceptions of Gypsy culture shared by members of the minority group, and the generalized and distorted representations which result inevitably from interpreting visible elements of the minority culture in the context of world views characteristic of the dominant society.

The romantic, the deviant and the other

In cultural geography, there is a growing concern with difference and otherness, with a recognition that relationships with other social groups and the environment are conditioned by shared perspectives which are quite diverse. This reflects a wider concern, evident particularly in feminist and post-modern literature, that general descriptive categories used in social science, such as 'class' or 'woman', neglect significant social cleavages and forms of oppression. Michelle Barrett (1987, p. 30), for example, has argued to this effect, suggesting that to treat a category like class as essential or universal does violence to the range of collective experiences which are actually or potentially significant in a political sense. She suggests that 'the claims of nation, region and ethnicity, as well as age, sexual orientation, disability and religion are being pressed as important and politically salient forms of experiential diversity'. An increased sensitivity to difference is necessary if experience is to be represented authentically, and this sensitivity is apparent in some academic writing, for example, where feminist theory has engaged with postmodern social anthropology (Mascia-Lees *et al.*, 1989). However, it is more generally the case that difference is viewed as deviance because it is set against some notion of the 'normal'. This is evident, for example, in responses to travelling people in Britain (a term which includes both Gypsies and Irish and Scottish Travellers). A commonly held view of travelling people as not just different but deviant is expressed in a comment on Irish Travellers in a letter to an English local newspaper, the *Walsall Observer*: 'Why, in heaven's name, don't [these] members of a foreign republic stay in their own country and live in houses there, like normal people?' (Sibley, 1981, p. 23).

Acknowledging that there are a number of 'salient forms of experiential diversity', as Barrett puts it, or differences in world views, it is still difficult to register these differences because the world views of others are in varying degrees inaccessible or muted. Others may communicate in a different idiom and employ different categories to make sense of their world (Ardener, 1975), and even without a language barrier it may be difficult to represent world views authentically. If the world views of others are partly hidden, there will be a danger of misrepresenting them and constructing stereotyped images. Clearly, this can work both ways. A minority's perspective on the larger society will also be partial and distorted, although in a practical sense this is not a problem in the way that it is for the majority. It is State agencies and antagonistic communities in the dominant society who have the power, the capacity to affect the lives of minority groups, and State policies for minorities may be oppressive because they are informed by partial and stereotyped views. This is the case for current policies for British Gypsies, for example, as I will attempt to demonstrate in this chapter.

The misrepresentation of Gypsies is evident in academic writing, novels and the media. They are portrayed both as romantic and deviant. The romantic image, which appears in cultural forms as different as opera (*Carmen*) and tourist brochures advertising the 'natural' attractions of the Camargue in the south of France (wild bulls, white horses, flamingoes and Gypsies) fits a world view in which Gypsies are seen as a part of nature or of an imagined pre-industrial rustic existence. The deviant consists of visible elements of Gypsy culture, associated with work, shelter and so on, which are seen out of context.

That is to say, in deviant representations there is no understanding of the practical needs of a semi-nomadic people whose survival depends partly on recycling materials discarded by the dominant society. The people and their material culture are viewed as malignant and polluting. They comprise 'matter out of place', as Mary Douglas (1966) puts it. The romantic image is essentially mythical, associating nomadism with freedom, with escape from the constraints of settled society and 'the Gypsy personality' with passion, colour and mystery. This is expressed, for example, in Hermann Hesse's poem, 'Glorious World':

> Sultry wind in the tree at night, dark Gypsy woman
> World full of foolish yearning and the poet's breath

and rather more prosaically in advertising and the presentation of consumer goods. For example, a picture in a recent catalogue for Monsoon clothes, a firm with shops in trendy locations like Covent Garden, London, shows models dressed in 'ethnic' fashions draped around a bow-top Gypsy wagon (Figure 14.1), and the same romantic image has been used in a British advertisement for a bra and on the wrapping of Gypsy Cream biscuits.

Ironically, a mythical, romantic Gypsy culture is identified as real in popular responses, as distinct from the 'they are not real Gypsies' reaction to those actually encountered. Visible features of modern Gypsy culture, such as modern, chrometrimmed trailers parked on waste ground in cities and surrounded by piles of scrap metal and wrecked cars, pram wheels and milkchurns for storing water (Figure 14.2), do not fit the romantic stereotype, so, in this sense, the people observed are not 'real'. At the same time, they violate accepted notions of the appropriate use of land in cities. The 'real' Gypsy is seen as belonging in the past and usually in rural surroundings, part of a cosy image of rural life (Figure 14.3), whereas the people camped on waste ground are perceived as violating urban space, the world of the majority population. This is suggested in characteristic reports in English local newspapers, describing opposition to urban Gypsy sites. Consider for example 'City could be gipsy dump' (*Hull Daily Mail*, 7 November 1990), and similarly: 'A spokesman for [York] corporation said it was a long standing policy to clear the site and tipping refuse was part of that policy. "If you don't tip, you will get more gipsies", he said' (*The Guardian*, 4 September 1975). There is an association implicit in these media representations between residual matter, refuse and a residual population. In Britain, the urban Gypsy population, a large majority of the total Gypsy population, is often referred to in coded terms which signify their perceived deviance and illegitimacy, particularly 'tinker' and 'itinerant', and these ascriptions reinforce the view of the group as residual.

In popular perceptions of the Gypsy presence in modern English cities, the appropriate context for understanding Gypsy culture, that is, the world views which Gypsies articulate themselves, remain largely hidden. Gypsy beliefs about social organization, about work and cleanliness, which make their use of land comprehensible, are viewed negatively because they do not correspond to

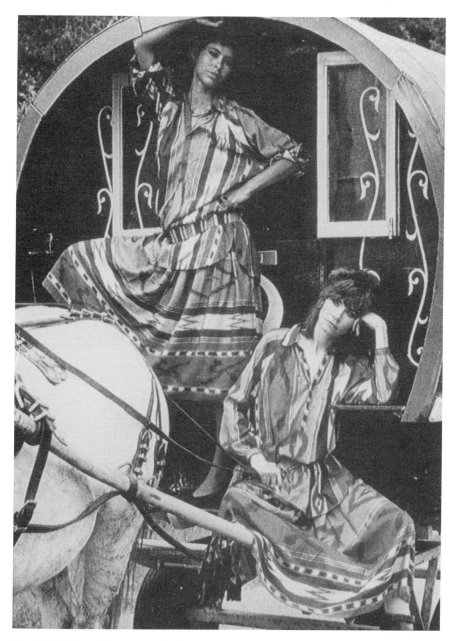

Fig. 14.1 Use of the romantic Gypsy image in advertising (courtesy of the author). Advertisement produced by Phyllis Walters Ltd, London, for Monsoon Fashion Catalogues

Fig. 14.2 Illegal Gypsy encampment in Hull, 1979 (courtesy of the author)

Fig. 14.3 Gypsy encampment near Hull, 1972 (courtesy of the author)

notions of social and spatial order which prevail in the larger society. Their behaviour is viewed as 'anti-social', rather than reflecting an alternative conception of social order.

It is notable that in many respects the values of the dominant society are reversed in Gypsy culture, providing an instance of symbolic reversal associated with many minority cultures (Cohen, 1985). Thus, the integration rather than separation of work, residence and recreation are valued; ritual taboos about cleanliness require defecation in an outside toilet or in the open air, not in a trailer; some domestic animals valued as pets by gaujes (non-Gypsies), cats for example, are considered mochadi (unclean). Thus, the boundary between Gypsy society and the larger society is confirmed through a series of reversals. While Gypsies are seen as polluting spaces controlled by the dominant society, gauje practices pollute Gypsy space. While the boundary is strong, the social distance between Gypsies and others is maintained and it remains difficult to uncover the hidden areas of Gypsy culture.

This is not to say that relations between Gypsies and the dominant society are entirely static or polarized. Some British Gypsies interact freely with gaujes and there is a long history of intermarriage. In the recent past, that is, since the early 1970s in England and Wales, there has been some recognition of the demands of Gypsies for education and secure settlements (with the gradual implementation of Part 2 of the Caravan Sites Act since 1970), and programmes designed to increase the social welfare of Gypsy families have prompted research which may have increased the awareness of Gypsy culture among officers of local authorities (Worrall, 1979; Hyman, 1989). In conflict situations, however, where the presence of Gypsies is perceived as some kind of threat to property or amenity, a different kind of knowledge – the partial, distorted view of Gypsy culture – is commonly articulated. The media, particularly the local press, continue to represent Gypsies as a deviant group.

This example demonstrates an important general point in regard to the mutedness of some social groups. Because they are muted, they remain partly invisible. This partial perspective on the 'other' renders them deviant in the sense that they do not fit into the categorical schemes of the dominant groups in society. This applies to some aspects of the relationships between adult and child, women and men, the able-bodied and the physically disabled, for example, where children, women and the physically disabled may be represented as 'other', as well as to instances of cultural difference defined by race or ethnicity. Lack of awareness of other world views is not only a question of knowledge, however. It is also a source of oppression.

Landscapes of exclusion

Space is implicated in the cultural construction of outsiders in two respects. First, marginal, residual spaces, places with which groups like Gypsies are often associated (Figure 14.4), confirm the outsider status of the minority. They may be places which are avoided by members of the dominant society because they appear threatening – a fear of the 'other' becomes a fear of place.

Fig. 14.4 Gypsies camped under a motorway in Arles, south of France, 1990 (courtesy of the author)

Associations are made between place and the minority community, and both the image of the place and the image of the group are founded on mythologies. This is evident in press reporting of events in British inner cities, for example, with the effect that 'inner city' itself becomes a coded term for the imagined deviance of black minorities (Keith, 1987; Smith, 1989). The labelling of places as threatening confirms the otherness of the minorities with whom the places are associated, and relegation to marginal spaces serves to amplify deviance. Press reporting of supposedly deviant behaviour similarly has an amplifying effect (Cohen, 1973). If social and spatial distance are maintained by the exclusion of the minority, it is likely that stereotyped views will persist.

A second role for space in the constitution of the outsider group concerns the arrangement of spaces in the built environment. Spatial structures can strengthen or weaken social boundaries, thus accentuating social division or, conversely, rendering the excluded group less visible. In order to understand the role of space in this process, it is necessary to think about space in relation to the exercise of power. Space represents power in that control of space confers the power to exclude, but some spatial configurations are easier to control than others. I will first examine this general problem, and then consider the outsider issue as one instance of the exercise of power over space.

Historically, we can recognize an association between priestly, military and civil power, and built form. The design of cities has in various periods had an instrumental role in the exercise of power. Thus, in early urban societies, such as the meso-American civilizations, in cities like Teotihuacan in Mexico, the bounded, enclosed, central space was the centre of priestly power and one which could not be profaned. Similarly, Neusner (1973) suggests that in ancient Israel, the rabbis could proscribe a wide range of things as polluting and this effectively gave them the power to exclude from the temple and from the land of Israel. The list of pollutants included some animals, women after childbirth, skin ailments, and other bodily conditions deemed unclean. More recently, military power was expressed in the extensive central spaces of the Baroque city. Challenges to authority in the form of popular uprisings were conspicuous if they violated the purified spaces of authority and were more effectively put down than they would be in the winding alleys of pre-Baroque cities (Mumford, 1961, pp. 369–70). These symbolic forms are echoed in the modern city in the highly ordered spaces in centres of government power, whether in Bucharest under Ceauèscu, Canberra, Brasilia, Washington DC, or the centre of Baghdad. Power is expressed in grand designs and a simple geometry.

More generally, spaces which are homogeneous or uniform, from which non-conforming groups or activities have been expelled or have been kept out through the maintenance of strong boundaries, can be termed pure in the sense that they are free from polluting elements and the purification of space is a process by which power is exercised over space and social groups (Sibley, 1988). The significance of such purified spaces in the construction of the 'other' is basically that difference is more visible than it would be in an area of mixed land use and social diversity. Residents in a socially and economically homogeneous suburb, for example, may erect barriers to those who are different because they pose a threat to the homogeneity which the residents have been conditioned to value. Dear (1980) examines this problem with specific reference to the rejection of the mentally ill and mentally handicapped by North American suburban communities, and the issue is discussed in sociopsychological terms by Richard Sennett in *The uses of disorder* (1970), where he argues that the North American suburb, as an ideal type of social area, is both exclusive and repressive. I think that the problem is more general than Sennett recognized, however. We can begin to understand it by looking at an analogous problem in education.

Spaces, boundaries and control

In an attempt to understand the relationship between the content of school curricula and control systems in education, Basil Bernstein (1967) has developed a number of schemata which focus on subject boundaries and content. As a control problem, the structuring and organization of the transmission of knowledge is analogous to the question of regulating spatial boundaries and locating objects or social groups in spatial units. In 'Open schools, open society' (1967), Bernstein distinguishes between an open curriculum, which emphasizes the interconnections between different branches of knowledge and thus the blurring of boundaries, and a closed curriculum in which knowledge is compartmentalized and boundaries between subjects are clearly defined. The former he associates with a democratic approach to learning, where students participate in making decisions about what is taught, and the latter with a hierarchical, centralized system where decisions are made at the top and transmitted downwards, with little opportunity for reconstituting knowledge through interdisciplinary work. In fact, it is in the interest of those in control of the closed curriculum to encourage the maintenance of boundaries between subjects. Their position is secured by the retention of strong boundaries around 'pure' subjects because this discourages new thinking across traditional subject boundaries which would present a challenge to authority.

Bernstein later formalized these ideas, describing the organization of knowledge in terms of its classification and framing (Bernstein, 1971). Classification, according to Bernstein, can be either strong or weak. With strong classification, boundaries are clearly defined and the knowledge contained within the boundaries is identified in unambiguous terms. Homogeneity is valued and a blurring of boundaries would be seen as a threat to the integrity of the subject. Thus, strong classification is characteristic of the closed curriculum. Weak classification, by contrast, signifies weakly defined subject boundaries and a concern for the integration of knowledge. Similarly, within subject areas, strong framing means that there are clear rules about what may and may not be taught, whereas weak framing means that many possible relationships and interconnections are explored.

Open/closed or strongly classified/weakly classified curricula could also be seen as alternative models for society, one where power is diffuse and the other where power is concentrated in the hands of a few at the top of a political hierarchy. In applying Bernstein's ideas to the organization of space, it is the connection with the distribution of political power which should be recognized.

Strongly classified spaces have clear boundaries, their internal homogeneity and order are valued and there is, in consequence, a concern with boundary maintenance in order to keep out objects or people who do not fit the classification. Weakly classified spaces will have weakly defined boundaries because they are characterized by social mixing and/or mixed land uses. Difference in this instance will not be obvious and if mixture and diversity are accepted, policing of the boundaries will be unnecessary. Generally, strongly classified spaces will also be strongly framed, in that there will be a concern with separation and order, as there is, for example, in many middle-class suburbs. Weak framing would suggest more numerous and more fluid relationships between people and the built environment than occur with strong framing. Buildings may have multiple uses, either simultaneously or at different times of day, for example. Using this schema, it is possible to see how space contributes to the social construction of the outsider.

The spatial context of the outsider problem refers to the presence of a non-conforming group in strongly classified space or the fear that such a group will intrude into a space which is strongly classified. To give an example of the latter, Sennett (1971, pp. 280–305) describes a middle-class suburban community in Chicago in the late nineteenth century, 'Union Park', where there was a panic following a spate of armed robberies in the city. Whatever the real circumstances of these crimes, in Union Park 'everyone knew immediately what was wrong, and what was wrong was overwhelming: it was nothing less than the power of the "foreigner", the outsider who had suddenly become dominant in the city'. The 'folk-devils' in this case were Italian anarchists. In response to this imagined threat, 'only a state of rigid barriers, enforced by a semi-military state of curfew and surveillance, would permit [the suburban community] to continue to function'. External threat, however, may also lead to internal cleansing, an urge to expel anyone who appears not to represent collective values. This need to purify space and society is evident both in Sennett's example of the threatened suburban community and in earlier cases of witch crazes, such as the infamous Salem witch trials in seventeenth-century Massachusetts, when any woman behaving in a way which appeared to depart from an ever more narrowly defined set of community values was in danger of being accused of witchcraft.

I would argue, therefore, that there is a connection between the strong classification of space and the rejection of social groups who are non-conforming. Further, there is evidence that minorities who are obliged to live in strongly classified and strongly framed environments characteristic of planned settlements, which includes approximately half the Gypsy population in England and Wales and many groups of indigenous peoples in the Arctic and sub-Arctic, in Canada, Greenland and the former Soviet Union (Osherenko and Young 1989), may find the organization of space in settlements, or on official sites in the case of English Gypsies, constraining and alienating. This is implied in a comment by a Dene (Canadian Indian) at Fort Macpherson, a planned settlement in sub-Arctic Canada (Berger, 1977, cited in Sibley, 1981, p. 72):

> Look at the housing where the transient government staff live. And look at housing where the Indian people live. . . . Look at how the school and hostel, the Royal Canadian Mounted Police and government staff houses are right in the centre of the town dividing the Indian people into two sides. . . . Do you think this is the way the Indian people chose to have this community?

To summarize, space is an integral part of the outsider problem. The way in which space is organized affects the perception of the 'other', either as foreign and threatening or as simply different. The strong classification of space, as in the archetypal homogeneous suburb, implies a rejection of difference so the presence of minority groups in such spaces accentuates their difference and outsiderness and the likelihood of exclusion is increased. Similarly, when a minority which does not make separations between activities like home and work is relegated to a strongly classified space and subjected to socio-spatial controls, its cultural practices are likely to appear deviant to the control agencies in the dominant society. In weakly classified space, minorities will be less visible, they may not be identified as non-conforming and, consequently, the potential for conflict over the use of space is reduced. Because behaviour is less likely to be recognized as deviant, control will not be so much of an issue. Thus, we can generally anticipate an association between the strong classification of space and the identification of outsiders as a social category.

Exclusion and adaptation: relationships between Gypsies and the dominant society

The aspects of Gypsy culture cited in this chapter so far have referred primarily to communities in the British Isles and I will make more detailed reference to a British example later in this essay. It would be inappropriate to generalize from these cases to the whole Gypsy population, however, because Gypsies exhibit considerable cultural diversity. Gypsies comprise a minority population in all European countries, parts of the Middle East, including Egypt and Iran, and in India and Pakistan. In addition, they have dispersed to the Americas, particularly Brazil and Argentina, the United States and Canada, and to Australia and New Zealand as a part of the large-scale intercontinental migrations in the nineteenth and early twentieth centuries. Thus, they have had to adapt to a variety of dominant cultures. These adaptations have been one source of difference within the Gypsy population.

Although Gypsies have an ethnic identity secured by language, economy and other cultural attributes, they have intermarried with other nomadic groups and with the settled population. Indeed, it is meaningless to talk about a racial identity although Gypsies have been racialised in the sense that aspects of their way of life viewed negatively have been described as racially inherent. This has provided legitimation for discrimination and exclusion.

In Britain and Holland, in particular, there are also culturally distinctive semi-nomadic groups with whom Gypsies compete for resources but who are similarly seen as outsiders by the dominant society. These are Irish and Scottish Travellers, living in England and Wales as well as in their native countries, and Woonwagenbevoners (caravan dwellers) in Holland. Within the European Gypsy population, communities distinguish themselves by kin-ties, place associations and occupational traditions which have contributed to the emergence of distinctive cultural identities, although migrations have complicated any regional patterns which might have existed. Some of the larger groups include the Kalderas, traditionally metal-workers from Russia but subsequently settled in Paris, Gothenburg and other West European cities, and in the United States, notably in the San Francisco Bay area and Los Angeles; the Boyash, from Hungary and Romania, but also settled in Western Europe and North America and with strong traditions in entertainment; the Sinti and Manus, in Southern Europe; and the Vlach in Hungary. However, self-ascriptions are complex and refer to different groupings within Gypsy society and different national identities. Also, Gypsies may not refer to themselves as Gypsy because of the pejorative use of the word by gaujes. It is for this reason that most British Gypsies usually refer to themselves as Travellers while Rom or Roma, meaning 'the people' in Romany, are self-ascriptions more commonly used by continental European Gypsies. As Liegeois (1986, p. 46) observes: 'Gypsies . . . are defined as such by the views and attitudes of others'.

The Gypsy economy is one of the most significant features distinguishing the minority as a distinctive culture. It is not occupations which are particularly distinctive but attitudes to work. Thus, it is possible to talk about the Gypsy economy as an aspect of culture, while recognizing that the particular niches in dominant economies occupied by Gypsies in different places and at different times vary considerably. In general, Gypsies avoid wage labour where possible and try to maintain a dominant position in any transaction as a matter of ethnic pride. They value flexibility and opportunism, with several money-making activities often being pursued simultaneously within one family, such as scrap metal dealing, horse trading and hawking. To some extent, the economy confirms the boundary between Gypsies and gaujes. Okely (1979, p. 20) suggests that self-employment is crucial in defining this boundary but there are circumstances in which this may not be possible. In Hungary under the Communist government, for example, men were obliged to work in factories, but the Vlach Gypsies combined factory employment with horse trading, scavenging and cultivating their own plots of land. Even social security payments can be viewed as one acceptable source of income, for example, in the United States and England (Sutherland, 1975; Okely, 1979), because taking money from the gaujes does not signify dependency. It is essentially no different from begging, which is still practised by Gypsies in Spain and by Travellers in the Republic of Ireland, for example. Whatever their transactions with the dominant economy, however, Gypsies see gauje society as exploitable.

Living on the margin allows Gypsies to exploit the residual products of the dominant economy, such as domestic scrap, and to provide services where mobility and minimal capital outlay are advantageous. Examples include the repair of supermarket trolleys or car bumpers (fenders) by Kalderas in the United States (Sutherland, 1975). These occupations put Gypsies on the outside but, at the same time, they are highly dependent on urban society. Theirs is an urban culture which popular imagery locates elsewhere, in rural settings. This false image has important consequences for Gypsy communities, creating opportunities but also constraining their activities. If Gypsies are not thought of as an urban culture, it may be possible for them to pass as non-Gypsy traders in the city. In some occupations, a Gypsy stereotype of unreliability would be bad for business so the failure of gaujes to recognize the ethnic identity of urban Gypsies – who 'belong' in the countryside – can be economically advantageous.

The Kalderas in the eastern suburbs of Paris, for example, find that presenting themselves as gaujes, which is made easier by living in small houses or bungalows (pavillons) in working-class districts, helps in getting contracts for building repairs and other work which is not usually associated with Gypsies (Williams, 1982). By contrast, when Gypsies are a highly visible urban minority living in trailers, the rural stereotype accentuates their 'deviance' in the eyes of antagonistic house-dwellers. In this sense, they are polluting because they do not belong in an urban setting and hostile communities attempt to exclude them. Gypsies are not accepted in rural areas either, however, because the visible features of their culture, the chrome-trimmed trailers, piles of scrap and so on, still render them deviant. There is no 'proper place' for Gypsies because, according to the romantic stereotype, they are always distant in space and time.

Prejudice in practice: separation, containment and control

In Europe, there is a long history of attempts by the State, or by local groups with government sanction, to remove Gypsies from national territory. The Nazi government in Germany was the last to attempt this, through genocide. In modern industrialized societies, the more general objective is to settle and contain Gypsies, to remove them from locations where they are perceived as a non-conforming outsider group, violating space valued by the settled society, particularly residential space. Separation rather than integration is the unstated goal of most settlement policies (Sibley, 1987). An alternative response, evident in several East European countries, has been to deny that Gypsies have a cultural identity and to house them with other workers. In Romania, for example, Gypsies are not recognized as a 'nationality' or minority group, although the country has the largest Gypsy population in Eastern Europe.

Liegeois (1986) documents attempts by European states to eliminate or remove Gypsies. In the seventeenth and eighteenth centuries, sanctions included the hanging of Gypsy men, in Slovakia in 1710 and Prussia in 1721, for example; the mutilation of women and children; flogging, branding, forced labour and banishment, including deportation from Britain to North America and Australia. In France, a common sentence for being a Gypsy in the seventeenth century was to be sent to the galleys for life. The harshest penalties were eventually seen to be ineffective, however, and other measures were substituted, with the same objective of removing Gypsies from sight, through physical expulsion to remote locations, cultural annihilation or assimilation.

Local responses: the case of Gypsies in Hull

There is a connection between this history of exclusion and response to Gypsies in modern societies. Attitudes to Gypsies in the developed world still suggest that the minority constitutes a threat to social order and, in some countries, a threat to spatial order. Thus, in a country like Britain, where the land use planning system reflects widely accepted notions of spatial order and amenity, unregulated Gypsy settlements constitute deviant landscapes. The response of the State to this deviance is to impose order on Gypsy communities through the medium of official sites, to isolate and transform in a controlled environment. The way in which these controls are exercised locally can be demonstrated with reference to the recent history of the Gypsy population in Hull, in north-east England.

Gypsies have lived in Hull for at least one hundred years. In the 1970s, old people recalled spending the winter months during their childhood in rented houses in the inner city, and migrating for agricultural work in the summer. While some families maintained this pattern of movement and settlement until about 1975, most had by this time settled in the city. They camped, illegally, on roadsides or in fields close to a large peripheral housing estate, or on land cleared of housing in the inner city.

This was a period of persistent conflict. Evictions by the local authority were frequent, and antagonistic comments by local politicians were publicized in the local press in a series of alarmist articles. One demonstration in the summer of 1973 by local authority tenants demanding the removal of a Gypsy camp close to their estate illustrated the enduring negative image of Gypsies projected by hostile communities. Some placards referred to the deviant form of settlement: 'How much longer do we have to put up with this shanty town on our estate?'. Others alluded to unregulated industrial activity: 'Smokeless zone – Gypsies burn car tyres, we would be fined'. Residents interviewed by the local press at this time made adverse comments about the Gypsies' lifestyle: 'They smell, they have rats, they make a noise'. This particular protest had all the elements of a moral panic but there were also more routine acts of violence and harassment, like bricks and iron bars thrown through caravan windows.

The conflict was defused by the construction of two sites in the city, both locations reflecting the local authority's desire to distance the Gypsies from the rest of the population in order to minimize conflict. The first was built in a heavily polluted industrial area which had been cleared of residential development. The second site was built in an old quarry, used for dumping rubbish, on the edge of the city. It could be argued that, through site development, Gypsies were consigned to residual space – a morally polluting minority was associated with physically polluted places. In a change of policy, a third site is now planned for a residential location in the inner city. The attitude of the settled population has not changed, however: 'Anger over Gypsy camp decision: estate residents plan protest to MP' (*Hull Daily Mail*, 13 March 1991).

Existing sites have reinforced the boundary between the Gypsy community and the rest of the city's population. The isolation of existing sites is coupled with site designs which represent a geometry of control, or strong classification, in Bernstein's terms. Both site layouts are based on models developed by a central government department (the Department of the Environment). Spaces for trailers are arranged in regular rows and this residential space is clearly separated from the warden's space. There are no work areas or play areas, although these are included in the model designs. Single-use zoning, characteristic of the Hull sites and most others built in England by local authorities, is important as a means of controlling residents. Families have been evicted from one site for 'misusing' space, for example, by erecting sheds in the residential zone. This kind of boundary enforcement causes discontent because the boundaries and imposed by authority and they are not those recognized as important in the Gypsy community, where work, play and residence are spatially integrated. A frequent comment by site residents is: 'You might as well be in a house as living on this site'. Boundary enforcement depends on effective policing. On the other site, the boundaries have been blurred through the construction of chicken runs, dog kennels and storage sheds around some of the trailers. Wardens have not attempted to maintain the separation of uses and, probably because of this, there appears to be a higher level of satisfaction with the site. Thus, while it seems legitimate to characterize official Gypsy sites as landscapes of control, at least in intention, it must be acknowledged that the dominated minority can act subversively and frustrate the efforts of the social control agencies.

These sites have been the only home for about forty Hull Gypsy families for a decade. Although there is some evidence of social change which may be attributed to site environments, they do not appear to have fundamentally affected the Gypsies' way of life. Extended families still interact intensively, usually occupying adjacent pitches, but less time is spent outside, talking around a fire, for example. Fires are banned but, in practice, they are simply lit less frequently. More time is spent watching television and videos. Satellite dishes and decoders have widened the range of viewing for a few families but with no noticeable effect on family values. There has been no transformation of Gypsy culture but it is clear that sites are constraining. They limit work opportunities and discourage social interaction beyond the family. They contribute to a resentment of authority, but it is the warden and other council officials rather than the police who serve as the agents of control. The Gypsies are occupying gauje space and have only limited success in making it their own.

Conclusion

The socio-spatial construction of certain groups as outsiders is a complex process but I have suggested that the problem can best be understood by focusing on boundary processes, the ways in which distinctions are made between the pure and the defiled, the normal and the deviant, the same and the other. Drawing on social anthropological concepts developed by Mary Douglas (1966), outsiders can be defined as those groups who do not fit dominant models of society and are therefore seen as polluting. In social space, such groups disturb the homogeneity of a locality, and a common reaction of the hostile community will be to expel the polluting group, to purify space. For Gypsies, both their unregulated occupation of land and the controlled environments to which they are increasingly relegated, as in Britain and Holland, constitute 'deviant' landscapes which confirm their outsider status and reinforce the boundary between the minority and the dominant society.

Mythology plays an important part in the representation of the minority as deviant and not belonging to 'society'. In order to establish the threatening nature of the outsider group, it is necessary to attribute to it mythical characteristics which dehumanize and legitimate exclusion or expulsion. If the group is distinguished by culture and physical characteristics, racist myths become an important part of the negative representation of the minority. The case of European Gypsies demonstrates the importance of racism, but the sense of non-conformity is magnified by a fear of the nomad, notwithstanding the fact that many Gypsies are sedentary.

Perceptions of an outsider group, however, are also conditioned by its visibility. While an inability to gain a complete understanding of the world view of the minority is part of the problem of stereotyping which academic research may hope to rectify, to remain hidden, out of sight of the dominant society, may also be to the advantage of the minority. In the case of Gypsies, attempting to survive in a modern urban society, to maintain an economic system without state regulation, depends on retaining a degree of advantage. In the city, the myths may help them to disappear. Visibility is also affected by structural factors, however, because to assume outward conformity depends on opportunities related to the management of the housing market and the built environment, and these opportunities vary over space and time. Because their relationship to place varies and because of their cultural diversity, there can be no single representation of Gypsies as an outsider group. Gypsy territory might be 'invisible', a house or an apartment in the city, or it might be highly visible, a patch of waste land or an official site – a landscape of exclusion. While a consciousness of the boundary with the gauje world is a defining characteristic of Gypsy cultures, this boundary takes many shapes.

References

Ardener, E. 1975: The problem revisited. In Ardener, S. (ed.), *Perceiving women*. Andover: Routledge & Kegan Paul, 19–27.

Barrett, M. 1987: The concept of difference. *Feminist Review* 26, 29–41.

Berger, T. R. 1977: *Northern frontier, northern homeland*. Ottawa: Ministry of Supply and Services.

Bernstein, B. 1967: Open schools, open society. *New Society*, 14 September, 351–3.

Bernstein, B. 1971: *Class, codes and control*, vol. 1. Andover: Routledge & Kegan Paul.

Boime, A. 1990: *The art of exclusion: Representing blacks in the nineteenth century*. London: Thames & Hudson.

Cohen, A. 1985: *The symbolic construction of community*. London: Tavistock Publications.

Cohen, S. 1973: *Folk devils and moral panics*. St Albans: Paladin.

Dear, M. 1980: The public city. In Clark, W. and Moore, E. (eds), *Residential mobility and public policy*. Beverly Hills: Sage, 219–41.

Douglas, M. 1966: *Purity and danger*. Andover: Routledge & Kegan Paul.

Guardian, 4 September 1975.

Hesse, Herman. 1975: *Wandering*. London: Picador.

Hull Daily Mail, 7 November 1990, 13 March 1991.

Hyman, M. 1989: *Sites for travellers*. London: London Race and Housing Research Unit.

Keith, M. 1987: Something happened: the problems of explaining the 1980 and 1981 riots in British cities. In Jackson, P. (ed.), *Race and racism*. London: Allen & Unwin, 275–301.

Liegeois, J.-P. 1986: *Gypsies: An illustrated history*, London: Al Saqi Books.

Mascia-Lees, F., Sharpe, P. and Cohen, C. B. 1989: The post-modern turn in anthropology: cautions from a feminist perspective. *Signs* 15(1), 7–33.

Mumford, L. 1961: *The city in history*. London: Secker & Warburg.

Neusner, J. 1973: *The idea of purity in ancient Judaism*. Leiden: E.J. Brill.

Okely, J. 1979: Trading stereotypes: the case of English Gypsies. In Wallman, S. (ed.), *Ethnicity at work*. Basingstoke: Macmillan, 17–36.

Osherenko, G. and Young, O. 1989: *The age of the Arctic*. Cambridge: Cambridge University Press.

Philo, C. 1989: Enough to drive one mad: the organization of space in 19th century lunatic asylums. In Wolch, J. and Dear, M. (eds), *The power of geography*. London: Unwin Hyman, 258–90.

Sennett, R. 1970: *The uses of disorder*. Harmondsworth: Penguin Books.

Sennett, R. 1971: Middle class families and urban violence: the experience of a Chicago community in the 19th century. In Haravan, T. K. (ed.), *Anonymous Americans*. Englewood Cliffs, NJ: Prentice-Hall, 280–305.

Sibley, D. 1981: *Outsiders in urban societies*. Oxford: Basil Blackwell.

Sibley, D. 1987: Racism and settlement policy: the state's response to a semi-nomadic minority. In Jackson, P. (ed.), *Race and racism*. London: Allen & Unwin, 74–89.

Sibley, D. 1988: Survey 13: purification of space. *Environment and Planning D: Society and Space* 6, 409–21.

Smith, S. J. 1989, *The politics of 'race' and residence*. Cambridge: Polity Press.

Sutherland, A. 1975, *Gypsies: The hidden Americans*. London: Tavistock.

Williams, P. 1982, The invisibility of the Kalderas in Paris. *Urban Anthropology* 11(3–4), 315–46.

Wolch, J. and Dear, M. 1987, *Landscapes of despair*. Cambridge: Polity Press.

Worrall, D. 1979, *Gypsy education: A study of provision in England and Wales*. Walsall: Council for Community Relations.

---

15 Peter Jackson,
'Street Life: The Politics of Carnival'

Reprinted in full from: *Environment and Planning D: Society and Space* 6, 213–27 (1988)

Introduction

In this paper, I aim to bring together some themes from Caribbean history and social anthropology with some ideas from contemporary social geography about the territorial basis of British racism (see Jackson, 1987). I develop Cohen's notion of Carnival as a socially contested event whose political significance is inscribed in the landscape (Cohen, 1980, 1982) and argue that London's Notting Hill Carnival is a contemporary British event with deep roots in the colonial past. Understanding its contemporary significance requires a knowledge of Caribbean history and of the changing geography of British racism. Although the present-day form of Carnival originated in the Caribbean, its meaning has changed over time. Like racism itself (Sivanandan, 1983), Carnival has changed shape according to the material circumstances and social relations of black people both in Britain and in the Caribbean. The meaning of Carnival in Trinidad and in Notting Hill is as different as the meaning of Rastafarianism in Jamaica and in Brixton. Neither Carnival nor Rastafarianism can be understood as a passive cultural import from the Caribbean. Both involve 'a creative construction of a new cultural tradition, saturating and modifying culture symbols and practices from [the Caribbean] with a specifically English experience' (Miles, 1978, p. 2).[1]

Also following Cohen, I shall argue that the ritual and symbolic aspects of

Carnival are not autonomous from, or independent of, their political and economic context, while at the same time they are not reducible to it. The cultural is not separable from or in opposition to the political; it is fundamentally political. Carnival is a contested event that expresses political and ideological conflict. It therefore makes considerable sense to refer to Carnival in terms of the 'cultural politics' of British racism (Gilroy, 1987) and as an aspect of the social construction of 'race' in general (Jackson, 1987).

Indeed, the Notting Hill Carnival has been associated with some of the key events in the politicization of 'race' in Britain. The 'race riots' in Nottingham and Notting Hill in 1958 were central to the ideological construction of 'race relations' as a political phenomenon in the period leading up to the imposition of immigration controls in the 1960s (Miles, 1984). The empirical evidence presented below suggests that the Carnival riots in 1976 had a similar significance, reflecting a radical shift in representations of black people in the British press and a similarly dramatic shift in relations between black people and the police. This is not to suggest that the riots themselves redefined British 'race relations' but that representations of the riots form a kind of prism through which the broader context of social change can be observed. Together with the social construction of 'mugging' as a 'racial' crime in the mid-1970s (Hall *et al.*, 1978), the Carnival riots presented an opportunity for the ideological construction of 'black youth' as an implicitly male, homogeneous, and hostile group, leading to the subsequent 'criminalization' of black people in general (see Gutzmore, 1983; Gilroy, 1987). The political context in Britain is therefore at least as important to an understanding of the contemporary symbolic form of Carnival as its Caribbean origins. In order to reflect this dialectical structure, the analysis will tack back and forth between Britain and the Caribbean, starting with a discussion of the changing significance of Carnival in Trinidad.

Carnival in Trinidad

Trinidad's Carnival has been described by one Trinidadian as 'the greatest annual theatrical spectacle of all time' (Hill, 1972, p. 3). Although the event has been greatly commercialized since then, Hill's account from the mid-1970s reports how, each year, more than 100,000 people participated in masked parades on the streets (playing *mas*), dancing, feasting, and engaging in general revelry, playing steel drums (beating steel), drinking, and smoking marijuana (*ganja*). Before the abolition of slavery in 1834, Carnival was celebrated in Trinidad exclusively by the white élite, particularly by the French-speaking Catholic middle class. Blacks were present, if at all, only as spectators (Pearse, 1956). After emancipation, the liberated slaves took over Carnival as a way of celebrating their delivery from slavery and, in the words of one contemporary observer, it 'degenerated into a noisy and disorderly amusement for the lower classes' (Pearse, 1956, p. 539). Carnival then gradually began to represent all the social, political, and 'racial' tensions of Trinidadian society. As one recent commentator expresses it, 'in bringing normally distinct and distant groups of the population together, carnival serves only to highlight the differences and hostilities between them' (Burton, 1986, p. 8).

To the extent that Carnival has persistently attracted official opposition, it has always been a political event. Throughout the 150 years prior to Trinidadian independence in 1962, Carnival was regarded by the British colonial authorities with disdain bordering on fear. Its participants were viewed as disreputable, their behaviour condemned as morally reprehensible. In 1883, a municipal ordinance was passed restricting the playing of drums in public places. Contemporary newspaper reports commenting on the ban convey the authorities' highly ambiguous attitudes towards such revelry, condemning its 'barbarity' but subconsciously expressing a certain respect for its potency ('muscular vigour') and its obvious potential for social disruption:

> To the ear of the European philharmonist there is no music in it but a dull monotonous reiteration of sound rendered the more objectionable by the distance to which it is carried by the muscular vigour of the performer and the immense reverberating capacity of the instrument. The state of civilization of people whose members can be set in movement by the repetition of such barbarous sounds can easily be gauged.
> (*Trinidad News*, March 1883, quoted in Hill, 1972, p. 44).

Such accounts go well beyond the expression of aesthetic judgments. The perceived threat to 'civilization' is clear, as is the territorial basis of that threat. The association between black musicality, sexuality, and social unrest was clearly already well established by the nineteenth century. It has remained a persistent theme in British 'racial' discourse (see Mair, 1986), reflected today in the writings of people like Kerridge whose comments on the squalour, drabness, and ghastliness of Carnival barely disguise his disquiet concerning its allegedly 'unruly' and 'harmful' social effects (Kerridge, 1983).

Official opposition to Carnival has been a consistent feature of its history both in Trinidad and in Britain. In 1846, for example, the Governor of Trinidad expressly forbade the wearing of masks in the street. In 1858, masquerade was banned again after criticisms in the press that wearing masks had become 'a pretext to other nuisances and offences against decency' (Pearse, in Horowitz, 1971, p. 534). In 1881, the Canboulay riots occurred, which involved pitched battles between police and masqueraders.[2] In 1895, cross-dressing (a form of symbolic reversal common during Carnival) was also banned. During the 1890s, in an effort to restore Carnival's tarnished reputation, the celebration of Canboulay was halted; stick-fighting was forbidden; pierrots were required to obtain a police licence; transvestism and obscene language were again prohibited (p. 548). There were also official sanctions against the celebration of Carnival throughout the Second World War. There is nothing new about police surveillance of Carnival or official attempts to intervene in the interest of maintaining 'public order'.

The latent conflict that pervades Carnival runs counter to those who would interpret it as a social leveller, a harmless release of tension, and a force for social integration. Few of the symbols employed in Carnival can be satisfactorily understood in this way. The great majority are *oppositional*: symbolic reversals of social status mirrored in the opposition between night and day, male and female, black and white, good and evil, master and slave. Other ritual aspects of Carnival have a similar intent: the ironic names of calypsonians like Mighty Sparrow, Attila the Hun, Black Stalin, and Mighty Chalkdust; the tradition of stick-fighting, ritualized battles between rival sound systems and their toasters; and even the election of Carnival Kings and Queens that produces such bitter conflict between different sections of Trinidad's allegedly plural society. When, after 1956, for example, the ruling political party in Trinidad, the PNM (People's National Movement), attempted to promote Carnival as a national cultural heritage, it did so to the virtual exclusion of the East Indian population, exacerbating the schism between them and the Creole majority (see Lewis, 1968; Oxaal, 1968; Ryan, 1972).

Such symbolic reversals are meaningful only in circumstances where a rigid social hierarchy is the norm. Carnival offers a temporary respite from normal relations of subordination and domination, when the sacred is (briefly) profaned (Leach, 1961). This has been a common feature of carnivals and other saturnalia at least since the Middle Ages (Burke, 1978; Darnton, 1984). In his discussion of Carnival in Romans in sixteenth-century France, for example, Le Roy Ladurie argues that one should not confuse inversion with subversion: 'If men exchanged roles during Carnival it was only to reaffirm the strength and permanence of the social hierarchy' (1981, p. 184).[3] Carnival is normally defined as a cultural rather than a political event, however, precisely because these reversals occur in a ritualized or symbolic form rather than in a directly instrumental manner (Hall and Jefferson, 1976). Conversely, much of its political power derives from the ambiguities of its symbolic form.

Despite similarities of symbolic form, the actual content of Carnival in the Caribbean has altered significantly over time. Calypso was introduced to Carnival in the 1890s, steel bands in the 1930s, gradually giving way to reggae and sound systems in the 1960s and 1970s.[4] The character and meaning of Trinidad Carnival was established in the early nineteenth century, but has gradually adapted to changing circumstances and social conditions, until, today, it is locally regarded principally as a rather debased and commercialized event whose principal advantage is as a means of attracting tourist dollars. As I attempt to demonstrate in the next section, the Notting Hill Carnival can be treated in a broadly comparable way.

The Notting Hill Carnival

Cohen has described the evolution of the Notting Hill Carnival from its origins in the 1950s as an 'English Fayre', characterized by polyethnic amity, to its contemporary form in the 1970s and 1980s, characterized by a variety of conflicts between police and people, black and white, young and old, Jamaican and Trinidadian (Cohen, 1980, 1982). Carnival was established in the 1950s with the deliberate aim of reversing Notting Hill's declining fortunes when the area had become associated with poor housing, prostitution, and, particularly after 1958, with 'racial' conflict. During the 1960s the festival enabled the working-class residents of the area to mobilize against bad housing and social conditions, opposing urban renewal and protesting about the construction of the M40 flyover. After the arrival of a large Afro-Caribbean ('West Indian') population in the 1960s, Carnival began to take on its contemporary form and range of associations. Conflict with the police began in this period, centred on the Mangrove restaurant in All Saints Road, which transects the area of North Kensington popularly known as Notting Hill.[5] Carnival was also 'commercialized' in 1975 with the participation of Capital Radio and a variety of other sponsors (see Owusu, 1986).

According to Cohen's (1980) periodization, Carnival can be said to have assumed a more clearly Trinidadian identity in the early 1970s as the polarization between blacks and whites increased in a period of rising unemployment and intensifying social conflict. Carnival began to be used as an organizing mechanism for protest and opposition. Then, towards the end of the 1970s, with the rise of the second-generation, British-born, Afro-Caribbean population, a new period in the history of Carnival can be identified, associated with youth and, increasingly, with Jamaica. Many second-generation 'West Indians' had grown up to feel alienated and disillusioned with British society. They experienced London as 'Babylon' and their disaffection came to be expressed through the symbols and styles of Rastafarianism and reggae. The potential for conflict increased until, in 1976, violence finally erupted.

Gilroy has argued that the Carnival 'riot' of 1976 was 'a watershed in the history of conflict between blacks and the police' (1987, p. 93), marking the period at which black people began to be 'criminalized' *en masse*. Before then, Gilroy argues, British 'racial' discourse centred on conflicts around issues of immigration, housing, and sexuality (see Reeves, 1983). Prior to 1976 the policing of black Britain was not generally perceived to be a serious problem, even by the police themselves. When, in 1972, a Home Affairs Select Committee on Race Relations and Immigration received evidence on the 'difficult and explosive' state of relations between black people and the police, the rank-and-file police officers' organization, the Police Federation, replied that there was 'no serious problem in police/immigrant relations' (Gilroy, 1987, pp. 88–9). Indeed, with the exception of robbery, 'immigrant crime rates were, if anything, a little lower than those for the indigenous population' (HMSO, 1972, p. 23). By 1976, all this had changed. In responding to criticisms about the policing of the Notting Hill Carnival, Metropolitan Police Commissioner Sir Robert Mark referred back to evidence he had given earlier that year to the Select Committee. Then, he had argued, the 'potential for conflict' was present in every law-enforcement situation between the police and black people (HMSO, 1976, quoted in Gilroy, 1987, p. 94). Again, according to Sir Robert Mark, some forty incidents had occurred in the preceding twelve months that had the potential for large-scale disorder.

Although the police may be said to have anticipated the Carnival disturbances in 1976 (if they did not in fact provoke them by an eightfold increase in the number of officers at Carnival compared with the previous year), the same cannot be said of the media, which were, in general, caught completely unawares. Although the *Sun* had just launched a special four-part investigation of 'Black Britain', its commentary on the 'Hate. Violence. Suspicion. And an ocean of misunderstanding' that characterized contemporary 'race relations' (30 August 1976) made no special reference to Carnival. When the riots occurred the following day, the *Sun*'s headlines concentrated on Sir Robert Mark's press conference remarks about his refusal to 'quit black areas': 'It's No to No-Go' (1 September 1976). Immediately before and even during the first two days of Carnival, several newspapers had run stories about the socially integrative aspects of the 'calypso Carnival' and its potential for improving community relations. Under its 'Carnival Time' headline, the *Daily Mirror* described the 'irresistible explosion of West Indian colour and music' that was about to hit 'the grey pavements of London this holiday weekend' (28 August 1976). Heavy showers on the Sunday night had failed to dampen Carnival's 'sunshine spirit', as the obligatory photographs of the 'laughing policeman' bore witness, 'Dancing in the Rain' with a black woman (*Daily Mirror*, 30 August 1976). Other papers carried similar stories: 'It's a cop festival' (*Daily Mail*, 30 August 1976), illustrated with similar photographs. Even *The Times* had a photograph of police 'Dancing in the Streets' (30 August 1976). The *Evening News* was, in fact, virtually alone in sounding a note of warning: 'the pickpockets are having a carnival' (30 August 1976).

The level of violence that occurred on the night of August Bank Holiday Monday clearly took the press by surprise. More than 250 people were injured as Carnival transformed into riot: sixty-eight arrests were made as the police sustained heavy casualties, with twenty-six officers detained in hospital. There was widespread looting and several police cars were burned. The immediate causes of the riot were never precisely established, as the call for an official inquiry was rejected by the Home Secretary, Roy Jenkins. Police accounts of the outbreak of violence, which seems to have begun about 4.30 p.m. at the junction of Portobello and Acklam Roads, were contradictory. According to different reports, the police had moved in to rescue a mugging victim or to break up two gangs of fighting youths, or, in the most popular account, to arrest pickpockets. Whatever happened, the situation got rapidly out of control and the police tried to restore order by repeated baton charges. The ensuing chaos is nicely satirized by Owusu (1986, p. 3):

> Then the police Mas arrived, more than 300 men in blue costumes and helmets. They carried no instruments except one percussive item, a baton concealed in their costumes. They started their ritual dance in silence, except for the radios and sirens.

Subsequent deliberations in the press about the causes of the 1976 Carnival riot foreshadow the way that the 1981 riots would be reported (Burgess, 1985). Headlines were full of violent military analogies: 'Battle at the Carnival' (*Daily Mail*, 31 August 1976); 'Behind the Frontline of Fury' (*Daily Mirror*, 1 September 1976). Extravagant parallels were drawn with violence in Northern Ireland ('Ulster in Portobello Road', *Daily Mail*, 31 August 1976) and, when arrest figures were released, 'outsiders' were blamed for causing all the trouble (*Evening Standard*, 1 September 1976). The media were charged with their portion of the blame in an 'astonishing attack on the BBC' by Tony Benn in which he accused them of boosting racism by reporting black immigrants as scapegoats ('Benn Blasts the Beeb', *Sun*, 4 September 1976).

Although Sir Robert Mark was prepared to admit that the violence had been a demonstration against the police rather than a 'race riot', some newspapers drew no such distinctions. The *Daily Telegraph* headlined the event: 'Carnival Ends in Race Riot', beginning its report 'Fierce race riots broke out in Notting Hill last night' (31 August 1976). The *Telegraph* went on to describe the battle between police and 'black youths', referring to the riots as 'inexplicable violence' and lamenting the problems of 'lawlessness' and 'black crime and disaffection' (1 September 1976).[6]

Only the *Daily Mirror*, in a feature article by columnist John Pilger (1 September 1976, p. 5), referred to racism as an explicit cause of the riots. Other papers merely acknowledged 'problems, prejudices and misunderstandings' (*Sun*, 31 August 1976) or simply reflected their own internalized racism in references to 'calypso mobs' (*Daily Express*, 31 August 1976), 'savage hatred' (*Daily Mirror* 31 August 1976), and 'animal spirits' (*Daily Express*, 1 September 1976). The deputy leader of Kensington and Chelsea Council, who had tried to ban Carnival from the streets of Notting Hill, claiming that it had outgrown the area, reminded the public that 'This is not Trinidad' (*Guardian*, 1 September 1976), and the *Daily Telegraph* (31 August 1976) included a front-page interview with Mr Robert McIntyre, a 6 ft 2 in ex-soldier, who had been present at the riot and admitted to having been 'bloody scared, though I'm half Scots, half Irish and can throw a punch as anyone'.

Readers later contributed their own interpretations of events and putative causes through the correspondence pages. In the *Evening News* (2 September 1976) readers blamed the violence on 'teachers, social workers, and others who have told the young blacks to do their own thing', and called for 'an immediate halt to further immigration'. There was praise for 'these brave men', 'our boys in blue', and calls for proper anti-riot gear, though Sir Robert Mark himself declared that 'under no conditions would his force call for special anti-riot equipment' (*Daily Telegraph*, 1 September 1976). Other letters suggested that 'the instability of the West Indian family' was the basic underlying cause of the riots (*Daily Telegraph*, 2 September 1976), an analysis that was given a more sophisticated twist by the editor of the *Caribbean Post*: 'While the State has a lot to answer for, so too have West Indian parents. The Asians have, in contrast, maintained a strong family discipline and motivated their children in the direction of material success. But West Indian parents for the main part have lost control over their children' (*Evening News*, 1 September 1976, page 6).

It was, however, the question of policing that was most widely debated after the 1976 riots. Although several commentators, including Haringey Community Relations Officer, Jim Crawford, criticized the level of policing at Carnival itself, others looked to the deterioration of police–community relations in general. The Commission for Racial Equality asserted its newly established authority by arguing that the Carnival riot was further evidence that 'many young West Indians have no confidence whatever in the police' (quoted in the *Sun*, 1 September 1976). The *Evening News* suggested that 'the quality of relations between London's young blacks and London's policemen has declined to such an extent that the mere sight of a white bobby is enough to induce paranoid relations in some disaffected West Indian minds' (31 August 1976). This symbolic opposition between the lone 'white bobby' and 'paranoid West Indians' is highly characteristic of racist news reporting as further examples, quoted below, confirm.

Several papers questioned the justification for increasing the police presence at Carnival from 200 in 1975 to around 1600 in 1976 ('Police commissioner defends use of 1598 men at Notting Hill', *The Times*, 1 September 1976). In the column referred to above, John Pilger condemned the police actions as 'a calculated act of police overkill, criticizing 'the bloated presence of a police force which, by waiting for trouble, cause trouble' (*Daily Mirror*, 1 September 1976, p. 5). The *Sun* asked simply whether there had not been too many police on the spot (1 September 1976), while the *Evening Standard* gave a lengthier assessment (quoted in Gilroy, 1987, p. 96):

> All the reports suggest that Scotland Yard was far too heavy-handed on Monday. It should not have sent 1500 uniformed men to police the Carnival in the Notting Hill area. A force seven times as large as the one that attended last year's festivities must surely have contributed to the tension in a part of London in which, as the Yard knows very well, the police are regarded by many inhabitants as the natural enemy. The whole exercise was an error of judgement.

Statistical evidence from the police themselves certainly casts doubt on the effectiveness of their strategy. Although sixty-eight people were arrested on the Monday night of the riots, the majority were charged with offences arising directly from the disturbances: twenty-eight for carrying an offensive weapon, twenty for threatening behaviour, and sixteen for assault or obstructing the police. Citing the small numbers arrested for theft and robbery, *Guardian* described the police operation as 'singularly unsuccessful' (2 September 1976).

The actions of the Metropolitan Police were given unqualified support by the *Daily Express*, which asked 'Are police, then, to keep a "low profile" in black areas of our own capital city?' (1 September 1976). It raised the spectre of 'race war in Britain', arguing that 'young blacks' had simply 'run riot' and that there was no evidence of police provocation. The revealing contrast that the *Express* draws here in its juxtaposition of 'our own' (implicitly white) metropolis and the (implicitly hostile) 'black areas' within it was paralleled in Sir Robert Mark's remarks at the press conference on the day after the riots. He claimed that his methods were justified in order to protect 'decent black people' from 'young black hooligans'. He painted a heroic picture of the police, refusing to abdicate their responsibilities, not prepared to buy 'an illusory peace' by creating 'no-go areas' in London's inner cities (*The Times*, 1 September 1976). He argued that a larger police presence was necessitated at the 1976 Carnival because of the high level of crime at the previous year's event and because of the fact that Carnival was being held over a much wider area. To support these contentions about the high level of street crime, the police displayed a cache of several hundred handbags and purses that they had retrieved from the pick-pockets in the days immediately after Carnival. The *Daily Mirror* supported these claims by citing some highly dubious figures suggesting that, during the previous year, 80 per cent of street crimes, muggings, attacks, and snatches were committed by blacks, whereas over 60 per cent of their victims were white (31 August 1976). Finally, Sir Robert Mark maintained that fewer police had been used in relation to the estimated attendance of 150,000 people at Carnival than at comparable events, such as the Football Association Cup Final at Wembley.

References to hooligans and comparisons with soccer violence were commonplace (see Pearson, 1983; Walvin, 1986). The *Guardian* referred to 'an element of hooligan violence and vandalism familiar from other occasions' (1 September 1976), singling out Manchester United fans for special mention. In denying a racial motive to the violence, the *Sun* argued that 'A crowd which happened to be predominantly black got out of hand – as white football crowds have been known to do' (1 September 1976). At the press conference, Sir Robert Mark himself drew 'a kind of rough comparison' between Carnival and a visiting Manchester United football crowd ('Mark Warns the Riot Hooligans', *Evening Standard*, 31 August 1976). He went on to argue that, among the 150,000 people attending Carnival, 'a hard core of 800 young hooligans' had been present ('Mark Blames 800 Hooligans', *Daily Telegraph*, 1 September 1976).

These comparisons between Carnival and football hooliganism confirm the impression that, for the British press at least, the threatening nature of Carnival derives in part from its association with particular forms of unrestrained 'masculine' behaviour. 'Carnival mobs' and 'black youth' are implicitly masculine phenomena, just as in the Caribbean it was the 'muscular vigour' of drumbeating that was considered objectionable. Images of women at Carnival are usually confined to pictures of them dancing cheerfully with male police officers. Their wider participation in Carnival, though still subject to a rigid gender division of labour, is generally neglected.[7]

In concluding this review of how the press reported the 1976 riots it is worth drawing attention to the territorial aspects of the policing of Carnival. It is clear that, for the police, the mobility of Carnival is one of its most problematic elements. In an interview published shortly before the 1976 Carnival, Superintendent Ron Paterson of Chelsea police station maintained that:

Last year's carnival was disorganised and potentially explosive.. . . The bands meadered around, going to unexpected places and blocking streets, pedestrians couldn't walk where they wanted to. Confusion was the order of the day.

(*Evening Standard*, 27 August 1976, p. 15)

In the same article, Selwyn Baptiste, Chair of the Carnival Development Committee, took up the theme: 'What we want is organized chaos . . . with space for freedom of movement. The emphasis is on mobility'. The police insisted, however, on a strategy of dividing Notting Hill into six areas, controlling movement between them.[8] The police had previously tried to ban Carnival from the streets of Notting Hill altogether, suggesting that it be located in a variety of sports stadia from White City to Chelsea Football Ground.[9] After the 1976 riot, Sir Robert Mark repeated this idea, saying that the police were not opposed to Carnival in principle but wanted it held in future 'under more controlled conditions such as in a stadium' (*Daily Mirror*, 1 September 1976). As the *Mirror*'s columnist Keith Waterhouse suggested the following day: 'The authorities do not like street life: it offends their sense of order and it makes them nervous' (2 September 1976).

Nervousness was not confined to the police. Columnist Lynda Lee-Potter betrayed similar anxieties in her musings on the 'thuggery and vindictive hooliganism' of Carnival. Drawing exaggerated comparisons between Notting Hill and Belfast and Chicago, she associated the riot with other events that had been in the news during the summer: squatting, social security 'spongers', and the illegal occupation of land for rock festivals. The common factor, from her point of view, was the collapse of 'law and order' and, specifically, the lack of respect for property and land: 'In our safe, comfortable homes in the provinces we're all beginning to know fear' (*Daily Mail*, 1 September 1976, p. 7).

As I have attempted to show in the foregoing analysis, the 1976 Carnival was a watershed in relations between black people and the police, marking the transition from a period when 'cultural diversity' and 'harmonious race relations' were still the stated goal of public policy to a period in which the brute fact of institutional racism could no longer be disguised (Carter, 1986). It also represents the period when, in Gutzmore's words, the culture of black people in Britain, always 'pregnant with rebellion', became 'inescapably one of resistance' (1982, p. 33).

Howe (1977) provides a valuable commentary on the ideological battle that developed for the control of Carnival in the period following the violence of 1976. Two rival organizations vied for control of the event, disputing its cultural and political significance. The Carnival and Arts Committee (CAC) saw Carnival as an explicitly political event, arguing that it should be used as a political lever to press for social reform and economic concessions. The Carnival Development Committee (CDC), with which Howe was himself associated, argued that Carnival was an essentially creative event that would be destroyed by overt exploitation for political and economic ends.[10] Only if Carnival remained overtly non-political could it be politically effective and culturally successful. Indeed, Howe argued that the very presence of a quarter of a million people, black and white, on the streets of Notting Hill, despite opposition from the police and the local council, and despite internal divisions, was a political event of the first order.

Since 1976, the symbolic meaning of Carnival in Britain has followed its Caribbean precursor into 'the domain of threatening culture' (Owusu, 1986, p. 8). Interpreting this turn of events, Cohen concludes that Carnival has immense political and cultural potentialities, but that the cultural dimension of Carnival is 'structured by the political . . . not determined by it' (1980, p. 79). His assessment of the irreducible in culture, despite its political significance, can now be reviewed in terms of the central paradox of Carnival: its integrative functions (in the creation of a specifically 'West Indian' identity in Britain, for example) versus its potential as a vehicle of protest, opposition, and resistance. Following the pattern established earlier in the paper, the analysis now returns to the Caribbean, where there is a substantial literature on the cultural politics of resistance. As this analysis reveals, symbolic resistance is often inherently territorial. When this point has been established for the Caribbean, it will then be possible to reapply it in the British context where it will be argued that the changing forms of Carnival as well as the strategies of containment and control employed by the police are fundamentally spatial.

Cultures of resistance

One of the central paradoxes of Carnival is its potential to serve both a socially integrative function and as a vehicle for the expression of protest, opposition, and resistance. Indeed, this ambiguity within the cultural form of Carnival is the source of much of its political significance. There are those, however, who maintain that Carnival's essential function is cathartic, ritualizing potentially disruptive social conflict. Craton represents an extreme version of this 'bread and circuses' theory of Caribbean history, as the following quotation suggests 1982, p. 238:

> The long history of Trinidad Carnival shows how festivals can be used as a safety valve or an anodyne by a ruling class, releasing harmlessly, or damping down, the energies of popular discontent so that actual revolution is averted or indefinitely postponed.

What this fails to explain, however, is why resistance takes the precise form it does and why the authorities evidently take these 'symbolic' protests so seriously. Why, for example, does Carnival dramatize and enact particular types of social and political conflict and why have there been such strenuous attempts to abolish Carnival if it is, in fact, no more than a harmless release of energy? Here, two anthropological studies (Wilson, 1973; Abrahams, 1983) allow us to take the analysis one stage further and to build up a social geography of Carnival as a specific form of cultural resistance with a distinctive spatial constitution.

In his account of the English-speaking Caribbean, Wilson (1973) makes the distinction between *respectability* and *reputation* as two key organizing principles of Caribbean social structure. He builds up an array of contrasting social attributes associated with each of these polar principles. He associates 'respectability' with high class, sexual propriety, good manners, the ideal of the nuclear family, church membership, premarital chastity (for women), and sober living (for men). By contrast, he associates 'reputation' with masculinity, virility, 'sweet talk' (boasting), music, and singing, and with the display of closely related sexual and verbal skills. He goes on to suggest that these social distinctions can be associated with distinctive and mutually exclusive spatial domains: the private domestic sphere of the home (in the case of respectability) and the public sphere of the rum shop and the crossroads (in the case of reputation) (see Table 15.1).

Table 15.1 Symbolic oppositions between the yard and the crossroads

Yard/home	Crossroads/street
Respectability	Reputation
Private world	Public world, keeping company
Family (generational organization)	Friendship networks (crew organization)
Order, acting sensible	Licence, being sporty, talking nonsense
Decorum, being behaved	Rudeness
Stability, passivity	Mobility, activity
Enclosed, protected	Free, adventurous
Circumspection	Gregariousness, flash, keeping company
Quiet, harmony	Noise to annoy, vextation, boderation (arguments, usually playful), making mock, giving fatigue (badinage)
Truth, honesty, cooperation, loyalty	Getting on fas', untrustworthiness, playful trickery, deceit

Source: Wilson (1973); Abrahams (1983).

Abrahams (1983) extends Wilson's distinction between household-based respectability and street-based reputation in his analysis of the role of performance in the emergence of Creole culture. His research on the Caribbean island of St Vincent shows how these two principles of social organization, and their respective spatial domains, are associated with the festivals of Christmas and Carnival. In St Vincent, everyone celebrates Christmas. It is a respectable festival, marking the birth of God's son and celebrated by families in their homes. Only the rude play Carnival, however, it being the devil's holiday, celebrated outdoors and concerned with the acquisition of reputation (often by disreputable means). Abrahams continues (1983, p. 100, emphasis added):

> Christmas provides for an orderly invasion of the yard, where the seasonal performances of singing and speech-making are carried out. *Carnival must be kept to the road*, however, because it is an overt and constant threat to the social order, and therefore to yard values.

The significance of these remarks is reinforced by a return to Pearse's discussion of Carnival in nineteenth-century Trinidad. Here, he argues that the political significance of Carnival was increased by the residential proximity of rich and poor. The 'singers, drummers, dancers, stickmen, prostitutes, matadors, bad-johns, dunois, makos and corner-boys' united in their celebration of Carnival in what he describes unequivocally in class terms (Pearse, 1956, in Horowitz, 1971, p. 551):

> It must be borne in mind that barrack-yard society was not isolated in one quarter of town, but back to back with the houses of the middle and upper classes. Its members were not only constantly confronted with the display of cultural standards of the higher social ranks, and thus aware of their distance from them, but paradoxically closely associated with them, especially through the women who were servants and often the predominant influence in the lives of the children. On the other hand,

middle-class men would seek liaisons with the women of – and on the fringes of – the jamette world, and some of them became patrons of yard bands and even stickmen themselves.

The parodic element in Carnival and its characteristic inversions of social convention depended to some extent on the mutual knowledge of different classes in Trinidadian society, even if relations between them were still very much of the 'paternalistic' variety (see van den Berghe (1967) on 'paternalistic' versus 'competitive' models of 'race relations').

Although this analysis has much to commend it, particularly in terms of its sensitivity to the spatial constitution of Carnival, the extreme gender division of society and space that Abrahams and Wilson assert should not be allowed to pass without comment. The gender roles that they ascribe to men and women are, as ever, socially constructed and no doubt vigorously contested. Furthermore, the association which these authors draw between Carnival and the public domain of 'masculine' values might be taken to imply that the symbolic power of Carnival as a ritualized form of protest is an exclusively 'masculine' phenomenon. This would certainly not be true of the contemporary celebration of Carnival in Notting Hill, even if media representations continue to portray events in these terms. Indeed, the structure of gender relations at Carnival represents a particularly rich field for further research (see also note 7).

These reservations aside, Abrahams (1983) goes on to identify the various 'symbolic landscapes' that emerge in the dramatization of social difference. Rather than focusing purely on elements of 'theatre', 'play', or 'spectacle', in the present analysis. I focus on the political significance of these different landscape forms, interpreting them as a symbolic expression of competitive social relations physically inscribed in space. As such, Carnival provides a test case for exploring the intersection of culture and politics in the creation of a specific geography of protest or resistance. It remains to be seen how far these remarks on the spatial constitution of Carnival as symbolic resistance can be applied in the British context and whether they can be extended to any broader theoretical conclusions about the 'carnivalization' of society in general.

Conclusion: the carnivalization of society

> Carnival . . . knows no spatial boundaries. During Carnival time it is possible to live only according to its laws, that is, to the laws of carnivalesque *freedom*.
> Mikhail Bakhtin, *The art of François Rabelais*

The literary critic Bakhtin describes the 'carnivalization' of society in medieval popular culture. He divides the folk culture of the Middle Ages and the Renaissance into ritual spectacles, comic verbal compositions, and various forms of billingsgate. These different cultural forms are united by their common evocation of a second world and a second life outside officialdom. Bakhtin's analysis of the literary works of François Rabelais illustrates the potential of popular cultural forms for displaying, mocking, contesting, and transforming social relations of power by forcing them 'out of the wings and onto the stage' (Hirschkop, 1986, p. 92). There are clear parallels here with the preceding analysis of Carnival, in terms both of the dramatic/territorial metaphor and of its political meaning.

Bakhtin describes the social and cultural logic of Carnival and its exploitation of the central political contradiction between a ruling group and the people. Although his particular concern is with the potential of specific linguistic forms to subvert and ridicule the social order, his analysis of drama as *performance* also suggests a means of analysing the subversive potential of Carnival. Bakhtin shows how Carnival distorts the normal relationship between actors and spectators, dissolving the distinction between participant and observer (1968, p. 7).

> carnival does not know footlights, in the sense that it does not acknowledge any distinction between actors and spectators. Footlights would destroy a carnival, as the absence of footlights would destroy a theatrical performance. Carnival is not a spectacle seen by the people; they live in it, and everyone participates because its very idea embraces all the people. While carnival lasts, there is no life outside it.

Not only does Carnival occur at a particular period in time that is set apart symbolically from the humdrum affairs of the mundane world as a time of feasting and general revelry,[11] but it *takes place*, literally, in a world apart, in the marketplace of medieval Europe, for example, or on the streets of Notting Hill, not in the bourgeois space of conventional theatre. Bakhtin goes on to show how the spatial world of medieval Carnival is demarcated by specific linguistic conventions (1968, p. 154, emphasis added):

> the unofficial culture of the Middle Ages and even of the Renaissance *had its own territory* and its own particular time, the time of fairs and feasts. This territory, as we have said, was a peculiar second world within the official medieval order and was ruled by a special type of relationship, a free, familiar, marketplace relationship. Officially the palaces, churches, institutions and private homes were dominated by hierarchy and etiquette, but in the marketplace a special kind of speech was heard, almost a language of its own, quite unlike the language of Church, palace, courts and institutions.

During the time of Carnival, existing forms of coercive social relations are temporarily suspended and this temporal 'world apart' is reflected spatially in the marketplace or on the streets (1968, p. 255, original emphasis).

> The carnivalesque crowd in the marketplace or in the streets is not merely a crowd. It is the people as a whole, but organized *in their own way*, the way of the people. It is outside of and contrary to all existing forms of the coercive socioeconomic and political organization, which is suspended for the time of the festivity.

All this may seem a long way from Notting Hill. But similar dramatic and spatial metaphors can clearly be applied both to the policing of Carnival in

Notting Hill, where territorial strategies of containment and control are fundamental, and to the symbolic form of Carnival itself, where the freedom and mobility of the streets is as central to Carnival as the symbolic reversals and relative anonymity of masquerade. As an exercise in social control from the point of view of the police, and as a form of symbolic protest from the viewpoint of the participants, Carnival is an intensely spatial event.

The link with medieval Carnival is made even more explicit by Gilroy's application (1987) of Bakhtin's ideas to the cultural politics of 'race' and nation in Britain. Employing Bakhtin's metaphor of the 'carnivalization' of society, Gilroy describes the power of black music 'to disperse and suspend the temporal and spatial order of the dominant culture' (1987, p. 210). Not surprisingly, the places where such music is played, like Carnival itself, become the focal point of hostile attention from the police.[12] Gilroy suggests that these venues comprise a symbolic space 'beyond the reach of racism' (p. 73). They represent a locus of struggle against the dominant society because they are associated with a symbolic rejection of work by black people. Time that should be devoted to rest and recuperation in order to be ready for work is pointedly and provocatively spent in the pursuit of leisure and pleasure (and of a particularly 'riotous' kind). This 'carnivalization' of life is naturally resented by the forces of law and order, who define their role in terms of social control. Conversely, the street protests and 'riots' of the 1980s are reported to have generated, for some participants at least, an atmosphere of Carnival (Gilroy, 1987, pp. 238–9). The association between the political and the cultural is once more reaffirmed. Carnival is, like rioting and war, the continuation of politics by other means.

Notes

1   Whether to speak of 'English' or 'British' racism is a complex political question that rests on rival historical accounts. Dummett is unequivocal in her book *A portrait of English racism* (1973), a usage which Smith (1987) has also followed, although the colonial experience was a British one. Elsewhere, Miles has criticized the view that racism is an English (as opposed to a Scottish) problem, choosing instead to write about the Scottish dimension of British racism (Miles and Dunlop, 1987). It is this latter usage that will be followed here.

2   The festival of Canboulay, a torchlight procession on the eve of Carnival, took its name from *cannes brûlées* (or burnt cane), recalling the practice of lighting fires in the cane fields during slave revolts and marking the occasion of the emancipation of the slaves. It was celebrated by the *jamette* class or underworld, below the 'diameter' (*diamètre*) of respectability (Pearse, in Horowitz, 1971, pp. 546 and 551).

3   The quotation from Le Roy Ladurie inadvertently raises the question as to whether some aspects of role reversal were gender-specific, such that the cross-dressing of men as women, for example, was more common than female transvestism. It would certainly be surprising if male and female transvestism were charged with equal significance in a society where other aspects of gender relations were fundamentally unequal.

4 Likewise in Notting Hill today, the 'traditional' music of calypso and reggae is combined with Latin American salsa and the scratch and hip-hop music that originated in the black ghettos of New York and Washington, DC (Hebdige, 1987).

5 Police raids on the Mangrove restaurant led to the arrest of the so-called 'Notting Hill nine' in 1970 on charges of riot, conspiracy, affray, and assault, culminating in the much-publicized 'black power' trial at the Old Bailey in 1971 (see Carter, 1986, pp. 105–8).

6 When violence recurred during the Notting Hill Carnival in 1987, press accounts were, superficially, much more sensitive to questions of 'race'. None of the major newspapers headlined events in directly 'racial' terms. By 1987, it seems, the word 'riot' was sufficient to connote 'race' and papers focused instead on policing issues. The *Daily Telegraph*, for example, headlined its report: 'Riot Police Battle with Mobs in Notting Hill'; the *Daily Mirror* led with: 'Carnival Riot Cops Storm In'; and the *Daily Express* headline read: 'Carnival Terror as Riot Police Charge Stone-Hurling Mobs' (all 1 September 1987).

7 Women are more likely than men to be involved in manufacturing costumes for the Carnival parades, in child-minding and in the preparation and sale of food. Men continue to dominate the musical events as calypsonians and toasters. Although this gender division of labour clearly merits further research, the present analysis deals mainly with *representations* of Carnival in the British media, where sexism and racism are combined in roughly equal measure.

8 Traditionally, of course, masquerade facilitated people's mobility by increasing their anonymity. It may still have a similar function in view of the increasingly sophisticated forms of technical surveillance employed in policing the Notting Hill Carnival.

9 The history of New York City's 'West Indian' Carnival is broadly comparable. Following a number of disturbances, the police withdrew their permission to hold Carnival on the streets of Harlem in 1964. It now takes place in Brooklyn, with most of the events confined within the grounds of the Brooklyn Museum, culminating in a parade along Eastern Parkway (Kasinitz, 1987a, pp. 232–4). The parallel between Carnival and 'ethnic' parades in US cities is discussed by Davis (1986) and Marston (1987), among others.

10 A similar attempt by Jesse Jackson to use New York's Carnival for overtly political ends was resented by many participants and led to considerable ill-feeling between Afro-Caribbean and 'West Indian' political activists (Kasinitz, 1987b).

11 The timing of Carnival has its own particular significance. Associated originally with the beginning of Lent and later with the emancipation of the slaves in Trinidad, the celebration of Carnival outside the Caribbean nowadays tends to coincide with major public holidays such as Labor Day in New York and August Bank Holiday in London.

12 The 1980 riot in Saint Paul's, Bristol, began after a police raid on the Black and White Cafe (Joshua *et al.*, 1983). The Mangrove restaurant in Notting Hill has a similar symbolic significance following the events described in note 5.

References

Abrahams, R. D. 1983: *The man-of-words in the West Indies: Performance and the emergence of Creole culture*. Baltimore: Johns Hopkins University Press.

Bakhtin, M. 1968: *Rabelais and his world*. Cambridge, MA: MIT Press.

Burgess, J. 1985: News from nowhere: the press, the riots and the myth of the inner city. In Burgess, J. and Gold, J. R. (eds), *Geography, the media and popular culture*. Beckenham: Croom Helm, 192–228.

Burke, P. 1978: *Popular culture in early modern Europe*. New York: New York University Press.

Burton, R. D. E. 1986: Cricket, carnival and street culture in the Caribbean. Paper presented at the Caribbean Societies seminar, Institute of Commonwealth Studies, University of London; copy available from the Institute.

Carter, T. 1986: *Shattering illusions: West Indians in British politics*. London: Lawrence & Wishart.

Cohen, A. 1980: Drama and politics in the development of a London Carnival. *Man* 15, 65–87.

Cohen, A. 1982: A polyethnic London Carnival as a contested cultural performance. *Ethnic and Racial Studies* 5, 23–41.

Craton, M. 1982: *Testing the chains: Resistance to slavery in the British West Indies*. Ithaca, NY: Cornell University Press.

Darnton, R. 1984: *The great cat massacre and other episodes in French cultural history*. New York: Basic Books.

Davis, S. G. 1986: *Parades and power: Street theatre in nineteenth century Philadelphia*. Philadelphia: Temple University Press.

Dummett, A. 1973: *A portrait of English racism*. Harmondsworth, Middx: Penguin Books.

Gilroy, P. 1987: *There ain't no black in the Union Jack: The cultural politics of race and nation*. London: Hutchinson.

Gutzmore, C. 1982: The Notting Hill Carnival. *Marxism Today*, August, pp. 31–3.

Gutzmore, C. 1983: Capital, 'black youth' and crime. *Race Today* 25, 13–30.

Hall, S. and Jefferson, T. (eds), 1976: *Resistance through rituals*. Centre for Contemporary Cultural Studies. London: Hutchinson.

Hall, S., Critcher, S. Jefferson, T., Clarke, J. and Roberts, B. 1978: *Policing the crisis: Mugging, the state and law and order*. London: Macmillan.

Hill, E. 1972: *The Trinidad Carnival: Mandate for a national theatre*. Austin, TX: University of Texas Press.

Hebdige, D. 1987: *Cut 'n' mix: Culture, identity and Caribbean music*. London: Comedia.

Hirschop, K. 1986: Bakhtin, discourse and democracy. *New Left Review* no. 160, 92–113.

HMSO. 1972: Police–immigrant relations. Select Committee on Race Relations and Immigration, 1971–72 Session. London: HMSO.

HMSO. 1976: The West Indian community. Select Committee on Race Relations and Immigration, 1975–76 Session. London: HMSO.

Horowitz, M. M. (ed.) 1971: *Peoples and cultures of the Caribbean*. Garden City, NY: The Natural History Press.

Howe, D. 1977: *The road make to walk on Carnival day*. Race Today Publications, 165 Railton Rd, London SE24.

Jackson, P. 1987: The idea of 'race' and the geography of racism. In Jackson, P. (ed.), *Race and racism: Essays in social geography*. Hemel Hempstead: Allen & Unwin, 3–21.

Joshua, H., Wallace, T. and Booth, H. 1983: *To ride the storm: the 1980 Bristol 'riot' and the State*. London: Heinemann Educational Books.

Kasinitz, P. 1987a: West Indian diaspora: race, ethnicity and politics in New York City.

Unpublished PhD dissertation. New York: Department of Sociology, New York University.

Kasnitz, P. 1987b: The minority within: the new black immigrants. *New York Affairs* 10, 44–58.

Kerridge, R. 1983: *Real wicked, guy: A view of black Britain*. Oxford: Basil Blackwell.

Le Roy Ladurie, E. 1981: *Carnival in Romans: A people's uprising at Romans, 1579–1580*. Harmondsworth: Penguin Books.

Leach, E. 1961: Time and false noses. In *Rethinking anthropology*. LSE Monographs on Social Anthropology 22. London: London School of Economics, 132–36.

Lewis, G. K. 1968: *The growth of the modern West Indies*. London: Monthly Review Press.

Mair, M. 1986: Black Rhythm and British Reserve: interpretations of Black Musicality in British racist ideology since 1750. Unpublished PhD dissertation. University of London: Department of Geography.

Marston, S. A. 1987: *Contested territory: An ethnic parade as symbolic resistance*. DP-87-4. University of Arizona, Tucson: Department of Geography and Regional Development.

Miles, R. 1978: Between two cultures? The case of Rastafarianism. Working Papers on Ethnic Relations 10. Bristol: Research Unit on Ethnic Relations/Social Science Research Council.

Miles, R. 1984: The riot of 1958: the ideological construction of 'race relations' as a political issue in Britain. *Immigrants and Minorities* 3, 252–75.

Miles, R. and Dunlop, A. 1987: Racism in Britain: the Scottish dimension. In Jackson, P. (ed.), *Race and racism: Essays in social geography*. Hemel Hempstead: Allen & Unwin, 119–41.

Owusu, K. 1986: *The struggle for black arts in Britain*. London: Comedia.

Oxaal, I. 1968: *Black intellectuals come to power*. Cambridge, MA: Schenkman.

Pearse, A. 1956: Carnival in nineteenth century Trinidad. *Caribbean Quarterly* 4, 176–93; reprinted 1971 in Horowitz, M. M. (ed.), *Peoples and cultures of the Caribbean*. Garden City, NY: The Natural History Press, 528–52.

Pearson, G. 1983: *Hooligan: A history of respectable fears*. London: Macmillan.

Pilger, J. 1976: Behind the frontline of fury. *Daily Mirror*, 1 September, 5.

Reeves, F. 1983: *British racial discourse*. Cambridge: Cambridge University Press.

Ryan, S. D. 1972: *Race and nationalism in Trinidad and Tobago: A study of decolonization in a multiracial society*. Toronto: University of Toronto Press.

Sivanandan, A. 1983: Challenging racism: strategies for the '80s. *Race and Class* 25, 1–11.

Smith, S. J. 1987: Residential segregation: a geography of English racism? In Jackson, P. (ed.), *Race and racism: Essays in social geography*. Hemel Hempstead: Allen & Unwin, 25–49.

van den Berghe, P. 1967: *Race and racism: A comparative perspective*. New York: John Wiley.

Walvin, J. 1986: *Football and the decline of Britain*. London: Macmillan.

Wilson, P. J. 1973: *Crab antics: The social anthropology of English-speaking Negro societies of the Caribbean*. New Haven, CT: Yale University Press.

16 Mike Davis,
'City of Quartz'

Excerpt from: M. Davis, *City of Quartz*. London: Verso (1991)

The revolutionary lumpenproletariat

The drug-taking, apathetic young Black people we bemoan today are the result of our failure to protect and cherish the Black Panthers during the Sixties.

Sonya Sanchez[1]

It is time to meet LA's 'Viet Cong'. Although the study of barrio gangs is a vast cottage industry, dating back to Emory Bogardus's 1926 monograph, inspired by the Chicago school, *The city boy and his problems*, almost nothing has been written about the history of Southcentral LA's sociologically distinct gang culture. The earliest, repeated references to a 'gang problem' in the Black community press, moreover, deal with gangs of *white* youth who terrorized Blacks resident along the frontiers of the southward-expanding Central Avenue ghetto. Indeed, from these newspaper accounts and the recollections of oldtimers, it seems probable that the first generation of Black street gangs emerged as a defensive response to white violence in the schools and streets during the late 1940s. The *Eagle*, for example, records 'racial gang wars' at Manual Arts High in 1946, Canoga Park High (in the Valley) in 1947, and John Adams High in 1949, while Blacks at Fremont High were continuously assaulted throughout 1946 and 1947. Possibly as a result of their origin in these school integration/transition battles, Black gangs, until the 1970s, tended to be predominantly defined by school-based turfs rather than by the microscopically drawn neighborhood territorialities of Chicano gangs.[2]

Aside from defending Black teenagers from racist attacks (which continued through the 1950s under the aegis of such white gangs as the 'Spookhunters'), the early Southcentral gangs – the Businessmen, Slausons, Gladiators, Farmers, Parks, Outlaws, Watts, Boot Hill, Rebel Rousers, Roman Twenties, and so forth – were also the architects of social space in new and usually hostile settings. As tens of thousands of 1940s and 1950s Black immigrants crammed into the overcrowded, absentee-landlord-dominated neighborhoods of the ghetto's 'Eastside', low-rider gangs offered 'cool worlds' of urban socialization for poor young newcomers from rural Texas, Louisiana and Mississippi. Meanwhile, on the other side of Main Street, more affluent Black youngsters from the 'Westside' bungalow belt created a status-oriented simulacrum of the ubiquitous white 'car club' subculture of Los Angeles in the 1950s. As J. K. Obatala would recall, 'besides the territorial factor, there was an element of class warfare in the 1950s':

Members of gangs such as the Flips and the Slausons were Westsiders whose families usually had a little more money and who considered themselves more socially sophisticated than their Eastside counterparts. The Eastsiders, in turn, looked upon their rivals to the West as snobs and sometimes deliberately ventured into their sphere of influence to break up parties or other social events.[3]

While 'rumblin" (usually non-lethally) along this East–West socioeconomic divide, or sometimes simply in extension of intermural athletic rivalries, the Black gangs of the 1950s also had to confront the implacable (often lethal) racism of Chief Parker's LAPD. In the days when the young Daryl Gates was driver to the great Chief, the policing of the ghetto was becoming simultaneously less corrupt but more militarized and brutal. Under previous police chiefs, for example, Central Avenue's boisterous, interracial night scene had simply been shaken down for tribute; under Parker – a puritanical crusader against 'race mixing' – nightclubs and juke joints were raided and shuttered. In 1954 John Dolphin, owner of Los Angeles's premier R&B record store near the corner of Vernon and Central, organized a protest of 150 Black business people against an ongoing 'campaign of intimidation and terror' directed at interracial trade. According to Dolphin, Newton Division police had gone so far as to blockade his store, turning away all white customers and warning them that 'it was too dangerous to hang around Black neighborhoods'.[4]

After smashing interracial 'vice' on Central Avenue, Chief Parker launched his own 'all-out war on narcotics' in Southcentral and East LA, alleging that heroin and marijuana were being exported to white neighborhoods. He charged in the press that 'the Communists furthered the heroin and marijuana trade, because drug use sped the moral degeneration of America'. Prefiguring Gates's call years later for the invasion of Colombia, Parker demanded the closing of the Mexican border, while his principal newspaper supporter, the *Herald-Express*, called for the execution of drug dealers.[5]

Chief Parker also did his bit to support the *Times*'s crusade against 'socialistic' public housing by using phoney crime statistics to paint lurid images of 'jungle life' in the projects – a political manipulation of police data which some critics feel has continued through the present. Like his protégé-successors, Chief Parker invoked racialized crime scares to justify his tireless accumulation of power. As one of his retiring subordinates observed in 1981, Parker constantly and self-servingly projected the specter of a vast criminal reservoir in Southcentral LA ('all Blacks as bad guys'), held in check by an outnumbered but heroically staunch 'blue line'. Accordingly, any diminution of the police budget or questioning of Parker's authority would weaken the dike and release a Black crime deluge on peaceful white neighborhoods.[6] Consider, for example, the Chief's extraordinary testimony before the US Commission on Civil Rights in early 1960:

A belligerent Parker characterized the LAPD as the real 'embattled minority' and argued that the tensions between LA's minority communities and the cops had simply to do with the fact that Blacks and Latinos were statistically many times more likely than Whites to commit crimes. Indeed Parker assured the Commission that the 'established [read White] community thinks cops aren't hard enough on Black vice'. Parker sparked a 500-strong protest rally in East Los Angeles when he went on to offer his insight into the high crime rate in the *barrios*, explaining that the people who lived there were only one step removed from 'the wild tribes of Mexico'.[7]

Since 'wild tribes' and gang perils were its golden geese, it is not surprising that Parker's LAPD looked upon the 'rehabilitation' of gang youth in much the same way as the arms industry regarded peace-mongering or disarmament treaties. Vehemently opposed to the extension of constitutional rights to juveniles and loathing 'social workers', Chief Parker, a strict Victorian, 'launched a concerted attack on the Group Guidance Unit of the Probation Department', a small program that had emerged out of the so-called 'Zoot Suit Riots' of 1943. The original sin of Group Guidance, in the Chief's opinion, was that they 'gave status to gang activity' by treating gang members as socially transformable individuals. Like the contemporary rhetoric of the HAMMER or 'Black-Lash', the LAPD in the 1950s and early 1960s dichotomized youth offenders into two groups. On one hand were mere 'delinquents' (mainly white youth) susceptible to the shock treatment of juvenile hall; on the other hand were 'juvenile criminals' (mainly Black and Chicano) – miniature versions of J. Edgar Hoover's 'mad dogs' – destined to spend their lives within the state prison system. Essential to the LAPD worldview was the assertion that ghetto gang youth were composed of the latter: a residuum of 'hardcore', unrehabilitable criminality. Moreover, as Black nationalist groups, like the Muslims, began to appear in the ghetto in the late 1950s, Parker, like Hoover, began to see the gang problem and the 'militant threat' as forming a single, overarching structure of Black menace.[8]

The LAPD's own abuses, in fact, were a self-fulfilling prophecy, radicalizing gang subculture in Southcentral. After the LAPD's unprovoked attack on a Nation of Islam Mosque in April 1962, which left one Muslim killed and six wounded, a community uprising against Parker's 'army of occupation' became envisioned as justified and virtually inevitable. Thus in May 1964 Howard Jewel memoed his boss, California Attorney General Stanley Mosk, that 'soon the "long, hot summer" will be upon us. The evidence from LA is ominous'. Jewell blamed Chief Parker for inciting racial polarization and predicted widespread violence.[9]

At the same time the Black version of the Southern California Dream, which had lured hundreds of thousands of hopeful immigrants from the Southwest, was collapsing. Excluded from lucrative construction and aerospace jobs, Black youth experienced the 1959–65 period – the white kids' 'endless summer' – as a winter of discontent. The absolute income gap between Black and white Angelenos dramatically widened. Median incomes in Southcentral LA declined by almost a tenth, and Black unemployment skyrocketed from 12 per cent to 20 per cent (30 per cent in Watts). Despite deceptive palm-lined streets and cute bungalow exteriors, the housing stock of Southcentral was dilapidated: the 'largest blighted area of any US city', according to the Regional Planning Commission.[10] But every attempt by civil rights groups to expand job or housing opportunities for Blacks was countered by fierce white resistance, culminating in the 75 per cent white vote in 1964 (Proposition 14) to repeal the Rumford Fair Housing Act.

Yet, unlike today's social polarization, this was also the heroic age of the Civil Rights Movement, of epic debates about strategies of liberation. Southcentral gang youth, coming under the influence of the Muslims and the long-distance charisma of Malcolm X, began to reflect the generational awakening of Black Power. As Obatala describes the 'New Breed' of the 1960s, 'their perceptions were changing: those who formerly had seen things in terms of East and West were now beginning to see many of the same things in Black and White'. As the gangs began to become politicized, they became 'al fresco churches whose ministers brought the gospel [of Black power] out into the streets'.[11]

Veteran civil rights activists can recall one memorable instance, during a protest at a local whites-only drive-in restaurant, when the timely arrival of Black gang members saved them from a mauling by white hotrodders. The gang was the legendary Slausons, based in the Fremont High area, and they became a crucial social base for the rise of the local Black Liberation movement. The turning-point, of course, was the festival of the oppressed in August 1965 that the Black community called a rebellion and the white media a riot. Although the 'riot commission' headed by old-guard Republicans John McCone and Asa Call supported Chief Parker's so-called 'riff-raff theory' that the August events were the work of a small criminal minority, subsequent research, using the McCone Commission's own data, proved that up to 75,000 people took part in the uprising, mostly from the stolid Black working class.[12] For gang members it was 'The Last Great Rumble', as formerly hostile groups forgot old grudges and cheered each other on against the hated LAPD and the National Guard. Conot cites examples of old enemies, like the Slausons and the Gladiators (from the 54th Street area), flashing smiles and high signs as they broke through Parker's invincible 'blue line'.[13]

This ecumenical movement of the streets and 'hoods lasted for three or four years. Community workers, and even the LAPD themselves, were astonished by the virtual cessation of gang hostilities as the gang leadership joined the Revolution.[14] Two leading Slausons, Alprentice 'Bunchy' Carter (a famous 'warlord') and Jon Huggins, became the local organizers of the Black Panther Party, while a third, Brother Crook (aka Ron Wilkins, created the Community Alert Patrol to monitor police abuse. Meanwhile, an old Watts gang hangout near Jordan Downs, the 'parking lot', became a recruiting center for the 'Sons of Watts' who organized and guarded the annual Watts Festival.[15]

It is not really surprising, therefore, that in the late 1960s the doo-ragged, hardcore street brothers and sisters, who for an extraordinary week in 1965 had actually driven the police out of the ghetto, were visualized by Black Power theorists as the strategic reserve of Black Liberation, if not its vanguard. (A similar fantasy of a *Warriors*-like unification of the gangs was popular among sections of the Chicano Left.) There was a potent moment in this period, around 1968–9, when the Panthers – their following soaring in the streets and high schools – looked as if they might become the ultimate revolutionary gang. Teenagers, who today flock to hear Eazy-E rap, 'It ain't about color, it's about the color of money. I love that green',[16] then filled the Sports Arena to listen to

Stokely Carmichael, H. Rap Brown, Bobby Seale and James Forman adumbrate the unity program of SNCC and the Panthers. The Black Congress and the People's Tribunal (convened to try the LAPD for 'the murder of Gregory Clark') were other expressions of the same aspiration for unity and militancy.

But the combined efforts of the FBI's notorious COINTELPRO program and the LAPD's Public Disorder Intelligence Division (a super-Red Squad that until 1982 maintained surveillance on every suspicious group from the Panthers to the National Council of Churches) were concentrated upon destroying Los Angeles's Black Power vanguards. The February 1969 murders of Panther leaders Carter and Huggins on the UCLA campus by members of a rival nationalist group (which Panther veterans still insist was actually police-instigated) was followed a year later by the debut of LAPD's SWAT team in a day-long siege of the Panthers' Southcentral headquarters. Although a general massacre of the Panther cadre was narrowly averted by an angry community outpouring into the streets, the Party was effectively destroyed.

As even the *Times* recognized, the decimation of the Panthers led directly to a recrudescence of gangs in the early 1970s.[17] 'Crippin', the most extraordinary new gang phenomenon, was a bastard offspring of the Panthers' former charisma, filling the void left by the LAPD SWAT teams. There are various legends about the original Crips, but they agree on certain particulars. As Donald Bakeer, a teacher at Manual Arts High, explains in his self-published novel about the Crips, the first 'set' was incubated in the social wasteland created by the clearances for the Century Freeway – a traumatic removal of housing and destruction of neighborhood ties that was the equivalent of a natural disaster. His protagonist, a second-generation Crip, boasts to his 'homeboys': 'My daddy was a member of the original 107 Hoover Crip Gang, the original Crips in Los Angeles, OG [original gangster] to the max'.[18] Second, as journalist Bob Baker has determined, the real 'OG' number one of the 107 Hoovers (who split away from an older gang called the Avenues) was a young man powerfully influenced by the Panthers in their late sixties heyday:

> He was Raymond Washington, a Fremont High School student who had been too young to be a Black Panther but had soaked up some of the Panther rhetoric about community control of neighborhoods. After Washington was kicked out of Fremont, he wound up at Washington High, and something began to jell in the neighborhood where he lived, around 107th and Hoover streets.[19]

Although it is usually surmised that the name Crip is derived from the 107 Hoovers' 'crippled' style of walking, Bakeer was told by one 'OG' that it originally stood for 'Continuous Revolution In Progress'.[20] However apocryphal this translation may be, it best describes the phenomenal spread of Crip sets across the ghetto between 1970 and 1972. A 1972 gang map (Figure 16.1) released by the LAPD's 77th Street Division, shows a quiltwork of blue-ragged Crips, both Eastside and Westside, as well as miscellany of other gangs, some descended from the pre-Watts generation.[21] Under incessant Crip pressure, these independent gangs – the Brims, Bounty Hunters, Denver Lanes, Athens Park Gang, the Bishops, and, especially, the powerful Pirus – federated as the red-hankerchiefed Bloods. Particularly strong in Black communities peripheral to the Southcentral core, like Compton, Pacoima, Pasadena and Pomona, the Bloods have been primarily a defensive reaction-formation to the aggressive emergence of the Crips.[22]

It needs to be emphasized that this was not merely a gang revival, but a radical permutation of Black gang culture. The Crips, however perversely, inherited the Panther aura of fearlessness and transmitted the ideology of armed vanguardism (shorn of its program). In some instances, Crip insignia continued to denote Black Power, as during the Monrovia riots in 1972 or the LA Schools busing crisis of 1977–9.[23] But too often Crippin' came to represent an escalation of intra-ghetto violence to *Clockwork orange* levels (murder as a status symbol, and so on) that was unknown in the days of the Slausons and anathema to everything that the Panthers had stood for.

Moreover, the Crips blended a penchant for ultra-violence with an overweening ambition to dominate the entire ghetto. Although, as Bakeer subtly sketches in his novel, Eastside versus Westside tensions persist, the Crips, as the Panthers before them, attempted to hegemonize an entire generation. In this regard, they achieved, like the contemporary 'Black P-Stone Nation' in Chicago, a 'managerial revolution' in gang organization. If they began as a teenage substitute for the fallen Panthers, they evolved through the 1970s into a hybrid of teen cult and proto-Mafia. At a time when economic opportunity was draining away from Southcentral Los Angeles, the Crips were becoming the power resource of last resort for thousands of abandoned youth.

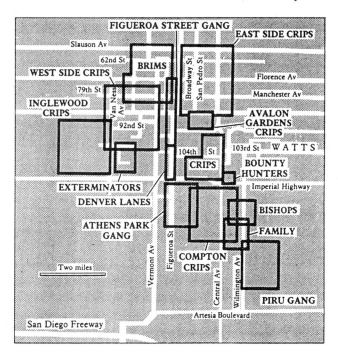

Fig. 16.1 Gang territories, 1972

Expendable youth

> Gangs are never goin' to die out. You all goin' to get us jobs?
>
> 16-year-old Grape Street Crip[24]

What would the Crips and Bloods say about the carnage if they could talk? It is, of course, a tactical absolute of 'anti-terrorism' – whether practiced in Belfast, Jerusalem or Los Angeles – to deny terrorism a public voice. Although terrorism is always portrayed precisely as inarticulate male violence, authorities expend enormous energy to protect us from its 'ravings', even at the cost of censorship and restriction of free speech. Thus the LAPD has vehemently (and usually successfully) opposed attempts by social workers and community organizers to allow gang members to tell 'their side of the story'.

A major exception was in December 1972, just as Cripmania was first sweeping Southside schools in an epidemic of gang shootings and street fights. The Human Relations Conference, against the advice of the police, gave a platform to sixty Black gang leaders to present their grievances. To the astonishment of officials present, the 'mad dogs' outlined an eloquent and coherent set of demands: jobs, housing, better schools, recreation facilities and community control of local institutions.[25] It was a bravura demonstration that gang youth, however trapped in their own delusionary spirals of vendetta and self-destruction, clearly understood that they were the children of deferred dreams and defeated equality. Moreover, as 'hard-core' Black and Chicano gang leaders have always affirmed, in the handful of other instances over the past eighteen years when they have been allowed to speak, decent jobs are the price for negotiating a humane end to drug-dealing and gang violence.[26]

So, what has happened to the jobs? It is necessary to recall that the revolutionary rhetoric of the 1960s was sustained by the real promise of reformism. While the Panthers were mesmerizing the campuses, civil rights politics gained new momentum with the rise of the Bradley coalition of Blacks, Jews and liberals. Moreover, in the superheated summit of the Vietnam boom, young Black men at last began to find their way, in some substantial number, into factory and transportation jobs, while Black women thronged into the lower levels of the pink-collar workforce. And, for teenagers and the younger unemployed, the federal government supplied a seasonal quota of temporary 'weed-pulling' jobs and bogus training schemes to cool out the streets during the long summers.

But the illusion of economic progress was shortlived. By 1985 – the tenth anniversary of the Watts Rebellion and year two of the Bradley era – a special report by the *Times* found that the 'the Black ghetto is not a viable community . . . it is slowly dying'. In the face of double-digit unemployment (1975 was a depression year for Southland Blacks), overcrowded schools, high prices, and deteriorating housing, 'the fighting mood of the 1960s has been replaced by a sick apathy or angry frustration'. With rebellion deterred by the paramilitarization of the police and the destruction of the community's radical fringe, *Times* writer John Kendall described despair recycled as gang violence and Black-on-Black crime.[27]

Seen from a perspective fifteen years further on, it is clear that the *Times*, and other contemporary observers, did not fully appreciate the complexity of what was happening in Southcentral Los Angeles. Although the image of over-all community demoralization was accurate enough, a sizable minority was actually experiencing moderate upward mobility, while the condition of the majority was steadily worsening. In simplified terms, Los Angeles's Black community became more internally polarized as public-sector craftworkers, clericals and professionals successfully entrenched themselves within city, county and federal bureaucracies, while the semi-skilled working class in the private sector was decimated by the dual impact of job suburbanization and economic internationalization.

Paradoxically it may be equally true that Black political leadership in Los Angeles County has sponsored significant economic advance and contributed to the community's benign neglect at the same time. Critics who accuse the Bradley administration of 'killing Southcentral LA' usually ignore its achievements in integrating the public workforce. It has been a dynamic Black public-sector job base (together with smaller-scale Black professional advances in the aerospace, financial and entertainment industries) that is responsible for the prosperity visible on the Black 'new Westside': the *nouveaux riches* hilltops of Ladera Heights and Baldwin Hills, and the tidy tractlands of suburban Inglewood and Carson..

At the same time, *community* economic development has been a total failure. As we have seen, the Bradley administration chose to accommodate the redevelopment agenda of the Central City Association, not the NAACP or the Mexican–American Political Association. Working-class Blacks in the flatlands – where nearly 40 per cent of families live below the poverty line – have faced relentless economic decline. While city resources (to the tune of $2 billion) have been absorbed in financing the corporate renaissance of Downtown, Southcentral LA has been markedly disadvantaged even in receipt of anti-poverty assistance, 'coming in far behind West Los Angeles and the Valley in access to vital human services and job-training funds'.[28] Black small businesses have withered for lack of credit or attention from the city, leaving behind only liquor stores and churches.

Most tragically, the unionized branch-plant economy toward which working-class Blacks (and Chicanos) had always looked for decent jobs collapsed. As the Los Angeles economy in the 1970s was 'unplugged' from the American industrial heartland and rewired to East Asia, non-Anglo workers have borne the brunt of adaptation and sacrifice. The 1978–82 wave of factory closings in the wake of Japanese import penetration and recession, which shuttered ten of the twelve largest non-aerospace plants in southern California and displaced 75,000 blue-collar workers, erased the ephemeral gains won by blue-collar Blacks between 1965 and 1975. Where local warehouses and factories did not succumb to Asian competition, they fled instead to new industrial parks in the South Bay, northern Orange County or the Inland Empire – 321 firms since 1971.[29] An investigating committee of the California legislature in 1982 confirmed the resulting economic destruction in Southcentral neighborhoods:

unemployment rising by nearly 50 per cent since the early 1970s while community purchasing power fell by a third.[30]

If Eastside manufacturing employment made a spectacular recovery in the 1980s, it offered little opportunity for Blacks, as the new industry overwhelmingly consisted of minimum-wage sweatshops, super-exploiting immigrant Latino labor in the production of furniture or non-durables like clothes and toys. (Borrowing the terminology of Alain Lipietz, we might say that a 'bloody Taylorism' now operates within the ruined shell of 'Fordism'.)[31] This extinction of industrial job opportunities has had profound gender as well as socioeconomic ramifications for the Black labor force. Young Black women have been partially able to compensate for community deindustrialization by shifting into lower-level information-processing jobs. Young Black working-class men, on the other hand, have seen their labor-market options (apart from military service) virtually collapse as the factory and truck-driving jobs that gave their fathers and older brothers a modicum of dignity have been either replaced by imports, or relocated to white areas far out on the galactic spiral arms of the LA megalopolis – fifty to eighty miles away in San Bernardino or Riverside counties.

Equally, young Blacks have been largely excluded from the boom in suburban service employment. It is a stunning fact – emblematic of institutional racism on a far more rampant scale than usually admitted these days – that most of California's 1980s job and residential growth poles (southern Orange County, eastern Ventura County, northern San Diego County, Contra Costa County, and so on) have Black populations of 1 per cent or less. At the same time, young Blacks willing to compete for more centrally located, menial service jobs find themselves in a losing competition with new immigrants, not least because of clear employer opinions about labor 'docility'. As a result, unemployment among Black youth in Los Angeles County – despite unbroken regional growth and a new explosion of conspicuous consumption – remained at a staggering 45 per cent through the late 1980s.[32] A 1985 survey of public housing projects in the ghetto discovered that there were only 120 employed breadwinners out of 1060 households in Nickerson Gardens, 70 out of 400 at Pueblo del Rio, and 100 out of 700 at Jordan Downs.[33] The scale of pent-up demand for decent manual employment was also vividly demonstrated a few years ago when *fifty-thousand* predominantly Black and Chicano youth lined up for miles to apply for a few openings on the unionized longshore in San Pedro.

This deterioration in the labor-market position of young Black men is a major reason why the counter-economy of drug dealing and youth crime has burgeoned. But it is not the whole story. Correlated to the economic peripheralization of working-class Blacks has been the dramatic *juvenation of poverty* among all inner-city ethnic groups. Statewide, the percentage of children in poverty has doubled (from 11 per cent to 23 per cent) over the past generation. In Los Angeles County during the 1980s, a chilling 40 per cent of children either lived below, or hovered just above, the official poverty line. The poorest areas in the County, moreover, are invariably the youngest: of sixty-six census tracts (in 1980) with median family incomes under $10 000, over 70 per cent had a median age of only 20–24 years (the rest, 25–29).[34] As the political muscle of affluent homeowners continues to ensure residential segregation and the redistribution of tax resources upwards, inner-city youth have been the victims of a conscious policy of social disinvestment. The tacit expendability of Black and brown youth in the 'city of the angels' can be directly measured by the steady drainage of resources – with minimum outcry from elected officials – from the programs that serve the most urgent needs.

Most telling, perhaps, have been the successive attacks on youth employment schemes, beginning with the Nixon administration's decision, echoed by then-Governor Reagan, to roll back Great Society community activism and redirect urban aid from the cities to the suburbs. The dismantling of the Neighborhood Youth Corps, followed under Reagan by the termination of the Comprehensive Employment and Training Act (CETA) and the evisceration of the Jobs Corps, were the landmarks in this retreat from the inner city. In Los Angeles the major, current source of public youth employment is the Los Angeles Summer Job Program – a typical 'fire insurance' scheme that is a pale shadow of its abolished federal predecessors. Ironically, at the very moment in 1987–88 when the klieg-light scrutiny of Hollywood and all the media was focused on illicit youth employment, the Summer Job Program was cut back by the City Council.[35]

Job alternatives for gang members have been almost non-existent, despite widespread recognition that jobs are more potent deterrents to youth crime than STEP laws or long penitentiary sentences. As Charles Norman, the veteran director of Youth Gang Services, observed in 1981: 'You could pull 80 per cent of gang members, seventeen years old or younger, out of gangs, if you had jobs, job training and social alternatives'.[36] State Senate President Pro Tem David Roberti, the top Democrat from Hollywood, acknowledged eight years later that 'Proposition 13 had ripped inner-city neighborhoods apart', preventing Norman's strategic expenditures on gang prevention.[37] Finally, as the LAPD's budget crept above $400 million in 1988, the City Council begrudgingly approved a $500 000 pilot program to create one hundred jobs for 'high-risk' youth. In the vast escalation of hostilities since the mid-1980s, this pathetic program is the only 'carrot' that the City has actually offered to its estimated 50 000 gang youth.[38]

The school system, meanwhile, has been travelling backwards at high speed. At the state level, California's celebrated educational system has been in steep decline, with per capita student expenditure falling from ninth to thirty-third place, or merely a third of the per capita level of New York. The Los Angeles Unified School District, the nation's second largest serving 600,000 students, has classrooms more crowded than Mississippi's and a soaring dropout rate of 30–50 per cent in its inner-city high schools. The term 'Unified' is a misnomer, as for many years the District has operated *de facto* separate systems for Blacks, Latinos and whites. One result is that Black males from Southcentral are now three times more likely to end up in prison than at the University of California. As the NAACP has charged in a major lawsuit, segregation remains rampant and school quality is directly reflective of the socioeconomic levels of neighborhoods. Moreover, as NAACP attorney Joseph Duff has explained, racial isolation in schools has been ramified by historic rental discrimination against families with children:

> Certain areas of the city with high-density, low-cost apartments and older, large single-family homes have become veritable 'children's ghettoes'. Public schools have been burdened by the concentration of school-age children in these family areas. The racial isolation has assumed an overlay of class isolation.[39]

Ill served by an overburdened and separate-but-unequal school system, low-income youth fare even worse after school. In Los Angeles County there are an estimated 250,000 to 350,000 'latch-key' kids between the ages of 5 and 14 who have no adult supervision between the final school bell and their parents' return from work. In the meantime the Bradley administration, applying triage to city programs in the wake of fiscal austerity, has virtually abandoned public recreation. In 1987 it allocated a paltry $30,000 in recreational equipment for 150 centers serving hundreds of thousands of poor children. It has also adopted the principle of apportioning its reduced park budget through a formula based on park size, while encouraging parks to operate as 'businesses' based on user fees. Since the wealthy areas of the city have disproportionate shares of park area and fee-generating facilities, this has entailed a regressive redistribution of park resources. The result is 'recreational apartheid' and a calamitous deterioration of public space in the inner city as parks become increasingly run down, unsupervised and dangerous.[40]

There has been desultory political mobilization against the hollowing out of the economic and social infrastructures of Southcentral or the pauperization of a generation of inner-city youth. Of the leadership generation of the Watts Rebellion only a handful have continued to raise hell about the fate of the community. Thus Assembly member Maxine Waters and Watts Labor Action leader Ted Watkins did pressure the legislature to finally hold hearings on local plant closures and economic distress (no comparable City Council initiative was taken). Despite a harrowing accumulation of testimony, the legislature, so keen to succor law enforcement, did nothing to address the economic decline that was obviously fueling crime rates.

Bolder action has been advocated by the surviving cadre of Los Angeles's 1960s Black Power movement, particularly Michael Zinzun of the Committee Against Police Abuse and Anthony Thigpen of Jobs with Peace. But their dogged attempts to build precinct-level organization in the community and to develop a grassroots agenda of 'critical needs' have been repeatedly sabotaged by various power structures, including ostensibly 'liberal' Democrats. Thus the Jobs with Peace campaign for a citywide assessment of the impact of military spending on local communities was countered by a vicious propaganda barrage from the political consultants to the Westside 'Berman–Waxman–Levine' machine. Zinzun's efforts, meanwhile, to expose police brutality led to a savage, unprovoked beating by Pasadena police and the loss of an eye. It is no criticism of the courageous dedication of these inner-city organizers to point out the David and Goliath character of their struggle. Unlike Chicago in 1986, where economic devastation in the ghetto could be laid neatly at the door of white political supremacy, in Los Angeles the Bradley regime, with its inner circle of Southside ministers and cronies, has been a powerful deterrent to the coalescence of Black protest or electoral insurgency.

Without the mobilized counterweight of angry protest, Southcentral LA has been betrayed by virtually every level of government. In particular, the deafening public silence about youth unemployment and the juvenation of poverty has left many thousands of young street people with little alternative but to enlist in the crypto-Keynesian youth employment program operated by the cocaine cartels. Revisiting Watts nearly a generation after a famous pioneering study of its problems, UCLA industrial relations economist Paul Bullock discovered that the worsening conditions described by the *Times*'s 'Watts: 10 Years Later' team in 1975 had deteriorated still further, and that endemic unemployment was at the core of the community's despair. Bullock observed that the last rational option open to Watts youth – at least in the neoclassical sense of utility-maximizing economic behavior – was to sell drugs.[41]

The political economy of crack

What's right? If you want something, you have the right to take it. If you want to do something, you have the right to do it.

Bret Easton Ellis, *Less than zero*[42]

Since the late 1970s, every major sector of the southern California economy, from tourism to apparel, has restructured around the increasing role of foreign trade and offshore investment. Southcentral LA, as we have indicated, has been the main loser in this transformation, since Asian imports have closed factories without creating compensatory economic opportunities for local residents. The specific genius of the Crips has been their ability to insert themselves into a leading circuit of international trade. Through 'crack' they have discovered a vocation for the ghetto in LA's new 'world city' economy.

Peddling the imported, high-profit rock stuff to a bipolar market of final consumers, including rich Westsiders as well as poor street people, the Crips have become as much lumpen capitalists as outlaw proletarians. If this has only underwritten their viciousness with a new competitive imperative, it has added to their charisma the weight of gold-braided neck chains and showy rings. In an age of narco-imperialism they have become modern analogues to the 'gunpowder states' of West Africa, those selfish, rogue chieftaincies who were middlemen in the eighteenth-century slave trade, prospering while the rest of Africa bled. The Latino Eastside gangs, by contrast, are still trying to catch up. Dealing largely in homegrown drugs, such as PCP, amphetamines and marijuana, with relatively low turnover values in a market consisting almost entirely of other poor teenagers, they are unable to accumulate the fineries or weaponry of the Crips. They have yet to effectively join the world market.

The contemporary cocaine trade is a stunning example of what some political economists (after the MIT duo of Sabel and Piore) are now calling 'flexible accumulation', on a hemispheric scale. The rules of the game are to combine maximum financial control with flexible and interchangeable deployment of producers and sellers across variable national landscapes. At the primary producer end, of course, coca has been the major economic adaptation of the Andean economies to the bank-imposed 'debt depression' of the 1980s. Tens of thousands of peasants have migrated to 'coke rush' frontiers like the famous Huallaga Valley of Peru, where they increasingly enjoy the protection of the 'Inca-Maoists' of Sendero Luminoso against the Green Berets and the Peruvian Army. In the late 1980s, the Colombian overlords tried to ensure the continuity of their supply, as well as their ability to impose a buyer's price on peasant producers, by opening their own auxiliary coca plantations using wage labor. Like oil production, however, the strategic instance is the refining process, centralized in Colombian laboratories under the personal supervision of the Medellín Cartel (or its Cali-based rival).

In popular imagination the Medellín Cartel has replaced the Mafia as the symbol of a super-criminal conspiracy of almost occult power; indeed, Bush and Bennett often talk as if America is fighting a 'war of the worlds' against extra-terrestrial invaders. The reality, of course, has always been more prosaic. Washington wages war on the same invisible hand that it otherwise deifies. As *Fortune* pointed out a few years back, the Medellín group have always been distinguished by their 'businesslike mentality' and their success 'in turning cocaine trafficking into a well-managed multinational industry'.[43] Eric Hobsbawm, an *aficionado* of bandits and imperialists, made the same point several years ago in a review:

> Left to themselves and the principles of Adam Smith, the consortia of Medellín investors would no more see themselves as criminals than did the Dutch or English venturers into the Indies trade (including opium), who organized their speculative cargoes in much the same way . . . the trade rightly resents being called a mafia. . . . It is basically an ordinary business that has been criminalized – as Colombians see it – by a US which cannot manage its own affairs.[44]

Like any 'ordinary business' in an initial sales boom, the cocaine trade had to contend with changing relations of supply and demand. Over production, due both to the cartels' deliberate promotion of supply and to the peasants' desperate stampede toward a saleable staple, has been endemic since the mid-1980s. Despite the monopsonistic position of the cartels *vis-à-vis* the producers, the wholesale price of cocaine fell by half. This, in turn, dictated a transformation in sales strategy and market structure. The result was a switch from *haute cuisine* to fast food, as the Medellin Cartel, starting in 1981 or 1983 (accounts differ), designated Los Angeles as a proving-ground for the mass sales potential of rock cocaine or crack.

Shortly before its demise in 1989, the *Herald-Examiner* published a sensationalized overview of 'Cartel LA' that synthesized law enforcement viewpoints on the history and organization of the crack economy. According to this account, the Colombian cartels responded to the militarization of federal drug enforcement in south Florida after 1982 by rerouting cocaine through Mexico with the aid of the 'Guadalajara Mafia' run by Miguel Gallardo (the 'godfather' presumed to have ordered the torture–murder of Drug Enforcement Authority (DEA) agent 'Kiki' Camarena in 1985). Upon its arrival in southern California via couriers or light aircraft (the DEA claims there are 'over 100 clandestine airstrips' in the California desert), the cocaine – by 1988 estimated to total 450,000 pounds annually – is supposedly warehoused and processed for wholesale distribution by Colombian nationals bound to the cartels by unbreakable *omertà*. Originally estimated to number a few hundred, the Colombians in 1989 suddenly became an 'invading army . . . thousands strong' organized into as many as '1000 cells'. (An Internal Revenue Service official described cell workers as 'soldiers coming into this country who are doing their tours of duty and then getting out'.[45]) Alarmed by news of the 'invasion', nervous southern California residents were put on the lookout for 'suspicious' Latin Americans, especially 'polite, well-dressed' families or individuals with penchants for quiet suburban neighborhoods.[46]

In any event, the financial turnover in LA's rock and powder markets appears easier to estimate than the number of Cartel 'foot soldiers'. Los Angeles has been described by the Justice Department as 'an ocean of drug-tainted cash'. Between 1985 and 1987 (the real take-off years for crack) the 'cash surplus' in the Los Angeles branch of the Federal Reserve system increased 2300 per cent to $3.8 billion – a sure index, according to federal experts, of the volume of illicit coke dollars.[47] In early 1989 a small army of Feds overwhelmed Downtown LA's Jewelry Mart in 'Operation Polar Cap' – a spectacular attack on 'La Mina' ('the Gold Mine'), a billion dollar per year money-laundering operation supposedly run on behalf of the Medellín Cartel by several dozen immigrant Armenian gold-dealers.[48] The disclosure of La Mina seemed to confirm earlier assertions by US Attorney (now federal judge) Robert Bonner that LA had surpassed Miami as 'the principal distribution center for the nation's cocaine supply' – a claim that the Justice Department officially recognized in August 1989.[49]

The vast, three-volume 'Dun and Bradstreet Primer on the Pervasiveness of Drugs in America' that Attorney General Thornburgh presented that month to drug czar William Bennett also proclaimed that LA drug gangs were firmly allied with the Medellín Cartel in a plot to flood American inner cities with crack. Quoting copiously from LAPD sources, the report pictured LA overrun by Colombians and the USA overrun by their Crip henchmen:

> Los Angeles street gangs now dominate the rock cocaine trade in Los Angeles and elsewhere, due in part to their steady recourse to murderous violence to enforce territorial dealing supremacy, to deter cheating and to punish rival gang members . . . the LAPD has identified 47 cities, from Seattle to Kansas City to Baltimore, where Los Angeles street gang traffickers have appeared.[50]

Washington's official adoption of the LAPD's characterization of LA street gangs as highly organized mafias in cahoots with the Colombians (a view also embraced by the California attorney general's office) was challenged by two

University of Southern California (USC) professors who had been carefully analyzing arrest records of crack dealers over the previous two years. In studying 741 cases in 'five gang-infested sections of Los Angeles County', they discovered that only 25 per cent of the alleged dealers were active gang members. Although acknowledging that the direct role of gangs might have substantially increased since their 1984–85 data, the USC team stood by their principal conclusions:

> The explosion in cocaine sales was engaging a number of street gang members but was in no way dominated by gang involvement. The drug parameters simply overwhelmed the gang parameters . . . the cohesiveness of the gangs themselves is very low . . . To expect a group like that to take on Mafia characteristics seems very • unlikely.[51]

Responding to this study, the LAPD's 'gang-drug czar', Deputy Chief Glenn Levant, admitted that 64 per cent of the 7000 suspected dealers arrested through his Gang-Related Active Trafficker program were not identifiable as gang members. But he denied that the Department had 'overstated the problem' since '36 per cent gang membership is very significant', and many, if not a majority, of the other arrestees were older ex-gang members.[52] But Levant's revision of the USC study – that is, a more significant direct participation of gang members and a large, if not dominant, role played by adult 'OGs' – still seemingly leaves in place the USC team's key finding that the gang role in drug distribution is too 'incoherent' to qualify for the 'organized crime network' badge that Levant's boss, Chief Gates, and most other law-enforcement officials want to pin on the Crips and Bloods.

All of which is to say that the Southcentral gangs are definitely in the drug business, but as small businessmen not crime corporations, and usually under the supervision of older dealers who, in turn, answer to a shadowy wholesale hierarchy of middlemen and cartel representatives. On the other hand, the very diffuseness of a crack trade organized through hundreds of competing gang sets and small-time dealers, while it belies the demonic power that the gangbusters would attribute to it, also defies all efforts to deliver the decisive 'knockout' blow. In the ghetto itself there are hundreds of independent rock house franchises, each turning over (according to LAPD estimates) about $5000 per day ($25,000 on welfare and social security check days). The constant attrition of such outlets to LAPD raids (like the one Nancy Reagan used as a media picnic) has become an ordinary business cost. Moreover, if Levant's estimate of 10,000 gang members making their livelihood from the drug trade is anywhere near correct, then crack really is the employer of last resort in the ghetto's devastated Eastside – the equivalent of several large auto plants or several hundred McDonalds.[53]

Of course this is 'reindustrialization' through disease and the redistribution of poverty. When $25 rock hit the streets of LA in volume during 1984–85, hospital and police statistics registered the cataclysmic impact: doubling of emergency room admissions for cocaine trauma, 15 per cent of newborns in public hospitals diagnosed drug-addicted, quintupling of juvenile arrests for coke-dealing, and so on.[54] It is important to remember that crack is not simply cheap cocaine – the poor man's version of the glamor drug stuffed up the noses of the marina and country club crowd – but a far more lethal form. Whether or not it is actually the most addictive substance known to science, as originally claimed, it remains an absolute commodity enslaving its consumers, 'the most devastating of all the monster drugs to afflict any American adolescent generation thus far'.[55]

For this epidemic bred out of despair – which, like heroin, inevitably turns users into petty dealers – the only treatment on demand is jail. In Los Angeles County, where infant mortality is soaring and the County trauma-treatment network has collapsed, it is not surprising that medical care for crack addiction – which experts agree requires long-term treatment in a therapeutic community – is generally unavailable. Thus Skid Row, Downtown's nightmarish 'Nickle', has the largest single concentration of crack addicts – young and old – in the city, but not a single treatment facility. Wealthy Pasadena is fighting crack-based gang activity in its Northwest ghetto with its own version of the HAMMER, including humiliating stripsearches in the field and a drug-tenant eviction policy, without spending a single cent on drug rehabilitation.[56] The examples could be depressingly multiplied, as drug treatment is filed in the same bottom drawer of forgotten liberal nostrums as youth employment or gang counseling.

In the meantime gang members have become the Stoic philosophers of this cold new reality. The appearance of crack has given the Crip subculture a terrible, almost irresistible allure. Which is not simply to reduce the gang phenomenon, now or in the past, to mere economic determinism. Since the 1840s when tough young Irishmen invented the modern street gang in the slums of the Bowery, Five Points and Paradise Alley (making the Bowery Boys and the Dead Rabbits just as dreaded as the Crips and Bloods are today), gang bonding has been a family for the forgotten, a total solidarity (like national or religious fervor) closing out other empathies and transmuting self-hatred into tribal rage. But the Crips and Bloods – decked out in Gucci T-shirts and expensive Nike airshoes, ogling rock dealers driving by in BMWs – are also authentic creatures of the age of Reagan. Their world view, above all, is formed of an acute awareness of what is going down on the Westside, where gilded youth practice the insolent indifference and avarice that are also forms of street violence. Across the spectrum of runaway youth consumerism and the impossible fantasies of personal potency and immunity, youth of all classes and colors are grasping at undeferred gratification – even if it paves the way to assured self-destruction.

There is little reason to believe that the crack economy or the new gang culture will stop growing, whatever the scale of repression, or stay confined to Southcentral Los Angeles. Although the epicenters remain in the ghetto zones of hard-core youth unemployment – like Watts–Willowbrook, the Athens district, or the Escher-like maze of the Crenshaw 'Jungle' – the gang mystique has spread (as Bakeer documents in *CRIPS*) into middle-class Black areas, where parents are close to panic, or vigilantism.

Meanwhile, as Southcentral itself undergoes an epochal (and surprisingly peaceful) ethnic transition from Black to new immigrant Latino (Mexican and Central American), the kids of the *mojados* look jealously at the power and notoriety of Cripdom.[57] In the absence of any movement towards social justice, the most explosive social contradiction in Los Angeles may become the blocked mobility of these children of the new immigrants. As a 1989 UCLA study revealed, poverty is increasing faster among Los Angeles Latinos, especially youth, than any other urban group in the United States.[58] While their parents may still measure the quality of life by old-country standards, the iron rations of Tijuana or Ciudad Guatemala, their children's self-image is shaped by the incessant stimuli of LA consumer culture. Trapped in dead-end low-wage employment, amid what must otherwise appear as a demi-paradise for white youth, they too are looking for short cuts and magical paths to personal empowerment.

Thus they also enter the underground economy with guns blazing. Some of the Black gangs (especially the Eastside Crips) have accommodated the aspirations of the new immigrants by integrating Latino members (the police estimate at least 1000 of these) or licensing crack-dealing franchises. In the MacArthur Park area, on the other hand, the upstart Salvadoreans of Mara Savatrucha have had to fight a bloody war against the established power of the 18th Street Gang – the largest and fastest-growing Chicano gang which threatens to become the Crips of East LA. But simultaneously in East LA, and throughout all the barrios old and new, traditional gang topography is being radically redrawn by the emergence of a myriad of micro-gangs, more interested in drug sales territories than neighborhood turf in the old-fashioned sense.

Aside from the 230 Black and Latino gangs which the LAPD have identified in the Los Angeles area, there are also 81 Asian gangs, and their numbers are also rapidly growing. In Long Beach, gangs of wild, parentless Cambodian boatchildren terrorize their elders and steal their hoarded gold. While the Filipino Satanas favor Chicano gang styles, the role-model of the Viet Crips (supposedly robbery specialists) is obvious. In Pasadena some Chinese high-school dropouts – unwilling to spend lifetimes as busboys and cooks – ambushed and killed a carload of crack DEA agents, before they too were cut down by a vengeful posse of nearly a hundred crops.[59]

These particular contradictions are rising fast, along a curve asymptotic with the mean ethos of the age. In a post-liberal society, with the gangplanks pulled up and compassion strictly rationed by the federal deficit and the Jarvis Amendment, where a lynchmob demagogue like William Bennett reigns as 'drug czar' – is it any wonder that poor youths are hallucinating on their own desperado 'power trips'? In Los Angeles there are too many signs of approaching helter-skelter: everywhere in the inner city, even in the forgotten poor-white boondocks with their zombie populations of speed-freaks, gangs are multiplying at a terrifying rate, cops are becoming more arrogant and trigger-happy, and a whole generation is being shunted toward some impossible Armageddon.

Notes

1 *Guardian* (New York), 18 May 1988.

2 *Eagle*, 20 March 1946 (Fremont), 25 July 1946 (Manual Arts), 30 January 1947 (Canoga Park), 20 March 1947 (Fremont), 25 September 1947 (Fremont), and 6 October 1949 (John Adams). It should be emphasized that this partial list includes only major incidents or 'riots'.

3 J. K. Obatala, The sons of Watts. Los Angeles *Times, West Magazine*, 13 August 1972.

4 Quoted in Sophia Spalding, The constable blunders: police abuse in Los Angeles's Black and Latino communities, 1945–1965. UCLA, Department of Urban Planning, 1989, unpublished, p. 7.

5 Joseph Woods, The progressives and the police: urban reform and the professionalization of the Los Angeles police, PhD thesis, Department of History, UCLA, 1973, p. 443.

6 Joe Dominick quotes Chief Parker warning a 1965 television audience: 'It is estimated that by 1970 45 per cent of the metropolitan area of Los Angeles will be Negro; if you want any protection for your home and family . . . you're going to have to get in and support a strong police department. If you don't do that, come 1970, God help you.'

7 Spalding, p. 11.

8 Cf. Robert Conot, *Rivers of blood, years of darkness*, New York, 1967, pp. 114–19 (on 'junior criminal' theory); and *Frontier*, July 1958, pp. 5–7 (on Group Guidance); and October 1965, p. 9 (on Parker's elimination of gang counselling); Woods, pp. 494–5, 611 (n. 159).

9 Conot, pp. 97–8; California Advisory Committee to the United States Commission on Civil Rights, *Report on California: Police–Minority Group Relations in Los Angeles and the San Francisco Bay Area*, August 1963, pp. 3–19.

10 Ibid., p. 101; *Times*, 22 October 1972.

11 Obtala.

12 See Robert Fogelson, 'White on Black: Critique of the McCone Commission Report on the Los Angeles riots', in Fogelson, R. (ed.), *Mass violence in America*, New York, 1969, pp. 120–1.

13 Conot, p. 244; the oral history project associated with 'Watts '65: To the Rebellion and Beyond' organized by the Southern California Library for Social Studies and Research is gathering new eye-witness testimony about the Rebellion.

14 *Times*, 19 March and 23 July 1972 (renewal of gang warfare in 1972 contrasted to post-Watts riot period). James O'Toole argues that until the Watts Rebellion politicized the young male gang leadership, 'there was no indigenous political activity within the ghetto except for the matriarch-preacher organizations'. He also claims that the Black vote was 'packaged and delivered from the outside' by middle-class Democratic activists loyal to Jesse Unruh. See *Watts and Woodstock: Identity and culture in the United States and South Africa*, New York, 1973, pp. 87, 89, 91.

15 Obatala; personal reminiscences.

16 Eazy-E quoted in *Times*, Calendar, 2 April 1989.

17 *Times*, 23 July 1972.

18 Donald Bakeer, *CRIPS: The story of the LA street gang from 1971–1985*, xeroxed, Los Angeles, 1987, pp. 12–13.

19 Bob Baker in the *Times*, 26 June 1988.

20 Ibid.

21 Ibid., 24 December 1972.

22 Ibid.

23 On the display of Crip insignia during the Monrovia riots, see ibid. (San Gabriel Valley edition), 2 April 1972. Seven months after the riots (during which one Black seventeen-year-old had his eye shot out by whites), a thirteen-year-old Black child was found hung in his cell in the city jail. (Ibid., 16 November 1972.)

24 Quoted in ibid., 10 April 1988.

25 Ibid., 15 December 1972.

26 For example, at the 1988 'End Barrio War' Conference sponsored by Father Luis Valbuena in Pacoima, twenty-four Valley gangs demanded less police harassment, and more job opportunity and youth recreation as a solution to increasing teenage violence (see ibid., 7 December 1988.)

27 Ibid., 'Watts, 10 years later: a special report', 23 March 1975.

28 Ron Curran, 'Malign neglect: the roots of an urban war zone', *LA Weekly*, 30 December to 5 January 1989, p. 2. Also see the Economic Justice Policy Group, 'Policy memorandum – economic state of the city', presented to the City Council, 25 January 1990, p. 4.

29 See Mark Ridley-Thomas, 'California commentary', *Times*, 29 January 1990. Ridley-Thomas argues that neither the 'office-based' nor 'shopping center-based' models of community redevelopment can compensate for a healthy industrial base.

30 California, Joint Committee on the State's Economy and the Senate Committee on Government Organization, *Problems and opportunities for job development in urban areas of persistent unemployment*, Sacramento, 1982, pp. 29, 50, 58, 94, 108, 111, 115.

31 For a typology of contemporary industrial regimes, see Alain Lipietz, *Mirages and miracles*, London, 1987.

32 This is the official estimate of the church-sponsored South Central Organizing Committee in 1988. For Watts, which has been more regularly surveyed than other areas of the community, youth joblessness (16–24 years old) has stayed near the 50 per cent mark since the early 1970s. (See data collected by UCLA's Institute of Industrial Relations.)

33 *Times*, 16 May 1985. Hundreds of women in the projects who desperately wanted to work were unable to because of the absence of childcare.

34 1983 LA Roundtable for Children; Policy Analysis for California Education, *The conditions of children in California*, Sacramento, 1989.

35 *Times*, 19 April 1988; Paul Bullock, *Youth training and employment from the New Deal to the new federalism*, Institute of Industrial Relations, UCLA, 1985, p. 78.

36 Quoted in ibid., 30 January 1981.

37 Ibid., 30 January 1989.

38 *Times*, 3 August 1988.

39 Ibid., 28 June, 18 October, and 25 November 1987; M. J. Wilcove, 'The dilemma of LA schools', *LA Weekly*, 6–12 November 1987.

40 Cf. *Times*, 20 March 1988; and Jack Foley, 'Leisure Rights' Policies for Los Angeles Urban Impact Parks, Paper presented to the People for Parks Conference, Griffith Park, 4 February 1989.

41 Cf. Paul Bullock, Youth in the labor market, PhD dissertation, UCLA, 1972; *Youth training*; and interview, 1983 (Southern California Library for Social Research). UC Berkeley sociologist Troy Duster has estimated that Black youth unemployment nationally was *four times higher* in 1983 than in 1960. (See social implications of the 'new' Black urban underclass. *Black Scholar*, May–June 1988, p. 3.)

42 New York, 1986, p. 189.

43 Louis Kraar, The drug trade, *Fortune*, 20 June 1988, p. 29.

44 Murderous Colombia, *New York Review of Books*, 20 November 1986, p. 35.

45 Cartel LA series, *Herald-Examiner*, 28 August to 1 September 1989. Also see the *Times*'s account of the 1989 Justice Department report (a 'Dun and Bradstreet primer') – 4 August 1989.

46 The *Herald-Examiner* reassured its readers that 'the 63,000 Colombians living in the Los Angeles area do not all work in cocaine distribution cells' – 'only 6000'.

47 Ibid., 28 August 1987.

48 *Times*, 30 March 1989; Evan Maxwell, Gold, drugs and clean cash. *Los Angeles Times Magazine*, 18 February 1990.

49 *Times*, 15 May and 12 June 1988; 4 August 1989.

50 Ibid.

51 Malcolm Klein and Cheryl Maxson quoted in ibid., 8 September 1988.

52 Quoted in ibid.

53 Ibid. Earnings of the youthful employees of the illicit drug industry have been vastly exaggerated by the police and media, with the inadvertent or deliberate effect of discouraging employment schemes as a realistic alternative to repression. Judging from the most detailed study available (based on extensive surveys among the street trade in Washington DC), youth are more likely to make $700 per month than per day, as usually depicted. See Jack Katz (op-ed.), ibid., 21 March 1990.

54 Ibid., 25 November 1984; 13 February 1989.

55 Novelist Claude Brown quoted in ibid., 17 May 1988.

56 Pasadena *Star-News*, 17 September 1989.

57 The Black population of Southcentral has fallen by 30 per cent since 1980 as families flee crime and economic decay for Inglewood, the Inland Empire or even back to the South. The Latino population, on the other hand, has increased at least 200 per cent (Mayan Indians now live in the Jordan Downs projects) and Black youth are suddenly minorities in the four major high schools. The old Slauson turf of Fremont High, for example, was 96 per cent Black in 1980; it is now 71 per cent Latino (*Times*, 30 March 1990).

58 See Paul Ong (project director), *The widening divide: Income inequality and poverty in Los Angeles*, UCLA, June 1989.

59 *Times*, 1 September 1988. Inter-ethnic gang warfare, surprisingly, remains rare in the gang-saturated Los Angeles inner city. One of the insidious deceits of the film *Colors* is its portrayal of a Black gang attacking Chicanos. Except for an outbreak in the Oakwood section of Venice in the late 1970s (which gang members blamed on the instigation of the LAPD), such a thing has never happened. On the other hand, antagonisms have mounted between Black youth and Asian adults. There have been bloody exchanges between Korean storekeepers and Black teenagers, and in May 1988 there was a pitched battle between Cambodians and local Bloods at the Pueblo del Rio housing project. The Bloods threw Molotov cocktails, while Cambodian men replied with fusillades from M1s and AK47s (ibid., 13 May 1988).

SECTION FOUR

GEOGRAPHICAL REPRESENTATIONS

Editors' introduction

Geographers have traditionally been strong realists, convinced that geographical writings and illustrations objectively portray the world and its workings. Others – artists, poets – might have produced entertaining and fanciful images of landscapes, but these are merely subjective impressions, which might be corrected by comparison with a reliably factual geographical account. The contributions in this section put this confident distinction into doubt. They consider academic geography as one of a number of discourses about the world, from novels to foreign-policy documents. Many of these discourses make factual claims; all are representations which powerfully influence attitudes and actions, including those which physically shape the world (Barnes and Duncan, 1992). There is a politics connoted in the very concept of representation, of speaking on behalf of certain people as well as about parts of the world.

In 'Geography's empire: histories of geographical knowledge', **Felix Driver** considers the 'imaginative geographies' produced in European writings about colonial territories, taking his cue from Edward Said's enormously influential book *Orientalism* (Said, 1978). If parts of Africa were imagined as a 'dark continent' in need of Christian enlightenment, so were the poorer quarters of English cities. What do geographical texts tell us about the contexts in which they were produced? How complicit was geographical theory and practice with colonialism, with heroic forms of masculinity? How should we make sense of the history of geography, its complex links with both practical and poetic endeavours? Driver's essay contributes to a new historiography of geography which looks beyond the usual progressive narratives of professional development to focus on broader contextual issues (see also Livingstone, 1992; Matless, 1992). History for Driver is 'less . . . a prop for the present, than . . . a means of understanding the *distanced* relationship between past and present . . . history as a series of spaces, rather than a single, seamless narrative'.

In 'Geopolitics and discourse: practical geopolitical reasoning in American foreign policy', **Gearóid ÓTuathail** and **John Agnew** look anew at the concept of geopolitics, a concept largely disused and discredited in

Anglo-American academic geography since its use to legitimize the terri-torial ambitions of the Nazi state. Geopolitical reasoning has neverthe-less persisted, in the foreign policies of nation states, notably the United States. ÓTuathail and Agnew analyse geopolitics as a form of discourse or rhetoric in which intellectuals acting for the state powerfully represent the world in stereotypical terms. If the crude us-and-them binaries of the Cold War have fallen with the collapse of the Berlin Wall, others are produced in the face of new developments. The 'imaginative geogra-phies' of Orientalism are being reactivated in the Middle East theatre of conflict. 'Merely to designate an area as "Islamic" is to designate an implicit foreign policy'.

Geography is a highly visual discipline, and maps are arguably its most potent form of depiction. In 'Maps, knowledge and power', **J. B. Harley** considers the role of cartography in representing and regulating the world. Harley's work has been central not only to a revisionary view of cartography, but to the iconographic study of many geographical images (Cosgrove and Daniels, 1988; Barnes and Duncan, 1992). Maps have proved powerful instruments in the acquisition and control of territory, from estates to empires. How might the social meanings and ideological purposes of maps be interpreted? Harley offers a guide to decoding the symbolism of maps from a variety of periods and places, to look critically at such conventions as scale, projection, settlement signs, colouring, and to watch for what is *not* shown, the social landscapes which are erased by the cartographer's art. Maps, in Harley's account, are oppressive, authoritarian representations. But can the power of maps be harnessed for popular ends (Wood, 1992)? The one-inch Ordnance Survey map may have been surveyed with the military in mind, but this century it has been used by ramblers in their thousands, often to gain access to places once the preserve of the rich and powerful. The Ordnance Survey has been an integral part of geographical education for the majority of British schoolchildren. Recently, innovative 'parish maps' have been produced to portray a popular sense of place, to counter the official cartography of domination and development (Crouch and Matless, 1996).

The study of literature by geographers (Pocock, 1981; Mallory and Simpson-Housely, 1987) has unlocked a valuable source, if it has often treated novels and poems in a somewhat myopic way, overlooking the structure of their texts and contexts, for either factual reportage or pro-jections of sensitive feelings. In 'Mapping the modern city: Alan Sillitoe's Nottingham novels', **Stephen Daniels** and **Simon Rycroft** analyse the texts of novels in terms of a wider discursive and social world. In parti-cular they examine the intersection of novel writing with cartography. Sillitoe's portrayal of modernizing, post-war Nottingham is mediated by his passion for maps. This connects the city in his writing with a network of other places, past and present, near and far, real and imaginary. This portrayal of working-class neighbourhoods, especially in *Saturday night and Sunday morning* (1958), finds echoes in many other media representations, particularly the British television soap opera *Coronation Street*. In Sillitoe's novels modern Nottingham appears a place of conflict, even a battleground, not least in relations between men and women. Sillitoe's portrayal of the city is pitted against that produced in official and academic geographies of Nottingham, the image of a coherent, progressive civic community.

The geographical study of pictorial imagery has broadened from maps and paintings to television, film and photography (Burgess and Gold, 1985; Ryan, 1994). In 'Contested global visions: *One-World, Whole-Earth*, and the Apollo space photographs', **Denis Cosgrove** examines two of the most powerful geographical representations in modern times, the photographs of the earth taken during the Apollo space missions of 1968 and 1972. These photographs have been endlessly reproduced in a variety of contexts. They are international icons of the age. Their meanings have proved highly mutable, but two broad symbolic configurations are apparent: an imperial vision of "One World"; an ecological vision of 'Whole Earth'. This double meaning is traced through an 'intertextual' methodology, tracking back and forth between the image on the photograph and other discourses about global thinking. As geographers who study specific places on the ground chart wider worlds of significance, so do geographers who study places in pictures. The challenge is to combine both perspectives, to chart both the material and the imaginary geographies of places (Cosgrove, 1992).

References and further reading

Alfrey, N. and Daniels, S. (eds) 1990: *Mapping the landscape: Essays on art and cartography*. Nottingham: University of Nottingham.

Barnes, T. J. and Duncan, J. S. (eds) 1992: *Writing worlds: Discourse, text and metaphor in the representation of landscape*. London: Routledge.

Burgess, J. and Gold, J. R. (eds) 1985: *Geography, the media and popular culture*. Beckenham: Croom Helm.

Cosgrove, D. 1992: *The Palladian landscape*. Leicester: Leicester University Press.

Cosgrove, D. and Daniels, S. (eds) 1988: *The iconography of landscape: Essays on the symbolic representation, design and use of past environments*. Cambridge: Cambridge University Press.

Crouch, D. and Matless, D. (1996) Refiguring geography: Parish maps of common ground. *Transactions of the Institute of British Geographers* NS 21(1).

Daniels, S. 1993: *Fields of vision: Landscape imagery and national identity in England and the United States*. Cambridge: Polity Press.

Duncan, J. and Ley, D. (eds) 1993: *Place/culture/representation*. London: Routledge.

Gregory, D. 1994: *Geographical imaginations*. Oxford: Basil Blackwell.

Livingstone, D. 1992: *The geographical tradition: Episodes in the history of a contested enterprise*. Oxford: Basil Blackwell.

Matless, D. 1992: A modern stream: water, landscape, modernism, and geography. *Society and Space* 10, 569–88.

Mallory, W. E. and Simpson-Housely, P. (eds) 1987: *Geography and literature: A meeting of the disciplines*. Syracuse, NY: Syracuse University Press.

Pocock, D. C. D. (ed.) 1981: *Humanistic geography and literature*. London: Croom Helm.

Ryan, J. R. 1994: Visualizing imperial geography: Halford Mackinder and the Colonial Office Visual Instruction Committee 1902–11. *Ecumene* 1(2), 157–76.

Said, E. 1978: *Orientalism*. Andover, Hants: Routledge, Chapman & Hall.

Short, J. R. 1991: *Imagined country*. London: Routledge.

Wood, D. 1992: *The power of maps*. London: Routledge.

Wilson, A. 1992: *The culture of nature: North Amerian landscape from Disney to the 'Exxon Valdez'*. Oxford: Basil Blackwell.

17　Felix Driver,
'Geography's Empire: Histories of Geographical Knowledge'

Reprinted in full, save for one illustration, from: *Environment and Planning D: Society and Space* 10, 23–40 (1992)

Although geography has a long and varied past, the idea of a history of geographical knowledge is of relatively recent date. The idea of a critical history of geography is still more recent; indeed, some might argue that it is yet to be formulated. By 'critical history', I mean simply an account which is sensitive to the various ways in which geographical knowledge has been implicated in relationships of power. In this paper, I explore the possibilities and hazards of such a perspective by examining the interplay between colonial power and modern geography during the 'age of empire' (Hobsbawm, 1987). This theme is of more than antiquarian interest, I shall argue, for the age of empire constituted a significant moment in the making of modernity.

Geography's empire: exploring a world in transition

In his essay 'Geography and some explorers', first published in 1924, Joseph Conrad charted three epochs in the history of exploration. The first epoch, of *Geography Fabulous*, he describes as a 'phase of circumstantially extravagant speculation'. It encompasses the fantastic visions of medieval cartography, which, Conrad tells us, 'crowded its maps with pictures of strange pageants, strange trees, strange beasts, drawn with amazing precision in the midst of theoretically-conceived continents' (Conrad, 1926a, p. 3). The coming of the second epoch, of *Geography Militant*, is marked by a rigorous quest for certainty about the geography of the earth; according to Conrad, Captain Cook is its most perfect embodiment. During the nineteenth century, Geography Militant turned from the navigation of the seas to the exploration of landmasses: central Asia, the Polar regions, and the heart of Africa. Initially, Conrad insists, this had the effect of expanding rather than contracting the geographical imagination; in place of 'the dull imaginary wonders of the dark ages' (p. 9) the maps of Geography Militant charted 'exciting spaces of white paper' in the innermost regions of unexplored continents. Yet, as the white spaces succumbed to the dominion of science, the mystery faded; and Geography Militant gave way to *Geography Triumphant*.

Conrad thus describes the genealogy of modern geographical science in the language of both romance and tragedy. Romance, because the explorers of Geography Militant are portrayed as 'adventurous and devoted men . . . conquering a bit of truth here and a bit of truth there, and sometimes swallowed up by the mystery their hearts were so persistently set on unveiling' (1926a, pp. 19–20). And tragedy, because the passage from Geography Militant to Geography

Triumphant marks the irreversible closure of the epoch of open spaces; the end of an era of unashamed heroism. Later explorers are 'condemned to make [their] discoveries on beaten tracks' (Conrad, 1926b, p. 134); or worse, to find their romantic illusions shattered by mere opportunists and fortune hunters. Conrad's description of his own journey to one of the blank spaces which had so inflamed his youthful imagination (the basin of the Congo River, which he navigated in 1890), provides an instance of this sense of disenchantment: 'there was no shadowy friend to stand by my side in the night of enormous wilderness,' he recalls, 'no great haunting memory, but only the unholy recollection of a prosaic newspaper "stunt" and the distasteful knowledge of the vilest scramble for loot that ever disfigured the history of human conscience and geographical exploration' (Conrad, 1926a, p. 25).[1]

Conrad's picture of the history of geography may strike the informed reader as rather too bold in its outline. Yet despite, or perhaps because of, its historical impressionism, his essay does highlight some characteristic features of the modern geographical imagination. The focus on exploration has the virtue of highlighting both the technical dimensions of geography – notably, the arts of triangulation, navigation, and cartography – and its cultural dimensions – notably, the rhetoric and iconography of discovery. These emphases are shared in some of the most innovative of recent writing on the history of the discourses of modern geographical knowledge (compare Cosgrove, 1985; Bann, 1990). Yet Conrad is rather more ambivalent than many of today's commentators when it comes to the political dimensions of modern geography. On the one hand, he is at pains to distance the quest for science from mere lust for commercial or political power (which is not to say he does not recognize science as another form of power). On the other hand, he draws attention to the irony of his own quest for truth in central Africa, during which (according to this story) his youthful dreams of heroism evaporated in the face of other, more harsh realities. This tension between faith in the ideals of the Enlightenment and disenchantment with their wordly, desacralizing effects is an irreducible feature of Conrad's essay. He is not simply writing in praise of a robust, 'manly' science (as one historian of geography has recently interpreted him; Stoddart, 1986, p. 142), but rather in memoriam; for such a science was only possible when there remained open spaces to explore, a horizon to conquer, and an absolute faith in science to cherish. The closing decades of the nineteenth century, as Conrad was keen to emphasize, brought into being an altogether different world.

The world to which Conrad addressed his writing was a rapidly changing one; new technologies, new aspirations, and new relationships were impressing themselves upon the social, economic, and cultural landscapes of the globe. The 'age of empire' was marked by a number of transformations; indeed, during the *fin de siècle*, transformation seemed to be the only constant in a world obsessed by change. In a moment of 'extraordinary uncertainty and indecision on endless questions', as H. G. Wells put it (1902, p. 13), the imagined horizons of time and space were being reshaped.[2] The cultural consequences of this implosion of modernity have recently been explored by a number of geographers and historians (Kern, 1983; Kearns, 1984; Hobsbawm, 1987; Harvey, 1989; Soja, 1989). For some, the rise of modernism between 1880 and 1920 – Conrad's era – was contemporaneous with the subordination of space to time in social theory (Soja, 1989, pp. 31–5). This indictment of the space-devouring 'historicism' of modern social theory finds an echo in current debates over geography and the social sciences. Yet it leaves relatively unexamined the role of space in a whole variety of modern aesthetic, cultural, and political discourses beyond a narrow definition of 'social theory' – in architecture, in the visual and plastic arts, in literature, and in geopolitics, for example (compare Gregory, 1990). In this context, Harvey's bold account of the condition of postmodernity (1989) provides a somewhat less restricted view of the intersections between modernity and the changing experience of space and time. Yet here too, the richness and diversity of these intersections are compromised, by a Marxism which seeks to reduce the cultural dimensions of modernity to the workings of capitalism. The approach here is reminiscent of a remark made by Mandel in his *Delightful murder: A social history of the crime story*. 'Historical materialism', Mandel insists, 'should be applied to all social phenomena. . . . The majesty of this theory – and the proof of its validity – lies precisely in its ability to explain them all' (Mandel, 1984, p. viii). If modernism (never mind postmodernism) has taught us anything it is that such claims must always be viewed with suspicion; no theory is immortal. As has been well observed, 'the universalizing habit by which a system of thought is believed to account for everything too quickly slides into a quasi-religious synthesis' (Said, 1985, p. 143).

The present concern with the cultural shifts of the last *fin de siècle* provides an opportunity for geographers to reconsider the role of their discipline within the various projects of modernity. Whereas Soja claims this period as the decisive moment of geography's subordination, I would suggest an alternative focus on the place that geographical knowledge has had in the construction of modernity. This perspective may lead us to Conrad and Le Corbusier, as well as to Mackinder and to Ratzel; and it will certainly extend beyond the world of the academy, towards the various points where geographical discourse intersects with strategies of power. Such a view embraces more than simply (say) the political and economic functions of colonial geography during the age of empire. For, to take one example, Mackinder's famous account of the geopolitical dilemmas posed by a shrinking globe – in which (by the turn of the century) scarcely a region was left 'for the pegging out of the claim of ownership' (1904, p. 421) – finds parallels in Conrad's speculations on the cultural condition of this inward-looking world. In 1923 Conrad observed that 'Nowadays, many people encompass the globe. . . . The days of heroic travel are gone' (Conrad, 1926b, p. 128). Such remarks frame a wider perspective on the cultural consequences of modernity itself, in an age of 'time–space compression' (Harvey, 1989, p. 240); 'the glance of the modern traveller contemplating the much-surveyed earth beholds in fact a world in a state of transition' (Conrad, 1926b, p. 130).

Conrad explored the nature of this modern 'world in transition' in his novel

Heart of darkness, first published in 1899. This tells the story of a quest (for Kurtz, the mysterious figure who has 'gone native' in the heart of the Congo) which is simultaneously an escape (from the decorous certainties of European civilization). According to one popular reading, the novel is a meditation on the associations of colonial philanthropy and power – the 'merry dance of death and trade' (Conrad, 1988, p. 17) – which commanded the attention of critics of the 'new' imperialism at the turn of the century (Porter, 1968; Brantlinger, 1988). Yet *Heart of darkness* is far from a straightforwardly anti-imperialist novel. Although Conrad lampoons the 'noble enterprise' of the Eldorado Exploring Expedition ('To tear treasure out of the bowels of the land was their desire, with no more moral purpose at the back of it than there is in burglars breaking into a safe'; pp. 31–2), his writing is replete with ambiguities and evasions. The 'horror' of which Kurtz speaks in his dying breath, for example, is never precisely named; in fact, Conrad conspicuously avoids naming names throughout the story. Through its deceptions and mirages, its multiplication of narrators, and above all its impressionist style (Watt, 1976, pp. 48–9), the novel represents the condition of modernity. *Heart of darkness* portrays a world of impressions and illusions, in which conventional certainties (not least the integrity of the narrator) are radically disturbed (Jameson, 1981, pp. 219–24). But, crucially, its vision of modernity also has a space; a space located not within the salons of European culture and civilization, but in the colonial encounter between Europe and the rest of the world (compare Parry, 1983).

Modern geography unmasked?

Delineating the origins of modern geography (as of modernity itself) is no easy task. Some of geography's historians focus on the scientific revolutions of the sixteenth and seventeenth centuries (Livingstone, 1990), whereas others emphasize the philosophers and geographers of the Enlightenment, such as Kant and Humboldt (Glacken, 1967). Here I am concerned with a third moment in the history of geographical knowledge: the institutionalization of geography during the late nineteenth century. This is not to argue that others have misconceived the genealogy of 'modern' geography; modernity surely as a multiplicity of 'origins' which are irreducible to each other (a point which is sometimes forgotten in current debates over postmodernism). Yet the focus on the closing decades of the nineteenth century is particularly appropriate in the present context, as it requires us to acknowledge the practical role of a discipline which found itself embroiled in a world of contracting spaces and expanding ambitions.

The relationships between geography and imperialism have attracted remarkably few historians, particularly where the British empire is concerned (compare Mackay, 1943). The reasons for this neglect are difficult to detect, given the considerable efforts that have made to reappraise the colonial past of allied disciplines, especially anthropology (Leclerc, 1972; Asad, 1973; Stocking, 1987; Said, 1989). Some might regard the lack of sustained critical reflection on geography and empire, in Britain at least, as a sign of the strong hold that the colonial frame of mind has upon the subject. It is as if the writings of our predecessors were so saturated with colonial and imperial themes that to problematize their role is to challenge the very status of the modern discipline. Yet this is perhaps the very thing that needs to be done if geographers are to exploit present intellectual and political opportunities. Such a critique need not result in mere handwringing; indeed, it might point us towards alternative roles for geographers in the future. What better justification for our historians?[3]

One of the few explicitly critical attempts to wrestle with geography's colonial past (in the English-speaking world) is Hudson's essay 'The new geography and the new imperialism' (Hudson, 1977). In this paper, Hudson notes the close chronological correspondence between the birth of modern geography and the emergence of a new phase of capitalist imperialism during the 1870s (compare Schneider, 1990). The relationship between geography and empire is defined in starkly instrumental terms; the new geography, Hudson argues, was promoted largely 'to serve the interests of imperialism in its various aspects including territorial acquisition, economic exploitation, militarism and the practice of class and race domination' (1977, p. 12). European geographers frequently associated their discipline with the perceived needs of empire; geography was claimed as an aid to statecraft. Representatives of the leading geographical societies were not slow to pronounce upon the worldly significance of their discipline. In 1899 Thomas Holdich (a military surveyor and future President of the Royal Geographical Society) declared (Holdich, 1899, p. 466).

> Truly, this period in our history has been well defined as the boundary-making era. Whether we turn to Europe, Asia, Africa or America, such an endless vista of political geography arises before us, such a vast area of land and sea to be explored and developed; such a vision of great burdens for the white man to take up in far-off regions, dim and indefinite as yet.

Geographical knowledge was thus represented as a tool of empire, enabling both the acquisition of territory and the exploitation of resources. In addition, Hudson maintains, geographical science lent ideological credibility to ideologies of imperialism and racism, especially through the discourses of environmental determinism. The latter claim has been developed by Peet, in his wide-ranging essay on 'the social origins of environmental determinism' (Peet, 1985). For Peet, the notion of environmental determinism (particularly in its neo-Lamarckian form) functioned to legitimize both the ideological claims of imperialism and the scientific claims of geography itself. The geography of Semple, Mackinder, and Ratzel, he argues, served primarily to 'legitimate the expansionary power of the fittest' (p. 327); only when it became 'dysfunctional' to capitalist imperialism, Peet maintains, did environmental determinism lose its sway over geographical thought.

The writings of Hudson and Peet issue an important challenge to those who would tell the story of geography's past in naively idealistic terms. They locate this history firmly in the material world; geographical ideas are put firmly in their place, interpreted as merely reflections or functions of material needs.

Yet such accounts beg a variety of important questions. Any viable attempt to place geographical knowledge within the discourses of colonialism must surely acknowledge that the 'age of empire' was constituted in complex ways, culturally and politically, as well as economically. As Hobsbawm has remarked, 'economic development is not a sort of ventriloquist with the rest of history as its dummy' (1987, p. 62). Geography during the 'age of empire' was more than simply a tool of capitalism, if only because imperialism was never merely about economic exploitation. There are significant aspects of the culture of imperialism – its representations of masculinity, for example – which deserve much more attention from the historians of modern geography than they have yet received. The fears and fantasies surrounding the notion of masculinity during the age of empire have recently been explored by a number of cultural historians (Green, 1980; Mangan, 1986; Mangan and Walvin, 1987, Richards, 1989). The heroes of the colonial landscape – the explorer, the hunter, the soldier, the missionary, the administrator, the gentleman – were all gendered in particular ways, providing moral models for a generation of empire builders. Geographical knowledge, in the broadest sense, was inevitably shaped by and through such figures. Conrad's ideal of Geography Militant, for example, was hypnotized by a particular vision of manly heroism under threat. The spectre of physical and moral degeneration in the modern, urban world was also an important stimulus for Mackinder; his obsession wth the training of 'manpower' fused a concern about the enfeeblement of race with the geopolitics of empire (Mackinder, 1905). Baden-Powell's Boy Scout movement (Geography Militant on a small scale?) was yet another response to this overwhelming sense of malaise (Warren, 1987; Jeal, 1989). These attempts to negotiate the contemporary crises of masculinity had very different origins; yet they converged in important ways upon questions of geography. Contemporary writings on 'geography' were infused with assumptions about gender, as well as empire; to ignore the former is necessarily to misinterpret the latter.

Broadening the scope of the critical history of geography during the age of empire would allow us to consider more directly the cultural and political dimensions of geographical knowledge during this period. This is not necessarily to abandon a materialist approach; the development of 'knowledge' would instead be grasped as a situated social practice rather than a spontaneous reflex of the imperatives of economic development. Peet's (1985) analysis of the new geography is in fact mainly concerned with the ideas of 'great men' rather than the contexts in which they lived and worked; Herbert Spencer, for example, is described as the 'godfather' of modern geography. In this account, concepts such as 'social Darwinism' appear to tower like storm clouds over the discursive practices of humble geographers. Yet, notwithstanding the current vogue for 'contextual' history, comparatively little is known about the ways in which geographical knowledge was socially constituted. There remains considerable scope for more contextually sensitive studies of geographical societies and related institutions, both metropolitan and peripheral (compare Schneider, 1990; MacKenzie, 1992). The activities of the Royal Geographical Society (RGS), to take one example, were clearly shaped, in a general sense, by Britain's imperial role. However, one ought not to prejudge the nature and extent of this role simply by referring to the most quotable pronouncements of prominent Fellows. At the very least, these statements need to be set alongside the activities of armies of anonymous cartographers, navigators, surveyors, and explorers, whose practical labours in Europe and at the imperial frontier were vital to the projects of colonialism.

The irony of Peet's apparently materialist account of the concept of environmental determinism is that it presents the history of ideas in an excessively abstract, disembodied way, leaving an enormous gulf between the level of the theoretical and the level of the practical. This seems to reflect a particular interpretation of what a 'contextual' approach demands. The 'context' envisaged by both Peet and Hudson is provided by a version of the theory of imperialism as a 'higher stage' of capitalism, refracted through contemporary social thought. The problem, as they see it, is to show how geography was 'functional' to the evolution of capitalism; all else is secondary. This approach reproduces many of the more general problems encountered by functionalism in social theory. It tends to neglect the antecedents of particular ideas (environmental determinism, racism, etc.), portraying them instead as functional responses to the needs of the moment; it homogenizes whole domains of knowledge, reducing them to a single function, or family of functions (such as the reproduction of capitalism); and it fails to ask how (and whether) particular knowledges actually do fulfil the claims made for them (compare Bridges, 1982). It is certainly important to recognize the extent to which geographical knowledge was represented in instrumental terms towards the end of the nineteenth century, although the supposed novelty of these associations might be questioned. After all, the scientific empire commanded by institutions such as the RGS during the mid-nineteenth century was truly global in its scope. Stafford's recent study of Roderick Murchison, for example, suggests that science and empire were so intertwined in his career that it is difficult to say where one ended and the other began (Stafford, 1989). The RGS had long provided the government with intelligence for the management and defence of the empire. As one perspicacious observer of '*scientific London*' put it in 1874 (Becker, 1874, pp. 332–3).

> the military and civil servants of Her Majesty well appreciate the value of the Society's map room. No sooner does a squabble occur – in Ashanti, Abyssinia or Atchin – than government departments make a rush to Savile Row and lay hands on all matter relating to that portion of the globe which happens to be interesting for the moment.

Yet this is not to say that geography served one and only one function; nor that its colonial fantasies were uncontested (compare Driver, 1991). Indeed, we cannot specify in advance the extent to which geographical knowledge (as opposed to other kinds of knowledge or power) actually was instrumental within the imperial project.

These arguments raise broader issues concerning the nature of 'contextual' interpretation which are of fundamental importance for historians of geography.

As Livingstone has recently observed, what once served as a flag of convenience for the new history of geography now cries out for further elaboration (Livingstone, 1990, p. 368). My own comments above are concerned with a particularly mechanistic view of the relationship between texts and their contexts, whereby texts simply reflect and reproduce some more fundamental, non-textual reality. There are many possible alternatives to this approach, which veers towards a now discredited base–superstructure model of culture (compare Bennett, 1987; Daniels 1989). There are those, inspired by the models of poststructuralist literary theory (and the work of Derrida in particular), who would abandon altogether the attempt to correlate texts with some non-textual reality. This position – adopted in some, but by no means in all, postmodernist quarters – commonly attracts the criticism that by confining itself within the bounds of textuality, it creates its own version of internal functionalism (Said, 1983, pp. 44–57). One escape route from the self-referential world of the text is provided by Jameson, who represents texts as socially symbolic acts, creating imaginary resolutions of determinate material contradictions. Jameson's oft-quoted injunction 'Always historicize!' (1981, p. 9) is intended not as a licence for a crude materialism, but as a reminder of the historicity both of texts and of interpretations (compare Gregory, 1990). Texts are read as unstable reworkings of historical contexts which they themselves help to generate. Jameson's 'history' is emphatically not just another text, even though it may not be directly accessible to us (Jameson, 1981). This insistence on historicity is echoed in the work of Said (to be discussed below), although he is far more sceptical than Jameson about the theoretical self-sufficiency of Marxism. Said insists that texts cannot be isolated from the circumstances which made them possible and which render them intelligible: 'My position is that texts are worldly, to some degree they are events, and, even when they appear to deny it, they are nevertheless a part of the social world, human life, and of course the historical moments in which they are located and interpreted' (Said, 1983, p. 4).

Imaginative geographies and worldly texts

I have suggested that we need to do more thinking about the way geographical knowledge is constituted, and the various forms it takes, before we venture, if we do at all, on to the treacherous terrain of functional argument. Said's work is of particular interest in this context, not least because his extraordinary book *Orientalism* (1978) is so full of insights for historians of geographical knowledge. Said highlights some of the key dilemmas facing those who wish to maintain a critical attitude towards the history of European knowledge about the non-European world. On the one hand, his critique of the discourse of Orientalism represents Western humanism itself as an accomplice in the project of colonialism. On the other, he refuses to abandon the critical legacy of the Enlightenment altogether, always in his writings emphasizing the possibility of emancipation. (No wonder, then, that he responds to the word 'humanist' with 'contradictory feelings of affection and revulsion' (Said, 1985,

p. 135).) Said is thus of considerable interest to critical historians of geography. Although he shares the suspicion towards metanarratives that we now (too readily?) associate with postmodernism, he refuses to abandon that emancipatory impulse we associate with the Enlightenment.

Once it is accepted that texts do not merely 'reflect' the demands of the material world, the problem of representation becomes an important issue. It provides the starting point for Said's *Orientalism*, in which he attempts to map the 'imaginative geography' of the Orient as it has been represented in a range of scholarly, administrative, and popular texts. The recurring motif of the discourse of Orientalism, he argues, is an opposition between Europe ('the West') and the Orient; the one rational, mature, and normal, the other irrational, backward, and depraved. For Said, the construction of this discourse is in itself a process of appropriation, of colonization, which inspires (as much as it 'reflects') more worldly forms of colonial expansion. Significantly, in the present context, he argues that geographical knowledge constitutes a critical axis of the entire colonial process. 'We would not have had empire itself', he has claimed, 'without important philosophical and imaginative processes at work in the production as well as the acquisition, subordination and settlement of space' (1989, p. 216). The process of exploration, for example, did not merely overcome distance; it created 'imaginative geographies'. The explorers 'conquered' truth (to borrow one of Conrad's most telling formulations) not because they exposed the inner secrets of the regions in which they travelled, but rather because they established particular ways of reading these landscapes.

At one level, *Orientalism* provides a critique of what one might call geographical essentialism: the idea that 'there are geographical spaces with indigenous, radically "different" inhabitants who can be defined on the basis of some religion, culture, or racial essence proper to that geographical space' (Said, 1978, p. 322; cf. Ashley, 1987). The essential Orient, Said argues, is a myth, the product of a variety of discourses originating in the West; a 'stage on which the whole East is confined' (1978, p. 63). *Orientalism* reminds us that the representation of the Other (places, people, races, gender) is intimately bound up with notions of the self; Europe defines itself through its representation of the Orient. Furthermore, this process of representation is simultaneously cultural and political; it thus renders impossible any absolute distinction between 'knowledge' (ideas, concepts, texts) and 'power' (strategies, institutions, contexts). Scholars created imaginative geographies which themselves implied and depended upon a relationship of power between Europe and its other; statesmen were able to speak about the Orient in the way they did because it had already been represented in the texts of scholars. 'To say that Orientalism was a rationalization of colonial rule is to ignore the extent to which colonial rule was justified in advance by Orientalism, rather than after the fact' (Said, 1978, p. 39). The cultural and scientific supports of the 'new imperialism' were, after all, not so new (Brantlinger, 1988; Stafford, 1989).

A number of recent studies have been concerned with the production of 'imaginative geographies' (Pratt, 1985; Brantlinger, 1988; Bishop, 1989;

Heffernan, 1989; Youngs, 1990). Many of these have examined the processes by which images and fantasies about the colonial world were created within the texts of geographers, soldiers, missionaries, anthropologists, novelists, and administrators. Of particular concern are the idioms, figures, and styles employed within these texts, as well as the different genres to which they belonged; for these defined what could be said (and how) in particular fields. Thornton (1983), for example, distinguishes between the monographs of anthropologists in the metropole and the ethnographical narratives on which they depended. Whereas the former were generally modelled on the 'objective' pattern of the natural sciences, the latter depended on the fiction of a more direct relationship between narrator and reader. Equally, some themes clearly cut across different genres of colonial writing. The myth of Darkest Africa, to take one example, permeated a vast range of literature in the colonial period and beyond. In his analysis of its genealogy, Brantlinger pays particular attention to the duplicity of the rhetoric of 'exploration'; as he remarks, 'Africa grew "dark" as Victorian explorers, missionaries and scientists flooded it with light' (Brantlinger, 1985, p. 166; cf. Curtin, 1965). The iconography of light and darkness, which embodied powerful images of race, science, and religion, portrayed the European penetration of the continent of Africa as *simultaneously* a process of domination, Enlightenment, and liberation. The rhetoric of the 'dark continent' was not without its ironies, however, as Conrad (among others) recognized.[4] Indeed, the metaphor of lightness–darkness could occasionally be turned against itself:

> You may say that by our commercial relations with African tribes we must surely have let in light. I reply, if it be so, it is the blaze of the burning village, or the flash of the Winchester rifle – at best it is the glare from the smoke-stack of the Congo steamer bearing away tons upon tons of ivory.
>
> (Waller, 1891, cited in Driver, 1991, p. 164).

For the vast majority of the world's population, Thornton argues, 'the discovery of Africa . . . was a discovery on paper' (1983, p. 505). Alongside the written word, however, visual representations played an important role in the construction of these 'imaginative geographies'. Explorers' tales were lavishly illustrated with images of fabulous creatures, awe-inspiring landscapes, and daring deeds. Exhibitions of colonial booty and travellers' ephemera quite literally staged the drama of empire, constructing a symbolic geography which simultaneously reinforced the distance between the subjects and consumers of these images (Greenhalgh, 1988). The camera itself was an important agent of this process of colonial appropriation (Banta and Hinsley, 1986; Tagg, 1988), not simply recording the experiences of travellers, but bringing them into the drawing rooms of the Home Counties. Photographs captured the sites and scenes of empire for permanent display, and technological innovation allowed for the mass production and distribution of relatively cheap colonial images.[5] In *The Queen's Empire*, a vast photographic tribute celebrating Victoria's Diamond Jubilee in 1897, readers could see for themselves the moral and economic geography of empire; from 'Treaty-making in East Africa', 'Dressing cane in

Malaya', 'Drying cocoa in Trinidad', and 'Cutting bananas in Jamaica', to 'The playing fields of Eton' (Arnold-Foster, 1897). Such images claimed to represent the world as it really was; each person, each race, in their own place.

Said's *Orientalism* is probably the single most important inspiration for recent work on the genealogy of such 'imaginative geographies'. In large measure, the popularity of the book (and indeed notoriety, in some circles) may be attributed to Said's attempt to repoliticize the apparently unpolitical. Although Said admits that 'most attempts to rub culture's nose in the mud of politics have been crudely iconoclastic' (1978, p. 13), he consistently warns against the analytical compartmentalization of culture and power. In the context of the discourses of Orientalism, for example, 'Europe was always in a position of strength, not to say domination. There is no way of putting this euphemistically' (1978, p. 40). This frankness echoes a famous remark in Conrad's *Heart of darkness*; 'The conquest of the earth, which means taking it away from those who have a different complexion or slightly flatter noses than ourselves, is not a pretty thing when you look into it too much' (Conrad, 1988, p. 10). Said acknowledges that it is not enough just to say this; 'it needs to be worked through analytically and historically' (1978, p. 123). Yet Said's attempt to do just this, for all its brilliance and audacity, faces a number of fundamental dilemmas. First, there is a problem of *representation*, in the political sense of speaking on behalf of others. On the one hand, the argument of *Orientalism* amounts to a passionate restatement of the values of liberal humanism; by exposing the consequences of Orientalism, the critic is able to build new and less oppressive visions of the oriental other. On the other hand, however, *Orientalism* undermines the very foundations on which (Western) humanism was built; namely, the power of the enlightened self to speak the truth of the Other in the name of science. The second problem, of *agency*, emerges in Said's treatment of the role of the individual author within the discourse(s) of Orientalism. On the one hand, he emphasizes the singular importance of the writings of particular figures (Ernest Renan, Gustave Flaubert, and Richard Burton, for example); on the other hand, he appears to deny them the possibility of escape from the swamps of Orientalism. (It should be noted that these problems of representation and agency are acknowledged, often highlighted, by Said himself. Indeed, some would regard them less as failings of method than as inescapable features of the modern human sciences as a whole.)

To speak of Said's work in these terms is immediately to raise the issue of his relationship to the philosophical discourses of postmodernism.[6] The postmodern challenge has frequently been expressed as a revulsion against metanarratives (such as those found within Orientalism) which dissolve the flux of social life in the name of totalizing theory. Suspicious of transcendental themes such as the Progress of History, the Destiny of the West, or the Inevitability of Revolution, it reinstates local differences, divergences, and misunderstandings; it celebrates the collision of levels and desires, rather than their resolution (Guattari, 1984). Postmodernists would thus interpret Orientalism as one of the master narratives of modernity. They are faced, however, with an immediate problem: how is it possible to write a critical history of

Orientalism which avoids the very essentialism it seeks to expose? For Said's own account of Orientalism might itself be (mis)conceived as a grand narrative, drawing local and individual differences into its vision of a governing structure of cultural power. There is an intriguing parallel to be drawn between this reading of *Orientalism* and a common (mis)reading of Foucault's account of 'panopticism' in *Discipline and punish* (1977). In both cases, the authors' emphasis on the heterogeneity of modern discursive regimes is compromised by readings which portray their effects as emanations of an essential master discourse. It should be admitted that such readings cannot entirely be dismissed as misreadings. In *Discipline and punish*, as Said himself points out, Foucault's account of panopticism appears to sweep all the different modalities of power – such as the normative structures of modern law – before it (Driver, 1985, pp. 436–8; cf. Said, 1983, pp. 244–6; Habermas, 1987, pp. 288–90; Fraser, 1989).

Debates over Foucault's method and politics thus have important implications for our reading of the work of Said. If Foucault's critique of totalizing models of power is taken at all seriously, it is necessary to maintain a distinction between different kinds of domination. Read in this light, the subject of *Orientalism* would not be power in general, but a variety of powers, geopolitical, authorial, disciplinary, cultural, and military. The force of Said's argument demands that the boundaries between these powers be occasionally blurred; but to erase them altogether would surely remove our capacity to make necessary and important distinctions. We also need to be more sensitive to the specific features of discursive regimes in different periods and places; 'Orientalism' (just as much as 'panopticism') must not serve as a flag of convenience, in place of contextually sensitive historical and geographical research. Said recognizes the differences between the French and the English models of Orientalism, for example; we might also consider the various ways in which discursive regimes diffuse across the boundaries of particular spaces, whether these are institutional, political, or cultural (cf. Driver, 1990). There is also the question of (internal) 'resistance' to the canons of Orientalism, which I would regard as a special case of a more general characteristic of such discursive regimes; namely, their heterogeneity. Although it is true, as Said maintains, that the very existence of Orientalism is inseparable from the unequal (colonial) relationship between Europe and the Orient (which is why Orientalism is not matched by an equally powerful discourse of Occidentalism), this does not mean that all orientalists shared the same visions and ideals. The history of European discourse about the non-European world was punctuated by successive controversies over the purposes and effects of colonialism, and the differences these disputes reveal are more than simply tangential to the history of colonialism. At one level, Said suggests, they may be portrayed as differences over means rather than ends,[7] in so far as the right of the European to speak for the colonized is so rarely questioned. Yet there is surely a violence done to the history of the colonial encounter when such divergences are suppressed altogether. Methodologically, the study of particular moments of domestic controversy, such as those concerning the bloody suppression of the Jamaican insurrection by Governor Eyre in 1865 (Semmel, 1962), the violence of Stanley's methods of exploration in central Africa (Driver, 1991), or the missionary debate over Islam in Africa during the late 1880s (Prasch, 1989), may be particularly illuminating, precisely because they expose important contradictions and tensions within the contemporary scientific, political, and philanthropic discourses of colonialism.

In considering the impact of Said's work upon the history of geography, it is also necessary to acknowledge our relative ignorance about the processes by which 'imaginative geographies' become commercialized and popularized. Recent studies of geography and popular culture (Burgess and Gold, 1985) have established a new agenda for the historian of geographical knowledge; and the postmodern concern with popular knowledges gives this agenda particular currency (cf. McRobbie, 1989). Although we are beginning to learn a lot about the production of geographical images, stereotypes, and myths, especially in the context of imperialism (cf. Curtin, 1965; Glendenning, 1973; Bell, 1982; MacKenzie, 1984; Richards, 1989), we know far less about the ways in which such images are handled by their 'consumers'. To speak of 'production' and 'consumption' is particularly appropriate in the present context, because the age of empire was so closely associated with the intensification of mass consumption and commodification in general. Explorers such as Henry Morton Stanley (significantly, a journalist turned geographer) promoted the exploitation of Africa in directly commercial and populist terms. In *How I found Livingstone*, for example, Stanley (1872, pp. 681–2) asserts that:

> It is simply a question of money, which is the sinew of all enterprises. With a sufficient supply of it all Africa can be explored easily. Not only explored, but conquered and civilized. Not only civilized, but intersected by railroads from one end to the other, through and through.

Stanley's imaginative geographies sold very well indeed. Even the title of his last major work, *In darkest Africa*, 1890, became a much sought-after commodity, repackaged in a dozen different forms from *Darkest England* to *Darkest New York* (Stanley, 1909, p. 411; see Nord, 1987). During 1890 Stanley's own (adopted) name was used to promote an impressive range of more mundane commodities, from Bovril to soap (Opie, 1985). There is surely a need for historical studies of the diverse ways in which such images were represented and reinterpreted; in Stanley's case, for example, it is clear that although he was a 'household name', he was certainly not universally admired. 'Dr Livingstone I presume?' became a popular joke rather than (as Stanley had intended in 1871) a momentous symbol; and his subsequent attempts to portray himself as almost the archetype of what Conrad later called Geography Militant were undermined by those who chose to represent his exploits in comic rather than heroic terms. The story of Stanley's mixed reputation (Driver, 1991) has more general implications for historians of geographical knowledge. The terms 'popularization' and 'commercialization' in fact stand for complex processes which remain almost entirely neglected. My suspicion is that there is much more to be said about the ways in which individuals remake the symbolic geographies they are sold. What is needed, in sum, is greater attention to the ways in which geographical knowledge is presented, represented, and misrepresented.

Choosing histories: some general questions

In much of this paper I have been concerned with a particular moment in the making of modern geographical knowledge. By way of a conclusion, I should like to consider some of the more general political and epistemological issues raised in the writing of the history of geography.

Why are histories of geographical knowledge necessary at all, in these (post)modern times? Some critics would complain that disciplinary histories all too frequently serve to legitimize the present. The concerns of the present are thus given historical roots, or even an evolutionary justification; those of the past, so the argument goes, are either co-opted as 'precursors' of their successors, or dismissed as products of a discarded prescientific imagination. This is, admittedly, to caricature the standard disciplinary history; yet it is remarkable just how much of the history of geography has been written in this way. The story of exploration, for example, has frequently been interpreted as the gradual triumph of modern (European) geographical science over the mysteries of the earth, the great explorers synthesizing the fragments of knowledge gathered by their predecessors. Critics of Whiggish histories of exploration have been among the keenest advocates of alternative 'contextual' perspectives (Livingstone, 1984). This term suggests a rather different vision of the history of geography; less as a prop for the present, than as a means of understanding the *distanced* relationship between past and present. In place of the continuous lines of progressivist history, it substitutes a landscape of discontinuity; history as a series of spaces, rather than a single, seamless narrative. The contextual approach to the history of geography is thus more concerned with mapping the lateral associations and social relations of geographical knowledge than with constructing a vision of the overall evolution of the modern discipline. It demands a far more historically (and geographically) sensitive approach to the production and consumption of knowledge than that provided by more conventional narrative histories.

The apparent triumph of the 'contextual' approach has not met with universal acclaim among historians of geography, however. As I have suggested in this paper, there is considerable room for debate over the precise nature of the 'contexts' which are supposed to give meaning to geography's past. In similar vein, Livingstone has recently argued against any attempt to 'privilege' either side of the 'equation' between text and context (Livingstone, 1990, page 368). Here, he objects to a very particular version of 'contextual' history, in which ideas and concepts are regarded as unproblematic reflections or functions of some extratextual real world. Others, perhaps in the name of poststructuralism, might abandon the 'equation' altogether, refusing any attempt to move 'beyond' the text. The polemical confrontation between conventional Marxism and poststructuralism has entrenched such alternatives, as if texts *either* fulfilled a narrow range of determinate functions transparently dictated by the workings of capitalism *or* belonged to some pure space of discourse beyond the world, beyond history and geography. Such a polarity places false limits on the ways in which 'contextual' history might be written and read, because it represents the problem of interpretation in terms of a choice for or against 'history'. In reality, however, the choice we face is not whether to historicize, but *how* to do so (Bennett, 1987).

It is at this point that we must grasp a rather different nettle; less the world of the text than the worldly role of the historian. It is in the narrating of history that 'equations' between texts and contexts are drawn up and dissolved, an imaginative process which always involves choices of various kinds. Representing geography's past is inevitably an act of the present, however much we attempt to commune with the past.[8] Indeed, the idea of mapping the historical landscape depends on the construction of perspective, a view from the present, around which the panoramas of history are made to revolve. Yet 'contextual' history sometimes appears to deny this fact. Indeed, it might be argued that the ultimate fiction of 'contextual' history consists less in its separation of 'texts' and 'contexts', than in its continual silence on the mediating role of the historian. This is all the more surprising in view of the role that historical writing has played in the formation and legitimation of political projects of many kinds during the twentieth century. E. P. Thompson, for example, has famously argued that history is all about choices, in its writing as well as in its making (Thompson, 1978, p. 234).

> 'Our vote [as historians] will change nothing. And yet, in another sense, it may change everything. For we are saying that these values, and not those other values, are the ones which make this history meaningful *to us*, and that these are the values which we intend to enlarge and sustain in our own present. If we succeed, then we reach back into history and endow it with our own meanings: we shake Swift by the hand'.

It is difficult to imagine a more eloquent defence of the modern version of a critical history. In the context of the history of geography, similar stances have been taken up by those who would rescue individuals such as Kropotkin and Reclus from the 'enormous condescension of posterity' (Thompson, 1968, p. 12; see Stoddart, 1986, p. 128; Soja, 1989, p. 4; Lowe and Short, 1990, pp. 5–6).

Postmodernists would wish to qualify, perhaps reject, such a stance. Does it replay the old game of legitimizing present projects by reference to authoritative ancestors? Does it treat figures like Kropotkin and Reclus as totems of an 'alternative' contemporary geography of which they are hardly prophets? Should we be suspicious of all attempts to construct countertraditions in which the very notion of a 'tradition' remains unchallenged? Such questions deserve attention, particularly in the light of the changing fortunes of Marxist social history in Great Britain and elsewhere. The grand narratives of conventional Marxist history seem quite simply to have fallen apart in the wake of the political and intellectual shifts of the past fifteen years. Of all the critics of

Marxist history, it is probably the most reluctant – Foucault – who has had the greatest impact in Britain and North America. In his writing, the past is no longer a continuous terrain in which the historian can shake hands with the subjects of history; it is instead a surface of discontinuities, radical breaks, and fissures; it lacks depth, roots, or underlying structures, and there is no privileged vantage point from which to survey the whole; only a cloud darkening the brightness of the Enlightenment project. Foucault's history, like Nietzsche's, is tragic; it tells a story of domination in the name of emancipation.

And yet, this critique of critiques ultimately leaves us no basis on which to choose or to act. It refuses to tell us what should be valued (a moral question) or what should be done (a political question). At its extreme, as others have shown (Fraser, 1989), it can disable the very idea of a critical project. In hailing the end of a particular history, it risks lending credence to clearly ideological pronouncements about 'The end of history' (Fukuyama, 1989), as if the failure of one orthodoxy amounted to the erasure of all other historical possibilities. Fukuyama's paean to the 'triumph of the West' demands a response from those who emphasize the possibility and necessity of emancipatory politics. The work of Said is particularly relevant in this context, not least because his writings unashamedly embrace moral and political questions, in a way rarely emulated elsewhere in the world of the academy. In one respect, Said's writings belong to the philosophical discourses of postmodernity, in the sense that he is so critical of the worldly role of the modern humanities, the heirs of the Enlightenment (Said, 1985), and is so keen for us to listen to other voices. Equally, however, he is frankly suspicious of what he calls the 'aesthetic response' which has characterized the postmodern turn in many of the human sciences, especially anthropology (Said, 1989). Not all would agree with Said that 'poetics [are] a good deal easier to talk about than politics' (1989, pp. 220–1); yet his insistence on the need to make political choices provides a powerful counterpoint to current drifts within postmodernist writing. One suspects that for Said, as much as for Habermas (1985), modernity is 'an incomplete project'.

Geography's history, like historical writing of all kinds, presents us with various choices, both in its execution and in its interpretation. The choice between these various routes through geography's past cannot be an absolute one, and it would be wrong to see them as mutually exclusive in all circumstances. As Habermas laments, postmodernism (in its more abandoned moments) 'exacts a high price for taking leave of modernity' (1987, p. 336); and yet its critiques of the master narratives of the Enlightenment (including Orientalism) have the effect of vastly enlarging our vision of possible geographies and their histories. Retaining and exploiting the tension between these alternatives is one of the most challenging tasks faced by contemporary historians of geographical knowledge.

Notes

1 Here Conrad refers to the publicity surrounding Stanley's search for Livingstone, and his subsequent role in the scramble for Africa (see also Golanka, 1985; Driver, 1991).

2 Wells's hope that science might conquer even the future – an 'impenetrable, incurable, perpetual blackness' (1902, p. 34) – evokes the symbolism of Conrad's *Heart of darkness*, without its sense of irony.

3 Some postmodernists might object to such a modern justification for the practice of history. I will discuss this in the concluding section.

4 Conrad's attitude to race is, however, the subject of fierce debate: see Achebe (1988); Brantlinger (1988).

5 Alloula describes the colonial postcard as the 'poor man's phantasm' (Alloula, 1987, p. 4).

6 I return to this question in the concluding section below.

7 This was Said's response to a question at his Raymond Williams Memorial Lecture in October 1989 (Said, 1990).

8 Thus exhibition or museum displays which represent other people, times, and places inevitably raise (political) questions about who is being represented by whom (see Karp and Lavine, 1991).

References

Achebe, C. 1988: An image of Africa: racism in Conrad's *Heart of darkness*. In Kimbrough, R. (ed.), Conrad, J. *Heart of darkness*, New York: W. W. Norton, 251–62.

Alloula, M. 1987: *The colonial harem*. Manchester: Manchester University Press.

Arnold-Foster, H. 1987: *The Queen's Empire*. London: Cassell.

Asad, T. (ed.) 1973: *Anthropology and the colonial encounter*. London: Ithaca.

Ashley, R. K. 1987: The geopolitics of geopolitical space. *Alternatives* 12, 403–34.

Bann, S. 1990: From Captain Cook to Neil Armstrong: colonial exploration and the structure of landscape. In Pugh, S. (ed.), *Reading landscape: Country – city – capital*. Manchester: Manchester University Press, 214–30.

Banta, M. and Hinsley, C. 1990: *From site to sight: Anthropology, photography and the power of imagery*. Cambridge, MA: Peabody Museum Press.

Becker, B. 1874: *Scientific London* (Henry King, London)

Bell, L. 1982: Artists and empire: Victorian representation of subject peoples. *Art History* 5, 73–86.

Bennett T, 1987: Texts in history: the determinations of readings and their texts. In Attridge, D., Bennington, G. and Young, R. (eds), *Post-structuralism and the question of history*. Cambridge: Cambridge University Press, 63–81.

Bishop, P. 1989: *The myth of Shangri-La*. London: Athlone Press.

Brantlinger, P. 1985: Victorians and Africans: the genealogy of the myth of the Dark Continent. *Critical Inquiry* 12, 166–203.

Brantlinger, P. 1988: *Rule of darkness: British literature and imperialism, 1830–1914*. Ithaca, NY: Cornell University Press.

Bridges, R. C. 1982: The historical role of British explorers in East Africa. *Terrae Incognitae* 14, 1–21.

Burgess, J. and Gold, J. (eds) 1985: *Geography, the media and popular culture*. Andover: Croom Helm.

Conrad, J. 1926a: Geography and some explorers. In Curle, R. (ed.), *Last essays*. London: Dent, 1–31.

Conrad, J. 1926b: Travel. In Curle, R. (ed.), *Last essays*. London: Dent, 121–34.

Conrad, J. 1988: *Heart of darkness*. Kimbrough, R. (ed.) New York: W. W. Norton, 7–76.

Cosgrove, D. 1985: Prospect, perspective and the evolution of the landscape idea. *Transactions of the Institute of British Geographers* 10, 45–62.

Curtin, P. 1965: *The image of Africa: british ideas and action, 1780–1850*. London: Macmillan.

Daniels, S. 1989: Marxism, culture and the duplicity of landscape. In Peet, R. and Thrift, N. (eds), *New models in geography*. London: Unwin Hyman, 2, 196–220.

Driver, F. 1985: Power, space, and the body: a critical assessment of Foucault's *Discipline and punish*. *Environment and Planning D: Society and Space* 3, 425–446.

Driver, F. 1990: Discipline without frontiers? *Journal of Historical Sociology* 3, 272–93.

Driver, F. 1991: Henry Morton Stanley and his critics: geography, exploration and empire. *Past and Present* 133, 134–66.

Foucault, M. 1977: *Discipline and punish: The birth of the prison*. London: Allen Lane.

Fraser, N. 1989: *Unruly practices: power, discourse and gender in contemporary social theory*. Cambridge: Polity Press.

Fukuyama, F. 1989: The end of history? *The National Interest*, Summer, 3–18.

Glacken, C. 1967: *Traces on the Rhodian shore: nature and culture in Western thought from ancient times to the end of the eighteenth century*. Berkeley, CA: University of California Press.

Glendenning, F. 1973: School history textbooks and racial attitudes, 1804–1911. *Journal of Educational Administration and History* 5, 33–44.

Golanka, M. 1985: Mr Kurtz, I presume? Livingstone and Stanley as prototypes of Kurtz and Marlow. *Studies in the Novel* 17, 194–202.

Green, M, 1980: *Dreams of adventure, deeds of empire*. Andover: Routledge, Chapman & Hall.

Greenhalgh, P. 1988: *Ephemeral vistas: the Expositions Universelles, Great Exhibitions and World's Fairs, 1851–1939*. Manchester: Manchester University Press.

Gregory, D. 1990: Chinatown, Part Three? Soja and the missing spaces of social theory. *Strategies: A Journal of Theory Culture and Politics* 3, 40–104.

Guattari, F. 1984: *Molecular revolution: psychiatry and politics*. Harmondsworth: Penguin Books.

Habermas, J. 1985: Modernity: an incomplete project. In Foster, H. (ed.), *Postmodern culture*. London: Pluto Press, 3–15.

Habermas, J. 1987: *The philosophical discourse of modernity*. Cambridge: Polity Press.

Harvey, D. 1989: *The condition of postmodernity*. Oxford: Basil Blackwell.

Heffernan, M. 1989: The limits of utopia: Henri Duveyrier and the exploration of the Sahara in the nineteenth century. *Geographical Journal* 155, 342–52.

Hobsbawm, E. 1987: *The age of empire*. London: Weidenfeld & Nicolson.

Holdich, T. 1899: The use of practical geography illustrated by recent frontier operations. *Geographical Journal* 13, 465–80.

Hudson, B. 1977: The new geography and the new imperialism, 1870–1918. *Antipode* 9, 12–19.

Jameson, F. 1981: *The political unconscious: Narrative as a socially symbolic act*. Andover: Methuen.

Jeal, T. 1989: *Baden-Powell*. London: Hutchinson Education.

Karp, I. and Lavine S. (eds) 1991: *Exhibiting cultures: the poetics and politics of museum display*. Washington, DC: Smithsonian Institution Press.

Kearns, G. 1984: Closed space and political practice: Frederick Jackson Turner and Halford Mackinder. *Environment and Planning D: Society and Space* 2, 23–34.

Kearns, G. 1985: Halford John Mackinder, 1861–1947. *Geographers Biobibliographical Studies* 9, 71–86.

Kern, S. 1983: *The culture of time and space, 1880–1918*. Cambridge, MA: Harvard University Press.

Leclerc, G. 1972: *Anthropologie et colonialisme: Essai sur l'histoire de l'africanisme*. Paris: Editions du Seuil.

Livingstone, D. 1984: History of science and the history of geography. *History of Science* 22, 271–302.

Livingstone, D. 1990: Geography and modernity: past and present. *Transactions of the Institute of British Geographers* 15, 359–73.

Lowe, M. and Short, J. 1990: Progress in human geography. *Progress in Human Geography* 14, 1–11.

Mackay, D. 1943: Colonialism in the French geographical movement, 1871–1881. *Geographical Review* 33, 214–32.

Mackay, D. 1985: *In the wake of Cook: Exploration, science and empire*. Andover: Croom Helm.

MacKenzie, J. (ed.), 1984: *Propaganda and empire*. Manchester: Manchester University Press.

MacKenzie, J. (ed.), 1990: *Imperialism and the natural world*. Manchester: Manchester University Press.

MacKenzie, J. 1992: Geography and imperialism: British Provincial geographical societies. In Driver, F. and Rose, G. (eds), *Nature and science: essays in the history of geographical knowledge*. RP28, Historical Geography Research Group, c/o Charles Withers, Department of Geography, Cheltenham and Gloucester College of Higher Education, Cheltenham GL50 3PB, 49–62.

Mackinder, H. 1904: The geographical pivot of history. *Geographical Journal* 23, 421–44.

Mackinder, H. 1905: Man-power as a measure of national and imperial strength. *National Review* 45, 136–43.

McRobbie, A. 1989: Postmodernism and popular culture. In Appignanesi, L. (ed.), *Postmodernism: ICA documents*. London: Free Association Books, 165–79.

Mandel, E. 1984: *Delightful murder: A social history of the crime story*. London: Pluto Press.

Mangan, J. 1986: *The games ethic and imperialism: aspects of the diffusion of an ideal*. Harmondsworth: Viking Penguin.

Mangan, J. and Walvin J. (eds) 1987: *Manliness and morality: Middle-class masculinity in Britain and America, 1800–1940*. Manchester: Manchester University Press.

Nord, D. 1987: The social explorer as anthropologist: Victorian travellers among the urban poor. In Sharpe, W. and Wallock, L. (eds), *Visions of the modern city*. Baltimore, MD: Johns Hopkins University Press, 122–34.

Opie, R. 1985: *Rule Britannia: trading on the British image*. Harmondsworth: Viking Penguin.

Parry, B. 1983: *Conrad and imperialism: ideological boundaries and visionary frontiers*. London: Macmillan.

Peet, R. 1985: The social origins of environmental determinism. *Annals of the Association of American Geographers* 75, 309–33.

Porter, B. 1968: *Critics of Empire: British radical attitudes to colonialism in Africa, 1895–1914*. London: Macmillan.

Prasch, T. 1989: Which God for Africa? The Islamic–Christian missionary debate in late-Victorian England. *Victorian Studies* 33, 51–73.

Pratt, M. L. 1985: Scratches on the face of the country; or, What Mr Barrow saw in the land of the Bushmen. *Critical Inquiry* 12, 119–43.

Richards, J. (ed.) 1989: *Imperialism and juvenile literature*. Manchester: Manchester University Press.

Said, E. 1978: *Orientalism*. Andover: Routledge, Chapman & Hall.

Said, E. 1983: *The world, the text and the critic*. Cambridge, MA: Harvard University Press.

Said, E. 1985: Opponents, audiences, constituencies and community. In Foster, H. (ed.), *Postmodern culture*. London: Pluto Press, 135–59.

Said, E. 1989: Representing the colonized: anthropology's interlocutors. *Critical Inquiry* 15, 205–25.

Said, E. 1990: Geography, narrative, literature. *New Left Review* 180, 81–97.

Schneider, W. 1990: Geographical reform and municipal imperialism in France, 1870–1880. In MacKenzie, J. (ed.), *Imperialism and the natural world*. Manchester: Manchester University Press, 90–117.

Semmel, B. 1962: *The Governor Eyre Controversy*. St Albans: MacGibbon & Kee.

Soja, E. 1989: *Postmodern geographies: the reassertion of space in critical social theory*. London: Verso.

Stafford, J. 1989: *Scientist of empire: Sir Roderick Murchison, scientific exploration and Victorian imperialism*. Cambridge: Cambridge University Press.

Stanley, D. 1909: *The autobiography of Sir Henry Morton Stanley*. London: Sampson, Low & Co.

Stanley, H. M. 1872: *How I found Livingstone*. London: Low, Marston and Searle.

Stocking, G. 1987: *Victorian anthropology*. New York: The Free Press.

Stoddart, D. 1986: *On geography*. Oxford: Basil Blackwell.

Tagg, J. 1988: *The burden of representation: essays on photographies and histories*. London: Macmillan.

Thompson, E. P. 1968: *The making of the English working class*. Harmondsworth: Penguin Books.

Thompson, E. P. 1978: *The poverty of theory*. London: Merlin Press.

Thornton, R. 1983: Narrative ethnography in Africa, 1850–1920: the creation and capture of an appropriate domain for anthropology. *Man* 18, 502–20.

Warren, A. 1987: Popular manliness: Baden-Powell, scouting and the development of manly character. In Mangan, J. and Walvin, J. (eds), *Manliness and morality*. Manchester: Manchester University Press, 199–219.

Watt, I. 1976: Impressionism and symbolism, in *Heart of darkness*. In Sherry, N. (ed.), *Joseph Conrad*. London: Macmillan, 37–53.

Wells, H. G. 1902: *The discovery of the future*. London: Fisher Unwin.

Youngs, T. 1990: My footsteps on these pages: the inscription of 'self' and 'race' in H. M. Stanley's *How I found Livingstone*. *Prose Studies* 13, 230–49.

18 Gearóid Ó Tuathail and John Agnew,
'Geopolitics and Discourse: Practical Geopolitical Reasoning in American Foreign Policy'

Reprinted in full from: *Political Geography* 11, 190–204 (1992)

The Cold War, Mary Kaldor recently noted, has always been a discourse, a conflict of words, 'capitalism' versus 'socialism' (Kaldor, 1990). Noting how

Eastern Europeans always emphasize the power of words, Kaldor adds that the way we describe the world, the words we use, shape how we see the world and how we decide to act. Descriptions of the world involve geographical knowledge, and Cold War discourse has had a regularized set of geographical descriptions by which it represented international politics in the post-war period. The simple story of a great struggle between a democratic 'West' against a formidable and expansionist East has been the most influential and durable geopolitical script of this period. This story, which today appears outdated, was a story which played itself out not in Central Europe but in exotic 'Third-World' locations, from the sands of the Ogaden in the Horn of Africa, to the mountains of El Salvador, the jungles of Vietnam and the valleys of Afghanistan. Of course, the plot was not always a simple one. It has been complex and nuanced, making the post-war world a dynamic, dramatic and sometimes ironic one – ironies such as Cuban troops guarding Gulf Oil facilities against black UNITA forces supported by a racist South African government. Yet the story was a compelling one which brought huge military–industrial complexes into existence on both sides of the 'East–West' divide and rigidly disciplined the possibilities for alternative political practices throughout the world. All regional conflicts, up until very recently, were reduced to its terms and its logic. Now with this story's unravelling and its geography blurring it is time to ask, how did the Cold War in its geopolitical guise come into existence and work?

This paper is not an attempt directly to answer such questions. Rather it attempts to establish a conceptual basis for answering them. It seeks to outline a reconceptualization of geopolitics in terms of discourse and apply this to the general case of American foreign policy. Geopolitics, some will argue, is, first and foremost, about *practice* and not discourse; it is about actions taken against other powers, about invasions, battles and the deployment of military force. Such practice is certainly geopolitical but it is only through discourse that the building up of a navy or the decision to invade a foreign country is made meaningful and justified. It is through discourse that leaders act, through the mobilization of certain simple geographical understandings that foreign-policy actions are explained and through ready-made geographically infused reasoning that wars are rendered meaningful. How we understand and constitute our social world is through the socially structured use of language (Franck and Weisband, 1971; Todorov, 1984). Political speeches and the like afford us a means of recovering the self-understandings of influential actors in world politics. They help us understand the social construction of worlds and the role of geographical knowledge in that social construction.

The paper is organized into two parts. The first part attempts to sketch a theory of geopolitics by employing the concept of discourse. Four suggestive theses on the implications of conceptualizing geopolitics in discursive terms are briefly outlined. The second part addresses the question of American geopolitics and provides an account of some consistent features of the practical geopolitical reasoning by which American foreign policy has sought to write a geography of international politics. This latter part involves a detailed analysis of two of the most famous texts of the origins of the Cold War: George Kennan's 'Long Telegram' of 1946 and his 'Mr X' article in 1947. The irony of these influential geopolitical representations of the USSR is that they were not concrete geographical representations but overdetermined and ahistorical abstractions. It is the anti-geographical quality of geopolitical reasoning that this paper seeks to illustrate.

Geopolitics and discourse

Geopolitics, as many have noted, is a term which is notoriously difficult to define (Kristof, 1960). In conventional academic understanding, geopolitics concerns the geography of international politics, particularly the relationship between the physical environment (location, resources, territory, etc.) and the conduct of foreign policy (Sprout and Sprout, 1960). Within the geopolitical tradition the term has a more precise history and meaning. A consistent historical feature of geopolitical writing, from its origins in the late nineteenth century to its modern use by Colin Gray and others, is the claim that geopolitics is a foil to idealism, ideology and human will. This claim is a long-standing one in the geopolitical tradition, which from the beginning was opposed to the proposition that great leaders and human will alone determine the course of history, politics and society. Rather, it was the natural environment and the geographical setting of a state which exercised the greatest influence on its destiny (Mackinder, 1890; Ratzel, 1969). Karl Haushofer argued that the study of *Geopolitik* demonstrated the 'dependence of all political events on the enduring conditions of the physical environment' (Bassin, 1987, p. 120). In a 1931 radio address he remarked:

> geopolitics takes the place of political passion and development dictated by natural law reshapes the work of the arbitrary transgression of human will. The natural world, beaten back in vain with sword or pitchfork, irrepressibly reasserts itself in the face of the earth. This is geopolitics!
>
> (Haushofer translated in Bassin, 1987, p. 120)

By its own understandings and terms, geopolitics is taken to be a domain of hard truths, material realities and irrepressible natural facts. Geopoliticians have traded on the supposed objective materialism of geopolitical analysis. According to Gray (1988, p. 93), 'geopolical analysis is impartial as between one or another political system or philosophy'. It addresses the base of international politics, the permanent geopolitical realities around which the play of events in international politics unfolds. These geopolitical realities are held to be durable, physical determinants of foreign policy. Geography, in such a scheme, is held to be a non-discursive phenomenon: it is separate from the social, political and ideological dimensions of international politics.

The great irony of geopolitical writing, however, is that it was always a highly ideological and deeply politicized form of analysis. Geopolitical theory from Ratzel to Mackinder, Haushofer to Bowman, Spykman to Kissinger was never an objective and disinterested activity but an organic part of the political philosophy and ambitions of these very public intellectuals. While the forms of geopolitical writing have varied among these and other authors, the practice of producing geopolitical theory has a common theme: the production of knowledge to aid the practice of statecraft and further the power of the State.

Within political geography, the geopolitical tradition has long been opposed by a tradition of resistance to such reasoning. A central problem that has dogged such resistance is its lack of a coherent and comprehensive theory of geopolitical writing and its relationship to the broader spatial practices that characterize the operation of international politics. This paper proposes such a theory by reconceptualizing the conventional meaning of geopolitics using the concept of discourse. Our foundational premise is the contention that geography is a social and historical discourse which is always intimately bound up with questions of politics and ideology (Ó Tuathail, 1989). Geography is never a natural, non-discursive phenomenon which is separate from ideology and outside politics. Rather, geography as a discourse is a form of power/knowledge itself (Foucault, 1980; ÓTuathail, 1989).

Geopolitics, we wish to suggest, should be critically reconceptualized as a discursive practice by which intellectuals of statecraft 'spatialize' international politics in such a way as to represent it as a 'world' characterized by particular types of places, peoples and dramas. In our understanding, the study of geopolitics is the study of the spatialization of international politics by core powers and hegemonic states. This definition needs careful explication.

The notion of discourse has become an important object of investigation in contemporary critical social science, particularly that which draws inspiration from the writings of the French philosopher Michel Foucault (MacDonell, 1986). Within the discipline of international relations, there has been a series of attempts to incorporate the notion of discourse into the study of the practices of international politics (Alker and Sylvan, 1986; Ashley, 1987; Shapiro, 1988; Der Derian and Shapiro, 1989). Dalby (1988, 1990a, b) and Ó Tuathail (1989) have attempted to extend the concept into political geography. Discourses are best conceptualized as sets of capabilities people have, as sets of socio-cultural resources used by people in the construction of meaning about their world and their activities. They are *not* simply speech or written statements but the rules by which verbal speech and written statements are made meaningful. Discourses enable one to write, speak, listen and act meaningfully. They are a set of capabilities, an ensemble of rules by which readers/listeners and speakers/audiences are able to take what they hear and read and construct it into an organized meaningful whole. Alker and Sylvan (1986) articulate the distinction this way:

> As backgrounds, discourses must be distinguished from the verbal productions which readers or listeners piece together. As we prefer to use the term people do not read or listen to a discourse: rather, they employ a discourse or discourses in the processes of reading or listening to a verbal production. Discourses do not present themselves as such; what we observe are people and verbal productions.

Discourses, like grammars, have a virtual and not an actual existence. They are not overarching constructs in the way that 'structures' are sometimes represented. Rather, they are real sets of capabilities whose existence we infer from their realizations in activities, texts and speeches. Neither are they absolutely deterministic. Discourses enable. One can view these capabilities or rules as permitting a certain bounded field of possibilities and reasoning as the process by which certain possibilities are actualized. The various actualizations of possibilities have consequences for the further reproduction and transformation of discourse. The actualization of one possibility closes off previously existent possibilities and simultaneously opens up a new series of somewhat different possibilities. Discourses are never static but are constantly mutating and being modified by human practice. The study of geopolitics in discursive terms, therefore, is the study of the socio-cultural resources and rules by which geographies of international politics get written.[1]

The notion of 'intellectuals of statecraft' refers to a whole community of State bureaucrats, leaders, foreign-policy experts and advisors throughout the world who comment upon, influence and conduct the activities of statecraft. Ever since the development of the modern State system in the sixteenth century there has been a community of intellectuals of statecraft. Up until the twentieth century this community was rather small and restricted, with most intellectuals also being practitioners of statecraft. In the twentieth century, however, this community has become quite extensive and internally specialized. Within the larger States at least, one can differentiate between types of intellectuals of statecraft on the basis of their institutional setting and style of reasoning. Within civil society there are 'defense intellectuals' associated with particular defense contractors and weapons systems. There is also a specialized community of security intellectuals in various public think-tanks (e.g. the RAND Corporation, the Hoover Institute, the Georgetown Center for Strategic and International Studies) who write and comment upon international affairs and strategy (Cockburn, 1987; Dalby, 1990b). One finds a different form of intellectualizing from public intellectuals of statecraft such as Henry Kissinger or Zbigniew Brzezinski who, as former top governmental officials, command a wide audience for their opinions in national newspapers and foreign-policy journals. Within political society itself there are different gradations amongst the foreign-policy community from those who design, articulate and order foreign policy from the top to those actually charged with implementing particular foreign policies and practicing statecraft (whether diplomatic or military) on a daily basis. All can claim to be intellectuals of statecraft for they are constantly engaged in reasoning about statecraft though all may not have the funtion of intellectuals in the conventional sense, but rather in the sense of Gramsci's 'organic' intellectuals (Gramsci, 1971).

We wish to propose four theses which follow from our preliminary observations on reasoning processes and intellectuals of statecraft. The first of these is that the study of geopolitics as we have defined it involves the *comprehensive* study of statecraft as a set of social practices. Geopolitics is not a discrete and relatively contained activity confined only to a small group of 'wise men' who speak in the language of classical geopolitics. Simply to describe a foreign-policy problem is to engage in geopolitics, for one is implicitly and tacitly normalizing a particular world. One could describe geopolitical reasoning as the creation of the backdrop or setting upon which 'international politics' takes place, but such would be a simplistic view. The creation of such a setting is itself part of world politics. This setting itself is more than a single backdrop but an active component part of the drama of world politics. To designate a place is not simply to define a location or setting. It is to open up a field of possible taxonomies and trigger a series of narratives, subjects and appropriate foreign-policy responses. Merely to designate an area as 'Islamic' is to designate an implicit foreign policy (Said, 1978, 1981). Simply to describe a different or indeed the same place as 'Western' (e.g. Egypt) is silently to operationalize a competing set of foreign-policy operators. Geopolitical reasoning begins at a very simple level and is a pervasive part of the practice of international politics. It is an innately political process of representation by which the intellectuals of statecraft designate a world and 'fill' it with certain dramas, subjects, histories and dilemmas. All statespersons engage in the practice; it is one of the norms of the world political community.

Our second thesis is that most geopolitical reasoning in world politics is of a practical and not a formal type. Practical geopolitical reasoning is reasoning by means of consensual and unremarkable assumptions about places and their particular identities. This is the reasoning of practitioners of statecraft, of statespersons, politicians and military commanders. This is to be contrasted with the formal geopolitical reasoning of strategic thinkers and public intellectuals (such as those found in the 'geopolitical tradition') who work in civil society and produce a highly codified system of ideas and principles to guide the conduct of statecraft. The latter forms of knowledge tend to have highly formalized rules of statement, description and debate. By contrast, practical geopolitical reasoning tends to be of a common-sense type which relies on the narratives and binary distinctions found in societal mythologies. In the case of colonial discourse there are contrasts between white and non-white, civilized and backward, Western and non-Western, adult and child. The operation of such distinctions in European foreign policy during the age of empire is well known (Kiernan, 1969; Gates, 1985). US foreign policy towards the Philippines and Latin America during the latter half of the nineteenth century and the beginning of the twentieth century is also replete with such distinctions (Hunt, 1987; Black, 1988; Karnow, 1989). In Cold War discourse the contrast was, as Truman codified it in his famous Truman Doctrine statement of March 1947, between a way of life based upon the will of the majority and distinguished by free institutions, representative government, free elections, guarantees of individual liberty, freedom of speech and religion, and freedom from political oppression versus a way of life based on the will of a minority forcibly imposed upon the majority. This latter way of life relied upon terror and oppression, a controlled press and radio, fixed elections and the suppression of personal freedoms. Such were the criteria by which places were to be judged and spatially divided into different geographical camps in the post-war period.

Our third thesis is that the study of geopolitical reasoning necessitates studying the production of geographical knowledge within a particular State and throughout the modern world-system. Geographical knowledge is produced at a multiplicity of different sites throughout not only the nation-state, but the world political community. From the classroom to the living-room, the newspaper office to the film studio, the pulpit to the presidential office, geographical knowledge about a world is being produced, reproduced and modified. The challenge for the student of geopolitics is to understand how geographical knowledge is transformed into the reductive geopolitical reasoning of intellectuals of statecraft. How are places reduced to security commodities, to geographical abstractions which need to be 'domesticated', controlled, invaded or bombed rather than understood in their complex reality? How, for example, did Truman metamorphose the situation in Greece in March 1947 – it was the site of a complex civil war at the time – into the Manichean terms of the Truman Doctrine? The answer, we suspect is rather ironic given the common-sense meaning of geography as 'place facts': geopolitical reasoning works by the active suppression of the complex geographical reality of places in favor of controllable geopolitical abstractions.

Our fourth thesis concerns the operation of geopolitical reasoning within the context of the modern world-system. Throughout the history of the modern world-system, intellectuals of statecraft from core States – particularly those States which are competing for hegemony – have disproportionate influence and power over how international political space is represented. A hegemonic world power, such as the United States in the immediate post-war period, is by definition a 'rule-writer' for the world community. Concomitant with its material power is the power to represent world politics in certain ways. Those in power within the institutions of the hegemonic state become the deans of world politics, the administrators, regulators and geographers of international affairs. Their power is a power to constitute the terms of geopolitical world order, an ordering of international space which defines the central drama of international politics in particularistic ways. Thus not only can they represent in their own terms particular regional conflicts, whose causes may be quite localized (e.g. the Greek civil war), but they can help create conditions whereby peripheral and semi-peripheral States actively adopt and use the geopolitical reasoning of the hegemon. Examples of this range from the institutionalization of laws to suppress 'Communism' in certain States (even though the State may not have an organized Communist movement; the laws are simply ways to suppress a broad range of dissent; e.g. the case of El Salvador) to the slavish parroting of approved Cold War disccourse in international organizations and forums.

Practical geopolitical reasoning in American foreign policy

Given our reconceptualization of geopolitics, any analysis of American geopolitics must necessarily be more than an analysis of the formal geopolitical reasoning of a series of 'wise men' of strategy (Mahan, Spykman, Kissinger and others). American geopolitics involves the study of the different historical means by which US intellectuals of statecraft have spatialized international politics and represented it as a 'world' characterized by particular types of places, peoples and dramas. Such is obviously a vast undertaking and we wish to make but three general observations on the contours of American geopolitical reasoning. Before doing so, however, it is important to note two factors about the American case. First, we must acknowledge the key role the presidency plays in the assemblage of meaning about international politics within the United States (and internationally since the US became a world power). In ethnographic terms, the US president is the chief 'bricoleur' of American political life, a combination of storyteller and tribal shaman. One of the great powers of the presidency, invested by the sanctity, history and rituals associated with the institution – the fact that the media take their primay discursive cues from the White House – is the power to describe, represent, interpret and appropriate. It is a formidable power but not an absolute power for the art of description and appropriation (e.g. President Reagan's representation of the Nicaraguan *contras* as the 'moral equivalents of the founding fathers') must have resonances with the Congress, the established media and the American public. The generation of such resonances often requires the repetition and recycling of certain themes and images even though the socio-historical context of their use may have changed dramatically. One has the attempted production of continuity by the incorporation of 'strategic terms' (Turton, 1984), 'key metaphors' (Crocker, 1977) and 'key symbols' (Herzfeld, 1982) into geopolitical reasoning. Behind all of these is the assumption of a power of appropriateness in the use of certain relatively fixed terms and phrases (Parkin, 1978).

Second, we must recognize that American involvement with world politics has followed a distinctive cultural logic or set of presuppositions and orientations, what Gramsci called 'Americanismo' (De Grazia, 1984–85). In particular, economic freedom – in the form of 'free' business activity and the political conditions necessary for this – has been a central element in American culture. This has given rise to an attempt to reconstruct foreign places in an American image. US foreign-policy experiences with Mexico, China, Central America, the Caribbean and the Philippines all bear witness to this fundamental feature of US foreign policy (Agnew, 1983; Karnow, 1989).

The first of our three observations on practical geopolitical reasoning in American foreign policy is that representations of 'America' as a place are pervasively mythological. 'America' is a place which is at once real, material and bounded (a territory with quiddity) yet also a mythological, imaginary and universal ideal with no specific spatial bounds. Ever since early modern times, North America and the Caribbean have had the transgressive aura of a place 'beyond the line', as Dunn (1972, ch. 1) terms it, where might made right and the European treaties did not apply. By its own lore, the origins of the country are mythic and its location divine. In his famous pamphlet *Common sense*, written in 1776 in support of the American rebellion, Thomas Paine (1969, pp. 39, 40–1), wrote:

This new world hath been the asylum for the persecuted lovers of civil and religions liberty from *every part* of Europe. Hither have they fled, not from the tender embraces of the mother, but from the cruelty of the monster. . . . Everything that is right or natural pleads for separation. The blood of the slain, the weeping voice of nature cries 'TIS TIME TO PART'. Even the distance at which the Almighty hath placed England and America, is a strong and natural proof, that the authority of the one, over the other, was never the design of Heaven. The time likewise at which the continent was discovered, adds weight to the argument, and the manner in which it was peopled encreases [*sic*] the force of it. The reformation was preceded by the discovery of America, as if the Almighty graciously meant to open a sanctuary to the persecuted in future years, when home should afford neither friendship nor safety.

The dramatic hyperbole of Paine's geopolitical reasoning is part of the mythological origins of the American state. In the popular imagination 'America' was 'discovered'; it was a new, empty, pristine place, a New World. Despite the obvious inadequacies of this view, such an imaginary geography can still be found in contemporary American political culture and in the articulation of US foreign policy. Speaking over 210 years later on 2 February 1988 in an address to the nation supporting the Nicaraguan *contras*, President Ronald Reagan (1988, p. 35) remarked:

My friends, I have often expressed my belief that the Almighty had a reason for placing this great and good land, the 'New World', here between two vast oceans. Protected by the seas, we have enjoyed the blessings of peace – free for almost two centuries now from the tragedy of foreign aggression on our mainland. Help us to keep that precious gift secure. Help us to win support for those who struggle for the same freedoms we hold dear. In doing so, we will not just be helping them; we will be helping ourselves, our children, and all the peoples of the world. We will be demonstrating that America is still a beacon of hope, still a light unto the nations. Yes, a great opportunity to show that hope still burns bright in this land and over our continent, casting a glow across centuries, still guiding missions – to a future of peace and freedom.

The continuity between the two texts is evidence of the durability of particular narratives in American political discourse. It is a structuralist fallacy to think of this narrative as having a 'deep structure' or a primordial set of binary oppositions – e.g. Old World : New World, despotism/totalitarianism : freedom – to which everything else can be reduced. As a discourse its existence is virtual, not actual, and is assembled and reassembled differently by presidents and other intellectuals of statecraft. Such discourse freely fuses fact with fiction and reality with the imaginary to produce a reasoning where neither is distinguishable from the other.[2] Both narratives read like primitive ethnographic tales: the origins of a tribe from the wanderings of persecuted members of other tribes, the flight from persecution, the chosen land, divine guidance, blessings, precious gifts, beacons and monsters. America's first leaders are known even today in American political culture as the 'founding fathers'.

Second, there is a tension between a universal omnipresent image of 'America' and a different spatially bounded image of the place. On one hand,

American discourse consistently plays upon the unique geographical location of 'America' yet simultaneously asserts that the principles of this 'New World' are universal and not spatially confined there. The geography evoked in the American Declaration of Independence was not continental or hemispheral but universal. Its concern was with 'the earth', the 'Laws of Nature and of Nature's God', and all of 'mankind'. In this universalist vision, 'America' is positioned as being equivalent with the strivings of a universal human nature. 'The cause of America', Paine (1969, p. 23) proclaimed, 'is in a great measure the cause of all mankind'. The freedoms it struggles for are in Reagan's terms, the freedoms desired by 'all the peoples of the world'. 'America' is at once a territorially defined State and a universal ideal, a place on the North American continent and a mythical homeland of freedom.

For the late eighteenth and most of the nineteenth century, the spatially bounded sense of 'America' was the one that predominated in US foreign-policy rhetoric. Even though the United States had closer economic, cultural and political ties with Europe than any other place, its foreign-policy rhetoric defined it as a separate and distinct sphere. 'Europe', George Washington observed in his farewell address of 1796, 'has a set of primary interests which to us have none or a very remote relation. Hence she must be engaged in frequent controversies, the causes of which are essentially foreign to our concerns' (Richardson, 1905, vol. 1, p. 214). Washington's geopolitical reasoning was largely a negative one which defined the American sphere as extra-European (like Persia and Turkey) rather than a system complete and to itself. For others, notably Thomas Jefferson, Henry Clay and John Quincy Adams, there was a distinct 'American system'. Jefferson, writing in 1813 to the geographer Alexander von Humboldt on the five Spanish–American colonies in rebellion (which the US recognized in 1822: earlier recognition moves were defeated), noted:

> But in whatever government they end, they will be *American* governments, no longer to be involved in the never-ceasing broils of Europe. The European nations constitute a separate division of the globe; their localities make them a part or a distinct system: they have a set of interests of their own in which it is our business never to engage ourselves. America has a hemisphere to itself. It must have its separate system of interests; which must not be subordinated to those of Europe.
>
> (Quoted in Whitaker, 1954, p. 29)

The 'American system' was not, however, to be a multi-lateralist, pan-American affair or a 'counterpose' to the Holy Alliance as Henry Clay had suggested in 1821. John Quincy Adams, who actively opposed such a policy, did not advocate isolationism so much as oppose any multi-lateral moves on the US's part (in concert with Great Britain or the South American republics). His position was unilateralist not isolationist. In 1820 he wrote to President Monroe:

> As to an American system, we have it; we constitute the whole of it; there is no community of interests or of principles between North and South America. Mr

Torres and Bolivar and O'Higgins talk about an American system as much as the Abbé Correa, but there is no basis for any such system.

(Quoted in Bemis, 1945, p. 367)

The unilateral declaration of what later became known as the Monroe Doctrine affirmed such a position, stating that the political system of the European powers is different from that of America. Therefore, the United States would 'consider any attempt on their part to extend their system to any portion of this hemisphere as dangerous to our peace and safety'. An 'American hemisphere', of course, was an arbitrary social construct – for the United States can be located in many different hemispheres, depending on where one decides to center them (e.g. a Northern hemisphere, a so-called Western hemisphere or a predominantly land hemisphere: see Boggs, 1945). Such geopolitical reasoning was imaginary, and the putative bonds of affinity between the Latin republics of South America and the white Anglo-Saxon republic of the North equally imaginary.

By the late nineteenth century, the increasing wealth and power of the US State, together with the scramble for colonies among the European powers, produced a foreign policy which subordinated the hemispheral identity of the United States to universalist themes and identities concerning race, civilization and Christianity. McKinley, acting under divine inspiration, saw it as the task of the United States to uplift and civilize the Philippines (while simultaneously preventing it from falling into the hands of commercial rivals France and Germany: Lafeber, 1963), while Roosevelt's famous 'corollary' of 1904 declared:

> Chronic wrongdoing, or an impotence which results in a general loosening of the ties of civilized society, may in America, as elsewhere, ultimately require intervention by some civilized nation, and in the Western Hemisphere the adherence of the United States to the Monroe Doctrine may force the United States, however reluctantly, in flagrant cases of wrongdoing or impotence, to the exercise of an international police power.
>
> (Richardson, 1905, vol. 9, p. 7053).

The geopolitical reasoning by which domestic slavery and continental US expansionism worked – i.e. those concerning civilized versus uncivilized territories, superior and inferior races, adult and child identifications of peoples with white Anglo-Saxon males as the adults – were drawn upon to help write global political space. The United States was beginning to consider itself a 'world power' with 'principles' that were no longer qualified as contingently applicable to the 'American hemisphere'. McKinley and Theodore Roosevelt's racial script was followed by Woodrow Wilson's crusade for what he and US political culture took to be democracy. That Wilsonian internationalism did not succeed was partly due to the reinvigoration of the mythology that an isolationist 'America' is the true and pure 'America'. Yet while the United States in the 1930s steered clear of political alliances with the rest of the world, its business enterprises continued their long-standing economic expansionism overseas. By the time of the Truman Doctrine, the USA no longer conceptualized itself as *a* world power but as *the* world power. The geopolitical reasoning of Truman, as noted earlier, was abstract and universal. Containment had no clearly conceptualized geographical limitations. Its genuine space was the abstract universal isotropic plane wherein right does perpetual battle with wrong, liberty with totalitarianism and Americanism with the forces of un-Americanism.

A third feature of American discourse is the strong lines it draws between the space of the 'Self' and the space of the 'Other' (Todorov, 1984; Dalby, 1988, 1990a,b). Like the cultural maps of many nations, American political discourse is given shape by a frontier which separates civilization from savagery in Turner's (1920) terms or an 'Iron Curtain' marking the free world from the 'evil empire'. Robertson (1980, p. 92) notes:

> Frontiers and lines are powerful symbols for Americans. The moving frontier was never only a geographical line: it was a palpable barrier which separated the wilderness from civilization. It distinguished Americans, with their beliefs and their ideals, from savages and strangers, those 'others' who could not be predicted or trusted. It divided the American nation from other nations, and marked its independence.

While such a point is valid, one can overstate the uniquely American character of this practice. Early European experiences, particularly the Iberian *reconquista* against the 'infidel' and the English colonial experience with 'heathens' in Ireland, were factors in the formation of imperialism as a 'way of life' in the United States (Williams, 1980; Meinig, 1986). European discourses on colonialism, we have already noted, found their way into US foreign-policy practice not only in Theodore Roosevelt's time but even in determining the shape of the post-war world. The processes of geopolitical world ordering in US foreign policy in the late 1940s are worthy of some detailed examination. Taylor (1990) provides an account of the practical geopolitical reasoning of British intellectuals of statecraft (chiefly Churchill, Bevin and the British Foreign Office) during 1945. Let us consider the case of the two most famous *American* texts of that period, the 'Long Telegram' and 'Mr X' texts of George Kennan.

The figure of George Kennan looms large in the annals of American foreign policy, for it was Kennan who helped codify and constitute central elements of what became Cold War discourse. Kennan himself was, as Stephanson (1989, p. 157) observes, a man of the North, one to whom the vast heterogeneous area of the Third World was 'a foreign space, wholly lacking in allure and best left to its own no doubt tragic fate'. The crucial division in the world for Kennan and the many others who made up the Atlanticist security community was that between the West and the East, between the world of maritime trading democracies and the oriental world of xenophobic modern despotism. Trained at Princeton and in Germany and Estonia, Kennan developed something of an Old World *Weltanschauung* and brought this to bear in his early analyses of the USSR and world politics when working at the US Embassy in Moscow and later as Head of the Policy Planning Staff in Washington, DC. In Kennan's two texts one can find at least three different strategies by which the USSR is represented. Each is worth exploring in detail.

The USSR as oriental

Orientalism is premised, as Said (1978, p. 12) notes, on a primitive geopolitical awareness of the globe as composed of two unequal worlds, the Orient and the Occident. For Kennan and the Cold War discourse he helped codify, the USSR is part of the 'Other' world, the oriental world. In his famous 'Long Telegram' Kennan describes the Soviet Government as pervaded by an 'atmosphere of oriental secretiveness and conspiracy'. In the 'Mr X' article published in *Foreign Affairs* in July 1947 he expounds on his thesis that the 'political personality of Soviet power' is 'the product of ideology and circumstances', the latter being the stamp of Russia's history and geography (Kennan, 1947, p. 574):

> The very teachings of Lenin himself require great caution and flexibility in the pursuit of Communist purposes. Again, these precepts are fortified by the lessons of Russian history: of centuries of obscure battles between nomadic forces over the stretches of a vast unfortified plain. Here caution, circumspection, flexibility and deception are the valuable qualities, and their value finds natural appreciation in the Russian or oriental mind.

In an earlier passage, Kennan had noted the paranoia of Soviet leaders. 'Their particular brand of fanaticism', he noted, 'was too fierce and too jealous to envisage any permanent sharing of power'. In a revealing sentence he then noted: 'From the Russian–Asiatic world out of which they had emerged they carried with them a scepticism as to the possibilities of permanent and peaceful coexistence of rival forces' (Kennan, 1947, p. 570). Pietz (1988) notes that the Cold War discourse Kennan helped shape was 'post-colonialist' in the sense that it drew upon and was assembled from many familiar and pervasive colonial discourses such as Orientalism and the putative primitiveness of non-Western regions and spaces. Totalitarianism, the theoretical anchor of Cold War discourse, came to be known as 'nothing other than traditional Oriental despotism plus modern police technology' (Pietz, 1988, p. 58).[3]

The USSR as potential rapist

Another pre-existent source from which Cold War discourse and representations of the USSR were assembled was patriarchal mythology – particularly that concerning fables of female vulnerability, rape and guardianship. In the descriptions being constructed around the USSR and Communism at this time the image of penetration was frequently evoked.[4] The leaders of the USSR were a 'frustrated' and 'discontented' lot who 'found in Marxist theory a highly convenient rationalization for their own instinctive desires' (Kennan, 1947, p. 569). Marxism was only a 'fig leaf' of moral and intellectual responsibility which cloaked essentially naked instinctive desire. These instinctive desires produced Soviet 'aggressiveness' (another favorite Cold War description of the USSR) and 'fluid and constant pressure to extend the limits of Russian police power which are together the natural and instinctive urges of Russian rulers' (Kennan, 1946 p. 54).

In the face of this instinctive behavior, the USA needed to be aware that the USSR 'cannot be charmed or talked out of existence' (Kennan, 1947, p. 576). The USSR was a wily and flexible power that would employ a variety of different 'tactical maneuvers' (e.g. peaceful coexistence) to woo the West, particularly a vulnerable and psychologically weakened Western Europe which was disposed to wishful thinking. Given this situation, the policy of the United States needed to be 'that of a long-term, patient but firm and vigilant containment of Russian expansive tendencies' (Kennan, 1947, p. 575). The United States needed to act as the tough masculine guardian of Western Europe. If the policy of 'adroit and vigilant application of counter-force at a series of constantly shifting geographical and political points, corresponding to the shifts and maneuvers of Soviet policy' was patiently followed by the United States, then the weaknesses of the Soviet Union itself would become apparent. Turning the sexual grid of intelligibility on the USSR itself, Kennan (1947, p. 578) wrote that as long as the deficiencies that characterize Soviet society are not corrected, 'Russia will remain economically a vulnerable, and in a certain sense an impotent, nation, capable of exporting its enthusiasms and of radiating the strange charm of its primitive political vitality but unable to back up those articles of export by the real evidence of material power and prosperity'. A testimony to the durability of this image is the rhetoric of the early Bush administration where Gorbachev's foreign policy was spoken of as a 'charm offensive' aimed at the 'seduction' of Western Europe.

The Red flood

In tandem with the patriarchal mythology described above, one also had the recurring representation of Soviet foreign policy and Communism as a flood. The image of the Red flood was a particularly powerful element in fascist mythology during the inter-war period where, as Theweleit (1987, p. 230) chronicles in Weimar Germany, the powerful metaphor 'engenders a clearly ambivalent state of excitement. It is threatening but also attractive . . .'. Many different elements are at play here: situations and boundaries are fluid, solid ground becomes soft and swampy, barriers are breached, repressed instincts come bursting forth – water and sea as symbolic of the unconscious, the undisciplined id – and conditions are unrestrained, anarchic and dangerous. The response of the Freikorps, in Theweleit's account, is to act as firm, erect dams against this anarchic degeneration of society. With both feet securely planted on solid ground, they contained the Red flood and brought death to all that flowed. The very foundations of society, after all, were under attack. Switching to Kennan's 'Mr X' article, we find the following graphic passage which defines the very nature of the Soviet threat to Western Europe:

Its [the USSR's] political action is a fluid stream which moves constantly, wherever it is permitted to move, towards a given goal. Its main concern is to make sure that it has filled every nook and cranny available to it in the basin of world power. But if it finds unassailable barriers in its path, it accepts these philosophically and accommodates itself to them. The main thing is that there should always be pressure, unceasing constant pressure, towards the desired goal. (Kennan, 1947, p. 575).

The image of the flood, which has also a sexual dimension (unrestrained, gushing desire, etc.), is critical, for it is by this means that the geography of containment becomes constituted. If the Soviet threat has the characteristics of a flood then one needs 'firm and vigilant containment' along *all* of the Soviet border. Containment is thus constituted as a virtually global and not singularly Western European task. Effective containment in Western Europe, so the scenario goes, will lead to increasing Soviet pressure on the Middle East and Asia which eventually could result in the USSR spilling out into one or more of these regions. Such an image is easily reinforced by appropriate cartographic visuals featuring bleeding red maps of the USSR spreading outwards, or menacingly penetrating arrows busily trying to break out. The explanation of why US security managers instinctively read the North Korean invasion of South Korea as an act of Soviet expansionism certainly must address the power of such pre-existent images and scenarios. The formal geopolitical reasoning found in the different strategies of containment (Gaddis, 1982) rested, we suspect, on the flimsy foundations of widely shared practical geopolitical preconceptions.[5]

Conclusion

The Cold War as a discourse may have lost its credibility and meaning as a consequence of the events of 1989 but it is clear from the Gulf crisis that intellectuals of statecraft in the West at least, and the military–industrial complex behind them, will try to create a 'new' set of enemies (the 'irrational Third World despot') in a restructured world order. The reductive nature of the practical geopolitical reasoning used in the 1990–91 Gulf crisis by President Bush and Prime Minister Thatcher looks all too familiar. The character of foreign places and foreign enemies is represented as fixed. In 1947 when George Kennan declared that 'there can be no appeal to common mental approaches' (1947, p. 574) in US dealings with the USSR he was effectively negating his own profession, namely diplomacy. The possibility of an open dialogue between the USSR and the United States was excluded a priori because the character of the USSR was already historically and geographically determined and thus effectively immutable. The irony of practical geopolitical representations of place is that, in order to succeed, they actually necessitate the abrogation of genuine geographical knowledge about the diversity and complexity of places as social entities. Describing the USSR then (or Iraq today) as Orientalist is a work of geographical abstractionism. A complex, diverse and heterogeneous social mosaic of places is hypostatized into a singular, overdetermined and predictable actor.

As a consequence, therefore, the United States was put in the ironic situation of being simultaneously tremendously geographically ignorant of the USSR (and today Iraq) yet fetishistically preoccupied with that state and its influence in world politics.

The global economic and political restructuring of the contemporary age has been both a consequence and a generator of changing geographical sensibilities. The marked 'time–space compression' wrought by modern telecommunications and the globalization of capital, ideologies and culture has bound the fate of places more intimately together but has also opened up a series of possibilities for new types of subjectivities and new forms of political solidarity between places (Agnew and Corbridge, 1989). Globalization has enabled certain critical social movements to make connections between their struggles and the struggles of other critical social movements in very different places (see, for example, Kaldor and Falk, 1987; Walker, 1988). Contemporary geography in deconstructing its own vocabulary and critically exploring the forms of practical geopolitical reasoning that circulate within states can be an ally to these critical social movements. It can help create descriptions of the world based not on reductive geopolitical reasoning but on critical geographical knowledge.

Notes

1 In attempting to use Foucault and critical international-relations theories in political geography, there is a tendency to speak loosely of the 'discourse of geopolitics' or 'geopolitical discourse'. Such phrases can be unhelpful, for they suggest that geopolitics is a discrete discourse itself. This is not our contention. We prefer to use the term 'geopolitical reasoning' to describe the spatialization of international politics that results from the employment of discourses in foreign-policy practice.
2 Jean Baudrillard (1988, p. 7) has termed America 'the only remaining primitive society', a society of ferocious ritualism and hyperbolic primitivism that has 'far outstripped its own moral, social or ecological rationale'. For a discussion of the political and economic realities of living in American mythology, see Davis (1986).
3 Kennan's successor as Head of the Policy Planning Staff was Paul Nitze. In urging that the USA develop the H-Bomb or 'Super' as it was known in security discourse, Nitze argued that the 'threat to Western Europe seemed to me singularly like that which Islam had posed centuries before, with its combination of ideological zeal and fighting power' (Nitze, quoted in Talbott, 1989, p. 52). The influence of a classical education on intellectuals of statecraft (see Luttwak, 1976), with its narratives of fights between civilization and barbarian hordes, seems worthy of further exploration. Inquiry in this area may help explain the appeal of Mackinder's ideas to elements of the security community in this period.
4 In volume 1 of his memoirs, Kennan (1967), who by this time had supposedly repudiated many of his earlier conceptions of the USSR, nevertheless repeatedly returns to the image of penetration in discussions of Soviet power.
5 There are a series of other strategies by which the USSR is represented in the early Cold War discourse codified by Kennan and numerous others. The writing of territory and states in organic terms prompted a medicalization of certain regions (e.g. Western Europe as a weak patient needing aid against disease) and the use of psychological terms to describe the Other (e.g. the USSR as a paranoid personality). See Yannas (1989).

References

Agnew, J. A. 1983: An excess of 'national exceptionalism': towards a new political geography of American foreign policy. *Polical Geography Quarterly* 2, 151–66.

Agnew, J. A. and Corbridge, S. 1989: The new geopolitics: the dynamics of geopolitical disorder. In Johnston, R. J. and Taylor, P. J. (eds), *A world in crisis?: Geographical perspectives*. Oxford: Basil Blackwell, 266–88.

Alker, H. and Sylvan, D. 1986: Political discourse analysis. Paper presented at the Annual Meeting of the American Political Science Association, Washington, DC, September.

Ashley, R. 1987: The geopolitics of geopolitical space: towards a critical social theory of international politics. *Alternatives* 14, 403–34.

Augelli, E. and Murphy, C. 1988: *America's quest for supremacy and the Third World: An essay in Gramscian analysis*. London: Pinter.

Bassin, M. 1987: Race contra space: the conflict between German *Geopolitik* and national socialism. *Political Geography Quarterly* 6, 115–34.

Baudrillard, J. 1988: *America*. New York: Verso.

Bemis, S. 1945: *John Quincy Adams and the foundations of American foreign policy*. New York: Alfred A. Knopf.

Black, G. 1988: *The good neighbor: How the United States wrote the history of Latin America*. New York: Pantheon.

Boggs, S. 1945: This hemisphere. *Department of State Bulletin*, 6 May.

Cockburn, A. 1987: The defense intellectual: Edward N. Luttwak. *Grand Street* 6(3), 161–4.

Crabb, C. 1982: *The doctrines of American foreign policy*. Baton Rouge: Louisiana State University Press.

Crocker, J. C. 1977: The social functions of rhetorical forms. In Sapir, J. D. and Crocker, J. C. (eds), *The social use of metaphor: Essays on the anthropology of rhetoric*. Philadelphia: University of Pennsylvania Press, 33–66.

Dalby, S. 1988: Geopolitical discourse: the Soviet Union as Other. *Alternatives* 13, 415–42.

Dalby, S. 1990a: American security discourse: the persistence of geopolitics. *Political Geography Quarterly* 9, 171–88.

Dalby, S. 1990b: *Creating the Second Cold War: The discourse of politics*. London: Pinter.

Davis, M. 1986: *Prisoners of the American dream*. London: Verso.

De Grazia, V. 1984–85: Americanismo d'Esportazione. *La Critica Sociologica* 71–72, 5–22.

Der Derian, J. and Shapiro, M. (eds) 1989: *International/intertextual relations*. Lexington, MA: Lexington Books.

Dunn, R. S. 1972: *Sugar and slaves: The rise of the planter class in the English West Indies, 1624–1713*. New York: Norton.

Etzold, T. and Gaddis, J. 1978: *Containment: Documents on American policy and strategy. 1945–1950*. New York: Columbia University Press.

Foucault, M. 1980: *Power/knowledge*. New York: Pantheon.

Franck, T. M. and Weisband, E. 1971: *Word politics: Verbal strategy among the superpowers*. New York: Oxford University Press.

Gaddis, J. L. 1982: *Strategies of containment*. New York: Oxford University Press.

Gates, H. L. (ed.) 1985: 'Race', writing and difference. *Critical Inquiry* 12(1).

Gramsci, A. 1971: *Selections from the prison notebooks*. New York: International Publishers.

Gray, C. 1977: *The geopolitics of the nuclear era*. Beverly Hills, CA: Sage Publications.

Gray, C. 1988: *The geopolitics of superpower*. Lexington: University of Kentucky Press.

Herzfeld, M. 1982: The etymology of excuses: aspects of rhetorical performance in Greece. *American Ethnologist* 9, 644–63.

Hunt, M. 1987: *Ideology and US foreign policy*. New Haven, CT: Yale University Press.

Kaldor, M. 1990: After the Cold War. *New Left Review* 80, 25–37.

Kaldor, M. and Falk, R. 1987. *Dealignment: A new foreign policy perspective*. New York: Basil Blackwell.

Karnow, S. 1989: *In our image: America's empire in the Philippines*. New York: Random House.

Kennan, G. 1946: The 'Long Telegram'. In Etzol, T. and Gaddis, J. (eds), *Containment: Documents on American policy and strategy, 1945–1950*. New York: Columbia University Press, 50–63.

Kennan, G. ['Mr X'] 1947: The sources of Soviet conduct. *Foreign Affairs* 25, 566–82.

Kennan, G. 1967: *Memoirs 1925–1950*. Boston: Little, Brown.

Kiernan, V. 1969: *The lords of human kind*. Boston: Little, Brown.

Kristof, L. 1960: The origins and evolution of geopolitics. *Journal of Conflict Resolution* 4, 15–51.

Lafeber, W. 1963: *The new empire: An interpretation of American expansionism, 1860–1898*. Ithaca, NY: Cornell University Press.

Luttwak, E. 1976: *The grand strategy of the Roman Empire*. Baltimore: Johns Hopkins Press.

MacDonell, D. 1986: *Theories of discourse: An introduction*. New York: Basil Blackwell.

Mackinder, H. 1890: The physical basis of political geography. *Scottish Geographical Magazine* 6, 78–84.

Meinig, D. 1986: *The Shaping of America*. Vol. 1: *Atlantic America, 1492–1800*. New Haven, CT: Yale University Press.

Ó Tuathall, G. 1989: Critical geopolitics: the social construction of place and space in the practice of statecraft. Unpublished PhD thesis, Syracuse University.

Paine, T. 1969: *The essential Thomas Paine*. New York: Mentor.

Parker, G. 1985: *Western geopolitical thought in the twentieth century*. New York: St Martin's Press.

Parkin, D. 1978: *The cultural definition of political response*. London: Academic Press.

Pietz, W. 1988: The 'post-colonialism' of Cold War discourse. *Social Text* 19/20, 55–75.

Ratzel, F. 1969: The laws of the spatial growth of states. In Kasperson, R. and Munghi, J. (eds), *The structure of political geography*. Chicago: Aldine, 17–28.

Reagan, R. 1988: Peace and democracy for Nicaragua. Address to the Nation on 2 February 1988. *Department of State Bulletin* 88(2133), 32–5.

Richardson, J. 1905: *A compilation of messages and papers of the presidents, 1789–1902*, 12 vols. Washington. DC: Bureau of National Literature and Art.

Robertson, J. O. 1980: *American myth, American reality*. New York: Hill & Wang.

Said, E. 1978: *Orientalism*. New York: Vintage Books.

Said, E. 1981: *Covering Islam*. New York: Pantheon Books.

Shapiro, M. 1988: *The politics of representation*. Madison: University of Wisconsin Press.

Sprout, H. and Sprout, M. 1960: Geography and international politics in an era of revolutionary change. *Journal of Conflict Resolution* 4, 145–61.

Stephanson, A. 1989: *George Kennan and the art of foreign policy*. Boston: Harvard University Press.

Talbott, S. 1989: *The master of the game: Paul Nitze and the nuclear peace*. New York: Vintage Books.

Taylor, P. J. 1989: *Political geography: World-economy, nation-state and locality*, 2nd edn. London: Longman.

Taylor, P. J. 1990: *Britain and the Cold War: 1945 as geopolitical transition*. London: Pinter.

Theweleit, K. 1987: *Male fantasies*. Vol. 1: *Women, floods, bodies, history*. Minneapolis: University of Minnesota Press.

Todorov, T. 1984: *The conquest of America: The question of the other*, trans. R. Howard. New York: Harper Torchbooks.

Turner, F. J. 1920: *The frontier in American History*. New York: Henry Holt.

Turton, A. 1984: Limits of ideological domination and the formation of social consciousness. In Turton, A. and Tanabe, S. (eds), *History and peasant consciousness in South-East Asia*. Senri Ethnological Studies, No. 13. Osaka: National Museum of Ethnology, 19–73.

Walker, R. 1988: *One world, many worlds: struggles for a just world peace*. Boulder, CO: Lynne Rienner.

Whitaker, A. 1954: *The Western hemisphere idea: its rise and decline*. Ithaca, NY: Cornell University Press.

Williams, W. A. 1980: *Empire as a way of life*. Oxford: Oxford University Press.

Yannas, P. 1989: Containment discourse and the making of 'Greece'. Paper presented at the joint annual ISA and BISA Conference, London, 28 March–1 April.

19 J. Brian Harley,
'Maps, Knowledge, and Power'

Excerpts from: D. Cosgrove and S. Daniels (eds), *The Iconography of Landscape*. Cambridge: Cambridge University Press (1988)

> Give me a map; then let me see how much
> Is left for me to conquer all the world, . . .
> Here I began to march towards Persia,
> Along Armenia and the Caspian Sea,
> And thence unto Bithynia, where I took
> the Turk and his great empress prisoners.
> Then marched I into Egypt and Arabia,
> And here, not far from Alexandria
> Whereas the Terrene and the Red Sea meet,
> Being distant less than full a hundred leagues
> I meant to cut a channel to them both
> That men might quickly sail to India.
> From thence to Nubia near Borno lake,
> And so along the Ethiopian sea,
> Cutting the tropic line of Capricorn,
> I conquered all as far as Zanzibar.
>
> Christopher Marlowe, *Tamburlaine*, Part II (V.iii.123–39)

Although maps have long been central to the discourse of geography they are seldom read as 'thick' texts or as a socially constructed form of knowledge. 'Map interpretation' usually implies a search for 'geographical features' depicted on maps without conveying how as a manipulated form of knowledge maps have helped to fashion those features.[1] It is true that in political geography and the history of geographical thought the link is increasingly being made between maps and power – especially in periods of colonial history[2] – but the particular role of maps, as images with historically specific codes, remains largely undifferentiated from the wider geographical discourse in which they are often embedded. What is lacking is a sense of what Carl Sauer understood as the eloquence of maps.[3] How then can we make maps 'speak' about the social worlds of the past?

My aim here is to explore the discourse of maps in the context of political power, and my approach is broadly iconological. Maps will be regarded as part of the broader family of value-laden images.[4] Maps cease to be understood primarily as inert records of morphological landscapes or passive reflections of the world of objects, but are regarded as refracted images contributing to dialogue in a socially constructed world. We thus move the reading of maps away from the canons of traditional cartographical criticism with its string of binary oppositions between maps that are 'true and false', 'accurate and inaccurate', 'objective and subjective', 'literal and symbolic', or that are based on 'scientific integrity' as opposed to 'ideological distortion'. Maps are never value-free images; except in the narrowest Euclidean sense they are not in themselves either true or false. Both in the selectivity of their content and in their signs and styles of representation, maps are a way of conceiving, articulating, and structuring the human world which is biased towards, promoted by, and exerts influence upon particular sets of social relations.[5] By accepting such premises it becomes easier to see how appropriate they are to manipulation by the powerful in society.

Political contexts for maps

Even a cursory inspection of the history of mapping will reveal the extent to which political, religious, or social power produce the context of cartography. This has become clear, for example, from a detailed study of cartography in prehistoric, ancient and medieval Europe, and the Mediterranean. Throughout the period, 'mapmaking was one of the specialized intellectual weapons by which power could be gained, administered, given legitimacy, and codified'.[6] Moreover, this knowledge was concentrated in relatively few hands and 'maps were associated with the religious elite of dynastic Egypt and of Christian medieval Europe; with the intellectual elite of Greece and Rome; and with the mercantile elite of the city-states of the Mediterranean world during the late Middle Ages'.[7]

Nor was the world of ancient and medieval Europe exceptional in these respects. Cartography, whatever other cultural significance may have been attached to it, was always a 'science of princes'. In the Islamic world, it was the caliphs in the period of classical Arab geography, the Sultans in the Ottoman Empire, and the Mogul emperors in India who are known to have patronized map-making and to have used maps for military, political, religious, and propaganda purposes.[8] In ancient China, detailed terrestrial maps were likewise made expressly in accordance with the policies of the rulers of successive dynasties and served as bureaucratic and military tools and as spatial emblems of imperial destiny.[9] In early modern Europe, from Italy to the Netherlands and from Scandinavia to Portugal, absolute monarchs and statesmen were everywhere aware of the value of maps in defence and warfare, in internal administration linked to the growth of centralized government, and as territorial propaganda in the legitimation of national identities. Writers such as Castiglione, Elyot, and Machiavelli advocated the use of maps by generals and statesmen.[10] With national topographic surveys in Europe from the eighteenth century onwards, cartography's role in the transaction of power relations usually favoured social elites.

The specific functions of maps in the exercise of power also confirm the ubiquity of these political contexts on a continuum of geographical scales. These range from global empire building, to the preservation of the nation state, to the local assertion of individual property rights. In each of these contexts the dimensions of polity and territory were fused in images which – just as surely as legal charters and patents – were part of the intellectual apparatus of power.

Maps and empire

As much as guns and warships, maps have been the weapons of imperialism. In so far as maps were used in colonial promotion, and lands claimed on paper before they were effectively occupied, maps anticipated empire. Surveyors marched alongside soldiers, initially mapping for reconnaissance, then for general information, and eventually as a tool of pacification, civilization, and exploitation in the defined colonies. But there is more to this than the drawing of boundaries for the practical political or military containment of subject populations. Maps were used to legitimize the reality of conquest and empire. They helped create myths which would assist in the maintenance of the territorial status quo. As communicators of an imperial message, they have been used as an aggressive complement to the rhetoric of speeches, newspapers, and written texts, or to the histories and popular songs extolling the virtues of empire.[11]

In these imperial contexts, maps regularly supported the direct execution of territorial power. The grids laid out by the Roman *agrimensores*, made functional in centuriation, were an expression of power 'rolled out relentlessly in all directions . . . homogenizing everything in its path',[12] just as the United States rectangular land survey created 'order upon the land' in more senses than merely the replication of a classical design.[13] The rediscovery of the Ptolemaic system of coordinate geometry in the fifteenth century was a critical cartographic event

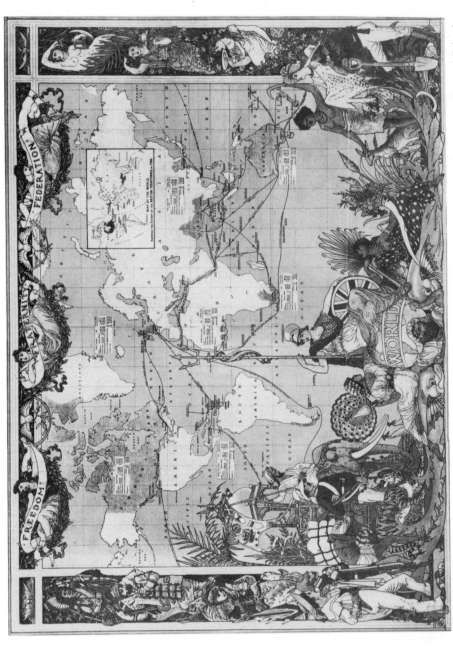

Fig. 19.1 *Imperial Federation – map of the world showing the extent of the British Empire in 1886* was first published as a supplement to the *Graphic* newspaper. Mercator's projection, a pink tint for Empire territory, and decorative emblems showing Britannia seated on the world are used to articulate the message of the 'New Imperialism'. By courtesy of the Mansell Collection

privileging a 'Euclidean syntax' which structured European territorial control.[14] Indeed, the graphic nature of the map gave its imperial users an arbitrary power that was easily divorced from the social responsibilities and consequences of its exercise. The world could be carved up on paper. Pope Alexander VI thus demarcated the Spanish and Portuguese possessions in the New World.[15] In the partitioning of North America, itself 'part of a vast European process and experiment, an ongoing development of worldwide imperialism', the

> very lines on the map exhibited this imperial power and process because they had been imposed on the continent with little reference to indigenous peoples, and indeed in many places with little reference to the land itself. The invaders parceled the continent among themselves in designs reflective of their own complex rivalries and relative power.[16]

In the nineteenth century, as maps became further institutionalized and linked to the growth of geography as a discipline, their power effects are again manifest in the continuing tide of European imperialism. The scramble for Africa, in which the European powers fragmented the identity of indigenous territorial organization, has become almost a textbook example of these effects.[17] And in our own century, in the British partition of India in 1947, we can see how the stroke of a pen across a map could determine the lives and deaths of millions of people.[18] There are innumerable contexts in which maps became the currency of political 'bargains', leases, partitions, sales, and treaties struck over colonial territory and, once made permanent in the image, these maps more than often acquired the force of law in the landscape.

Maps and the nation state

The history of the map is inextricably linked to the rise of the nation State in the modern world. Many of the printed maps of Europe emphasized the estates, waterways, and political boundaries that constituted the politico-economic dimensions of European geography.[19] Early political theorists commended maps to statesmen, who in turn were among their first systematic collectors.[20] The State became – and has remained – a principal patron of cartographic activity in many countries.[21]

Yet while the State was prepared to finance mapping, either directly through its exchequer or indirectly through commercial privilege, it often insisted that such knowledge was privileged. In Western Europe the history of cartographic secrecy, albeit often ineffective, can be traced back to the sixteenth-century Spanish and Portuguese policy of *siglio*.[22] It was the practice to monopolize knowledge, 'to use geographic documents as an economic resource, much as craft mysteries were secreted and used'.[23]

A major example of the interaction between maps and State polity is found in the history of military technology. In military eyes, maps have always been regarded as a sensitive sort of knowledge, and policies of secrecy and censorship abound as much today in the 'hidden' specifications of defence and official map-making agencies as in the campaign headquarters of the past.[24] At a practical level, military maps are a small but vital cog in the technical infrastructure of the army in the field. As the techniques of warfare were transformed from siege tactics to more mobile strategies, especially from the eighteenth century onwards, so too were the maps associated with them transformed.[25] Even in these active contexts, however, there were subtler historical processes at work. Map knowledge allows the conduct of warfare by remote control so that, we may speculate, killing is that much more easily contemplated.[26] Military maps not only facilitate the technical conduct of warfare, but also palliate the sense of guilt which arises from its conduct: the silent lines of the paper landscape foster the notion of socially empty space.

Not all military maps are silent; many stridently proclaim military victory. Just as there were military parades, songs, and poems, so too, at least from the fifteenth century onwards in Europe, there have been battle plans designed to commemorate the sacred places of national glory.[27]

Maps and property rights

Cadastral or estate maps showing the ownership of property reveal the role of mapping in the history of agrarian class relations. Here the map may be regarded as a means by which either the State or individual landlords could more effectively control a tenant or peasant population.[28] In Roman society, the codified practices of the *agrimensores* may be interpreted not just as technical manuals of land division in a theoretical sense but also as a social apparatus for legally regulating appropriated lands and for exacting taxation.[29] The maps themselves, whether cast in bronze or chipped in stone, were designed to make more permanent a social order in which there were freemen and slaves and for which the territorial division of land was the basis of status.[30] In early modern Europe, too, though the sociological context of mapping was different, some of the same forces were at work. The extent to which the mapping of local rural areas was locked into the process of litigation can leave us in no doubt about its socio-legal context and as a means by which conflict between lords and peasants over private rights in land could be more effectively pursued.[31] Maps fitted as easily into the culture of landed society as they had into the courtly diplomacies and the military manoeuvres of European nation States in the Renaissance.

In similar terms, maps can be seen to be embedded in some of the long-term structural changes of the transition from feudalism to capitalism. The world economy and its new geographical division of labour were produced with the aid of geographical documents, including maps.[32] Accurate, large-scale plans were a means by which land could be more efficiently exploited, by which rent rolls could be increased, and by which legal obligations could be enforced or tenures modified. Supplementing older, written surveys, the map served as a graphic inventory, a codification of information about ownership, tenancy, rentable values, cropping practice, and agricultural potential, enabling capi-

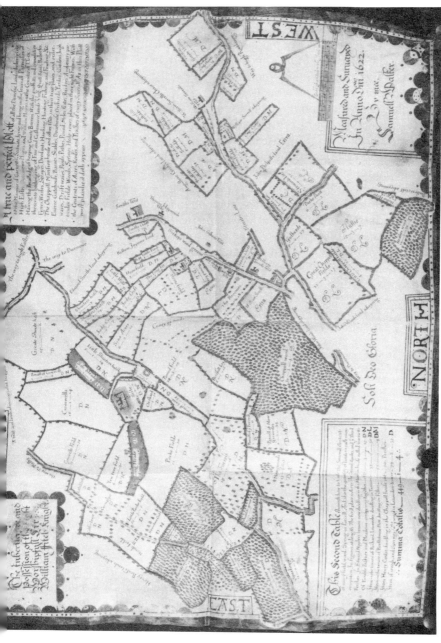

Fig. 19.2 Large-scale estate maps, and the written cadastres they accompanied, became a tool in the rise of agrarian capitalism in England from the sixteenth century. In this example of Samuel Walker's map of the estate of Garnett's, Essex (1622), details of ownership (DN = Edward Naylor's desmesne, DL = Richard Lavender's demesne, etc.), precise delineation and accurate measurement (in acres, roods, perches) translate property rights into a tangible and legally binding image. By permission of the British Library

talist landowners to see their estates as a whole and better to control them.[33] Seeing was believing in relation to the territorial hierarchies expressed in maps. Whether in the general history of agricultural improvement, of enclosure, of the draining or embankment of fens and marshes, or of the reclamation of hill and moor, the surveyor ever more frequently walks at the side of the landlord in spreading capitalist forms of agriculture.[34]

Maps impinged invisibly on the daily lives of ordinary people. Just as the clock, as a graphic symbol of centralized political authority, brought 'time discipline' into the rhythms of industrial workers,[35] so too the lines on maps, dictators of a new agrarian topography, introduced a dimension of 'space discipline'. In European peasant societies, former commons were now subdivided and allotted with the help of maps, and in the 'wilderness' of former Indian lands in North America, boundary lines on the map were a medium of appropriation which those unlearned in geometrical survey methods found impossible to challenge. Maps entered the law, were attached to ordinances, acquired an aureole of science, and helped create an ethic and virtue of ever more precise definition. Tracings on maps excluded as much as they enclosed. They fixed territorial relativities according to the lottery of birth, the accidents of discovery, or, increasingly, the mechanism of the world market.

Map content in the transaction of power

'Is that the same map?' Jincey asked. She pointed to the large map of the world that hung, rolled up for the summer, above the blackboard behind Miss Dove. 'Is China still orange?' 'It is a new map,' Miss Dove said. 'China is purple.' 'I liked the old map,' Jincey said. 'I like the old world.' 'Cartography is a fluid art,' said Miss Dove.

Frances Gray Patton, *Good morning, Miss Dove*

Cartographers and map historians have long been aware of tendencies in the content of their maps that they call 'bias', 'distortion', 'deviance', or the 'abuse' of sound cartographic principles. But little space in cartographic literature is devoted to the political implications of these terms and what they represent, and even less to their social consequences. Such 'bias' or 'distortion' is generally measured against a yardstick of 'objectivity', itself derived from cartographic procedure. Only in deliberately distorted maps, for example in advertising or propaganda, are the consequences discussed.[36] 'Professional' cartography of the Ordnance Survey, the USGS, Bartholomew or Rand McNally or their predecessors would be regarded as largely free from such politically polluted imagery. That maps can produce a truly 'scientific' image of the world, in which factual information is represented without favour, is a view well embedded in our cultural mythology. To acknowledge that all cartography is 'an intricate, controlled fiction'[37] does not prevent our retaining a distinction between those presentations of map content which are deliberately induced by cartographic artifice and those in which the structuring content of the image is unexamined.

Deliberate distortions of map content

Deliberate distortions of map content for political purposes can be traced throughout the history of maps, and the cartographer has never been an independent artist, craftsman, or technician. Behind the map-maker lies a set of power relations, creating its own specification. Whether imposed by an individual patron, by State bureaucracy, or the market, these rules can be reconstructed both from the content of maps and from the mode of cartographic representation. By adapting individual projections, by manipulating scale, by over-enlarging or moving signs or typography, or by using emotive colours, makers of propaganda maps have generally been the advocates of a one-sided view of geopolitical relationships. Such maps have been part of the currency of international psychological warfare long before their use by Nazi geopoliticians. The religious wars of seventeenth-century Europe and the Cold War of the twentieth century have been fought as much in the contents of propaganda maps as through any other medium.[38]

Fig. 19.3 Even simple thematic maps can carry subtle propaganda messages. This school atlas map, from *Geschichtsatlas . . . Deutsch* (1933), represents Germanic elements in Europe and (inset) overseas but omits a key to the values of the three sizes of symbol. While the distribution pattern is realistic, German minorities in European countries were usually very much smaller (under 4 per cent of total population) than the use of ranked symbols suggest. By permission of the British Library

Apparently objective maps are also characterized by persistent manipulation of content. 'Cartographic censorship' implies deliberate misrepresentation designed to mislead potential users of the map, usually those regarded as opponents of the territorial status quo. We should not confuse this with deletions or additions resulting from technical error or incompetence or made necessary by scale or function. Cartographic censorship removes from maps features which, *other things being equal*, we might expect to find on them. Naturally this is less noticeable than blatant distortion. It is justified on grounds of 'national security', 'political expediency', or 'commercial necessity' and is still widely practised. The censored image marks the boundaries of permissible discourse, and deliberate omissions discourage 'the clarification of social alternatives', making it 'difficult for the dispossessed to locate the source of their unease, let alone to remedy it'.[39]

The commonest justification for cartographic censorship has probably always been military. In its most wholesale form it has involved prohibiting the publication of surveys.[40] On the other hand, settlement details on eighteenth-century maps were left unrevised by Frederick the Great to deceive a potential enemy, just as it has been inferred that the towns on some Russian maps were deliberately relocated in incorrect positions in the 1960s to prevent strategic measurements being taken from them by enemy powers.[41] Since the nineteenth century, too, it has been almost universal practice to 'cleanse' systematically evidence of sensitive military installations from official series of topographical maps.[42] The practice now extends to other features where their inclusion would be potentially embarrassing to the government of the day; for example, nuclear waste dumps are omitted from official USGS topographical maps.

Deliberate falsification of map content has been associated with political considerations other than the purely military. Boundaries on maps have been subject to graphic gerrymandering. This arises both from attempts to assert historical claims to national territory,[43] and from the predictive art of using maps to project and to legitimate future territorial ambitions.[44] For example, disputed boundaries, whether shown on official maps, in atlases, or in more ephemeral images such as postage stamps, have been either included or suppressed according to the current political preference.[45] Nor do these practices apply solely to political boundaries on maps. It is well documented how the geographies of language, 'race', and religion have been portrayed to accord with dominant beliefs.[46] There are the numerous cases where indigenous place-names of minority groups are suppressed on topographical maps in favour of the standard toponymy of the controlling group.[47]

'Unconscious' distortions of map content

Of equal interest to the student of cartographic iconology is the subtle process by which the content of maps is influenced by the values of the map-producing society. Any social history of maps must be concerned with these hidden rules of cartographic imagery and with their accidental consequences.[48] Three aspects of these hidden structures – relating to map geometry, to 'silences' in the content of maps, and to hierarchical tendencies in cartographic representation – will be discussed.

Subliminal geometry

The geometrical structure of maps – their graphic design in relation to the location on which they are centred or to the projection which determines their transformational relationship to the earth[49] – is an element which can magnify the political impact of an image even where no conscious distortion is intended. A universal feature of early world maps, for example, is the way they have been persistently centred on the 'navel of the world', as this has been perceived by different societies. This '*omphalos* syndrome',[50] where a people believe themselves to be divinely appointed to the centre of the universe, can be traced in maps widely separated in time and space, such as those from ancient Mesopotamia with Babylon at its centre, maps of the Chinese universe centred on China, Greek maps centred on Delphi, Islamic maps centred on Mecca, and those Christian world maps in which Jerusalem is placed as the 'true' centre of the world.[51] The effect of such 'positional enhancing'[52] geometry on the social consciousness of space is difficult to gauge and it would be wrong to suggest that common design features necessarily contributed to identical world views. At the very least, however, such maps tend to focus the viewer's attention upon the centre, and thus to promote the development of 'exclusive, inward-directed worldviews, each with its separate cult centre safely buffered within territories populated only by true believers'.[53]

A similarly ethno-centric view may have been induced by some of the formal map projections of the European Renaissance. In this case, too, a map 'structures the geography it depicts according to a set of beliefs about the way the world should be, and presents this construction as truth'.[54] In the well-known example of Mercator's projection it is doubtful whether Mercator himself – who designed the map with navigators in mind to show true compass directions – would have been aware of the extent to which his map would eventually come to project an image so strongly reinforcing the Europeans' view of their own world hegemony. Yet the simple fact that Europe is at the centre of the world on this projection, and that the area of the land masses are so distorted that two-thirds of the earth's surface appears to lie in high latitudes, must have contributed much to a European sense of superiority. Indeed, the fact that the 'white colonialist States' appear on the map relatively larger than they are while 'the colonies' inhabited by coloured peoples are shown 'too small' suggests how it can be read and acted upon as a geopolitical prophecy.[55]

The silence on maps

The notion of 'silences' on maps is central to any argument about the influence of their hidden political messages. It is asserted here that maps – just as much as examples of literature or the spoken word – exert a social influence through their omissions as much as by the features they depict and emphasize.

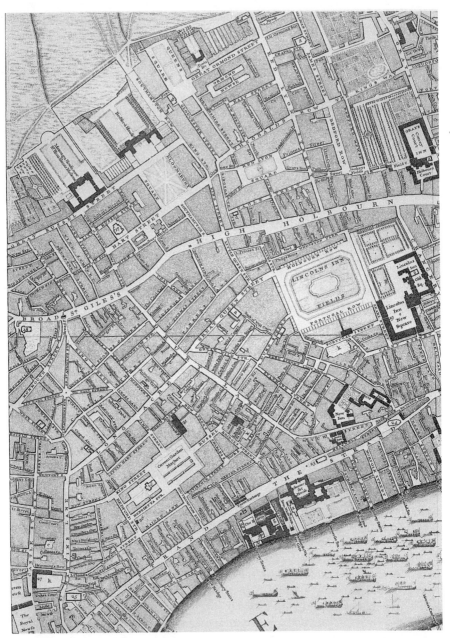

Fig. 19.4 Silences on maps: part of John Rocque's 'Plan of the Cities of London and Westminster . . .' (1955) showing the built-up area west of the City of London and the prestigious new green-field developments of Bloomsbury. While districts to the north of Covent Garden and around Broad Street and St Giles were rapidly becoming slums, the cartographer has produced an idealized view of the city which emphasizes the gracious rurality of the main squares but fails to convey urban squalor. By permission of the British Library

So forceful are the political undercurrents in these silences that it is some-times difficult to explain them solely by recourse to other historical or technical factors. In seventeenth-century Ireland, for example, the fact that surveyors working for English proprietors sometimes excluded the cabins of the native Irish from their otherwise 'accurate' maps is not just a question of scale and of the topographical prominence of such houses, but rather of the religious tensions and class relations in the Irish countryside.[56] Much the same could be said about omissions on printed county surveys of eighteenth-century England: the exclusion of smaller rural cottages may be a response as much to the ideal world of the map-makers' landed clients as to the dictates of cartographic scale.[57] On many early town plans a map-maker may have unconsciously ignored the alleys and courtyards of the poor in deference to the principal thoroughfares, public buildings and residences of the merchant class in his conscious promotion of civic pride or vaunting commercial success.[58] Such ideological filtering is a universal process. In colonial mapping, as in eighteenth-century North America, silences on maps may also be regarded as discrimination against native peoples. A map such as Fry and Jefferson's of Virginia (1751) suggests that the Europeans had always lived there: where 'Indian nations' are depicted on it, it is more as a signpost to future colonial expansion than as a recognition of their ethnic integrity.[59] In this way, through-out the long age of exploration, European maps gave a one-sided view of ethnic encounters and supported Europe's God-given right to territorial appro-priation. European atlases, too, while codifying a much wider range of geo-graphical knowledge, also promoted a Eurocentric, imperialist vision, including as they did a bias towards domestic space which sharpened Europeans' perception of their cultural superiority in the world system.[60] Silences on maps – often becoming part of wider cultural stereotypes – thus came to enshrine self-fulfilling prophecies about the geography of power.

Representational hierarchies

The role of the map as a form of social proclamation is further strengthened by the systems of classification and modes of representation – the so-called 'con-ventional' or cartographic signs[61] – which have been adopted for landscape features. It has long been one of the map-maker's rules that the signs for towns and villages – whether depicted iconically or by abstract devices – are shown proportionally to the rank of the places concerned. Yet the resulting visual hierarchy of signs in early modern maps is often a replica of the legal, feudal, and ecclesiastical stratifications. Indeed, the concept of a tiered territorial society was by no means lost on contemporary map-makers. Mercator, for example, had hoped in his 1595 atlas to show 'an exact enumeration and designation of the seats of princes and nobles'.[62] Like other map-makers before him, he designed a set of settlement signs which, just as truly as the grids which have already been discussed, reify an ordering of the space represented on the map by making it visible. On other maps, towns occupy spaces on the map – even allowing for cartographic convention – far in excess of their sizes on the ground.[63] Castle signs, too, signifying feudal rank and military might, are sometimes larger than signs for villages, despite the lesser area they occupied on the ground. Coats of arms – badges of territorial possession – were used to locate the *caput* of a lordship while the tenurially dependent settlements within the feudal order were allocated inferior signs irrespective of their population or areal size. This was particularly common on maps of German territory formerly within the Holy Roman Empire. Such maps pay considerable attention to the geography of ecclesiastic power. The primary message was often that of the ubiquity of the Church. Whether in 'infidel' territory held by the Turk, in lands under the sway of the Papacy, in areas dominated by Protestants in general, or by particular sects such as the Hussites, maps communicated the extensiveness of the temporal estate within the spiritual landscape. As a secondary message, not only do these maps heighten the perception of the power of the Church as an institution within society as a whole, but also they record the spatial hierarchies and conflicting denominations within the Church itself. On the former point, we may note that on Boazio's map of Ireland (1599), an exaggerated pictorial sign for 'a Bishopes towne' is placed at the head of its key,[64] just as on the regional map of Reformation England the signs for church towers and spires often rose far above the requirement of a notional vertical scale. On the matter of hierarchy, individual signs for archbishoprics and bishoprics, in arrays of single or double crosses, or croziers, mitres, and variations in ecclesiastical headgear, testify to the social organisation of religion.[65] Here again, the selective magnifications of cartographic signs were closely linked to the shifting allegiances of opposing faiths. They survive as expressions of the religious battlegrounds of early modern Europe.

Conclusion: cartographic discourse and ideology

I have sought to show how a history of maps, in common with that of other culture symbols, may be interpreted as a form of discourse. While theoretical insights may be derived, for example, from literary criticism, art history, and sociology, we still have to grapple with maps as unique systems of signs, whose codes may be at once iconic, linguistic, numerical, and temporal, and as a spatial form of knowledge. It has not proved difficult to make a general case for the mediating role of maps in political thought and action nor to glimpse their power effects. Through both their content and their modes of representation, the making and using of maps has been pervaded by ideology. Yet these mechanisms can only be understood in specific historical situations.

Notes

1　Historians are also primarily concerned with the extent to which the evidence of maps can be evaluated as a 'true' record of the facts of discovery, colonization, exploration, or other events in space.

2　On this view Margarita Bowen, *Empiricism and geographical thought from Francis Bacon to Alexander von Humboldt* (Cambridge, 1981); and D. R. Stoddart (ed.), *Geography, ideology and social concern* (Oxford, 1981), esp. pp. 11, 58–60.

3 Carl O. Sauer, The education of a geographer. *Annals of the Association of American Geographers* 46, 287–99, (1956), esp. p. 289.

4 W. J. T. Mitchell, *Iconology: Image, text, ideology* (Chicago, 1986), pp. 9–14.

5 Cf. the analysis of art in 'Art as ideology', in Janet Wolff, *The social production of art* (London, 1981), p. 49.

6 J. B. Harley and David Woodward, Concluding remarks. In J. B. Harley and David Woodward (eds), *The history of cartography*. Vol. 1: *Cartography in prehistoric, ancient, and medieval Europe and the Mediterranean* (Chicago, 1987), p. 506.

7 Ibid.

8 Islamic cartography is most authoritatively described in E. van Donzel, B. Lewis and Ch. Pellat (eds), *Encyclopaedia of Islam* (Leiden, 1978), vol. 4, pp. 1077–83.

9 Joseph Needham, *Science and civilisation in China*, vol. 3, sec. 22 (Cambridge, 1959).

10 B. Castiglione, *The courtier* [1528], transl. George Bull (Harmondsworth, 1967), p. 97; Thomas Elyot, *The boke named the gouernour*, ed. from the first edn of 1531 by H. H. S. Croft, 2 vols (London, 1880), vol. 1, pp. 45, 77–8; Machiavelli, *Arte della guerra* [1521], ed. S. Bertelli (Milan, 1961), pp. 457–8.

11 For the classical empires, see O. A. W. Dilke, *Greek and Roman maps* (London, 1985), pp. 41–53 (on Agrippa's map) and pp. 169–70 (on the world map of Theodosius II). Maps of the British Empire became popular during the Victorian era: see Margaret Drabble, *For Queen and country: Britain in the Victorian age* (London, 1978), where the map by Maclure & Co., London, 1886, is reproduced. The geopolitical message of such maps and globes is unequivocally conveyed by G. K. Chesterton, Songs of education: II Geography.

12 Samuel Y. Edgerton, Jr, From mental matrix to *mappamundi* to Christian empire: the heritage of Ptolemaic cartography in the Renaissance. In David Woodward (ed.), *Art and cartography* (Chicago, 1987), p. 22.

13 Hildegard Binder Johnson, *Order upon the land: The US rectangular land survey and the upper Mississippi country* (New York, 1976).

14 Claude Raffestin, *Pour une géographie du pouvoir* (Paris, 1980), p. 131.

15 Alexander's bull regarding the demarcation line is given in Anne Fremantle (ed.), *The papal encyclicals in their historical context* (New York, 1956), pp. 77–81.

16 D. W. Meinig, *The shaping of America: A geographical perspective on 500 years of history*. Vol. 1: *Atlantic America, 1492–1800* (New Haven, 1986), p. 232. A similar point is made by Robert David Sack, *Human territoriality: Its theory and history* (Cambridge, 1986), p. 11.

17 See P. A. Penfold (ed.), *Maps and plans in the Public Record Office*. Vol. 3: *Africa* (London, 1982), *passim*; J. Stengers, King Leopold's imperialism. In Roger Owen and Bob Sutcliffe (eds), *Studies in the theory of imperialism* (London, 1972), pp. 248–76.

18 For a vivid reconstruction of Radcliffe's partition of India employing relatively small-scale maps, see Larry Collins and Dominique Lapierre, *Freedom at midnight* (London, 1982), pp. 245–8.

19 Chandra Mukerji, *From graven images: Patterns of modern materialism* (New York, 1983), p. 83. See also Giuseppe Dematteis, *Le metafore della terra: La geografia umana tra mito e scienza* (Milan, 1985), pp. 54–9.

20 On early map collections, see R. A. Skelton, *Maps: A historical survey of their study and collecting* (Chicago, 1972), pp. 26–61; Harley, The map and the development of the history of cartography. In Harley and Woodward (eds), *History of cartography*, op. cit. (note 6), pp. 6–12.

21 For early examples of state involvement in topographical mapping, see Lloyd A. Brown, *The story of maps* (Boston, 1949), esp. pp. 241–71.

22 Daniel J. Boorstin, *The discoverers* (New York, 1983), pp. 267–9; on the Dutch East India Company's policy, see Gunter Schilder, Organization and evolution of the Dutch East India Company's hydrographic office in the seventeenth century. *Imago Mundi* 28, 61–78 (1976); for an English example, Helen Wallis, The cartography of Drake's voyage. In Norman J. W. Thrower (ed.), *Sir Francis Drake and the famous voyage, 1577–1580* (Los Angeles and London, 1985), pp. 133–7.

23 Mukerji, *From graven images*, op. cit. (note 19), p. 91; see also Chandra Mukerji, Visual language in science and the exercise of power: the case of cartography in early modern Europe. *Studies in Visual Communications* 10(3), 30–45 (1984).

24 Official map-making agencies, usually under the cloak of 'national security', have been traditionally reticent about publishing details about what rules govern the information they exclude, especially where this involves military installations or other politically sensitive sites.

25 Christopher Duffy, *Siege warfare: The fortress in the early modern world 1494–1660* (London, 1979), esp. p. 81; and *The fortress in the age of Vauban and Frederick the Great 1660–1789.* (London, 1985), esp. pp. 29, 72, 142. On the effect of cartography on more mobile warfare, see R. A. Skelton, The military surveyor's contribution to British cartography in the 16th century. *Imago Mundi* 24, 77–83 (1970).

26 Phillip C. Muehrcke, *Map use: Reading, analysis, and interpretation* (Madison, WI, 1978), pp. 299–301.

27 Probably the majority of published battle plans and campaign maps issued 'after the event' in Europe down to the end of the eighteenth century fall either into this category or illustrated histories justifying the conduct of warfare.

28 A comparison can be made here with written documents; see, for example, M. T. Clanchy, *From memory to written record: England 1066–1307* (London, 1979), esp. pp. 149–265.

29 O. A. W. Dilke, *The Roman land surveyors: An introduction to the Agrimensores* (Newton Abbot, 1971).

30 P. Anderson, *Passages from antiquity to feudalism* (London, 1974), esp. pp. 147–53, 185, 188–9, 207–8.

31 P. D. A. Harvey, *The history of topographical maps: Symbols, pictures and surveys* (London, 1980), *passim*.

32 Mukerji, *From graven images*, op. cit. (note 19), p. 84; Immanuel Wallerstein, *The modern world-system.* Vol. 2: *Mercantilism and the consolidation of the European world economy, 1600–1750* (New York, 1980) offers many clues to this process. Appropriately enough, the frontispiece to the volume is a world map by Jan Blaeu (1638).

33 J. R. Hale, *Renaissance Europe 1480–1520* (London, 1971), pp. 52–3.

34 F. M. L. Thompson, *Chartered surveyors: The growth of a profession* (London, 1968).

35 David S. Landes, *Clocks and the making of the modern world* (Cambridge, MA, 1983), pp. xix, 2, 25, 228–30, 285–6; and Stephen Kern, *The culture of time and space* (London, 1983), pp. 10–35.

36 There is an extensive literature on maps in the pre-war German school of geopolitics. See, for example, Hans Speir, Magic geography. *Social Research* 8, 310–30 (1941); Louis O. Quam, The use of maps in propaganda. *Journal of Geography* 42, 21–32 (1943); Louis B. Thomas, Maps as instruments of propaganda. *Surveying and Mapping* 9, 75–81 (1949); and John Ager, Maps and propaganda. *Bulletin of the Society of University Cartographers* 11, 1–14 (1977).

37 Muehrcke, *Map use*, op. cit. (note 26), p. 295.

38 Geoffrey Parker, *The thirty years' war* (London, 1984), plates 10, 13.

39 T. J. Jackson Lears, The concept of cultural hegemony: problems and possibilities. *American Historical Review* 90 (1985), 567–93.

40 Harry Margary, *The old series Ordnance Survey maps*, vol. 3 (Lympne Castle, 1981), p. xxxiv.

41 Speir, Magic geography, op. cit. (note 36), p. 320; F. J. Ormeling, Jr, Cartographic consequences of a planned economy – 50 years of Soviet cartography. *American Cartographer* 1(1), 48–9 (1974); Soviet cartographic falsifications, *Military Engineer* 62(410), 389–91 (1970).

42 For 'security' reasons not even the existence of these practices is reported, although in Britain, for example, in recent years they have been unearthed by investigative journalism: see *New Statesman*, 27 May 1983, p. 6, which reported that 'Moles within the Ordnance Survey have sent us a most interesting secret manual which lists and defines the places in Britain which do not officially exist, and therefore cannot appear on maps'.

43 For example, in West Germany, the publishers of atlases have been obliged to obey a set of detailed ministerial regulations relating to political boundaries for maps that are to be used in schools. These did not receive approval for publication unless they showed the 1937 boundaries of Germany as well as those of today: K. A. Sinnhuber, 'The representation of disputed political boundaries in general atlases.' *Cartographic Journal* 1(2), 20–8 (1964).

44 Numerous examples occur in the eighteenth-century British and French maps of North America: Percy G. Adams, *Travelers and travel liars 1660–1800* (New York, 1980), pp. 64–79, who, however, misses the ideological significance of the cartographic falsification he describes. See also J. B. Harley, 'The bankruptcy of Thomas Jefferys: an episode in the economic history of eighteenth century map-making. *Imago Mundi* 20, 28–48, (1968), esp. pp. 33–40. For a nineteenth-century example, see Charles E. Nowell, *The rose-coloured map: Portugal's attempt to build an African empire from the Atlantic to the Indian Ocean* (Lisbon, 1982).

45 For political aspects of carto-philately, see Bruce Davis, Maps on postage stamps as propaganda. *Cartographic Journal* 22(2), 125–30 (1985).

46 H. R. Wilkinson, *Maps and politics: A review of the ethnographic cartography of Macedonia* (Liverpool, 1951).

47 F. J. Ormeling, *Minority toponyms on maps: The rendering of linguistic minority toponyms on topographic maps of Western Europe* (Utrecht, 1983).

48 The idea of the hidden rules of cartography comes from Michel Foucault, *The order of things: An archaeology of the human sciences* (London, 1966; repr. 1970).

49 These geometrical elements also include the manipulation of scale and orientation and the use of cartographic grids to organize space. On the wider social significance of these geometries, see Robert Sack, *Conceptions of space in social thought: A geographic perspective* (London, 1980), *passim*.

50 The phrase is that of Edgerton, 'From mental matrix to *mappamundi*', p. 26.

51 On European examples see Harley and Woodward, *The history of cartography*, vol. 1; on Chinese maps, Needham, *Science and civilisation in China*, op. cit., vol. 3; and on Islamic maps, *Encyclopaedia of Islam*, op. cit. (note 8), vol. 4.

52 The concept is E. H. Gombrich's *The sense of order* (Ithaca, 1979), pp. 155–6.

53 Edgerton, From mental matrix to *mappamundi*', op. cit., (note 12), p. 27. For potential insights into how maps could have contributed to the infrastructure of social cosmologies, see Michael Harbsmeier, On travel accounts and cosmological strategies: some models in comparative xenology. *Ethnos* 50(3–4), 273–312 (1985).

54 Denis E. Cosgrove, *Social formation and symbolic landscape* (London, 1984), p. 8.

55 Arno Peters, *The new cartography* (New York, 1983), p. 63; see also Terry Cook, A reconstruction of the world: George R. Parkin's British Empire map of 1893. *Cartographica* 21(4), 53–65 (1984) for the deliberate use of Mercator's projection in a map promoting the 'New Imperialism' of the pan-Britannic world of the late nineteenth century. The recent reaction of cartographers towards the 'unscientific' nature of the alternative 'Peters' projection', which adjusts some of these distortions in favour of the Third World, provides a contemporary gloss on the entrenched scientism among map-makers which still gives credibility to the mathematically constructed map while ignoring the possibility of the social and political effects of its imagery. For example, see the comments by John Loxton, The Peters' phenomenon. *Cartographic Journal* 22(2), 106–8 (1985), which attempt to discredit Peters as a 'Marxist' and 'socialist'. 'The so-called Peters' projection', in ibid., pp. 108–10, which is presented as the considered view of the German Carto-graphical Society, is in some respects more polemical than Peters in its 'defence of truthfulness and pure scientific discussion'. See also A. H. Robinson, Arno Peters and his new cartography, *American Cartographer* 12, 103–11 (1985), and Phil Porter and Phil Voxland, Distortion in maps: the Peters' projection and other devilments. *Focus* 36, 22–30 (1986).

56 J. H. Andrews, *Plantation acres: An historical study of the Irish land surveyor and his maps* (Belfast, 1985), pp. 157–8.

57 J. B. Harley, The re-mapping of England 1750–1800. *Imago Mundi* 19, 56–67 (1965); Paul Laxton, The geodetic and topographical evaluation of English county maps, 1740–1840. *Cartographic Journal* 13(1), 37–54 (1976).

58 Cf. Juergen Schulz, Jacopo de' Barbari's view of Venice: map making, city views and moralized geography before the year 1500. *Art Bulletin* 60, 425–74 (1978); J. B. Harley, Meaning and ambiguity in Tudor cartography. In Sarah Tyacke (ed.), *English map-making 1500–1650: Historical essays* (London, 1983) pp. 28–32.

59 For the development of this argument, see J. B. Harley, Society, ideology, and the English geographical atlas in the eighteenth century. In John A. Wolter (ed.), *Images of the world: The atlas through history* (Washington, DC, forthcoming).

60 James R. Akerman, National geographical consciousness and the structure of early world atlases. Paper presented at the Eleventh International Conference on the History of Cartography, Ottawa, Canada, July 1985.

61 I am indebted to Catherine Delano Smith for discussion and the sight of a draft manuscript; 'Cartographic signs in the Renaissance', to be published in J. B. Harley and David Woodward (eds), *The history of cartography*. Vol. 3: *Cartography in the age of Renaissance and discovery* (Chicago, forthcoming).

62 Catherine Delano Smith, Cartographic signs on European maps and their explanation before 1700. *Imago Mundi* 37, 9–29, (1985), where Mercator's *Advice for the use of maps: Atlas sive cosmographicae. Meditationes de fabrica mundi et fabricati figura* (1595) is quoted, pp. 25–6.

63 See Christian Sgrothen's maps of the Netherland (1573), where towns such as Bruges, Brussels, and Ghent are depicted in high oblique in such a way – and with so large a sign – as to ensure ample scope for the detailed display of the attributes of their commercial success and civic pride.

64 Edward Lynam, Boazio's map of Ireland. *British Museum Quarterly* 11, 92–5, (1937).

65 François de Dainville, *Le langage des géographes: Termes, signes, couleurs des cartes anciennes, 1500–1800* (Paris, 1964), pp. 236–44.

20 Stephen Daniels and Simon Rycroft, 'Mapping the Modern City: Alan Sillitoe's Nottingham Novels'

Excerpts from: *Transactions of the Institute of British Geographers* NS 18, 460–480 (1993)

As a literary form, the novel is inherently geographical. The world of the novel is made up of locations and settings, arenas and boundaries, perspectives and horizons. Various places and spaces are occupied or envisaged by the novel's characters, by the narrator and by audiences as they read. Any one novel may present a field of different, sometimes competing, forms of geographical knowledge and experience, from a sensuous awareness of place to an educated idea of region and nation. These various geographies are co-ordinated by various kinds of temporal knowledge and experience, from circumscribed routines to linear notions of progress or transformation (Kestner, 1978; Tuan, 1978; Barrell, 1982; Said, 1989).

From its formulation in the eighteenth century, the novel has been a speculative instrument for exploring and articulating those material, social and mental transformations we call modernization. The novel was first associated with the transformation of London into a world metropolis, representing the capitalist city to its bourgeois citizens as 'accessible, comprehensible and controllable' (Bender, 1987, p. 65). Its scope was not confined to the city; early novelists charted transformations in the countryside and colonies too. The refinement of the novel as a genre was commensurate with the refinement of a number of geographical discourses, such as town planning, estate improvement, cartography and topographical painting, which surveyed and reordered the spaces of the modernizing world (Alfrey and Daniels, 1990; Varey, 1990; Daniels, in press). From the time of Defoe the novel has been fashioned and refashioned as an instrument for representing various geographies in different phases, forms and sites of modernization (Watt, 1957; Williams, 1973; Bradbury, 1976; Seidel, 1976; Berman, 1983, pp. 173–286; Said, 1993).

In this article we examine the geographies of novels by Alan Sillitoe (1928–) set in and around Nottingham. We consider how the novels explore conflicts in the modernization of working-class areas of the city from the 1920s to the 1950s, in particular the clearance of slums, the building of new housing estates and the emergence of a consumer culture. It was a time when the city corporation, proud of its progressive social and economic planning, promoted Nottingham as 'the modern city'. We focus on the geographies of the novels' Nottingham-born male protagonists: local rebel Arthur Seaton in *Saturday night and Sunday morning* (1958/1976[1]), RAF conscript Brian Seaton in *Key to the door* (1961) and *The open door* (1989) and internationalist guerilla Frank Dawley in *The death of William Posters* (1965). These novels take us beyond transformations of mid-century Nottingham to transformations overseas, to the violent ending of colonial rule in Malaya and Algeria.

We situate these novels in terms of a number of Sillitoe's other writings: autobiography, travel writing, literary criticism, poetry, political journalism.[2] We also consider a range of other cultural discourses which bear upon the novels, including aerial photography, urban sociology and classical mythology. Above all, we wish to show the importance of maps, map-reading and map-making to the geographies of the novels. This was the subject of a main source of this article, an interview we conducted with Alan Sillitoe in 1991.[3]

First, we will examine the issue of mapping in relation to Sillitoe's life and work, his literary influences and the modernization of Nottingham. Second, we will consider the connections between mapping, modernism and masculinity. The third and largest part of the article analyses the texts and contexts of the novels. Finally we compare the geographies of Nottingham in these novels with geographies of the city in official and academic publications of the time.

In this article we try to re-vision the relationship between 'geography and literature' (Pocock, 1981; Mallory and Simpson-Housley, 1987) in a way which takes account of some recent developments in cultural geography and literary criticism (Said, 1983; Barnes and Duncan, 1992; Barrell, 1992; Driver, 1992; Daniels, 1993). We consider geography and literature not as the conjunction of two essentially distinct, coherent disciplines, or orders of knowledge – objective and subjective, real and imaginative, and so on – but as a field of textual genres – the novel, the poem, the travel guide, the map, the regional monograph – with complex overlaps and interconnections. We have brought out both the worldliness of literary texts and the imaginativeness of geographical texts. The imaginativeness of texts consists in the images they express and in the way they construct, through modes of writing or composition – however empirically – particular and partial views of the world. The worldliness of texts consists in the various contexts – biographical, economic, institutional, geographical – which are entailed by texts and make them intelligible.

Maps and the man

Alan Sillitoe was born and raised in the Radford area of Nottingham, a nineteenth-century working-class suburb to the west of the city centre. Sillitoe recalled the Radford of his childhood as a labyrinthine world:

> Even when you knew every junction, twitchell and double entry (a concealed trackway which, connecting two streets, figured high in tactics of escape and manoeuvre) you never could tell when a gas lamp glowed that someone in the nearby dark was not using its light as an ambush pen. Neither did you know what waited behind the corner it stood on. . . . You invented perils, exaggerated pitfalls, occasionally felt that you even called them up. Potholes became foxholes, and foxholes as often or not turned into underground caverns full of guns and ammunition, food, and later, more gold than Monte Cristo ever dreamed of. In such streets you could outdream everybody.
>
> (Sillitoe, 1987b, p. 3)

As a child, Sillitoe envisaged his neighbourhood in terms of the underground worlds of the novels which then dominated his reading: *The Count of Monte Cristo* and, more strongly still, *Les misérables*.

> *Les misérables* took me through the prolonged crisis of childhood . . . I read the book again and again . . . till most of it was fixed firmly in.. . . From an early-age I was more familiar with the street names of Paris than those of London.. . . Exotic though it was in many ways, *Les misérables* seemed relevant to me and life roundabout . . . Gavroche, the street urchin who reminded me vividly of one of my cousins . . . the revolutionary fighting in the streets of Paris . . . when Jean Valjean rescues one of the wounded fighters from one of the about-to-be overrun barricades by carrying him through the sewers.
>
> (Sillitoe, 1975a, p. 156; 1975b, p. 12; 1987a, p. 12)

The physiography of Nottingham and its attendant folklore gave credence to the Parisian connection. Under the city, carved out of a cave system is a complicated network of chambers dating back to medieval times. These were used for storage, dwelling, gambling and, during the Second World War, as air raid shelters. Their occasional occupation throughout Nottingham's history by outlaws and rebels sustained a local mythology of a clandestine underworld, much like that of Paris as set out in *Les misérables* (Kempe, 1988, pp. 185–190).

In *Les misérables* the counterpoint of the underworld is the spacious, systematic new city planned by Baron Haussmann for Napoleon III (Hugo, 1982, esp. 399–410). Haussmann's plan was a city-wide vision which directly opposed the Parisian underworld, clearing poor districts to make way for a system of broad boulevards, public buildings, parks, parades and classical perspectives. It was a spectacular vision, planned from a height, in a new survey of the city from especially constructed towers and best seen in panoramic views (Pinkney, 1958; Clark, 1984, pp. 23–78). Haussmann's Paris is in many ways the vantage point of Hugo's novel. The narrator looks back to events of 1815–32 from the perspective of the 1860s, reconstructing, with the help of old maps, the social geography which Haussmann erased. Hugo's 'aerial observer' does not always have a clear view, peering down into the 'silent, ominous labyrinth' of the insurrectionary districts (as the reader 'peered into the depths' of another 'labyrinth of illusion', the conscience of the fugitive Valjean) (Hugo, 1982, pp. 945–7, 208). While sympathetic to the plight '*Les misérables*', the novel tracks them with a consciously cartographic eye.

In Sillitoe's Nottingham novels, the urban underworld is similarly counterpointed by a newly planned, systematic, self-consciously modern city. From the 1920s, the city corporation promoted Nottingham as 'the modern city' with 'wide thoroughfares, well proportioned buildings, and an entire absence of the smoke and grime usually associated with industry . . . creating a broad spaciousness that other cities envy and seek to emulate'. In official guides and publications, the structure of this modern city was displayed in aerial photographs: the new city hall (the Council House) and civic square, bright new factories, broad boulevards and spacious suburban estates (Figure 20.1). The corporation was particularly keen on its new aerodrome outside the city, built in 1928, the second in Britain to be licensed: 'the city of Nottingham

Fig. 20.1 The attractively laid-out Aspley Housing estate, with the William Crane Schools in the centre, viewed from an aeroplane. From *Nottingham official handbook* (10th edn, 1939)

has always been in the forefront in the matter of aviation' (British Association for the Advancement of Science, 1937, pp. 9–18; Nottingham, Corporation, 1939, pp. 25, 35–7, 62–5; Chambers, 1945, pp. 43–53).

During Sillitoe's youth the country beyond Radford, estate land developed with a mixture of parkland, plantations, collieries, allotments and cottages, was comprehensively modernized. The corporation purchased a large swathe of this land and built a spacious zone of boulevards, public parks and housing estates (Figure 20.2). The 2800 houses of the Aspley estate (1930–32) (Figure 20.1) were intended for newly married couples from Sillitoe's Radford or to rehouse families from cleared slum areas. There was a school at the centre of the estate, a showpiece of the city's enlightened educational policy, but few other social facilities or places of work. The new working-class suburb contrasted pointedly with the old: its elegant curves, crescents and concentric circles served to emphasize Radford's intricate network of terraces, back streets and alleys (Mellors, 1914, pp. 25–60; Chambers, 1945, pp. 47–8; Thomas, 1966, 1971; Silburn, 1981, pp. 30–3). Sillitoe's autobiographical story of childhood gang-fights is set on this modern frontier:

> Our street was straggling line of ancient back-to-backs on the city's edge, while the enemy district was a new housing estate of three long streets which had outflanked us and left us a mere pocket of country in which to run wild.

(Sillitoe, 1985, p. 156)

Fig. 20.2 Enlarged detail of north-west Nottingham. Reproduced from the 1946 1:63,360 Ordnance Survey map with the permission of the Controller of HMSO. © Crown copyright

Despite, or perhaps because of, the fact that his family remained in Radford, Sillitoe sought a heightened consciousness of Nottingham in a passion for maps as well as books. He taught himself to read maps as he learned to read novels and made maps as he learned to write. Born into a poor family, suffering the insecurities of chronic unemployment, Sillitoe 'latched onto maps in order to pull myself into the more rarefied and satisfying air of education and expansion of spirit'. Maps helped make sense of Nottingham, clarified its character and development. And they connected the city to a wider world. 'The first time I saw a map I wanted to leave home' (Sillitoe, 1972, p. 98). Sillitoe collected maps of all kinds. A large-scale estate map from his grandfather's cottage on the fringe countryside beyond Radford became a 'dream landscape' as this land began 'to be covered by houses and new roads'. An inch-to-the-mile Ordnance Survey map of the Aldershot area marked with tactical exercises, a gift from a retired guardsman next door, 'gave a picture I could relate to the land in my own district. Every cottage and copse was marked, every lane and footpath'. At school he watched 'with wonder and fascination' as the teacher took a wheeled metal cylinder and rolled gleaming outlines of Europe or North America on the page: 'it was the action of a magic wand', (Sillitoe, 1975c, p. 62–3; Rycroft, 1991, 10.)

The magic of maps was not just conceptual but technical, maps as artefacts not just images. As a child, Sillitoe made maps of all kinds, of both real and imaginary places, drawn on wallpaper, in the flyleaves of books, drawn 'with the same attention to detail as my lace-designer uncle put into his intricate patterns before they were set up on Nottingham machines'. Sillitoe esteemed maps as agents of modern, material transformation, 'a highway built where one had not existed before . . . a new town settled on the edge of sandy or forest wastes' (Sillitoe, 1972, pp. 98–9). Wartime conditions heightened Sillitoe's map consciousness. With signposts removed and street maps torn out of city guides, the war 'turned everyone into a spy and me into my own surveyor'. With the aid of a War Office manual, Sillitoe taught himself triangulation and 'with a simple compass and the expedient of pacing' made a detailed map of his neighbourhood (Sillitoe, 1975c, p. 68; 1987a, p. 9; Rycroft, 1991, pp. 11–12).

During the war, Sillitoe joined the Air Training Corps based at the local aerodrome. Here he acquired a military–geographical education, learning radiotelegraphy, flight theory, meteorology and photogrammetry. The vertical viewpoint offered on training flights over Nottingham from a de Havilland biplane was a revelation. The oblique panorama of the topographical observer gave way to a broader, more penetrating vision:

This bird's-eye snapshot appeared to be just as valuable as the dense intricacies that came with lesser visibility on the ground.. . . It was easy to pick out factories and their smoking chimneys, churches and park spaces, the Castle and the Council House, as well as the hide-outs and well-trodden streets that had seemed so far apart but that now in one glance made as small and close a pattern as that on a piece of lace.. . . From nearly two thousand feet the hills appeared flat, and lost their significance, but the secrets of the streets that covered them were shown in such a way that no map could have done the job better.

(Sillitoe, 1975c, p. 70; 1987a, p. 10)

During and immediately after the war, progressive experts, including professional geographers, hoped that increased flying experience and familiarity with aerial photography would reorder ordinary people's perceptions of the world and their place in it. In 1946 David Linton told the Geographical Association 'the air view of the ground . . . has become a familiar thing to us all' (Linton, 1947, p. 3).

> Direct flying experience . . . has been extended to a great body of service personnel, ATC cadets and others, and war films and war photographs have brought some appreciation of the airman's point of view to virtually the whole adult population.

The advantages of the airman's point of view were cumulative (ibid., p. 5):

> As we leave the ground our visual and mental horizon expands, and we have direct perception of space-relations over an ever widening field, so that we may see successively the village, the town, the region, in their respective settings. The mobility of the aircraft makes our range of vision universal . . . We may fly to the ends of the earth.

This expanding field of vision was seen to be potentially one of international citizenship, connecting the local with the global in a new post-war world order (Taylor, 1945).

Sillitoe's internationalism maintained its leftward bearing. He saw his air training as preparation for 'the fight against fascism', but the war ended too soon for Sillitoe to participate and he was posted by the RAF to Malaya, to take part in the fight against communist insurgents in 1948. Here as a wireless operator he was required 'against my political beliefs' to give bearings to bombers trying to 'hunt out the communist guerrillas in the jungle' and maintained his 'accustomed accuracy' with 'lessening enthusiasm' (Sillitoe, 1975d, p. 56).

Returning to Nottingham in 1950, Sillitoe wrote a few short stories, some published in a local magazine, and a long novel, 'a vainglorious mishmash of Dostoevsky, D. H. Lawrence and Aldous Huxley' promptly rejected by a London publisher (Sillitoe, 1975b, p. 26). In a second-hand bookshop he met Ruth Fainlight, an American writer and poet and the woman he was to marry. Because of Sillitoe's illness [tuberculosis], they decided to move to the sunnier climate of southern Europe, subsisting on Sillitoe's air force pension. Expecting to be away for six months, they stayed six years, by which time Sillitoe had established his vocation as a writer.

In southern Europe, Sillitoe and Fainlight 'were culturally severed from England'. The magazines we read, the people we met, the books we got hold of, came from Paris, or New York or San Francisco' (Sillitoe, 1987a, p. 10). Sillitoe was part of a great post-war migration to the Mediterranean of English writers and artists (Mellor, 1987, pp. 69–70). Robert Graves, then working on *The Greek myths*, lived nearby in Majorca and gave Sillitoe and Fainlight access to his library. Sillitoe wrote some poems on classical heroes and a fantasy novel but Graves suggested he 'write a book set in Nottingham, which is something you know about'. From a series of unpublished short stories and sketches centring on the character of Arthur Seaton, 'a young, anarchic roughneck', Sillitoe completed the first draft of *Saturday night and Sunday morning* in 1956–57 (Sillitoe, 1975b, pp. 19–33).

> The factory and its surrounding area ascended with a clarity that might not have been so intense had I not looked out over olive groves, lemons and orange orchards . . . under a clear Mediterranean sky.
>
> (Sillitoe, 1975b, p. 30)

Writing the novel, Sillitoe was reminded of the clear view of his first training flight over Nottingham but felt, at the dawn of the space age, launched further into orbit:

> I re-drew my maps and made my survey as if from a satellite stationed above that part of the earth in which I had been born.
>
> (Sillitoe, 1975c, p. 70; 1987a, p. 13; Rycroft, 1991, pp. 16–17).

Mapping, modernity and masculinity

To emphasize the mapping impulse in Sillitoe's work and life, and its pre-war roots, is to revise the conventional interpretation of his writing. Sillitoe is concerned accurately to document local characters and their environment but he cannot simply be grouped with consciously English, realist contemporaries like Larkin, Amis and Osborne (Lodge, 1977, p. 213). In its Continental allusions, cosmopolitan vantage point and mythological register, Sillitoe's writing may be situated in an earlier modernist tradition, one which includes authors he esteems: Hugo, Lawrence, Conrad and Joyce.

The very conventions of mapping which help to fix Nottingham's geography also release the author and his subject from purely local, vernacular associations, co-ordinate Nottingham to other cities and their cultural traditions. Sillitoe exploits both the documentary aspect of mapping and its metaphorical aspect, the transposition of cultural meanings and associations from one place to another. Mapped on to the modernization of Nottingham, the upheaval and reconstruction of its urban fabric, are epic geographies of insurgent Paris and Stalingrad.

In Sillitoe's Nottingham novels, as in *Les misérables*, the process of surveying proceeds vertically as well as horizontally, in excavations or transects of the urban underworld. Sillitoe quotes from Hugo's novel in characterizing the authorial view as stratigraphic, both documenting, as if from a mountain top, the 'external facts' of culture and, as if in the depths of a cavern, its 'hearts and souls' (Sillitoe, 1975a, p. 152). This vertical axis has long been a central trope in

European literature. In Ovid's *Metamorphosis* it is the separation of the world of the labyrinth, occupied by the Minotaur, the beast-man, from that of the air, occupied by Daedalus, the bird-man. The development of ballooning, the building of skyscrapers and the invention of the aeroplane activated this vertical axis as a defining trope of modernism. As authors upheld a civilized superstructure of spirit and vision, populated by figures like Joyce's Stephen Daedalus (Joyce, 1956) or Geddes's heroic aviator, so they also excavated a primitive substructure of unreason and bodiliness, populated by figures like Hugo's *Les misérables* or D. H. Lawrence's coal-miners (Kern, 1983, pp. 242–7; Schleier, 1986, pp. 5–68; Cunningham, 1988, pp. 168–73, 241–65; Grant, 1989, pp. 385–6; Matless, 1990a, b; Williams, 1990, pp. 51–81; Faris, 1991).

Sillitoe's main characters in his Nottingham novels are variously positioned on this vertical axis. While Brian Seaton transcends Nottingham to achieve a cerebral, cosmopolitan vision, one vested like Sillitoe's in maps and air-mindedness, his brother Arthur remains local and visceral, prowling the warren of streets. Daedalus and Minotaur. The third character, Frank Dawley, never achieves a fully aerial view. After speculating 'what Nottingham looked like from the air, he fell like a stoned and frozen bird back near the middle of it' (Sillitoe, 1965, p. 73). But Dawley does escape the city on an internationalist underground quest, as a guerrilla fighter in North Africa.

As Alison Light has pointed out, there is a distinctly masculine positioning and scope to this radical mode of literary modernism, in its heroic, worldly visions of free movement, political liberation, sexual autonomy and economic independence (Light, 1991, p. 24). Such visions were occasionally awarded to women, in the air-mindedness of some of Virginia Woolf's free-spirited female characters (Beer, 1990) and in the educated, panoramic visions of some of D. H. Lawrence's. The opening of Lawrence's *The rainbow* (1915/1989[4]) has men archaic and earthbound, women modern and outward looking:

> The women looked out from the heated, blind intercourse of farm life, to the spoken world beyond.. . . She [*sic*] stood to see the far-off world of cities and governments and the active scope of men, the magic land to her, where secrets were made known and desires fulfilled . . . to discover what was beyond, to enlarge their own scope and freedom.
>
> (Lawrence, 1989, pp. 42–3)

Sillitoe's Nottingham novels are, by contrast, comprehensively masculine, structured almost entirely on the expression or repression of male desire, whether in its more visceral or more educated forms. Indeed, what aligns Sillitoe's novels with the gritty realism of his English contemporaries is the hardness of their male positioning and address, in their aggressive, misogynistic heroes, individuated largely by running battles with women.

The very belligerence of Sillitoe's heroes, and the portrayal of Nottingham as a sexual battleground, does at least make his women characters a force to be reckoned with. There is a local context for this. The prevailing mythology of modern Nottingham is feminine. The industrialization of the city in the lace, hosiery and clothing industries, with a conspicuous increase of female workers, was accompanied by a new urban folklore of formidable, independent women, economically, politically and sexually (Bryson, 1983, pp. 150–61). This was famously mobilized by D. H. Lawrence in *Sons and lovers* (1913/1983[5]) in the figure of the hero's lover, lace worker Clara Dawes, a ten-year veteran of the women's movement. Moreover, the myth was incorporated in the regal figure which imaged the 'City Beautiful' modernism in official civic publicity, 'Queen of the Midlands'. Guidebooks used this feminine image to promote Nottingham as progressively pure and healthy, free from the grime and drabness usually associated with coalfield areas (Nottingham Corporation, 1927) (Figure 20.3). All local manufacturing industries employed a large proportion of women, and promotional literature was keen to show them working in bright, spacious surroundings. In contrast, Sillitoe's novels evoke a harsher, grimier, more masculine world, the carboniferous industrialization which shadows both Lawrence's novels and city guides. The factory floor, and work generally, is represented almost entirely as a male preserve, as are most public spaces in the novels. It is not just that Sillitoe's male characters rebel against the authority of women; the texts of his Nottingham novels rebel against authoritative texts of the city.

Angry young man

Saturday night and Sunday morning charts a year in the life of Arthur Seaton, machinist in a Nottingham bicycle factory, and young urban rebel. The longer

Fig. 20.3   Cover, *Nottingham 'The queen city of the Midlands' guide* (6th edn, 1921)

part of the novel, 'Saturday night', describes Arthur's work and, more extensively, his escapes from work, his drinking bouts, sexual conquests, street fights, fishing trips and belligerent fantasies. The brief and more reflective 'Sunday morning' finds Arthur recovering from one Saturday night's excess and contemplating, reluctantly, the 'safe and rosy path' to marriage, family and suburban life.

First published in 1958, *Saturday night and Sunday morning* helped frame its cultural moment. It appeared at the time of a spate of accounts of urban working-class life by academics, playwrights, novelists and documentary film makers. Many were concerned with the effect of a burgeoning consumer culture on working-class life. The very idea of 'community' was counterpointed by the emergence of a new working-class affluence and individualism (Hewison, 1981, pp. 163–80; Price, 1987).

Saturday night and Sunday morning was aligned to a male-centred genre of plays and novels, including John Osborne's *Look back in anger* (1956) and John Braine's *Room at the top* (1957), authored by and largely featuring so-called 'Angry Young Men' (Atherton, 1979, pp. 15–21; Hitchcock, 1989, pp. 22–49). In contrast to politely accented literature set in the Oxbridge–London belt and its overseas outliers, the Angries' work was riveted in lower-class quarters of provincial towns and cities, and largely articulated by aggressive, straight-talking, often foul-mouthed, male heroes. The Angries' world seemed at the time shockingly visceral, short on wit and irony and long on sex and violence and general bodiliness. *Saturday night and Sunday morning* opens with Arthur Seaton in a drinking match, knocking-back seven gins and ten pints of beer in quick succession, falling down the pub stairs and vomiting over a nicely dressed middle-aged man and his wife. *Saturday night and Sunday morning* made *Room at the top* 'look like a vicarage tea-party' announced the *Daily Telegraph*; it was, claimed the *New Statesman*, 'very much the real thing' (Marwick, 1984; Segal, 1988).

The popular reputation of *Saturday night and Sunday morning* was established with the release in 1960 of a film of the novel (Sillitoe, 1974). Scripted by Alan Sillitoe and directed by Karel Reisz, it starred Albert Finney as Arthur Seaton and featured the Nottingham streets, factories, pubs, canals and housing estates described in the novel (Figure 20.4). Switching between high-angled long shots and darker, short-focused scenes, sometimes accompanied by Arthur's thoughts, the film opened up the gap between the panoramic and labyrinthine worlds of the text. This was, as Terry Lovell notes, 'a point of enunciation' in a number of British films and television programmes of working-class life of the time, one especially suited to the position of the adult working-class male looking back on the world he had left.

Within the familiar landscape, such a viewer is offered a potent figure of identification in the young, sexually active male worker, because he may identify in him a fantasy projection of the self he might have become had he remained.

(Lovell, 1990, p. 370)

Fig. 20.4 Arthur Seaton cycles home. From *Saturday night and Sunday morning* (1960). BFI stills archive

Tied into the film's release was a million-selling paperback edition of the novel. This was issued by Pan (regarded, in contrast to Penguin, as a distinctly low-brow publisher), marketed in the lurid 'sex and violence' style associated with American pulp fiction and sold largely from the racks of newsagents. The front cover (Figure 20.5) features an illustration of a tough-looking Arthur Seaton against the mean streets of Nottingham. The back cover shows a still from the film of Arthur seducing a workmate's wife and, in the wake of the controversial publication of *Lady Chatterley's lover*, the announcement of a new author 'from Lawrence country . . . who might well have startled Lawrence himself'. Readers were promised 'a raw and uninhibited story of a working-class district of Nottingham and the people who live, love, laugh and fight there'. In giving a transatlantic gloss to the novel, Pan made connections with American works with rebellious male heroes, like Jack Kerouac's *On the road* which they issued in 1958 (although there was no disguising that Arthur Seaton was a very English rebel, a rebel without a car) (Price, 1987, pp. 162–5; Hitchcock, 1989, pp. 75–8).

Saturday night and Sunday morning does not dwell on material deprivation, moral improvement or community spirit. In a world of accelerated industrial production, full employment and rising wages, the novel traces the pursuit of

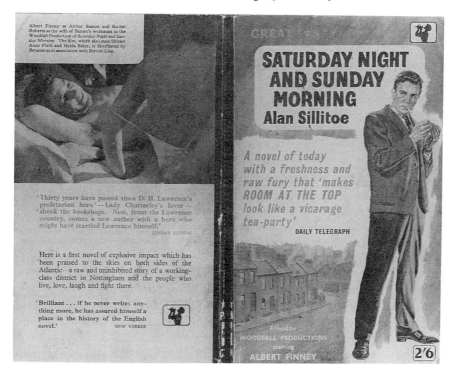

Fig. 20.5   Cover, paperback edition of *Saturday night and Sunday morning* (1960), Pan Books

pleasure and a new consumer passion among the working class. The bicycle factory is booming, with the introduction of piece-work and streamlined production. The thousands who work there take home good wages.

> No more short-time like before the war, or getting the sack if you stood ten minutes in the lavatory reading your *Football Post* – if the gaffer got on to you now you could always tell him where to put the job and go somewhere else . . . With the wages you got you could save up for a motor-bike or even an old car, or you could go for a ten-day binge and get rid of all you'd saved.
>
> (Sillitoe, 1958/1976, p. 27)

Television aerials are 'hooked on to almost every chimney, like a string of radar stations, each installed on the never-never'. Seaton's father has sufficient money to chain-smoke Woodbines in front of the television all evening, his mother to hold her head high in the Co-op and nonchalantly demand 'a pound of this and a pound of that', now 'she had access to week after week of solid wages that stopped worry at the source'. The new affluence has not subdued the 'empty-bellied pre-war battles'; it has aggravated and enlarged them: 'feuds merged, suppressed ones became public' (pp. 26–8, 48, 130).

Arthur Seaton spends much of his wage packet on himself. For a weekend night out he chooses from 'a row of suits, trousers, sports jackets, shirts, all suspended in colourful drapes and designs, good-quality tailor-mades, a couple of hundred quid's worth, a fabulous wardrobe' (p. 174). Described as a Teddy boy, Arthur seems to fit the newly affluent image of working-class youth which alarmed commentators of both right and left (Pearson, 1983, pp. 12–24). He comes close to Raymond Williams's contemporary definition of a 'consumer', a word with imagery drawn from 'the furnace or the stomach' which 'materializes as an individual figure (perhaps monstrous in size but individual in behaviour)' (Williams, 1965, p. 322). Yet in many ways Arthur is a traditional, even anti-modern urban delinquent, the bloody-minded freeborn Englishman whom left-wing writers recruited as makers of the English working-class (Thompson, 1963, pp. 77–101). Arthur's leisure pivots on the pub: 'I'm a six foot pit prop that wants a pint of ale'. He is contemptuous of many modern commodities, notably television, with its implications of passive, domesticated manhood (cf. Spigel, 1992), and cars, with their associations of suburban living (he physically attacks the only car to appear in the novel). The consumer good Arthur values most is the one he helps to produce: the bicycle.[6]

Arthur Seaton is confident, 'cocksure' (p. 45). He has a mind to take on all figures of authority, 'fighting every day until I die . . . fighting with mothers and wives, landlords and gaffers, coppers, army, government' (p. 224), and all monuments of authority, the factory in which he works, the city hall, the castle which broods over the city. Arthur is against all authority, except the authority of men over women (Gray, 1973, pp. 123–7; Dollimore, 1983; Segal, 1988, pp. 80–1). In this he has a local ancestry in D. H. Lawrence's working class heroes, notably the men in Nottingham and the mining country (1930), figures whose roving 'physical, instinctive' masculinity, cultivated at work underground, is trapped and tamed by women no less than by schools, cinemas or machines (Lawrence, 1981, p. 117). But Arthur also has a more contemporary connection in the comicstrip culture of the time, in the war comics of rugged individualists taking on the enemy single-handed and in the tough, street-wise boy-heroes of the *Beano* and *Dandy*, forever in scrapes with authority figures: teachers, policemen and strong-armed mothers (Perry and Aldridge, 1975, p. 5; Segal, 1988, p. 87).

Arthur Seaton's world is a labyrinthine zone, recurrently described as a 'jungle' or 'maze'. Arthur prowls the backstreets of the city, or the footpaths of the adjacent country, part guerrilla, part predatory beast 'caught in a game of fang-and-claw' (Ogersby, 1966, p. 217; Rycroft, 1991, pp. 21–2). At the fairground, Arthur passes up the aerial thrill of the Big Wheel for the subterranean thrill of the Ghost Train. 'Assailed by black darkness and horrible screams from Hell', Arthur tangles with Death in the form of 'the luminous bones of a hanging skeleton', 'kicking and pummelling until his arms emerged from the heavy black cover, glistening skeleton bones looking like tiger-streaks over his back, head and shoulders' (Sillitoe, 1976, pp. 167–8). Each outing was 'an expedition in which every corner had to be turned with care, every pub considered for the ease of tactical retreat in terms of ambush' (p. 209).

If Arthur haunts the streets of *Saturday night and Sunday morning*, domestic interiors are a woman's realm, inhabited by his mother, aunt, mistresses and fiancée, in which men are either absent or marginalized. A formidable female challenge to Arthur's authority, and a main target of his abuse, is a more public figure who surveys the streets. Stationed at the end of his yard, *en route* to the factory, is the gossip, Mrs Bull, 'ready to level with foresight and backsight at those that crossed her path in the wrong direction' (p. 121):

Deep-set beady eyes traversed the yard's length from streets to factory, were then swivelled back from the factory wall to where she was standing, ranging along upstairs and downstairs windows, no point of architecture or human movement escaping her. It was rumoured that the government had her name down for a reconnaissance unit in the next war.

Mrs Bull controls networks of knowledge which Arthur can barely discern. Her 'malicious gossip travelled like electricity through a circuit, from one power-point to another, and the surprising thing was that a fuse was so rarely blown' (p. 121). Arthur attempts to sabotage the system. Playing the role of sniper, he shoots Mrs Bull with an air rifle, bruising her cheek, stinging her into wild gesticulation, confirming her as the slapstick figure of boy's comics.

'Once a rebel, always a rebel', Arthur Seaton pleads at the end of the novel before he dons 'suit, collar and tie' to meet his fiancée Doreen one cold spring Sunday morning 'on the outskirts of the housing estate' where they are destined to live (pp. 207, 209). If Arthur's industrial neighbourhood offered him a measure of snug security, the new modern estates on the edge of the city are bleak, aerial landscapes. '[Up] Broxtowe, on the estate, I like living in them nice new houses,' announces Doreen. 'It's a long way from the shops, but there's plenty of fresh air.' 'My sister married a man in the air force . . . and they've got a house up Wollaton. She's expecting a baby next week' (p. 154). Arthur and Doreen 'take a long walk back to her house, by the boulevard that bordered the estate', the 'safe and rosy path' to domesticity (p. 160). To a disinterested observer they 'seemed like a loving and long-engaged couple only kept back from marriage by the housing shortage'. But to Arthur the 'new pink-walled houses gave an even gloomier appearance than the black dwellings of Radford'. The very image of 'the modern city' in official publicity (Figure 20.1), the spacious new housing estate is, for Arthur, a trap (p. 161):

Arthur remembered seeing an aerial photo of it: a giant web of roads, avenues and crescents, with a school like a black spider lurking in the middle.

New man

In a 1965 sequel to *Saturday night and Sunday morning*, *The death of William Posters*, a political extension of Arthur Seaton, Frank Dawley, rebel turned revolutionary, strives to break out of Arthur's world and his view of it (Rycroft,

1991, pp. 20–1). Through twelve years of factory work and marriage Dawley 'had brooded and built up the Bill Posters legend' (Sillitoe, 1965, p. 16), the legend of a local social bandit (p. 18):

> There's been a long line of William Posters, a family of mellow lineage always hoved up in some cellar of Nottingham Streets. His existence explains many puzzles. Who was General Ludd? None other than the shadowy William Posters, stockinger, leading on his gallant companies of Nottingham lads to smash all that machinery. . . . Who set fire to Nottingham Castle during the Chartist riots? Later, who spat in Lord Roberts' face when he led the victory parade in Nottingham after the Boer War? Who looted those shops in the General Strike?

Frank 'wondered what Nottingham looked like from the air, but fell like a stoned and frozen bird back near the middle of it' (p. 73). He eventually breaks out of the labyrinth of Nottingham, or rather, through its demolition during redevelopment, has it broken for him (pp. 73–4):

> One street funnelled him into space, a view across rubble that a few months ago had been a populous ghetto of back-to-backs and narrow streets. He lit a fag, to absorb the sight of all these acres cleared of people, smashed down and dragged to bits. It wasn't unpleasant, this stalingrad of peace.

As the labyrinth had been cleared, so had William Posters been unearthed, exposed and destroyed. 'Bill Posters, thank God, had died at last in the ruins of Radford–Stalingrad . . . crushed to death under the slabs and bricks, beams and fireplaces' (p. 309):

> [Dawley] walked into space, few paces taking him across a clearly marked street plan on which as a kid each moss-dewed corner and double entry had seemed miles from each other. . . . Streets in all directions had been clawed and grabbed and hammered down, scooped up, bucketed piled, sorted and carted off. Where had all the people gone? Moved onto new estates, all decisions made for them, whereas he also wanted to uproot himself but must make his own moves. (p. 74)

'Exploding out of life so far', Dawley leaves 'wife, home, job, kids' and the place 'where he had been born bred and spiritually nullified' (p. 16). First he heads east for the Lincolnshire wolds. 'His mind had changed with the land-scape since leaving Nottingham; surprising him at times by its breadth' (p. 11), Dawley's broad-mindedness is framed by the copy of *Dr Zhivago* he carries, its evocation of the 'big country' and 'wide open spaces' of Russia (p. 38, 55), and enlarged by his affair with a middle-class woman and his introduction to her library.

Criss-crossing the country like a fugitive, Dawley heads south, for north London, and another conquest of another middle-class wife, Myra Bass-ingfield. As Dawley's horizons expand, those of the jilted husband, George, close in. George Bassingfield is a professional geographer, lecturer at the LSE, author of *New aspects of geography*. 'Few people knew the land of England as well as George, or had a deeper feeling for it . . . the subtleties of land and people were profoundly fascinating, and George was lord of all he surveyed when their composite reactions to land and air tied in with his knowledge and sympathy'. But in middle age 'his visionary eyes did not seek harmony any more, but fixity into which people and the three elements slotted with neatness and safety' (pp. 199–200). Frank and Myra

> left him standing, looking into the tall drawn curtains that opened onto the back garden. . . . Life had always seemed a straight road, and he hadn't even been foxed by a simple dead-end or caught in a false cul-de-sac. Instead he was now trapped in an unsurveyable maze of footpaths darkened by tall hedges. Such a labyrinth was extreme torment for a mind that could exist only on order and calm, which wanted everything measured and shaped, reduced to a beautiful design and set down on paper. The last few days had drawn him into the labyrinth, like a doomed fly fixed in helpessness until the spider-god came out for him. (pp. 243–4)

Frank and Myra leave the cramped world of England, heading south for France, Spain, Morocco, eventually Algeria. Here Dawley enlists as a guerrilla fighter with the FLN during the Algerian War of Independence.

This novel and its sequel *A tree on fire* (1967) appear to be shaped by Sillitoe's reading of the theory and practice of guerrilla warfare, some in preparation for his script for a projected film about 'Che' Guevara (Sillitoe, 1975e, p. 121). The spatiality of guerrilla warfare, 'drifting and subtle . . . arabesques', 'the spider's web of revolution' (Sillitoe, 1965, p. 308; 1967, p. 427) characterize Frank Dawley's tactics throughout his journeying. His quest evokes Che Guevara's notion of the socialist 'new man', evolving from the 'wolfman' of capitalist competition (Lowy, 1973, pp. 25–8), and also the hightech ideology of Khrushchev's Soviet Union. Dawley envisages a modernist, machine-tooled utopia.

> All I believe in is houses and factories, food and power stations, bridges and coalmines and death, turning millions of things out on a machine that people can use. It's no use harping back to poaching rights and cottage industries. We've got to forget all that and come to terms with cities and machines and moon landings. We're going to become new men, whether we like it or not, and I know I am going to like it.
> (Sillitoe, 1965, p. 259)

Airman

It is Brian Seaton, Arthur's elder brother, who acquires an airborne cartographic view of the world in *Key to the door* (1961b) and its sequel *The open door* (1989). The course of Brian Seaton's life parallels Alan Sillitoe's own, from factory work in Nottingham, to National Service in Malaya to embarking, as a writer, for the south of France. It is these novels which challenge the prevailing stereotype of Sillitoe's Nottingham as a 'northern' province of a London-centred nationalist culture. For Brian Seaton 'London didn't exist' (Rycroft, 1991, p. 9); it was a place you passed over in a more global vision. South of the River Trent is not southern England but southern Europe, the Trent is a 'magic band of water' separating 'oak from olive, mildew from hot pines and baking rock' (Sillitoe, 1989, p. 335).

Key to the door begins in 1930s Nottingham with the destitute Seaton family on the run from the bailiffs and the slum clearance programme of 'a demolishing council'. While some slum dwellers take 'the benefit of new housing estates', father Harold Seaton 'clung to the town centre because its burrow was familiar' (Sillitoe, 1961, p. 17). Eventually they are forced out by the bulldozers and bombardment from the air. One area of 'broken and derelict maze' is set aside 'to be the target of bombs from buzzing two-winged aeroplanes, the sideshow of a military tattoo whose full glory lay on the city's outskirts' (p. 17). The Seaton family take refuge in cottage in a still-rough, semi-rural, warren-like area at the edge of the city. It is a frontier zone about to feel the turbulent force of modernization, to be turned into a 'tipscape', filled with rubble from the old slums, levelled and developed. 'Then they'll make an aerodrome', Brian speculates, 'to bomb old houses like ourn was on Albion Yard' (p. 78).

What they actually make is a bright new estate, lit by electricity, 'magically blessed' with a mains water supply, marked out with broad boulevards and the first new houses:

> Pink houses of new estates were spilling into the countryside. Men with black and white poles and notebooks came across the new boulevards into lanes and fields; they set theodolites and dumpy levels pointing in sly angles at distant woods . . . invading Brian's hideouts, obliterating his short-cuts and concealed tracks. (p. 191)

Brian is enthralled with the men and machines:

> Instead of woods and fields, houses would appear along new roads, would transform the map in his mind. The idea of it caught at him like fire (p. 192)

Brian Seaton grows up with Alan Sillitoe's passion for books and maps. 'Moulded by an addiction to *Les misérables*' he envisages war in the streets of Nottingham with barricades and sandbag parapets. On a huge war-map of Europe he follows the progress of the Red Army on the Eastern Front. Brian Seaton works in a claustrophobic factory world, in the 'underground burrow' (p. 251) of boiler room, having to dig out soot from flues.

> Having to work in the dark set him thinking of coalmines and pit ponies, and the fact that he would go crackers if he didn't get out and prove he wasn't buried a thousand feet underground. Jean Valjean traipsing through the sewers was better than this, though I expect Edmond Dantes in *his* tunnels didn't feel too good either. . . . This is how you get TB, he thought, by breathing black dust like this for hour after hour. (p. 243)

Brian pulls himself out of this subterranean world, to join the air force as a wireless operator in Malaya, and a life of 'morse and mapmaking' (p. 301), doing guard duty in a 'worn out part of the British empire' (p. 433).

The open door (1989) finds Brian Seaton negotiating the labyrinth of the Malayan jungle. It was 'a place where you could be as much at home as in any maze of streets', but for Seaton, the imperial outsider, it remains intractable, a heart of darkness. 'The jungle had inflicted a deadly bite by drawing him through the valley of the shadow' (p. 75). With map and compass, he struggles unsuccessfully through this predatory world towards the summit of a 4000 foot peak, Gunong Barat. And writing it up, from his diary notes, he remains gripped by the experience. 'Unable to sleep, he dreamed of creepers and decomposing trees, and blades of water waving down cliff-faces enlarged my memory's infallible magnifying glass' (p. 74).

Returning to Nottingham, Seaton deploys his cartographic intelligence on a more pliant subject, the woman he seduces by tracing 'a map upon her back' (p. 167) and embarking on an exotic travelogue, 'looking at the Beautiful Horizon, plodding through Bangkok, eating the Sandwich Islands, swimming off Madagascar, trekking the five-fingered forests of Gunong Barat' (p. 174). He tries it on his younger brother Arthur too, in offering the lad the kind of educated, reflective prospect of Nottinghamshire that Arthur will, as the rebellious youth in *Saturday night and Sunday morning*, never achieve. Brian takes Arthur on a bus-ride beyond the city for a spot of fraternal bonding on Misk Hill.

> 'Who showed yer where it was?'
> 'I found it on a map. The top's over five hundred feet above sea level.'
> 'Will I be able to breathe?' He ran on to the plateau of a large field, arms in front like pistons . . .
> Suburbs started three miles away, houses and factories under mountainous cloud. Faint haze emphasized the rich squalor of memorable dreams, his past in a semicircle from north to south.. . . .
> 'It's smashin' up 'ere.' Arthur hurled a stick . . .
> A shunting train was pinpointed by feathers of smoke. Brian held him tight. 'Don't ever leave it. It's your hill.'
> 'Eh, fuck off!' Arthur broke away. 'Are yo' trying to fuck me, or summat?'
> Brian laughed. 'Come on loony, let's get down.' (p. 291)

East Midland geographies

Sillitoe's novels chart the modernization of Nottingham in a way which combines and competes with official and academic geographies of the city and its region. In this article we have presented the novels as a field of different, sometimes conflicting forms of geographical knowledge and experience. To do so we have shown how the narratives are interleaved with a variety of discourses on Nottingham and its region, on other modernizing cities, in fact and fiction, on an internationalist politics of citizenship and, pre-eminently, on geography, specifically maps and map-reading. In so doing we hope to further the recent broadening of the history of geography beyond the usual internal, linear, professional histories, to take account of those 'lateral associations and social relations of geographical knowledge' (Driver, 1992, p. 35; see also Livingstone, 1992).

In the period covered by the novels, the city corporation's publications represented Nottingham as a model 'modern city'. Here, through careful planning, economic and social development was orderly and integrated, creating the framework for a prosperous, enlightened city and citizenry. From 1954 this progressive view was endorsed and extended to the city's hinterland by the regional journal, *The East Midland Geographer*. Under the founding editorship of K. C. Edwards, himself active in local regional planning and policy making, the journal charted infrastructural developments in the city and its region: the modernization of the mining industry, the rationalization of the railways, the building of municipal estates, the construction of motorways (Freeman, 1979, pp. 95–6). The region's representativeness in landscape and human activity made it 'an epitome of the English scene'. 'Its importance in the economic development of the country moreover is continually growing and is likely to increase vastly in the future' (Edwards, 1954, p. 2). This was not just a forward-looking view; developments in the past were narrated as part of the same progressive story. In a series of public lectures on the development of Nottingham, from the mid-1930s to mid-1960s, Edwards charted the expansion and consolidation of the city into 'a coherent, closely-knit economic and social entity' (Edwards, 1937, 1965; p. 747; 1966).

In the year, 1958, that K. C. Edwards told this story of Nottingham, in Nottingham, in his address to the conference of the Institute of British Geographers, the first edition of Alan Sillitoe's *Saturday night and Sunday morning* was published. Like professional planners and geographers, Sillitoe framed land and life in terms of maps, but charted a different, darker story. Sillitoe's image of the city and its citizenry is not one of coherence and continuity, of community building, but one of conflict and upheaval, of explosive physical and social change. As on a military map, the city is envisaged as a field of battle. There are, as we have shown, many mediations in this vision, including representations of insurgent Stalingrad, Petrograd, Paris and Nottingham itself during the Luddite and Reform riots. If official and academic versions of Nottingham's geography were written in that progressive, optimistic, enlightened discourse of modernism, Sillitoe's version was written in modernism's counter-discourse of violence, oppression and exclusion (Hall and Eieben, 1993, p. 14).

It is not surprising that City officials responded coolly to the international success of *Saturday night and Sunday morning*, moreover accused Sillitoe of stirring up the trouble the novel described (Price, 1987; Rycroft, 1991, p. 18). Now both parties stand condemned. The City Corporation is accused of pulling down 'Victorian and Edwardian treasures' to make way for 'modern monstrosities'; Sillitoe is condemned for tarnishing the world that remained standing. The renovation of Nottingham's derelict textile district, the Lace Market, as a heritage spectacle promised a more stylish future. 'Ten years ago the Queen of the Midlands had a slightly dowdy look . . . [now] it is no longer the dirty city of Alan Sillitoe's *Saturday night and Sunday morning*' (*Nottingham Evening Post Supplement*, 1988). It is too soon to say whether post-industrial planning will erase the memory of Arthur Seaton, or the mythology which sustained him. He was recently spotted, in the summer of 1993, in Albert Finney's scowling portrait, printed on the T-shirts of protesters against the closure of local collieries (Figure 20.6).

Fig. 20.6 T-shirt with portrait of Albert Finney as Arthur Seaton. Trades Council May Day Rally, Nottingham, 1993

DON'T LET THE BASTARDS GRIND YOU DOWN

Notes

1 The first edition was published in 1958, but the edition used as a source for this paper was published in 1976.
2 Sillitoe's many works are catalogued in Gerard (1988) along with many works of criticism and commentary. This has proved a valuable resource for the article. Also valuable is the Sillitoe collection at the Central Library, Nottingham, especially the file of newspaper cuttings on his early career. The most comprehensive work of criticism on Sillitoe is Atherton (1979). A study of Sillitoe with points of connection with this article is Daleski (1986).
3 An edited transcript of this interview is provided in Rycroft (1991).

4 The first edition was published in 1915, but the edition used as a source for this paper was published in 1989.
5 The first edition was published in 1913, but the edition used as a source for this paper was published in 1983.
6 Sillitoe has said that because he was out of the country for most of the 1950s, 'what I was doing, I think, was really bringing my experience from the Forties up into the Fifties' (Sillitoe, 1975–76, p. 176). Sillitoe's Nottingham seems in some respects more like 1960 'Worktown' (Bolton), about which Mass Observation commented:

> Despite the telly, despite increased working class car ownership, despite the whole complex of commodity fetishism which *looks* as if it is changing the way ordinary people in England live . . . the pub still persists as a social institution. Qualitatively and quantitatively. Never having had it so good doesn't mean only washing machines and holidays abroad; it is also more beer.
>
> (Harrisson, 1961, p. 194)

Selected References

Alfrey, N. and Daniels, S. (eds) 1990: *Mapping the landscape: Essays on art and cartography*. Nottingham: University of Nottingham.

Atherton, S. 1979: *Alan Sillitoe: A critical assessment*. London: W. H. Allen.

Barnes, T. J. and Duncan, J. S. (eds) 1992: *Writing worlds: Discourse, text and metaphor in the representation of landscape*. London: Routledge.

Barrell, J. 1982: Geographies of Hardy's Wessex. *Journal of Historical Geography* 8, 347–61.

Barrell, J. (ed.) 1992: *Painting and the politics of culture: New essays on British art*. Oxford: Oxford University Press.

Beer, G. 1990: The island and the aeroplane. In Bhaba, H. (ed.), *Nation and narration*. London: Routledge.

Bender, J. 1987: *Imagining the penitentiary: Fiction and architecture of mind in eighteenth-century England*. Chicago: University of Chicago Press.

Berman, M. 1983: *All that is sold melts into air: The experience of modernity*. London: Verso.

Bradbury, M. 1976: The cities of modernism. In Bradbury, M. and McFarlane, J. (eds), 1971: *Modernism*. Harmondsworth: Penguin Books, 96–104.

British Association for the Advancement of Science (1937) *A scientific survey of Nottingham*. London: BAAS.

Bryson, E 1983: *Portrait of Nottingham*. London: Hale.

Chambers, J. D. 1945: *Modern Nottingham in the making*. Nottingham: Nottingham Journal.

Clark, T. J. 1984: *The painting of modern life: Paris in the art of Manet and his followers*. London: Thames and Hudson.

Cunningham, V. 1988: *British writers of the thirties*. Oxford: Oxford University Press.

Daleski, H. M. 1986: The novelist as map maker. In Bock, H. and Wertheim, A. (eds), *Essays on the contemporary British novel*. Munich: Max Hueber, 137–52.

Daniels, S. 1993: *Fields of vision: Landscape imagery and national identity in England and the United States*. Cambridge: Polity.

Daniels, S. 1994: 'Re-visioning Britain: mapping and landscape painting 1750–1820'. In Katharine Baetjer (ed.), *Glorious nature: British landscape painting 1750–1850*. New York: Hudson Hills, 61–72.

Dollimore, J. 1983: The challenge of sexuality. In Sinfield, A. (ed.) *Society and literature 1945–70*. London: Methuen, 51–85.

Driver, F. 1992: Geography's empire: histories of geographic knowledge. *Society and Space* 10, 23–40.

Edwards, K. C. 1937: Nottingham and its region. In British Association for the Advancement of Science, *A scientific survey of Notthingham*. London: British Association for the Advancement of Science.

Edwards, K. C. 1954: Editorial introduction. *East Midland Geographer* 1, 2.

Edwards, K. C. 1965: Nottingham: Queen of the Midlands. *Geographical Magazine*, September: 329–47.

Edwards, K. C. 1966: The geographical development of Nottingham. In Edwards, K. C. (ed.), *Nottingham and its region*. London: British Association for the Advancement of Science.

Faris, W. B. 1991: The labyrinth as sign. In Caws, M. A. (ed.), *City images: perspectives from literature, philosophy and film*. New York: Gordon & Breach, 33–41.

Freeman, T. W. 1979: Twenty-five years of 'The East Midland Geographer' 1954–79. *East Midland Geographer* 7, 95–9.

Gerard, D. 1988: *Alan Sillitoe: a bibliography*. London: Mansell.

Grant, M. 1989: *Myths of the Greeks and Romans*. London: Weidenfeld & Nicolson.

Gray, N. 1973: *The silent majority: a study of the working class in post-war British fiction*. London: Vision.

Hall, S. and Eieben, B. 1993: *Formations of modernity*. Cambridge: Open University and Polity Presses.

Harrisson, T. 1961: *Britain revisited*. London: Victor Gollancz.

Hewison, R. 1981: *In anger: culture in the cold war*. Weidenfeld & Nicolson.

Hitchcock, P. 1989: *Working-class fiction in theory and practice: a reading of Alan Sillitoe*. London: UMI Research Press.

Hugo, V. 1982: *Les misérables*. Harmondsworth: Penguin Books.

Joyce, J. 1956: *A portrait of the artist as a young man*. London: Jonathan Cape.

Kempe, D. 1988: *Living underground: a history of cave and cliff dwelling*. London: Herbert Press.

Kern, S. 1983: *The culture of time and space 1880–1914*. Cambridge, Mass.: Harvard University Press.

Kestner, J. A. 1978: *The spatiality of the novel*. Detroit: Wayne State University Press.

Lawrence, D. H. 1913/1989: *Sons and lovers*. Harmondsworth: Penguin.

Lawrence, D. H. 1915/1989: *The rainbow*. Harmondsworth: Penguin.

Lawrence, D. H. 1981: Nottingham and the mining country. In *Selected essays*. Harmondsworth: Penguin Books, 114–22.

Light, A. 1991: *Forever England: femininity, literature and conservatism between the wars*. London: Routledge.

Linton, D. L. 1947: *The interpretation of air photographs*. London: Geographical Association.

Livingstone, D. N. 1992: *The geographical tradition: episodes in the history of a contested enterprise*. Oxford: Basil Blackwell.

Lodge, D. 1977: *The modes of modern writing: metaphor, metonymy and the typology of modern literature*. Ithaca, NY: Cornell University Press.

Lovell, T. 1990: Landscapes and stories in 1960s British realism. *Screen* 31, 357–76.

Lowy, M. 1973: *The marxism of Che Guevara: philosophy, economics and revolutionary warfare*. London: Monthly Review Press.

Mallory, W. E. and Simpson-Housley, P. (eds) 1987: *Geography and literature: A meeting of the disciplines*. Syracuse University Press.

Marwick, A. 1984: *Room at the top, Saturday night and Sunday morning* and the 'cultural revolution' in Britain. *Journal of Contemporary History* 19, 127–52.

Matless, D. 1990a: Ordering the land: the 'preservation' of the English countryside 1918–39. Unpubl. PhD thesis, Department of Geography, University of Nottingham.

Matless, D. 1990b: Preservation, modernism and the nature of the nation. *Built Environments* 16, 179–91.

Mellor, D. 1987: *A paradise lost: the neo-romantic imagination in Britain 1935–55* London: Lund Humphries in association with the Barbican Art Gallery.

Mellors, R. 1914: *Old Nottingham suburbs: then and now*. Nottingham: J. and H. Bell.

Nottingham Corporation 1927: *Nottingham, 'The Queen City of the Midlands'. The Official Guide*. Cheltenham and London: E. J. Burrow.

Nottingham Corporation 1939: *Nottingham official handbook*. Cheltenham and London: E. J. Burrow.

Ogersby, J. R. 1966: Alan Sillitoe's *Saturday night and Sunday morning*. In Hibbard, G. R. (ed.), *Renaissance and modern essays*. London: Routledge & Kegan Paul.

Pearson, G. 1983: *Hooligan: a history of respectable fears*. London: Macmillan.

Perry, G. and Aldridge, A. 1975: *The Penguin book of comics*. Harmondsworth: Penguin Books.

Pinkney, D. 1958: *Napoleon III and the rebuilding of Paris*. Princeton, NJ: Princeton University Press.

Pocock, D. C. D. (ed.) 1981: *Humanistic geography and literature*. London: Croom Helm.

Price, T. 1987: The politics of culture: *Saturday night and Sunday morning*. Unpublished PhD thesis, University of Nottingham.

Rycroft, S. 1991: *Ordinance and order in Alan Sillitoe's fictional topography* Department of Geography, University of Nottingham Working Paper No 13.

Said, E. 1983: *The world, the text, and the critic*. London: Faber & Faber.

Said, E. 1989: Jane Austen and empire. In Eagleton, T. (ed.), *Raymond Williams: critical perspectives*. Cambridge: Polity, 150–64.

Said, E. 1993: *Culture and imperialism*. New York: Knopf.

Schleier, M. 1986: *The skyscaper in American art, 1890–1931*. New York: Da Capo Press.

Segal, L. 1988: Look back in anger: men in the fifties. In Chapman, R. and Rutherford, J. (eds), *Male order: unwrapping masculinity*. London: Lawrence & Wishart, 68–96.

Seidel, M. 1976: *Epic geography: James Joyce's 'Ulysses'*. Princeton, NJ: Princeton University Press.

Silburn, R. 1981: People in their places. In *One hundred years of Nottingham*. Nottingham: University of Nottingham, 16–35.

Sillitoe, A. 1958/1976[1] *Saturday night and Sunday morning*. London: Grafton.

Sillitoe, A. 1961: *Key to the door*. London: W. H. Allen.

Sillitoe, A. 1965: *The death of William Posters*. London: W. H. Allen.

Sillitoe, A. 1967: *A tree on fire*. London: W. H. Allen.

Sillitoe, A. 1972: *Raw material*. London. W. H. Allen.

Sillitoe, A. 1974: 'Saturday night and Sunday morning' screenplay. In Taylor, J. R. (ed.), *Masterworks of the British cinema*. London: Lorimer, 267–328.

Sillitoe, A. 1974–5: A sense of place. *Geographical Magazine* 47, 685–9.

Sillitoe, A. 1975a: Mountains and caverns. In Sillitoe, A. *Moutains and caverns*. London: W. H. Allen, 152–60.

Sillitoe, A. 1975b: The long piece. In Sillitoe, A. *Mountains and caverns*. London: W. H. Allen, 9–49.

Sillitoe, A. 1975c: Maps. In Sillitoe, A. *Mountains and caverns*. London: W. H. Allen, 59–73.

Sillitoe, A. 1975d: National service. In Sillitoe, A. *Mountains and caverns*. London: W. H. Allen, 50–8.

Sillitoe, A. 1975e: 'Che' Guevara. In Sillitoe, A. *Mountains and caverns*. London: W. H. Allen, 121–7.

Sillitoe, A. 1975–6: An interview with Alan Sillitoe. *Modern Fiction Studies* 21, 175–89.

Sillitoe, A. 1983: Alan Sillitoe. *Author*, Autumn, 28–30.

Sillitoe, A. 1985: The death of Frankie Butler. In Sillitoe, A. *The loneliness of the long-distance runner*. London: Grafton, 154–74.

Sillitoe, A. 1987a: We all start from home. *Bulletin de la Société des Anglicistes de l'Enseignment Supérieur* no. 3. Sept., 6–16.

Sillitoe, A. 1987b: *Alan Sillitoe's Nottinghamshire*. London: Grafton.

Sillitoe, A. 1989: *The open door*. London: W. H. Allen.

Spigel, L. 1992: The suburban home companion: television and neighbourhood in post-war America. In Colomina, B. (ed.) *Sexuality and space*. Princeton, NJ: Princeton Architectural Press.

Taylor, E. G. R. 1945: *Geography of an air age*. London: Royal Institute of International Affairs.

Thomas, C. J. 1966: Some geographical aspects council housing in Nottingham. *East Midland Geographer* 4, 88–98.

Thomas, C. J. 1971: The growth of Nottingham since 1919. *East Midland Geographer* 5, 119–32.

Thompson, E. P. 1963: *The making of the English working class*. New York: Vintage Books.

Tuan, Y. F. 1978: Literature and geography. In Ley, D. and Samuels, M. (eds), *Humanistic geography prospects and problems*. London: Croom Helm, 194–2.

Varey, S. 1990: *Space and the eighteenth-century English novel*. Cambridge: Cambridge University Press.

Watt, I. 1957: *The rise of the novel*. Harmondsworth: Penguin.

Williams, R. 1965: *The long revolution*. Harmondsworth: Peliccan.

Williams, R. 1973: *The country and the city*. London: Chatto & Windus.

Williams, R. 1990: *Notes on the underground: an essay on technology, society and the imagination*. Cambridge, MA: MIT Press.

21 Denis Cosgrove,

'Contested Global Visions: *One-World, Whole-Earth,* and the Apollo Space Photographs'

Excerpts from: *Annals of the Association of American Geographers* 84, 270–94 (1994)

At 05:33 Eastern Standard Time on 7 December 1972, one of the three United States astronauts aboard the spaceship Apollo 17 on its coast towards the Moon shot a sequence of eleven color photographs of Earth with a handheld Hasselblad camera. Twelve hours after the spacecraft's splashdown on Christmas Eve, the film sequence was developed at the Manned Space Center in Houston. Doug Ward, National Aeronautics and Space Administration's (NASA) Director of Public Affairs, examined the printed sequence with a view to issuing part of the mission's three- to four-thousand frame photographic record for the waiting press. One of the images – number AS17-148-22727, taken at some 21,750 nautical miles from the Earth (Figure 21.1) – caught his photojournalist's eye.[1] It captured, center-frame and with perfect resolution, the full terraqueous disk without a solar shadow or 'terminator'. The whole Earth, geography's principal object of study, had been photographed by a human eyewitness.

My intention here is to examine that photographic image, *22727*, together with an earlier and equally familiar Apollo photograph of Earth rising over a lunar landscape, *Earthrise* (Figure 21.2), with the intention of placing them in

Fig. 21.1 *The whole earth* (NASA AS17-148-22727). Apollo 17 photograph of Earth from space, December 1972

the cultural and historical context of Western global images and imaginings. I shall argue that representations of the globe and the whole Earth in the twentieth century have drawn upon and reconstituted a repertoire of sacred and secular, colonial and imperial, meanings, and that these representations have played an especially significant role in the self-representation of the post-war United States and its geo-cultural mission. While the Apollo lunar project signified the achievement of the technocratic goals and universalist rhetoric of Modernism, the project's most enduring legacy is a collection of *images* whose meanings are contested in post-colonial and postmodernist discourses. In order to analyze and contextualize these Apollo images, I bring to bear the intertextual approach developed in contemporary cultural analysis, here applied to the primary object of geographical representation: the surface of the Earth. The photographs are interpreted by reference to various texts, some written about them, others referring less directly to imagined and actual views and representations of the globe but providing context for Apollo readings.

The Apollo Earth photographs, though receiving very limited formal attention within geography, have been widely used as cover illustrations for texts and journals (for example, in *Geography*, the journal of the Geographical Association in Britain). They have been enormously significant, however, in altering the shape of the contemporary *geographical imagination*. This essay thus contributes to the growing interest in the histories of geographical knowledge, in which geography as a formal academic discipline is merely one

Fig. 21.2 *Earthrise* (NASA AS8-14-2383). Apollo 8 photograph of Earth taken from lunar orbit, December 1968

element (Driver, 1992; Livingstone, 1992). And by examining terms that are so closely associated with the Apollo images (*One-world* and *Whole-earth*), we provide perspective also on geography's engagement in contemporary cultural debate.

The Apollo program and Earth photography

The Apollo space program was aptly named. Greek Apollo combined the strength and beauty of male youth with the severe purity of reason. As a sun god he circled the Earth, his dispassionate vision encompassing the pathetic doings of mortals. On the shoulders of similarly youthful male heroes, NASA's Saturn rockets carried the imaginative vision of a modern superpower beyond the confines of Earth. The program's appeal, while spectacular, was short-lived. Apollo 17 was the last in a series of American-manned flights to the Moon. Indeed, the two expeditions planned to follow it had already been cancelled before its launch. The entire period of the Apollo space program thus spanned little more than a decade from its inception in 1961. Apollo 8, the first to escape Earth orbit and encircle the Moon, returned during Christmas 1968 with *Earthrise*. With it came the earliest eyewitness pictures taken from suffi-cient distance to capture the whole terraqueous globe, albeit as a partial and shadowed disk suspended over the lunar landscape (Figure 21.2). *Earthrise* was the subject of immediate commentary and speculation about a reformed view of the world. But soon after the objective of a lunar landing was achieved in 1969, public interest and official support for the Apollo program waned rapidly. Since 1972, NASA has confined astronautical activities to Earth orbit. Two photographs, *Earthrise* and *22727*, define therefore a historical moment in which the curtain opened on the theater of the world and the human eye pretended to Apollo's heritage.

Oddly enough, the only major American newspaper to carry *22727* was the *Chicago Tribune* in its edition of Sunday, 24 December 1972, while the *National Geographic* magazine failed to reproduce the image in its lavishly illustrated 1973 summary of 'mankind's greatest adventure' (Grosvenor *et al.*, 1973). Under the headline 'One Last View of Earth', the *Tribune* noted presciently that not only was this 'the first time the full Earth has been photographed,' but that it might also be the last. What neither journalists nor other commentators anticipated, however, was the enormous popularity of this image. As an icon of the Earth, *22727* would largely replace the cartographer's globe with its delineation of lands and seas on a graticule of latitude and longitude. The fact that both *Earthrise* and *22727* are in the public domain[2] accounts, in part, for their ubiquitous reproduction as advertizing and publicity copy. But that does not tell us why these images have become such powerful and ambiguous icons, their meaning apparently malleable enough for deployment in behalf of diverse and often opposing ideological positions. More than any other images, *Earthrise* and Photo *22727* now serve as visual signifiers for the terms *Whole-earth* and *One-world*, especially in American culture.[3]

Earthrise

Apollo 8 produced the photograph of a partially shadowed Earth rising over the lunar surface (Figure 21.2) The shot was a sensation, despite the fact that full-Earth images from mechanical cameras predated the Apollo 8 mission by two years. In 1966, Lunar Orbiter I, an unmanned lunar vehicle, sent back a full-Earth photograph that had been processed in space and electronically recomposed back on the ground; and in July 1967 a color photograph of the full earthly disk was received from a United States Navy Dodge satellite. These images were not widely publicized, however, because their quality was poor. *Earthrise* was, by contrast, witnessed by a mass television audience prior to the publication of this stunning still-color photograph. Given the appeal of *Earthrise*, the formal aspects of its composition are worthy of more detailed examination.

The still photograph (AS8–14–2383) is tripartite in composition. A section of the lunar surface 'grounds' the image; it is light gray in color, dusty in texture, and the outlines of craters are visible from color contrast. This portion of the photograph occupies some 25 per cent of the frame and contains an uninterrupted horizon line sloping gently from left to right. The rest of the image consists of the deep black of unexposed film enshrouding the semicircle of Earth slightly right of center. The Earth is composed of swirls of white against a blue background in the color print or black in the monochrome. Patches of brown at the lower edge, where the clear definition of the upper arc gives way to the haze of the terminator line, are scarcely traceable on the monochrome. They can, with close attention, be recognized on the color print as the western edge of the African continent. The sloping horizon and position of the Earth give the picture a directional sense, while the orientation of the planet on an east–west axis, the swirling pattern of cloud, and the shading of the land mass into darkness all suggest its revolution.

The most striking aspect of the photograph is its inversion of an intensely familiar representational theme: a nocturnal landscape illuminated by a half-moon. But here the 'landscape' element is the inorganic moon while color is reserved to the cool oceanic and atmospheric earth. A secondary challenge to familiar assumptions is the lack of any other illumination – the night sky is bereft of stars. Combined with the deathly lunar surface, the photograph suggests the complete isolation of terrestrial life in a black, sepulchral universe. In the words of Buckminster Fuller, the Earth appears to float in 'x-trillions of time years of nothingness (whose incredible depths appear to us as pure no-light, a quality of blackness never before experienced)' (Fuller, 1969, p. 37). By no stretch of the imagination could we call *Earthrise* a cartographic image; it is, however, intensely *geographical*, drawing on powerful conventions of cosmographic and chorographic representation in the Western geographical imagination (Cosgrove, 1984) and opening it to the range of interpretations discussed below.

22727

The Apollo 17 mission's plan called for photographic sequences of lunar earthshine photographs to be taken during the trans-lunar coast (TLC), but other shots were 'targets of opportunity.' The sequence of eleven Earth photographs (22725–22735), taken after a shot of the falling away of the final stage of the Saturn V rocket, varied in quality because of problems of exposure and framing. The *Preliminary Science Report* following the mission paid little attention to these Earth photographs. It reproduced Photo *22727* accompanied by a bland caption: 'For the first time on an Apollo mission, the Antarctic icecap was visible during the Apollo 17 TLC. This full disk view encompasses much of the South Atlantic Ocean, virtually all the Indian Ocean, Antarctica, Africa, a part of Asia, and, on the horizon, Indonesia and the western edge of Australia' (NASA SP-330, 1973, pp. 4–9).

The popular response was, by contrast, rather more enthusiastic. Indeed, the very ubiquity of *22727*, endlessly reproduced on postcards, lapel buttons, flags, calendars, political manifestos, commercial advertizements, and T-shirts (Gaarb, 1985), serves to deflect close scrutiny of the image's content. In some cases its reproducers have unconsciously and unobservedly reversed the image as, for example, when BBC TV News used *22727* as the logo for their week-long coverage of the Rio Earth Summit in 1992 (Figure 21.3). All of this

Fig. 21.3 *Attractive detached residence.* Poster published by Friends of the Earth, London (courtesy of Friends of the Earth)

suggests that the formal qualities of the image outweighed its cartographic content. To be sure, examination of the image's composition and content suggests a density and an aesthetic harmony that are remarkable in a photograph taken almost at whim. Undoubtedly these artistic qualities have played a significant, if little noted, role in the photograph's dissemination and reception.

22727 locates a perfectly circular Earth image within a square frame. When the terrestrial disk is centered by minor cropping of the original shot, the image attains the mandala form of circle and square whose completeness and geometrical unity are familiar from the cross-cultural history of cosmic images and which Carl Jung (1959) regarded as a key archetype. This may account, in part, for the quasi-mantric status of the image among *Whole-earth* enthusiasts. As in *Earthrise*, the surrounding space is a deep black void. The floating Earth seems to merge into nothingness, an impression that is conveyed by the faint edging haziness of its outline, which is produced by the globe's encircling belt of atmosphere, and which is delineated most clearly against the land mass at the top left. Within the circular frame are secondary and more complex geometrical shapes: a major triangle of land, a series of arcs dividing the disk into bands, and a number of minor circles giving weight to the lower part. These downward curving arcs together with the atmospheric haze, the cloud forms, and the colors produce a *watery* image of almost tearful intensity.

The dominant colors are blue, white, and brown. The brown and blue are easily recognizable to anyone familiar with the conventional world map as the land masses of Africa and the Arabian Peninsula and the South Atlantic and Indian Oceans, respectively. The desert and savannah regions of Africa and Arabia, Earth's largest cloud-free region, occupy the frame. The Gulf of Aden and the Red Sea cut a deep gash into the patch of ocher so that the Horn of Africa and Arabian desert peninsula are clearly etched. Patches of white clouds wreathe the rest of the Earth, save for the dense mass of the Antarctic continent, whose outline is readily apparent.

Since the photograph orients the globe according to the cardinal points, the warm browns of the cloud-free Sahara at the top (north) are perfectly balanced by the cold white of the icy Antarctic mass on the lower (southern) edge. A broadly circular area of ocean defined by the coast of Mozambique, the island of Madagascar and the northern edge of the densest cloud mass provides a central focus to the design. Given the time of year, close to the winter solstice, and the trajectory of the spaceship, the east–west diameter of the global disk lies almost exactly along the Tropic of Capricorn, while the equatorial line is identifiable by the broken cloud cover of the Intertropical Convergence Zone. The largest visible oceanic area lies east of Africa in the western part of the Indian Ocean whose high productivity renders it intensely blue on a photographic plate. Any monotony of marine tones is relieved, however, by the pattern of clouds in the southern oceans: a series of swirling sickle shapes formed by depressions passing from west to east and giving the impression of rotational dynamism. This impression is further emphasized – and the picture rendered three-dimensional – by the equatorial arc of broken clouds. Thus, when these compositional elements are taken as a whole, photograph *22727* is readily correlated with modern cartographic representations of the world.

At the upper edge of the photograph, the eastern part of the Mediterranean Sea is just discernible. To Western eyes this is the 'oldest' part of the world, cartographic center of Ptolemy's ecumene. Or, as an American commentator speaking about an earlier space photograph put it, 'much of our commonly taught history centers around that little sea, a mere patch in the hemisphere, which once seemed to its inhabitants the whole world' (quoted in Nicks, 1970, p. 3). At the base of *22727*, meanwhile, is Antarctica, the 'youngest' part of the known world, 'globalized' under the Treaty of 1959. Between lies Africa. Although now widely regarded as the birthplace of mankind, Africa has been seen as the 'dark' continent in conventional Western imagination and it has been consistently diminished in Eurocentric cartographic practice (Rabasa, 1985, p. 14, footnote 6; Driver, 1992). *22727*, by contrast, gives Africa an unaccustomed centrality in the representation of the world. Indeed, the *South* dominates the image to the exclusion of Europe, the Americas, and Australasia.

For Western observers, the image *22727* challenges received notions of continental scale by exaggerating precisely those regions – Africa, the southern oceans, Antarctica – that, through the cartographer's choice of map projections, normally appear so small on world maps, and so correspondingly insignificant in Western geographical consciousness. Above all, the picture lacks both the co-ordinating system of the graticule and text. In the first instance, the graticule has been so taken for granted in cartographic representation since the Renaissance that we register only subliminally its organizing lattice. In the second, placing names on the world map has been such an important cartographic expression of European knowledge-power that their absence from *22727* constitutes a radical challenge to the Modern geographical imagination. Freed of graticule, names, and human boundaries, *22727* represents an Earth liberated from cultural constrictions and apparently at liberty to clothe itself anew in the natural hues of water, earth, and the softest veils of atmosphere.

Modernist global images and visions

While the formal qualities of *Earthrise* and *22727* and the narrow context of their origin in the Apollo space program served to increase the cultural significance of the photographic images, these factors fall short of a full account. Critical interpretation requires us to delve further by examining the broader aspects of Modern culture in which the images were addressed. In this section, I turn to twentieth-century interrelations between photography, the aerial vision, global representations, and geopolitics as they played themselves out within Modernist discourse, especially in the United States. This approach more directly addresses the cultural assumptions that engaged interpretations of the Apollo Earth images, both initially and in the ensuing quarter century.

I have already noted photography's role in completing the planetary cartographic project entrained during the European Renaissance. The influence of photography in structuring the Western geographical imagination is only now beginning to receive the critical attention it deserves. Photography's close relations with landscape painting in the era of the diorama and the American conquest of the West have been noted often enough (Galassi, 1981; Daniels, 1993), but photography played an equally significant role in imperialist representations of the cultural Other within the late nineteenth-century discourses of European sciences such as anthropology and geography (Harraway, 1991; Ryan, 1994). That same period also marks the origin of photography's powerful claim to mimetic truth, a claim only successfully challenged during the past two decades (Shapiro, 1988; Bolton, 1989). Bureaucratic and judicial acceptance of photography as documentary and legal evidence in the 1890s fostered the assumption that the camera cannot lie (Tagg, 1988). The photograph implied a human eye behind the camera and thus a 'witness' whose image testified to the veracity of the recorded event. The significance of the eyewitness in establishing the truth of images resurfaced in the history of space photography as well: John Glenn's 1962 pictures of Earth, shot with a 35 mm camera, had much greater public impact than the hundreds of terrestrial images taken by automatic cameras and sensors – and the same applies to the *Whole-earth* images discussed here, also predated by automatically generated photographs.[4] The claim that *Earthrise* and *22727* offered the first pictures of the Earth 'as it really is' depended upon this armature of assumptions that defended the objectivity of the photographic image.

The airman's vision

However, the Apollo images emerge from a history that is much more specific than that of photography in general. This history deals with the intimate relations between the camera and aerial flight and with the status attributed to the eyewitness behind the aerial camera, the airman himself, that developed during the course of the twentieth century. The revolutionary perspective afforded by the aerial view of the Earth encouraged balloon photography from the earliest days of the new medium and that view also appealed to the Modernist imagination in the interwar years. This appeal was especially strong in those nations – Italy, Germany, and the United States – that most enthusiastically adopted Modernism's futuristic aesthetic. The Italian Futurist painter Marinetti, for example, proclaimed the aerial view as the artistic perspective of the future; and in 1928, the *National Geographic* published a series of articles on geography from the air. These articles celebrated, among other things, the achievement of the 'Italian Argonauts', the long-distance pilots organized by the Fascist air ace, geopolitical strategist, and later governor of Italy's Libyan empire, Italo Balbo (Dreikhausen, 1985; Segre, 1987; Atkinson, 1993).

The airborne camera simultaneously realized geography's mission – to provide accurate description of the entire global surface – as it bore witness to a new perspective on that surface: 'the airman's vision', which served as the foundation of twentieth-century geopolitical thought that would, in turn, influence some of the earliest commentaries on the Apollo photographs. 'The airplane', in Antoine de Saint-Exupéry's words, 'has unveiled for us the true face of the earth' (Bunkse, 1990). The pilot's Olympian perspective was privileged, however. Only a 'few' – Charles Lindbergh in the United States, Balbo in Italy – were mythologized as modern Apollos, youthful gods whose missions took them above and beyond the mundane life of earthbound mortals and gave them a uniquely modern *vision*. The romance and power attached to the aerial view at this time are menacingly apparent in the opening scenes of Leni Riefenstahl's Nazi propaganda movie, *Triumph of the Will*, in which an airborne camera follows the Fuhrer's plane through the clouds, providing our's and Hitler's mastering gaze with quasi-cartographic glimpses of the German landscape below.

The romantic association of (generally male) youth, power, and will with the Apollonian perspective offered by air flight allowed for an heroic construction that attributed the airman with distinctively Modern qualities of scientific objectivity, technical mastery, global vision and, ultimately, *mission*. The last of these terms has been closely associated, of course, with the interlocking discourses of religious conversion and military rule that have long structured the imperial imagination in the West.[5] These attributes were further reinforced by the aerial engagements of the Second World War (Gruffudd, 1991) and later informed the selection and public personae of American astronauts throughout the space race in the 1960s. As Michael Smith (1983) has pointed out, the alliance of technology and gender loomed prominently in the representation of early American astronauts (all of them test pilots) as 'helmsmen'. *Time* portrayed John Glenn as 'a latter day Apollo' and Alan Shepard as the new Lindbergh; and the ubiquitous use of 'mission' resonates through the entire Apollo program.

Global airlines

Rapid development of commercial jet airplanes and the falling real cost of air travel in the post-war years enabled growing numbers of Americans and Europeans to experience the aerial perspective. By the late 1950s, the DC8 and Boeing 707 were bringing long-distance flight within the range of business and recreational travelers in the rich countries of the world. By the early 1970s, wide-bodied 'jumbo' jets, the Boeing 747 for example, further reduced the cost of air travel; and, flying at altitudes up to 45,000 feet, they offered extended views of the Earth's surface to ordinary families in the West. The Olympian perspective on the Earth which just thirty years earlier had been the privilege of a small number of cultural heroes was now becoming commonplace. Although the slow-moving panorama visible from the window of a jet is not recognizable cartographically unless we are already acquainted with a regional map of the area, air travel has familiarized none the less large numbers with the synoptic, high-altitude gaze over the Earth and enabled many others to share vicariously the astronaut's perspective on our planet. But even these experiences did not fully prepare people for the global views provided by *Earthrise* and *22727*.

Whatever the role of the post-war airline corporations in elevating the *image* of the globe to a more central place in American cultural consciousness, America's fascination with the globe as a symbol of modernity was already apparent in the period between the world wars. There has been a long history of using globes as an emblem of empire. The vast globes constructed in the late nineteenth century consciously signified the universalist claims of European imperialism, whether commercial, as in their emblematic usage in Universal Exhibitions in the 1890s, or spiritual, as in their popularity among Christian missionary societies.[6] Similarly, the use of globes on colonial postage stamps signified a world unified by postal and telegraph communications. And technical advances early in this century – advances that permitted accurate inscription of the entire pattern of land and sea areas on the globe's surface – further enhanced the globe's appeal as an icon of progress for institutions and corporations, sacred or secular, that claimed worldwide links.

The media, communications, and transportation were obviously attracted to the emblematic significance of the globe. Newspapers, especially in North America, used the words 'world' and 'globe' in their titles and constructed globes in or on their buildings (Domosh, 1989). In the 1930s, a revolving aluminum globe, measuring 12 feet in diameter and weighing 2 tons (at a scale of 1 : 3 480 000), was mounted on the top of the *New York News* building. It became one of the landmarks of New York's Modernist skyline, as familiar to New Yorkers as was the *Daily Planet* to readers of Marvel Comics' *Superman*. In the same decade, the American Bible Society and the Christian Science Publishing House in Boston, both dedicated to world-wide evangelism, commissioned large globes (50 inches and 30 feet respectively) to signify the geographical scope of their 'mission'. The links between the globe and Modernism in the 1930s were strengthened also by usage of the globe as a logo by Hollywood movie studios, while the identification of the globe with Modernist culture received its ultimate imprimatur with the construction of a hollow globe, 13.5 feet in diameter, for the Museum of Modern Art in New York which the public was invited to enter to view the world from a central stage (Fisher and Muller, 1944). The post-war period continued the theme: the central structure of the New York World's Fair in 1964/65, the vast Unisphere, consisted of an open global frame formed by the graticule to which relief maps of the continents were attached, while Disneyworld's seventeen-story silver geosphere, 'Spaceship Earth,' traced the history of communications.

International airlines in the post-war years were likewise captivated by globes and world maps as visual descriptors of their commercial activities. Not only did globes graphically demonstrate the scope of their route systems, they conveyed also a sense of scale and importance, regardless of the density of the route network. Thus the globe, together with the national flag, became a favored logo for airlines. During the 1940s and 1950s, the first truly international airlines, predominantly American, erected gigantic globes as decorative and declarative statements at their head offices. Pan American, for example, commissioned a globe 10 feet in diameter and 1:4 million in scale for its Miami office. In the late 1950s, Trans World Airways (TWA) established an 'air-world' education department with the declared aim of increasing passenger traffic by removing the fear of flying and making Americans air-minded. Addressing the first International Globe Conference in Vienna in 1962, Trans World's chief officer, Paul L. Dengler, described one of its programs which carried selected university education majors to Europe on a 'flying seminar'. Lectures were delivered in front of a large globe illuminated from within and carrying the letters TWA. The seminar's theme, 'air-mindedness,' invoked a vision of global citizenship that would overcome American isolationism and provincialism and induce understanding of 'the consequences of the daily shrinking process of time and space on our globe'. 'Of course', continued Dengler, 'you should remain good patriots of your own nation . . . but at the same time you must try to think globally.. . . Let yourself be convinced that we are, all of us, in the same boat, for better or worse, whether you like it or not' (Dengler, 1962, p. 94).

Dengler's emphasis on the threat of the A-bomb and total war as the compelling reasons for TWA's initiative imparted a significance well beyond commercial promotion; and his terminology anticipated language and terms that would be used later in connection with the Apollo photographs: 'our globe, formerly the image of a mysticism and unknown remoteness, shrinks before our eyes to a tiny apple' (Dengler, 1962, p. 95).

Textualizing Apollo's *Whole-Earth* images

The post-war years witnessed both the dismemberment of the European empires and the full panoply of America's global power. Replacing European dominion while retaining so many of the old continent's sacred and secular cultural assumptions, the United States inherited the European *mission civila-trice*. A combination of commercial acumen and a universalist vision projected the American way as the model of enlightened civic virtue to which all the world's peoples should naturally aspire. America's own constitutional principles and its deep ideological opposition to the one remaining territorial empire, the USSR, denied the United States traditional forms of imperial domination in territorial acquisition. The American empire required a new structure and a new language of *imperium* (McDougall, 1985). The structure was economic, based on America's total domination of immediate post-war industrial production and international trade; the language was triumphal, and predicated on American democracy as a universalist model that, in the eyes of many in the establishment, had proven its moral virtue by defeating fascism and uniting the diverse peoples of the world into one nation (*e pluribus unum*).

'The idea of one world', wrote Freidrich Tenbruch in tracing the emergence of 'one worldism' as a totalizing discourse informing America's post-war sense of mission, 'could only spring from the ground of Christendom' (Tenbruch, 1990, p. 198). Given that versions of Islam also have universalist proselytizing aspirations (as does Marxism), Tenbruch's claim may perhaps more accurately be made for Judeo-Christian monotheism rather than Christendom alone. The United States, none the less, has been the heir to a universalizing culture that is embodied in the Enlightenment principles of its constitutional philosophy.

Appropriately, therefore, the globe has served as the graphic motif for American empire, and it has been deployed not only by American corporations and missionary groups, but also by American-sponsored international agencies such as the United Nations. But in one key respect, this totalizing iconography was different. The globe was newly – and subtly – interpreted as a sign of spatial and social *incorporation* rather than of direct imperial domination.

The Apollo space program was inextricably linked to this American sense of planetary imperial mission (McDougall, 1985; Logsdon, 1970). Lyndon Johnson, speaking in the debate which led to NASA's establishment in 1958, proclaimed: 'The Roman Empire controlled the world because it could build roads . . . the British Empire was dominant because it had ships. In the air age we were powerful because we had airplanes. Now the Communists have established a foothold in outer space'. While competition with the Soviet Union certainly resonated in John F. Kennedy's May 1961 address to Congress committing the nation 'to achieving the goal, before this decade is out, of landing a man on the moon and returning him safely to the earth', the dominant rhetoric of Apollo spoke of an incorporative vision of global human mission rather than of dominion or territorial control; and as such, that rhetoric was unremarkably consonant with much of post-war American foreign policy. Imperial expansion, henceforth, was to be directed peacefully beyond the Earth for the benefit of 'all mankind' rather than into the territories of other human cultures.

Apollo 8 was launched on 21 December 1968, and returned to Earth on 27 December. Its spectacular success in escaping earth orbit, coasting to the Moon, orbiting it and returning to a safe splashdown gained added impact from the fact that the journey spanned the Christmas holiday. Not only did this timing maximize a global television audience made possible by recently established satellite links, but it also ensured the harnessing of the various associations of Christmas, both sacred and secular, with the mission's representation.[7] A new star was in the heavens, with a message of peace and goodwill to all mankind. The news media capitalized on these poetic opportunities to align traditional Christian universalism to the American vision of global harmony already articulated by Dengler, among others. As NASA's news clippings file reveals, American newspapers exploited the sacred meanings of Christmas as a time of rebirth, harmony and peace in stressing the venture's pan-human themes.

While American patriotism was evident in American news coverage, the patriotic theme was largely subordinated to a humanist rhetoric of peace and harmony, influenced perhaps by the reports of heavy American casualties sustained in Vietnam. The three astronauts themselves – Frank Borman, James Lovell, and William Anders – reinforced the religious theme by transmitting on Christmas morning an unscheduled reading of the cosmogonic narrative from the Book of Genesis, a selection that unknowingly echoed Renaissance cosmographers who related the cartographic image of the world to the Christian narration of its creation (Rabasa, 1985, p. 6). In his commentaries to Mission Control during the ten lunar orbits, Lovell compared the

Moon's dead surface, 'essentially gray, with almost no color . . . much like plaster of Paris or a grayish beach sand', with the appearance of a living Earth, visible as a bright silver ball to television viewers and as a swirl of blues, browns, and whites to the astronauts: 'a grand oasis in the big vastness of space'. Frank Borman's response to this view of *Earthrise* once again echoed, albeit with less grace, Seneca's words in Abraham Ortelius's world atlas: 'Is this that pinpoint which is divided by sword and fire among so many nations? How ridiculous are the boundaries of mortals'. In Borman's rendering (quoted in *Newsweek*, 23 December 1968):

> When you're finally up at the moon looking back at earth, all those differences and nationalistic traits are pretty well going to blend and you're going to get a concept that maybe this is really one world and why the hell can't we learn to live together like decent people.

These responses to the Apollo 8 mission refocused the public mind, shifting its attention from the project's official objective (a Moon landing) toward the astronauts' view of their 'home planet'. This was dramatically reinforced with publication of *Earthrise* two days after splashdown.

Spacewalkers

In an interview given soon after the Apollo 8 mission, William Anders, who shot the *Earthrise* photograph, described his experience at the time. The capsule was returning from the lunar shadow after the first orbit of the Moon. The three astronauts were acutely conscious of being literally on the dark side of the lunar landscape, beyond any possible contact with Earth, utterly isolated in the blackness of space:

> The Earth looked so tiny in the heavens that there were times during the Apollo 8 mission when I had trouble finding it. If you can imagine yourself in a darkened room with only one visible object, a small blue-green sphere about the size of a Christmas-tree ornament, then you can begin to grasp what the Earth looks like from space. I think that all of us subconsciously think that the Earth is flat or at least almost infinite. Let me assure you that, rather than a massive giant, it should be thought of as the fragile Christmas-tree ball which we should handle with care.
>
> (quoted in Nicks, 1970, p. 14)

Although Anders's words rework the significance of the coincidence between Christmas and the timing of the flight, their meaning extends beyond reference to universal peace and human goodwill derived from its historic religious associations to embrace the more secular, rooted, and domestic interpretation of American popular culture (McGreevy, 1990). The Christmas tree, of course, is more domestic than sacred, more evocative of images of home and family than of church and faith. The ornament suggests a child's innocent excitement, while the concluding statement insists on fragility and the possibility of irreparable damage by childish clumsiness. The metaphor can, of course, have the opposite effect of that intended: it can trivialize Earth, making it a mere plaything. Whichever way we choose to understand his metaphor, Anders invokes an association that is more local and homely and less visual, a more tactile sense of feeling and holding the Earth rather than of simply seeing it. It was a sense that resonated oddly with the contrapuntal response of proponents of progressive one-worldism and Christian mission.

These divergent ways of interpreting the image of a floating Earth at the turn of the 1970s capture at once the Modernist technological faith that had launched the Apollo project ten years earlier and the gnawing sense of mistrust in that faith that was increasingly apparent in the closing years of the 1960s. *Spaceship Earth*, for example, was a term originated by another arch-progressive and Modernist thinker, Buckminster Fuller. By entitling his late-1969 essay 'Vertical is to live – horizontal is to die', Fuller conveys the spirit of progress that he saw as embodied in the space project. His conclusion, while acknowledging the limitations imposed by Earth's isolation in an organically dead space, draws upon a series of engineering metaphors to underwrite a sense of technological optimism: 'our space-vehicle Earth and its life-energy-giving Sun and tide-pumping Moon can provide ample sustenance and power for all humanity's needs' (Fuller, 1969, p. 38). But such optimism was increasingly less secure. In the three years that had elapsed between the moon landing and the final Apollo mission that produced *22727*, the cultural currency of the Modernist notion of progress through technology had been devalued, as indeed had faith in America's global mission. Once the objective of a Moon landing had been achieved, public interest returned rapidly to terrestrial matters. As one recent writer observes, the four years that separate *Earthrise* from *22727*, 1968–1972, mark the era of the 'prophets of doom', when a spate of gloomy futurologies heralded the global environment movement (McCormick, 1989).

Press commentary on the final Apollo launch consistently weighed the costs of the mission, as against its human benefits, and found them too high. *Time* captured the dramatic change in mood. In 1968, *Time's* editors heralded the Apollo 8 crew as 'men of the year' against a backdrop of the *Earthrise* photograph and the simple caption 'Dawn'. The award was 'not merely for the dazzling technology of their achievement, but for the larger view of our planet and the fundamental unity of man' (*Time*, 1968). On the return of Apollo 17, things had changed. In December 1972, *Time* published a retrospective essay that regarded the night launch as 'a triumph of spectacle' orchestrated by NASA to revive flagging public interest. The result 'may have been as much theatrical effect', the correspondent continued, 'as spiritual experience', a feature, parenthetically, that we often associate with postmodern cultural events.[8] The tone of the essay was reflective and its theme humility. It cautioned against claims of having conquered space and appealed instead for reshaping our attitudes toward 'the tired Earth'.

Although Apollo 17 returned with *22727*, that fact was inundated in a rising tide of self-questioning, about limits to growth and the population explosion, about global pollution and poverty, about social injustice. A tired and battered

America had begun the last pull-out of troops from Vietnam, and *Time's* essay accurately reflected the prevailing media response to the Apollo program and to the political pressures on NASA to bring the project to a premature end. *22727* and *Earthrise* thus sit ambiguously between two textual constructions: the progressive *One-worldism* of late American Modernism and a *Whole-earth* environmentalism which, though historically deep-rooted, is such a significant aspect of postmodern culture (Cosgrove, 1990; Oelschlaeger, 1991).

One-world/Whole-earth

Through television reports and pictures, many younger observers detected a reality of violent oppression beneath the universalist and humanist rhetoric of the American *imperium*. For them, the airman's inheritance was a B52 bomber wreaking indiscriminate destruction on the fields and forests of South East Asia. For others, especially for women, MacLeish's images of 'men' 'taking' America, and indeed the Earth, 'brutally' meant just that – and in the most violent ways. They responded to an alternative representation, less synoptic and distanced, articulated in the astronauts' own sensibilities. Consider Michael Collins's very personal record of isolation as he circled the Moon's dark side, the single occupant of the Command Module during the Apollo 11 landing: 'I am alone now, truly alone, and absolutely isolated from any known life . . . I am it. If a count were taken, the score would be three billion plus two on the other side of the Moon, and one plus God only knows what on this side . . .'. Then, as the earth rose over the lunar horizon: '[It seemed] so small I could blot it out of the universe simply by holding up my thumb. . . . It suddenly struck me that that tiny pea, pretty and blue, was the earth . . . I didn't feel like a giant. I felt very, very small' (quoted in Ferris, 1984, p. 106).

Collins's emphasis on *feeling* rather than seeing, his recognition of limits to the power inherent in the gaze which the technological miracle of his craft allowed him, his reflections on humility and the vulnerable fragility of the earth, and his visions of intense *localism* resonated with the sensibilities of earthbound environmentalists such as Aldo Leopold, Fraser Darling, and Rachel Carson (Worster, 1988). Seen from 200,000 miles, Earth showed no signs of brotherhood or common humanity, nor even human agency. *Man* seemed no more central to existence than any other creature. In fact, what life there was seemed to inhere in the planet as a *lifeworld* rather than in some ordained hierarchy of creatures on its surface.

The astronauts' words articulated the *sublimity* of the Apollo photographs, their graphic representation of the world as 'a whole, animated and moved by inward forces' (Humboldt, 1847, p. xviii), forces so balanced, intricate, and powerful that in their presence the only valid human responses were awe, wonder, and humility. Here the sense of sight is subordinated to more visceral responses. Like the imperial reading of the globe, this vitalist interpretation of earth has a long and distinguished historical pedigree (Glacken, 1967; Livingstone, 1992), but for much of the twentieth century it largely seems to have been suppressed in the geographical imagination, defeated by the empiricist and technological imperatives of Modernism (but see Matless, 1992a, b). In the 1960s, however, certain scientific developments anticipated a vitalist revival. The scholarly acceptance of plate tectonics and of historical variation in global magnetic polarity signalled new scientific perspectives on the Earth. These would gain enormous stimulus with the publication of James Lovelock's Gaia hypothesis in the 1970s.[9]

In popular culture too, life on Earth was read in new ways. Computer-based global inventories, made possible through the very agencies and technologies that an optimistic Modernism had generated, seemed to reveal a nature that had been scarred and brutalized by human activity rather than 'improved' for a common humanity, an Earth despoiled rather than adorned by human achievement. In the four years between *Earthrise* and *22727*, a spate of texts predicted environmental doomsday as a consequence of global human activity: Paul Ehrlich's *Population bomb* (1968), Barry Commoner's *The closing circle* (1971), the Club of Rome's *Limits to growth* (1972), and *The Ecologist's A Blueprint for survival* (1972). It was their reading of the Earth as a unitary and fragile organism that placed *Earthrise* on the dustjacket of James Lovelock's text *Gaia* (1978), and *22727* on the cover of *The whole earth review*. Testimony to the impact of the message conveyed by these texts was the celebration of the first 'Earth Day' in the United States in 1970.

Emphasis on the loneliness of Earth in the blackness of space, so powerfully represented in *22727*, drew upon a reading of America as old as William Bradford and the Puritan Fathers, of the New World as mankind's last best hope, of a people cut off from the rest of life, required to attend to their own redemption and to seek moral renewal within the confines of its separate space (Worster, 1988). It was an attitude against which *One-world* advocates like Dengler and the poet and playwright Archibald MacLeish had struggled – and prevailed – in the early years of the Second World War. But three decades hence, in the 1970s, that attitude resurfaced as an alternative projection of American culture, to the *Whole-earth*.

Since the middle years of the 1970s, the demand for the Apollo photographs has been continuous and strong. In 1990 alone, 90 per cent of the photographic requests to the Johnson Space Center were for *22727* and 1280 copies were mailed (M. Gentry 1991, personal communication). Its public use continues to reflect the two readings identified here. The post-war sense of *One-world* as America's salvational mission, though more difficult to sustain in an era of American economic decline, the passing of the bipolar conflict that provided the ideological foundation for that mission, and some two decades of post-colonialist criticism, this global vision has not entirely disappeared as a mastering gaze. High-technology industries, largely concerned with communication (computers, telecommunications, media, and transportation), have dominated global economic trends over the past decade, and for them *22727* serves as an appropriate successor to the global corporate symbols of the post-war years. They persist in the *One-world* reading in which the Apollo image signifies secular mastery of the world through spatial control (Figure 21.4). By contrast, for *green* environmental organizations (alternative political

Fig. 21.4   *One-world and high technology.* Advertizement for TRW Engines Inc., Cincinnati using composite of *Earthrise* and *22727* appearing in *Fortune* magazine, 23 April 1990. © TRW Inc., 1990

parties, ecological pressure groups, educational agencies), *Earthrise* and *22727* represent a quasi-spiritual interconnectedness and the vulnerability of terrestrial life. For them the *Whole-earth* reading signifies the necessity of planetary stewardship, best practiced from an insider's localist position. In Western culture both readings originate in Genesis, the text that captioned the first televised pictures of *Earthrise*. They continue to intersect today in the varied uses of the Apollo space images.

Conclusion

Analyses of the Apollo photographs, of their composition, color and content, the conditions of their production, the contexts of their reproduction, and the texts that accompanied their cultural reception, give some support to both these interpretations of the *Whole-earth* image even as they draw attention to an alternative, and still popular, *One-world* reading. These two discourses associated with the photographs draw upon and extend ideas of human territoriality that have deep historical, geographical, and cultural roots in Western imaginings. *One-world* is a geopolitical conception coeval with the European and Christian sense of *imperium*. It signifies the expansion of a specific socio-economic order across space. Throughout Western history, this has been based in large measure on military and political power. Today's *imperium* is primarily an economic and technological order of which *22727*'s erasure of political boundaries allows representation in the networks of financial, media, or communications links etched across an unbounded globe. *Whole-earth* is, by contrast, an environmentalist conception that appeals to the organic and spiritual unity of terrestrial life. Humans are incorporated through visceral bonds between land and life (individual, family, community), bonds that have traditionally been localized, frequently as mystical ties of blood and soil. Despite this rhetoric of localism, *Whole-earth* readings of the Apollo images have difficulty keeping faith with the local because the photograph's erasure of human signs implies the extension of organic bonds across all humanity and the entire globe. In this too we might note the echoes of Western Christianity's traditional missionary imperative. A *Whole-earth* interpretation seems drawn, like so many Renaissance globe gazers, toward a transcendental vitalism as a basis for universal order and harmony.

It is highly questionable whether the conceptions of space, environment, and humanity drawn from these images can reconcile such divergent but equally totalizing tendencies in Western discourse. An alternative approach might avoid the 'visualist assumption' underlying the idea of the world as a globe and replace it with an older notion of the world as *sphere*, a body that *contains* life, including human life-worlds and that is itself contained within greater spheres beyond (Ingold, 1992) – spheres that are completely absent from the Apollo photographs. Such a perspective, in addition to immediately localizing us within the world rather than beyond it, might, in John Kennedy's words and Michael Collins's hopes, 'return us safely to the earth'.

Notes

1 The distance is approximate since it was not recorded by the crew. It is also worth mentioning that the actual photographer remains unknown. The three crew members aboard Apollo 17, Gene Sherman, Ron Evans, and Jack Schmitt, have refused to state which of them took the sequence. I do not deal in this essay with Soviet space photographs. The quality of their film was much lower than that available to American crews; pictures appeared red-tinged and muddied, with poor color resolution. Also, they produced no whole Earth photographs taken by hand, and none of their pictures achieved the widespread cultural impact of the images discussed here.

2 The 1958 Space Act establishing NASA directed the agency to place all of the information that it gathered into the public domain, unless specifically excluded for reasons of national security. Any citizen of the United States may therefore request and reproduce the Apollo space photographs without fee.

3 This paper deals only with American and European receptions of the Apollo images. Beyond the Western world they may have been understood rather differently. I am aware that the photographs have been widely reproduced in Islamic countries and beyond, but explication of the meanings that other cultures attach to them would require detailed cultural analysis.

4 NASA used John Glenn's photography of Earth to support its case for manned space flight on the grounds that the human photographer was much more flexible in identifying good targets than pre-set mechanical cameras. The debate is discussed in detail in Mack (1990). On the significance given to the graphic representation of the

eyewitness account as historical evidence in an earlier period, see Fortini-Brown's (1988) discussion of Venetian narrative painting.

5 While a significant number of inter-war pilot heroes were women, Amy Johnston being the most famous, the pilot was characteristically *gendered* male, and certainly the *fighter* pilot was male.

6 The French geographer Elisée Reclus was responsible for the design of one of the largest globes ever produced; he designed it for the Paris Universal Exhibition of 1900. The great globe produced for the headquarters of the (British) Society for Promoting Christian Knowledge at the height of Britain's imperial domination now graces the entrance to the Cambridge University Library.

7 On the cultural significance of Christmas in the United States, see McGreevy (1990). For a poetic description of the universal celestial harmony associated with Christmas, see John Milton's 'Ode on the morning of Christ's nativity'. The cosmographical associations of Christmas are profound, and relate not only to its occurrence at the winter solstice, but also the astrological associations of the Magi.

8 Turning important events into dramatic public spectacles, especially designed for large television audiences, has been regarded by many commentators as a characteristic feature of postmodernism. While I am not suggesting causation, it is worth noting that the period of the lunar space flights, and thus of *Whole-earth* photography (1968–1972), corresponds exactly with the years most often cited as the critical moment in the emergence of postmodern society (Harvey, 1989). Michael Smith's (1983) essay emphasizes the consumerist features of the entire Apollo project and relates it to the growing significance of 'commodity scientism' in American culture after 1950 (see also Sack, 1992, pp. 1–26).

9 The revival of vitalist theories of Earth is one facet of modern environmentalism, itself stimulated by the Apollo photographs (Lovelock, 1978; Cosgrove, 1990). There are intriguing historical parallels here with the fifteenth-century European recovery of Ptolemy's method of projecting the globe and a concurrent revival of vitalism (Schmitt and Skinner, 1988, pp. 199–300). The first published (1482) Italian version of Ptolemy's *Geography* was a verse translation by Francesco Berlinghieri, a member of the Platonic Academy in Florence and close associate of its founder, the humanist and neo-Platonist Marsilio Ficino, who wrote the dedication for the work.

Selected references

All NASA references are to materials held in The History Office at the Lyndon B. Johnson Space Center (JSC), Houston.

Atkinson, D. 1993: The discourses of geography and geopolitics in Fascist Italy. Paper presented at the annual conference of the Institute of British Geographers. London: Royal Holloway College.

Bolton, R. (ed.) 1989: *The contest of meaning: Critical histories of photography*. Cambridge, MA: MIT Press.

Bunkse, E. V. 1990: Saint-Exupéry's geography lesson: art and science in the creation of landscape values. *Annals of the Association of American Geographers* 80, 96–108.

Club of Rome. 1971: *The limits to growth; A report for the Club of Rome's project on the predicament of mankind*. New York: Universe.

Commoner, B. 1971: *The closing circle*. New York: Bantam.

Cosgrove, D. 1984: *Social formation and symbolic landscape*. London: Croom Helm.

Cosgrove, D. 1990: Environmental thought and action: pre-modern and post-modern. *Transactions of the Institute of British Geographers*, NJ, 15, 344–58.

Daniels, S. 1993: *Fields of vision: Landscape imagery and national identity in England and the United States*. Princeton, NJ.: Princeton University Press.

Dengler, P. L. 1962: Education towards global thinking. *Der Globusfreund* 11, 91–5.

Domosh, M. 1989: A method for interpreting landscape: a case study of the New York World Building. *Area* 21(4), 347–55.

Dreikhausen, M. 1985: *Aerial perception: The Earth as seen from aircraft and spacecraft and its influence on contemporary art*. Philadelphia: Art Alliance Press.

Driver, F. 1992: Geography's empire: Histories of geographical knowledge. *Environment and Planning D: Society and Space* 10, 23–40.

Ehrlich, P. 1968: *The population bomb*. London: Pan.

Ferris, T. 1984: *Spaceshots: The beauty of nature beyond Earth*. New York: Pantheon Books.

Fisher, I. and Muller, O. M. 1944: *World maps and globes*. New York: Essential Books.

Fortini-Brown, P. 1988: *Venetian narrative painting in the age of Carpaccio*. New Haven, Yale University Press.

Fuller, B. 1969: Vertical is to live – horizontal is to die. *American Scholar*, Winter, 27–47.

Gaarb, Y. J. 1985: The use and misuse of the *Whole Earth Review*, March, 18–25.

Galassi, P. 1981: *Before photography*. New York: Museum of Modern Art.

Glacken, C. 1967: *Traces on the Rhodian shore; Nature and culture in Western thought from ancient times to the end of the eighteenth century*. Berkeley: University of California Press.

Grosvenor, G. M. *et al.* 1973: Summing up mankind's greatest adventure. *National Geographic* 144(9), 289–331.

Gruffudd, P. 1991: Reach for the sky: The air and English cultural nationalism. *Landscape Research*, 16(2), 19–24.

Harraway, D. 1991. *Symians, cyborgs, and women: The reinvention of nature*. London: Free Association Books.

Harvey, D. 1989. *The condition of postmodernity*. Oxford: Basil Blackwell.

Humboldt, A. von. 1847. *Cosmos: A sketch of a physical description of the universe*. London: Longmans.

Ingold, T. 1992. Globes and Spheres: The Topology of Environmentalism. Paper presented to the Conference of the Association of Social Anthropologists: Anthropological Perspectives on Environmentalism, Durham, UK.

Jung, C. G. 1959: *The archetypes and the collective unconscious*. London: Routledge & Kegan Paul.

Katz, C. and Kirby, A. 1991: In the nature of things: The environment and everyday life. *Transactions of the Institute of British Geographers*, NS 16, 259–71.

Livingstone, D. 1992: *The geographical tradition*. Oxford: Basil, Blackwell.

Logsdon, J. M. 1970: *The decision to go to the Moon: Project Apollo and the national interest*. Cambridge, MA: MIT Press.

Lovelock, J. 1978. *Gaia: A new look at Earth*. London: Pan.

Mack, P. 1990: *Viewing the Earth: The social construction of the landsat satellite system*. Cambridge, MA: MIT Press.

Matless, D. 1992a: Regional surveys and local knowledges: the geographical imagination in Britain 1918–39. *Transactions of the Institute of British Geographers* 17(4), 464–80.

Matless, D. 1992b: A modern stream: water, landscape, modernism and geography. *Environment and Planning D: Society and Space* 10, 569–88.

McCormick, J. 1989: *The global environmental movement*. London: Belhaven.

McDougall, W. A. 1985: *The heaven and the earth: A political history of the space age*. New York: Basic Books.

McGreevy, P. 1990: Place and the American Christmas. *Geographical Review* 80, 32–42.

NASA SP-330 1973: *Apollo 17, Preliminary science report*. Apollo Collection, Houston: JSC.

Nicks, O. W. (ed.) 1970. *This island earth*. Washington, DC: NASA Science and Technical Information Division.

Oelschlaeger, M. 1991. *The idea of wilderness*. New Haven, CT, and London: Yale University Press.

Rabasa, J. 1985. Allegories of the *Atlas*. In Barker, F. *et al.* (eds), *Europe and its others*, vol. 2. Chichester: University of Essex, 1–16.

Ryan, J. 1994. Visualising imperial geography: Halford Mackinder and the Colonial Office Visual Instruction Committee. *Ecumene* 1(2), 157–76.

Sack, R. D. 1992. *Place and the consumer's world: a relational framework for geographical analysis*. Baltimore: Johns Hopkins University Press.

Schmitt, C. B. and Skinner, Q. 1988. *The Cambridge history of Renaissance philosophy*. Cambridge: Cambridge University Press.

Segre, C. G. 1987: *Italo Balbo: A fascist life*. Berkeley and Los Angeles: University of California Press.

Shapiro, M. 1988: *The politics of representation: Writing practices in biography, photography, and policy analysis*. Madison: University of Wisconsin Press.

Smith, M. 1983: Selling the Moon: the US manned space program and the triumph of commodity scientism. In Fox, R. W. and Lears, T. J. J. (eds), *The culture of consumption: Critical essays in American history 1880–1980*. New York: Pantheon, 177–209.

Tagg, J. 1988: *The burden of representation: Essays on photographies and histories*. London: Macmillan.

Tenbruch, F. H. 1990: The dream of a secular ecumene: the meaning and limits of policies of development. In Featherstone, M. (ed.), *Global culture: Nationalism, globalization and modernity*. London: Sage, 193–206.

The Ecologist (1972): *A Blueprint for Survival*.

Time, 1968: Men of the year. 31 December.

Worster, D. (ed.) 1988: *The ends of the Earth: Perspectives on modern environmental history*. New York: Cambridge University Press.

SECTION FIVE
RE-VISIONING HUMAN GEOGRAPHY

Editors' introduction

The contributors to this section survey the scope and purpose of geography a century after its formalization as an academic discipline. From different intellectual and ideological perspectives, associated with Karl Marx on the one hand and Carl Sauer on the other, **David Harvey** and **David Stoddart** reaffirm a broad integrative vision for geography, of theoretical coherence and social purpose, in the face of trends which they see as threatening to fragment the discipline into a myriad of fashionable ideas and narrow proficiencies.

In 'Between space and time: reflections on the geographical imagination', David Harvey examines struggles over the meaning of the basic dimensions of social life to rethink an intellectual and political vision for geography. This would be a revivified 'historical geography' examinining horizons of time and space in human affairs and their intersection in social development. On one co-ordinate Harvey identifies progressive forces of transformation, the domain of much social theory, including Marx's historical materialism, on the other co-ordinate conservative forces of rootedness and nostalgia, the domain of much aesthetic theory including 'the mythologies of landscape geography'. Resituating geography at the conjunction of these perspectives would bring together 'understandings that give space priority over time with those that give time priority over space'. 'Can we build a language – even a whole discipline – around a project that fuses the environmental, the spatial and the social within a sense of the historical geography of space and time?'

In 'To claim the high ground: geography for the end of the century', David Stoddart locates geography (and not just human geography) at the intersection of 'land and life' (Sauer, 1967). This is an explicitly environmental vision, and one that recognizes the elemental role of the the physical world. Stoddart finds that many human geographers have persuaded themselves that the physical world does not exist 'have forgotten – it is extraordinary to have to say so – that some parts of the Earth are high, others low; some wet, others dry; some desert, others covered by forest and grassland and ice'. He draws their attention to Bangladesh, 'a very physical place' and 'a very human place' whose people struggle with the combined power of the Ganges and Brahmaputra Rivers.

These manifestos for a committed and unified geography might be read in the context of their author's book-length studies (Stoddart, 1986; Harvey, 1989) which locate issues of geographical knowledge in terms of broader cultural and historical developments. They might also be read in the context of a strain of recent geographical writing which is sceptical of, sometimes hostile to, such grand visions, especially when surveyed from the high ground of the man's world of Anglophone geography (Deutsche, 1991; Massey, 1991; Pile and Rose, 1992; Rose, 1993).

Mona Domosh is no less concerned than Harvey or Stoddart to affirm vision and purpose for geography but mobilizes a postmodernist perspective to deconstruct the clubbable world of high imperial Anglo-American geography. Women have been written out of the formative history of academic geography, and in 'Towards a feminist historiography of geography' she sets out to reclaim their voices, their vision. The allure of far-away places, the thrill of discovery, energized female as well as male explorers in the late nineteenth and early twentieth centuries. Excluded from the formal institution of geography, women yet wrote and published compelling accounts of their travels. These women were, not surprisingly, complicit in many of the social and racial structures of European imperialism, but Domosh discerns in their work an alternative way of seeing the land as compared with their male counterparts, less possessive and exploitative, more revealing of themselves and their feelings, sensitive to their role as an outsider in an alien culture. There is now a wealth of empirical and theoretical material from other disciplines on postmodernism and the gendering of knowledge and landscape which may be revealing if brought to bear on human geography (Rose, 1993), but 'we do not need to look far afield . . . it is in our own backyard, if we would only step outside'.

References and further reading

Bondi, L. and Domosh, M. 1992: Other figures in other places: on feminism, postmodernism and geography. *Environment and Planning D; Society and Space* 10, 199–213.

Deutsche, R. 1991: Boys' town. *Environment and Planning D: Society and Space* 9, 5–30.

Gregory, D. 1994: *Geographical imaginations.* Oxford: Basil Blackwell.

Harvey, D. 1989: *The condition of postmodernity.* Oxford: Basil Blackwell.

Harvey, D. 1992: Postmodern morality plays. *Antipode* 24(4), 300–26.

Massey, D. 1991: Flexible sexism. *Environment and Planning D: Society and Space* 9, 31–57.

Pile, S. and Rose, G. 1992: All of nothing? Politics and critique in the modernism–postmodernism debate. *Environment and Planning D: Society and Space* 10, 123–36.

Rose, G. 1993: *Feminism and geography: The limits of geographical knowledge.* Cambridge: Polity Press.

Sauer, C. 1967: *Land and life: A selection of the writings of Carl Ortwin Sauer,* Leighly, J. (ed.). Berkeley, CA: University of California Press.

Stoddart, D. 1986: *On geography and its history.* Oxford: Basil Blackwell.

22 David Harvey,

'Between Space and Time: Reflections on the Geographical Imagination'

Reprinted in full from: *Annals of the Association of Geographers* 80, 418–34 (1990)

The question I wish to consider is the construction of a historical geography of space and time. Since that sounds and indeed is a double play on the concepts of space and time, the idea requires some initial elaboration. I shall then explore the implications of the idea in relation to the historical geography of everyday life and the social practices of those who call themselves geographers.

The spaces and times of social life

Durkheim pointed out in *The elementary forms of the religious life* (1915) that space and time are social constructs. The writings of anthropologists such as Hallowell (1955), Lévi-Strauss (1963), Hall (1966) and, more recently, Bourdieu (1977) and Moore (1986) confirm this view: different societies produce qualitatively different conceptions of space and time (see also Tuan, 1977). In interpreting this anthropological evidence, I want to highlight two features.

First, the social definitions of space and time operate with the full force of objective facts to which all individuals and institutions necessarily respond. For example, in modern societies, we accept clock time, even though such time is a social construct, as an objective fact of daily life; it provides a commonly held standard, outside of any one person's influence, to which we turn again and again to organize our lives and in terms of which we assess and judge all manner of social behaviors and subjective feelings. Even when we do not conform to it, we know very well what it is that we are not conforming to.

Second, the definitions of objective space and time are deeply implicated in processes of social reproduction. Bourdieu (1977) shows, for example, how in the case of the North African Kabyle, temporal and spatial organization (the calendar, the partitions within the house, etc.) serve to constitute the social order through the assignment of people and activities to distinctive places and times. The group orders its hierarchies, its gender roles and divisions of labor, in accordance with a specific mode of spatial and temporal organization. The role of woman in Kabyle society is, for example, defined in terms of the spaces occupied at specific times. A particular way of representing space and time guides spatial and temporal practices which in turn secure the social order.

Practices of this sort are not foreign to advanced capitalist societies. To begin with, space and time are always a primary means of both individuation and social differentiation. The definition of spatial units as administrative, legal or accounting entities defines fields of social action which have wide-ranging impacts on the organization of social life. Indeed, the very act of naming geographical entities implies a power over them, most particularly over the way in which places, their inhabitants and their social functions get represented. As Edward Said (1970) so brilliantly demonstrates in his study of Orientalism, the identity of variegated peoples can be collapsed, shaped, and manipulated through the connotations and associations imposed upon a name by outsiders. Ideological struggles over the meaning and manner of such representations of place and identity abound. But over and beyond the mere act of identification, the assignment of place within a sociospatial structure indicates distinctive roles, capacities for action, and access to power within the social order. The when and where of different kinds of social activity and of different manners of relating convey clear social messages. We still instruct children, for example, in the idea that there is 'a time and a place for everything' and all of us, at some level of meaning, know what our place is (though whether or not we feel comfortable with it is another question). We all know, furthermore, what it means to be 'put in one's place' and that to challenge what that place might be, physically as well as socially, is to challenge something fundamental in the social order. Sit-ins, street demonstrations, the storming of the Bastille or the gates of the US embassy in Tehran, the striking down of the Berlin Wall, and the occupation of a factory or a college administration building are all signs of attack against an established social order.

Sufficient accounts of these phenomena exist to render further proof of their generality superfluous, though the exact manner in which concepts of space and time operate in social reproduction is so subtle and nuanced as to require, if we are to read it right, the most sophisticated apparatus of inquiry we can muster. But the evidence is solid enough to support the following proposition: *each social formation constructs objective conceptions of space and time sufficient unto its own needs and purposes of material and social reproduction and organizes its material practices in accordance with those conceptions.*

But societies change and grow, they are transformed from within and adapt to pressures and influences from without. Objective conceptions of space and time must change to accommodate new material practices of social reproduction. How are such shifts in the public and objective conceptions of time and space accomplished? In certain instances, the answer is simply given. New concepts of space and time have been imposed by main force through conquest, imperial expansion or neocolonial domination. The European settlement of North America imposed quite alien conceptions of time and space upon the Plains Indians, for example, and in so doing altered forever the social framework within which the reproduction of these peoples could, if at all, take place. The imposition of a mathematically rational spatial order in the house, the classroom, the village, the barracks and even across the city of Cairo itself, Mitchell (1988) shows, were centerpieces of a late-nineteenth-century project to bring Egypt into line with the disciplinary frameworks of European capitalism. Such impositions are not necessarily well received. The spread of capitalist social relations has often entailed a fierce battle to socialize different peoples into the common net of time discipline implicit in industrial organization and into a respect for partitions of territorial and land rights specified in mathematically rigorous terms (see Sack, 1986). While rearguard actions against such impositions abound, it is nevertheless true that public definitions of time and space throughout much of the contemporary world have been imposed in the course of capitalist development.

Even more interesting problems arise when the public sense of time and space is contested from within. Such contestation in contemporary society in part arises out of individual and subjective resistance to the authority of the clock and the tyranny of the cadastral map. Modernist and postmodernist literature and painting are full of signs of revolt against simple mathematical and material measures of space and time, while psychologists and sociologists have revealed, through their explorations, a highly complicated and often confused world of personal and social representations which departs significantly from dominant public practices. Personal space and time do not automatically accord with the dominant public sense of either and, as Tamara Hareven (1982) shows, there are intricate ways in which 'family time' can be integrated with and used to offset the pressing power of the 'industrial time' of deskilling and reskilling of labour forces and the cyclical patterns of employment. More significantly, the class, gender, cultural, religious, and political differentiation in conceptions of time and space frequently become arenas of social conflict. New definitions of what is the correct time and place for everything as well as of the proper objective qualities of space and time can a rise out of such struggles.

A few examples of such conflict are perhaps in order. The first comes from the chapter in *Capital* called 'The working day', in which Marx (1967, pp. 233–5) sets up a fictitious conversation between capitalist and worker. The former insists that a fair day's work is measured in relation to how much time a worker needs to recuperate sufficient strength to return to work the next day and that a fair day's wage is given by the money required to cover daily reproduction costs. The worker replies that such a calculation ignores the shortening of his life which results from unremitting toil and that the measure of a fair day's work and wage looks entirely different when calculated over a working life. Both sides, Marx argues, are correct from the standpoint of the laws of market exchange, but different class perspectives dictate different time horizons for social calculation. Between such equal rights, Marx argues, force decides.

The gendering of 'Father Time' yields a second example. It is not only that time gets construed quite differently according to gender roles through the curious habit of defining working time as only that taken up in selling labor power directly to others. But, as Forman (1989) points out, the reduction of a woman's world to the cyclical times of nature has had the effect of excluding women from the linear time of patriarchal history, rendering women 'strangers in the world of male-defined time'. The struggle, in this case, is to challenge the traditional world of myth, iconography and ritual in which male dominion over time parallels as 'natural beings'. When Blake, for example, insisted that 'Time and Space are Real Beings. Time is a Man, Space is a Woman, and her masculine Portion is Death' (quoted in Forman, p. 4), he was articulating a widespread allegorical presumption that has echoes even unto the present day. The inability to relate the time of birthing (and all that this implies) to the masculine preoccupation with death and history is, in Forman's view, one of the deeper psychological battlegrounds between men and women.

The third example derives from a conversation between an economist and a geologist over the time horizon for optimal exploitation of a mineral resource. The former holds that the appropriate time horizon is set by the interest rate and market price, but the geologist, holding to a very different conception of time, argues that it is the obligation of every generation to leave behind an aliquot share of any resource to the next. There is no logical way to resolve that argument. It, too, is resolved by main force. The dominant market institutions prevailing under capitalism fix time horizons by way of the interest rate and, in almost all arenas of economic calculation (including the purchase of a house with a mortgage), that is the end of the story.

We here identify the potentiality for social conflict deriving entirely from the time horizon over which the effect of a decision is held to operate. While economists often accept the Keynesian maxim that 'in the long run we are all dead' and that the shortrun is the only reasonable time horizon over which to operationalized economic and political decisions, environmentalists insist that responsibilities must be judged over an infinite time horizon within which all forms of life (including that of humans) must be preserved. The opposition in the sense of time is obvious. Even when, as in Pigouvian economics, longer time horizons are introduced into economic calculation, the effective means is through a discount rate which is set by economic rather than ecological, religious or social calculation (see, for example, the report by Pearce *et al.* (1989) on a entitled *Blueprint for green economy*, which insists that all environmental impacts can be monetized and that the discount rate is a perfectly adequate means by which to take account of long-term environmental impacts). The whole political–economic trajectory of development and change depends upon which objective definition we adopt in social practice. If the practices are capitalistic, then the time horizon cannot be that to which environmentalists cleave.

Spatial usages and definitions are likewise a contested terrain in both practical and conceptual realms. Here, too, environmentalists tend to operate with a much broader conception of the spatial domain of social action, pointing to the spillover effects of local activities into patterns of use that affect global warming, acid rain formation and global despoliation of the resource base. Such a spatial conception conflicts with decisions taken with the objective of maximizing land rent at a particular site over a time horizon set by land price and the interest rate. What separates the environmental movement (and what in many respects makes it so special and so interesting) is precisely the conception of time and space which it brings to bear on questions of social reproduction and organization.

Such deep struggles over the meaning and social definition of space and time are rarely arrived at directly. They usually emerge out of much simpler conflicts over the appropriation and domination of particular spaces and times. It took me many years, for example, to understand why it was that the Parisian communards so readily put aside their pressing tasks of organizing for the defense of revolutionary Paris in 1871, in order to tear down the Vendôme column. The column was a hated symbol of an alien power that had long ruled over them; it was a symbol of that spatial organization of the city that had put so many segments of the population 'in their place', by the building of Haussmann's boulevards and the expulsion of the working class from the central city. Haussmann inserted an entirely new conception of space into the fabric of the city, a conception appropriate to a new social order based on capitalistic (particularly financial) values. The transformation of social relations and daily life envisaged in the 1871 revolution entailed, or so the communards felt, the reconstruction of the interior spaces of Paris in a different, non-hierarchical image. So powerful was that urge that the public spectacle of toppling the Vendôme column became a catalytic moment in the assertion of communard power over the city's spaces (Ross, 1988). The communards tried to build an alternative social order not only by reoccupying the space from which they had been so unceremoniously expelled but by trying to reshape the objective social qualities of urban space itself in a non-hierarchical and communitarian image. The subsequent rebuilding of the column was as much a signal of reaction as was the building of the Basilica of Sacré-Coeur on the heights of Montmartre in expiation for the Commune's supposed sins (see Harvey, 1985 and this volume).

The 1989 annual convention of the Association of American Geographers in Baltimore likewise took place in what is for me, a resident of that city for some eighteen years, alien territory. The present carnival mask of the inner harbor redevelopment conceals a long history of struggle over this space. The urban renewal that began in the early 1960s was led by the property developers and financial institutions as they sought to recolonize what they saw as a strategic but declining central city core. But the effort was stymied by the unrest of the 1960s that had the downtown dominated by anti-war demonstrations, countercultural events and, most devastating of all for investor confidence, street uprisings mainly on the part of impoverished African–Americans. The inner city was a space of disaffection and social disruption. But in the wake of the violence that rocked the city after Martin Luther King's assassination in 1968, a coalition sprang to life to try to restore a sense of unity and belonging to the city. The coalition was broad; it included the Churches (the Black Ministerial Alliance in particular), community leaders of all kinds, academics and downtown lawyers, politicians, trade unionists, bureaucrats, and, bringing up the rear in this instance, the business community, which was plainly at a loss as to what to do or where to turn. The struggle was on to try to put the city back together again as a cohesive social entity, as a working and living community alert to racial and social injustice.

One idea that emerged from that effort was to create a city fair in the inner city, a fair that would celebrate 'otherness' and difference by being based on the city's distinctive religious, ethnic and racial composition but which would also celebrate the theme of civic unity within that diversity. In 1970 the first fair took place, bringing a quarter of a million people over a weekend, from all neighborhoods of the city, into the inner city space of disaffection. By 1973, nearly two million came and the inner harbor was reoccupied by the common populace in ways which it had been impossible to envisage in the 1960s. It became a site of communal affirmation of unity within difference.

During the 1970s, in spite of considerable popular opposition, the forces of commercialism and property development recaptured the space. It became the site of a public–private partnership in which vast amounts of public moneys were absorbed for purposes of private rather than civic gain. The Hyatt-Regency Hotel, headquarters for the AAG meetings, was built with $5 million of private money, a $10 million Urban Development Action Grant, and a complicated deal of city investment in infrastructures and shell which took some $20 million of a city bond issue. The inner city space became a space of conspicuous consumption, celebrating commodities rather than civic values. It became the site of 'spectacle' in which people are reduced from active parti-cipants in the appropriation of space to passive spectators (Debord, 1983). This spectacle diverts attention from the awful poverty of the rest of the city and projects an image of successful dynamism when the reality is that of serious impoverishment and disempowerment (Levine, 1987). While all that money was pouring into the inner-city redevelopment, the rest of the city gained little and in some instances lost much, creating an island of downtown affluence in a sea of decay (Szanton, 1986). The glitter of the inner harbor diverts the gaze from the gathering tragedy of injustice in that other Baltimore, now safely (or so it seems) tucked away in the invisible neighborhoods of despair.

The point of these examples is to illustrate how social space, when it is contested within the orbit of a given social formation, can begin to take on new definitions and meanings. In both Paris and Baltimore, we see the struggle for command over strategic central city spaces as part of a broader struggle to replace a landscape of hierarchy and of pure money power with a social space constructed in the image of equality and justice. While both struggles were unsuccessful, they do illustrate how dominant and hegemonic definitions of social space (and time) are perpetually under challenge and always open to modification.

Materialist perspectives on the historical geography of space and time

If space and time are both social and objective, then it follows that social processes (including social conflicts of the sort already outlined) have a role to play in their objectification. How, then, would we set out to study the ways in which social space and time get shaped in different historical and geographical contexts? There is no answer to that independent of the explicit character of our ontological and epistemological commitments. My own are, as is well known, explicitly Marxist, which means the organization of inquiry according to the basic principles of historical geographical materialism. The objective definitions must in the first instance be understood, not by appeal to the world of thoughts and ideas (though that study is always rewarding), but from the study of material processes of social reproduction. As Smith (1984, p. 77) puts it, 'the relativity of space [is] not a philosophical issue but a product of social and historical practice'.

Let me illustrate such a principle at work. I often ask beginning geography students to consider where their last meal came from. Tracing back all the items used in the production of that meal reveals a relation of dependence upon a whole world of social labor conducted in many different places under very different social relations and conditions of production. That dependency expands even further when we consider the materials and goods used in the production of the goods we directly consume. Yet we can in practice consume our meal without the slightest knowledge of the intricate geography of production and the myriad social relationships embedded in the system that puts it upon our table.

This was the condition that Marx (1967, pp. 71–83) picked upon in developing one of his most telling concepts: *the fetishism of commodities*. He sought to capture by that term the way in which markets conceal social (and, we should add, geographical) information and relations. We cannot tell from looking at the commodity whether it has been produced by happy laborers working in a co-operative in Italy, grossly exploited laborers working under conditions of apartheid in South Africa, or wage laborers protected by adequate labor legislation and wage agreements in Sweden. The grapes that sit upon the supermarket shelves are mute; we cannot see the fingerprints of exploitation upon them or tell immediately what part of the world they are from. We can, by further inquiry, lift the veil on this geographical and social ignorance and make ourselves aware of these issues (as we do when we engage in a consumer boycott of non-union or South African grapes). But in so doing we find we have to go behind and beyond what the market itself reveals in order to understand how society is working. This was precisely Marx's own agenda. We have to get behind the veil, the fetishism of the market and the commodity, in order to tell the full story of social reproduction.

The geographical ignorance that arises out of the fetishism of commodities is in itself cause for concern. The spatial range of our own individual experience of procuring commodities in the marketplace bears no relationship to the spatial range over which the commodities themselves are produced. The two space horizons are quite distinct, and decisions that seem reasonable from the former standpoint are not necessarily appropriate from the latter. To which set of experiences should we appeal in understanding the historical geography of space and time? Strictly speaking, my answer will be both because both are equally material. But it is here that I insist we should deploy the Marxian concept of fetishism with its full force. We will arrive at a fetishistic interpretation of the world (including the objective social definitions of space and time) if we take the realm of individual experience (shopping in the supermarket, traveling to work and picking up money at the bank) as all there is. These latter activities are real and material, but their organization is such as to conceal the other definitions of space and time set up in accordance with the requirements of commodity production and capital circulation through price-fixing markets.

A pure concern for the material base of our own daily reproduction ought to dictate a working knowledge of the geography of commodity production and of the definitions of space and time embedded in the practices of commodity production and capital circulation. But in practice most people do without. This also raises important moral issues. If, for example, we consider it right and proper to show moral concern for those who help put dinner on the table, then this implies an extension of moral responsibility throughout the whole intricate geography and sociality of intersecting markets. We cannot reasonably go to church on Sunday, donate copiously to a fund to help the poor in the parish, and then walk obliviously into the market to buy grapes grown under conditions of apartheid. We cannot reasonably argue for high environmental quality in the neighborhood while still insisting on living at a level which necessarily implies polluting the air somewhere else (this is, after all, the heart of the ecologists' argument). Our problem is indeed precisely that in which Marx sought to instruct us. We have to penetrate the veil of fetishisms with which we are necessarily surrounded by virtue of the system of commodity production and exchange and discover what lies behind it. In particular, we need to know how space and time get defined by these material processes which give us our daily bread. It is to this world that I now turn.

The historical geography of space and time in the capitalist epoch

Consideration of the historical geography of space and time in the era of Western capitalism illustrates how conceptions and practices with respect to both have changed in accordance with political–economic practices. The transition from feudalism to capitalism, Le Goff (1980, 1988) argues, entailed a fundamental redefinition of concepts of space and time which served to reorder the world according to quite new social principles. The hour was an invention of the thirteenth century, the minute and the second became common measures only as late as the seventeenth. While the first of these measures had a religious origin (illustrating a deep continuity between the Judeo-Christian view of the world and the rise of capitalism), the spread of adequate measures of time-keeping had much more to do with the growing concern for efficiency in production, exchange, commerce and administration. It was an urban-based revolution 'in mental structures and their material expressions' and it was 'deeply implicated', according to Le Goff (1980, p. 36), 'in the mechanisms of class struggle'. 'Equal hours' in the city, Landes (1983, p. 78) confirms, 'announced the victory of a new cultural and economic order'. But the victory was partial and patchy, leaving much of the Western world outside of its reach until at least the mid-nineteenth century.

The history of cartography in the transition from feudalism to capitalism has, like the history of time-keeping, been very much about refinement of spatial measurement and representation according to clearly defined mathematical principles. Here, too, the interests of trade and commerce, of property and territorial rights (of the sort unrecognizable in the feudal world), were of paramount importance in reshaping mental structures and material practices.

When it became clear that geographical knowledge was a vital source of military and economic power, then the connection between maps and money, as Landes (1983, p. 110) shows, followed not far behind. The introduction of the Ptolemaic map into Florence in 1400 and its immediate adoption there as a means to depict geographical space and store locational information was arguably the fundamental breakthrough in the construction of geographical knowledge as we now know it. Thereafter it became possible in principle to comprehend the world as a global unity.

The political significance of this cartographic revolution deserves consideration. Rational mathematical conceptions of space and time were, for example, a necessary condition for Enlightenment doctrines of political equality and social progress. One of the first actions of the French revolutionary assembly was to ordain the systematic mapping of France as a means to ensure equality of political representation. This is such a familiar constitutional issue in the democracies of the world (given the whole history of gerrymandering) that the intimate connection between democracy and rational mapping is now taken for granted. But imagine attempting to draw up an egalitarian system of representation armed only with the Mappa Mundi! The Jeffersonian land system, with its repetitive mathematical grid that still dominates the landscape of the United States, likewise sought the rational partitioning of space so as to promote the formation of an agrarian democracy. In practice this proved admirable for capitalist appropriation of and speculation in space, subverting Jefferson's aims, but it also demonstrates how a particular definition of objective social space (in this case strictly interpreted in rationalistic Enlightenment terms) facilitated the rise of a new kind of social order.

Accounts of the sort which Le Goff and Landes provide illustrate beyond doubt that concepts of space and time and the practices associated with them are far from socially neutral in human affairs. Precisely because of such political and economic implications, the sense of space and time remains contested and more problematic than we are wont to admit. Helgerson (1986) points out, for example, the intimate connection between the Renaissance maps of England (by Speed, Nordon, Caxton, and the others), the fight with dynastic privilege and the latter's ultimate replacement by a politics in which the relation between individual and nation became hegemonic. Helgerson's point is that the new means of cartographic representation allowed individuals to see themselves in terms that were more in accord with these new definitions of social and political relations. In the colonial period, to take a much later example, the maps of colonial administrations had very distinctive qualities that reflected their social purposes (Stone, 1988).

Since I have taken up the above themes elsewhere (Harvey, 1985, 1989a), I shall here merely assert that the construction of new mental conceptions and material practices with respect to space and time were fundamental to the rise of capitalism as a particular socioeconomic system. These conceptions and practices were always partial (though they became more hegemonic as capitalism evolved), and they were, in any case, always subject to social contestation in specific places and times. But social reproduction of the capitalist sort required their deep implantation in the world of ideas as well as in the realm of social practices.

Capitalism is, however, a revolutionary mode of production, always restlessly searching out new organizational forms, new technologies, new lifestyles, and new modalities of production and exploitation. Capitalism has also been revolutionary with respect to its objective social definitions of time and space. Indeed, when compared with almost all other forms of innovation, the radical reorganizations of space relations and of spatial representations have had an extraordinarily powerful effect. The turnpikes and canals, the railways, steamships and telegraph, the radio and the automobile, containerization, jet cargo transport, television and telecommunications, have altered space and time relations and forced us to new material practices as well as to new modes of representation of space. The capacity to measure and divide time has been revolutionized, first through the production and diffusion of increasingly accurate timepieces and subsequently through close attention to the speed and co-ordinating mechanisms of production (automation, robotization) and the speed of movement of goods, people, information, messages, and the like. The material bases of objective space and time have become rapidly moving rather than fixed datum points in human affairs.

Why this movement? Since I have explored its roots in greater detail elsewhere (Harvey, 1982, 1989a) I simply summarize the principal argument. Time is a vital magnitude under capitalism because social labor time is the measure of value and surplus social labor time lies at the origin of profit. Furthermore, the turnover time of capital is significant because speed-up (in production, in marketing, in capital turnover) is a powerful competitive means for individual capitalists to augment profits. In times of economic crisis and of particularly intense competition, capitalists with a faster turnover time survive better than their rivals, with the result that social time horizons typically shorten, intensity of working and living tends to pick up, and the pace of change accelerates. The same sorts of proposition apply to the experience of space. The elimination of spatial barriers and the struggle to 'annihilate space by time' is essential to the whole dynamic of capital accumulation and becomes particularly acute in crises of capital overaccumulation. The absorption of surpluses of capital (and sometimes labor) through geographical expansion into new territories and through the construction of a completely new set of space relations has been nothing short of remarkable. The construction and reconstruction of space relations and of the global space economy, as Henri Lefebvre (1974) acutely observes, has been one of the main means to permit the survival of capitalism into the twentieth century.

The general characteristics (as opposed to the detailed where, when and how) of the historical geography of space and time which results are not accidental or arbitrary, but implicit in the very laws of motion of capitalist development. The general trend is towards an acceleration in turnover time (the worlds of production, exchange, consumption all tend to change faster) and a shrinking of space horizons. In popular terms, we might say that Toffler's (1970) world of 'future shock' encounters, as it were, Marshall McLuhan's

(1966) 'global village'. Such periodic revolutions in the objective social qualities of time and space are not without their contradictions. It takes, for example, long-term and often high-cost fixed capital investments of slow turnover time (like computer hardware) to speed up the turnover time of the rest, and it takes the production of a specific set of space relations (like a rail network) in order to annihilate space by time. A revolution in temporal and spatial relations often entails, therefore, not only the destruction of ways of life and social practices built around preceding time–space systems, but the 'creative destruction' of a wide range of physical assets embedded in the landscape. The recent history of deindustrialization is amply illustrative of the sort of process I have in mind.

The Marxian theory of capital accumulation permits theoretical insights into the contradictory changes that have occurred in the dimensionality of space and time in Western capitalism. If, as is the case, the temporal and spatial world of contemporary Wall Street is so very different from that of the nineteenth-century stock exchange and if both depart from that of rural France (then and now) or of Scottish crofters (then and now), then this must be understood as a particular set of responses to a pervasive aggregate condition shaped by the rules of commodity production and capital accumulation. It is the contradictions and tensions implied therein that I want to examine.

Cultural and political responses to the changing dimensionality of space and time

Rapid changes in the objective qualities of social space and time are both confusing and disturbing, precisely because their revolutionary implications for the social order are so hard to anticipate. The nervous wonderment at it all is excellently captured in the *Quarterly Review* for 1839:

> Supposing that our railroads even at our present simmering rate of travelling were to be suddenly established all over England, the whole population of the country would, speaking metaphorically at once advance *en masse*, and place their chairs nearer to the fireside of their metropolis.. . . As distances were thus annihilated, the surface of our country would, as it were, shrivel in size until it became not much bigger than one immense city.
>
> (cited in Schivelbusch, 1978, p. 32)

The poet Heine likewise recorded his 'tremendous foreboding' on the opening of the rail link from Paris to Rouen:

> What changes must now occur, in our way of looking at things, in our notions! Even the elementary concepts of time and space have begun to vacillate. Space is killed by the railways. I feel as if the mountains and forests of all countries were advancing on Paris. Even now, I can smell the German linden trees; the North Sea's breakers are rolling against my door.
>
> (cited in Schivelbusch, 1978, p. 34)

The German theatre director Johannes Birringer (1989; pp. 120–38) records a similar sense of shock in a contemporary setting. On arrival in Dallas and

Houston, he felt an 'unforeseen collapse of space', where 'the dispersion and decompositions of the urban body (the physical and cultural representation of community) have reached a hallucinatory stage'. He remarks on:

> the unavoidable fusion and confusion of geographical realities, or the interchangeability of all places, or the disappearance of visible (static) points of reference into a constant commutation of surface images.

The riddle of Houston, he concludes:

> is one of community: fragmented and exploded in all directions. . . . The city impersonates a speculative disorder, a kind of positive unspecificity on the verge of a paradoxical hyperbole (global power/local chaos).

I shall call this sense of overwhelming change in space–time dimensionality 'time–space compression' in order to capture something of Heine's sense of foreboding and Birringer's sense of collapse. The experience of it forces all of us to adjust our notions of space and time and to rethink the prospects for social action. This rethinking is, as I have already argued, embedded in political–economic struggles. But it is also the focus of intense cultural, aesthetic and political debate. Reflection on this idea helps us understand some of the turmoil that has occurred within the fields of cultural and political production in the capitalist era.

The recent complex of movements known as 'postmodernism' is, for example, connected in the writings of authors as diverse as Jameson (1984), Berman (1982) and Daniel Bell (1976) to some new experience of space and time. Interestingly, having advanced the idea, none of them tells us exactly what they might mean by it. And the material basis upon which these new experiences of space and time might be built, and its relation to the political economy of capitalist development, remains a topic lost in the shadows. I am particularly interested to see how far postmodernism can be understood simply by relating it to the new experiences of space and time generated out of the political–economic crisis of 1973 (Harvey, 1989a).

Much of the advanced capitalist world was at that time forced into a major revolution in production techniques, consumption habits and political–economic practices. Strong currents of innovation have focused on speed-up and acceleration of turnover times. Time horizons for decision-making (now a matter of minutes in international financial markets) have shortened and lifestyle fashions have changed rapidly. And all of this has been coupled with a radical reorganization of space relations, the further reduction of spatial barriers, and the emergence of a new geography of capitalist development. These events have generated a powerful sense of time–space compression which has affected all aspects of cultural and political life. Whole landscapes have had to be destroyed in order to make way for the creation of the new Themes of creative destruction, of increased fragmentation, of ephemerality (in community life, of skills, of lifestyles) have become much more noticeable in literary and philosophic discourse in an era when restructuring of everything from industrial production techniques to inner cities has become a major topic of concern. The transformation in 'the structure of feeling' which the move towards postmodernism betokens seems to have much to do with the shifts in political–economic practices that have occurred over the past two decades.

Consider, glancing backwards, that complex cultural movement known as modernism (against which postmodernism is supposedly reacting). There is indeed something special that happens to writing and artistic representation in Paris after 1848 and it is useful to look at that against the background of political–economic transformations occurring in that space and at that time. Heine's vague foreboding became a dramatic and traumatic experience in 1848, when for the first time in the capitalist world, political economy assumed an unlooked for simultaneity. The economic collapse and political revolutions that swept across the capitals of Europe in that year indicated that the capitalist world was interlinked in ways that had hitherto seemed unimaginable. The speed and simultaneity of it all was deeply troubling and called for some new mode of representation through which this interlinked world could be better understood. Realist modest of representation which took a simple narrative structure as their model simply could not do the job (no matter how brilliantly Dickens ranged across space and time in a novel like *Bleak House*).

Baudelaire (1981) took up the challenge by defining the modernist problematic as the search for universal truths in a world characterized by (spatial) fragmentation, (temporal) ephemerality and creative destruction. The complex sentence structure in Flaubert's novels and the brushstrokes of Manet defined totally new modes of representation of space and time that allowed new ways of thinking and new possibilities for social and political action. Kern's (1983) account of the revolution in the representation of space and time that occurred shortly before 1914 (a period of extraordinary experimentation in fields as diverse as physics, literature, painting and philosophy) is one of the clearest studies to date of how time–space compression generates experiences out of which new conceptions are squeezed. The avant-garde movements in the cultural field in part reflected but in part also sought to impose new definitions of space and time upon a Western capitalism in the full flood of violent transformation.

A closer look at the contradictions built into these cultural and political movements illustrates how they can mirror the fundamental contradictions in capitalist political economy. Consider the cultural response to the recent speed-up and acceleration of capital turnover time. The latter presupposes, to begin with, a more rapid turnover in consumption habits and lifestyles which consequently become the focus of capitalist social relations of production and consumption. Capitalist penetration of the realm of cultural production becomes particularly attractive because the lifetimes of consumption of images, as opposed to more tangible objects like autos and refrigerators, is almost instantaneous. In recent years, a good deal of capital and labor has been applied to this purpose. This has been accompanied by a renewed emphasis upon the production of controlled spectacles (of which the Los Angeles Olympic Games was a prime example) which can conveniently double as a means of capital accumulation and of social control (reviving political interest in the old Roman formula of 'bread and circuses' at a time of greater insecurity).

The reactions to the collapse of spatial barriers are no less contradictory. The more interrelations become, the more internationalized our dinner ingredients and our money flows, and the more spatial barriers disintegrate, so more rather than less of the world's population clings to place and neighborhood or to nation, region, ethnic grouping, or religious belief as specific marks of identity. Such a quest for visible and tangible marks of identity is readily understandable in the midst of fierce time–space compression. No matter that the capitalist response has been to invent tradition as yet another item of commodity production and consumption (the re-enactment of ancient rites and spectacles, the excesses of a rampant heritage culture), there is still an insistent urge to look for roots in a world where image streams accelerate and become more and more placeless (unless the television and video screen can properly be regarded as a place). The foreboding generated out of the sense of social space imploding in upon us (forcibly marked by everything from the daily news to random acts of international terror or global environmental problems) translates into a crisis of identity. Who are we and to what space/place do we belong? Am I a citizen of the world, the nation, the locality? Not for the first time in capitalist history, if Kern's (1983) account of the period before the First World War is correct, the diminution of spatial barriers has provoked an increasing sense of nationalism and localism, and excessive geopolitical rivalries and tensions, precisely because of the reduction in the power of spatial barriers to separate and defend against others.

The evident tension between *place* and *space* echoes that fundamental contradiction of capitalist political economy to which I have already alluded: that it takes a specific organization of space to try to annihilate space and that it takes capital of long turnover time to facilitate the more rapid turnover of the rest. This tension can be examined from yet another standpoint. Multinational capital should have scant respect for geography these days precisely because weakening spatial barriers open the whole world as its profitable oyster. But the reduction of spatial barriers has an equally powerful opposite effect: small-scale and finely graded differences between the qualities of places (their labor supply, their infrastructures and political receptivity, their resource mixes, their market niches, etc.) become even more important because multi-national capital is in a better position to exploit them. Places, by the same token, become much more concerned about their 'good business climate' and inter-place competition for development becomes much more fine-tuned. The image-building of community (of the sort which characterizes Baltimore's inner harbor) becomes embedded in powerful processes of interurban competition (Harvey, 1989b). Concern for both the real and fictional qualities of place increases in a phase of capitalist development in which the power to command space, particularly with respect to financial and money flows, has become more marked than ever before. The geopolitics of place tend to become more rather than less emphatic. Globalization thus generates its exact opposite motion into geopolitical oppositions and warring camps in a hostile world. The threat of geopolitical fragmentation in global capitalism – between geopolitical power blocks such as the European Common Market, the North American Common Market, and the Japanese trading empire – is far from idle.

It is for these reasons that coming to terms with the historical geography of space and time under capitalism makes so much sense. The dialectical oppositions between place and space, between long- and short-term time horizons, exist within a deeper framework of shifts in time–space dimensionality that are the product of underlying capitalist imperatives to accelerate turnover times and to annihilate space by time. The study of how we cope with time–space compression illustrates how shifts in the experience of space and time generate new struggles in such fields as aesthetics and cultural representation, how very basic processes of social reproduction, as well as of production, are deeply implicated in shifting space and time horizons. In this regard, I find it intriguing, if I may make the aside, that the exploration of the relations between literature and geography that have so far emanated from the geographers' camp have almost without exception concentrated on the literary evocation of place (see, for example, Mallory and Simpson-Housley, 1987) when the far more fundamental question of spatiality in, say, the novels of Flaubert and Joyce (a topic of great import for literary historians) has passed by unremarked. I also find it odd that geographers have concentrated so much more upon the importance of locality in the present conjuncture, leaning, as it were, to one side of the contradictory dynamic of space and place, as if they are separate rather than dialectically related concepts.

Geography in relation to social and aesthetic theory

Armed with such epistemological and ontological commitments as historical–geographical materialism provides, we can begin to unravel the theoretical and philosophical conceptions of space and time which sustain (explicitly or implicitly) particular social visions and interpretations of the world. In so doing, it is useful to begin with consideration of a major divide in Western thought between aesthetic and social theory.

Social theory of the sort constructed in the diverse traditions of Adam Smith, Marx or Weber tends to privilege time over space in its formulations, reflecting and legitimizing those who view the world through the lenses of spaceless doctrines of progress and revolution. In recent years, many geographers have sought to correct that defective vision and to reintroduce the concept of space as not only meaningful but vital to the proper understanding of social processes (see Gregory and Urry, 1985; Soja, 1989). To some degree that effort has been rewarded by the recognition on the part of some social theorists that space indeed does matter (for example, Giddens, 1984). But that task is only partly complete. Getting behind the fetishism of commodities challenges us to integrate the historical geography of space and time within the frame of all our understandings of how human societies are constructed and change. Our interventions in social theory stand to be strengthened even further by the exploration of that theme, though this presupposes, as always, the training of geographies with a powerful command over social theory and seized intellectually by the challenge to explore the difficult terrain of interface between society and the social construction of space and time.

But there is, curiously, another terrain of theoretical intervention which remains largely unexplored, except in that unsatisfactory and partial manner that always comes with nibbling at hidden rather than struggling over overt questions. I refer here to the intersection between geographical work and aesthetic theory. The latter, in direct contrast to social theory, is deeply concerned with 'the spatialization of time' albeit in terms of how that experience is communicated to and received by knowing, sensuous individuals. The architect, to take the most obvious case, tries to communicate certain values through the construction of a spatial form. Architecture, suggests Karsten Harries (1982), is not only about domesticating space, wresting and shaping a livable place out of empty space. It is also a deep defense against 'the terror of time'. The 'language of beauty' is 'the language of a timeless reality'. To create a beautiful object is 'to link time and eternity' in such a way as to redeem us from time's tyranny. The aim of spatial constructs is 'not to illuminate temporal reality so that [we] might feel more at home in it, but . . . to abolish time within time, if only for a time'. Even writing, comments Bourdieu (1977, p. 156), 'tears practice and discourse out of the flow of time'.

There are, of course, as many varieties of aesthetic theory as there are of social theory (see, for example, Eagleton's (1990) brilliant treatise on the subject). But I quote these comments from Harries to illustrate one of the central themes with which aesthetic theory grapples: how spatial constructs are created and used as fixed markers of human memory and of social values in a world of rapid flux and change. There is much to be learned from aesthetic theory about how different forms of produced space inhibit or facilitate processes of social change. Interestingly, geographers now find even more support for their endeavours from literary theorists (Jameson, 1984; Ross, 1988) than from the social theorists. Conversely, there is much to be learned from social theory concerning the flux and change with which aesthetic theory has to cope. Historical geography, in so far as it lies at the intersection of those two dimensions, has an immense potentiality to contribute to understanding them both. By playing these two currents of thought off against each other, we may even aspire to create a more general theoretical framework for interpreting the historical geography of space and time while simultaneously figuring how cultural and aesthetic practices – spatializations – intervene in the political–economic dynamic of social and political change.

Let me illustrate where the political significance of such an argument might lie. Aesthetic judgments (as well as the 'redemptive' artistic practices that attach thereto) have frequently entered in as powerful criteria of political and social action. Kant argued that independent aesthetic judgment could act as a mediator between the worlds of objective science and of subjective moral judgment. If aesthetic judgment gives space priority over time, then it follows that spatial practices and concepts can, under certain circumstances, become central to social action.

In this regard, the German philosopher Heidegger is an interesting figure. Rejecting the Kantian dichotomies of subject and object, and fearing the descent into nihilism that Nietzschean thought seemed to promote, he proclaimed the permanence of *being* over the transitoriness of *becoming* and attached himself to a traditionalist vision of the truly aesthetic political state (Chytry, 1989). His investigations led him away from the universals of modernism and Judeo-Christian thought and back to the intense and creative nationalism of pre-Socratic Greek thought. All metaphysics and philosophy, he declared (Heidegger, 1959) are given their meaning only in relation to the destiny of the people. The geopolitical position of Germany in the interwar years, squeezed in a 'great pincer' between Russia and America, threatened the search for that meaning. 'If the great decision regarding Europe is not to bring annihilation', he wrote, the German nation 'must move itself and thereby the history of the West beyond the center of their future "happening and into the primordial realm of the powers of being" and 'that decision must be made in terms of new spiritual energies unfolding historically from out of the center'. Herein for Heidegger lay the 'inner truth and greatness of the National Socialist movement' (Blitz, 1981, p. 217).

That a great twentieth-century philosopher, who has incidentally inspired the philosophizing of Karsten Harries as well as much of the geographical writing on the meaning of place (see Relph, 1976; Seamon and Mugerauer, 1989), should so compromise himself politically and throw in his lot with the Nazis is deeply troubling. But a number of useful points can be made from the standpoint of my present argument. Heidegger's work is deeply inbued with an aesthetic sense which prioritizes *being* and the specific qualities of *place* over *becoming* and the universal propositions of modernist progress in universal space. His rejection of judeo-Christian values, of the myth of machine rationality, and of internationalism was total. The position to which he subscribed was active and revolutionary precisely because he saw the necessity for redemptive practices which in effect depended upon the restoration of the power of myth (of blood and soil, of race and fatherland, of destiny and place) while mobilizing all of the accoutrements of social progress towards a project of sublime national achievement. The application of this particular aesthetic sense to politics helped alter the historical geography of capitalism with a vengeance.

I scarcely need to remind geographers of the tortured history of geopolitical thinking and practices in the twentieth century and the difficulty geographers have had in confronting the thorny issues involved. I note that Hartshorne's (1939) *The nature of geography*, written in Vienna shortly after the *Anschluss*, totally rejects aesthetics in geography and reserves its most vitriolic condemnations for the mythologies of landscape geography. Hartshorne, following Hettner, seems to want to expel any opening for the politicizing of academic geography in an era when geography was suffused with politics and when sentiments of place and of aesthetics were being actively mobilized in the Nazi cause. The difficulty, of course, is that avoiding the problem does not eliminate it, even in academic geography.

This is not to say that everyone who, since Hartshorne, has sought to restore an aesthetic dimension to geography is a crypto-Nazi, for, as Eagleton (1990, p. 28) points out, the aesthetic has ever been 'a contradictory, double-edged concept'. On the one hand 'it figures as a genuinely emancipatory force – as a community of subjects now linked by sensuous impulse and fellow feeling' while on the other it can also serve to internalize repression, 'inserting social power more deeply into the very bodies of those it subjugates and so operating as a supremely effective mode of political hegemony'. The aestheticization of politics has, for this reason, a long history, posing both problems and potentialities in relation to social progress. There are left and right versions (the Sandinistas, after all, aestheticize politics around the figure of Sandino, and Marx's writings are full of references to an underlying project of liberation of the creative senses). The clearest form the problem takes is the shift in emphasis from historical progress and its ideologies towards practices which promote national (or even local) destinies and culture, often sparking geopolitical conflicts within the world economy. Appeals to mythologies of place, person and tradition, to the aesthetic sense, have played a vital role in geopolitical history.

Herein, I think, lies the significance of conjoining aesthetic with social theoretic perspectives, bringing together understandings that give space priority over time with those that give time priority over space. Historical geography in general, and the study of the historical geography of space and time, lies exactly at that point of intersection and therefore has a major intellectual, theoretical, political and practical role to play in understanding how human societies work. By positioning the study of geography between space and time, we evidently have much to learn and much to contribute.

The geographical imagination

I conclude with a brief commentary on the implications of such a perspective for the study of geography and for that relatively small group of scholars occupying a niche labeled 'geographer' within the academic division of labor.

The latter is a product of late-nineteenth-century conditions and concerns. It is by no means self-evident that the disciplinary boundaries then drawn up (and subsequently fossilized by professionalization and institutionalization) correspond to contemporary conditions and needs. Partly in response to this problem, the academy has moved towards an increasing fragmentation in the division of labor within disciplines, spawned new disciplines in the interstices and looked for crosslinks on thematic topics. This history resembles the development of the division of labor in society at large. Increasing specialization of task and product differentiation, increasing roundaboutness of production and the search for horizontal linkages are as characteristic of large multinational corporations as they are of large universities. Within geography this process of fragmentation has accelerated since the mid-1960s. The effect has been to make it harder to identify the binding logic that is suggested by the word 'discipline'.

The turnover time of ideas in academia has also accelerated. Not so long ago, to publish more than two books in a lifetime was thought to be over-ambitious. Nowadays, it seems, leading academics have to publish a book every two years if they are to prove they are still alive. Definitions of productivity and output in academia have become much more strictly applied and career advancement is more and more measured simply in such terms. There is, of course, a certain intersection here between research and corporate/nation State requirements, between academia and the publishing trade, and the emergence of education as one of the big growth sectors in advanced capitalist societies. Speed-up in the production of ideas parallels a general push to accelerate turnover time within capitalism as a whole. But greater output of books and journals must rest on the production of new knowledge, and that implies the much fiercer competitive search for new ideas, a much greater proprietary interest in them. Such frenetic activity can converge upon some consensual and well-established 'truth' only if Adam Smith's hidden hand has all those effects in academia that it plainly does not have in other markets. In practice, the competitive marketing of ideas, theories, models, topic thrusts, generates color-of-the-month fashions which exacerbate rather than ameliorate conditions of rapid turnover, speed-up and ephemerality. Last year it was positivism and Marxism, this year structurationism, next year realism and the year after that constructivism, postmodernism, or whatever. It is easier to keep pace with the changes in Benetton's colors than to follow the gyrations of ephemeral ideas now being turned over within the academic world.

It is hard to see what we can do to resist such trends, even when we bewail their effects. Our job descriptions do not encompass those of 'intellectual geographer' but much more typically specify ever-narrower proficiencies in everything from mere command of techniques (remote sensing and Geographical Information Systems (GIS)) to specialists in transport modeling, industrial location, groundwater modeling, Soviet geography or flavor of the month topic (sustainable development, chaos theory, fractal geometry or whatever). The best we can do is appoint specialists and hope they have an interest in the discipline as a whole. Our seeming inability or unwillingness to resist fragmentation and ephemerality suggests a condition in which something is being done to us by forces beyond our control. I wish, for example, that those who now so loudly proclaim the power of individual agency in human affairs could demonstrate how their or our specific agencies have produced this macroshift in our conditions of working and living. Are we mere victims of social processes rather than their real progenitors? If here, too, I prefer the Marxian conception of individuals struggling to make history but not under conditions of their own making, it is because most of us have a lifetime of exactly that kind of experience behind us.

This same question comes to mind when we consider the resurgent interest in aesthetics, landscape geography and place as central to the concerns of many human geographers. The claim that the place of geography in academia is to be secured by attaching the discipline to a core concept of place (even understood as a unique configuration of elements) has strengthened in a phase of capitalist development when the particular qualities of place have become of much greater concern to multinational capital and when there has simultaneously been a renewed interest in the politics and image of place as an arena of supposed (even fictional) stability under conditions of powerful time–space compression. The social search for identity and roots in place has re-entered geography as a leitmotif and is in turn increasingly used to provide the discipline with a more powerful (and equally fictitious) sense of identity in a rapidly changing world.

A deeper understanding of the historical geography of space and time sheds considerable light on why the discipline might cultivate such arenas of research in this time and place. It provides a critical perspective from which to evaluate our reactions to the social pressures that surround us and suffuse our lives. Do we, in unthinkingly accepting the significance of place to our discipline, run the danger of drifting into subconscious support for a re-emergence of an aestheticized geopolitics? The question does not imply avoidance of that issue but a proper confrontation of it through a conception of geography that lies at the intersection between social and aesthetic theory.

The historical geography of space and time facilitates critical reflection on who we are and what it is we might be struggling for. What concepts of space and time are we trying to establish? How do these relate to the changing historical geography of space and time under capitalism? What would the space and time of a socialist or ecologically responsible society look like? Geographers, after all, are contributors (and potentially powerful and important ones at that) to the whole question of spatiality and its meanings. Historical geographers with their potential interests in both space and time have unbounded potentiality to reflect back not only on the history of this or that place and space relations but the whole conundrum of the changing experience of space and time in social life and social reproduction.

Critical reflection on the historical geography of space and time locates the history of ideas about space and time in their material, social and political setting. Hartshorne did not write *The nature of geography* in a political vacuum but in post-*Anschluss* Vienna, and that fact (though never mentioned in consideration of that work) is surely present in its manner of construction and intervention in the world of ideas. This text of mine is likewise constructed in the light of a certain experience of time–space compression, of shifting mores of social reproduction and political argument. Even the great Kant did not develop his ideas on space and time, his distinctions between aesthetic, moral and scientific judgments, in a social vacuum. His was the grand attempt to codify and synthesize the evident contradictions inherent in the bourgeois logic of Enlightenment reason as it was then unfolding in the midst of the revolutionary impulses sweeping Europe at the end of the eighteenth century. It was a very distinctive product of that society with its particular and practical interests in commanding space and time with rational and mathematical precision, while experiencing all the frustrations and contradictions of initiating such a rational order given the nascent social relations of capitalism. If Hegel attacked Kant (on everything from aesthetics to his theory of history) and if Marx attacked both Hegel and Kant (again, on everything from aesthetics to basic conceptions of materiality and history), then these debates had everything to do with trying to redefine the paths of social change. If I, as a Marxist, still cling to that quest for an orderly social revolution that will take us beyond the contradictions, manifest injustices and senseless 'accumulation for accumulation's sake' logic of capitalism, then this commits me to a struggle to redefine the meaning of space and time as part and parcel of that quest. And if I am still so much in a minority in an academy in which neo-Kantianism dominates (without, it must be said, most people even knowing it), then this quite simply testifies to the persistence of capitalist social relations and of the bourgeois ideas that derive therefrom, including those defining and objectifying space and time.

Attachment to a certain conception of space and time is a political decision, and the historical geography of space and time reveals it so to be. What kind of space and time do we, as professional geographers, seek to promote? To what processes of social reproduction do those concepts subtly but persistently allude? The current campaign for geographical literacy is laudable, but what language is it that we teach? Do we simply insist that our students learn how many countries border on Chad? Do we teach the static rationality of the Ptolemaic system and insist that geography is nothing more than GIS, the contemporary version of the Hartshornian rule that if it can be mapped, then it is geography? Or do we teach the rich language of the commodity, with all its intricate history of social and spatial relations stretching back from our dinner table into almost every niche of labor activity in the modern world? And can we go on from that to teach the rich and complex language of uneven geographical development, of environmental transformations (deforestation, soil degradation, hydrological modifications, climatic shifts) whose historical geography has scarcely begun to be reconstructed? Can we go even further and create a deep awareness of how social processes can be given aesthetic forms in political debate (and learn to appreciate all the dangers that lurk therein)? Can we build a language – even a whole discipline – around a project that fuses the environmental, the spatial and the social within a sense of the historical geography of space and time?

All such possibilities exist to be explored. But whatever course we take entails a political commitment as to what kind of space and time we wish to promote. We are political agents and have to be aware of it. And the politics is an everyday question. The marketing head of a US, communications firm in Europe commented (*International Herald Tribune*, 9 March 1989) on conversations with senior bankers in which he sought to go beyond the banter about it being the warmest January on record and talk seriously about the long-term effects of global warming. His clients all reacted in such a way as to suggest they thought about the environment 'in the same way we practice a hobby, in the comfort of our homes' and at weekends, when we should really think about it all the time, 'especially at work'. But how can international bankers think about such things when their time horizon is minutes? If twenty-four hours is a very long time in financial markets, and if finance capital is today the most powerful force in international development, then what kinds of long-term decisions can we expect from that quarter that make any sense from the standpoint of even long-term planning of investments, let alone of environmental regulation? When the commander of the *Vincennes* had to make the life-and-death decision on whether an image on a screen was a diving fighter or an Iranian airbus, he was caught in the terror of time–space compression which ultimately dissolves everything into ephemera and fragments such that the devil takes not the hindmost but the global totality, the whole social fabric of an internationalizing society that is more closely linked than ever before and in which the pace of change has suddenly accelerated.

Geographers cannot escape the terrors of these times. Nor can we avoid in the broad sense becoming victims of history rather than its victors. But we can certainly struggle for a different social vision and different futures with a conscious awareness of stakes and goals, albeit under conditions that are never of our own making. It is by positioning our geography between space and time, and by seeing ourselves as active participants in the historical geography of space and time, that we can, I believe, recover some clearer sense of purpose for ourselves, define an arena of serious intellectual debate and inquiry and thereby make major contributions, intellectually and politically, in a deeply troubled world.

References

Baudelaire, C. 1981: *Selected writings on art and artists*. Cambridge: Cambridge University Press.

Bell, D. 1976: *The cultural contradictions of capitalism*. New York: Basic Books.

Berman, M. 1982: *All that is solid melts into air*. New York: Simon and Schuster.

Birringer, J. 1989: Invisible cities/transcultural images. *Performing Arts Journal* 12, 33–34, 120–38.

Blitz, M. 1981: *Heidegger's being and time: The possibility of political philosophy*. Ithaca, NY: Cornell University Press.

Bourdieu, P. 1977: *Outline of a theory of practice*. Cambridge: Cambridge University Press.

Chytry, J. 1989: *The aesthetic state: A quest in modern German thought*. Berkeley: University of California Press.

Debord, G. 1983: *Society of the spectacle*. Detroit: Black and Red Books.

Durkheim, E. 1915: *The elementary forms of the religious life*. London: Allen and Unwin.

Eagleton, T. 1990: *The ideology of the aesthetic*. Oxford: Basil Blackwell.

Forman, F. J., with Sowton, C. (eds) 1889: *Taking our time: Feminist perspectives on temporality*. Oxford: Pergamon Press.

Giddens, A. 1984: *The constitution of society*. Oxford: Polity Press.

Gregory, D. and Urry, J. (eds) 1985: *Social relations and spatial structures*. London: Macmillan.

Hall, E. T. 1966: *The hidden dimension*. Garden City, NY: Doubleday.

Hallowell, A. 1955: *Culture and experience*. Phildelphia: University of Pennsylvania Press.

Hareven, T. 1982: *Family time and industrial time*. Cambridge: Cambridge University Press.

Harries, K. 1982: Building and the terror of time. *Perspecta: The Yale Architectural Journal* 19, 59–69.

Hartshorne, R. 1939: *The nature of geography*. Lancaster, PA: Association of American Geographers.

Harvey, D. 1982: *The limits to capital*. Chicago: University of Chicago Press.

Harvey, D. 1985: *Consciousness and the urban experience*. Baltimore: Johns Hopkins University Press.

Harvey, D. 1989a: *The condition of postmodernity*. New York: Basil Blackwell.

Harvey, D. 1989b: From managerialism to entrepreneurialism: the transformation in urban governance in late capitalism. *Geografiska Annaler* 71 (Series B), 3–17.

Heidegger, M. 1959: *An introduction to metaphysics*. New Haven, CT: Yale University Press.

Helgerson, R. 1986: The land speaks: cartography, chorography, and subversion in Renaissance England. *Representations* 16, 51–85.

Jameson, F. 1984: Postmodernism, or the cultural logic of late capitalism. *New Left Review* 146, 53–92.

Kern, S. 1983: *The culture of time and space, 1880–1918*. London: Weidenfeld & Nicolson.

Landes, D. 1983: *Revolution in time: Clocks and the making of the modern world*. Cambridge, MA: Harvard University Press.

Lefebvre, H. 1974: *La production de l'espace*. Paris: Anthropos.

Le Goff, J. 1980: *Time, work and culture in the middle ages*. Chicago: University of Chicago Press.

Le Goff. J. 1988: *Medieval civilisation*. Oxford: Basil Blackwell.

Levine, M. 1987: Downtown redevelopment as an urban growth strategy; a critical appraisal of the Baltimore renaissance. *Journal of Urban Affairs* 9(2), 103–23.

Lévi-Strauss, C. 1963: *Structural anthropology*. New York: Random House.

McLuhan, M. 1966: *Understanding media: The extensions of man*. New York: McGraw-Hill.

Mallory, W. F. and Simpson-Housley, P. (eds) 1987: *Geography and literature: A meeting of the disciplines*. Syracuse, NY: Syracuse University Press.

Marx, K. 1967: *Capital,* vol. 1. New York: International Publishers.

Mitchell, T. 1988: *Colonising Egypt*. Cambridge: Cambridge University Press.

Moore, B. 1986: *Space, text and gender*. Cambridge: Cambridge University Press.

Pearce, D. Markandya, A. and Barbier, E. 1989: *Blueprint for a green economy*. London: Earthscan Publications.

Relph, E. 1976: *Place and placelessness*. London: Pion.

Ross, K. 1988: *The emergence of social space: Rimbaud and the Commune*. Minneapolis: University of Minnesota Press.

Sack, R. 1986: *Human territoriality: Its theory and history*. Cambridge: Cambridge University Press.

Said, E. 1978: *Orientalism*. New York: Random House.

Schivelbusch, W. 1978: Railroad space and railroad time. *New German Critique* 14, 31–40.

Seamon, D. and Mugerauer, R. eds 1989: *Dwelling, place and environment*. New York: Columbia University Press.

Smith, N. 1984: *Uneven development: Nature, capital and the production of space*. Oxford: Basil Blackwell.

Soja, E. 1989: *Postmodern geographies*. London: Pluto.

Stone, J. 1988: Imperialism, colonialism and cartography. *Transactions of the Institute of British Geographers* NS 13(1), 57–64.

Szanton, P. 1986: *Baltimore 2000*. Baltimore: Goldseker Foundation.

Toffler, A. 1970: *Future shock*. New York: Bodley Head.

Tuan, Yi-Fu. 1977: *Space and place*. Minneapolis: Minnesota University Press.

23   David Stoddart,

'To Claim the High Ground: Geography for the End of the Century'

Reprinted in full from: *Transactions of the Institute of British Geographers* NS 12, 327–36 (1987)

It is a particular privilege to give this Ninth Carl Sauer Memorial Lecture for several reasons. First, it is always a privilege to come to Berkeley. I first came here more than twenty years ago, on the way to my first Pacific expedition in the Solomon Islands: I saw something then and have since come to know much more of the unparalleled scholarly resources and surroundings which this university [the University of California at Berkeley] offers. Second, it is a privilege to honour Sauer himself. He was away from Berkeley during my earlier visits, and it was not until 1971 that I tracked him down: I still have the extensive notes I made on that occasion of our conversation. He died, of course, in 1975, and it was a privilege to occupy his old office when I taught in Berkeley in 1980. I make no secret of the fact that, all my life, I have been deeply sympathetic to Sauer's views: indeed, his *Land and life* is perhaps the most prominent of a very small group of books that I have turned to over the years to restore one's faith in the subject we profess.[1]

The two of us worked, it is true, in very different fields, he in the historical geography of Mexico and the South-West, I in the study of the geomorphology and biogeography of coral reefs and islands. There is, however, in the Sauer archive in the Bancroft Library a note by him saying he knew nothing whatever about corals, but that he wished to know more.[2] Today that kind of remark from an historical or cultural geographer would be almost unthinkable; for an economic or political geographer it would be out of the question. The walls have been built between us, and too many of us devote our time to despising the intellectual validity of what our colleagues are concerned with. It is the implications of this state of affairs that I want to talk about today.

Let me start my remarks with a paradox that seems to me to be quite astonishing.

In the English-speaking world we are just completing the first centenary of Geography as a formal academic discipline. Of course the subject is of vast antiquity. We all know about Strabo and Eratosthenes and Ptolemy. We know of people like the Venerable Bede and Albertus Magnus, who as Clarence Glacken[3] has shown us helped set the medieval frame. We know of Hakluyt, Varenius, Humboldt, who brought our history to the dawn of modern times. None of these men was a *professional* geographer, because for them geography existed largely as a body of knowledge rather than as a professional activity. The transformation is surprisingly recent.

It was exactly one hundred years ago that John Scott Keltie wrote his report on geographical education in Britain for the Royal Geographical Society.[4] He drew a dismal picture. The schools and universities were dominated by the classics, mathematics and religion. The natural world and the study of man in society and history were uniformly ignored. Keltie was able to point to a quite different situation in Europe. In Germany, the Kaiser had ordained the institution of chairs in geography throughout Prussia in the 1870s, and subsequently in the rest of Germany.[5] Richthofen in 1883 had laid down the framework of geography as an academic discipline, in his inaugural address in Leipzig.[6] The French did not take long to learn the same lesson, particularly after the humiliation of the Franco-Prussian War.[7] Keltie called for a similar transformation in Britain. He was mainly interested in the mechanics of the situation: the creation of chairs and formal courses in the universities, training geographers who could teach in the schools and thus maintain a continuous flow of undergraduate students. But what were they to teach and investigate? It was to be Richthofen's geography, brilliantly and polemically interpreted by Halford Mackinder in a lecture given to the Royal Geographical Society in January 1887, 'On the scope and methods of geography'.[8] Its impact was remarkable. Within months teaching positions had been established at both Oxford and Cambridge, and geography began its career as a university discipline in Britain.[9] It followed rather later in the United States, though it is again almost exactly a century since William Morris Davis introduced the idea of the cycle of erosion,[10] which launched geomorphology into academic prominence.

In the decades that followed, departments of geography were created throughout the university systems of Europe, the Americas, and the rest of the world. The first honours degrees in geography were instituted early in this century (my own professor, Alfred Steers, who has taught at Berkeley, took the first first-class honours degree in Cambridge in 1921). The PhD became established as a badge of professional competence (the first Cambridge doctorate in geography was earned by Clifford Darby, a former Sauer Lecturer, in 1931). We know that in all the readily measurable parameters – numbers of professional societies, publications, first degrees, higher degrees – professional geography has expanded at the same rate as that of the academic endeavour in general.[11] The situation is rather more complicated in the United States, but in Britain geography remains one of the most popular subjects both in national school examinations and also in university entry and first-degree specialization.[12]

There has, of course, been a lot more to this progress than simply counting heads. The technical achievement has been remarkable; the advance in conceptual sophistication equally so. Had it not been so, needless to say, we would all have been out of business. Much of this has been enormously exciting. I well remember the impact made by William Bunge's 'Theoretical geography',[13] and the transformation in the way we thought about things produced by Peter Haggett's *Locational analysis in human geography*[14] and Richard Chorley's introduction of systems analysis to physical geography,[15] all of which occurred as I joined the ranks of professional geographers in the mid-1960s. It was the time of high excitement of the so-called 'new geography' – the first new geography since Mackinder's, eighty years before.[16]

And the paradox? The paradox is this: that instead of riding the crest of this wave, celebrating the past century, building on these achievements, I find many of our colleagues despondent, morose, disillusioned, almost literally devoid of hope, not only about geography as it is today but as it might be in the future. Indeed, there are those who have already given up the ghost: you probably have seen that sad and dismal piece by Eliot Hurst which he chose to title 'Geography has neither existence nor future' – what a clarion call to sound![17] And all of you will know that he is not alone: that our libraries are being taken over by pessimistic and often autobiographical confessions of failure by many of the leading practitioners of the past thirty years.[18] At the same time, many of those who continue to toil in the vineyard seem unable to agree as to whether they are harvesting the grapes or chopping down the vines. Instead of tending the fine centenary vintages we might expect, we appear to be overrun by the metaphorical prohibitionists and teetotallers of the profession.

I want to say quite frankly tonight that it is time to call a halt. We need to spell out the fact that geography is alive and well, that the disaffected speak only for themselves, that we are custodians of one of the great traditions of intellectual inquiry going back to remote antiquity and powerfully and vibrantly reinforced by the developments of the past hundred years which I have just outlined.

Very well, you might say: why should this be so? How has this situation come about? Why are so many of the leading members of the discipline abandoning what we have all collectively worked for during the course of our professional lives? Let me offer you, first, diagnosis, and then, prognosis.

First, diagnosis. There is one fundamental reason for the present discontents. It is a reason that many of the discontented will not wish to hear, and doubtless one that some may never be able to accept. It is simple and straightforward, and it comes down to the fact that the intellectual horizon that these people recognize as geography is to me no longer recognizable as geography at all. These are fighting words, and they are meant to be, but in stating them I want to be clear that I am very far from making accusations of deviation from any kind of rigid rubric about what geography is and what it is not (Sauer in particular would rise from his grave were I to suggest anything so crass[19]). Rather I am arguing that the reasons geography in the 1980s finds itself in the miserable position that it does is that too many of our colleagues have either abandoned or failed ever to recognize what I take to be our subject's central intent and indeed self-evident role in the community of knowledge.

Let me expand on this, because if my argument is in any sense correct the difficulties we now face are both more profound than the discontents of some of our ageing, tired and disillusioned colleagues, but also – another paradox – more easily soluble.

I take as the intellectual core of geography that structuring of the world in a comparative and analytic frame which characterized the philosophers and scholars of the Enlightenment.[20] Men were exploring the world in which we live in a completely new way, collecting, measuring, comparing, generalizing, with the new tools of rationalism. Pre-eminent among these were the Forsters, father and son, naturalists on Cook's second voyage. Johann Reinhold, the father, was a cantankerous, difficult, objectionable, brilliant man,[21] and it is to him that geography owes its subsequent emergence in the nineteenth century. Georg, the son, is to some extent the better known, for it was with Georg that the young Humboldt travelled down the Rhine and on to England in 1790, and it was Georg's narrative ethnography of the Pacific that excited Humboldt to his great South American expedition and thus ultimately to the *Kosmos*.[22]

For me, Johann Reinhold's book is the more impressive: *Observations made during a voyage round the world, on physical geography, natural history, and ethic philosophy, especially on 1. The earth and its strata, 2. Water and the ocean, 3. The atmosphere, 4. The changes of the globe, 5. Organic bodies, and 6. The human species*.[23] His subtitle specifies his agenda for research: the circumference of his geography. It is, you might say, simply physical geography. Yes, of course, except for number 6. The point is that for Forster the bounds of geography were set by the world about him – its land and peoples, or, as Carl Sauer's book has it, both *Land* and *Life*. Forster's philosophical framework was set by Immanuel Kant – a framework which had a profound influence on geography throughout its recent history, especially in Hartshorne's *Nature of geography*.[24] It is a framework I am not attempting to revive. The point I wish to make is that when Kant wrote his lectures on physical geography, he saw a subject very far from confined to the facts of the physical earth.[25] His physical geography, and that of Forster, was not opposed to a human geography, as it is today – in fact it encompassed it. Physical geography for Kant was simply a field of knowledge quite distinct from, for example, history or politics.

This I might call the great tradition of our subject. Let us not get distracted by the endless debates of a nascent academic discipline about regions, landscape, determinism, possibilism, or, even more to the point, about phenomenology, structuralism, behaviouralism, and all the rest: I suspect that in a decade or so these labels will seem as trivial and pedantic to us as Hartshorne and his concerns seemed to Sauer nearly half a century ago.[26] For Forster there was *geography, a* geography, *the* geography. And not just for Forster. For Humboldt, for Ritter, Ratzel, Richthofen, Hettner, the Chinese walls sundering our subject did not exist. Each of these men worked equally and equally successfully across the diversity of land and life.

For many – perhaps most – geographers today, this is no longer so. We call ourselves not just physical or human geographers, but biogeographers, historical geographers, economic geographers, urban geographers, geomorphologists. We each develop our own expertise, our own techniques, our own theoretical constructs. Necessarily so, if we are to make our mark in scholarship. It is not the fact of this specialization within the field that I object to – we cannot all be polymaths – but its consequences. And the chief of these is that for too many of us the central idea of geography – a geography, *the* geography – has disappeared.

There are many explanations for this, apart from simply academic divisions of labour. One was the essentially political act of getting geography established in the universities. In England its champions were natural scientists, especially zoologists. It had to tread particularly warily with geology, because of the obvious area of overlap. Above all, it had to be intellectually respectable, which meant scientific. Hence the early emphasis on geomorphology and climate and the de-emphasis on man. After all, the conceptual apparatus was on hand to cope with the scientific sides of the subject, whereas ideas and procedures in the human sciences were in a much flimsier and preliminary state.[27] Likewise in France, Vidal de la Blache had to carve out an autonomous role for his kind of geography in competition with Durkheim and social science on the one hand and the historians on the other. Febvre told us all about that in his *Geographical introduction to history*, a book which the geographers have consistently misread, both then and ever since:[28] perhaps if we had understood what Febvre was saying so loud and clear we would have avoided the elephant traps that he and many others were digging along the way. And the two sides were driven yet further apart by an early insistence on a simplistic environmentalism yoked to nineteenth century ideas of causality, especially in the United States, a situation brilliantly analysed by John Leighly.[29]

The result is clear enough. Across geography we speak separate languages, do very different things. Many have abandoned the possibility of communicating with colleagues working not only in the same titular discipline but also in the same department. The human geographers think their physical colleagues philosophically naive; the physical geographers think the human geographers lacking in rigour. *Geography* – Forster's, Humboldt's, Mackinder's – is abandoned and forgotten. And inevitably we teach our students likewise. Small wonder then that the world at large wonders what we are about.

Lest you think I exaggerate it is a simple matter to illustrate and expand what I have said from the current literature. It is hardly necessary to do so because you all know it to be true. Take but one example – R. J. Johnston's history of Anglo-American human geography since 1945.[30] Johnston omits any consideration of physical geography and gives his reasons. First, he finds the links between it and human geography 'tenuous'. Second, he says he is not competent to write about physical geography, which may well be true. And third, he believes that physical geography is of no importance in American university departments of geography, which is a purely marketing consideration. He concludes that to a considerable extent, therefore, human and physical geography are separate, if not independent disciplines. And it is a very short step before he is announcing that for him the terms geography and human geography are both synonymous and interchangeable. Suddenly through this sleight of hand physical geography disappears altogether.[31]

There is a double danger in this situation. The first is that outside a more general framework physical geography loses its coherence. We become specialists in pedology, climatology, geomorphology, bio-geography, drawn more to cognate disciplines than to any common core. Geography in Forster's and Humboldt's sense simply disappears. Of course there have been great efforts to avoid this by making physical geography 'applied'; it is not difficult to demonstrate the practical usefulness of studies of slope failure, coastal erosion, flood control. But the fact is that this kind of justification speaks pragmatically to the world at large and not in any intellectual sense to the human geographers: it does nothing to solve the problems with which as *geographers* we are faced.

The second danger is even greater. Human geography as an exclusively social science loses its distinctive identity – it competes with sociology, economics, anthropology – but on their ground, not on ours. No wonder that the human geographers are suddenly talking in the language and the categories of Giddens – they have abandoned their own.[32]

Somewhere along this road we have lost sight of the world in which we live. Thirty years ago it was our central concern. That remarkable symposium *Man's role in changing the face of the earth*[33] was published in the year in which I began my undergraduate work at Cambridge. Carl Sauer played a major role in organizing it, and in high degree it reflected the values and concerns of geography at Berkeley at that time. It was a book about the physical earth and man's relationship with it, on a vast and panoramic scale. Reading it you feel the dust in your eyes, the sand between your toes, the salt spray on your face. It is a palpable, tangible real world, peopled by the real men and women who have transformed it.

I am astonished to pick-up books and journals today, calling themselves geographical and often making enormous claims for this or that particular kind of geography, and find them completely devoid of any similar impact. Often they deal with space rather than with place, with what they call human agency rather than with people, with abstract categories and numerical symbols rather than with specific situations and what is often harsh reality. Many of these studies are restricted to the narrow horizon of Anglo-American urban and industrial situations, where perhaps it is easier for the authors to persuade themselves that the physical world does not exist. Geographers have forgotten – it is extraordinary to have to say so – that some parts of the earth are high, others low; some wet, others dry; some desert, others covered by forest and grassland and ice. No one ever seems to mention these days that two-thirds of the surface of the planet is covered by the sea. These are the elemental categories of human existence in which geography must deal. They are Forster's categories too. And then there is Forster's sixth. Some parts of the world are virtually empty of people, others are desperately overcrowded and becoming more so. Geography is about precisely this: earth's diversity, its resources, man's survival on the planet.

Vidal de la Blache once wrote that he could not conceive of a geography without man.[34] I agree. But equally I cannot conceive of a geography without the earth and man's relationship to it. All the world is not like Omaha, Nebraska, or Luton, England. If it were, geography would be a vastly less interesting subject than it is. Pretending that everywhere is like Omaha or Luton has brought geography to its present state. It is losing its distinctiveness, its historic function, its appeal. No one can be surprised that people find no use for a geography which tells them nothing of the world in which they live, and that one by one the great universities of the country are reaching the same conclusion. Such a path for geography simply reinforces public ignorance of the world in which we live, encourages national and international prejudice, and wastes our opportunities for improving the qualities of all our lives: it is a path we cannot afford to take.[35]

Fine words, you may say. How to do something about it? Is this just another call for a return to regional geography? If it were, it would not be the first, from others (such as Robert Steel, John Fraser Hart and B. H. Farmer[36]) who have made the same diagnosis. Did we not struggle long enough to get away from the barren didacticism of capes and bays? In point of fact I see no harm – indeed positive advantage – in knowing where one is in the world. We learn the alphabet, vocabulary, syntax, grammar, without protest, simply in order to be able to communicate. I have heard no advocates for giving these up.[37] Location, position, distance, area: these are *our* basic building-blocks. Everything depends on what you do with them, but you cannot do very much if you do not know what they are and what they mean.

We assemble them in order to know the world in which we live. To build regional geography. To show the distinctiveness of places. I do not, however, think that regional description is necessarily the goal of our endeavours, as it is usually said to be. Everyone recognizes the quality of Vidal de la Blache's *Tableau de la géographie de la France* or Mackinder's *Britain and the British seas*, for example.[38] I have myself a special affection for Cressey's *China's geographic foundations*, for Trewartha's *Japan*, for Spate's *India and Pakistan*.[39] But having written them – and the scope for such achievement must be relatively finite – what does one do with them? I think we have a more important job to do, for which such regional accounts really serve as an ordering framework. The task is to identify geographical problems, issues of man and environment within regions – problems not of geomorphology or history or economics or sociology, but geographical problems: and to use our skills to work to alleviate them, perhaps to solve them. Regional geography helps to identify and specify such problems; it is, however, the beginning rather than the end.

Let me illustrate my meaning with reference to the geography of Bangladesh – a very physical place. This small country occupies the combined deltas of the Ganges and the Brahmaputra Rivers, the land being intersected by distributary channels which may be up to 30 km wide but which are frequently less than 5 m deep. The rivers have a combined mean annual discharge of 31,000 m^3/s, the second largest in the world after the Amazon. Because of the monsoon the seasonal variability is enormous, by a factor of 20 in the case of the Ganges and a factor of 60 in the case of the Brahmaputra. When discharge is high the rivers flow at up to 5 m/s, and vast areas of the lower delta are completely water-covered, with villages appearing as islands on slight elevations. With a suspended sediment discharge estimated at 2.2×10^9 t/yr, the combined rivers rank first in the world in terms of load, and it is this of course which has formed the delta. Much of the western part of the coastline is still covered with mangroves (the Sundarbans, covering 420,000 km^2, being the world's largest mangrove forest), but in the east the mangroves have long since been removed for firewood, construction, and to provide agricultural land. The coastline itself is both high-energy and macrotidal, with highest tidal ranges reaching up to 9 m at springs. It is affected, too, by catastrophic cyclonic storms which bring with them storm surges that inundate the low-lying coastal lands. The cyclone of 1970, which generated a 10 m storm surge, resulted in 280,000 deaths, and has claim to be the world's greatest natural disaster in terms of human impact; such an event in Bangladesh has a recurrence interval of about 300 years. Such an environment gives point to the remark attributed to Charles Fisher: that academic debates about environmental determinism have a somewhat different flavour if you are working on the Burma Road (as he did) than if you are standing at the bar of the Raffles Hotel in Singapore (of which doubtless he also had experience).

But Bangladesh is also a very human place – one of the poorest countries in the world. With a per caput GNP of less than US$100 a year, it ranks 126th in the world, according to UN statistics. The key to this situation lies in population growth. For centuries the population hovered between fifteen and twenty million people, kept at this level by the classic Malthusian checks of famine and disease. It proved, characteristically, easier to control the death rate than the birth rate. The former fell from 40–45 per 1000 in 1920 to 18 per 1000 in 1977: the birth rate has remained high and stable at 45–50 per 1000. The result has been uncontrollable increase in numbers, at rates approaching 3 per cent per annum, implying a doubling of the population every 25 years. More than 100 million more people will live in the area of Bangladesh at the end of this century compared with the beginning:

Date	Population, millions	Density per km^2
1900	30	215
Today	100	740
2000	130	950
2020	170	1250

Put another way, in 1900 each person had an area measuring 59 × 59 m to support him; today that has shrunk to 30 × 30 m; and by 2020 it will be only 25 × 25 m. In the medium term the population increase is literally uncontrollable: age statistics show that at present 53 per cent of the population, or 45 million people, are less than 19 years old and are moving into reproductive age groups. Government projections indicate that numbers in the major reproductive age class of 20–49 years old will treble by the year 2000; and these people are already born.[40]

Meanwhile, the total cropped land in the country remains essentially static at ten million hectares. The country is kept from collapse only by foreign aid, which now exceeds US$1 billion a year. Small wonder that the Minister of Planning ended his introduction to a recent interim plan 'So help us God'. For Bangladesh this is more than a ritual Islamic injunction: God truly seems to be looking the other way.

These are the elements of traditional geography. If I were writing a regional geography of Bangladesh I would certainly include them all, though not in the traditional order.[41] But as geographers we need to do more: it is not enough to stand by and describe. We need to ask what can be done.

Let me describe a project in the coastlands, the area most susceptible to devastation by cyclone and storm surge, where lives need to be protected and croplands safeguarded from saline flooding. The initial attempt to do this was by what might be termed the Dutch solution, through the creation of enormous polders surrounded by earth banks, which average 5 m in height and have a total length of 3650 km. Collectively they constitute the greatest earth construction in the world, and it is sobering to realize that the whole of it was put in place on women's heads: what kind of quality of life is it that requires this kind of toil, and what kind of relationship between man and land where such occupations are essential simply to give people by the millions something to do? The scheme was carried through with foreign aid, and it proved too massive for Bangladeshi villagers in the most remote parts of the country to maintain. The banks were too long and too expensive to repair; even simple sluice gates were too complex to operate. And the heart went out of it in 1970 when the storm surge overtopped the banks, turned the polders into saltwater lakes, and drowned many of those who thought their lives had been made safe.

It was then suggested that the coastline would be substantially protected if the natural belt of fringing mangroves could be restored. The mangroves would offer physical protection against waves, wind and storm surge; they would provide a source of timber products, notably sawlogs and firewood (and in the case of the latter releasing cowdung for direct use as a nitrogen fertilizer); they would stabilize accreting land, promote sedimentation, and ultimately allow a transition from timber to paddy; and the mangroves themselves would generate abundant by-products in the form of honey, prawns and fish. The Bangladesh Department of Forestry established that *Sonneratia apetala* was the most appropriate species to use for afforestation: its seeds were collected, germinated in seed beds, and then planted out in exactly the same manner as paddy by local farmers. Since 1980 some 10,000 ha a year have been planted, with the total now standing at 65,000 ha. As an exercise in plantation forestry the project has been an enormous success.

The problems are certainly immense. There are short-term problems of land tenure, particularly at the time of the transition to agriculture, when those hallmarks of the Bangladesh rural scene – power, money and corruption – will be at their height. There is the possibility that, as in other mangrove reclamation projects, acid sulphate soils will develop which will be useless for agriculture. There is the long-term fear that as the project is successful more and more people will be lured to live in the coastal areas at highest risk from cyclones, and that the cyclone warning and protection facilities might not prove adequate to the demands placed on them in such remote areas. More acutely, such a project, while providing a source of timber, fuel and food, and ultimately even new agricultural land – that scarcest of all commodities – makes no impact whatever on the main problem of all, that of population out of control.

This remains insoluble for a variety of reasons. Some are social, to do with the acceptance of population control procedures in a largely Islamic, predominantly rural, virtually illiterate and inaccessible population, in which the status of women determines that those most in need of assistance are the least receptive to it. Some are technical, to do with as yet unresolved methods by which control might be affected. Some are managerial, to do with the provision and even more the utilization of funds for control purposes. In the First Five Year Plan population control programmes accounted for only US$20.50 per head of the population. This has risen to US$2 per head by the Third Plan, but even this meagre sum was structurally impossible to spend: in some years 25 per cent of available funds for population control remained undisbursed. In some coastal districts as a result, Plans provide for less than 0.5 condoms per head of the population per annum. Even the mangrove scheme cannot rescue Bangladesh from this disaster.[42]

So the geography of Bangladesh is literally a geography of life and death. It is dominated by the universals of birth, reproduction, mortality; by the need to find enough food to survive; by constant disease: leprosy, elephantiasis, diarrhoea, malnutrition, starvation.[43] It is a country largely dominated by prejudice and tradition (depending on your point of view), by corruption, cruelty, desperate poverty, and human degradation. But it is also a country of heroic efforts to gain a living, chiefly by managing and changing the face of the Bangladeshi earth.

My argument from this bare rehearsal is that there is no such thing as a physical geography of Bangladesh divorced from its human geography, and even more so the other way round. A human geography divorced from the physical environment would be simply meaningless nonsense.

Even more to the point, the geography I advocate is a geography well worth while, and it leads to another strand in my argument for the historical continuity of what we are concerned about. It is slightly over a century since Peter Kropotkin, nephew of the tsar and prominent anarchist, wrote while in prison in France his remarkable essay 'What geography ought to be'.[44] It must be a subject which provides a means of creating feelings worthy of humanity; it must fight against racialism, war, intolerance and oppression; it must disperse the lies resulting from ignorance, presumption and egotism.

My vision, again perhaps paradoxically, is thus a very conservative one, rooted in the past. But it is the very opposite of obsolete. It is of a *real* geography – a reasserted *unified geography*, built on Forster and Humboldt, and at the same time a *committed geography*, seeking to honour Kropotkin's resolve. It is a geography which reaches out to the future, and the future is even conditional on how well we do it. It is a geography which will teach us the realities of the world in which we live, how we can live better on it and with each other. It is a geography which will teach our neighbours and students and our children how to understand and respect our diverse terrestrial inheritance. These are, of course, familiar words, part of Sauer's teaching during his Berkeley years and giving point and significance to *Man's role in changing the face of the earth*.

Sauer thought these issues urgent then, three, four and five decades ago. They are vastly more urgent now. If as geographers we can get our heads out of the sands of our various minute concerns we will see the crisis which has overtaken us all during our own professional lives. The history of world population is that of Bangladesh writ large: in 1750, the time of Cook, 730 million; 1850, the time of Darwin, 1200 million; 1950; *Man's role*, 2500 million; 1986 – today – 5000 million; the end of the century, 6000 million. As the total grows so the distribution changes, with by far the greatest proportion of twentieth-century increase supplied by the continent of Asia.

What is to be done? The old traditional control mechanisms of disaster, epidemic and famine are scarcely viable policy options for stabilizing the situation, and neither are the prospects of nuclear war or viral pandemics. The numbers need to be fed if social upheaval is to be averted. There are possible technological solutions of the kind that Sauer himself so suspected. Meanwhile, environmental equilibrium is itself disturbed. The tropical rainforest is being destroyed at the rate of 1200 ha an hour. Acid rain kills the temperate woodlands and renders lakes and rivers toxic. Because of the greenhouse effect the polar ice is melting and sea-level around the world will rise at between 0.5 and 2 m during the next hundred years. These are facts which dictate our professional concerns as geographers.

Quite frankly I have little patience with so-called geographers who ignore these challenges. I cannot take seriously those who promote as topics worthy of research subjects like geographic influences in the Canadian cinema, or the distribution of fast-food outlets in Tel Aviv. Nor have I a great deal more time for what I can only call the chauvinist self-indulgence of our contemporary obsession with the minutiae of our own affluent and urbanized society: housing finance, voting patterns, government subsidies for this and that, and how to get the most from them. We cannot afford the luxury of putting so much energy into peripheral things. Fiddle if you will, but at least be aware that Rome is burning all the while.

Our subject has thus emerged as a formal intellectual discipline during a period of salient changes in the transformation of our world. These have been conceptual, professional, organizational, technological and social, and they have been of startling recency and set against the inescapable background of population spiralling out of control. It is frightening to recall that only thirty years ago, in the very first chapter of *Man's role*, E. A. Gutkind denounced as 'megalomaniac' the idea of orbiting satellites surveying the earth[45] – he preferred the technology of Wright's biplane, with which he was more familiar; it was only a year before Sputnik first went into space.

It follows that the people who founded our discipline – men like Griffith Taylor, Ellsworth Huntington, L. Dudley Stamp, to mention but three – lived in a world quite different to our own. Perhaps by present standards they *were* conceptually naive and technically unsophisticated: it would be disastrous if we had made no advance since then. Sauer himself would have been the first to recognize the obsolescence of his conjectures on agricultural origins with the advent of ^{14}C dating, tropical palynology, and increasing awareness of the complexity of Pleistocene climatic changes. But these advances do not justify the amused contempt with which too many regard these pioneers – as amiable old dodderers at best, certainly not half as clever as us. Yet they dared to do something that we, in our sophistication, rarely do. They asked the big questions, about man, land, resources, human potential. No one exemplified this more than Sauer, with his daring speculations about fire, the role of the seashore, and the origins of agriculture. We need to remember that science is about asking daring questions like these.

We no longer ask these questions: but the questions remain. It is largely people other than geographers who are asking – and answering – them now. It is astonishing that it is Ladurie and the *Annales* school who have commandeered the whole field of the relations of climate and history.[46] Braudel writes what is in effect geography (though without maps) and calls its history: the historical geographers tag along in dutiful homage.[47] One could multiply the examples endlessly.

We need to claim the high ground back: to tackle the real problems: to take the broader view: to speak out across our subject boundaries on the great issues of the day (by which I do not mean the evanescent politics of Thatcher, Reagan and Gorbachev). We need to forget the trivia and the tedium of much that has passed for geographical research and erudition over the past twenty years. We need to forget especially the disillusion of many of our colleagues which saps away at our professional self-respect and the enthusiasm of our students.

Land and life is what geography has always been about. It is time we got out again into the great wide world, met its challenges, and met them in a way that Forster, Humboldt and Carl Sauer himself would have approved.

Notes

1 Leighly, J. (ed.) 1963: *Land and Life: a selection from the writings of Carl Ortwin Sauer* (Berkeley).
2 Sauer, C. O., letter to Edwin Doran, 20 November 1952: Bancroft Library, University of California, Berkeley, Sauer Archive.
3 Glacken, C. 1967: *Traces on the Rhodian shore: Nature and culture in western thought from ancient times to the end of the eighteenth century* (Berkeley).
4 Keltie, J. S. 1886: Geographical education – report to the Council of the Royal Geographical Society. *Supplementary Paper of the Royal Geographical Society* 1, 439–594. See also Stoddart, D. R. 1980: The RGS and the 'New Geography': changing aims and changing roles in nineteenth century science, *Geographical Journal*, 146, 190–202; Wise, M. J. 1986: 'The Scott Keltie Report 1885 and the teaching of geography in Great Britain'. *Geographical Journal* 152, 367–82.
5 Taylor, P. J. 1985: 'The value of a geographical perspective', in Johnston, R. J. (ed.), *The future of geography* (London), pp. 92–110, ref. on p. 98.
6 Von Richthofen, F. 1885: *Aufgaben und Methoden der heutigen Geographie* (Leipzig).
7 Broc, N. 1977: La géographie francaise face a la science allemande (1870–1914), *Annales Geographical* 86, 71–94.
8 Mackinder, H. J. 1887: On the scope and methods of geography. *Proceeds of the Royal Geographical Society* NS 9, 141–60.

9 Stoddart, D. R. 1975: The RGS and the foundations of geography at Cambridge. *Geographical Journal* 141, 216–39; Scargill, D. I. 1976: The RGS and the foundations of geography at Oxford. *Geographical Journal*, 142, 438–61.

10 Davis, W. M. 1885: 'Geographic classification, illustrated by a study of plains, plateaus, and their derivatives'. *Proc. Am. Ass. Adv. Sci.*, 33, 428–32.

11 Stoddart, D. R. 1967: Growth and structure of geography. *Transactions of the Institute of British Geographers* 41, 1–19.

12 Stoddart, D. R. 1981: Geography, education and research. *Geographical Journal* 147, 287–97.

13 Bunge, W. 1962: Theoretical geography. *Lund Studies in Geography* C 1, 1–210.

14 Haggett, P. 1965: *Locational analysis in human geography* (London); to appreciate the response see the ecstatic review by Gould, P. 1967: *Geographical Review* 57, 292–4.

15 Chorley, R. J. 1962: Geomorphology and general systems theory. *Professional Papers of the US Geographical Survey* 500-B, 1–10.

16 It was so identified, perhaps for the first time, in a review of Chorley, R. J. and Haggett, P. 1967: *Frontiers in geographical teaching* (London), by G. Manley, *Guardian* 37228 (18 March 1966), 8.

17 Eliot Hurst, M. E. 1985: Geography has neither existence nor future. In Johnston, R. J. (ed.), *The future of geography* (London), 59–91.

18 Billinge, M. D., Gregory, D. J. and Martin, R. L. (eds) 1984: *Recollections of a revolution: Geography as spatial science* (London).

19 Sauer, C. O. 1941: Foreword to historical geography. *Annals of the Association of American Geographers* 31, 1–24, ref. on p. 4; compare Steers, J. A. 1954: The coast and the geographer. *Advances in Science* 11, 171–81, ref. on p. 172.

20 Stoddart, D. R. 1982: Geography – a European science. *Geography* 67, 289–96.

21 Alas, qualities which no longer seem to be appropriate in today's regimented and bureaucratic universities.

22 Stoddart, D. R. 1985: Humboldt and the emergence of scientific geography. In Alter, P. (ed.), *Humboldt* (London).

23 Forster, J. R. 1778: *Observations made during a voyage round the world* (London).

24 Hartshorne, R. 1939: The nature of geography: a critical survey of current thought in the light of the past. *Annals of the Association of American Geographers* 29, 171–658.

25 See Adickes, R. 1911: *Untersuchungen zu Kants physischer Geographie* (Tübingen), and May, J. A. 1970: *Kant's concept of geography and its relation to recent geographical thought* (Toronto).

26 There is an interesting exchange between Hartshorne and Sauer in 1946 over the latter's presidential address to the Association of American Geographers (Sauer, C. O., op. cit., note 19) in the Bancroft Library, University of California, Berkeley, Sauer archive. Sauer clearly thought Hartshorne's points of little significance, and the exchange ended with a note by his secretary saying, appropriately enough, that Sauer had gone to Mexico.

27 Stoddart, D. R., op. cit. (notes 4 and 12).

28 Febvre, L. 1925: *A geographical introduction to history* (London). For alternative views of Febvre's message, see Baker, A. R. H. 1984: Reflections on the relations of historical geography and the *Annales* school of history. In Baker, A. R. H. and Gregory, D. J. (eds), *Explorations in historical geography* (Cambridge), 1–27, 195–203; and Andrews, H. F. 1984: The Durkeimians and human geography: some contextural problems in the sociology of knowledge. *Transactions of the Institute of British Geographers*. NS 9, 315–36.

29 Leighly, J. 1955: What has happened to physical geography. *Annals of the Association of American Geographers*. 45, 309–18.

30 Johnston, R. J. 1979: *Geography and geographers: Anglo-American human geography since 1945* (London).

31 Johnston, R. J., op. cit. (note 30), 2.

32 See Giddens, A. 1984: *The constitution of society: outline of the theory of structuration* (Berkeley), and compare Gregory, D. J. 1978: The discourse of the past: phenomenology, structuralism and historical geography. *Journal of Historical Geography*. 4, 161–73, and Gregory, D. J. 1982: Action and structure in historical geography. In Baker, A. R. H. and Billinge, M. D. (eds), *Period and place: Research methods in historical geography* (Cambridge) 244–50, 352–3.

33 Thomas, W. L. Jr (ed.) 1956: *Man's role in changing the face of the Earth* (Berkeley). For a commentary see Williams, M. 1987: Carl Sauer and *Man's role. Geographical Review* 77, 218–31.

34 Vidal de la Blache, P. 1926: *Principles of human geography* (London), 1.

35 But there are signs of a revival of geography in school education, both in the United States (see Selholz, E. 1986: The forgotten subject: geography is finding its way back onto the map. *Newsweek*, 8 September 1986, p. 55), and in Britain, where the Minister for Education has included geography in his 'core curriculum' for school education (April 1987).

36 Farmer, B. H. 1973: Geography, area studies and the study of area. *Transactions of the Institute of British Geographers* 60, 1–15; Steel, R. W. 1982: Regional geography in practice. *Geography* 67, 2–8; Hart, J. F. 1982: The highest form of the geographer's art. *Annals of the Association of American Geographers* 72, 1–29.

37 Though note the catastrophic collapse in elementary literacy in the public education systems of both our countries.

38 Vidal de la Blache, P. 1911: *Tableau de la géographie de la France* (Paris); Mackinder, H. J. 1902: *Britain and the British seas* (London).

39 Cressey, G. B. 1934: *China's geographic foundations: A survey of the land and its people* (New York): Trewartha, G. T. 1945: *Japan: A physical, cultural and regional geography* (Madison); Spate, O. H. K. 1954: *India and Pakistan: A general and regional geography* (London).

40 See the annual *Statistical yearbook of Bangladesh* (Dhaka).

41 For traditional regional geographies of Bangladesh, see Johnson, B. L. C. 1975: *Bangladesh* (London), and Er Rashid, H. 1977: *Geography of Bangladesh* (Dhaka).

42 For a fuller treatment, see Stoddart, D. R. and Pethick, J. S. 1984: Environmental hazard and coastal reclamation: problems and prospects in Bangladesh. In Bayliss-Smith, T. P. and Wanmali, S. (eds), *Understanding green revolutions: Agrarian change and development planning in South Asia* (Cambridge), 339–61, and for commentary on the argument presented here see Faaland, J. and Parkinson, J. R. 1976: *Bangladesh: The test case of development* (London) and Faaland, J. (ed.), *Aid and influence: The case of Bangladesh* (London).

43 During my first visit to Bangladesh the then president (since assassinated) declared open the new International Centre for Diarrhoeal Disease, and referred almost with pride to Dhaka as 'the diarrhoeal capital of the world'.

44 Kropotkin, P. 1885: What geography ought to be. *Nineteenth Century* 18, 940–56.

45 Gutkind, E. A. 1956: Our world from the air: conflict and adaptation. In Thomas, W. L., Jr (ed.), op. cit. (note 33), 1–44.

46 Le Roy Ladurie, E. 1967: *Histoire du climat depuis l'an mil* (Paris); and Le Roy Ladurie, E. 1985: The history of climate. In Le Goff, J. and Nora, P. (eds), *Constructing the past: essays in historical methodology* (Cambridge) 81–98.

47 Braudel, F. 1980: *On history* (London), and Baker, A. R. H., op. cit. (note 28).

24   Mona Domosh,
'Towards a Feminist Historiography of Geography'

Reprinted in full from: *Transactions of the Institute of British Geographers* NS 16, 95–104 (1991)

It is, too, a matter for pride that our history contains such a record of achievement at the farthest ends of the earth. Let us salute with Conrad, men great in their endeavour and in hard-won successes of militant geography; men who went forth each according to his lights and with varied motives . . . but each bearing in his heart a spark of the sacred fire. If that spark ever dies, then our geography will indeed have become a dry and bloodless thing.

(Stoddart, 1986, p. 157)

Such as it is, Estes Park is mine. It is unsurveyed, 'no man's land', and mine by right of love, appropriation, and appreciation; by the seizure of its peerless sunrises and sunsets, its glorious afterglow, its blazing noons, its hurricanes sharp and furious, its wild auroras, its glories of mountain and forest, of canyon, lake, and river, and the stereotyping them all in my memory.

(Bird, 1879, p. 120)

If, as Stoddart suggests, many of the more heroic episodes in the history of geography are the results of a spark in men's hearts that set them out on voyages, then geography truly is the inheritor of the Enlightenment tradition, a tradition that energized and legitimized that 'spark' that would bring light to the world. And, as the second quotation makes clear, that spark for exploration was as evident in the accounts of women explorers as of their male counterparts. Although a contemporary reading of Isabella Bird's travels in the Rocky Mountains may suggest a political agenda in her ability to appropriate through love a land that no man has yet controlled, it cannot be denied that her thrill of discovery and wonder at what she has found places her well within the confines of the male exploratory tradition, as outlined by Stoddart (1986). The 'sirens' that, in J. K. Wright's words (1947), lure people to unknown lands were surely at work in motivating Bird to leave her family in Scotland and venture by herself, and on horseback, into the Rocky Mountains. Yet the accounts of Isabella Bird, and the many other women travellers, are not included in the histories of geography, not even in Stoddart's book, which attempts to recover the exploratory tradition for geographic historiography. Certainly we are not to deny that the excitement of discovery, whether it be of new lands or new ideas, is a spark that should not be doused, and geography's roots in the exploratory tradition are indeed, as Stoddart indicates, quite inspiring and should act as sources of pride. It becomes problematic, however, when only part of that tradition is remembered and recorded in the official histories of the discipline. This being the case, geography loses some of its history, and in a time when geographers are looking far afield for sources of ideas about reconstructing geographic thinking (Cosgrove, 1988; Dear, 1988; Daniels, 1992), this loss becomes even more problematic.

Given the recent attempts to rewrite and contextualize geographic history (Driver, 1988; Livingstone, 1988), it would behove us to recover from our own history the stories that have gone unnoticed. Recent work on women travellers has opened an entirely new chapter on the history of geography from which we can recapture sources for a post-modern reconstruction (Middleton, 1962; Birkett, 1989; Tinling, 1989). It is in pointing to these possible sources that this essay is directed. This essay will draw on the writings of Victorian and post-Victorian women travellers to suggest what a 'women's way of knowing' (Belenky *et al.*, 1986) could contribute to our rewriting of the history of geography, and, by implication, to a feminist historiography of geography.

By focusing on the experiences of these women explorers, I am not implying that they are the only group to be systematically excluded from the histories of geography. Many individuals, both male and female, have been ignored in our institutional accounts of geography because their views and activities did not accord with the standards of 'scientific' geography. What I am suggesting, however, is that the experiences of Victorian women travellers were different from those of their male counterparts. This does not imply any statement of essential differences between men and women, only that Victorian women explorers could not escape the contexts in which they lived – contexts that were, in significant and well-documented ways, quite distinct from those of men. And those contexts shaped not only their outlook on personal matters and the structure of their social networks, but operated in very material ways, by limiting the resources and support networks available to women in their travels.

This essay draws much of its inspiration from recent discussions both within geography and the other social sciences concerning what has come to be called the post-modern turn. The issue of post-modernism is a complex one, providing differing critiques and constructions as it has been filtered through the lenses of the humanities and sciences. In its questioning of the assumptions that have supported our deeply embedded philosophical systems since the Enlightenment, it throws open doors to ways of thinking that we have yet to explore fully. The issues raised by the post-modern turn go way beyond those that can be addressed here, so I have chosen to outline only those directly relevant to my discussion of a feminist historiography in geography. Although I recognize the tensions that exist between feminist theory and post-modernism,[1] I have chosen to concentrate on those aspects of post-modernism that have allowed us to hear and appreciate the voices of these women travellers. Specifically, a reassessment and deconstruction of the Enlightenment notions of knowledge, objectivity and language has provided the space through which women like Isabella Bird can be seen and heard. Although here I can provide only the briefest of discussions, an outline of the particular elements of post-modernism that inform this essay should help us to understand the importance of retelling the stories of Victorian women travellers.

Simply stated, the post-modern deconstruction has allowed us to understand that knowledge is both ideologically and socially constructed and therefore cannot be separated from its specific context. Accordingly, there can be no universal truths nor universalizing discourses since knowledge is dependent on the contingencies of social relations. The very idea of a perspectiveless knowledge is revealed as a product of a specific time and place, and therefore is seen as both reflecting and legitimizing the social conditions and relations of power from which it was derived (including those of gender).

The idea that there exists a world somehow separate from the subject, that is, an abstracted, objective world, is exposed as an assumption on which a perspectiveless knowledge is built. We can investigate the world only from a perspective of the contingencies of our self, which includes our physical, social and historical experiences. To explore the world, both figuratively and literally, involves the active participation of the subject as observer. Language embodies and embellishes that participation, giving form to the observation. That form is not a direct representation of a separate reality – language is not transparent – but instead reflects a particular way of seeing that world. A post-modern critique allows us to see both words and objects as socially constructed. The following discussion of women explorers is grounded within this perspective of a post-modern view of knowledge, objectivity and the use of language.

The context of women explorers

To start, it is worth considering why the stories of these women have been omitted from the official histories of geography. Many of these women travellers were born into the British upper-middle classes of the Victorian era, at the time of the professionalization of the academic disciplines. Denied access to the academic training that would confer on them the appropriate status as 'scientists', women like Mary Kingsley, Mary Gaunt, Isabella Bird, and Marianne North found that fieldwork in the sense of exploration was as open to them as to anyone with adequate resources. Yet as the disciplines in general were professionalized, and geography in particular came to be rigorously defined, these women were removed from the newly defined label of 'geographer'. The fieldwork of 'professional' geographers was codified and regulated in order to advance scientific learning. Fieldwork as geographic inquiry was limited to a few elite, white males and was fostered in the male club atmosphere of the Royal Geographic Society (RGS) in England and the American Geographical Society in the United States.

It was not until 1915 that women were elected to membership in the RGS, and the thirty-year story of that battle reveals the predilections and prejudices of Victorian male culture (Middleton, 1982). Women had been elected to membership earlier, but only as exceptions to the rule. When it became apparent that the few women members might represent a trend, the doors to their membership were effectively shut. Such ferment followed the election of twelve women as fellows in 1893 that membership to others was immediately closed. As Birkett points out, much of the objection to women began to be voiced in terms of proper geographic knowledge. Women travellers, it was thought, were not truly adding to geographic knowledge, that is they were not surveying new lands and therefore could not qualify for membership, although such a requirement of 'new' geographic knowledge was never applied to men seeking membership. As one member inquired, were the ladies to be 'young and beautiful' or 'old and scientific' (Birkett, 1989, p. 219)? George Curzon, on his return from Asia, was a vehement speaker against women's membership: 'Their sex and training render them equally unfitted for exploration, and the genus of professional female globe-trotters with which America has lately familiarized us is one of the horrors of the latter end of the nineteenth century' (quoted in Middleton, 1982, p. 13). Curzon and his group were effective in preventing those 'professional globe-trotters' from becoming professional geographers.

Denied institutional support, Victorian women explored and travelled at their own expense and in their own contexts. Their lone travels were neither followed up with full-scale explorations nor sponsored by institutions (as was the case with their male counterparts). Thus their names survive, if at all, through their writings but not through their sanctioned deeds; their stores were, and are, not part of the institutional histories of geography. Stoddart is not alone in writing a man's story of geography, but by his celebrating the exploratory tradition in geography, his omission of women is even more blatant than many other authors. The 'spark' that energized many women explorers took them to places they themselves could not have imagined, and it contributed far more to geographic knowledge than we have heretofore recognized.

Women and geographical knowledge

If our post-Kuhnian critiques of science have taught us anything, it is that knowledge is socially and therefore ideologically constructed; it is as much a product of who defines it as of some objective reality. The case of the redefinition of 'exploration' mentioned above dearly makes the point for the field of geography, and one of the challenges for a post-modern geography is somehow to come to terms with the subjectivity of defining what constitutes knowledge. The stories of women travellers are incredibly diverse, yet they share some common threads, one of which is their quite explicit recognition of the personal goals of their travels. The so-called objective discoveries of new places were not separated from the discoveries of themselves.

Women travellers set out on their treks with some definite goals, but 'discovery' *per se*, in the sense of discovering new lands, was not one of them (Middleton, 1982; Birkett, 1989). Many of these women travellers were in middle age when they started to live the life they had only imagined in their youth. Most had grown up with family members who had been involved in some aspects of exploration, but they could only dream of setting out on voyages themselves. It was usually only after they had fulfilled their family 'duties' that they were free to set out on their own. Divorced from the institutions that served to legitimize travel for discovery, for fulfilling some objective purpose, women travellers were free to explore in the broadest sense. As Gertrude Bell states, 'My thoughts travelled forward, and I longed to follow the path they had taken' (quoted in Birkett, 1989, p. 62). If one were to draw their journeys on a map, their routes would not resemble the fairly direct lines to sources of rivers or tops of mountains, as was the case with most of their male counterparts. Instead, their routes were often circular, appearing to have no definite destinations. They often took the form of what Stoddart calls planned journeys, 'of which the aim is simply to proceed between known points, with no suggestion of adding to knowledge other than through traversing unfamiliar routes' (1986, p. 142). Yet the lack of such external and institutional support did not mean that these women were undirected. Their direction came from internal sources, for most were seeking places where they could live a type of life denied them at home. Growing up in worlds circumscribed by Victorian standards and expectations, their lives had been moulded for them. Their freedom came from living in places removed from that circumscription.

These women often spoke of the empowerment they felt when they were exploring, and their utter despair on losing that power when they returned home. It was felt most acutely when they were visiting regions that were located within the colonial power structure. Colonialism allowed women to be powerful as representatives of the white race; it created a structure for a type of power dependent on race, not on sex. In this light, we can begin to understand their political support for colonialism, and their belief in the essential nature of the differences between the races. Their power and control over their lives was based on their race; once those differences were eroded or erased, their power was drained. Overcoming the dangers encountered in their travels was also a source of empowerment for such women, and many wrote of these experiences with great pride. Dangerous situations allowed them to prove their abilities – abilities that could not be tested at home – and it provided testing grounds for their own strengths in controlling their life situations. These sources of empowerment certainly were not exclusive to women, but, given the general context of Victorian women's lives, they often provided the only sources of such intensely felt personal power and authority. For some women explorers, their empowerment when travelling often overcame physical disabilities. Isabella Bird, for example, was continually diagnosed with severe physical problems when she returned to Britain from her travels, only to find the symptoms disappear when she set out again. When speaking of her decision to travel through Japan, she claimed it was recommended for her health:

> Having been recommended to leave home, in April 1878, in order to recruit my health by means which had proved serviceable before, I decided to visit Japan, attracted less by the reputed excellence of its climate than by the certainty that it possessed, in an especial degree, those sources of novel and sustained interest which conduce so essentially to the enjoyment and restoration of a solitary health-seeker.
>
> (Bird, 1987, p. 1)

Women travelled then, for quite specific reasons, but what they were seeking was as much empowerment and self-knowledge as 'objective' knowledge. 'The women travellers followed invisible red lines across a map into a distant unknown. But the pot of gold they were chasing was not the mountain, the source of the river, or the oasis in the desert, but the long shadows, cast by the tropical sunlight and mountain glare, of themselves' (Birkett, 1989, p. 71). Their satisfaction was derived not in the external discovery of 'new' geographies, but in the process of exploring, in experiencing a world in which they could participate in their own definition.

In our questioning of the objectivity privileged by the scientific method and in our recognition that our choices of research topics, methodologies and results tell us as much about ourselves as of some objective reality, we might do well to reflect on a geographic heritage in which such goals were explicitly recognized. Certainly male explorers were also interested in self-exploration, but their contexts usually demanded that the external discovery of 'places' was given priority. Denied institutional context, women were in a sense more free in their travels, and more explicitly aware of their subjective goals.

Women as observers: the view from the outside

The process of exploration is by definition an ambiguous one. On the one hand, it involves the so-called 'opening up' of previously unknown lands and peoples (that is, the exploration of 'foreign' peoples by Western culture), while on the other, that 'opening up' itself changes and ultimately destroys those very societies that it 'discovers'. The role of the explorer also is by definition ambiguous: explorers are both outsiders and insiders, observers of, yet participants in, the lives and lands that they travel through. In the histories of exploration, these perspectives frequently conflicted, and the external demands of discovery so often a part of the male explorer's mission often meant that these conflicts were ignored. Yet many women explorers were arguably better suited to deal with their ambiguous role. They were outsiders in the everyday world virtue of their sex, and much of their energy throughout their lives had been spent dealing with that fact. The ambiguity of the role of explorer was not new to them. As women, their lives were created around that dilemma; they were certainly insiders and participants in their culture, yet they always stood outside the structures of power. Women carried that duality of identity into the field with them, and they found that such duality served them well. At home they were outsiders by virtue of their sex; in the field they were outsiders by virtue of their race. And they realized the precariousness of that position. Their authority in the field was derived from their role as outsiders – as representatives of the white race – yet the basis of that authority is what made them insiders in a culture in which they had no authority. Their skills at switching the basis of their authority must have been well honed, which, in turn, allowed them to accommodate the ambiguities of the role of 'observer'. 'Women travellers continually juggled their identities in the foreign lands to meet these turbulent emotions of sympathy yet distance, and found comfort in a role which did not necessitate the resolution of these seemingly insurmountable conflicts of interest' (Birkett, 1989, p. 176).

Many such women found that their inclinations as sympathetic observers could act as a basis for their authority within their own culture, and therefore they were keen supporters of the uniqueness of fieldwork. Isabella Bird made a point of noting that as a woman travelling alone, she was able to observe matters that others may have missed:

> As a lady travelling alone, and the first European lady who had been seen in several districts through which my route lay, my experiences differed more or less widely from those of preceding travellers; and I am able to offer a fuller account of the aborigines of Yezo, obtained by actual acquaintance with them, than has hitherto been given.
>
> (Bird, 1987, p. 1–2)

Fieldwork was based on subjective experience, and women could claim that they provided valuable insights that could not be gained from reading books or studying in the university, luxuries denied to many of them. Although herself highly educated, Gertrude Bell supported the preciousness of knowledge gained from direct experience:

> Often when one sets out on a journey one travels by all the roads according to the latest maps, one reaches all the places of which the history books speak. Duly one rises early and turns one's face towards new countries, carefully looks and laboriously one tries to understand, and for all one's trouble one might as well have stayed behind and read a few big archaeology books. But I would have you know that is not the way that I have done it. . . . Here is a world of history that one sees with the eye and that enters the mind as no book can relate it.
>
> (quoted in Birkett, 1989, p. 173)

Ironically, it is this very claim to knowledge that eventually was used to deny women's experiences and exclude them from the status as professional geographers. The subjectivity of fieldwork that women could claim as their special contribution to geographic knowledge was, as pointed out above, systematically taken out of the realm of scientific geography. The suppression of the subjective and the denial of the ambiguity of observation was part of the legitimation of the academy and the professionalization of the social sciences that occurred in the first decades of the twentieth century. Yet as anthropologists and other social scientists have recently argued, fieldwork and ethnographic studies are by definition exercises in metaphorical storytelling, and are as much constructions of the subjective realm as of the objective realm (Clifford and Marcus, 1986). Indeed, it is the very recognition of the blurring of distinctions between the subjective and the objective – between observer and participant – that is at the heart of recent critiques of science (Harding, 1986; Grosz, 1987; Sayers, 1987). The 'pre-scientific' experiences of women travellers at the turn of the century, therefore, are in one sense more relevant today for what they can tell us about the role of the outsider and the methods of observation than for any information about 'new' places.

Representing women's experiences

The inherent ambiguity in the experiences of women explorers necessitated forms of representation that differed from the scientific accounts of their male counterparts. At one level, their choice of language was circumscribed by the fact that they were women engaged in work that was male-defined. To utilize the discourse of exploration was to deny their gender and identify totally with the male explorer. To 'conquer' and 'penetrate' unknown lands was a male activity, and the exploratory routes had provided the grounds upon which men could prove their masculinity, suppressing foreign lands as they had suppressed women, imagining and describing those lands as female (Said, 1978). The tensions between being a women and being an explorer were made manifest in many ways, including how the women chose to dress themselves (whether they should dress like men in trousers or wear long dresses was always at issue), but in their choice of language these women were confronted directly with those tensions. Their search for a vocabulary that would lend legitimacy to their experiences was a search that brought them abruptly against the confines of the world circumscribed by a male-defined language.[2] In this, they could not take language for granted, and they undoubtedly were forced to recognize its opacity.

Many women travellers took to referring to themselves as men in order to better utilize the language of exploration. Identifying with the male exploratory tradition was empowering for these women, as it legitimized their own travels, and supported their claims to authority over different races. As Birkett points out, at times their identification with the masculine was so strong that their references to themselves as men were often unwitting, as when Mary Kingsley wrote, 'I have given into temptation and am the third Englishman to ascend the Peak' (quoted in Birkett, 1989, p. 124). Their (perhaps unconsciousness) recognition of the power of language was apparent in their acceptance of male titles for themselves, and in the fact that they often gave their male attendants female names.

The problematic of language was apparent to many women travellers at another level – the tension between the subjective and objective in the reports of their travels. When it became apparent that the objective mode of discourse was favoured in the 'scientific' world of professional geography, many women began to remove the 'I' from their writing. Although many wrote their first accounts as mixtures of personal reminiscence and factual observations, they soon learned to distinguish and separate what were becoming defined as different forms of knowledge (Middleton, 1982). Mary Kingsley originally intended to write one large volume of her West African voyages, but ended up writing two separate books: one factual the other more of a narrative (Frank, 1986). Mary Gaunt always wrote a factual travelogue and a novel of each of her trips (Birkett, 1989). In this, women were once again forced to confront the problem of language.

The issue of representation has been identified as one of the central concerns of a post-modern geography (Cosgrove, 1989; Cosgrove and Domosh, 1993), and post-modern social science (Clifford and Marcus, 1986). Whether the discussion centres on the reading and decoding of texts (Duncan and Duncan, 1988) or the proper use of drawings and travelogues (Quoniam, 1988), attempts to rid the discipline of a belief in the naivety of language will provide many challenges for reconstructing human geography. As explorers whose experiences lay outside the realm of acceptable discourse, women were forced to confront that dilemma early. Their recognition of the power of language, that it both encodes and represents a particular view of the world, and therefore can be used to support that view (as when women referred to themselves as men, and their male attendants as women) or challenge it, is a recognition that takes on new meaning in the recent debates and discussions about language, both within geography and feminist theory (Irigaray, 1974; Franklin, 1985).

Other explorers

Subsequent stories of women explorers and geographers are in many ways quite similar to those of their Victorian predecessors. Many of the same considerations informed the activities of the next generation of women explorers, those that were associated with the Society of Women Geographers. Although exploring in the post-Victorian period, these women were similar to their Victorian predecessors in their general life contexts, as well as their exclusion from the scentific community. The women explorers that Elizabeth Fagg Olds writes about in *Women of the four winds* (Annie Smith Peck, Delia J. Akeley, Marguerite Harrison, Louise Arner Boyd) form what Olds calls a transitional group between the Victorian lady travellers and modern women scientists (Olds, 1985). Still not accorded scientific status, and living lives often circumscribed by their sex, these women none the less set aside much of their Victorian past to embrace the new scientific community. For example, Louise Arner Boyd, an independently wealthy socialite from San Francisco, provided the funding herself for most of her polar expeditions in the 1920s and 1930s. Many of those expeditions, however, were officially sponsored by the American Geographical Society (AGS), and were undertaken with explicit scientific goals. Trained botanists, geologists and surveyors accompanied many of her voyages, and the AGS published in book form the results of the expeditions (Olds, 1985). Boyd enthusiastically embraced the professional credentials that sponsorship by the AGS afforded and made sure that she purchased for her trips the very best scientific equipment and instruments available.

Yet she herself was not a trained scientist, and accordingly was often treated with much disdain:

> Her emergence from a wealthy society background to become a significant explorer with serious credentials required that she buck up against even more derision than most women explorers of the day. Not only was she female and a wealthy socialite, but she was not a scientist. And as she would learn, even in the field of polar exploration she would not always be accepted by the snobbish band of specialists.
>
> (Olds, 1985, p. 236)

Although scientific activities were integral to her expeditions, Boyd's adventures were not explicitly meant to discover new lands. The so-called new lands that she did survey were discovered by accident:

> Louise had never set out to 'conquer' and 'discover'; she more or less stumbled upon what became Miss Boyd Land and the Louise Boyd Bank. So when she at last decided to go to the North Pole, her motive was curiosity and a need for emotional satisfaction rather than ambition.
>
> (Olds, 1985, p. 290)

Not hampered by the strict constraints of Victorian society, Boyd nevertheless had lived the life of a wealthy heiress, sponsoring social parties, and attending appropriate functions. We do not need to stretch our imaginations far to suggest what the adventures of polar expeditions offered in the way of 'emotional satisfaction'. And, like her Victorian predecessors, Boyd did not engage in many of the traditional practices of the male exploratory tradition. She only found out after the fact that part of an ice fiord that she had 'stumbled upon' had been named in her honour:

> I am not guilty of giving the name 'Miss Boyd Land' to the land that lies between the De Geer Glacier, which I had the good fortune to discover in 1931, and the Jaette Glacier . . . My first intimations that this land had been so designated came in a letter from Dr Lange Koch and on seeing the name of his published map.
>
> (quoted in Olds, 1985, p. 247)

This is not to say that Boyd was not deeply proud of her accomplishments, only that she did not position herself within a tradition that used naming as a form of recognition of accomplishments (a tradition associated with male explorers).

We can only speculate what women in the contemporary geographic community inherited from their Victorian and exploratory heritage. The professionalization of the discipline removed most geographers from the arena of exploration, and women from their histories of exploration. With the hindsight afforded by historical reflection, we can point to the potential contributions of Victorian women travellers with some degree of clarity; a discussion of gender and its implications for contemporary knowledge construction is far less certain (Goodchild and Janelle (1988) have presented us with some of the data to begin this discussion).

The study of gender and its contribution to the construction of knowledge has been undertaken in several other disciplines, and this work may help us suggest avenues for discussion in geography. The work of Evelyn Fox Keller (1985) in exploring the role of gender in the sciences is particularly enlightening, and her discussion of Barbara McClintock's research on plant genetics suggests several directions in which a women's science might differ from a science that operates totally within a patriarchal system.[3] Perhaps more relevant to geography is the discussion of the implications of women and gender in anthropology. In *Daughters of the desert: Women anthropologists and the Native American Southwest, 1880–1980*, Barbara Babcock and Nancy Parezo suggest how women anthropologists have shaped the history of the discipline:

Restless and rebellious women seeking freedom from their stays and from their drawing-room domesticity of Boston and New York found in the southwest not only topographical and psychological space, but an otherness that intrigued and nurtured ... As scientist, humanists, romanticists, and activists, they were to significantly shape anthropological understandings, public conceptions, and government policies, regarding the Native American Southwest.

(Babcock and Parezo, 1988, p. 2)

The stories of these women's lives sound amazingly familiar in light of my discussion of Victorian women explorers. Women anthropologists were often ignored in the official histories of the discipline, they were limited in what they could study and write about, and few held academic posts, though many worked in museums, work that anthropologist Clark Wissler thought was 'fitting for women since it resembled housekeeping' (Babcock and Parezo, 1988, p. 4). The stories of even the most prominent of these women anthropologists, Elsie Clews Parsons and Ruth Benedict, seem to parallel those of our Victorian travellers: 'They compartmentalized and compromised their discourse, wrote poetry under pseudonyms, and packed away their feminist writings under pressure to conform to male standards of "scientific" academic anthropology' (Babcock and Parezo, 1988, p. 4). Anthropologists have begun to use the self-reflexivity allowed by their post-modern turn to explore the implications of gender in shaping the construction of their knowledge. It is past time for us to do the same.[4]

Implications

Let me close this essay with suggestions for how we can begin to create a feminist historiography of geography. First, we need to broaden our definitions of geography so that in our histories we do not restrict ourselves to the canon of the 'great' Western thinkers – to what J. K. Wright called the 'relatively small core area' (1947, p. 81) of geography. Livingstone (1990) and Mitchell and Smith (1990) have made the same plea elsewhere; we have no excuses for continuing to write histories that are essentially an 'exclusionary chronological litany of white, male, aristocratic heroes' (Mitchell and Smith, 1990, p. 233). By discussing the contributions of Victorian women travellers, this essay has attempted to open the borders of geography, and is only one example of how we could construct a more inclusionary historiography.

Second, we must always be aware that gender relations and representations are integral to the social construction of knowledge. The story of professional geography has, for the most part, been a men's story – they have been the principal actors and writers. But those men have existed in a social fabric of gender relations, and that fabric serves as both context and text for the history of geography. Specifically, the social fabric enters our histories in at least three ways: (1) The practices of geography – for example, the practice of fieldwork as presented in this essay shows how its use, legitimation and de-legitimation were clearly linked to the social roles of women and their potential access to academic geography. (2) The discourse of geography – the formulation of research questions, and the development of particular methods, theories, descriptions and interpretations of results. For example, the history of professional geography is littered with metaphors and theories which suggest androcentric thinking: the 'invasion and succession' of urban development theories, the 'rational man' of consumer behaviour studies, the competing 'fronts' of climatic activity, the notion of 'virgin' forests. Felix Driver (1988) has shown how much of the thinking in late-nineteenth-century social sciences in general and, later, in geography was part of a moral attempt to order and thereby control the seemingly chaotic industrial city, and Sally Shuttleworth (1990) has suggested that such views of urban life and urban form were implicated in attempts to control women. Her analysis of the metaphors used to describe the female body in medical texts, and the urban 'body' found in social scientific literature, strikes a very loud and clear blow to those who believe in the value-free nature of urban geographic inquiry. (3) The types of knowledge deemed appropriate to geography. Geography's commitment to a value-free, perspectiveless, objective science must be questioned in light of feminist critiques, as has been suggested throughout this essay. Such a commitment is itself suspect, since the stories of women explorers raise the issue of how and why 'objective' knowledge was given priority over 'subjective' knowledge. If geographic practices, theories and language have been socially and therefore ideologically constructed, can they embody any objective claims to truth? If the structures of geography are the products of particular historical contexts, and embody the biases of those contexts, then those structures both reflect and legitimize those biases. Geography's commitment to one type of knowledge, 'scientific' knowledge, can itself be seen as an indication of androcentric thinking, as Sandra Harding (1986) has so persuasively shown us.

Third, we must be reflexive in our rewriting of the history of geography. Understanding the contemporary social construction of the field, and how that construction is shaping our practices and the writing of our histories must be part of a feminist historiography of geography. We must question, for example, why the post-modern discourse in geography has been a male-dominated discussion, and what our current commitment to Geographical Information Systems (GIS) tells us about contemporary gender relations.

Conclusions

The recent rewriting of the history of geography has ignored the gendered construction of that history, and the post-modern turn in geography has ignored feminist theory.[6] A feminist historiography of geography would require an exploration of the relationship between its social practices and the gender stereotyping of society as a whole, and a reassessment both of the particular historical reasons for the invisibility of women in the discipline, and the traditional belief that new scientific practices (such as codified fieldwork) are necessary by-products of the search for knowledge. Such a reconsideration might lead to an alternative categorization of geographic paradigms based on the accessibility of each of those practices to women (Kelly-Gadol, 1976). To contextualize the history of geographic ideas requires a full recognition of the gendered construction of many of its practices, theories, and methods.

Yet to dwell on why women were excluded from the discipline is to risk ignoring their potential contributions. Given recent attempts to reconceptualize human geography, it is worthwhile to reflect on what geography could have been and could be if it included women's experiences and women's ways of thinking into its own canon (Belenky *et al.*, 1986). Although Victorian women explorers are not the only group of geographers to be excluded from the accounts of 'scientific' geography, their well-documented experiences do provide us with a unique opportunity to recover from our own history sources for a more human geography. These were geographers who wrote novels and travelogues to help capture the richness of their journeys, who openly admitted that they were seeking knowledge as much of themselves as of the lands they explored, and who recognized explicitly the ambiguity of their role as outsider in an alien culture. We do not need to look far afield to reconstruct a postmoderm geography – it is in our own backyard, if we would only step outside.

Notes

1 The most thorough discussion of those tensions, and of the ambivalent relationship between feminism and post-modenism, is found in the essays in *Feminism and postmodernism*, edited by Linda Nicholson 1990.
2 Annette Kolodny has documented similar confrontations with a male-defined language in her study of women's experiences in the American West (Kolodny, 1984).
3 The discussion of feminism and the practices of science is a somewhat complicated and oftentimes obscure discourse, often revolving around a debate as to whether feminist analysis will bring about a better science, or the total deconstruction of science. For recent overviews, see Harding 1986, and the summer 1989 issue of *Women's Studies International Forum*.
4 Janice Monk has begun to examine the relationships between women geographers and the course of academic geography in America. For a preliminary view, see Monk 1989.
5 A critique of GIS that is informed by both a feminist and post-modern critique can be found in Curry 1990.
6 For an analysis of a similar circumstance in anthropology, see Mascia-Lees *et al.* 1989.

References

Babcock, B. A. and Parezo, N. J. 1988: *Daughters of the desert: women anthropologists and the Native American Southwest, 1880–1980*. Albuquerque: University of New Mexico Press.
Belenky, M. F., Clinchy, B. M., Goldberger, N. R. and Tarule, J. M. 1986: *Women's ways of knowing the development of self, voice and mind*. New York: Basic Books.
Bird, I. 1879: *A lady's life in the Rocky Mountains*. London: Murray.
Bird, I. 1987: *Unbeaten tracks in Japan*. Boston MA: Beacon Press, reprinted from an 1880 edition.
Birkett, D. 1989: *Spinters abroad: Victorian lady explorers*. New York: Basil Blackwell.
Clifford, J. and Marcus, G. (eds) 1986: *Writing culture: The politics and poetics of ethnography*. Berkeley: University of California Press.

Cosgrove, D. 1988: Ideas for a new world: Late Renaissance naturalism and its history. Paper presented at the conference, 'What is the Engine of History?' Texas A&M University.

Cosgrove, D. 1989: A terrain of metaphor: cultural geography 1988–89, *Progress in Human Geography*. 13, 506–15.

Cosgrove, D. and Domosh, M. 1991: Author and authority: writing the new cultural geography. In Duncan, J. and Ley, D. (eds), *Place/culture/representation*. London: Routledge, 25–38.

Curry, M. 1990: Morality and agency in geographical information systems. Paper presented at the departmental lecture series, Department of Geography, San Diego State University.

Daniels, S. 1992: Loutherbourg's chemical theatre: Coalbrookdale by Night. In Barrell, J. (ed), *Painting and the politics of culture*. Oxford: Oxford University Press, 195–230.

Dear, M. 1988: The postmodern challenge: reconstructing human geography. *Transactions of the Institute of British Geographers*, NS, 13, 262–74.

Driver, F. 1988: Moral geographies: social science and the urban environment in mid-nineteenth century England. *Transactions of the Institute of British Geographers*, NS, 13, 275–87.

Duncan, J. and Duncan, N. 1988: (Re)reading the landscape. *Society and Space* 6, 117–26.

Frank, K. 1986: *A voyager out: the life of Mary Kingsley*. New York: Ballantine Books.

Franklin, S. 1985: Luce Irigaray and the feminist critique of language. Women's studies occasional papers No. 6, Canterbury: University of Kent.

Goodchild, M. F. and Janelle, D. G. 1988: Specialization in the structure and organization of geography. *Annals of the Association of American Geographers* 78, 1–28.

Grosz, E. A. 1987: Feminist theory and the challenge to knowledges. *Women's Studies International Forum* 10, 475–80.

Harding, S. 1986: *The science question in feminism*. Ithaca: Cornell University Press.

Irigaray, L. 1974: *Speculum de l'autre femme*. Paris: Editions Minuit.

Keller, E. F. 1985: *Reflections on gender and science*. New Haven: Yale University Press.

Kelly-Gadol, J. 1976: The social relation of the sexes: methodological implications of women's history. *Signs: Journal of Women and Society* 1, 809–23.

Kolodny, A. 1984: *The land before her: fantasy and experience of the American frontier, 1630–1860*. Chapel Hill: University of North Carolina Press.

Livingstone, D. 1988: Science, magic and religion: a contextual reassessment of geography in the sixteenth and seventeenth centuries. *History of Science* 26, 269–94

Livingstone, D. 1990: Geography and modernity: past and present. Paper presented at the AAG meeting, Toronto.

Mascia-lees, F. E., Sharpe, P. and Ballerino, C. 1989: The postmodernist turn in anthropology: cautions from a feminist perspective. *Signs: Journal of Women and Society* 15, 1–29.

Middleton, D. 1982: *Victorian lady travellers*. Chicago: Academy Chicago.

Mitchell, O. and Smith, N. 1990: Bringing in race. *Professional Geographer* 42, 232–33

Monk, J. 1989: Women geographers and geographic institutions, 1900–1950. Paper presented at the 1989 AAG meeting, Baltimore.

Nicholson, L. J. (ed.) 1990: *Feminism and postmodernism*. New York: Routledge.

Olds, E. F. 1985: *Women of the four winds*. Boston: Houghton Mifflin.

Quoniam, S. 1988: A Painter, geographer of Arizona. *Society and Space* 6, 3–14.

Said, E. N. 1978: *Orientalism*. New York: Vintage Books.

Sayers, J. 1987: Feminism and science – reason and passion. *Women's Studies International Forum* 10, 171–79.

Shuttleworth, S. 1990: Female circulation: medical discourse and popular advertising in the mid-Victorian era. In Jacobus, M., Keller, E. F. and Shuttleworth, S. (eds), *Body/politics: women and the discourses of science*. New York: Routledge.

Stoddart, D. 1986: *On geography*. New York: Basil Blackwell.

Tinling, M. 1989: *Women into the unknown: a sourcebook on women explorers and travelers*. New York: Greenwood Press.

Women's Studies International Forum 1989: 12, 3.

Wright, J. K. 1947: Terrae incognitae: the place of the imagination in geography. *Annals of the Association of American Geographers* 37, 1–15.

INDEX

Page numbers with suffix 'n' refer to end-notes